Plants in the Landscape

Plants in the Landscape

Philip L. Carpenter

Theodore D. Walker

Frederick O. Lanphear

PURDUE UNIVERSITY

W. H. FREEMAN AND COMPANY
San Francisco

Frontispiece: *A sunken plaza at the base of the Crown Zellerbach Building in downtown San Francisco. In addition to the ground covers and Italian stone pines visible in the photo, plantings in this plaza include sycamore, magnolia, honey-locust, holly-oak, olive, and crabapple. The plaza occupies two-thirds of the site on which the building stands.*

Library of Congress Cataloging in Publication Data

Carpenter, Philip Lee, 1933–
    Plants in the landscape.

    Includes bibliographies and indexes.
    1. Landscape gardening.   2. Plants, Ornamental.
I. Walker, Theodore D., joint author.   II. Lanphear,
Frederick O., joint author.   III. Title.
SB472.C27   712   74-32292
ISBN 0-7167-0778-0

Printed in the United States of America

9 8 7 6 5 4 3 2

Contents

Preface

Plants have been with man since the beginning of time, and each generation has struggled to make the most efficient and effective use of plants for food, for clothing, and for housing. Plants are a comfort to both body and soul. *Plants in the Landscape* is meant for those who plan to make a career of working with plants. The primary focus of this book is on the landscape industry and on ways the various members of that industry use plants to improve man's physical environment aesthetically and functionally. Realizing the need for a book that would bring together balanced introductory discussions of landscape design, construction, and maintenance, the three of us drew from our different backgrounds and fields of expertise in order to write such a book. We hope that the book will lead to improved communication among the various occupations that make up the landscape industry. At present these occupations form separate segments. If that goal can be at least partially realized, then we will feel we have made a contribution toward a greener and more attractive environment.

Each of us is indebted to the large number of people with whom we have associated during many years of theoretical and practical training. It would be impossible to thank each person by name or to describe the influence each has had on our work. Encouragement came from many colleagues and acquaintances throughout the country, especially from those who work in the landscape industry. Many firms, research institutions, libraries, governmental agencies, and private individuals contributed drawings and photographs generously.

Finally, we wish to acknowledge the influence of the landscape itself. Through its constant renewal, the landscape inspires an optimism towards life; plants start life, grow and develop, flower, seed, and then repeat the life cycle. Plants help man physically, emotionally, and spiritually, and when man allows them to, plants imbue him with a greater sense of being and purpose.

February 1975

Philip L. Carpenter
Theodore D. Walker
Frederick O. Lanphear

Plants in the Landscape

I

Man and the Landscape

1

Plants in the Landscape

ABOUT THIS BOOK

It is difficult to envision a landscape without plants. Except in the most adverse climates, man is almost always in close association with plants. They cover the countryside in pastures, meadows, woodlands, and forests. They also adorn the diminishing spaces in suburbs and cities. Population pressures and urbanization have meant that the space allocated for the growth of plants has been decreasing rapidly, particularly in densely populated residential areas, but even as more land is paved or covered with houses and the other construction necessary for urban and suburban life, plants continue to be important features in the man-made landscape.

There are two primary reasons for the importance of plants in the landscape. First, they are necessary. Plants are an integral part of the Earth's biosphere and they perform a vital role in sustaining life. They are also naturally persistent, as anyone who has pulled weeds in a backyard or in a flower or vegetable garden will surely agree. Although this encourages man to define some plants as weeds, it is fortunate that plants are persistent, because they provide rapid revegetation of the many scars man has imposed on the landscape, along highways and at other construction projects where the soil has been cut away. The vegetation that invades these man-made scars naturally is important in reducing erosion. Man, if he is to be a proper caretaker of his environment, must also assist in the reestablishment of plants.

The second reason for the importance of plants in the landscape is that they are delight-

1-1

Figure 1-1. *Anyone who aspires to work in landscape development can benefit from studying the growth and features that occur on the land without human work. The photos in this chapter might seem at first glance to be examples of virgin land; in fact, all were taken in national forests or parks, where man does to some degree manage the landscape. This photo: blossoms of mountain-laurel (Kalmia latifolia) in Pisgah National Forest, North Carolina. Mountain-laurel is naturally profuse in the Appalachians and is a shrub frequently used in landscape plantings.*

ful. Man has a fascination with, and a desire for, association with plants. There are many possible explanations for this relationship, some of which will be discussed later in this chapter and in subsequent chapters. A quick trip through any suburban residential area will demonstrate the importance people place on plants in the landscape. A house seldom remains in a barren landscape for very long. Although many homes are sparsely planted, there is almost always evidence that an attempt at planting has been made.

What, precisely, is the role of plants in the landscape? What principles are effective and what practices necessary for the design, specification, installation, and maintenance of a good landscape? We hope this book will answer those questions. We have not attempted to provide a compendium of details on any one of the subjects, but we do provide a comprehensive and functional overview of each and show the interrelatedness of the subjects. A primary concern of the various specialists who comprise the landscape profession is to improve their communication and coordination. We hope this book will help to bridge the gaps that now segment the professional areas. The book contains enough information about each area to provide background for practical work in each profession.

The first part of this book provides a historical perspective of man's efforts to develop the landscape and a brief description of each of the segments of what has become known as the landscape industry: design, construction, maintenance, and the nursery.

The second part of the book provides an introduction to landscape plants. This information will be a useful background to the chapters that follow. Such subjects as plant communities (sometimes referred to also as plant ecology), the response of plants to their environments, and scientific classification and the origins of plants are explored and discussed.

Design is the focus of the third part, in which the reader will find an introduction to the basic principles of design with plants, discussion of functional and aesthetic values of plants when used in design, and information about how the architect or designer applies principles and values in the design process—in short, how he creates a work of art and function.

As a natural follow-up to design with plants, the preparation of plans, specifications, cost estimates, bidding, and many other contracting procedures comprise the fourth part of the book.

Part V is about landscape construction, starting with such subjects as soils, drainage, fertility, and irrigation systems, and progressing to the planting and establishing of woody plants, turf, ground covers, and herbaceous plants.

Once the planting is completed, maintenance is important, and this is the subject of Part VI, which provides an introduction to the physical care of woody plant material, the control of weeds, diseases, and insects, and other problems in maintaining the landscaped site.

To conclude the book, three chapters provide a summary in which all the ideas of the book are viewed in the context of work to be found in urban, suburban, and rural environments.

1-2

Figure 1-2. *Square Top Mountain, viewed across Green River Lake in Bridger National Forest, Wyoming.*

1-3

Figure 1-3. *Lake near Tuolumne Meadows in Yosemite National Park.*

At the end of most chapters selected references have been added as suggested additional reading.

PLANTS AS A REFLECTION OF ENVIRONMENTAL QUALITY

There is a growing concern nationwide and throughout the world about man's effect on the quality of his environment. The evidence of environmental decay has become apparent in all areas, whether urban or rural. The impact of increased population and technology on land use and on the quality of air, water, and soil can no longer be ignored.

For those who work to design and develop the landscape, man's struggle to maintain his environment at its best quality will never succeed as long as there is unrestrained removal of vegetation from the landscape. The effects of such removal can be shown with countless examples. Whether the land is to be used for highways or housing, the general practice is to bring in the bulldozers to scrape the land clear. Although planting may be done at a later date, the plants usually take from 10 to 20 years to reach a desirable size. All too often, much of the land being "developed" today is not replanted but is paved to provide more parking space for ever-increasing numbers of automobiles. Extensive paving prevents rain from replenishing the water table beneath the paving. The absence of vegetation in the paved areas is visually ugly; physical discomfort results from the higher temperatures of the nonshaded, heat-absorbing paved areas. In place of trees, utility poles and power lines continue to be installed, adding further to the ugliness.

Urban expansion and the destruction of existing vegetation has had a profound effect on a public that is apprehensive about the quality of its environment. As a result, some individuals, corporations, communities, and local and federal governmental bodies are taking greater interest in improving and beautifying their homes, industrial sites, communities, parks, and public facilities, and are gaining pride from doing so. New schools and industrial sites are generally provided planned landscapes as an integral part of the planning and construction program. In recent years, new high-density single- and multiple-unit residential developments have included land allocated for recreation and attractive landscaping. Even downtown shopping areas, whose merchants are faced with the commercial pressures to fit parking, buildings, and people into a limited space, are being enhanced through conversion of existing congested streets into attractively planted pedestrian malls because shoppers enjoy them. The importance of parks and other landscaped areas in crowded cities is apparent, the need for them is urgent, and recently a number of "mini-parks" and "vest-pocket parks" have been created in many of the nation's cities. This trend will most likely continue in the midst of continued urbanization and accelerated environmental change, as it should, for the number of small parks will need to increase.

The greater emphasis on using landscape planting to enchance man's environment has placed greater demands on the landscape industry than at any previous time. More plants are now being used, and in locations for which

1-4

1-5

they must be either selected or maintained with extreme care, or in which both selection and maintenance require special care. A specific example of this is the use of landscape plants in the Federal Highway Administration's Highway Beautification Program. The landscape contract for a particular interstate highway project may require as many as 10,000 plants per mile, usually specifying just a few species. Often the quantities of plants needed in their proper sizes for such a project are extremely difficult to obtain. Moreover, the adverse soil or weather conditions of many roadside development projects limit the type of plants that can be used to a select few.

PLANT SELECTION AND ARRANGEMENT

The initial selection and arrangement of plants is the crucial step in the ultimate success of any landscape plantings. Too often the same plants are used over and over again, sometimes without an understanding of the environmental differences between sites. In fact, fascination with particular plants prevents people from realizing their inappropriateness in certain locations. Unless ecological requirements are considered along with aesthetic characteristics, the chances of successfully establishing landscape plantings are rather poor.

The arrangement of plants in the landscape requires special attention that can usually be provided best by the landscape architect or landscape designer. Each landscape project should be considered separately, with recognition of the unique problems and possibilities for the site. After careful analysis and definition

Figure 1-4. *Grand Canyon National Park.*
Figure 1-5. *Rocky Mountain National Park.*

of specific needs, the architect or designer can consider solutions. Landscapes are created for people, and any planning should consider who those people are, what they are going to be doing, and how the landscape can have the most effective impact on the lives and the work of the people within that landscape. For best results the design of landscape plantings should begin during the initial planning stage of the project, before any construction or site-disturbance has occurred. Unfortunately, the quality of many landscape plantings is determined by purchasing a plant and then looking for a place to plant it. This is particularly true of residential landscapes. Where the landscape is planted more intensively, as in most urban sites, the design and plant-selection requirements must be more exact.

A popular misconception is that landscape plantings are only cosmetic. Too often plants have been used only to conceal blemishes on the landscape or to add decorative areas. Unfortunately, this misconception has been cited by some professionals and amateurs alike as the primary purpose of landscaping.

The real value and art of selecting and arranging plants in the landscape is achieved when the designer of the landscape has been able to integrate the man-made landscape, including all of its architectural features, with the natural landscape of the area. That is not to imply that the man-made landscape must duplicate or even simulate the natural landscape, only that the plants that have been selected and arranged should tend to "fit." This requires close attention to the selection of plants that are either native or adaptable to an area and to the sensitive grouping and placement of plants. More will be said about this later in the book, with illustrations to demonstrate what is otherwise difficult to describe effectively.

The selection of plants is both an art and a science. It is art because it requires sensitivity to elements of design, such as color, form, and texture, and the ability to judge these elements in each plant. And herein lies the primary difficulty, for in describing the design qualities of a plant, the designer must remember that the plant is not static but changes in texture, form, color, and so forth, with seasons as well as with age. It is science because it requires knowing the plant's environmental requirements before its health can be maintained. The proper selection of plants is dependent on the fulfillment of both artistic and scientific considerations.

PLANT PROCUREMENT

Suppose plants have been selected for a project. The next step in devising a landscape is to obtain the plants in the sizes and quantities specified. This is usually the responsibility of the landscape contractor, though the architect may also involve himself. Obtaining plants would seem at first to be a relatively easy task. However, locating plants that are the least bit unusual in terms of species or sizes, or in quantities, can become a major problem. This is particularly true of larger plants, which are not always readily available but which are in great demand for highway and urban redevelopment projects. Frequently, plant substitutions must be made, but substitution should be kept to a minimum and should be approved first by the architect.

1-6

1-7

The increasing production of container-grown plants, which include rather large trees, has extended the contracting season, and the designer of the landscape and the landscape contractor may now use many more hard-to-move species during any season than were available in the past. Nevertheless, planners of projects with planting deadlines need to anticipate possible difficulty in procurement so that sufficient time is available to investigate alternative possibilities.

The problems encountered in plant procurement necessitate close scrutiny of the extent to which the plants delivered to the project meet the specifications of the architect or designer. Along with the landscape contractor, he should assume responsibility for inspecting all plants. Species, size, and quality should all be included in the designer's specifications, which are a fundamentally important part of the landscape plan. The nurseries supplying the plants also have standards that specify the size of the root ball, number of branches, etc., for plants of specific sizes, and fulfillment of these standards should be inspected.

THE ESTABLISHMENT OF PLANTS IN THE LANDSCAPE

Once the selection and arrangement of the plants are complete, and the plants have been located and purchased, planting can begin. Many landscape plants fail because of improper and careless transplanting. Success begins with the adequate care of the plants before they are actually replanted. It will be worthwhile to give particular attention to site modification, so that

Figure 1-6. *South Fork of the Rio Grande River in Rio Grande National Forest, Colorado.*

Figure 1-7. *Mountain scenery and water reflections.*

the requirements of each plant species will be met and optimum performance of the plants will be obtained. Then, when the plants are established in the new landscape, it is imperative that the landscape contractor exercise sound judgment, particularly during the period immediately following transplanting. No formula will take into account unanticipated weather variations or other problems that influence the chances that a new plant will survive.

Landscape plantings are usually long-term investments. They may mature in a relatively short time or they may take 20 years or more to reach maturation. To protect that investment, a comprehensive management program is essential: cultural requirements have to be satisfied to insure the optimum performance of any plant. Moreover, pests or environmental stress problems usually need to be managed, by prevention, or with curative maintenance, or with both. The need for good maintenance of landscape plantings is often overlooked when landscape projects are planned, and the cost is sometimes underestimated. If provisions for maintenance will not be made, then it is essential to consider this in the planning stage.

INTERRELATIONSHIPS OF LANDSCAPE OPERATIONS

Although the operations we have just outlined are all distinct, it is imperative that they be interrelated from beginning to end. Not only is each operation dependent on the others for ultimate success, the ease and efficiency in accomplishing each step can be greatly facili-

1-8

Figure 1-8. *View of Devil's Tower, Wyoming.*

Figure 1-9. *View near the head of Miner's Creek from Suiattle Pass, Mt. Baker National Forest, Washington.*

1-9

tated by knowledge of, and coordination with, the other operations.

The dynamics of the interrelationships of the landscape architect, landscape contractor, landscape maintenance supervisor, and nurseryman are shown in a diagram at the beginning of Chapter 3, on page 41.

An effective understanding of the interrelationships is important and communication among the personnel who work at each job during these operations is of the utmost importance. For example, if the architect is unaware of maintenance requirements or limitations in a project of his design, it is unlikely that he will be able to anticipate them effectively. Conversely, a landscape maintenance supervisor who is unaware of the effect the architect desired when he drew the plans can completely defeat the architectural objective, as he most certainly would if he sheared plants the architect intended to allow to develop natural habits of growth. Similar problems in communication can exist between the nurseryman and the architect over the selection, availability, and substitution of plant materials. Specific examples of how all these operations are interrelated will be given in later chapters. To some degree nearly all the chapters will suggest methods of coordinating the various operations.

ECOLOGY OF LANDSCAPE PLANTINGS

Today's landscapes are hardly the natural countryside that existed before the age of technology. Indeed, through the history of civilization, the impact of man on the land has been negative more often than positive: witness the many ecological "disasters" in our own time. Man is finally beginning to realize that his technology cannot afford to ignore natural ecologies. Few are in a position to understand this so well as those who plan, construct, and maintain man's landscaped environments.

Technology is not necessarily incompatible with the landscape unless one assumes that the only acceptable landscape is one untouched by man—a wilderness—and clearly such an assumption is unrealistic. But man has become dominant in the landscape, and therefore he must assume responsibility for observing ecological principles, or he will suffer the consequences. Specifically, for those of us who choose to make a livelihood of fashioning and planting the landscape, this involves recognizing the natural features of an area and then selecting, arranging, establishing, and maintaining plants in the manner most favorable for that area. To do so requires consideration of relationships in natural plant communities, the role of plant succession in the long-term development of an area, macro- and microclimatic factors, as well as the most basic question an architect or designer may have to answer: Is the habitat actually suitable for landscape development. These factors have not always been considered in the past; the consequences have been unfortunate.

There is need, then, to approach planting design, construction, and maintenance comprehensively, and to consider ecological and technological principles as well as aesthetic considerations. Filling the need requires either that every member of the landscape profession have a very broad training in these areas or that a team effort be made of landscape projects.

The interrelationships of the disciplines involved in landscape work and the applicable principles and technology are the central focus of this book. The reader may decide, when he finishes the book, how best to make his mark on the land.

2

Landscape Development in Historical Perspective

A garden is man's idealized view of the world; and because most men are representative of the society of which they are a part, it follows that fashionable gardens of any community and any period betray the dream world which is the period's ideal. All history is one. Gardens cannot be considered in detachment from the people who made them.

Derek Clifford, *A History of Garden Design,* 1963

In making a sensitive, constructive use of plants in the landscape, it is helpful to understand the relationship of man to those parts of the landscape that he developed during the course of history, for man's gardening in any period reflects much about the cultural, economic, and political nature of people. A study of history can, furthermore, provide a better understand-ing of man today and how he is motivated to express himself in landscape development.

For ease, in this chapter we will talk of both "gardens" and "landscapes," even though, by origin, the two words have different origins. The meanings say quite a lot about man's relationship with plants in his environment. "Garden" originally referred to an enclosed area used for planting. "Landscape" is a word that meant, originally, a fashioning of land forms, and apparently the word first became useful when painters chose land forms as the subject of their paintings. Of course, today, the word landscape has a more general use. But so has "garden." The important distinction, perhaps—the distinction we mean to convey, at least—is that on the one hand, a garden is a private, intensively planted enclosure, and on the other, that a landscape is more open, more free, and more accessible to public use.

In pre-Christian gardens, religious significance was associated with plants. But in other eras, a simple desire for flowers and plants was sufficient reason to adorn the landscape with ornamental plants. Then, in another time, landscape plantings were treated as works of art by people who fulfilled a need to display their affluence by creating elaborate landscape scenes. The naturalist strove to make the design and creation of the managed landscape blend in harmoniously with the elements of nature. In some societies, work with features of the landscape was done to express a desire for a formal, controlled style of beauty. One of the prevailing reasons for landscape development was to provide attractive settings for imposing castles, villas, mansions, and public buildings; and providing attractive settings for imposing buildings continues to be the reason for much of the landscape development undertaken today. These uses of landscaping are not meant to suggest that any one of them was the only controlling factor in landscape development for a specific time in history, but that the importance of these various motives was closely related to the cultural, economic, and political values of various societies.

In addition to the values and motivations of people, certain geographical and functional factors exerted an influence on the style and extent of landscape development. Climate, topography, land, water, and the availability of suitable plants have all been important limiting factors in the form the land took. The purpose of the plantings was important too; plantings were used to provide privacy or to give protection from wind and sun. In every period of history, one of the major factors in landscape development was the availability of resources, financial and human, required for such endeavors, which were generally considered more of a luxury than a necessity, even as they often are today. Yet it is true that gardens are meager in societies struggling to survive and usually flourish once the basic necessities have been met, when extra time and energy are available for creative activities.

It would be impossible to survey the history of gardening adequately in one chapter. But our intention is to describe it briefly, instead, in order to place the relationship of man and ornamental plants in proper perspective. Plants are not the only landscape features important in gardens, but they are the primary concern of this book. Consequently, our historical overview will describe ways in which plants have been used, recognizing that each new period in gardening history is built upon the knowledge of the past and generally reflects, to some extent, earlier traditions.

ANCIENT LANDSCAPE DEVELOPMENT

Evidence of Egyptian gardens from about 2200 BC are the earliest record of man's activity in landscape development. Both useful and ornamental plants were planted then. Trees as well as vines of grapes and ivy, which were trained on rafters and arbors, were used for shade. Flowering plants were arranged symmetrically in well-maintained gardens. Simple formal gardens—primitive versions of the French *parterres*—included roses, jasmine, myrtle, and other plants that were grown either in the earth or in

Figure 2-1. *Tomb painting showing the garden estate of a wealthy Egyptian official, from the time of Amenhotep III (about 1400 BC).*

Figure 2-2. *Birdseye view of an Egyptian garden, as reconstructed from the painting shown in Figure 2-1.*

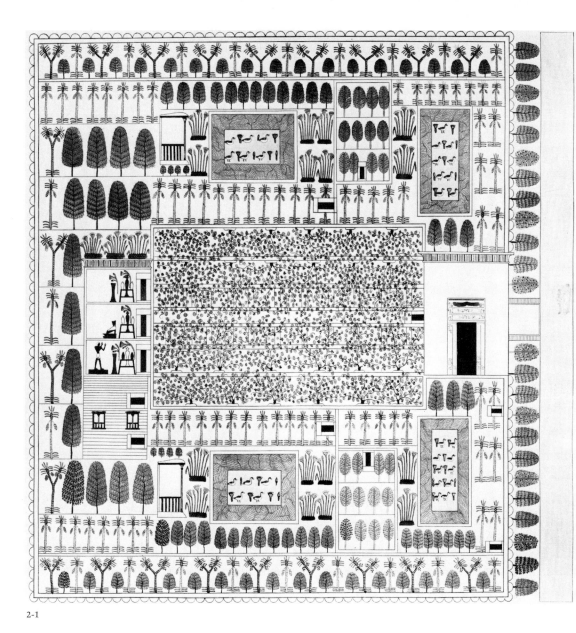

2-1

2-2

pots. The concept of enclosed gardens also originated at this time, primarily to provide privacy for the women in the household. It should be noted that not every Egyptian had his garden; these early gardens belonged mainly to the pharaohs and their officials or served as religious or sacred gardens.

The most famous gardens of ancient times were the Hanging Gardens of Babylon. Built about 600 BC at the beginning of the Persian dynasty, they were considered one of the legendary Seven Wonders of the World. These gardens were constructed in the form of a pyramid—an artificial hill—having a square or rectangular base with dimensions estimated to range from 400 to 1,400 feet. Steps were constructed on the base to create terraces, each one built upon arches, so that between each terrace was a cool promenade or series of rooms. Trees, shrubs, and flowers were planted on each terrace, giving the effect of a tree-covered manmade mountain. Although one is awed by the feat of building such a structure (the Babylonians were the first people to use arches to support the mass of a building), the horticulturist will be equally impressed by the knowledge that it was possible to establish large plants in what today he would call a roof garden. This was accomplished by covering the stone used in construction with a layer of reeds and asphalt mixed with brick and gypsum, and then by placing a layer of lead over this to provide a solid support for the soil. For large trees, the pillars on the next lower terrace were made hollow and filled with soil so that the roots could penetrate deeply. The wonder of the hanging gardens was not only their beauty, but also their size and complexity.

Any aspect of ancient history would not be complete without consideration of some contribution made by the Greeks during the period from 600 BC to the beginning of the Christian era. Before the Greeks came into close contact with other countries, their earliest gardens were very simple, usually consisting of an orchard or a kitchen garden. After 500 BC, pleasure gardens resembling those of Persia and Egypt evolved. These gardens were usually planted in small open courtyards—prototypes for the Roman peristyles—which were contained within houses in a town. In addition to many structural features, gardens contained low

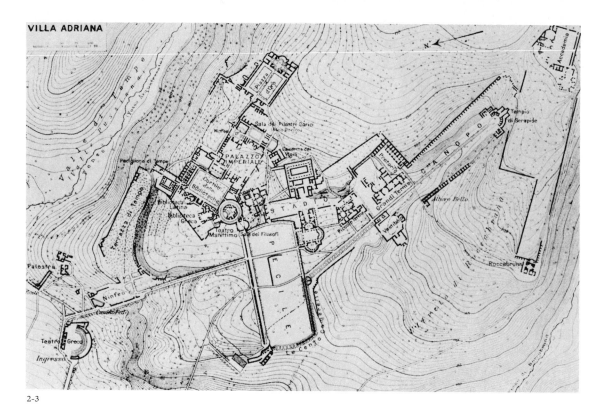

2-3

beds of exotic plants brought from foreign countries; their use is indicative of an early desire by man to surround himself with rare and unusual plants. There were also public gardens; so in ancient Greece one can see the beginning of public parks. Many of these park-gardens became meeting places for the Greek philosophers and their pupils, who would engage in discussion while pacing up and down garden walks lined with groves of elm and plane trees.

The ancient art of gardening reached its climax in the last period of Roman civilization, during the early years of the Christian era. In-

Figure 2-3. *Site map showing the remains of the villa of the emperor Hadrian, at Tivoli, near Rome. The buildings and grounds, laid out circa 125 AD, covered an area of some seven square miles. The grounds contained numerous monuments commemorating Hadrian's travels. A monument to the Egyptian city of Canopus is shown in the next figure; its location in this figure is toward the end of the long axis leading from the center to the upper right corner.*

2-4

2-5

Figure 2-4. *The remains of Hadrian's villa, Tivoli.*

Figure 2-5. *Trees at Hadrian's villa, Tivoli.*

deed, the influence of the classic traditions of Roman gardening has existed into the twentieth century. Yet, what the Romans achieved must also be viewed in terms of the ties that connected the Greek and Roman civilizations during the first century before Christ.

In Rome, as well as in the lesser cities and the towns of the Roman empire, landscape plantings were everywhere. Every house was adorned with flowers and plants. Public parks, "hanging" gardens borne on arches, and garden courts influenced by Greek precedents could all be found. When ground space was limited, the roofs of houses were converted to gardens with plantings and other garden features. A characteristic of the town gardens in the Roman regions was the use of raised beds two to three feet high; these may have been designed to hold friable soil in areas with rocky or poorly drained ground.

As Rome became crowded, people moved to the surrounding suburban and rural countryside, away from the heat and congestion of the city, and built villas where it was cooler. The villas were also status symbols. They provided more garden space in quiet, secluded locations. Courtyards fashioned after the Greek peristyle provided the primary setting for gardens. These gardens were embellished with a great variety of useful and ornamental objects in addition to the flower beds, which were carefully laid out to create effective patterns. Even kitchen gardens were planted with concern for details of design. Greenhouses built with panes of glass or translucent stone provided protection for tender and exotic plants introduced from the East. These greenhouses were also used to force certain plants to mature or bloom out of season.

As for the plants used, roses, lilies, and violets were the flowers probably admired most, along with narcissus, anemone, gladiolus, iris, poppy, amaranth, verbena, periwinkle, and crocus. Other herbaceous plants, such as basil, sweet marjoram, and thyme, were grown for their fragrance. Trees and shrubs were given special attention, either because they were considered sacred or because of the coolness they provided. Favorite trees and shrubs included pine, oak, laurel, myrtle, olive, and cypress. One interesting method of handling plants that developed during this period was the art of topiary or plant sculpture. Evergreen trees and shrubs were clipped into pyramids, cones, various animals, and even entire scenes. The lack of variation in shrub species was overcome by the diversity of these topiary forms. Junipers and rosemary were the most frequently used shrubs, along with boxwood, which was also considered the best shrub for edgings.

MEDIEVAL LANDSCAPE DEVELOPMENT

Northern European Gardens

With the fall of Rome, horticulture and other creative pursuits were lost. It was not until the beginning of the monastic era, in the sixth century AD, that horticulture began to be practiced to the north and west of Italy, in the countries to which monks carried Christianity. The Benedictine Order maintained large gardens tended by the monks and smaller ones tended by the abbots as a way of teaching that "work sanctified by prayer is the best thing a man can do." Flowers, which had been despised by earlier Christians as symbols of paganism, were now grown to decorate the churches. Roses were a favorite flower for this purpose. Nuns in convents maintained flower gardens for similar reasons. Little else is known about the gardens of this period than that the monasteries and convents were where the art of gardening was practiced for two centuries.

During the ninth and tenth centuries, monasticism declined and horticulture again became practically a lost art. In the eleventh century, with a revival of religious zeal followed by the Norman Conquest of England, monasteries were again to flourish. Gardening was always associated with these monasteries and gardens were often the greatest pride and glory of a monastic community. Although vegetables and aromatic or medicinal herbs were the primary crops, some flowers were included for fragrance and color and for use on the church altar. Cloisters, which were enclosed courtyards similar to the ancient peristyles, contained grass plots intermingled with beds of flowers and sometimes some shrubs. These areas served as places of refuge, seclusion, and meditation. Burial grounds or cemeteries were also planted with trees and shrubs, much as they had been in ancient times and continue to be today. Many of the monasteries in England, along with their gardens, were discontinued by Henry VIII in the sixteenth century. Their discontinuation has obscured this long era of gardening history. Today, at The Cloisters Museum in New York, one can see excellent re-creations of cloister gardens.

During the Dark Ages and through the Middle Ages there were also castle gardens. The earliest of these might have appeared during the brief Carolingian revival of the arts.

Figures 2-6, 2-7. *Moorish gardens in Granada, Spain. A pool before the Torre de las Damas in The Alhambra (2-6); a garden at The Generalife (2-7).*

2-6

2-7

roses climbed to cover a walk, and a maze designed in the shape of a knot and planted with shrubs. Enclosure was critical for privacy; this was often accomplished with hedges of privet, thorn, sweetbriar, and yew, in addition to stone walls and fences.

Orchards during this time were not planted apart from the gardens, but contained herbs and flowers as well as fruit trees.

Numerous manuscripts from the Middle Ages depict gardens of the period, including the *Book of Hours*, prepared for the Duke of Berry and illustrated with several views of his gardens.

Moorish Gardens in Spain

While most of Europe was struggling to regain the civilization lost with the disintegration of the Roman world, Spain was enjoying wealth and stability under Moorish rule. Luxurious villas were constructed, and the Moorish influence on gardening can still be observed in the gardens of the Alhambra and the Generalife at Granada, dating from the fifteenth century. The Alhambra contained four courtyards based on the style of Roman courtyards built 14 centuries earlier but with distinctive Moorish architecture. These courtyard gardens were developed as outdoor rooms; one contained simple hedge plantings; for variety, another was fully planted to provide shade. Because of the dry climate, water was an important feature, and a central theme of the gardens was the use of fountains and reflection pools. The Generalife, located a few hundred yards away on a higher hill overlooking the Alhambra, is a series of small terraced gardens that lead toward a palace. The coolness of shade from trees as

During the early ninth century, Charlemagne indicated his desire to have a garden with many kinds of plants; among those familiar to him were roses, lilies, poppies, and many fruit trees. In general, though, in most areas of Europe, gardening did not begin to flourish until late in the twelfth century; by that time the conflict and warfare of the Dark Ages had begun to subside. Then the "pleasance" was developed in France; it was a small garden enclosed by the towers and battlements of a castle but usually located in an outer extension of the ramparts and reached through a small door in them. These were used primarily for entertaining ladies. A typical pleasance might contain flowers in beds or in pots on the walls, clipped trees and shrubs, an arbor upon which vines and

well as the desire for color and the scent of flowers influenced the design of the Spanish-Moorish gardens. One horticultural oddity practiced during this period was the grafting of as many as a dozen different varieties of trees onto a tree of a single stock, or the grafting of vines onto fruit trees.

LANDSCAPE DEVELOPMENT DURING THE RENAISSANCE

Gardening as an art really became fully developed during the Renaissance period. Not only did the Renaissance revive the formal, classical ideals of ancient Roman and Greek civilizations, it created a distinctive style of gardening that has had influence in Europe and most of the rest of the world to this day. It serves as the transition between the ancient and the modern world.

Italy

As the need for security lessened, the design of gardens took on a more open, outward-looking mood. Gardens were frequently located on slopes so that one could look out over surrounding walls. Indeed, the awareness of extended space and of the relation of scale to distance—in short, perspective—were important innovations. Yet, with all the emphasis on lengthening views and creating an outward look, gardens were conceived in conjunction with buildings and were integrated with them to provide a pleasant and welcoming environment.

As one studies the elaborate villas erected in Italy during the Renaissance, the expressive artistry of the aristocracy is quite apparent. In fact, these gardens were often intended more for spectacle than as an area of retreat or privacy. A villa might typically be surrounded by from 10 to 15 acres of land, often a long and narrow property the major axis of which led down the slope of a hill. This slope was then divided into three or four terraces often retained behind stone walls. The lowest of these terraces usually served as the principal entrance and contained formal flower gardens. On the second level might be located a casino—a house apart from the residence that was used for social functions. The third level would likely be wooded and would serve as a secluded retreat.

The use made of plants and other landscape features is not much different from what has been described for ancient Greece and Rome, for there was a conscious desire to borrow from the civilizations that had lived on the same land and with the same climates and plants in the past. But new innovations were present too. So along with pergolas and porticoes, decorative containers emblazoned with the name or emblem of a family were used for growing flowers. Boxwood and rosemary were used for the edging of garden beds. Cypress and yew, in combination with ivy, were desirable plants. Trees were functionally important in providing shade, and oaks, cypress, stone pine, and chestnut were popular for this. Topiary was a much-used art in this period; its importance suggests that the art may never have been forgotten but was continuous from ancient times. The art of *espalier* (training plants flat against a wall or fence) was also practiced. During the Renaissance, plant materials were often grown because they could be used as

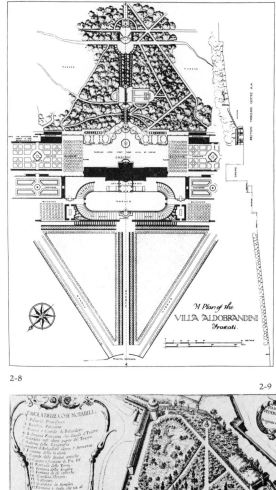

2-8

2-9

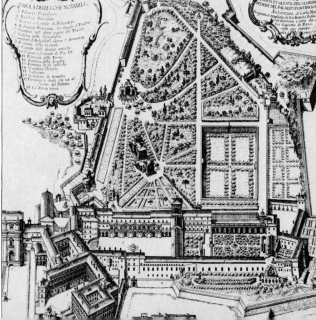

2-10

sculptured architectural features rather than for their natural beauty.

Often just as important as terracing in Italian gardens were the magnificent arrangements of staircases linking the terraces together. The use of terraces was a way to bring attention to horizontal features of the land as well as to provide effective control of steep hill slopes. When combined with steps, terracing made it possible to develop sites on steep slopes that had in the past often been avoided.

Also important in the gardens of this era was the use of statues and water. Gardens often took on the appearance of museums, with many statues (sometimes excavated from Roman sites) lining the paths and occupying choice locations on the terraces. Spectacular use was made of water, where this was available; in some gardens it rivalled the use of plant materials. Water was used with bold ingenuity at Villa d'Este, and at Villa Aldobrandini, where a torrent of water was directed from a source far up a hill down a long flight of steps.

Although the emphasis in the Italian gardens was on structural features, there is evidence of a desire for unusual plants in some of these gardens as well. Plant collectors were numerous during the Renaissance and a few gardens reflect surprising diversity in plant types. Plant exploration and importation became a fad, with both men and women aspiring for fame through horticultural achievement. As early as the fifteenth century the phrase "green thumb" was used to describe the ability of a person who could successfully grow exotic plants. In 1545 the University of Padua established the first botanic garden in Europe, an indication of the growing interest in plants.

Figure 2-8. *Plan of the Villa Aldobrandini at Frascati, near Rome, built about 1600. A section through the central axis of the grounds is shown at the right edge of the figure. It illustrates the sloping terrain on which the villa is built.*

Figure 2-9. *The gardens of the Vatican in Rome as they appeared in the late seventeenth century. An engraving by Falda.*

Figure 2-10. *Giardino all'Italiana, the Vatican, Rome.*

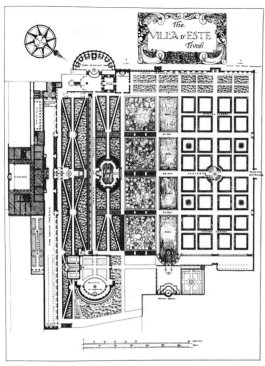

2-11

2-13

2-12

Figure 2-11. *Plan of the Villa d'Este at Tivoli, built about 1550. The villa occupies a slope that descends from left to right. The principal entrance is at the far right. The fountain shown in the next figure, one of many at the villa, is located in the lower left corner of this figure.*

Figure 2-12. *A fountain at the Villa d'Este, Tivoli.*

Figure 2-13. *A fountain in the Borghese Gardens, which date from the early 1600s, in Rome.*

Figure 2-14. *One of many palaces and villas at Lake Garda, in northern Italy. This villa is on the Isle of Garda.*

Figure 2-15. *View across Lake Como, in northern Italy, from a lakeside villa.*

Figure 2-16. *A seventeenth-century garden at Isola Bella, Lake Maggiore, in northern Italy.*

2-14

Although its main purpose was to establish a garden of medicinal herbs, the garden was soon expanded to include other plants introduced through exploration.

France

Elements of the Italian garden style were introduced to France at the turn of the sixteenth century and were applied to isolated formal gardens usually contained within chateau walls. As the spirit of the Renaissance pervaded France, the French began to develop their own distinctive styles. Gardening became an activity in which there was competition for excellence. Summer houses, for which converted corner towers were used, were an important landscape feature, as were man-made grottoes, the design of which became a primary source of competition. Topiary was practiced to a greater extent in French Renaissance gardens than it had been in any other time or place. Trees were planted close together and clipped uniformly to form solid walls of greenery. The time required for topiary and its difficulty are indicative of the importance the French placed on gardening art during this period.

Many French gardens were most spectacular if viewed from slightly above ground level, a fact attributable to, and enhanced by, the concept of the *parterre*—flower beds with paths of gravel or turf arranged in complicated patterns. The parterre was fully developed by French gardeners and the concept flourished during the sixteenth and seventeenth centuries. Initially the pattern of these flower beds had been primarily angular or rectangular, but later various ornate curves became fashionable. Low flowers such as violets, wallflowers, and

2-15

2-16

pintas were used extensively in these flower beds, the corners of which were punctuated with clipped evergreens.

Boxwood was used for edging and for high hedges between different areas of the French garden, or around parterres. The choice of flowers often reflected a desire for continuous bloom. Interest in flowers, particularly exotic flowers, began to spread throughout France.

One characteristic of most French gardens, whether large or small, was a sense of order. Gardens were usually compartmentalized and each part was accessible to the others. On estates, a garden was sometimes divided into one compartment for vegetables, another for the orchard, another for a fountain area, and one for a resting area.

No discussion of French Renaissance gardening would be complete without mention of André Le Nôtre (1613–1700) and his famous garden creations, of which the grounds of Vaux-le-Vicomte and Versailles are best known. Although he did not create a style, he adapted and refined the principles of earlier Renaissance gardeners and developed them, in France, on a grand scale. The gardens at Vaux-le-Vicomte were laid out in 1656–1661 and are considered Le Nôtre's best work. Work on the gardens at Versailles began in 1661 as part of the plan of King Louis XIV to convert his hunting lodge there into the location of the French court. Unaccounted millions were spent on its construction. Since the king wanted an immediate result, large trees had to be located and transported over great distances for the project. One shipment alone consisted of 25,000 trees. The garden was not limited to foliage but utilized water extensively. A total of 1,400

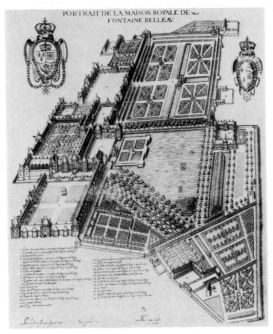

2-17

fountain jets operated at one time. Statuary was displayed extensively, and the grounds also contained the largest zoo of the time. The enormous project employed as many as 36,000 workers at one time and took a quarter of a century to develop. Understandably, Le Nôtre's influence was felt all over France, but certainly it did not stop there, as is evidenced by the work of his students in England, Holland, Austria, Germany, and even Russia.

Figure 2-17. *An example of sixteenth-century landscape design in France: the grounds at Fontainebleau, built by Francis I, show gardens that are enclosed by the wings of buildings or are separated from each other by walls.*

2-18

2-19

Figure 2-18. *Plan for the grounds at Vaux-le-Vicomte, designed by Le Nôtre shortly before he began work on the landscape at Versailles.*

Figure 2-19. *View north across the gardens of Vaux-le-Vicomte toward the chateau.*

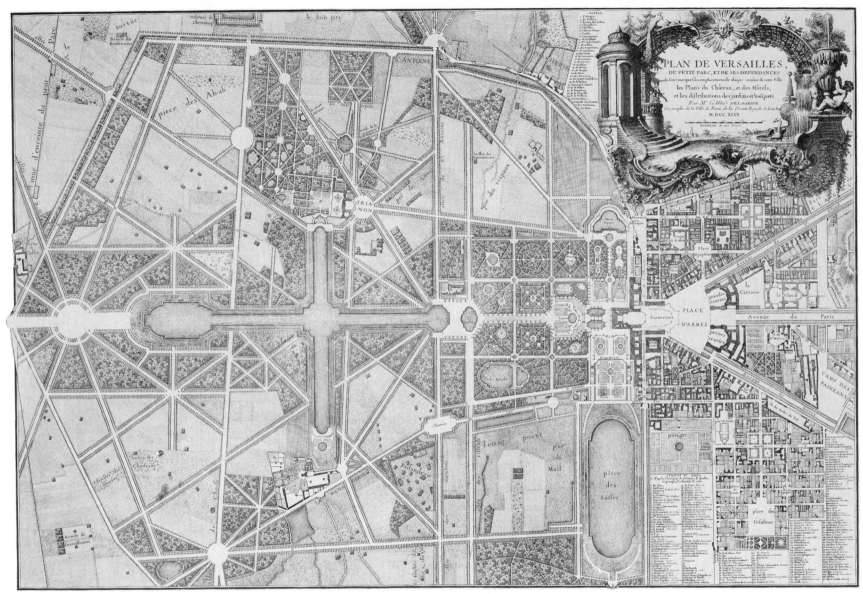

2-20

Figure 2-20. *Plan of Versailles, designed by Le Nôtre, as it appeared in 1746. An engraving by Delagrive.*

Figure 2-21. *Enlarged area of the map shown in the previous figure, showing the gardens adjacent to the facade of the palace at Versailles.*

Figure 2-22. *A view of the parterres du Midi at Versailles; beyond them is the Orangerie.*

Figure 2-23. *Plan of the Orangerie at Versailles.*

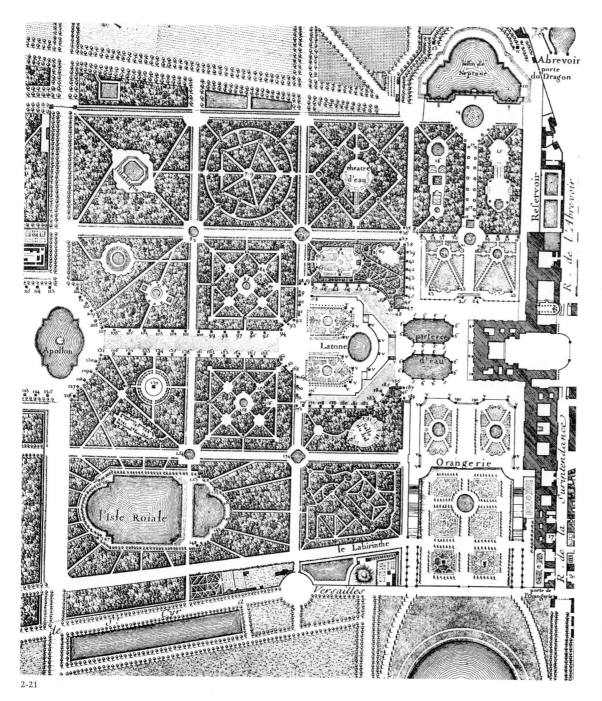

2-21

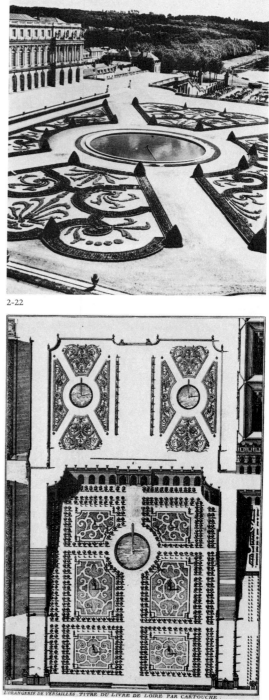

2-22

2-23

England

In England, a new era in gardening began during the Tudor period (1519–1558), following the end of the Wars of the Roses. The peace and stability of the period eliminated the need for barriers and restricted gardens and allowed for garden expansion. Yet, the style of these gardens was slow to change. They began to resemble in character the gardens of France and to some extent those of Italy, but remained rectangular and enclosed. Both ornamental and useful plants had their places in the English gardens of the period, with many flowers being arranged in fancy geometric patterns, around which boxwood or other low-growing plants were set. Clipped evergreens at the corners of these formal beds, arbors formed by trained trees or vines, and a variety of statues, sundials, and other artificial features, all were combined to create very formal garden settings. This formal style changed very little during the reign of Elizabeth I (1558–1603), except that more extensive use was made of topiary, patterned flower beds, and pools and fountains.

The development of a distinctly English style of garden began to evolve about the time of James I (1603–1625), the first ruler of the House of Stuart. The style was still formal and was used mainly by the wealthy. Increased spaciousness characterized the gardens during this period; but this was often accomplished by increasing the width of walkways through the gardens and by decreasing the space allocated to flower beds.

A new interest in exotic plants resulted in the importation of plants from Holland and America. At the same time, English gardeners

Martius, Aprilis, Maius, sunt tempora ueris · | VER Pueritie compar | Vere Venus gaudet florentibus aurea sertis ·

2-24

Figure 2-24. *The busy activity of spading, raking, planting, watering, and pruning, as performed by some sixteenth-century Flemish gardeners. An engraving by Brueghel.*

Figure 2-25. *A formal garden at Eastbury in Dorsetshire, England, designed by the eighteenth-century English landscape planner Charles Bridgeman.*

and botanists explored their own country for new and unusual plants. It is not surprising then that the first English botanical garden—the Hortus Botanicus of Oxford University—was established in the 1620s. Although it contained only five acres, these were used to the fullest: more than 1,600 varieties of plants were displayed in a formal garden, in greenhouses, and in an orangery—a building of stone or brick with a translucent roof that was used to house orange or lemon trees during the winter. In the summer the trees, which were grown in huge boxes, were moved outdoors to decorate the garden paths. Orangeries became a characteristic feature of large English gardens.

Whereas the interest in gardens had always previously been limited to the rich, during the seventeenth century common people began to take an interest in developing what has delightfully come to be known as the cottage garden. Even in the cities, where little or no ground space was available, anyone could express a love for flowers even if the only area available was a colorfully planted window box. The increased interest in gardening produced many books that helped to spread both knowledge and interest even further.

INFORMAL OR NATURALISTIC GARDENS IN ENGLAND

The extreme formalism of the Renaissance did not escape criticism. The emphasis on costly, showy designs in preference to natural beauty was severely attacked by critics first in this period, and more so in the eighteenth century. The criticism was based in part on evidence of the deteriorating quality of the formal gardens

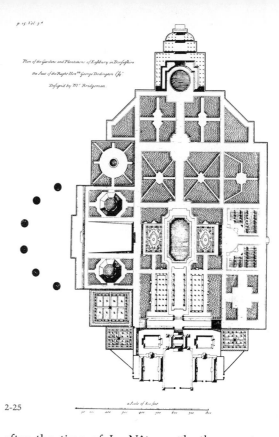

2-25

after the time of Le Nôtre and other master designers. It provides a lesson today to avoid extreme luxury and to provide financially for long-term maintenance in order to avoid deterioration of planting designs and diminished usability of a site. The inability of others to maintain the formal gardens, and a greater freedom in the life style of the people of the eighteenth century, ushered in a new era of naturalistic style. Changes that took place in England provide the best examples of this style.

Although there had earlier been considerable interest in applying "natural" designs to the landscape and some criticism of the formal designs, it was not until about 1720 that the first evidence of a natural style became appar-

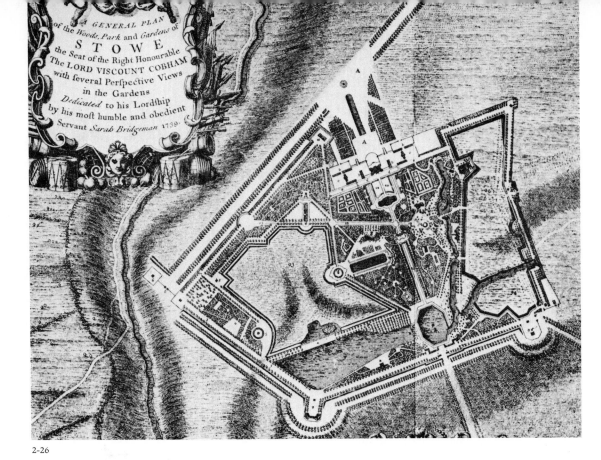

2-26

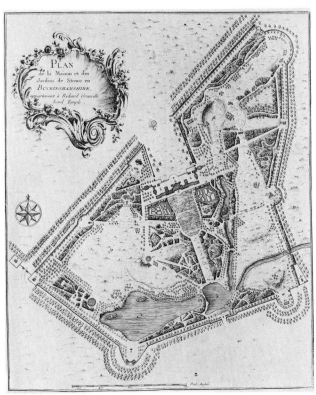

2-27

ent. The earliest attempts resulted in many absurdities, partly because the style of landscape painting was imposed on garden design, with poor results. Temples and "ruins" were often constructed in the middle of an informal garden. For romantic effect dead trees were used in these gardens to represent the decay found in nature. Straight lines and paths became unpopular, for they were considered "contrary to nature." In general, a total lack of order punctuated occasionally with ridiculous garden structures (called "follies") marked this initial period of naturalism.

Not only was the shift towards naturalism

evident in the development of new gardens; many of the finest formal gardens in England were ruthlessly destroyed, to be replaced by naturalistic gardens. Lancelot Brown (1715–1783), nicknamed "Capability" Brown, was one of the well-known designers who participated in this transformation of England's landscape during his career, which extended from 1749 to 1783. Brown designed over 100 gardens. In these, he increased the size of lawns, added belts of trees and shrubbery, and generally reshaped the topography of an area by lowering hillsides, elongating slopes, redirecting streams, and creating lakes.

Figures 2-26, 2-27. *The gardens at Stowe, in Buckinghamshire, England, show the transition of English gardens from formal to informal design: plan showing Stowe as it appeared in 1739, designed by Charles Bridgeman and Henry Wise (2-26); plan showing the gardens at Stowe, as later redesigned by William Kent in an informal style (2-27).*

Figures 2-28, 2-29. *The gardens at Blenheim, near Oxford, England: the gardens as first laid out by Henry Wise and Sir John Vanbrugh (2-28); the gardens as subsequently modified, by "Capability" Brown, for greater informality (2-29).*

Figure 2-30. *The formal gardens at Blenheim.*

Figure 2-31. *Harewood House, in Yorkshire, England, with its formal gardens.*

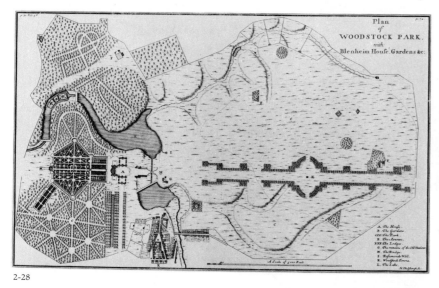

2-28

2-29

2-30

2-31

31

2-32

The naturalistic style received refinement by Sir Humphrey Repton (1752–1818), the first to call himself a landscape gardener. His career began in the 1780s. He moved beyond the simulation of landscape paintings in order to create expansive views in which animal life became a part of the scenery. He was primarily responsible for the English park concept, with broad lawns and meadows and balanced arrangements of trees, which greatly influenced the design of large parks throughout the world.

Oriental garden styles also had an influence on the English naturalistic gardens during the eighteenth century. Europeans impressed by gardens seen during visits to China returned to influence garden design in France and England. Sir William Chambers, who had earlier made a trip to China, was commissioned to design the Royal Botanic Gardens at Kew, for which he proposed some temples of oriental character. His "Dissertation on Oriental Gardening" greatly influenced subsequent garden design and became a classic in its field.

GARDENING IN THE ORIENT

No historical narrative of gardening would be complete without mentioning the unique use

Figure 2-32. *The informal, naturalistic English landscape at Valley Gardens, Windsor, Berkshire.*

Figure 2-33. *Garden of Ritsurin Park, Takamatsu, Japan.*

2-33

larly during the Tang dynasty (618–906 AD) and later during the Ming dynasty (1368–1644), garden art reached its highest development in China.

Religion greatly affected the art of gardening in China. Buddhism emphasizes an appreciation of the natural landscape; a picturesque natural style has dominated Chinese landscape design ever since the advent of Buddhism. Nature was imitated to the extent of creating hills and adding areas of water as early as 200 BC. Generally this would be accomplished by selecting some well-known natural landscape and reproducing it in a miniature scale within the dimensions of a limited area. The various features of the landscape, including trees, herbs, stones, etc., each took on symbolic meaning until the art of gardening became fixed under laws called *Fen-Shoi.* Every plant used in a garden had some specific symbolism—gardens were designed to be looked at, and as an environment for meditation, but not for walking through.

Although gardening was primarily an art of the aristocracy, there were also great public and temple gardens, in which trees were regarded with unusual respect. The reverence for trees was carried to family grave sites, where trees were planted in groves that had great permanence in the Chinese landscape. Frequently, only these sacred groves remain in the tree-stripped landscapes of twentieth century China.

Buddhist missionaries to Japan carried with them ideas of gardening that had developed on the Asiatic continent. Early gardening attempts in Japan were crude, consisting of little more than a pond with an island in imita-

made of plants in the oriental landscape. The gardening style that emerged in China and Japan reflects the intensive population pressures of those countries, and the miniaturization of oriental gardens owing to limited space may be of particular value in guiding the design of twentieth century urban areas where space is also quite limited.

The landscape garden had existed in China since 2600 BC, though at that time the emphasis was on medicinal plants and vegetables. As early as 200 BC, extensive areas of the countryside were allocated for gardens and parks, used chiefly for hunting, often at the expense of agricultural lands. In later centuries, particu-

tion of the Chinese style. Soon, the Japanese love of nature began to make an art of gardening that was distinctly Japanese.

In Japan, as in every culture, various periods of garden style show varying shifts in emphasis. The earliest periods were simple, becoming more substantial during the thirteenth century and reaching a peak in the Muromachi period (1333–1573). Symbolism and the expression of philosophical ideas in the landscape were characteristic elements of gardening up to this time. Later, gardening efforts became more ornamental and superficial.

Plants were important in the Japanese garden, but only after due consideration had been given to architectural features. In choosing plants, considerable attention was given to their unique suitability for achieving a desired effect in replicating nature, as well as to their symbolic meaning. Evergreens were used to a great extent because of their year-round beauty; they were also symbolic of long life. Flowering trees and shrubs were intermingled with the evergreens. But herbaceous flowering plants were not used extensively.

Special treatment of plants included clipping and training trees into various shapes for a particular effect and position in the garden. Similarly, the art of bonsai, which involved the cultivation of dwarf potted trees, was practiced as early as 1000 AD. For this purpose, small seedlings of maple, oak, pine, and cherry were bound and pruned into a carefully chosen shape and trained for many years until they grew gnarled and twisted in forms that looked as natural as those found in full-sized trees growing along a windswept stretch of seashore or on a barren outcropping in the mountains.

34

2-34

2-35

2-36

2-37

2-38

2-39

2-40

2-41

Figure 2-34. *Garden of Ginkakuji Temple, Kyoto, Japan.*

Figure 2-35. *Garden of Rengeji Temple, Kyoto, Japan.*

Figures 2-36 to 2-38. *Sixteenth-century styles of Japanese hill gardens:* shin, *or formal, style (2-36);* gyo,

or intermediate, style (2-37); so, *or informal, style (2-38).*

Figures 2-39 to 2-41. *Sixteenth-century styles of Japanese flat gardens:* shin *style (2-39);* gyo *style (2-40);* so *style (2-41). Figures 2-36–2-41 were published, with notes explaining them, in Jiro Harada's* The Gardens of Japan.

During the evolution of Japanese gardens, many concepts and garden features were developed that have no counterpart anywhere. In the Muromachi period, for example, the flat or dry garden was introduced. This particular garden feature, most vividly portrayed in the flat garden of the Ryoan-ji, a Zen Buddhist temple built circa 1500 at Kyoto, simulated the dried bed of a stream through use of rocks, pebbles, sand, and a few trees or shrubs. Stones took on special significance in such gardens, both for their intrinsic beauty and for their symbolic meaning, or as representations of mountains.

Many attempts have been made to transplant the Japanese garden style into other countries, but with only limited success. So much of the Japanese concept of gardening is entrenched in symbolism and so many of its practices actually follow ancient, strict laws that most efforts at imitation by other cultures fail. Yet, there is little question that this picturesque style has had a great influence on the gardens of other countries, and it is notable that the Japanese garden style has not experienced, during its evolution, the dramatic shifts so typical of other cultures.

LANDSCAPE DEVELOPMENT IN AMERICA

During the early settlement of America, there was very little time for the luxury of gardening, except as it related to the production of food, which could be grown in kitchen gardens. Yet, as early as 50 years after settlement on the East Coast there are records of a number of flowering plants that could only have come from Europe, such as hollyhocks and gilly flowers

35

(pinks), as well as barberry and roses. These familiar plants were obviously brought to the New World by the early colonists.

The attitude towards ornamental gardening in the United States as late as the middle of the nineteenth century was less than enthusiastic in many states. This is not very surprising when one reflects on the quality of life on the still unsettled frontier. Generally, cultural refinements such as landscaping receive scant attention when habitation on the land itself is uncertain and are developed only after the land has been conquered and people acquire leisure time and financial resources.

Eighteenth Century

Behind the frontier, along the Eastern Seaboard, colonial gardens were either quite formal, with boxwood-bordered geometrical plantings, or were without form, with plants growing freely. The average garden was modest and utilitarian, containing many fruit trees, vegetables, and herbs. A few ornamental plants such as lilacs, roses, lilies, tulips, hollyhocks, and some other annuals were used to a limited extent. However, there were also a number of carefully planted estates throughout the colonies during the eighteenth century, the gardens of which displayed a European flavor. The prevailing style of these estate gardens, both in the North and the South, was the formal patterned style of the English gardens. These are probably best represented today at Williamsburg, once the capital of colonial Virginia, where the gardens of the era have been re-created. Spanish influence was experienced in the Southwest and along the Pacific Coast.

The interest in horticulture and gardening during the eighteenth century led to the establishment of several plant collections, which ultimately became botanic gardens. One of the most notable was established near Philadelphia by John Bartram in 1728. Bartram made extensive collecting trips through the colonies and exchanged seeds and plant parts with his European counterparts. Initially, more plants were taken back to Europe than were brought to America. A number of nurseries were also established during this period; most concentrated on the growing of fruit trees. A few offered extensive collections of both native and foreign trees, shrubs, and flowering plants. The first commercial nursery was founded by Robert Prince in Flushing, New York, in 1737. Although fruit trees were the Prince family's primary stock, their catalogue in the later years of the century included such trees as smoke tree (*Cotinus coggygria*), goldenchain tree (*Laburnum anagyroides*), rose of Sharon (*Hibiscus syriacus*), Lombardy poplar (*Populus nigra* 'Italica') and common snowball (*Viburnum opulus* 'Sterile').

Nineteenth Century

The increased growth and prosperity in the United States during the nineteenth century resulted in the development of many beautiful gardens and fine parks. In the course of the century, landscape architecture became firmly established, and the value of the services of landscape architects became recognized. European design still exerted the greatest influence on the style of gardens, which sometimes exhibited a combination of the formal gardens of

2-42

2-43

2-44

Figures 2-42, 2-43. *Re-creations of eighteenth-century American gardens: the formal garden of Elkanah Deane, Irish coachmaker, in Colonial Williamsburg, Virginia (2-42); north half of the re-created formal garden of Alexander Craig, in Colonial Williamsburg, Virginia (2-43).*

Figure 2-44. *The gardens of Dumbarton Oaks in Washington, D.C., which were designed during the 1920s by Beatrix Farrand, one of the founding members of the American Society of Landscape Architects, organized in 1899.*

the Renaissance and the natural style of English gardens. It was the landscape designer Andrew Jackson Downing (1815–1852) who introduced the naturalistic style to the United States through his writings and his work in the second quarter of the nineteenth century.

Horticulture began to emerge from agriculture as people spent more time in gardening and took greater interest in it. Where there was wealth, interest in the art of gardening gave birth to a number of nurseries that catered to those interests. Usually this required a large stock of trees and shrubs, among which were many interesting new plants introduced from Asia or elsewhere. A number of botanical gardens and arboreta were established during the early part of the century, the most famous of which is the Longwood Gardens at Kennett Square, Pennsylvania, not far from Philadelphia. The gardens were established circa 1800 and were developed by Pierre Samuel du Pont. They were made public in 1921 and are still considered to be among the finest gardens in the country.

During the latter part of the century, plant exploration and collection increased in importance. Many species and varieties that had been introduced first into Europe found their way into America, but some collectors, such as George R. Hall, M.D. (1820–1899) and Professor Charles S. Sargent (1841–1927), introduced many new plants directly from Asia into America. Some of their introductions will be discussed in Chapter 6. Professor Sargent was the first Director of the Arnold Arboretum, which was established in 1872. Today the Arnold Arboretum contains over 6,000 species, varieties, and selections of ornamental trees and

37

shrubs. It is administered by Harvard University and is located at Jamaica Plain, Massachusetts, near Boston.

The development of parks in the United States signaled a transition, before which the work of a landscape planner was restricted mainly to small-scale residential gardens, and after which a larger landscape garden-style developed. Central Park, designed in 1858 by Frederick Law Olmsted, Sr. and Calvert Vaux, was the forerunner of the latter, and many were to follow. Some of the outstanding large public parks of this period include Prospect Park, Brooklyn (1866); Franklin Park, Boston (1886); Fairmount Park, Philadelphia (1855); Forest Park, St. Louis (1904); but there were many others, too. Even private residential landscapes were designed in large scale during this period for those who could afford them, at many estates on Long Island and along the Hudson River near New York, on Massachusetts Bay near Boston, at Lake Forest north of Chicago, and in many other places around the nation. These, of course, were a reflection of the wealth of their owners, who, like the ancient Romans, chose to move away from cities to more spacious suburbs. Some, like H. H. Hunnewell of Wellesley, Massachusetts, were also responsible for introducing many new plants to cultivation in the United States. Hunnewell introduced many plants from Europe during the third quarter of the century.

Frederick Law Olmsted, Sr. (1822–1903), is considered the father of landscape architecture since he was the first to use the title "Landscape Architect" in May, 1863, in conjunction with the work he and Vaux did at Central Park. His practice included a considerable number of

2-45

public rather than private clients, and large-scale design dominated his works. Notably, in planning his public parks, not only did Olmsted take care that plant materials and land forms were used to their best advantage, but that the needs of people using the parks were served well also.

Early in the nineteenth century, a number of horticulture and landscape societies were established, including the New York Horticultural Society in 1818, the Pennsylvania Horticultural Society in 1827, and the Massachusetts Horticultural Society in 1829. Later in the century, the American Society of Landscape Architects (1899) and the American Institute of Park

Figure 2-45. *Frederick Law Olmsted, Sr., "Landscape Architect."*

Executives (1898) were founded. In this period, also, a number of gardening magazines and books were being published, indicating that an interest in gardening, horticulture, and landscaping was increasing. However, most of the publications that were not supported by a society were not profitable; many journals had a short life and ceased publication within a few years. Flower shows also came into existence with the beginnings of horticultural societies such as those just mentioned. The first was held in 1829 in Philadelphia, sponsored by the Pennsylvania Horticultural Society.

Another important development during this century was the initiation of the State Agricultural Experiment Stations, which began testing new plants as well as defining their cultural requirements. Plant breeding had been developed in England in the eighteenth century but it wasn't until the nineteenth century that hybridization of ornamental plants was enthusiastically pursued by both professionals and amateurs. Although most of the newly hybridized ornamentals were developed in Europe, some notable exceptions were those American hybrids developed by Luther Burbank, who successfully bred superior lilies, poppies, clematis, shasta daisy, and coleus.

Design styles used in the United States today can be traced not only through the gardens of the eighteenth and nineteenth centuries in this country, but through the entire development of civilization, from ancient to modern times. Many periods of man's development have yielded design concepts and gardening practices that influence today's landscape design and horticulture practices. A designer of landscapes today may choose to use either a formal or a naturalistic style, depending upon such factors as the style of architecture at the site, limitations or opportunities of the site itself, and the desires of the client. Whatever the choice, the result is bound to reflect some of the influence of the past at the same time that it contributes to future landscape development.

FOR FURTHER READING

Berrall, J. S., 1966. *The Garden: An Illustrated History.* New York: Viking Press.

Clifford, D. P., 1963. *A History of Garden Design.* New York: Praeger. Revised edition, 1966.

Manks, D. S. (editor), 1967. *Origins of American Horticulture: A Handbook.* Brooklyn: Brooklyn Botanic Garden. Special edition of *Plants and Gardens*, Vol. 23, No. 3.

Newton, N. T., 1971. *Design on the Land: The Development of Landscape Architecture.* Cambridge (Mass.): Belknap Press.

Tobey, G. B., Jr., 1973. *A History of Landscape Architecture: The Relationship of People to Environment.* New York: American Elsevier.

3

The Landscape Industry

The landscape industry in the United States today depends upon the work done primarily by three kinds of skilled professionals: the landscape architect or designer, the landscape contractor, and the landscape maintenance supervisor. Because this book is concerned principally with plant material in the landscape, the role of a fourth participant in the industry, the nurseryman, will also be considered. The channels of communication between each of these professions should be well established and should remain open. The schematic diagram at Figure 3-1 shows those relationships.

The heavy arrows represent communication channels of prime importance. Sometimes these channels are not developed properly, however. Notice that ideally a strong relationship should link the landscape architect or designer and the landscape maintenance supervisor. But often the landscape maintenance supervisor is not hired when the project is

designed, or worse, the client may not understand that the maintenance supervisor should be part of the team. The light lines represent lines of communication less important but still vital to successful overall development of the landscape.

In describing the role of each member of the landscape industry generally, and in discussing their relationships, it should be pointed out here that frequently one man or firm may serve in one or more of the roles; i.e., a landscape contractor may operate his own nursery and may also employ a maintenance crew. Additionally, he may have as an employee a landscape architect or designer who will prepare plans for clientele.

Just as the development and subsequent management or maintenance of the landscape and its plant materials are all dependent on the team effort of the landscape architect, the landscape contractor, the landscape mainte-

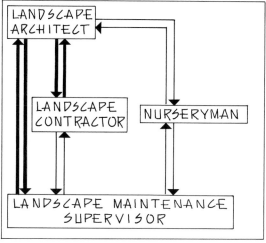

3-1

Figure 3-1. *Landscape architect, landscape contractor, landscape maintenance supervisor, and nurseryman all need to work together. The importance of communication between them is shown in this diagram and is discussed in this chapter.*

nance supervisor, and the nurseryman, each member of the team has a key role to play in the development of the landscape and, if the service performed by any one of the team is not satisfactory, the entire project suffers or may even fail completely. It is useful, therefore, to define the service provided by each team member and to demonstrate how the work each person does must interlock to achieve complete success in the development of the landscape.

THE LANDSCAPE ARCHITECT
OR THE LANDSCAPE DESIGNER

The landscape architect or designer is the planner on the team. It is unfortunate that so many people persist in a limited view of the profession and assume that it amounts to little more than arranging plant materials. The true role of the architect or designer may be best defined by describing what landscape architecture is, as John B. Frazier and Richard J. Julin do in their book, *Your Future in Landscape Architecture.* Notice that they say nothing directly, in the quotation used here, about "arranging plant materials."

> Landscape architecture is a profession that deals with the wide planning and sensitive design of land areas. It is the ability to not only change the very scene, but the mood of an environment, whether it be a city slum, suburban wooded or hillside area, undeveloped countryside, rolling prairie, or bottomland.*

*Frazier, J. B., and R. J. Julin, 1967. *Your Future in Landscape Architecture.* New York: Rosen Press. Page 15.

Landscape architecture then is a profession that deals with the aesthetic qualities of man's physical environment; to serve it adequately, the landscape architect must do more than deposit a few plants around a building. He must be concerned with the integration of a building and its immediate surroundings, which include facilities such as walks, roads, and parking areas, as well as elements that screen or enclose, expand, or enhance an area. Walls, fences, fountains, pools—and of course, plantings—are a few of the elements that contribute to an aesthetically pleasing environment. At the same time the landscape architect must maintain the efficient use of the building and its surrounding landscape. He is concerned—in short—with the planning of the *total* environment.

From this description it is apparent that what a landscape architect sells, when he has been engaged by a client, is really a *service,* that of advising the client about plans that can improve the client's environment. Therefore, he is a consultant. In practice, the landscape architect must always represent the best interests of his client and should be receptive to the needs of a client. If he owns a nursery or supplies plants for his landscape projects, he may become biased in his recommendations of what products to purchase or what plant materials to use on a particular project. A high level of professional integrity is one of the stipulations for membership in the American Society of Landscape Architects.

What is included in the landscape architect's professional planning service? As in all professions, a degree of specialization exists in landscape architecture. The services that a landscape architect may be called on to perform are so complex and varied that it is nearly impossible for one person to carry out in detail the planning phases of, for example, an entirely new community or the redevelopment of downtown urban areas. So it is useful for us to make the same distinction between "generalists" and "specialists" that many large landscape firms make. The overall planner on such a staff has been described as a generalist. He develops a master plan of the project. When an overall desirable effect has been described, the generalist's staff, or specialists in specific areas of landscape design will prepare the detailed plans and requirements for the completion of the project. The overall or master planner must be capable of selling his philosophy and the plan he prepares from it to his clientele, whether this be a city council, a school board, a large corporation, a housing developer, or the owner of a single residence. Often he must be able to communicate his recommendations to the public (who may be asked to pay for them) as well as to individual clients.

Such factors as soil types, drainage patterns, traffic flow (both vehicular and pedestrian), placement of structures (and in some instances designs of uninhabited structures), walks, roadways, swimming pools, and many others influence the preparation of the overall master plan and the detailed plans of a landscape site. So the landscape architect must be able to describe and often illustrate in some detail how a specific portion of the overall construction project must be carried out. He or the generalist on his staff will delegate to landscape architects who are specialists the job of preparing the detailed planning of each phase of the overall project.

When a specialist prepares the planting specifications for a design he identifies the plant materials and the planting techniques to be used. These specifications are his first communication with the landscape contractor. After contractors have been invited to examine the project they may want to discuss certain phases of it with the landscape architect before submitting a bid. After he opens their bids, the landscape architect may want to interview the bidders to determine that the bids are honest and realistic. He may then want to advise his client in making the decision as to which contractor to select (the lowest bid should not invariably be the controlling factor in awarding a contract—it is more important that the landscape architect have confidence in the contractor he recommends to his client). He may also want to suggest plant sources if doing so will insure that the plant material will meet the specifications fully.

The landscape architect should inspect the site after plant installation to insure that the work has been done according to his specifications. He may want also to consult with maintenance personnel at this time to insure that the maintenance sustains the plant materials in good health and that the maintenance personnel can implement practices that will not destroy the integrity of the design.

In serving as the consultant on the landscape team, the landscape architect sells a service to his client much as an attorney represents a client. It is the landscape architect's responsibility to insure that all other members of the landscape team perform within the specifications that he has prepared and that the client has accepted. In this way the landscape architect protects his client's interests even after he submits the landscape design.

Overview of the Profession
HISTORY AND SCOPE

Considering how many gardens have been created during human history and how many landscapes have been laid out with plantings, it seems surprising that the term "landscape architect" is only little more than a century old: it was first used by Frederick Law Olmsted in 1863 to describe his activity in land planning. Few would deny that Olmsted ought to be considered the father of the term by virtue of his talents and the excellence of his work. Since Olmsted's day the profession has retained his identification of it and there are today several thousand practitioners using the title "landscape architect" to describe their work.

The scope of the profession ranges from planning residential sites to the analysis, evaluation, and planning of areas spreading over thousands of acres, projects for which such names as "regional planning," "land-use planning," "natural resource analysis," etc., are appropriate. In between come such projects as the design of urban neighborhoods, schools and college campuses, church grounds, parks and recreation areas, subdivisions, housing developments, shopping centers, industrial parks, etc. Besides devising planting plans, landscape architects also provide such services as the preparation of master plans, feasibility studies, cost estimates, detailed site plans, grading plans, drainage plans, and specifications and details of the construction of walls, fences, walks, paving, fountains, outdoor benches, play equipment, lighting, sprinkling systems, etc.

EDUCATION

From four to five years of college training is generally required of those who intend to become landscape architects. In rare instances it is possible to acquire the skills in an apprenticeship arrangement. We think that one is not fully prepared to practice on his own until he has undertaken an additional period of internship following graduation.

In selecting a school offering a curriculum in landscape architecture, one should consult the listing of schools accredited by the Board of Landscape Architectural Accreditation, an agency of the National Commission on Accrediting. This list is distributed by the American Society of Landscape Architects.

CAREER OPPORTUNITIES

There are many diverse opportunities for those who are interested in design and planning. These range from employment as a designer for a local nurseryman to private practice either on one's own or as part of someone else's firm. There are several private firms in every major city; the yellow pages of a telephone book will offer the quickest means of counting and comparing the firms in any city. Opportunities are available also with city, county, and state governments and in several agencies of the federal government, through the U.S. Civil Service Commission.

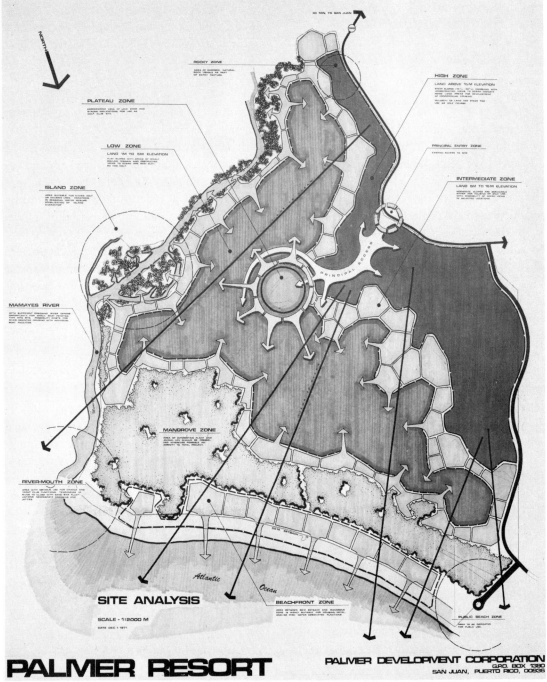

SITE ANALYSIS

SCALE - 1:2000 M

DATE DEC 1 1971

PALMER RESORT

PALMER DEVELOPMENT CORPORATION
G.P.O. BOX 1380
SAN JUAN, PUERTO RICO, 00936

3-2

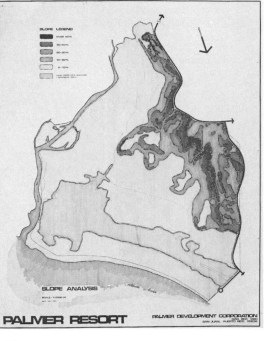

SLOPE ANALYSIS

SCALE - 1:2000 M

PALMER RESORT

PALMER DEVELOPMENT CORPORATION
G.P.O. BOX 1380
SAN JUAN, PUERTO RICO, 00936

3-3

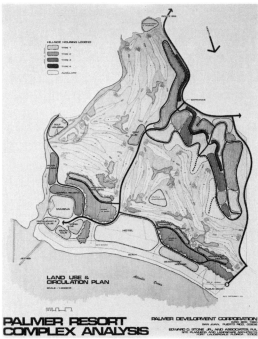

LAND USE &
CIRCULATION PLAN

PALMER RESORT
COMPLEX ANALYSIS

PALMER DEVELOPMENT CORPORATION
G.P.O. BOX 1380
SAN JUAN, PUERTO RICO, 00936
EDWARD D. STONE JR. AND ASSOCIATES, P.A.
SITE PLANNERS AND LANDSCAPE ARCHITECTS
FORT LAUDERDALE, FLORIDA 33301

3-4

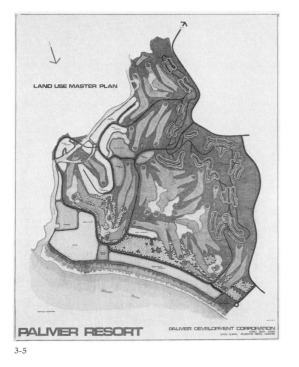

LAND USE MASTER PLAN

PALMER RESORT

PALMER DEVELOPMENT CORPORATION
G.P.O. BOX 1380
SAN JUAN, PUERTO RICO, 00936

3-5

SECTION A - A'

GOLF CLUB DEVELOPMENT

PALMER RESORT

PALMER DEVELOPMENT CORPORATION
G.P.O. BOX 1380
SAN JUAN, PUERTO RICO, 00936

3-6

Figures 3-2 to 3-5. *Drawings made for presentation to a client, showing a site analysis (3-2), a slope analysis (3-3), a land use and circulation plan (3-4), and a land use master plan (3-5), for a resort in Puerto Rico designed by Edward D. Stone, Jr., and Associates, Landscape Architects. Drawings such as these help the client to understand the methodology used by a landscape architect to solve design problems.*

Figure 3-6. *An enlarged plan for the golf club development of the resort project illustrated in Figure 3-5. The section in the upper left corner shows the slope of the terrain from the parking lot to the golf course (lower right corner of drawing). Edward D. Stone, Jr., and Associates, Landscape Architects.*

In recent years the interest in improving the quality of man's environment has meant that the demand for landscape architects has increased. Job openings have exceeded the ability of schools to produce the graduates to meet that demand.

REGISTRATION

A majority of states within the United States now require that landscape architects be registered or licensed before they can offer their services to the public. This does not include those who work under another licensed landscape architect as an apprentice or permanent employee. Registration is a relatively recent requirement. It was begun in California in 1953.

One reason for registration is the need for consumer protection. In some states all professionals who are registered as "landscape architects" must promise to adhere to minimum standards of work that are designed to promote safety and health. But registration varies from state to state, as do the titles that may be used. Reference will be made in some later chapters to "designer" when a discussion pertains to both those who may not have degrees in landscape architecture or who may not be licensed (the law allows them to call themselves "designers") and those who are landscape architects.

To qualify for a license requires taking an examination. Most states administer a uniform examination prepared by the Council of Landscape Architectural Registration Boards. The areas of coverage and time allowed are as follows: (1) history and theory of landscape architecture, 2 hours; (2) professional administration, 2 hours; (3) landscape construction, 10 hours; (4) planting design and plant mate-

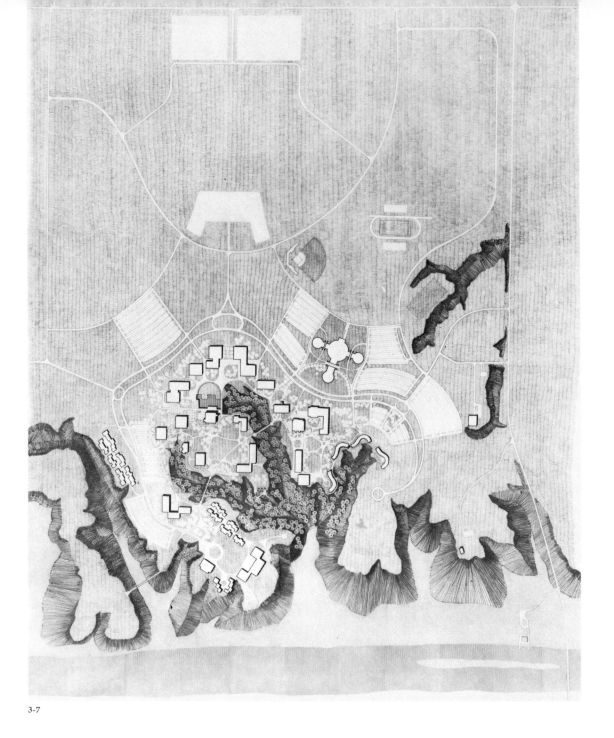

3-7

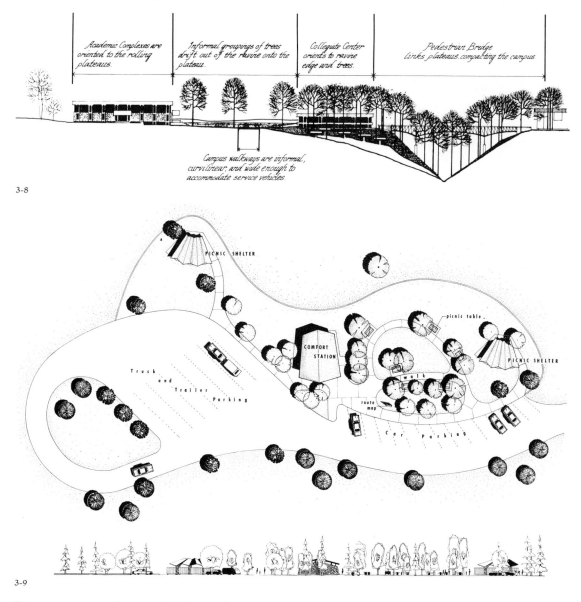

Academic Complexes are oriented to the rolling plateaus.

Informal groupings of trees drift out of the ravine onto the plateau.

Collegiate Center orients to ravine edge and trees.

Pedestrian Bridge links plateaus, compacting the campus.

Campus walkways are informal, curvilinear, and wide enough to accommodate service vehicles.

3-8

PICNIC SHELTER

COMFORT STATION

picnic table

PICNIC SHELTER

Truck and Trailer Parking

walk

route map

Car Parking

3-9

Figures 3-7, 3-8. *A master plan (3-7), and a general cross section (3-8), for Grand Valley State College, Allendale, Michigan, designed to take advantage of deep, natural ravines. Johnson, Johnson, and Roy, Landscape Architects.*

Figure 3-9. *A plan and cross-section for the landscaping of a roadside rest stop proposed by the California Department of Transportation.*

rials, 6 hours; (5) landscape architectural design, 12 hours. Because plant materials vary so widely throughout the United States, knowledge of plant materials is not tested as part of the uniform examination and requirements for background in plant materials are prepared separately by each state.

A current listing of states requiring registration, and the address of the Registration Board in each, can be secured from the Council of Landscape Architectural Registrations Boards, 1750 Old Meadow Road, McLean, Virginia 22101.

PROFESSIONAL ORGANIZATION

By far the largest and most prominent organization representing landscape architects in the United States is the American Society of Landscape Architects, whose headquarters are at 1750 Old Meadow Road, McLean, Virginia 22101. The Society was founded in 1899. It sponsors annual meetings, educational workshops and seminars, and represents landscape architects at various hearings before federal agencies in Washington, D.C. It publishes a monthly newsletter entitled *Land,* the monthly *Bulletin* (which describes Society policies and procedures) and a quarterly magazine, *Landscape Architecture.* The Society also issues a number of other miscellaneous publications.

Additional information about this professional organization and its activities can be obtained by writing to the American Society of Landscape Architects—ASLA—at the address mentioned above.

The ASLA is also a member of the International Federation of Landscape Architects, which has its headquarters in Lisbon, Portugal.

3-10

3-11

Figure 3-10. *A landscape architect may sometimes be called on to design a setting that will seem to have been created by nature, such as this hiking trail through a wooded area of a proposed park in Illinois.*

Figure 3-11. *Concept for proposed recreation facilities. The landscape architect used plants and landscape materials to create a "mood" for the entire area. Maas and Grassli, Landscape Architects.*

3-12

Figure 3-12. *Proposal for using street tree plantings in a downtown redevelopment concept. Sasaki, Dawson, DeMay, Associates, Landscape Architects.*

THE LANDSCAPE CONTRACTOR

The landscape contractor executes the plans of the landscape architect. He must obtain a copy of the landscape plans and specifications and from them determine what materials are needed, what labor is required for their installation, what the overhead will cost, and what profit can be anticipated. He then makes a bid on the landscaping project, and usually, if his is the low bid, he will receive the contract. So long as his calculations are correct and he does not encounter unforeseen plant losses, delays, and other misfortunes, he will make a profit on the job. However, if he makes an error in his cost determinations, or if the plant losses are excessive, he may lose a great amount of money (contracts can range from just a few hundred to many, many thousands of dollars). Likewise, if he always bids high to insure against loss he will not obtain work and hence will not be able to stay in business for long. A successful landscape contractor must be a good businessman, but he must also have an appreciation of landscapes and how plants grow in them.

Overview of Landscape Contracting
HISTORY AND SCOPE

With the shift of gardening from principally small-scale residential gardens to large-scale public and private areas, the landscape contractor came into existence. The opportunity to build the Hanging Gardens of Babylon would make any present-day landscape contractor's mouth water and it is apparent that persons performing duties that might be expected today

PICNIC

CREEK

FOOT BRIDGE

BASKETBALL

TENNIS

BIKES

PARKING

SOFTBALL & TOUCH FOOTBALL

EARTH SCULPTURE & SCREEN

BENCHES & SHELTER

SPRING PADS

SWINGS & CLIMBERS

SAND

FIREPOLE & SLIDE

EARTH SCULPTURE

3-13

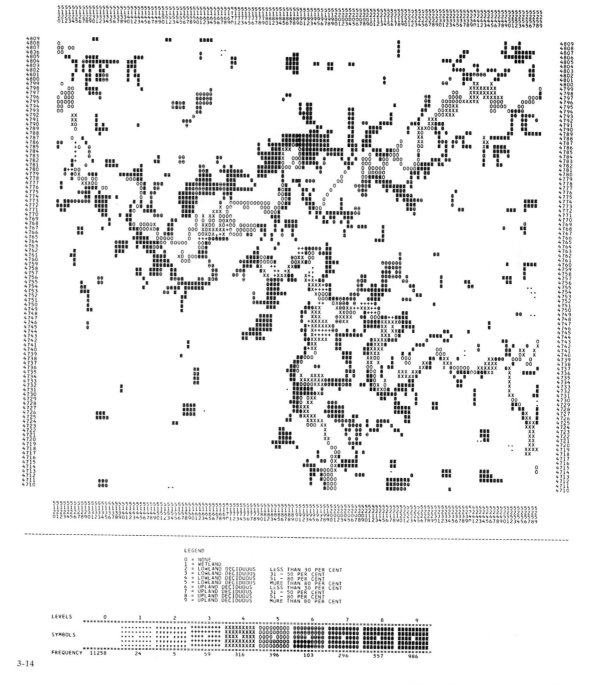

Figure 3-13. *Preliminary master plan proposals for recreation and playground facilities in a condominium development. The use of landscape plants and materials reflects the different uses of each kind of facility. Walker, Harris, Associates, Inc., Landscape Architects.*

Figure 3-14. *Regional planners study many factors of land use in a large land area. This is a computer analysis of vegetation in the east-central section of Tippecanoe County, Indiana.*

3-14

of the landscape contractor must have been present during the construction in Babylon. However, until the early part of the twentieth century most landscape contracting was done by employees of the person whose land was being developed. Landscape contracting firms came into existence in the United States on a large scale after World War II, primarily because of highway construction, suburbanization, and a general increase in the affluence of the public. In the 1960s the increased public attention to problems of environmental quality resulted in the expenditure of more public and private funds for landscape construction in order to provide aesthetically pleasing sites for roads, schools, industrial areas, parks, etc. The landscape construction business boomed during this period and continues to grow.

There is a tremendous range in the size of the business conducted by landscape contractors. A small contractor may operate with only a pickup truck and some small power equipment. For a labor force he may hire one or two people for part-time summer help and do much of the work himself. A large contractor, on the other hand, may have many thousands of dollars invested in equipment suitable for handling materials, and in trucks, power equipment, and so on. His labor force might then number 30 or more full-time, year-round employees; indeed, during the busy season he could expect that the number of employees he would need might increase by a factor of two or three. Of course, firms of varying sizes measure between the small and the large extremes. Every firm is different depending on the aims and needs of the contractor who owns it and of the area he serves.

The installation of plant material at the landscape site is the major function of the contractor. Correct installation is an absolute necessity if the plants are to develop to their fullest potential. Proper techniques of installation will also reduce potential problems of maintenance that could become real problems in the future. The most successful contractors give an extreme amount of attention to the details of plant installation, for it is their business to see that a satisfactory environment is established for continued plant growth. Such men will have nothing to do with the fly-by-night contractors who dig holes in the ground, put the plant in the hole, and hope it survives until their guarantee has expired. The good contractor will be able to exhibit his work with pride many years after installation; more immediately, he will be able to show it to prospective clients as evidence of the reliability of his work.

The landscape contractor, though primarily concerned with the installation of plant material, often has other obligations to his client. He may be responsible for the installation of irrigation systems, walks, patios, driveways, etc. This may require him to deal with subcontractors whose work he will have to supervise. In arrangements such as this he will be held responsible by his client for the quality of work of the subcontractor and therefore should know his subcontractors and the quality of their work before using them.

THE CONTRACTOR'S RELATIONSHIP TO OTHERS IN THE INDUSTRY

The contractor's most important relationship is direct communication with the landscape architect. This channel for communication

3-15

3-16

3-17

Figure 3-15. *The landscape contractor is responsible for site preparation, including the addition of fill soil and earth contouring. These preparations make possible the landscape shown, finished, in Figure 3-27.*

Figure 3-16. *Establishing initial grades and even slopes for water ways may also be the responsibility of the landscape contractor.*

Figure 3-17. *After grades have been established, the landscape contractor prepares a site for seeding or laying of turf.*

Figure 3-18. *Laying sod permits the landscape contractor to provide turf nearly instantaneously.*

3-18

many times is not as open as could be desired, so this is not always easy. The landscape contractor works at a definite disadvantage if he cannot or will not discuss the design and specifications for a project with the landscape architect. Being the consultant to his client, to serve the client properly the landscape architect must communicate the client's desires to the contractor who is to execute the plans that were prepared. Likewise, to serve the landscape architect properly, the contractor must discuss any problem or foreseeable difficulty with him. It is imperative that if the contractor has reservations about some aspect of the plans, he make his feelings known to the landscape architect *before* preparing his bid. Changes in the plans can be made after bids have been invited if there is time to notify all the invited bidders of the changes. But it is not ethical on the part of either the contracting authority or the contractor to let or obtain a contract and then attempt to change the design or specifications. Therefore most contracting authorities will not permit changes after the contract is let; the contractor must stand the loss if he cannot complete the project as specified.

Communication works in two directions, and another reason for good dialogue between contractor and landscape architect is that the landscape architect will learn some of the problems that may beset contractors and others in the industry; in future projects the landscape architect can avoid or ameliorate some of these problems. Many landscape architects hire experienced contractors as consultants in the hope that shared knowledge will lead to a lessening of difficulties.

The contractor must know his plant-material suppliers (nurserymen) well, too. He depends on the nurseryman to have the plant material required in the specified sizes and quantities. Delivery must be made at the proper time so as not to delay the installation of the landscape project. Delays can strain the relationship that ought to develop between the *general* contractor—who is responsible for the total project, including buildings and the site work (and who may find plant materials a nuisance to begin with)—and the *landscape* contractor. Unauthorized substitutions of plant material by a nurseryman or a landscape contractor will cause delays in completing the project. The landscape contractor must be able to communicate his needs and his schedules to a reliable nurseryman.

Except for rare instances the contractor will have little contact with landscape maintenance personnel. It is always helpful if the contractor supplies the landscape maintenance supervisor with special or unusual information about maintenance that can help during the period when new planted plants are being established. But sometimes the contractor himself must provide the required maintenance for a period of up to one year before turning the project over to the owner (or to the owner's maintenance people).

In summary, the landscape contractor executes the plans of the landscape architect. Toward this end he depends on good dialogue between himself and the landscape architect in order to complete the installation of plants and the development of the landscape site according to the architect's plans. He is a businessman who must understand how plants grow and what environmental factors must be present at the landscape site so that each plant he installs will develop in the way that is best and most natural for it.

EDUCATION

There is no commonly agreed upon formal education program for landscape contractors, and the amount of formal education varies among contractors. But formal training would be of great benefit to those who have no prior experience either in a family business or in work for another contractor. Both two- and four-year programs are offered by many junior colleges and universities; most of these programs are directly associated with horticulture or plant science departments. In general, the student should build a good background in woody plant materials, landscape construction, and horticulture methods for growing woody plants, and the stronger his background the better. Strong business-management background is of prime importance too.

Once the student has completed formal study he should, if possible, work for an established contractor for a few years to gain practical knowledge of the business. It will be easier to build a sound landscape-contracting business if one has had this practical experience.

NATIONAL ORGANIZATIONS

There are several organizations to which a landscape contractor may choose to belong. On a national scale are the Associated Landscape Contractors of America, 1750 Old Meadow Rd., McLean, Virginia 22101; and the National Landscape Association, 230 Southern Building, Washington, D.C. 20005.

Unlike the ASLA, these organizations do not have restrictive membership requirements. Instead, they have as their general, main requirement that members be landscape contractors with honest business reputations. Annual meetings are held; the emphasis at these is on education in landscape contracting matters that can be passed on to members. Business management and construction techniques are the subjects most frequently covered. Sometimes educational seminars are held separately from the annual meetings.

Many landscape contractors belong also to local and state organizations. Furthermore, many state and local nursery associations welcome landscape contractors as members.

EMPLOYMENT OPPORTUNITIES

With the continued interest in environmental improvement through active landscaping programs, employment opportunities are numerous for those interested in landscape contracting. Jobs exist throughout the business; the work ranges from being a crew chief to owning your own business and is limited only when an individual's ambition and foresight are limited.

THE LANDSCAPE MAINTENANCE SUPERVISOR

The final effectiveness of a landscape design rests in the hands of the landscape maintenance supervisor, for he will determine by his maintenance whether the design features the landscape architect desired will be achieved. He also controls to a great extent the future growth and development of plant material after it has been grown by the nurseryman and installed by the landscape contractor. Poor maintenance practices even for a short period of time can destroy much of the beauty of the plant material at a landscape site. Improper pruning is a prime example of how a plant's usefulness in the landscape may be completely destroyed inadvertently. And thoughtless replacement of one species with a different species might alter or perhaps drastically change the design. The necessity of minimizing environmental damage makes the correct use of pesticides extremely important. All things considered, maintaining landscaped areas requires the efforts of a trained professional.

Overview of Landscape Maintenance
HISTORY

When people plant gardens, they also have to care for them, so landscape maintenance has been in existence for as long as man has been gardening. However, of the special occupations within the landscape industry, landscape maintenance has been the last to develop into a full-fledged profession. A partial reason for this may be that in the past the owners of many estates hired private gardeners to maintain landscaped areas, of which there were fewer than there are today. Nurseries have often had, and continue to have, landscape maintenance crews that contract for small maintenance jobs. On a larger scale, arborists (tree maintenance firms) have been active for several generations in this country. Recently some arborists have undertaken maintenance of total landscape projects.

Considering the increased interest in landscaping that dates from the 1960s, it seems only logical that interest in maintenance should

3-28

3-29

3-30

also increase. Unfortunately, the fate of many projects landscaped then shows that the public was unaware that the well-landscaped site must also be well maintained to continue to be aesthetically pleasing. Since then, to try to close the gap between good intentions and good results, firms have been established that specialize in landscape management; maintenance budgets are increasing; and more attention is being given to obtaining qualified personnel to carry out the management required for a site. Also, consulting firms have been organized that develop programs of maintenance for specific sites and provide a source of information for the landscape maintenance supervisor.

SCOPE

The responsibilities of the landscape maintenance supervisor and his personnel may vary from mowing turf to cleaning swimming pools and removing snow, as well as maintaining healthy, vigorous plant material (which is the most significant duty). It may be necessary to repair a parking lot surface one day and prune a hedge the next.

The physical requirements for the growth and development of the plants in the landscape which must be met by the landscape maintenance supervisor include providing irrigation water as needed, fertilizing, and pruning. The water needs of landscape plants require the supervisor to have a knowledge of irrigation systems and their operation. He must also know when to apply water and how much to apply. A thorough understanding of soils and their moisture-holding capacity is necessary since this influences what watering techniques should be used.

Figure 3-28. *A well-landscaped residential lot must also be well maintained. These birches form a focal point in a design that has also been maintained with care.*

Figure 3-29. *Turf care is often a major part of the maintenance program at many landscape sites.*

Figure 3-30. *A view of Constitution Plaza, Hartford, Connecticut. Landscape maintenance here entails caring for plants in containers, pools, large paved areas, etc.*

Fertilizing trees and shrubs is no longer a simple process. There are many different fertilizer materials on the market. For example, materials that release nitrogen slowly are valuable for use on turf but their effectiveness for trees and shrubs has not been entirely proven. The timing of fertilizer applications is critical and this varies greatly with the plant species as well as with the climatic section of the country. Also, trying to establish plant material in other than its natural soil environment often requires the application of minor elements to the soil—for example, addition of iron around pin oaks (*Quercus palustris*) in the alkaline (high-*p*H) soils of the Midwest.

Pruning is another requirement for maintaining healthy, vigorous plant material in the landscape. Seldom is pruning properly carried out by people who are ignorant of pruning techniques. In their hands the plant may be permanently ruined. But correct pruning will increase the useful life of the plant material, so it is essential that a landscape supervisor train his employees and supervise the pruning operations.

Pest control has become a specific science. Use of the correct pesticide materials at the proper rates is essential. After all, it is not necessary to saturate the countryside with it; it is only the plant material that needs protection from specific pests. Labels must be read correctly and their recommendations followed exactly under penalty of the law. Many pesticides have trade or generic names that sound very much alike. Therefore it is extremely important that a *herbicide* not be substituted for a *fungicide* or *insecticide*. Such errors have occurred. Calibration (a check of the output-rates)

of equipment must be carried out on a regular basis.

The landscape maintenance supervisor must also have a knowledge of the equipment necessary for maintaining the landscape site. This includes the ability to purchase at the least cost the equipment that will do the job right and efficiently. And he must consider the durability (maintenance-needs) of the equipment, as well as the efficiency with which the equipment can complete the work for which it was designed. The equipment needs will vary depending on whether the landscape maintenance supervisor operates his own business or is in charge of a single landscape site, such as the grounds of an industrial site, a park, a small campus, etc. The independent businessman must transport his own equipment, so he is well advised to pick versatile equipment that can be used at many different sites.

Clearly, the landscape maintenance supervisor must be versatile in carrying out these responsibilities. If he is professional, he will be careful to become aware of and make use of the latest developments in landscape maintenance.

THE MAINTENANCE SUPERVISOR'S
RELATIONSHIP TO OTHERS IN THE INDUSTRY

Maintenance has been called the "stepchild of landscaping" by one writer.* Too often maintenance is an afterthought, following the completion of the landscape design and the installation of the plant material. The landscape architect needs to anticipate maintenance

*Gustin, Ray, Jr., 1970. "Maintenance—stepchild of landscaping." *Weeds, Trees and Turf,* 9(8): 16.

3-31

3-32

Figures 3-31, 3-32. *Maintenance of certain large landscape sites may require specialized power equipment. The equipment shown here is designed to remove stumps (3-31) and to convert tree remains to chips (3-32).*

3-33

3-34

3-35

Figures 3-33, 3-34. *Correct pruning and fertilizing of trees and shrubs requires professional skill. These men work for a professional tree-maintenance service.*

Figure 3-35. *It is absolutely essential for the landscape maintenance supervisor to make correct use of pesticides.*

needs. A poor design can make it impossible to maintain plants in optimum condition. Often the landscape architect or, more important, the owner of the site does not consider the maintenance budget. Provision for a satisfactory maintenance budget for future years should be a prime consideration of the landscape architect in his work with his client. This will make it possible for the landscape maintenance supervisor to carry out proper maintenance procedures. Sometimes, either for financial reasons or through failure to understand the needs of landscape maintenance, untrained persons are hired to carry out the maintenance program. The person in charge of building maintenance is rarely if ever qualified to maintain the landscape around that building. It is poor judgment in administration to trust the maintenance of grounds to personnel inadequately trained or lacking in experience.

It is extremely rare for the landscape maintenance supervisor to have direct contact with the landscape architect. The landscape architect could alter this unfortunate situation by suggesting that the client hire a maintenance supervisor during the construction of the landscape project and involve him in the total development of the landscape. The landscape supervisor should be aware of the installation techniques used, as these may be valuable information if problems develop in the growth of the plant material.

The supervisor should have some knowledge of the design since ultimately he may be the only one involved in replacing lost plant material, changing walks, enlarging parking lots, etc. Without contact with the landscape architect and a knowledge of his design objectives, the desired effects of the landscape can be destroyed with improper changes made by the landscape maintenance supervisor.

EDUCATION

There are no commonly agreed on formal educational requirements, but some training should be obtained either in a two-year or four-year program depending on one's goals. The schools offering programs in landscape maintenance are few but they are increasing as the demand for trained personnel increases.

In his plan of study, the landscape-maintenance student should emphasize a knowledge of woody plant materials, entomology, plant pathology, weed control, and horticultural production of woody plants. He must know how plants grow if he is going to manage a landscape site. Business training will also be of benefit even if he works for governmental agencies or other nonprofit organizations.

PROFESSIONAL ORGANIZATIONS

An organization of professional gardeners has been in existence for a long time and just recently it changed its emphasis to extend to all persons who work at landscape maintenance. The name and address of this national organization is: Professional Grounds Management Society, 1750 Old Meadow Road, McLean, Virginia 22101.

In a few larger cities groups have begun to organize in different areas of the country. They are primarily concerned with developing educational programs on landscape maintenance. Also there is a national arborist association that devotes consideration to matters of landscape maintenance.

EMPLOYMENT OPPORTUNITIES

As is true of other areas of the landscape industry, there is great demand for trained, qualified personnel. We suggest that employment be sought first with a firm that maintains several landscape sites, since good practical experience should be obtained before seeking employment where one would be in charge of a site. Prime employers are those who administer public parks, buildings, college campuses, and industrial parks.

In summary, the landscape maintenance supervisor is the "stepchild" of landscaping primarily because of a lack of communication with other members of the landscape industry. It is the obligation of the landscape architect to open the much-needed channels of communication both with the administrative personnel representing the owner of the facility being developed and with the landscape maintenance supervisor.

THE NURSERYMAN

The nurseryman, as the producer of the plant material used in the landscape, is an important member of the landscape industry. Though not one of the three primary members, he does supply the basic raw material used in the design—the plant material. The nurseryman has several obligations to his customers—the landscape contractor and the landscape maintenance supervisor. He is obliged to supply correctly labelled plant materials that are of the size and quality specified by the landscape architect. He should be able to deliver the required plant material within the time limits set by the landscape contractor.

The nurseryman controls the quality of the plant material used by the contractor from the time it is propagated until it reaches the desired size and is sold. Good-quality plant material requires constant attention before it is sold. A plant may never develop properly if it is kept too long as a liner (small plant) in a pot. A girdling root may form and the plant may actually strangle itself years later. As it grows tighter and tighter around the base of the stem, the root will eventually prevent the development of nutrient- and water-conducting tissues and destroy the plant. The same danger exists for larger container-grown plants that are kept too long in their containers.

Field-grown stock should be root-pruned frequently to develop a good compact root system. Attempts at some Christmas-tree plantations to move six- to eight-foot conifers that were not root-pruned proved to be largely unsuccessful: the purchase of conifers from the plantations thus turned out to be false economy.

Digging the plant and preparing the soil ball for shipping are of prime importance. A properly burlapped and tied soil ball will most likely arrive at the landscape site in good condition. Soil balls that are cracked or damaged will greatly endanger the plant's chances for survival. If a contractor discovers such damage in the plants he purchases from a nurseryman, he will be inclined to want to obtain plant materials from more reliable sources in the future.

The nurseryman supplies the key element —the plant material—used by the landscape architect. His role in the landscape industry is to provide good-quality plant material that meets the specifications of the landscape designer, at the time the contractor wants the material on the site.

SUMMARY

The full development of any landscape site requires a team approach by all the members of the landscape industry—the landscape architect, the landscape contractor, the maintenance supervisor, and the nurseryman. Each of these members of the team is concerned with the growth and development of the plant material used in the landscape project.

The remaining chapters of this book will deal with how such plants are used and maintained in the landscape. Chapters 10, 11, and 12 contain discussions of some of the business procedures used by landscape architects and landscape contractors. Then, in Chapter 16, recommendations are made about the business of maintaining the landscape.

FOR FURTHER READING

Frazier, J. B., and R. J. Julin, 1967. *Your Future in Landscape Architecture*. New York: Richard Rosen Press.

Sidney, H., 1969. *Agricultural, Forestry, and Oceanographic Technicians*. Chicago: J. G. Ferguson Publishing Company.

II

Landscape Plants

4

Plant Communities

There is a tendency in the planning and maintenance of landscapes to ignore the ecological relationships of plants and their natural environments. This is extremely unfortunate. The ultimate performance of a plant or group of plants is dependent on the extent to which the ecological requirements are fulfilled. In addition, the aesthetic qualities of landscape plantings are frequently enhanced when plants of the proper associations are grouped together just as they are found in natural communities. This chapter will briefly consider the interrelationships of plants, plant communities, and their natural environments, as well as the impact of man on natural plant communities.

PLANT GEOGRAPHY

Plants dominate the Earth. Over most of the land-surface there exists a layer of plants so complete and continuous that the soil is seldom visible. The only land-surfaces undisturbed by man that do not support plant life are certain high mountainous areas and parts of the desert. This plant cover, or "green mantle," as it is sometimes called, is a dynamic and variable feature of the land. Yet there are certain observable characteristics in any plant-supporting area that suggest a pattern. Further analysis of this pattern leads to certain conclusions that are important in understanding the ecological relationships and requirements of plants in both natural terrain and managed landscape.

What is obvious to anyone who has traveled from one region of the country to another is that the many different kinds of plants are restricted to many different regions and that there is considerable difference in the kinds of plants growing in each region. From these observations, as well as from additional evidence that we will discuss, it can be concluded that the kinds of plants growing in a particular area are related to the environment of that region. Generally the environmental differences that are most descriptive of a region are those of climate and soil. In addition, there is evidence that the migration of plants that occurred in the past still continues and that it greatly influences the type of plants in a region.

It is interesting to consider the significance of the term "migration" in reference to plants. Most plants are stationary in an area, in contrast to animals, which are mobile. Obviously, the migration of plants refers to a kind of plant or group of plants taken collectively. It is during the reproductive stage that migration takes place. The seeds or fruits of most plants are quite "mobile," utilizing such natural forces as wind, water, animals, man, gravity, and even propulsion. Generally the migration distance for a particular seed or fruit is limited to a few hundred feet or a few miles at most, although there may be exceptions. Accumulatively with time, short migrations ultimately extend a plant group over tremendous distances.

Plants in nature produce an excess of seeds each year, and some species produce over a million seeds annually. Yet, all that is needed is for a single seed to germinate and survive in order to maintain a constant population of a species. However, if only one seed were to be distributed by a plant in a year, the chances of that seed germinating and reaching maturity would be remote. Instead, many seeds are distributed and germinate, only to succumb ultimately sometime before maturity. For example, it has been estimated that a mature sugar maple (*Acer saccharum*) lives 350 years and occupies

400 square feet. Approximately 4,000 young trees sprout each year under a tree of this size in the forest, and during the total life of a sugar maple a total of 1,400,000 seedlings might sprout. Only about 70,000 persist into the second year; 1,400 live to be 10 years old; 35 grow into tall saplings that die at about 50 years of age due to the dense shade; two live to be 150–200 years old, and only one survives to become a mature tree. Therefore, in addition to withstanding adversities in climate and soil factors, plants have to live in constant competition with each other and frequently are unable to survive.

Even before plant competition becomes a factor in plant survival, germination of the dispersed seeds must occur. For germination and subsequent survival or establishment to occur, the seed must have a favorable environment. If one observes a bare spot in a lawn or a field, he will soon see a number of different kinds of plants sprouting there, even though the adjacent areas will not contain any of these plants. Obviously the surrounding areas were also seeded, but owing to unfavorable conditions the plants did not germinate there. This pattern is called *discontinuous distribution*.

There are at least two kinds of discontinuity that can be observed. First, very rarely does one kind of plant occupy an area of ground to the complete exclusion of other plants. Even in forests dominated by a single species, various kinds of shrubs and herbaceous understory plants will grow. Generally from 50 to 100 different species of plants will be found sharing an acre of land. Some will be more abundant than others, but no single species will have a monopoly of the space. The other type of discontinuity is the broken range of a particular kind of plant over any expanse of land. Within that expanse, the plant is limited to certain suitable habitats and is absent from other habitats in the same range. The suitability or unsuitability of the habitat may be related to microclimatic factors or to the presence of competing species.

The interaction of the migrating plants with the climatic and soil factors largely determines the kind of plants that grow in an area. The geographic distribution of plants then reveals the natural area or range of such a group of plants. For example, the sugar maple is widely distributed over the eastern United States. The appearance of boundaries indicates that some factor in the environment is limiting the sugar maple or is unfavorable to it, since migration generally does not otherwise have limits. To the east it is limited by a physical boundary, the Atlantic Ocean. The northern boundary indicates that a minimum temperature is the limiting factor, but to the south the lack of a temperature far enough below 40°F to overcome dormancy may be the limiting factor. The western boundary coincides with the beginnings of a region with insufficient rainfall (*Acer saccharum* requires at least 20 inches rainfall annually).

Although the geographic range and distribution of each species is very important, it would be very cumbersome to describe the distribution of each species in this way. This becomes apparent when one realizes there are at least 225,000 species of flowering plants, with more than 9,000 of these native to the United States. Consequently, the distribution of vegetation types is a more useful method

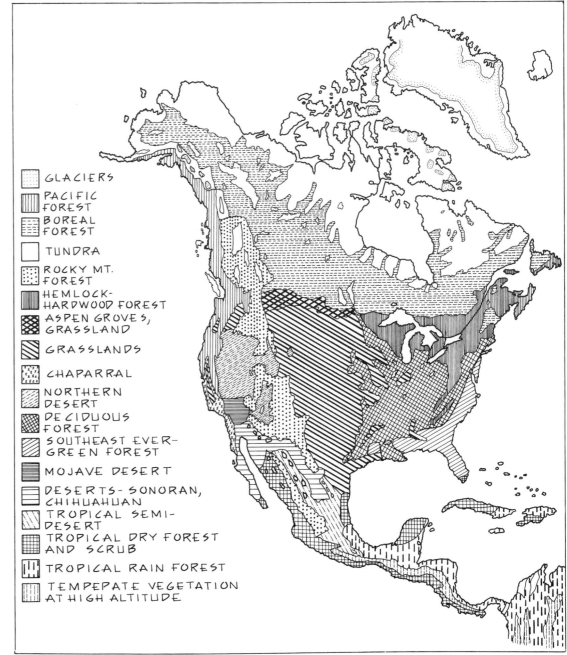

4-1

Figure 4-1. *Map of major plant associations in the United States, Canada, and Central America.*

4-2

Table 4-1 Vegetation types and the North American climax formations on which they are based.

Type of vegetation	Climax formation
Tundra	Tundra
Forest (coniferous)	Boreal forest
	Subalpine forest
	Montane forest
	Pacific coastal forest
Forest (deciduous)	Deciduous forest
Woodland and scrub	Broad sclerophyll
	Southwestern woodland
	Cold desert
	Warm desert
Grassland	Grassland
Tropics	Tropical

Figure 4-2. *Paper birch* (Betula papyrifera) *is a constant though secondary species throughout the Boreal forest formation. A pure stand such as this, near Shelburne, New Hampshire, often forms after an area has been burned or otherwise disturbed, eventually to be succeeded by climax vegetation.*

for presenting a comprehensive view of North America vegetation than are descriptions based on the range of each species.

There have been many methods of classifying vegetation types with varying degrees of differentiation. Probably the largest categories of vegetation types are desert, grassland, savanna, and forest. A classification as general as this has only limited usefulness in describing the plants of an area. In attempting to differentiate further between vegetation types, systems have been devised that recognize anywhere between 9 to 39 different types or classes. For the purpose of this discussion, the system of Henry J. Oosting, which classifies plants on the basis of climax formations, will be followed. *Climax formations* are relatively stable and distinctive plant communities characterized by one or more dominant species. The major climax formations of North America are listed in Table 4-1.

Climax Formations

TUNDRA

Tundra formation occurs either between the northern limit for trees and the area of perpetual ice and snow, or at high altitudes above the timber line. These are known as arctic and alpine tundra, respectively. Tundra vegetation is low-growing and usually includes many grasses and sedges. There are relatively few species in this vegetation type since they must endure environmental extremes.

CONIFEROUS AND DECIDUOUS FORESTS

Boreal forest formation spans the continent in a broad band just south of the tundra. As with the tundra, the climate is severe and is a limiting factor. This climax forest is characterized by the conifers, white spruce (*Picea glauca*) and balsam fir (*Abies balsamea*) being dominant species, and paper birch (*Betula papyrifera*) a constant secondary species.

Deciduous forest formation occupies most of the eastern United States, extending north to the conifer forest and west to the grasslands, where decreased rainfall becomes limiting. The climate is temperate, with distinct seasonal differences. Temperatures commonly go below freezing in the climate of these deciduous forests. There are a number of different associations included in this classification. The associations, which will be discussed in more detail later, are mixed mesophytic forest, beech-maple, maple-basswood, hemlock-hardwoods, oak-chestnut, and oak-hickory.

WESTERN MOUNTAIN VEGETATION, BY ALTITUDE

Rocky Mountain forest complex is characterized by distinct vegetation zones that extend over the great height of the mountains. The zones, and the climax vegetation of each, are as follows:

Alpine zone
    Tundra climax

Subalpine zone
    Engelmann spruce–alpine fir climax

Montane zone
    Douglas-fir climax
    Ponderosa pine climax

Foothills (woodland) zone
    Piñon–juniper climax
    Oak-mountain mahogany climax

The alpine zone, which is cold and dry, is characterized by the tundra vegetation described previously. It occurs at progressively lower altitudes as one moves north along the Rocky Mountain range.

Just below the tundra and forming the timber line is the subalpine spruce–fir complex, made up largely of Engelmann spruce (*Picea engelmannii*) and alpine fir (*Abies lasiocarpa*). The transition between the alpine tundra and subalpine zone is generally gradual and is characterized by sparse stands and dwarf, distorted trees known as *krummholz* at the upper limit. Sometimes, right at the timber line, species are found that cannot compete with the climax species below nor survive the tundra above. The famous bristlecone pine (*Pinus aristata*) is an example of this in the southern Rockies.

At the next lower level, Douglas-fir (*Pseudotsuga menziesii*) is the primary species, often at the exclusion of most other species. Below this can be found the ponderosa pine (*Pinus ponderosa*) climax, which is made up of this species and lodgepole pine (*P. contorta*), which species is dominant only in the northern Rockies, and related varieties and species in other parts of the Rockies. Both of these zones together make up the montane zone.

The other major vegetation zone is that of the foothills, consisting of the piñon-juniper climax and the oak–mountain mahogany climax. The former is an open coniferous woodland of different junipers and piñon pines with a grass cover between trees that are widely spaced. Such vegetation is prevalent in intermountain regions as well as in mountain foothills. The foothill zone also contains the oak-mountain mahogany climax, which acts as a

4-3

4-4

Figure 4-3. *The alpine vegetation zone at high altitude (11,000-foot elevation) in the Rocky Mountains, Montana.*

4-5

4-6

Figure 4-4. *Bristlecone pine (Pinus aristata), Inyo National Forest, California; an example of vegetation in the subalpine zone.*

Figure 4-5. *Mount Olympus, Washington, and the montane vegetation of the Cascade Mountains.*

Figure 4-6. *Scrubby vegetation at Sipapu Bridge, Natural Bridges National Monument, Utah. An example of Great Basin Desert area vegetation.*

transition between the conifer forest in the foothills and the treeless plains. The primary components of this climax are different oak species, which predominate in the southern parts of the Rockies, and mountain mahogany, which is dominant in the north. The vegetation in this climax occurs in dense groves or as individual plants separated by grass or desert vegetation.

Sierra Nevada forest complex, in which is included the area of the Cascade Mountains, is made up of vegetation zones that are similar to those in the Rockies, though different species are discernible. Although similar zones of vegetation occur on both the east and west slopes of the Sierra Nevada mountain range, each is definitely different; sometimes the zones bear no resemblance to each other.

Pacific conifer forest, another very important vegetation zone, parallels the coast from Alaska to central California. The climate is relatively mild with light to heavy precipitation. The forest is principally montane in character. The Puget Sound area contains the fullest array of species in the forest.

WOODLAND AND SCRUB

Broad sclerophyll formation is composed of evergreens that occur in both a forest climax and a shrub climax called chaparral. Both climaxes occur in the same range but in alternating patches, beginning in southern Oregon and extending beyond southern California, where the formation is best developed. The chaparral is widely distributed and characterized by low, dense thickets of evergreens which are often burned by fires during hot, dry summers. If the fires are not frequent, chaparral vegetation will sprout vigorously and return to normal within 10 years.

Desert vegetation covers an extensive area of the North American continent. The climate throughout this area has similar features, including low and erratic amounts of precipitation, widely divergent diurnal (day–night) and seasonal temperatures in both the air and the soil, and low humidity along with strong winds and bright sunlight. Yet, despite these similarities, there are distinct differences in the climate and vegetation of various regions within the area.

Four desert formations have been defined for North America, based on physiographic, climatic, and vegetational differences. One of these, the Great Basin Desert, can be distinguished from the other three because of its much lower temperatures. This desert, which extends north from southern Nevada and Utah, has two major plant communities: the sagebrush association in the north and at high elevations, and the shadescale association. The other three deserts, classified as warm deserts, include the Mojave Desert, the Sonora Desert, and—the most southern—Chihuahua Desert.

GRASSLANDS

Grassland formation is the most extensive of all climax forms in North America and consequently grows under a diversity of conditions. The climatic cycle that characterizes grasslands is a hot, dry spell in late summer following a spring and early summer during which adequate moisture has been acquired.

4-7

4-9

4-8

Figures 4-7, 4-8. *Examples of vegetation in the northern area of the Great Basin. Pink phlox and sagebrush (4-7), and arrowleaf balsamroot (Balsamorhiza sagittata) (4-8), in Malheur National Forest, Oregon.*

4-10

Figure 4-9. *Desert sand dunes. In the foreground grass is just beginning to establish itself.*

Figure 4-10. *Joshua-trees (Yucca brevifolia) in the Joshua Tree National Monument, California. This species of yucca is a prominent feature in the landscape of the Mojave Desert.*

Figure 4-11. *Yucca in the Coronado National Forest, near Tucson, Arizona.*

Figure 4-12. *Clumps of fescue, northern Arizona.*

Figure 4-13. *Panhandle National Grassland, Texas, famous as a dustbowl area in the 1930s.*

4-11

4-12

Grasses can tolerate the extended drought because of their long period of dormancy, whereas forest development is impeded by drought conditions. Although the entire grassland formation experiences this general climate, there are still distinct regional differences in climate and vegetation. The three most distinct grassland associations are tall-grass prairie, mixed-grass prairie, and short-grass plains. Tall-grass prairie, sometimes called "true prairie," receives the most rainfall and borders the deciduous forests. It has many dominant species, including a number of bunch grasses that grow in excess of six feet tall, as well as some sod-forming species. This formation once extended as far east as Illinois and Indiana. Short-grass plains are on the western edge of the grasslands, extending to the Rockies and consisting primarily of short grasses that tolerate low amounts of moisture. The mixed-grass prairie occupies the area between the other two major regions and contains dominants from both.

TROPICAL FORMATIONS

The only other major climax vegetation in the North American continent is the *tropical formation*. This grows primarily in southern Mexico and Central America and is beyond the scope of this discussion.

PLANT COMMUNITIES

Some groups or kinds of plants habitually live together. The reason communities of plants form is that they are able to grow and survive in a similar environment. That is not to say that all the plants living in a habitat must have

4-13

precisely the same environment. In fact, it is the modifying effect of the plants on their environment that creates distinctly different environments within the same habitat. These microclimatic differences make it possible for plants with different requirements to live together. Thus, it is the mutual interaction of plants and the interaction of plants with their environments that determine a plant community.

There are many factors interacting in a plant community that enable a particular group of plants to share the same habitat. The relationship between plants, including direct and indirect effects on each other, is very important. *Competition* among plants for light, nutrients, and water is a primary factor, particularly when demand exceeds supply. Individual plants of the species will be competing for some thing they all need, so if the supply is limited, some of the plants will ultimately die or become severely stunted. In forest management, thinning is practiced as a way of reducing the competition, thus ensuring more vigorous individual trees. In unmanaged plant communities, the plant population adjusts itself, through competition, so that the plants that survive share between them all the available resources, or nearly all.

Several species are generally involved in competition within a stand. If their needs are similar, they may occupy similar locations in the community. If their requirements differ, their arrangement within the community will not be equal. For example, tall-growing species form an overstory that controls the community, so they are called the *dominant* species. Shorter plants will survive only if they can tolerate the lesser light resulting from the shade created by the tall trees. This relationship among plants is known as *stratification.* For a species to maintain dominance in this community, the plants of the species must be able to reproduce themselves, and this entails competing successfully in all strata.

Although competition and stratification among plants act to exclude many plants, they also provide a favorable habitat for others. The *dependence* of one species on another for its survival is equally important in the composition of the plant community. Many of the organisms that are dependent on others are inconspicuous parasites that obtain their sustenance from other living organisms, or are saprophytes that exist on decaying dead plants. Others include plants that require the low amounts of light and the high humidity provided by the dominant and secondary plants.

Plant communities may be as simple as a single-layered community of grass or as complex as a multilayered, temperate deciduous forest. Communities can be described on the basis of the species observed, or by using some physical system based on plant form. For example, as one walks through a temperate zone woodland he will see an obvious vertical pattern made up of at least three or four distinct layers of vegetation. The upper layer consists of large, dominant, overstory trees. Below them is a layer formed by the crowns of shade-tolerant secondary or understory trees. Under these trees will be one or more layers of shrubs, below which will be yet one or more layers of herbaceous plants.

A plant community with natural or arbitrary boundaries is called a *stand.* Although no

4-14

Figure 4-14. *Vertical pattern of a woodland, showing overstory, understory, and ground plants. The pattern is visible in almost any temperate zone forest. Compare Figure 4-16, for example, in which the vertical layers are less clearly separated, with the photo of the coast redwoods shown in Figure 7-25, where the definition is distinct.*

4-15

Figure 4-15. *An area geographically near the original, ancient center of the deciduous forest formation, in the southern Appalachians: Chattahoochee National Forest, Georgia.*

two stands are exactly alike, there are stands that resemble each other. Because of the similarities in plant stands, they have been classified into vegetational types of *associations*. As indicated earlier, associations are climax communities that comprise a larger classification known as a formation. Regionally, associations exhibit climatic and vegetational differences, although there are several species that may occur in all the associations of a particular formation. To illustrate this relationship so that it will be better understood, we will describe the associations of the deciduous forest formation that covers the major portion of the eastern United States.

The center of dispersal for the deciduous forest appears to be in the southern Appalachians, an area that is known as a *mixed mesophytic forest association*. In it are numerous species that occur in various combinations depending on variations in the environment. The most representative of this association are the yellow buckeye (*Aesculus octandra*) and white basswood (*Tilia heterophylla*). In addition to being found in the southern Allegheny region, the association is sometimes found beyond this region in favorable habitats, which include high, moist areas farther south and the ravines and deep valleys to the west and east.

As one moves north and west from the Allegheny region to New York or to Ohio and even into Wisconsin, the *beech–maple association* is more prevalent. The dominant species, as indicated in the name, are American beech (*Fagus grandifolia*) and sugar maple (*Acer saccharum*).

As one moves to the northwest limits of the deciduous forest formation, beech is re-

4-16

4-18

4-19

4-20

4-17

4-21

Figure 4-16. *An example of the vegetation of the beech-maple forest association of the Midwest, in early spring: Stewart Woods, West Lafayette, Indiana. Figures 4-17 to 4-23 show some examples of the wide variety of forest plants to be found in this one association.*

Figure 4-17. *Wild geranium (Geranium maculatum).*

Figure 4-18. *Jack-in-the-pulpit (Arisaema triphyllum).*

Figure 4-19. *A ground cover of mayapple (Podophyllum peltatum).*

Figure 4-20. *Bloodroot (Sanguinaria canadensis).*

Figure 4-21. *Twinleaf (Jeffersonia diphylla).*

4-22

4-23

Table 4-2 Trees and shrubs in the beech-maple-hemlock association.

Botanical name	Common name
TREES	
Acer pensylvanicum	Striped maple
Acer saccharum	Sugar maple
Acer spicatum	Mountain maple
Betula alleghaniensis	Yellow birch
Betula pendula	White birch
Castanea dentata	American chestnut
Cornus florida	Flowering dogwood
Fagus grandifolia	American beech
Fraxinus americana	White ash
Liriodendron tulipifera	Tulip-tree
Tilia americana	American linden, or basswood
Tsuga canadensis	Canada hemlock
SHRUBS	
Amelanchier canadensis	Downy shadblow
Cornus alternifolia	Alternate-leaf dogwood
Hamamelis virginiana	Witch-hazel
Kalmia latifolia	Mountain-laurel
Taxus canadensis	Canadian yew
Viburnum dentatum	Arrow-wood
Viburnum lantana	Wayfaring-tree

Figure 4-22. *Fragile-fern (Cystopteris fragilis).*

Figure 4-23. *Lobel spleenwort (Asplenium pinnatifidum), growing in a crevice of a decaying log and surrounded by moss.*

placed by basswood for a *maple–basswood association.* This change begins in Wisconsin and continues into Minnesota. Oak and hickory may appear along with maple and basswood in this association but primarily on poor sites of rugged topography and along the edges of the prairie.

On the northern edge of the deciduous forest and below the northern coniferous forest lies a transitional association known as *beech–maple–hemlock association* or *hemlock-hardwood association.* Hemlock is a constant member of this association, which extends from northwestern Minnesota to Nova Scotia. This area supported great pine forests in the recent past; a few of them remain in this hardwood climax. Table 4-2 provides a relatively comprehensive picture of the trees and shrubs that occur in this association.

One of the interesting climax communities is the *oak association,* once known as the *oak–chestnut association.* This may take a different name in the future. The chestnut was eliminated by blight in a very short time and it will take some time to see if another species will become dominant in its place. Some indications are that northern red oak (*Quercus rubra*) and tulip-tree (*Liriodendron tulipifera*) are possibilities, along with red maple (*Acer rubrum*) as a secondary tree. None of the original association remains intact today because of lumbering and chestnut blight. The species characteristic of this association are indicated in Table 4-3.

Another plant community in this formation is the *oak–hickory association.* As one moves from the center of the deciduous forest formation, precipitation tends to decrease. Consequently, drought-resistant oak and hickory become dominant species and occur as a fringe around most of the formation except in the north. Since this association covers a wide territory, the dominants are not the same throughout.

DYNAMICS OF PLANT SUCCESSION

Plant communities are never completely stable and are generally characterized by constant change. Sometimes the change is dramatic, as when a prominent species is eliminated because of disease, or when natural vegetation is disturbed by cultivation or fire. Often the change is so gradual that it is generally not apparent to the untrained observer.

The changes in vegetation that occur naturally are known as *plant succession*. A frequently observed example of succession occurs when a cultivated field is permitted to revegetate naturally. Annual weeds will predominate at first, followed by numerous herbaceous perennials in subsequent years, eventually by woody perennials. Although there is always the element of chance in biological changes, plant succession in a particular climate and habitat is predictable. Similar habitats support similar plant communities and the sequence of plant succession usually occurs in the same order.

Plant succession occurs as the habitat changes. As plants become established and develop in an area, they will alter the habitat. Direct effects include modification of the microclimate, i.e., light, temperature, and humidity. Other effects include the modification of the soil environment caused by the accumu-

Table 4-3   Species of the oak association.

Botanical name	Common name
TREES	
Carya glabra	Pignut hickory
Carya ovata	Shagbark hickory
Carya tomentosa	Mockernut hickory
Cornus florida	Flowering dogwood
Liriodendron tulipifera	Tulip-tree
Morus alba	White mulberry
Ostrya virginiana	Hop-hornbeam
Prunus pensylvanica	Pin cherry
Prunus serotina	Black cherry
Quercus alba	White oak
Quercus coccinea	Scarlet oak
Quercus muehlenbergii	Chinkapin oak
Quercus prinus	Chestnut-oak
Quercus rubra	Red oak, or northern red oak
Quercus stellata	Post oak
Quercus velutina	Black oak
Sassafras albidum	Sassafras
Sorbus americana	American mountain-ash
Tilia americana	American linden, or basswood
SHRUBS AND VINES	
Amelanchier canadensis	Downy shadblow
Ceanothus americanus	New Jersey tea
Celastrus scandens	Bittersweet
Clematis verticillaris	Clematis
Cornus alternifolia	Alternate-leaf dogwood
Diervilla lonicera	Bush-honeysuckle
Gaylussacia frondosa	Huckleberry
Hamamelis virginiana	Witch-hazel
Ilex verticillata	Winterberry
Kalmia latifolia	Mountain-laurel
Lonicera sempervirens	Trumpet honeysuckle
Rhamnus cathartica	Common buckthorn
Rhododendron nudiflorum	Pinxterbloom azalea
Ribes cynosbati	Prickly gooseberry
Ribes rotundifolium	Gooseberry
Rosa setigera	Prairie rose
Rubus odoratus	Flowering raspberry
Staphylea trifolia	American bladdernut
Vaccinium angustifolium	Lowberry blueberry
Vaccinium stamineum	Deerberry
Viburnum dentatum	Arrow-wood
Vitis aestivalis	Summer grape
Vitis labrusca	Fox grape

lation of plant litter. Over extended periods, plant litter will greatly alter soil development, water relations, nutrient availability, and other soil factors. It is significant to note that as plants alter their habitat they generally make it less favorable for themselves and more favorable to species that could not have existed there without this alteration. Under the altered conditions, new species are able to compete with, and often replace, existing species.

Other changes may also alter the habitat and affect the process of succession. Physical changes in the soil environment such as soil erosion, flooding, or accumulation of salts greatly alter the habitat and affect the kinds of plants that will grow there.

There are two basic kinds of succession: primary, and secondary.

Primary succession occurs over barren areas where no vegetation has grown before. Such situations are relatively unusual in nature, occurring in areas of severe erosion, on newly deposited volcanic rock, or where a new island has been formed. Similar areas may be formed where drastic earth-moving occurs, such as in highway construction. The habitats for primary succession are usually unsuitable for all but a few plants. Plants that do become established are appropriately called *pioneers,* since they must be able to survive under extreme conditions. These pioneers tend to reduce the extremes and provide a more favorable habitat for other species. The primary effect of these pioneers is to make the improvements in soil conditions that must occur before succession can continue.

Secondary succession takes place when normal succession is upset by fire, cultivation, lumbering, or other disruption. The rate of plant succession depends on the extent of the disturbance. If the influence of previous vegetation on the habitat is eliminated, as happens after severe fire or cultivation, succession will be slow. But if the disturbance is less severe, as is true of lumbering or selective thinning of woodland, succession will be rapid and the original plant community will restore itself in a much shorter time.

Succession progresses in stages, from the pioneer stage through a series of more mature communities to a relatively stable community called a *climax*. Generally, pioneer stages are slow to establish themselves. Following the pioneer stage, successive communities replace each other rapidly and dramatic exchanges of species occur from year to year. As succession continues toward climax, the process slows down, and at climax the plant community is in relative equilibrium with the climate. The transition from one stage to another until climax reveals the infinite variety that exists in natural plant groupings. This can be illustrated by tracing what happens to an abandoned farm in the northeastern deciduous forest area when it is allowed to revegetate naturally.

The uncultivated field or meadow is quickly covered with a blanket of weeds—herbaceous flowering plants. Some of these same flowering weeds are well known and are used effectively as cultivated plants. Although all of the flowering plants thrive in what is described as the *open field association*, within that association will be considerable diversity in species depending on soil and moisture conditions. Also characteristic of open fields are the shrub plantings or hedgerows that form the boundaries of these fields. These are narrow planting strips that were undisturbed during the use of the field for farming. Now that the field has been abandoned, not only do they provide a picturesque enclosure for the flowering plants, they also serve as a seed source for woody plants that will begin to grow in the midst of the herbaceous plants.

If this open field remains undisturbed, the next association to develop will be the *juniper association*, which is also characteristic of dry, sunny, sometimes rocky hillsides. The prominent species in this group is the eastern redcedar (*Juniperus virginiana*). These rugged, columnar evergreens appear both as individuals and in groups, usually with considerable open space between groups. Interspersed among these upright junipers are the low spreading common juniper (*J. communis*) and various deciduous shrubs, including blackhaw (*Viburnum prunifolium*), common barberry (*Berberis vulgaris*), and many others. The remaining ground, somewhat barren, supports low herbaceous flowers and grasses, mosses, and lichens.

Shortly after the juniper association has made its appearance, the *gray birch association* forms in the midst of the junipers. The dominant species is the graceful gray birch (*Betula populifolia*), which grows in clumps and groves. Below the birches can be found a variety of ferns as well as many delicate flowering herbaceous species. The birch makes its appearance quickly because of its rapid rate of growth,

but it disappears almost as quickly because of its short life span.

The shade and protection provided by the gray birches enable seedling white pines to grow up and form the *pine association*, which quickly replaces the birch. A limited number of species are included in this group; the dominants are all pines—red (*Pinus resinosa*), pitch (*P. rigida*), and eastern white (*P. strobus*)—and the understory plants are all low-growing, shade-tolerant ferns and flowers. With time this association will be supplanted by the more variable, more permanent oak association, which has been described previously. Frequently, groups of old pines are found remaining among the oaks, revealing the transition that has taken place.

Other plant communities in the area of the deciduous forest formation also have distinctive topography that exerts a strong influence on the plant life. Topography is constantly changing as a result of plant succession and it in turn causes plant succession. For example, as ponds or bogs fill up because of accumulated vegetation, the species composition at the edges will change as the water level changes. And as water deepens a ravine, only those plants that can tolerate the increasing shade and coolness will be adaptable.

Fluctuating water levels are an important factor in the plant communities along a stream or river in a flood plain. These plants are sometimes classified as the *streamside association*. The higher water table and relative humidity dramatically influence the species that will be adaptable. The most prevalent trees include silver and red maple (*Acer saccharinum* and *A. rubrum*), box-elder (*A. negundo*), American

4-24

Figure 4-24. *A pond or bog filling up with accumulated vegetation.*

plane (*Platanus occidentalis*), American elm (*Ulmus americana*), shining and black willows (*Salix lucida* and *S. nigra*), and others. Just as much diversity exists among shrubs, which include various alders (*Alnus incana* and *A. rugosa*), dogwoods (*Cornus amomum* and *C. stolonifera*), viburnums (*Viburnum acerifolium*, *V. dentatum*, and *V. lentago*), and many others.

The *pond or bog association,* with its more stable water level, has somewhat similar diversity but has fewer species. Primary trees include the red maple (*Acer rubrum*), sour gum (*Nyssa sylvatica*), pin oak (*Quercus palustris*), and black willow (*Salix nigra*). These are outnumbered by species of shrubs, which include those found in the streamside association. These plants must tolerate an undrained waterlogged environment that is highly unfavorable for most plants.

The last grouping, of interest to those living along the seacoast, is the *seaside association.* These are plants that must tolerate excessively dry, barren soil; at the same time they must endure strong winds that sweep over them from the ocean, carrying toxic salt sprays in stormy weather. Despite these conditions, a wide diversity of plants will be found growing along the seaside. Some of them will also be found in the pond or bog association or the juniper association; their presence in all these associations indicates the extreme versatility of many native North American plants.

The versatility of certain native plants is a primary reason why a landscape planner should give them some priority over exotics, which, though interesting and unique, may not be nearly so adaptable to the wide range of conditions that may exist at a landscape site.

THE EFFECT OF MAN ON THE LANDSCAPE

As civilization has advanced, man has become a major force in shaping the land and the conditions for plant life that the land must support. The primary impact has been to shift the balance of natural systems by introducing completely managed ecosystems and to direct the evolution of the plant species grown in these new ecosystems. The advantage to man of managed ecosystems is well known and very evident if his ability to feed, clothe, and shelter himself are the criteria used in measuring success. The consequences, on the other hand, though not completely understood, must be continuously evaluated in terms of long-range effects on both man and the biological system that supports him.

The impact of man on the land can be traced through six successive stages that relate to the extent of development or civilization of society. They are gathering, hunting, herding, agriculture, industrialization, and urbanization. With each new stage of development, man's impact on the plant environments around him was more drastic, partly because the effects were cumulative. The shift from an agricultural to an industrial society did not relieve the pressures that agriculture exerted on natural resources, but rather added new pressures exerted by industry.

The earliest relationship of man to nature was similar to that of other animals, and consisted in *gathering* plants for food and shelter. Man also gathered fibrous plants for clothing. This practice had very little effect on plant environments and certainly had no greater effect than the impact made by other animals.

Even as hunter, man did not greatly alter the natural balance as long as he provided only for his own needs. The plains of North America once exhibited a balance between grasses and buffaloes. Certain low-growing grasses were maintained by the continued grazing of buffaloes. The arrival of Indian hunters did not alter this balance, because they killed only those buffaloes necessary to fill their own immediate, limited needs. However, the white settlers eliminated the buffalo, by exploiting this animal for economic gains, and thus drastically changed the balance.

Herding has exerted a pronounced effect on the land. Plant succession is frequently impeded or virtually arrested by the grazing patterns of such animals as sheep and goats. When man developed agriculture and domesticated animals and plants, the alterations of plant succession became quite significant. Overgrazing of natural grasslands in the southwestern United States resulted in an invasion of weeds and desert shrubs, and some areas ultimately became man-made deserts. Overgrazing is not limited to natural grasslands, however, and may constitute a problem in suburban and rural landscapes, too, if these are near areas in which deer live. Deer can usually find abundant food in natural undergrowth, unless their numbers increase where they are free from natural predators and where man is prohibited from hunting them. They then venture into landscaped areas in the winter to nibble on evergreens and other trees. In areas where this has occurred, a visible browse line usually indicates the maximum feeding height of the browsing animals. Young woody plants and the lower limbs of young trees and conifers are frequently eaten by deer.

The development of *agriculture* was at the expense of natural plant communities. Agricultural crops are generally unable to resist the natural processes of plant succession without the influence of man in creating favorable habitats. The altered habitats favored the production of introduced species for food and fiber and resulted in very high yields, but they created some less desirable effects as well. Large areas of soil normally covered with natural plant communities were laid bare, thus reducing the total biological productivity and exposing the soil to wind and water erosion. Soil structure and natural vegetation were disturbed and frequently new pests were introduced that were destructive to native vegetation.

Lumbering practices have affected woodland communities in a number of ways. Selective thinning is least disturbing, but clear-cutting creates a state not normally experienced in natural communities. The complete removal of the forest canopy above soil that is left unchanged results in a habitat in which reestablishment of vegetation proceeds at an advanced stage of succession. However, before regeneration occurs, soil erosion is a serious danger. If the commercial trees are the climax growth in the area, the method of cutting and the reforestation employed determine whether the return growth will also be climax or, if not climax, whether natural succession can be prevented and the desired species maintained.

Another factor associated with man, particularly in forest lands, is *fire*. Although fires

4-25

Figure 4-25. *The impact of urbanization on the landscape.*

4-26

Figure 4-26. *Evidence of the negative impact of man on his environment.*

caused naturally by lightning are believed to have maintained some land in grassland and savanna, fires are usually caused by the carelessness or thoughtlessness of man and are a primary factor in controlling vegetation of some regions. When fire is recurring, only fire-resistant species called *pyrophytes* predominate. These are plants that either resist burning, such as the coast redwood (*Sequoia sempervirens*) and many pines, or plants that are stimulated to sprout after a fire, such as aspen or various manzanitas (*Arctostaphylos* spp.). On the other hand, fire prevention can be *too* efficient, with detrimental effects. Occasional low-intensity fires help eliminate dry underbrush. Without elimination by small, controlled fires, large amounts of tinder and burnable brush accumulate to fuel enormous accidental holocausts that destroy total forests. Fire has to be managed, not eliminated.

Industrialization has a definite impact on the countryside. The impact may be noticed in the depletion of certain species as a raw material, but more likely it will be related to the effect of contaminants or other destructive forces imposed on the land. Air pollutants from a variety of industries have injured or completely destroyed vegetation in surrounding areas. Road systems and strip-mining have left tremendous scars. Likewise, the damming of waterways for industrial purposes alters the nature of the adjacent land dramatically, affecting particularly those plant species growing along the waterways.

The most recent impact of man on plant environments is related to *urbanization*. Plant environments in cities are apt to be very artificial, providing possibilities for protection but at the same time presenting adverse conditions that only the most durable plants can tolerate. Limits to the availability of land places additional restrictions on what kind of plant communities can be grown.

The *mobility* of man has had a great influence on the distribution of plants. Through his travels, he has consciously or accidentally transported many exotic species. Some of these exotics never become established unless they are planted and protected by man; an example is the Norway spruce (*Picea abies*). Others become naturalized and perpetuate themselves in habitats to which they are particularly adapted. Some exotics, such as the tree-of-heaven (*Ailanthus altissima*) from China, are commonly found along roadsides, railroad tracks, vacant lots, and other unused places. The majority of exotics, such as mustard, ox-eye daisy, and most common weeds, will naturalize in cultivated fields. A few of these exotics were first introduced for landscape plantings, only to become a serious pest when they were not controlled. An example of this is Hall's honeysuckle (*Lonicera japonica* 'Halliana'), a vine that grows vigorously and competes with other exotic as well as many native plantings. We mentioned a few plant introductions in Chapter 2 and will discuss the topic in Chapter 6.

SUMMARY

Although considerable destruction and disruption of the natural land has been because of man's activities, it does not mean that man cannot exist on the land without abusing it. In fact, in numerous ways man exerts a positive influence, either by preserving or by enhancing the countryside. The ultimate effect of man's presence is determined by the extent to which he understands and ultilizes ecological principles in his use of the land. This will be discussed in subsequent chapters.

FOR FURTHER READING

Dansereau, P., 1957. *Biogeography: An Ecological Perspective.* New York: The Ronald Press Co. 394 pages.

Oosting, H. J., 1948. *The Study of Plant Communities: An Introduction to Plant Ecology.* San Francisco: W. H. Freeman and Co. Second edition, 1956. 440 pages.

5

Plants and Their Environments

As environmental factors affect man and his existence, likewise there are many environmental factors that influence the growth and sometimes even the survival of the plant. It is important for those persons dealing with plants to understand what these factors are and how they influence the development of a plant once it has been planted in a landscaped site. The purpose of this chapter is to show how the environment influences the plants used in the landscape.

CLIMATIC FACTORS

Limiting factors in the distribution and range of plants in nature are frequently associated with climate. Even in the managed landscape, climatic factors are one of the most important considerations in plant selection. In this regard climate refers to a number of environmental factors acting simultaneously on a plant. These will of necessity be considered separately, though it cannot be overemphasized that the plant responds to an *interaction* of such climatic factors as light, temperature, and atmospheric conditions.

Light

The source of all the Earth's radiant energy is the sun. Part of the sun's energy is visible as light, though visible light is only a small part of the total spectrum. The characteristics of light that are most important for our purposes are intensity (measured in foot-candles), duration (measured as photoperiods), and quality (measured in wavelengths). The values these take are determined naturally by the changing position of the Earth relative to the sun, the direction and slope of the land surface, and other natural and man-made features on the land surface.

Light intensity is greatly affected by the atmosphere through which it is transmitted. Certain gases, such as nitrogen and oxygen, absorb small amounts of light at short wavelengths, and moisture in the air absorbs large amounts of light at longer, visible wavelengths. Clouds, therefore, may reduce light to 4 percent of normal intensity. Consequently, light intensity is greater at high elevations and in dry climates. Also, the angle at which the sun's rays hit the Earth's surface is directly related to the depth of the atmosphere through which the rays must pass; thus the angle of the sun controls daily, seasonal, and latitudinal variations in light intensity. In addition, light intensity can be greatly reduced by dust and smoke. In some metropolitan areas, as much as 90 percent of full sunlight has been absorbed by smoke. The light reaching plant surfaces is further reduced by smoke particles that settle out onto the part of the leaf where photosynthesis occurs.

Vegetation also exerts a significant effect on light intensity. The difference between the light intensity above and below a canopy of vegetation is great. Only about 10 percent of the light that strikes leaf surfaces passes through. In plant communities, such as a forest, only the tallest trees receive full sunlight; understory plants receive much lower intensities. In fact, light intensity may be reduced to 1 percent of full sunlight in a dense forest, though more generally it is reduced to 15 per-

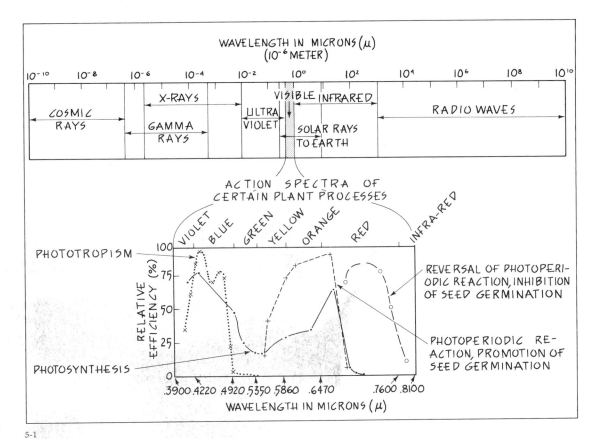

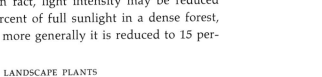

Figure 5-1. *The electromagnetic spectrum and the part of it in which certain plant processes are active.*

Figure 5-2. *Light filtering through the forest canopy in Muir Woods National Monument, California.*

cent or less under such a canopy. One must realize that light intensity is seldom constant; it varies with the movement of leaves and branches in the wind as well as with changes in the direction from which the sunlight comes.

The importance of light in photosynthesis by plants is a central fact in plant growth. A plant is uniquely capable of converting solar energy to its own use in the manufacture of carbohydrates and the process is called photosynthesis. The optimum light intensity for the occurrence of maximum photosynthesis in a single leaf is usually much lower than the intensity of full sunlight. However, most leaves seldom receive full sunlight because of shading and the orientation of leaves relative to the direction of the light. Consequently, these shaded leaves do not receive enough light for maximum photosynthesis even if the entire plant is in full sunlight. The overall effect, then, is that full sunlight is beneficial since it increases the likelihood that leaves within the canopy will have a high photosynthetic efficiency.

The above is true of plants that "perform" best in full sunlight. Some plants use light more efficiently and can grow at a much lower intensity of light. These plants are usually classified as shade tolerant. It is important to recognize that some shade-*tolerant* plants grow best in full sunlight, and that others actually *require*, or grow better in, light of lower intensities. There is some question whether these differences are due to light intensity or some other factor, such as temperature or relative humidity.

Not only does a difference in light requirements exist between plants; for some plants the light requirement will differ during the stages of development. Pine seedlings are more efficient in utilizing light for photosynthesis than a mature pine tree because of differences in the internal structure of the needles. The differences in light requirements of tree seedlings determines which species ultimately occupy a habitat. Plants with high light requirements, such as white pine, are able to dominate in an initial forest stand, if it is open and sunny, but as shade develops conditions become more favorable to shade-tolerant species such as hemlock, beech, or sugar maple, and less favorable to pine. A continuous stand of pine must be vigorously managed or it will be succeeded by native vegetation that is more tolerant of shade. Vegetation types succeed each other until that shade-tolerant species predominates which is able to reproduce and grow in its own shade. Shade-tolerant plants in the forests include most maples, beech, red oak, basswood, spruces, firs, and hemlocks. Pines, bur oak, willows, cottonwood, aspens, tulip-tree, birches, larches, and junipers require more light.

PHOTOPERIODISM

The photoperiod or relative duration of light and darkness in a 24-hour period exerts a great influence on plants, and the duration of the dark period is the critical factor. This was first recognized in 1920 as the factor controlling the time of flowering in certain species. Since then, photoperiodism has often been demonstrated to control the following processes in certain species: leaf abscission (leaf fall), dormancy, hardiness, leaf size, pigmentation, germination; and others too. Plants that develop and flower only under short photoperiods (usually less than 12 hours of light) are called short-day plants, and those requiring long photoperiods (usually 14 hours or more of light) are called long-day plants. Plants that initiate flowers under any length of photoperiod are called day-neutral.

The photoperiodic sensitivity of a species is an important factor in plant distribution. In equatorial (tropical) regions where there is little variation in photoperiod, the effects brought on by photoperiodic changes are not noticeable. On the other hand, in regions closer to the polar axes, plants must be long-day or day-neutral since the photoperiods are long throughout the entire growing season. In temperate zones, the plants that have adapted may be either long-day or short-day plants, in accordance with the photoperiods of the temperate zones. The plants can generally be distinguished by the time of year at which they flower; early spring or late summer flowering plants are usually short-day plants and those that flower between these times are mostly long-day plants.

Short-day plants that bloom in late summer are limited in their northern migration to those areas in which there is sufficient time for flowering between the arrival of short days and the occurrence of low temperatures. The migration of long-day plants toward the equator frequently reaches limits when the photoperiod is insufficiently long to induce flowering and the plants lose the ability to flower. Day-neutral plants are generally not limited by photoperiods in their migration.

Besides controlling flowering, and the distribution of flowering plants, photoperiods

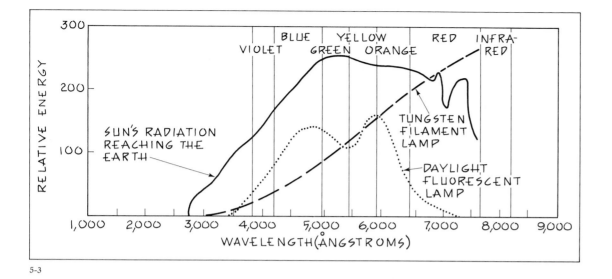

Figure 5-3. *Spectral emissions of tungsten filament and daylight fluorescent lamps as compared to the spectrum of sunlight reaching the Earth. The weak emission of the mercury vapor of fluorescent lamps is not shown here. The chart offers no quantitative comparison with respect to the energy output of the sources.*

influence the geographic distribution of woody plants by exerting control on a plant's hardening, or acclimation to winter conditions. Short photoperiods help to precondition many woody species to initiate acclimation. The critical photoperiod required before this process will begin varies with different segments of the population of a species. Through natural selection, plants of the same species have made different genetic adaptations to the variations in photoperiod throughout a region. Plants that differ this way within a species are called climatic races or, if geographically separated by some boundary such as mountains, they are described as an ecotype. There may be a lag of one to two months in the development of hardiness between races or ecotypes of a species when grown together.

LIGHT QUALITY

Although differences in light quality are important in controlling various plant processes, they do not seem to be critical in limiting the natural environment of plants. Quality varies largely because of the same factors that affect light intensity, such as absorption and diffusion owing to clouds, fog, smoke, and dust. Nevertheless, in some environments, such as high altitudes where ultraviolet light may be incoming in injurious amounts because it passes through less-dense atmosphere, light quality may be a limiting factor, along with other factors. But for the most part, light quality is generally of limited ecological importance. However, the increased use of indoor landscaping—sometimes in very large indoor areas and with plants of great diversity—makes it important to measure light quality and to study the effects of varying wavelengths on plants when installing artificial lights.

Temperature

SOURCE AND DISTRIBUTION OF HEAT ENERGY

Heat is another form of energy that is derived primarily from the sun and used by plants. Temperature changes are closely related to the daily, seasonal, and annual changes in the position of the sun relative to the Earth's surface. Daily, the sun rises and heats the Earth's surface faster than the Earth can reradiate the heat. As the surface temperature continues to rise during the day, a balance is reached between incoming energy that is absorbed as heat and the heat lost by reradiation and conduction. From the midafternoon on into the evening, the incoming energy declines but the Earth's surface continues to release heat energy, cooling steadily during the night until the sun rises again the next day.

As this process goes on daily, the Earth also moves through a seasonal cycle influenced by the angle of the sun's rays and the distance between the sun and Earth, both of which change seasonally as the Earth circles the sun. Although the daily process of warming and cooling is continuous through all seasons, the seasonal differences in temperature are measurable in the daily net gain or loss of heat energy. In the spring and summer the trend is one of net gain, but in the fall and winter the trend is one of net loss.

Any net gain is stored in the soil, which—like air temperature—undergoes daily as well as seasonal change. Except for the soil surface the maximal and minimal soil temperatures occur somewhat later than they do in air. This temperature-change lag relative to air temperature becomes greater with soil depth, amounting to a 4-hour delay at a 15-centimeter depth (5.9 inches) and as much as 80 hours at a 1-meter depth (3.2 feet).

MACROCLIMATE

Macroclimate refers to the weather of a relatively large area of the Earth's surface. Temperature is one of the most common macroclimatic indicators used to describe weather and climate. Variations in temperature are frequently expressed as absolute maximum or minimum temperatures that occur during a year, or the yearly mean temperature (the average of the daily maxima and minima—useful in contrasting seasonal mean temperatures), the yearly mean maximum temperature, and the yearly mean minimum temperature. Moreover, soil temperatures are sometimes recorded.

Since the total solar radiation reaching the Earth decreases as one moves away from the equator, temperature decreases as well. Therefore, the greater the latitude, the lower the temperature generally will be, but temperatures can be greatly altered by the presence of large bodies of water or differences in altitude too.

Large bodies of water act as a buffer to temperature extremes. Water requires more heat energy to raise its temperature in spring and summer than the atmosphere does, and is slower to release heat energy late in the fall and winter. The buffering quality of water is extremely effective in influencing plant distribution. Plants that normally will not survive at a particular latitude inland can survive more northern latitudes at locations along the Atlantic Coast or along the shores of the Great Lakes.

Temperatures change more dramatically within short distances through increasing altitudes than through increasing latitudes, however. Increasing altitudes in mountainous areas produce reductions in temperature of about 3°F for every 1,000 feet. Air at higher altitudes absorbs less heat and warm air loses heat more rapidly because of the expansion of the air at the reduced atmospheric pressures. These sharp differences in temperature are quite noticeable in mountains, where zones of vegetation can be readily observed without travelling great distances.

MICROCLIMATE

Microclimate refers to the more immediate climate experienced by vegetation. Among the many localized conditions that influence micro-

5-4

climate are topography, exposure, and surrounding vegetation. These microclimatic differences allow plants to grow beyond their normal geographic range.

The effect of altitude on temperature has already been described as a macroclimatic effect. Lesser changes in topography also exert important microclimatic influences on temperatures. Cold-air drainage at night into valleys is a well known phenomenon by which the heavier cold air sinks into an area from which lighter, warmer air has risen. This microclimatic condition exercises a dramatic limit on natural vegetation and influences the location of commercial crops and nurseries. The settling of heavier colder air into valley bowls to displace rising warm air causes a temperature inversion—a condition in which the air at ground level is cooler than the air overlaying it, and the warm air is held stationary by the cold air just over adjacent higher terrain. This may result in frost pockets that have microclimates markedly different from surrounding slopes and hilltops. Frost damage has been observed on sensitive plants such as azalea in a valley, yet the same species has been undamaged on a slope a short distance away.

Temperature inversions also occur if there is a rapid loss of heat by reradiation from soil surfaces at night so that the soil becomes cooler than the air just above. When this occurs, heat will be conducted from the air to the soil, reducing the temperature of the lower air layer until it is cooler than upper layers that earlier in the day had been heated by reradiation from the soil. This kind of temperature inversion is most likely to occur on clear, calm nights where there is no earthward radiation by clouds or fog

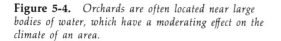

Figure 5-4. *Orchards are often located near large bodies of water, which have a moderating effect on the climate of an area.*

and little air movement to mix the warm and cool air.

Related to topographical differences in microclimate is the effect of slope exposure on temperature. The importance of the angle of the sun in microclimatic temperature differences during the day and seasonally has already been described. The angle of the sun's incidence—the angle at which the sunlight strikes the Earth's surface—is also related to the slope of the land or, as it is sometimes called, the aspect of the land. A south-facing slope receives more concentrated solar rays and thus becomes warmer than flat terrain. A north-facing slope receives even less and is the coldest. Slope exposure then becomes an important factor in determining temperatures.

Vegetation has an important effect on air temperature. Bare soils or other dark surfaces absorb heat quickly, but a plant cover reflects much of the incoming radiation and thus greatly reduces soil heating. Consequently, under full shade the temperature of the soil surface remains cooler than the air temperature, but on nonshaded surfaces the soil will be more heated than the air. The air under a plant canopy is also more humid than the air above unshaded surfaces and consequently more heat is needed to raise the air temperature beneath vegetation. This explains the sharp contrast between the low daytime air temperatures in woodlands or forests and the high daytime air temperatures of open fields or urban areas.

At night the plant cover actually reduces the rate of reradiation. Consequently, soil and air temperature under plant canopies generally do not decrease as much as they do in open areas. Thus, because of opposing influences through the day and night, vegetation acts as a buffer to temperature fluctuations. During the summer, daytime temperatures in the forest are commonly 10°F cooler than open areas; at night they may be 10°F warmer.

Vegetation also affects air temperatures by influencing air movement. If the air moves freely, there may be no difference between air temperature in the sun and in the shade. Yet the temperatures of sunny areas that are enclosed by vegetation are frequently warmer than open areas in which air movement mixes the warm and cool air. In enclosed areas the plant cover actually results in higher air temperatures by preventing the wind from blowing the heated air away.

EFFECTS OF TEMPERATURE ON PLANTS

The temperatures of plants, unlike the temperatures of warm-blooded animals, are closely related to the temperature of the surrounding environment. However, in bright sunlight leaf temperatures may rise much higher (20–30°F) than the air temperatures as a result of absorption of more radiant energy than is lost. Plant temperature is controlled by the exchange of energy that occurs at the surface of the leaf. Plants gain heat by absorption of radiation, by conducting from the surrounding environment, and by respiration. They lose heat by conduction and convection currents to the surrounding environment, by reradiation, or by the evaporation of water through transpiration—loss of water at the surfaces of leaves. The exchange of energy between the plant and its environment determines the plant's temperature and thus, the adaptability of a plant to a particular environment.

Plants differ considerably in their response to temperature and in their tolerance of temperature extremes. Each species has an average optimum temperature, but different functions of a plant may have different optimum temperatures. Thus, a plant usually requires a range of temperatures in order to complete its life cycle. For example, many woody plants require a long exposure to temperatures near 40°F during the winter before they can overcome dormancy, yet they develop optimally at much higher temperatures during the summer.

Plant distribution and adaptation are limited by temperatures in at least two ways. First, the temperature range must satisfy the plant's developmental requirements at all seasons, and second, temperatures must not exceed certain minimum and maximum limits during any one stage of development. The limits of the latter requirement are frequently exceeded, and in temperate climates this is usually associated with winter injury or low-temperature injury.

LOW-TEMPERATURE INJURY

The problem of maintaining woody plants through the winter—overwintering—has been one of the primary climatic limits to plant distribution and cultivation. It is not unique to northern states but appears to be just as critical in many southern states, for two reasons: (1) in any area there is a tendency to attempt to grow exotic species that are only marginally suited to that area by the degree of their cold hardiness, and (2) changing methods of growing plants in containers or raised planters expose roots to abnormal conditions.

Low-temperature injury may happen in widely varying circumstances. To aid in predicting when injury may occur, hardiness zones have been established that are based on average minimum temperatures. However, minimum temperatures are just one of the limiting factors in overwintering plants. Other important factors are the rate of temperature fluctuation, the season of the year at which the low temperature occurs, and the condition of the plant during the exposure.

For example, some arborvitaes that will tolerate temperatures lower than –100°F in winter have nevertheless been injured at temperatures *above* 0°F when exposed to a sudden drop in temperature as rapid as 17°F per minute. This rapid a drop occurs naturally on clear and sunny but cold days. The sun may have warmed the foliage to above freezing even though the air temperature has remained below freezing. Then, if the sun drops below the horizon or behind some structure, the foliage quickly comes to equilibrium with the surrounding air temperature in a rapid temperature drop. When this happens, ice forms within the plant cells, disrupting the plant's chemical processes and causing the death of the tissue. Rapid temperature fluctuations may also cause frost cracks or bark-splitting on the trunks of many trees. Such injury can be avoided by providing shade or by placing sensitive plants on the north or east exposures of a structure, where the sunlight will warm them less.

SEASONAL VARIATION IN HARDINESS

To understand seasonal variation in hardiness it is helpful to know when and how winter hardiness develops. In most woody plants, the first stage of hardiness starts with dormancy during the shorter days in the fall. Although this cool weather may enable the plant to withstand temperature changes in a range no greater than 10°F, this increased hardiness is enough to provide protection from early frosts and at the same time prepares the plant for the second stage of hardiness, which occurs during the first exposures to lower temperatures. It is during the second stage that hardiness may enable the plant to withstand temperatures from −50°F to −100°F or lower, depending on the species.

The exact timing of the onset of dormancy and hardiness depends largely on the particular plant. In fact, in some species there is considerable variation between the plants of different geographical strains that have evolved and adapted to a particular climate. These plants may continue to act as if they were in their natural habitat even when transplanted to a different climate. Consequently, some plants may be injured because they develop hardiness so much later in a new habitat that they are injured by early frosts. This suggests that the landscape contractor should consider the climate in which nursery stock has been grown when he selects plants for a project, particularly if the plants were propagated from seed or evolved in a warmer climate, or both.

Besides injury from early fall and late spring frosts, winter injury occurs in late winter or early spring. The temperatures may not be as low then as earlier but the plants have undergone changes during the winter which make them more susceptible to injury. In late winter, periods of warm temperatures above freezing will frequently be followed by a quick return to subfreezing temperatures. Although such warm spells may also happen early in the winter, plant injury usually does not occur then. The difference is in the condition of the plant at each time. In early winter most woody plants are still in a stage of dormancy or winter rest. During this period they retain their cold hardiness more effectively when there are warm periods than they do in late winter when sufficient chilling has occurred to overcome dormancy. It is during the period following the breaking of the winter rest that the plants lose their hardiness most rapidly during warm weather. Some plant species will never completely regain their hardiness, while other species do regain it, providing they have sufficient exposure once again to noninjurious low temperatures before they are subjected to very low temperatures.

WINTER INJURY TO ROOTS

Generally, the soil environment effectively buffers temperature extremes so that root injury is unlikely to occur. However, winter root injury may damage plants grown in containers or raised planters. Two possible explanations can be given. One is the inability of roots to withstand the subfreezing temperatures that surround the planter. This is particularly true if the soil mass is completely above ground but less so if the soil in the raised planter is in contact with the subsoil. Roots of woody plants cannot tolerate temperatures as low as the tops of the plant can. For example, although the stems and foliage of Japanese yew (*Taxus cuspidata*) can tolerate temperatures as low as –30°F when fully hardened, the mature roots can only survive temperatures as low as 0°F. It is even more significant that the active young roots do not develop hardiness and are easily killed by temperatures that drop below 20°F. This suggests that during most winters, plants in containers suffer some injury to active roots that may delay or inhibit growth the following spring until new active roots are regenerated to replace those injured.

The other type of winter injury in raised planters is desiccation (drying) or "winter burn," which is particularly prevalent among evergreens. Winter burn is associated with extended periods of cold during which time the soil is frozen and moisture is unavailable, conditions that are particularly serious during bright sunny days when water loss from the foliage may be great. Of course, direct exposure to sunlight or windy locations will increase the possibility of this type of injury.

HIGH-TEMPERATURE INJURY

Injury from high temperatures is frequently observed as desiccation, but death is the direct result after prolonged exposure to temperatures above 130°F. This is the maximum temperature that most plants can withstand, though certain alpine plants are injured at much lower temperatures.

Fortunately, temperatures seldom climb this high in the environment of the temperate zone, and when that heat has been recorded, it has usually been recorded right at the soil surface. Consequently, the most common form of heat injury is known as *stem girdle*, which is caused when the extremely high soil-surface temperatures kill stem tissue where it is in contact with the soil. Seedlings are most fre-quently injured by stem girdle; however, nearly all plant material used on landscape sites is not susceptible to this type of injury.

Leaves and roots are seldom injured by high temperatures, except where plants are grown in containers or planters. Injury to roots in containers may result when container walls lack insulation from high temperatures.

ATMOSPHERIC FACTORS

An environmental factor that is generally taken for granted (or even ignored) is the atmosphere that surrounds plants. Because gases are a rela-tively constant part of the atmosphere, they are not considered as a limiting factor in plant environments. Although nitrogen is the pri-mary atmospheric component (accounting for about 78 percent of the volume of the atmo-sphere), it is the oxygen (nearly 21 percent of the volume) and the carbon dioxide (about 0.03 percent) in the air that are essential for plant growth. The oxygen (O_2) is utilized in respira-tion, and the carbon dioxide (CO_2) is required for photosynthesis, which in turn releases O_2. The net effect, however, is to increase the per-centage of O_2 in the atmosphere, inasmuch as photosynthesis is more vigorous than respira-tion. The increase of atmospheric O_2 from photosynthesis is offset by animals that take in O_2 and liberate CO_2. The complementary metabolism of plants and animals is largely responsible for the balanced state of these gases in the atmosphere.

There is considerable variation in the atmospheric amounts of CO_2 with time and location, although its relative concentration remains at about 0.03 percent of the total atmosphere at sea level. Over cities and near the forest floor the CO_2 concentration tends to be somewhat higher, but at high altitudes it is less concentrated. There are daily localized reductions in CO_2 concentrations when photosynthesis is most active, but seldom is CO_2 a limiting factor in plant distribution even though daily fluctuations may limit photosynthesis.

A more important limiting atmospheric factor is the accumulation of various pollutants. Air pollution is definitely an environmental factor limiting the distribution of plants in the natural environment and must be taken into consideration particularly in urban areas.

Air Pollution

Air pollution is not a new problem. It was more apparent in many cities in the 1930s because of the increased use of coal and the large amount of coal smoke then. Today smoke has been greatly reduced, but increased industrial activity and the expanded use of internal combustion engines for transportation have meant that invisible gases injurious to plants are present at critical levels in the atmosphere over many areas of the country.

Damage to agricultural crops from air pollution has been estimated at 500 million dollars annually. This does not include the damage done to ornamental plants, which contribute greatly to the quality of everyone's environment. That damage is more difficult to assess. Disfigured foliage and stunted growth from air pollution are becoming more prevalent in many cities and even some rural areas. In any area with large population centers or numerous industrial installations citizens will soon have to cope with problems caused by air pollution, if they are not already doing so. The primary source of pollution is the use of cars and trucks, which continue to increase in number.

AIR POLLUTANTS MOST HARMFUL TO PLANTS

Contaminates in the polluted atmosphere are waste products that include gases and solid matter. Certain instances of dust injury to plants have been reported near cement and lime kilns. There have also been examples of injury from acid mists near certain industries. However, the most serious pollutants are invisible gases.

Plant injury attributed to sulfur dioxide was described over a century ago. This is not surprising since one of the primary sources of sulfur dioxide is the combustion of coal. Another serious pollutant is fluoride, which is not as abundant but constitutes a serious problem nonetheless since it causes injury at lower concentrations than does sulfur dioxide.

A group of pollutants that have been recognized only since the 1940s are the photochemical gases. These are produced in sunlight by the combination of nitrogen oxides and organic vapors, both of which are produced by vehicular exhaust emissions. One such gas is ozone. Ozone has been known to be phytotoxic—plant-injurious—for many years and the injury it causes has been observed on sensitive plants following electrical storms. It has become a serious pollutant only with the growth of gasoline-powered transportation. Along with related gases, ozone poses the most serious threat to plants now and in the future.

Table 5-1 General symptoms for diagnosing air-pollution injury to plants.

Pollutant	Symptoms	Sensitive indicator plants
Ozone	Reddish-brown stipple or bleached flecking on upper surface of the leaf; small areas merge to form irregular blotches and marginal rolling and scorching when severe. Conifers show tip burn or yellow-to-brown banding on the needles.	Lilac, white pine, Scots pine, locust, sycamore, green and white ash, tulip-tree, European larch, aster, salvia, and dahlia.
PAN (Peroxyacetyl nitrate)	Collapse of tissue on lower leaf surface, which appears silver or bronze either in bands or blotches. Chlorosis or bleaching in conifers.	Petunia, salvia, chrysanthemum, snapdragon, aster, and primrose.
Sulfur dioxide	Light blotches occurring between leaf veins and on the leaf margin; adjacent tissues chlorotic. Conifers show brown necrotic tips on the needles.	Larch, white pine, Douglas-fir, spruce, white fir, certain crabapples, scarlet hawthorn, violet, begonia, zinnia, verbena, and certain tulip varieties.
Fluorides	Tips and margins of leaves become necrotic, with scorched appearance; distinct boundary accented by a narrow, dark, reddish-brown or slightly chlorotic band. Conifers show brown-to-reddish-brown necrotic needle tips.	Pine, gladiolus, iris.

An important question for the plantsman is "What do pollutants do to plants and how can the injury be recognized?" This is not an easy question to answer, because the effects of pollutants are quite similar to many other plant disorders.

However, there are symptoms characteristic of particular pollutants. These symptoms and the plants that are known to be relatively sensitive to specific gases are described in Table 5-1.

The symptoms by themselves are not very revealing since they could be caused by other disorders such as insects, disease, or physiological disorders. Yet there are times when the symptoms are quite significant. If the plant is located near a source of pollution such as an industry or a heavily travelled expressway, the chances the plant has suffered pollution injury are great. Weather and prevailing winds should also be observed. Pollutants tend to concentrate during periods of still air, during a temperature inversion or during an overcast day. Symptoms of pollution injury will probably become evident a few days later. The times of year when pollution is most likely to result in injury are late spring or early summer, when the plants are in their most active stage of growth.

In diagnosing pollution injury, first rule out other disorders. Then consider the likelihood of pollution injury based on the location of the plant in relation to possible sources of pollution and prevailing winds, weather conditions, and the season. Next determine if the plant on which symptoms have been found, or adjacent plants, are known to be especially sensitive to the suspected pollutant, because such plants will be the first to show injury symptoms. But some plants that are not known to be particularly sensitive may nevertheless be severely injured if they are exposed to high concentrations of some pollutants. At best, the diagnosis will be an intelligent guess.

ACTION OF POLLUTANTS

Gaseous pollutants enter the plant in the same manner as carbon dioxide. As with carbon dioxide, the ports of entry are the stomata openings of the leaf. If gaseous pollutants do not enter here, they do not cause injury.

It takes a definite amount of the pollutant to cause injury and usually the plant must have endured a particular period of exposure. For example, sulfur dioxide can be tolerated indefinitely at low concentrations, but high concentrations for a few hours can cause serious injury. The sulfur content of the leaf is of little help in determining if sulfur dioxide is the cause of injury because greater amounts of sulfur may accumulate through long exposures to high concentrations. Unless the short exposure has resulted in injury, growth will continue. This is true of both sulfur dioxide and fluorides.

But unlike sulfur dioxide injury, the injury that results from fluoride poisoning is dependent on the accumulation of fluorides to toxic levels, and this explains in part why fluoride injury is localized in the leaf margin where the fluoride accumulates. Consequently, the leaf will store fluoride over long periods of exposure to low concentrations until the fluoride content becomes toxic; the toxicity can be detrimental to many plants.

High concentrations of ozone for a short period cause more serious injury than low concentrations over an extended period. However, there is reason to suspect that lower levels of ozone may also cause a type of "hidden injury" by suppressing the growth of some plants.

PREVENTION OF AIR-POLLUTION INJURY

It is a misconception that washing plants with water will overcome poisoning by pollution or remove the pollutants from the plants. Washing may help when salt used as a de-icer accumulates on evergreen foliage or when soot, dirt, and certain acid mists are a problem, but these are examples of particulate pollution; washing will be of little value in protecting plants against the phytotoxic gases.

Unfortunately, there is very little that can be done culturally to prevent pollution damage to plants. Presently, the only recommended practice is to grow pollution-resistant plants if a known or potential pollution problem exists.

The preparation of a list of resistant plants is not without problems since knowledge in this area is rather limited. Use caution with some of the sensitive plants listed in Table 5-1 if a particular pollution problem is suspected. Exact information is not available on tolerances of many important species of ornamentals, and further research is necessary before such guides will be trustworthy. The best evidence on resistant species is based on observation of

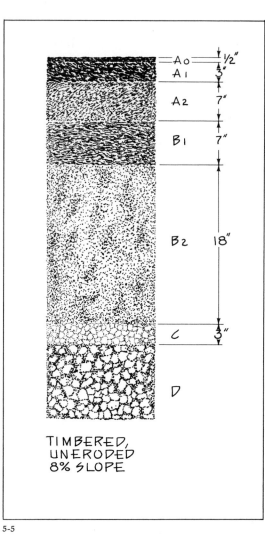

Labels in figure: Ao — ½″, A1 — 3″, A2 — 7″, B1 — 7″, B2 — 18″, C — 3″, D

TIMBERED, UNERODED 8% SLOPE

5-5

Figure 5-5. *A typical example of a soil profile. This profile is of Miami silt loam in virgin forest soil. The lowest horizon is unweathered bedrock.*

plants and their growth in urban or industrial areas.

THE ROOT-ZONE ENVIRONMENT

The environment to which the roots of the plant are subjected once the plant has been installed in the landscape project is as important to the survival and subsequent development of the plant as the environment provided by the atmosphere and climate. The soil conditions present at the landscape site are one of the key factors to be considered when studying the root-zone environment. The soil in which most woody ornamentals grow in native habitats is a complex, carefully balanced biological system. The woody plant contributes to this system and in return benefits from the system. The soil system supplies water, oxygen, and nutrients to the roots of the plant. The plant holds the soil in place, preventing erosion and sometimes changing the coarse structure of the total soil system. Because they are so important, it will be worth while to consider the physical and the chemical effects of the soil on the total environment of the plant, through the rest of this chapter.

Soil Composition

Undisturbed soil consists of many different layers varying greatly in composition. Figure 5-5 is a simplified diagram or profile of the composition of virgin forest soil. As can be seen, the upper layer (A horizons) are rich in organic matter (humus) and contain roots, bacteria, fungi, and small animals. The farmer calls these layers the topsoil. It is in the topsoil

that the root systems of most woody plants are most active in obtaining nutrients and moisture. The B horizons represent subsoil. Little or no organic matter is contained in the B layers since there is very little living matter present. Some roots of woody plant material penetrate these layers, deriving additional moisture and providing some physical support for the upper portions of the plant. But very little nutrient uptake is achieved since the B horizons are deficient in the soluble mineral elements that are used by the plant. The soil of the B horizons is not as friable (crumbly or loose) as that of the A horizons since the clay content is much greater in the lower horizons. The subsoil is less permeable to moisture penetration and aeration is poor.

The C and D horizons are the layers below the subsoil. These layers consist of the parent material of the soil (C) and the bedrock (D). Very little biological activity occurs here that has an immediate effect on the growth of woody species of the forest. However, the roots of certain species will penetrate to these depths to obtain moisture.

Realizing that the main root activity of most woody plant species occurs in the A and upper-B horizons—a depth of from 12 to 18 inches—let us examine what happens to the soil at a typical construction site before the plant material is installed. In modifying the site through grading, the topsoil is generally removed; sometimes at highway sites even the subsoil is removed. If not removed, the topsoil may be buried under heavy, thick layers of subsoil added to raise the ground level. Heavy construction equipment frequently compacts the soil, destroying its structure. Temporary roadways often are made at construction sites and consequently the structure of the soil is destroyed beneath the roadway. Then, as construction progresses, debris consisting of pieces of lumber, sand, gravel, cement, plaster board, asphalt, and much else is thrown aside on the ground. During the final grading these residues from construction are thoroughly mixed into the soil. Often as token restoration a thin layer of topsoil from four to six inches deep is spread over the disaster area to give the soil a normal appearance after the final grading. But what happened to the soil—that delicate biological system that is necessary for good plant growth? The soil profile has been altered so drastically that survival of the landscape plant—let alone its good health—may not be possible because of the changes in moisture retention and drainage of the soil, soil oxygen levels, and the addition of construction residues to the soil.

SOIL COMPONENTS

Soil consists of four major physical components: (1) mineral materials, (2) organic matter, (3) water, and (4) air. A silt loam soil in good condition and at a moisture of field capacity consists of 45 percent mineral material, 25 percent water, 25 percent air, and 5 percent organic matter. Later, in "Soil texture" and "Soil water" we will explain what is in a silt loam soil having a moisture of field capacity, but for the moment we are interested in it as a model soil (see Figure 5-6). What happens to the ideal structure during construction of a landscape site such as the one we just mentioned, for which temporary roads are built and through which

heavy equipment rolls? Compaction reduces the pore space of the soil and the result is a reduction in the amount of air and water held by the soil, both of which are essential to good plant growth and the development of root systems.

The importance of maintaining the pore structure of the soil cannot be overemphasized. The size of the pores and their number control the moisture-holding capacity of the soil and its aeration. The large pores hold the water only temporarily. As in a sponge, gravity drains the water from the large pores, and these then fill with air, giving the soil good aeration. The air then provides the oxygen required by the plant for respiration, by which carbohydrates are converted to the energy the plant requires for root growth.

If the soil structure has been destroyed by compaction during construction, the large pores collapse and aeration of the soil is drastically reduced. Respiration in the roots is slowed (or even stopped), and it is likely the plant will die. The packing effect is illustrated in Table 5-2.

Small soil pores retain the moisture more tightly, again, much the way a sponge holds water. From this reservoir of moisture, a plant obtains its water. Thus, a soil with good structure can have both good aeration (provided by large pore spaces) and good moisture-holding capacity (provided by small pore spaces).

Soil structure is very closely related to soil texture. Soil structure refers to the makeup of the total soil, including water and air. Soil texture refers to the makeup of only the solid portion of the soil—mineral materials and organic matter.

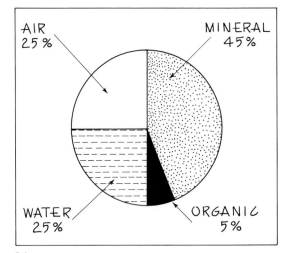

5-6

Figure 5-6. *The physical components of a silt loam soil, and the percentage of each by volume, when half of the pore space is filled with water.*

Table 5-2 Effect of traffic on soil aeration.

Pressure exerted	Soil density (g/ml)	Large pore space (%)
None	1.25	37.6
By tractor	1.32	35.0
By tractor and sprayer	1.46	27.0

There are three mineral particles and one organic particle that affect soil texture. The minerals are classified on the basis of their sizes, their overall contribution to soil structure, and their composition.

The largest of the mineral particles is sand, which is quite easily visible when a handful of soil is examined. Sand increases the pore space size and thus affects soil structure by increasing aeration. It contributes little to the moisture-holding capacity of the soil and does not provide a substantial reservoir for nutrients.

Silt is a smaller-sized particle that can be viewed with the aid of a microscope. The main function of silt in the soil structure is to increase the moisture-holding capacity, for the pores between particles of silt are smaller than between particles of sand and thus water is retained within the soil through capillary action. Silt has little or no influence on the nutrient retention of the soil.

Clay is the smallest of the soil particles and a single particle is visible only through the use of an electron microscope. The clay particle is platelike in structure and several particles will adhere tightly together when compacted. A soil in which the platelike particles are aligned in a flat manner is said to have "puddled," and puddling occurs when the soil is worked or compacted while wet. Soils that have a high clay-content are more susceptible to damage by compaction and puddling. Unlike sand and silt, clay increases the nutrient-holding capacity of the soil. Clays are active chemically; on their negatively charged surfaces they hold cations (positive charged ions) such as hydrogen, potassium, calcium, ammonium, magnesium; others too. In the film of water held tightly around the clay particle, these cations are in equilibrium with other cations in this water film. These are then exchanged, the plant root "taking up" from the water-film-clay complex those cations necessary for plant growth.

The organic nature of the soil texture is always changing because of the addition of more organic matter from plant and animal sources and the constant decomposition of the added organic matter. Organic matter accounts, on the average, for only from 3 to 5 percent of the topsoil by weight but contributes greatly to the overall soil structure by helping to keep the soil loose and porous. In this way organic matter helps in the aeration of the soil. It also possesses nutrient-holding capacity in a manner similar to clay. Moreover, organic matter is a source of energy for soil microorganisms, and when levels of organic materials have decreased to very low quantities the activity of microorganisms ceases. Such a deficiency of organic matter makes some soil barren at highway landscape sites and at other sites of heavy construction, where major changes have been made in the site's topography. Microorganisms are important in nitrogen fixation and other phases of the nitrogen cycle, which serves as a source of nitrogen for plants, and are important in other ways to the biochemical activity of the soil, functioning, for example, in the processes of oxidation and reduction of other mineral elements essential for plant growth.

Organic matter is classified on the basis of the degree of decomposition, not on particle size. Partially decomposed materials such as roots, leaves, pine needles, animal wastes, etc., are called simple organic matter. Fully decomposed organic matter is called humus; it is gelatinous (jellylike) in nature, and has greater nutrient and moisture-holding capacities than clay. Investigations have shown that humus is a major source of two of the essential elements for plant growth, phosphorus and sulfur.

SOIL TEXTURE

The amounts of sand, silt, and clay determine the soil's texture and to a great degree affect the overall structure of the soil. The term loam is used to describe a soil texture that is not dominated by the characteristics of any one of the three kinds of particles. A soil that consists of 40 percent sand, 40 percent silt, and 20 percent clay is considered a loam. The terms sandy loam and silt loam are often used to refer to certain soil types found in various sections of the country. A sandy loam consists, approximately, of 10 percent clay, 65 percent sand, and 25 percent silt. A silt loam will contain from 60 percent silt, 20 percent clay, and 20 percent sand. Any soil that contains over 55 percent clay is called a clay soil. Figure 5-7 shows the standard triangle used to classify soil texture on the basis of the quantities of the three kinds of particles.

What happens to the overall soil complex as the texture changes? If the sand content is too great (70–80 percent) the soil has a poor capacity for holding nutrients and moisture. Frequent fertilization and irrigation will be required to maintain optimum growth of many plant species if they are planted in such soil. But mixing sand into soils of high clay content will improve soil aeration.

Increasing the clay content of the soil will result in an increase in the capacity to hold nutrients, an increase in tightly held water (most of which will not be available to the plant) and a decrease in soil aeration. If the clay content of the soil is quite high, approaching 70 percent, aeration will often be so poor during periods of high moisture that insufficient oxygen will be present for the active roots of some plant species to survive.

Silt quantities have a less major effect on the overall soil condition. However, as the silt increases, moisture usable to the plant increases, and both the nutrient-holding capacity and aeration decrease. A soil that consists almost entirely of silt would be relatively nonproductive.

The term loam is often misused even when construction specifications are written for landscape projects. In specifications, it would be more appropriate to require a soil of good structure that has adequate aeration and moisture-holding capacity than to use the term loam. A balance of all three mineral particles plus adequate organic matter (3–5 percent) will provide the proper relationship of the solid portion of the soil complex.

SOIL WATER

It is generally common knowledge that water is essential for the existence of plant life. The amount of water available to the plant is controlled to some degree by the soil. Obviously if the water is never applied to the soil either by rainfall or irrigation the soil will have little influence on the availability of moisture to the plant. However, if water is available the soil texture will determine the rate of water pene-

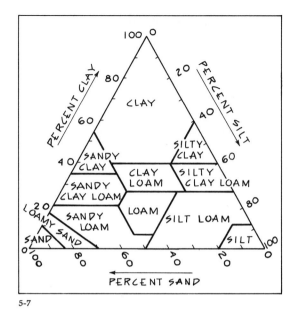

5-7

Figure 5-7. *Data from a mechanical soil analysis can be used in conjunction with this diagram to determine the textural name of the soil.*

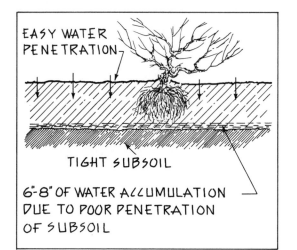

EASY WATER PENETRATION

TIGHT SUBSOIL

6"-8" OF WATER ACCUMULATION DUE TO POOR PENETRATION OF SUBSOIL

5-8

Figure 5-8. *An artificial water table develops if porous fill soil is placed on top of heavy, poorly drained subsoil. Plants may be injured by the excess water.*

tration to the root zone, the time of soil retention in the root zone, and the quantity of water available to the plant. Such terms as "saturated," "field capacity," "wilting coefficient," and "hygroscopic water" are used to describe how tightly the water is held by the soil. When a soil is saturated, all the pore spaces are filled with water. As the water drains by gravity from the soil, the soil is said to be at field capacity when the large pores are filled with air and drainage stops. A silt-loam soil that consists of 50 percent pore spaces will be at field capacity when half of the pores have drained (the large pores will drain first). As the plant utilizes water and surface evaporation occurs, the quantity of moisture is reduced to 25 percent of the pore space. This percentage in soils of varying moisture-holding capacity is called the wilting coefficient. It is significant because the only water then remaining in the soil is a film around the soil particle, which is called hygroscopic water. It occupies approximately 20 percent of the total pore space. This water is not available to the plant.

Water is the universal solvent, and the mineral nutrients necessary for plant growth must be dissolved in the soil water in order to be taken up by the plant roots. The hygroscopic water surrounding the clay particles serves as the solvent that holds the essential minerals required by the plant.

Man can alter the drainage patterns of a soil either intentionally or unintentionally. He can install drainage systems to increase the water movement through tight soils, from planters, and away from various landscape features, such as planting areas in parking lots and shopping centers.

He may add a porous fill soil on top of a tight subsoil or a compacted soil, and this may alter the drainage patterns, for what is known as an artificial water table may result. During periods of high moisture the porous soil will drain rapidly to the top of the layer of tight soil. There the water movement slows down drastically or stops altogether. In a short time the fill soil becomes saturated as a water table begins to form only a few inches below the surface. Aeration is reduced to nearly nothing and some plants may not survive the flooding.

An adequate amount of water is essential for plant growth. Either inadequate water or too much water is considered by many to be a prime cause for the loss of most landscape plant material. The problem of excess water for woody ornamentals at a landscape site is often compounded if turf is being installed, since both the seeding and sod techniques of turf installation require large amounts of water during their initial establishment. Some care should be taken in these circumstances to prevent overwatering of the trees and shrubs that have been installed at the same time as the turf. Watering techniques during both construction and subsequent maintenance will be discussed in detail in Chapters 13, 14, and 15.

SOIL AIR

Soil air differs markedly from the atmospheric air and there is even a variation within soil air depending on the soil's location. For example, the composition will vary in local pockets depending on the various chemicals and biochemical reactions occurring with surrounding particles. In pockets of substantial organic matter the CO_2 composition will be several hundred times more concentrated than the 0.03 percent found in the atmosphere. This is due to the decomposition of organic matter.

Accordingly, the amount of oxygen decreases to 10–12 percent; atmospheric air consists of 20 percent oxygen. The requirements for respiration in the root vary with the plant species and the stage of growth of the root system. Dormant roots require very little oxygen and this may account for the fact that some, such as the roots of the sugar maple, will tolerate a water saturated soil during their dormant season, but will not survive the condition during active growth periods.

Filling soil around existing trees alters the soil air and generally reduces the amount of air and particularly the amount of oxygen available to the roots. Also, changes occur in the level of soil moisture. Trees such as sugar maple, beech, and some oaks will not tolerate the addition of fill soils in the area extending from their trunks to the drip line (maximim spread of limbs), probably because of the changed oxygen concentration around the root system that is caused by the added fill.

Soil air moves into pore spaces not occupied by water. If the soil contains any moisture at all the air within it will constantly be near 100 percent relative humidity.

Poor soil aeration is one of the most critical soil factors faced by landscape contractors and maintenance personnel in areas that possess heavy or tight soils. Yews, dogwoods, rhododendrons, and many other species are noted for not tolerating tight, heavy soils. Poor aeration is the primary reason for their poor growth, and the lack of soil air is due to heavy soils, water saturation, and limited pore space. Certain woody species are adapted to soils with low concentrations of oxygen. Such species include some junipers, willows, and sycamore (*Platanus occidentalis*). Soils with low oxygen concentration may have a composition different from moist soils. As an example, hemlock will tolerate moist soils but not heavy soils with poor aeration. Apparently the moist soils also must have an adequate quantity of large pores, and hence, adequate aeration.

SOIL POLLUTANTS

Man is responsible exclusively for the soil pollutants that affect plant growth. Often the pollution is accidental, such as oil and gas leaks that saturate the soil and kill the plant life. These types of pollutants must be removed from the soil before the area can be relandscaped.

Pollution of the soil by salt is a common problem in the northern latitudes, occurring in landscape plantings along highways, parking lots, and sidewalks where the salt is used to remove ice from roadways and walkways during the winter. Salt injury to plant roots occurs because the addition of salt to the soil results in a movement of water from the root to the soil, which reverses the normal water movement. The roots become desiccated and are injured. The plant symptoms are nearly the same as when a plant is suffering from drought. Salt buildup in the soil will also result in degradation of the soil structure, since large quantities of sodium will replace the potassium and calcium in the internal structure of the clay particles, causing the particles to contract. This causes soil compaction.

Table 5-3 Relative "salt" tolerance of some woody plant species.

Low tolerance (injury prone)	Moderate tolerance	High tolerance
Abies balsamea	*Acer negundo*	*Elaeagnus angustifolia*
Acer saccharum	*Fraxinus pennsylvanica*	*Gleditsia triacanthos*
Alnus glutinosa	*Juniperus virginiana*	*Morus* spp.
Berberis thunbergii	*Lonicera japonica*	*Quercus alba*
Buxus sempervirens	*Malus baccata*	*Quercus borealis*
Carpinus betulus	*Pinus ponderosa*	*Quercus robur*
Euonymus alatus		*Rhus trilobata*
Fagus grandifolia		*Robinia pseudoacacia*
Picea glauca		*Salix alba*
Picea pungens		*Shepherdia argentea*
Pseudotsuga menziesii		*Tamarix gallica*
Rosa multiflora		
Salix purpurea		
Spiraea vanhouttei		
Tilia cordata		

Source: Information given in *Effects of De-icing Salts on Water Quality and Biota.* National Cooperative Highway Research Program. Report 91.

Plants vary in their susceptibility to salt injury. Table 5-3 gives a partial list of ornamental plants and their relative tolerance to salt buildup in the soil. In areas of danger from salt pollution, landscape architects should use plants that tolerate high concentrations of salt, if possible.

Herbicide accumulation or errors in herbicide application-rates will also cause soil pollution. Careful following of label directions, which include application techniques, rates, and plant tolerance, will reduce the danger from this type of soil pollution to a minimum. Caution should be exercised when using fill soil from agricultural lands because of the possibility of herbicide residues. Know the past history of the field before using fill soil taken from it.

SOIL NUTRIENTS

The soil is the source of all the essential mineral elements required for plant growth. Under most conditions these essential elements enter the plant through the root system. On some occasions, either when the soil is deficient in a specific element or when for some reason the plant is unable to take it up, applications of nutrients are made to the plant foliage. The efficiency of such techniques is generally marginal, however. Under normal soil-environmental conditions the plant will obtain the element from the soil, or if the soil is deficient, man will supply it to the soil.

Since man can supply all the essential mineral elements in the form of fertilizers, he can control the quantity of nutrients present in most soils at landscape sites. However, whether or not the elements are available to the plant is another matter. Nutrient availability is controlled to a great degree by the acidic or basic reaction of the soil—the soil pH. The term pH is used to describe the acidic or basic reaction of a certain material on a scale ranging from 1 to 14, with 7 being the neutral point. The more acidic the soil the lower the number below 7. At pH 7 the hydrogen ions (acidic) and hydroxyl ions (basic) are balanced. Above 7 the hydroxyl ions are present in greater quantities than acidic ions and the soil reaction is basic. Soils commonly range from 4.5 to 8.0 in pH reaction, though greater extremes have been recorded. Measurements of pH are based on a negative logarithmic scale, and a pH change from 7 to 8 means that the soil is 10 times more alkaline. Or a pH change from 6 to 5 is 10 times more acid; a change from 6 to 4 means the soil is 100 times more acid. For most plants used in the landscape a pH of from 6.0 to 6.5 is considered ideal. Acid-loving plants, for example the ericaceous family, prefer a soil pH of from 4.5 to 5.0.

At extremes on the soil pH scale some elements, such as iron and sulfur, but some others as well, are insoluble in water and the plant roots cannot absorb them. A deficiency results for the plant even though the soil contains an adequate quantity of the element. Figure 5-9 shows the relative availability of various elements at the pH range commonly found in soils.

It can be seen in that figure that at a high pH the solubility of iron decreases. Even though adequate iron is present in the soil, it is not available to the plant and iron chlorosis develops. The symptom of iron deficiency is a yellowing of the new plant growth. This may

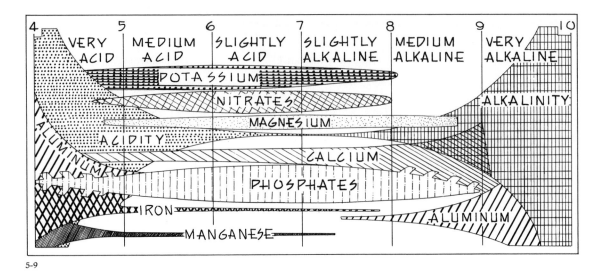

5-9

Figure 5-9. *The effect of soil pH in making various plant nutrients in the soil available to the plants.*

occur with the acid-loving plants at pH above 6.0. Pin oak suffers from iron chlorosis and poor growth when the soil pH is above 7.5. Addition of iron without a simultaneous reduction of the soil pH has little effect in remedying the condition.

It is most important that the landscape architect know what the soil pH is at the landscape site and that he use plant material adaptable to the soil pH present there. Modifying the soil pH will be discussed in detail in Chapter 13, "Site Modification."

It is essential that all the members of the landscape industry be aware of the factors essential for plant growth. If the landscape is designed with environmental factors for plant growth in mind, there is a much greater chance that the desired effect will be achieved with the plant material.

FOR FURTHER READING

Daubenmire, R. F., 1967. *Plants and Environment: A Textbook of Plant Autoecology.* New York: John Wiley and Sons, Inc. 422 pages.

Lyon, T. L., H. O. Buckman, and N. C. Brady. 1952. *The Nature and Properties of Soils.* New York: The Macmillan Co. 591 pages.

Janick, J. 1972. *Horticultural Science.* San Francisco: W. H. Freeman and Company. Second edition. 586 pages.

Janick, J., R. W. Schery, F. W. Woods, and V. W. Ruttan, 1974. *Plant Science.* San Francisco: W. H. Freeman and Company. Second edition. 740 pages.

6

The Classification and Origins of Landscape Plants

PLANT IDENTIFICATION

Although plant identification is largely beyond the scope of this book, the importance of proper identification of plants by the landscape architect, contractor, and maintenance supervisor warrants some consideration at this time. The landscape architect will need to identify existing plants on any project in order to recommend which ones should be saved. He will also be responsible for inspecting the plants used on his projects to make sure the proper plants were used. The landscape contractor will be responsible for implementing the plan, which requires that he identify the plants so that they will be placed where specified. And finally, maintenance personnel must be able to identify plants so that they will know what cultural practices are necessary for each plant.

The ability to identify plants is something like learning peoples' names. When you are introduced to someone by name you may concentrate on associating the name with particular features of that person, whether they are facial or other physical features. If you meet the person only once, you will probably soon forget who the person is. However, after you have been associated with a person for a long time and have called him by name a number of times, you will then be able to identify that person when you see him anywhere. If you do not see him for a few years you may find that you have forgotten his name, but it will only take a short reminder to refamiliarize yourself with that person. The same process is involved in identifying plants.

6-1

6-2

Figure 6-1. Sempervivum tectorum *(hen-and-chickens) is a succulent. It is often planted in rock gardens or on stone walls.*

Figure 6-2. Menispermum canadense *(common moonseed) is a woody vine. It spreads quickly by sending out underground runners.*

The significant difference between identifying plants and identifying people is that plants can't tell you who they are. Consequently, various guides have been prepared to assist in determining the identity of various plants. Three such manuals of particular value for identification of native and exotic species in the United States are the following:

Liberty Hyde Bailey
Manual of Cultivated Plants

Asa Gray
Manual of Botany

Alfred Rehder
Manual of Cultivated Trees and Shrubs

The actual identification of an unknown plant usually requires an *analytical key*, which is a part of most identification manuals. These keys list plant features, such as leaf arrangement, leaf shape, leaf color and hairiness, various twig features, and many other identifying characteristics of the plant that are evident at various times of the year. Usually the keys are based on vegetative features, even though the first separation of plants by species was based on differences in sexual structures. Unfortunately, the flowering stages do not last long enough to use this as a general means of identifying plants.

The use of keys requires some skill and does not always help in identifying certain varieties of plants. An alternative, when there is time, is to send the plant sample to an arboretum or botanical institute for proper identification. It is very important that any sample sent for identification be representative of the plant and as complete as possible. It is best to send a stem piece with leaves and flowers or fruits, if available.

Classification of Ornamental Plants

There are many ways of classifying or categorizing the thousands of plants that fall into the loosely defined category of ornamental plants. The validity of any system depends on consistency, clarity, and utility. For example, the classification of plants based on use, such as ornamentals in contrast to those that are edible, seems logical until you consider those species which are both ornamental and edible. Other ways of classifying plants, such as through the relationships of their growth habits, are also descriptive though frequently not a basis for easy differentiation; for example, differences between some trees and shrubs or between evergreen, semievergreen, and deciduous trees and shrubs may depend on geographical location. Throughout this book we will use classifications based on practical criteria such as use in landscape projects and the growth habit of a plant. These, along with the scientific classification, which we will also discuss in detail, ought to provide you with background to build upon as you become increasingly experienced.

A major division in ornamental plants occurs between those that are *succulent* or herbaceous and those that are *woody*. Herbaceous plants (those plants that do not produce woody stems) with self-supporting stems are known as *herbs*, and those that require support to grow upright or are trailing are *vines*. Woody plants are generally classified as *trees, shrubs,* or *woody vines (lianas)*. The distinction between trees and shrubs is not always apparent, but generally

6-3

6-5

6-6

6-7

6-4

Figure 6-3. Aesculus parvifolia *(bottlebrush buck-eye) is a deciduous shrub native to South Carolina and Alabama.*

Figure 6-4. Quercus palustris *(pin oak) is a deciduous tree native to the midwestern United States. The leaves turn a russet color before dropping in autumn. Branches are dense, and lower ones extend horizontally or droop to touch the ground. An excellent specimen tree, though its low spread may require too much space to make it practical as a street tree.*

Figure 6-5. Tsuga caroliniana *(Carolina hemlock) is a coniferous evergreen native to the mountains of the southeastern United States. It has a tolerance for city planting conditions.*

Figure 6-6. Viburnum × rhytidophylloides *is a broadleaf evergreen shrub. Its dense foliage makes it good for screen and background plantings.*

Figure 6-7. Pinus mugo *var.* mughus *(mugho pine) is native to the eastern Alps and the Balkan states. It is slow growing to about four feet and is a popular container plant.*

6-8

6-9

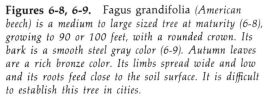

6-10

6-11

Figures 6-8, 6-9. Fagus grandifolia *(American beech) is a medium to large sized tree at maturity (6-8), growing to 90 or 100 feet, with a rounded crown. Its bark is a smooth steel gray color (6-9). Autumn leaves are a rich bronze color. Its limbs spread wide and low and its roots feed close to the soil surface. It is difficult to establish this tree in cities.*

Figure 6-10. Fagus sylvatica *'Fastigiata', a European beech cultivar, grows to a mature size of about 90 feet. The branches cluster in a fastigiate manner.*

Figure 6-11. Quercus imbricaria *(shingle oak, or northern laurel-oak because of its laurel-shaped leaves) grows to a mature height of about 60 feet, open, with a rounded crown. While young, the tree grows in a pyramidal habit.*

trees are characterized by a single upright stem or trunk and shrubs have several upright stems. In addition, trees are generally taller than shrubs. However, the distinctions may be obscured by such practices as pruning or training and by environmental conditions.

Among woody plants, a major distinction is made between those that lose their leaves during part of the year (*deciduous*) and those whose leaves persist during the entire year (*evergreen*). There are also those that hold their leaves late into the winter when others are leafless (*semievergreen*) but eventually lose their leaves or turn brown. In fact, even evergreen plants ultimately lose their leaves, though it is usually after new leaves have been formed. Some evergreens hold their leaves only one year, but many hold them two or more years.

Plants may also be classified on the basis of their life span. One group, *annual* plants, complete their life cycles in one growing season and must be planted new each year. Another category, *biennial* plants, complete their life cycles in two growing seasons, with only vegetative growth occurring the first year and flowering not taking place until the second year. The final category is *perennial* plants; these grow year after year. Although annuals and biennials are both herbaceous, perennials include both woody and herbaceous plants. Some woody plants such as abelia and some hydrangeas act like herbaceous plants in northern climates since they are killed to the ground each winter.

Landscape Categories

In addition to the very general horticultural classifications outlined above, plants are further differentiated for landscape purposes by size, growth habit, usage, and adaptability to specific environmental conditions.

Size is an extremely helpful classification system as it is one of the first considerations in selecting a plant for landscape purposes. Although size may seem to be the basis of the categories "trees" and "shrubs," these are grossly inadequate descriptions without further reference to size. The size ranges shown in Table 6-1 are helpful in differentiating within the general categories of trees and shrubs.

It is important to recognize that these are average or common sizes and not ultimate sizes. Mature or ultimate heights are frequently given in some manuals as an indication of size. This is not particularly helpful to the landscape architect, since during the major duration of the life of a plant mature size is rarely achieved. However, the time until maturity varies with the plant species. In addition to size, growth habit is a descriptive category that is quite useful. Besides the general categories of trees, shrubs, and vines already mentioned, each of these can be further divided. Some of the subdivisions are shown in Table 6-2.

Plants are frequently classified by their use in landscape designs, sometimes to the extent that the plant takes on the functional name. For example, privet (*Ligustrum* spp.) is often called hedge plant since it is almost always used as a hedge plant. Usage groups are listed for each major type in Table 6-3.

Finally plants are classified according to their ability to tolerate various environmental conditions, or on the basis of their requirement of them. This is particularly true of plants whose growth is unique to a specific habitat,

Table 6-1   Range of shrub and tree sizes, with examples.

	Example	
Range of size	Botanical name	Common name
SHRUB HEIGHT		
Dwarf: under 3 ft	*Viburnum opulus* var. *nanum*	Dwarf European cranberry-bush
Small: between 3 and 6 ft	*Kerria japonica*	Kerria
Medium: between 6 and 10 ft	*Viburnum dilatatum*	Linden-viburnum
Tall: between 10 and 15 ft	*Hamamelis virginiana*	Witch-hazel
Treelike: over 15 ft	*Cornus mas*	Cornelian-cherry
TREE HEIGHT		
Small: usually 30 ft	*Cornus florida*	Flowering dogwood
Medium: usually under 60 ft but more than 30 ft	*Carpinus caroliniana*	American hornbeam
Large: usually over 60 ft	*Acer saccharum*	Sugar maple

Table 6-2   Growth habits of trees, shrubs, and vines.

	Example	
Habit	Botanical name	Common name
TREES		
Columnar (fastigiate)	*Quercus robur* 'Fastigiata'	Columnar oak
Drooping (weeping)	*Salix* spp.	Weeping willows
Irregular (picturesque)	*Gingko biloba*	Gingko
Roundheaded (globular)	*Acer platanoides* 'Globosum'	
Pyramidal	*Quercus palustris*	Pin oak
Horizontally branching	*Nyssa sylvatica*	Tupelo, or Black gum
SHRUBS		
Drooping (weeping)	*Forsythia suspensa*	Weeping forsythia
Upright	*Hibiscus syriacus*	Rose of Sharon
Horizontally spreading	*Cotoneaster divaricata*	Spreading cotoneaster
VINES		
Clinging	*Parthenocissus tricuspidata*	Boston ivy
Twining	*Clematis* spp.	Clematis
Trailing	*Lonicera japonica* 'Halliana'	Hall's honeysuckle

Table 6-3 Various uses of trees, shrubs, and vines.

Trees	Shrubs	Vines
For shade	For screens	On walls
For street	For ground	On fences
plantings	covers	On trellises
For fruit	For flowers	For ground
For flowers	For hedges	covers
For windbreaks	(trimmed or	For flowers
As specimens	natural)	For fruit
For hedges		

6-12

6-13

6-14

Figure 6-12. Betula nigra *(river birch) is native to the southeastern United States, where it is found along streams. Seeds mature in the late spring when river banks are likely to be exposed by receding flood waters. Roots can withstand flooding.*

Figure 6-13. Carissa *spp., evergreen shrubs frequently used for hedges and screens in southern Florida and in southern California, are tolerant of seashore conditions.*

Figure 6-14. Cocos nucifera *(coconut palm) is widely distributed through tropical and subtropical regions and is sometimes used as a landscape plant in parts of Florida, California, and Hawaii.*

such as bog plants. Some of the environments that are singled out for classifying plants are the following:

Toleration of shade
Toleration of moist soil
Toleration of dry or poor, sterile soils
Toleration of the seashore
Toleration of city conditions

Major categories related to environment are:

Tropical
Subtropical
Temperate

Within each of these categories and locations, plants are classed either as hardy or tender, depending on whether or not the plant will survive the winter of a particular region.

Scientific Classification

Various methods of classifying plants have been used throughout history, including some of the approaches we have already mentioned, but it was the effort of Carolus Linnaeus (1707–1778) that revolutionized plant classification and gave form to the present scientific system. This system uses structural (morphological) similarities and differences particularly in the reproductive organs of the plant as a basis for classification. These parts of the plant are the least likely to be influenced by environmental conditions and therefore provide stable distinguishing features. Students of horticulture and landscape architecture frequently are overwhelmed by the Linnaean classification system; but it should be realized that it is only through a system such as this that order was created out of chaos and that a universal classification system came into being.

Taxonomy, the systematic classification of plants or other organisms, is not a fixed science. The principles of evolution proposed by Darwin had a profound effect on taxonomy, for the relationship of plants to each other through evolution provides a natural framework for plant classification. Of course, the validity of an evolutionary approach to taxonomy is related to how well evolutionary lines can be established. To help unravel these, plant scientists are utilizing genetic, ecological, and physiological-biochemical evidence. Thus, plant classification will continue to change as new information becomes available. That this happens continuously can be seen in relation to nomenclature, which must be adjusted to reflect changed thinking about plant lineage, as we will discuss.

Plant classification begins by dividing the plant kingdom into major divisions, separated on an evolutionary basis. Some of these divisions include such early evolutionary plants as algae, fungi, bacteria, and mosses. However, the division that will be of importance in this book is the most advanced division containing the so-called higher plants. This division, known as Tracheophyta, are plants with roots, stems, leaves, and vascular systems. We will illustrate further divisions by using as an example the pink flowering dogwood (*Cornus florida* var. *rubra*).

The pink flowering dogwood is described by each of the following categorizations. The precision of the description increases as the list descends.

Kingdom	Plant
Division	Tracheophyta
Class	Angiospermae
Subclass	Dicotyledoneae
Order	Cornales
Family	Cornaceae
Genus	*Cornus*
Species	*C. florida*
Variety	*C. f.* var. *rubra*

The two classes of primary concern in woody ornamental plants are gymnosperms and angiosperms. The gymnosperms, numbering less than 700 species, are primarily the evergreen species of the temperate zones. They are readily identifiable because of their naked seeds, which are usually borne on cones, in contrast to the seeds of angiosperms, which are fully enclosed in a fruit. Gymnosperms generally also have narrow or needlelike leaves, but angiosperms usually have broad leaves. There are over 250,000 species of angiosperms distributed all over the world.

Gymnosperms are further subdivided into three orders; Cycadales, Ginkgoales, and Coniferales, of which the latter two are most important for landscape plantings. Angiosperms are first subdivided into two major subclasses; the Dicotyledoneae and the Monocotyledoneae. The dicots, numbering about 200,000, include most of the broadleaf herbs, shrubs, and trees. Monocots, numbering about 50,000, include such orders as lilies, palms, and grasses.

The next lower grouping, called families, has very specific distinguishing characteristics that can be used for identification purposes. This is particularly true of reproductive (flower)

6-15

parts, but frequently holds true for nonreproductive structural features, such as leaf and bud arrangements. There are also definite cultural similarities that remain constant within families, such as the acid-soil requirement of the heath family (Ericaceae).

The genus is a very important classification grouping. Plants of a particular genus are strikingly similar morphologically. In fact, even before the Linnaean system was devised, the close relationship within such groups as roses (*Rosa*), oaks (*Quercus*), pines (*Pinus*), and maples (*Acer*) was recognized. Members of the same genus will generally cross-pollinate among themselves but not with members of other genera. Thus hybrids are generally crosses of species within the same genus.

The basic unit of this taxonomic system is the species. Individuals of a given species exhibit greater similarities morphologically than do the species of a genus. The proper designation of a species always requires using the name of its genus as well as the specific epithet. This binomial (two-name) system therefore allows a particular specific epithet to be used in combination with a number of generic names. For example, the white oak is *Quercus alba* and the tatarian dogwood is *Cornus alba*. There may be any number of genera containing similar specific epithets and any number of species within each genus, yet any given combination of a generic name and a specific epithet designates only one species.

Although the species is the basic taxonomic unit, there are further subclassifications that are extremely important to horticulturists. Some divisions are based on genetic differences, but others are related to ecological factors, and sometimes a subclassification will refer to both.

Plants that differ sufficiently in appearance within a species and that are similar in most other ways are classified as varieties. For example, the *pink* flowering dogwood (*Cornus florida* var. *rubra*) is a variety of the flowering dogwood (*C. florida*). The only visible difference between the variety and species is the color of the flower. This difference is genetic and occurs naturally.

A special type of variety is the horticultural variety, or cultivar, such as *Cornus florida* 'Pluribracteata'. Unlike the botanical variety, which occurs naturally, the cultivar is selected and maintained only in cultivation. Horticulturists depend heavily on cultivars for landscape use. With woody plants in particular, a cultivar usually indicates a particular clone that is propagated vegetatively (asexually) from a single plant; all plants from the propagation are identical genetically.

Subdivisions of the species based on ecological factors include ecospecies, the integrity of which is maintained by ecological barriers reinforced by genetic factors, and the ecotype, the integrity of which is dependent entirely on ecological barriers. Taxonomists have devised other subclassifications to handle other types of variation, but these will not be discussed in this text.

Scientific Nomenclature

The use of scientific names with plants causes much consternation among students and professionals, but use of them is the only way in which there can be any certainty as to the identity of a plant. Common names are helpful, but

Figure 6-15. Cornus florida *(flowering dogwood).*

there are so many plants with the same common name, as well as geographical differences in names, that they are not reliable. For example, if a landscape architect were to specify simply a "snowball bush," the nursery might supply *Viburnum plicatum*, *V. opulus* 'Roseum', *Hydrangea arborescens* 'Grandiflora', or any other plant that has been called a snowball bush. Consequently, it is absolutely essential that scientific names be utilized.

One difficulty encountered in specifying plants by scientific name arises from the discrepancies in scientific nomenclature. That is, plant names are sometimes changed if it is discovered that earlier some other name was given for that plant. Unfortunately, nurseries and designers are slow to change or update plant names. Catalogues will list a plant name incorrectly even though the name was changed 10 or 20 years ago. A good example of this is silver maple, which has been known or advertised as *Acer dasycarpum* or *A. saccharinum* var. *dasycarpum*, whereas authorities agree it is *Acer saccharinum*. For this reason there is some merit in using both scientific and common names as a double-check.

Scientific names of plants are usually designated by using italics or underlining. This is also true of the name of the variety, but not so of the cultivar. In the case of cultivars, the name does not have to be latinized, as the generic, specific, and varietal names should be. Instead, the cultivar name is capitalized and enclosed with single quotes, or the single quotes are dropped and the letters cv. inserted between the species and cultivar name. Thus, the cultivar lilac 'Mont Blanc' is designated either as *Syringa vulgaris* 'Mont Blanc' or as *S.v.* cv.

Mont Blanc, whereas a botanical or natural variety such as Sargent juniper would be *Juniperus chinensis* var. *sargentii*. Some cultivar names will be latinized, such as *Magnolia soulangeana* 'Lennei', because they were named before the International Code of Nomenclature for Cultivated Plants came into effect in 1954.

Plant nomenclature seems more difficult to learn than it really is. The binomial system is similar to the way people have named themselves for centuries. However, it is probably the unfamiliar latinized names that frighten people from feeling comfortable with plant taxonomy. It is helpful to recognize the meaning of some of the Latin names that are used most frequently because they are generally descriptive of some feature of that plant. For example, in the name for scarlet firethorn, which is *Pyracantha coccinea*, the *coccinea* is Latin for scarlet, which is the color of the fruit. Clues that may help decipher the meaning of specific plant names are listed in Table 6-4.

ORIGINS OF ORNAMENTAL PLANTS

Historical Origins

Plants have had a continuous association with man. At first, plants provided for such basic needs as food, clothing, and shelter. In addition to satisfying physical needs, they also fulfilled spiritual needs. Trees took on religious significance in ancient times, as mystical symbols and objects of worship. They were used as memorials in ancient Rome, as well as in the Far East, where memorial trees were planted during the Chou dynasty (circa 1100–250 BC) in China. There, use of officially designated memorial

6-16

6-17

Figure 6-16. Viburnum opulus *(European cranberrybush) has flower clusters in which fertile flowers form a center surrounded by infertile flowers. A cultivar,* V. o. *'Roseum', has flower clusters composed entirely of infertile flowers and is one of several "snowball" viburnums.*

Figure 6-17. Phellodendron amurense *(Amur corktree) takes its Linnaean name from the Greek "phellos" (cork) and "dendron" (tree) and is native to northern China. The tree is noted for its corklike bark and its broad rounded form, heavy trunk, and large open limbs.*

Table 6-4 Some helpful clues to the meaning of specific names of plants.

Note: The italicized terms in this table are Latin (or latinized terms of Greek origin). Some of them, such as *multi-*, always form compounds; others may or may not (for example, *albus* may stand alone or it may form compounds, such as *albiflorus*). The endings given here are masculine, but the ending of a Latin adjective changes according to the gender of the word it modifies: for example, the masculine *niger* (as in *Helleborus niger*) becomes *nigra* when it modifies a feminine noun (*Betula nigra*) and *nigrum* when it modifies a neuter noun (*Solanum nigrum*). A word of caution: Many familiar generic names with the characteristic masculine ending "*-us*" are actually feminine, notably *Cornus, Juniperus, Malus, Pinus, Populus, Prunus,* and *Quercus.* Thus, the correct name for the bristlecone pine is *Pinus aristata* (not *Pinus aristatus*).

KEYS TO PARTS OF PLANTS

-anthus:	flower
-carpus:	fruit
-caulis, cauli-:	stem
-florus, flori-:	flower
-folius, foli-:	leaf
-lobus:	lobe
-pes, -pedatus:	foot
-petalus:	petal
-phyllus:	leaf
-pus, -podus:	foot, stalk
-rhyzus:	root
-sepalus:	sepal
-spinus:	spine
-squamus:	scale

KEYS TO COLORS

albus, albidus:	white
argenteus:	silver
aurantiacus:	orange
aureus:	golden
azureus:	sky blue
caeruleus:	dark blue
caesius:	bluish gray
candicans, candidus:	white, shining
carneus:	flesh colored
cardinalis:	cardinal red
chromus:	color
chryseus:	golden yellow
cinereus:	ash colored
citrinus:	lemon yellow
coccineus:	scarlet
coelestinus:	sky blue
concolor:	similarly colored
croceus:	saffron
cyaneus:	dark blue
discolor:	of two or of different colors
flavus:	yellow

fulvus:	tawny, orange
incarnatus:	flesh toned
leuco-:	white
lilacinus:	lilac
luteus:	yellow
niger:	black
purpureus:	purple
roseus:	rosy
ruber, rubeus:	red
sanguineus:	blood red
verricolor:	variously colored
violaceus:	violet
viridis, virens:	green
xanthinus:	yellow

KEYS TO QUANTITIES

(Used here in compounds with words in the first section of this table.)

1:	*uniflorus; monophyllus*
2:	*biflorus; diphyllus*
3:	*trilobus; ternifolius*
4:	*quadrifolius; tetraphyllus*
5:	*quinqueflorus; pentanthus*
6:	*hexaphyllus*
7:	*heptaphyllus*
8:	*octopetalus*
9:	*enneaphyllus*
10:	*decapetalus*
100:	*centifolius*
1000:	*millefolius*
few:	*pauciflorus*
many:	*multiflorus; polyanthus*
various:	*heterophyllus*

KEYS TO SIZES AND SHAPES

altus:	tall
angularis:	angular
angustus:	narrow
brevis:	short
elongatus:	elongated
giganteus:	large, gigantic
gracilis:	slender
grandis:	large
nocturnus:	of night
perennis:	perennial
praecox:	very early
tardus:	late
vernus, vernalis:	of spring

KEYS TO DESIGNATIONS OF EMPHASIS OR DEGREE

atro-:	dark
pseudo-:	false
semper-:	ever, always
sub-:	somewhat
-bundus:	abundant
-escens:	becoming
-ferus:	bearing
-issimus:	very
-oides:	similar to
-osus:	with, bearing
-ulus:	somewhat
latus:	wide
longus:	long
macro-:	large
maximus:	very large
mega-:	large
micro-:	small
minimus:	very small
minor:	smaller
nanus:	dwarf, baby
ortho-:	straight

(continued)

Table 6-4 (continued)

parvus:	small
plenus:	full, double-flowered
pumilus:	dwarf
steno-:	narrow
tenuis:	slender

KEYS TO SEASONS OR TIMES

aestivus, aestivalis:	of summer
annuus:	annual
autumnalis:	of autumn
biennis:	biennial
diurnus:	of day
hyemalis:	of winter
majalis:	of May

KEYS TO REGIONS OR HABITATS

(Certain place names—*americanus, chinensis, germanicus, japonicus,* etc.—can be guessed.)

agrarius, agrestis:	of fields, wild
alpinus, alpestris:	alpine
aquaticus:	aquatic
australis:	southern
borealis:	northern
campestris:	of fields
exoticus:	foreign
hortensis:	of gardens
maritimus:	of shore or sea
montanus:	of mountains
niveus, nivalis:	of snow
occidentalis:	western
oceanicus:	of the sea
orientalis:	eastern
palustris:	of marshes
praetensis:	of meadows
riparius:	of river banks
rupestris:	of rocks
sativus:	cultivated
saxatilis:	of rocks
sinensis:	Chinese
sylvaticus, sylvestris:	of forests
terrestris:	of earth
vulgaris:	common

6-18

6-19

Figures 6-18, 6-19. Cedrus libani *var.* stenocoma. *The cedar of Lebanon is native to Asia Minor and is mentioned in the Bible as the tree used in the construction of Solomon's Temple. Var. stenocoma is the hardiest form. It is slow growing to 100 feet at maturity. While young, it has a narrow, pyramidal habit (6-18); at maturity its crown is flat. Needles are bright green in young trees (6-19), dark gray green in older trees.*

6-20

6-21

Figures 6-20, 6-21. *Cornus kousa (Japanese dogwood) is an introduction from Japan and Korea. It grows to about 20 feet (6-20), bearing flowers on the upper sides of horizontal branches (6-21). It is spectacular if planted so that it can be observed from above.*

trees depended on a person's station in life; pine trees were planted for kings, arborvitaes for princesses, pagoda-tree for high officials, goldenrain-tree for scholars, and poplars memorialized common people. The religious significance of trees arose because of the fruit they bore. Nut trees have had a longer association with man than most other woody plants.

In ancient Greece, some of the trees valued primarily for shade or ornament were elm, plane, yew, beech, and alder. The Romans made use of all the trees of Greece as well as their own favorites, such as pine and boxwood. The ancient Chinese, in addition to setting out memorial plantings, lined highways with such trees as pine, willow, pagoda-tree, chestnut, and elm.

Plant Introduction

One of the richest sources of plant materials in the United States has been through plant introductions. Like most immigrants in a new land, at first the early American colonists were more interested in familiar trees from their homeland than in native plants. Consequently, they made a concerted effort to introduce into America nearly all the important cultivated species of European trees and many shrubs, even though native American plants provided far greater variety and were also more suitable to the American climate. It wasn't until the eighteenth century that cultivation of native trees began to be practiced in America, and during the nineteenth century this became widespread.

Plant introduction has been going on for centuries and in all countries. The travels of some plants that are widely distributed in the United States today include stops in other countries before final arrival at the shores of America. Many of the plants brought to America from Europe were originally brought to Europe from Asia, having made the initial trip by way of the routes that had served traders for centuries, such as the "silk road" which connected the East and West.

By the eighteenth century Russia was sending out plant explorers to such places as Alaska, California, Siberia, Mongolia, Manchuria, and Persia. In the nineteenth century, Russian explorers included such men as Richard Maack (1825–1886, for whom the genus *Maackia* is named), Carl Johann Maximowicz (1827–1891, Japanese poplar or *Populus maximowiczii*), Eduard von Regel (1815–1892, the genus *Aregelia*), Baron A. von Schlippenbach (who collected *Rhododendron schlippenbachii* in 1854), and Alexander von Bunge (1803–1890, *Euonymus bungeanus*).

In the nineteenth century, plants were being introduced into Europe from the Orient as well as from America. The outstanding plant explorers during the first half of the nineteenth century include Allan Cunningham (1791–1839) from Kew Gardens, England, who made trips to Brazil, Australia, and New Zealand; Robert Fortune (1812–1880) who explored China, Formosa, Java, and the Philippines; and Carl Peter Thunberg (1743–1822) and Philipp Franz von Siebold (1796–1866), who collected plants in Japan.

During the last half of the nineteenth century and the early part of the twentieth, Ernest Henry Wilson (1876–1930) and Charles Sprague Sargent (1841–1927) were sent to various parts of the world by the Arnold Arboretum of Harvard University and established America as an active participant in the botanical exploration. Wilson, who became known as "Chinese" Wilson, made five trips to the Orient, bringing back hundreds of plants, among which were many of those that have since become the most popular plants in European and American gardens. As the result of just two of these trips, he sent 1,193 species and varieties to the Arnold Arboretum, where 918 were successfully grown, representing four new genera, 521 new species, and 356 new varieties.

When one considers the origin of the landscape plants used in America, one soon realizes the significance of plant introductions from other countries in enriching the American landscape. Of all the plants used in landscape development, the largest concentration of woody plants have come from eastern Asia. In the small area of Japan alone, there are more than 550 species of woody plants. In China, more than 900 genera of woody plants have been reported, which is more than three times the number of woody plant genera found in eastern North America. The reason for this is Asia's diversity in topography, climate, and ecological conditions. A list of some of the important cultivated shade trees originating in eastern Asia can be found in Table 6-5.

By comparison with the many landscape plants originating in eastern Asia, those native to Europe and to western or central Asia are few. Owing to the success of Europeans in colonizing different parts of the world, however, many European trees have been widely dispersed, and some have been present in

Table 6-5 Woody plants originating in Eastern Asia.

Botanical name	Common name	Region of origin
Acer buergerianum	Trident maple	Eastern China; Japan
Acer palmatum	Japanese maple	Korea; Japan
Ailanthus altissima	Tree of heaven	China
Albizia julibrissin	Silk-tree	Central China to Iran
Berberis thunbergii	Japanese barberry	Japan
Buddleia alternifolia	Fountain buddleia	Northwest China
Buxus microphylla	Littleleaf box	Japan
Castanea mollissima	Chinese chestnut	China; Korea
Cercidiphyllum japonicum	Katsura-tree	China; Japan
Cercis chinensis	Chinese Judas-tree or Chinese redbud	Central China
Chaenomeles japonica	Japanese flowering quince	Japan
Cornus alba 'Sibirica'	Siberian dogwood	Siberia to Manchuria
Cornus kousa	Japanese dogwood	Korea; Japan
Cornus officinalis	Japanese cornel	Korea; Japan
Cotoneaster divaricata	Spreading cotoneaster	Central and Western China
Cotoneaster horizontalis	Rock spray cotoneaster	Western China
Deutzia gracilis	Slender deutzia	Japan
Deutzia grandiflora	Early deutzia	Northern China
Elaeagnus umbellata	Autumn-olive	China; Korea; Japan
Euonymus alatus	Winged spindletree	Northeast Asia
Euonymus japonicus	Evergreen euonymus	Southern Japan
Forsythia ovata	Early forsythia	Korea
Forsythia suspensa var. *sieboldii*	Siebold forsythia	Japan
Hamamelis mollis	Chinese witch-hazel	Central China
Hibiscus rosa-sinensis	Chinese hibiscus	China
Hibiscus syriacus	Shrub-althea or Rose of Sharon	China; India
Hydrangea paniculata 'Grandiflora'	Peegee hydrangea	Japan
Ilex crenata	Japanese holly	Japan
Kalopanax pictus	Kalopanax or castor-aralia	China; Japan
Koelreuteria paniculata	Goldenrain-tree	China; Korea; Japan
Kolkwitzia amabilis	Beauty bush	Central China
Ligustrum amurense	Amur privet	Northern China
Ligustrum ovalifolium	California privet	Japan
Lonicera tatarica	Tatarian honeysuckle	Manchuria; Korea
Magnolia denudata	Yulan magnolia	Central China
Magnolia kobus var. *stellata*	Star magnolia	Japan
Magnolia liliflora	Lily magnolia	China
Morus alba	White mulberry	China
Paulownia tomentosa	Paulownia or empress-tree	China
Phellodendron amurense	Amur cork-tree	North China; Northeast Asia
Pieris japonica	Japanese andromeda	Japan
Prunus glandulosa	Dwarf flowering almond	China; Japan
Quercus acutissima	Sawtooth oak	Himalayas to Japan

Table 6-5 (continued)

Botanical name	Common name	Region of origin
Rhododendron obtusum	Hiryu azalea	Japan
Rosa chinensis 'Minima'	Fairy rose	China
Rosa hugonis	Father Hugo's rose	Central China
Rosa multiflora	Japanese rose or multiflora rose	Japan; Korea
Rosa rugosa	Rugosa rose	Northern China; Korea
Salix babylonica	Weeping willow	China
Salix matsudana	Hankow willow	China
Sophora japonica	Japanese pagoda-tree or Chinese scholar-tree	China; Korea
Spiraea prunifolia	Bridalwreath spirea	Japan; Central China
Spiraea thunbergii	Thunberg spirea	Japan; China
Styrax japonica	Japanese snowbell	China; Japan
Syringa reticulata (S. *amurensis* var. *japonica*)	Japanese tree-lilac	Japan
Syringa villosa	Late lilac	Northern China
Ulmus parvifolia	Chinese elm	Northern and Central China; Korea; Japan
Ulmus pumila	Siberian elm	Eastern Siberia; Northern China
Viburnum carlesii	Korean spice viburnum	Korea
Viburnum macrocephalum 'Sterile'	Chinese snowball	China
Weigela florida	Weigela	Korea; Northern China
Weigela praecox	Early weigela	Korea
Wisteria floribunda	Japanese wisteria	Japan
Zelkova serrata	Japanese zelkova	Japan

American landscapes since colonial times. None represents a new genera to North America, and with the exception of a few notable trees such as European beech and Norway maple, the introduced species do not thrive as well as the native ones.

Although woody plants from western to central Asia are among the earliest cultivated plants of the world, they are not widely planted in other parts of the world because they are not as hardy as other temperate species. Yet, this is the center of origin of such plants as grape, cherry, almond, pear, fig, walnut, and pomegranate. A list of some important woody plants originating either in Europe or in western to central Asia can be found in Table 6-6.

Finally, a discussion of the origin of woody plants would not be complete without consideration of the rich source of plants that are native to North America. Here woody plants originated primarily either in the east or along the Pacific coast. In general, these two major regions are dissimilar in climate as well as in geological makeup. Some species do extend all the way from the Pacific coast to the Atlantic coast, but the majority are found in one area or the other. A list of some native North American woody plants and of the regions from which they come is given in Table 6-7.

The origin of conifers in the various parts of the world are listed in Table 6-8.

Plant Selection and Improvement

During the time plants have been in cultivation, they have undergone continual improvement. Initially, this was accomplished by observing natural variations in plants and selecting those characteristics that were most desirable. One

Table 6-6 Woody plants originating in Europe to Western or Central Asia.

Botanical name	Common name	Region of origin
Acer campestre	Hedge maple	Europe: Caucasus
Acer platanoides	Norway maple	Europe; Western Asia
Acer pseudoplatanus	Sycamore-maple	Europe; Western Asia
Acer tataricum	Tatarian maple	Europe; Western Asia
Aesculus hippocastanum	Common horsechestnut	Balkan Peninsula
Alnus glutinosa	European black alder	Europe; Northern Africa to Central Asia
Alnus incana	Speckled alder	Europe; Asia Minor
Betula pendula	European white birch	Europe; Asia Minor
Buxus sempervirens	Common box	Southern Europe; Northern Africa; Western Asia
Calluna vulgaris	Scotch heather	Europe
Carpinus betulus	European hornbeam	Europe to Central Asia
Cornus mas	Cornelian-cherry	Central and Southern Europe; Western Asia
Cytisus scoparius	Scotch broom	Central and Southern Europe
Elaeagnus angustifolia	Russian-olive	Southern Europe to Western and Central Asia
Erica carnea	Spring heath	Central and Southern Europe
Fagus sylvatica	European beech	Central and Southern Europe
Fraxinus excelsior	European ash	Europe; Asia Minor
Hedera helix	English ivy	Europe
Ligustrum vulgare	Common privet	Europe
Lonicera tatarica	Tatarian honeysuckle	Southern Russia
Ostrya carpinifolia	European hop-hornbeam	Eastern Europe; Asia Minor
Philadelphus coronarius	Sweet mock-orange	Southern Europe
Platanus orientalis	Oriental plane-tree	Western Asia
Pyracantha coccinea	Scarlet firethorn	Italy to Western Asia
Quercus robur	English oak	Europe; Northern Africa; Western Asia
Ribes alpinum	Alpine currant	Europe
Rosa centifolia	Cabbage rose	Eastern Caucasus
Rosa damascena	Damask rose	Asia Minor
Syringa vulgaris	Common lilac	Southeast Europe
Tilia petiolaris	Pendant silver linden	Southeast Europe; Western Asia
Tilia tomentosa	Silver linden	Southeast Europe; Caucasus
Viburnum lantana	Wayfaring-tree	Europe; Western Asia

Table 6-7 Shrubs originating in North America.

Botanical name	Common name	Region of origin
Amelanchier canadensis	Juneberry, shadbush, or serviceberry	Maine to Minnesota, to Georgia and Louisiana
Chionanthus virginicus	Fringe-tree	New Jersey to Florida
Cornus stolonifera	Red-osier dogwood	Eastern United States
Cotinus obovatus	American smoke tree	Southeastern United States
Franklinia alatamaha	Franklinia	Georgia
Hamamelis virginiana	Common witch-hazel	Eastern and Central United States
Hydrangea quercifolia	Oak-leaved hydrangea	Georgia and Florida to Mississippi
Ilex glabra	Inkberry	Eastern United States and Canada
Ilex verticillata	Winterberry	Eastern United States
Leucothoë fontanesiana (L. catesbaei)	Drooping leucothoë or fountain leucothoë	Virginia to Georgia to Tennessee
Magnolia virginiana	Sweet-bay magnolia	Coastal Eastern United States
Mahonia aquifolium	Oregon-grape	British Columbia to Oregon
Myrica pensylvanica	Bayberry	Newfoundland to Maryland on Coast
Pachistima canbyi	Canby pachistima	Western North America
Parthenocissus quinquefolia	Virginia creeper	Eastern United States
Rhododendron calendulaceum	Flame azalea	Pennsylvania to Georgia and west to Kentucky
Rhododendron carolinianum	Carolina rhododendron	North Carolina
Rhododendron catawbiense	Catawba rhododendron	Virginia to Georgia
Rhododendron macrophyllum	Coast or California rhododendron	Pacific Coast
Rhus aromatica	Fragrant sumac	Eastern United States
Rhus glabra	Smooth sumac	Eastern United States
Robinia hispida	Rose-acacia	Virginia to Georgia and Alabama
Rosa virginiana	Virginia rose	Newfoundland to Alabama, Virginia, and Missouri
Viburnum trilobum	American cranberry-bush	Southern Canada; Northeastern United States
Vitis californica	California grape	Oregon to California
Yucca filamentosa	Adam's needle	Southern United States

plant may have had larger flowers or fruits, or been hardier and more vigorous than other plants of the same species or genus. The difference, which man then tried to cultivate, may have occurred first owing to natural crossbreeding, mutations, or other events that alter the genetic makeup of an individual plant. Genetic variation and plant selection have had a very significant effect on the characteristics of plants and their ultimate use in the landscape.

Variation in biological organisms is not surprising or unique, rather it is expected and common. Genetic variation is the basis of natural selection. Natural selection is the process by which one plant or species survives while another, with slightly different genetic composition, fails to survive. Man utilizes genetic variation when he selects the one plant out of a thousand that has certain characteristics that make it more desirable than others for landscape use. The process of selection and propagation of certain plants has been conducted for centuries, particularly with ornamentals like roses, tulips, and lilies. But the reason for variation did not begin to become clear until Gregor Mendel's work on the basis of heredity was recognized in 1900.

The dispersion of plants through exploration and through introduction of new plants into an area greatly affects the genetic variation in plant material. In addition to making the introduced species itself available, plant dispersion brings together geographically isolated but genetically related species, and these often produce hybrids. Examples of this can be found in *Aesculus*, the horsechestnuts, and in many other groups. Generally if hybrids breed

Table 6-8   Origins of conifers

Region of origin and botanical name	Common name
EUROPE	
Abies alba	Silver fir
Cupressus sempervirens	Italian cypress
Juniperus communis	Common juniper
Larix decidua	European larch
Picea abies	Norway spruce
Pinus mugo	Swiss mountain pine
Pinus nigra	Austrian pine, black pine
Pinus sylvestris	Scots pine
Taxus baccata	English yew
NORTH AFRICA	
Abies numidica	Algerian fir
Cedrus atlantica	Atlas cedar
Juniperus thurifera	Incense juniper
WESTERN ASIA	
Abies cilicica	Cilician fir
Abies nordmanniana	Nordmann fir (or Caucasian fir)
Cedrus libani	Cedar of Lebanon
Juniperus drupacea	Syrian juniper
Picea orientalis	Oriental spruce
HIMALAYAS	
Abies pindrow	Pindrow fir
Abies spectabilis	Himalayan fir
Cedrus deodara	Deodar cedar
Cupressus torulosa	Himalayan cypress
Picea smithiana	Himalayan spruce
Pinus wallichiana (*P. griffithii*)	Himalayan pine
CHINA	
Cephalotaxus fortunei	Chinese plum-yew
Cryptomeria japonica var. *sinensis*	Chinese cryptomeria
Cunninghamia lanceolata	China-fir
Cupressus funebris	Chinese weeping cypress

Region of origin and botanical name	Common name
Juniperus chinensis	Chinese juniper
Juniperus formosana	Formosan juniper
Keteleeria davidiana	Keteleeria
Larix gmelinii	Dahurian larch
Larix potaninii	Chinese larch
Metasequoia glyptostroboides	Metasequoia, dawn redwood
Pinus armandii	Armand pine
Pinus bungeana	Lacebark pine
Pinus massoniana	Masson pine
Pinus tabulaeformis	Chinese pine
Pseudolarix amabilis (*P. kaempferi*)	Golden-larch
Thuja orientalis	Oriental arborvitae
Torreya grandis	Chinese torreya
JAPAN	
Cephalotaxus harringtonia var. *drupacea*	Japanese plum-yew
Chamaecyparis obtusa	Hinoki false-cypress
Chamaecyparis pisifera	Sarawa false-cypress
Cryptomeria japonica	Cryptomeria
Juniperus chinensis var. *sargentii*	Sargent juniper (from Kuril Islands)
Larix kaempferi	Japanese larch
Pinus densiflora	Japanese red pine
Pinus thunbergii	Japanese black pine
Sciadopitys verticillata	Umbrella-pine
Taxus cuspidata	Japanese yew
Thuja standishii	Japanese arborvitae
Thujopsis dolabrata	Hiba false-arborvitae
Torreya nucifera	Japanese torreya
Tsuga sieboldii	Siebold hemlock
EASTERN NORTH AMERICA	
Abies balsamea	Balsm fir
Chamaecyparis thyoides	Atlantic white-cedar
Juniperus virginiana	Eastern red-cedar
Picea rubens	Red spruce
Pinus banksiana	Jack pine
Pinus palustris	Longleaf pine
Pinus resinosa	Red pine

Region of origin and botanical name	Common name
Pinus rigida	Pitch pine
Pinus strobus	Eastern white pine
Pinus taeda	Loblolly pine
Taxodium distichum	Bald-cypress
Thuja occidentalis	American arborvitae
Tsuga canadensis	Eastern or Canada hemlock
WESTERN NORTH AMERICA	
Abies concolor	White fir
Abies grandis	Grand fir
Abies lasiocarpa	Subalpine fir
Abies magnifica	California red fir
Abies procera	Noble fir
Chamaecyparis lawsoniana	Lawson false-cypress
Chamaecyparis nootkatensis	Nootka false-cypress
Cupressus macrocarpa	Monterey cypress
Juniperus pachyphloea	Alligator juniper
Juniperus scopulorum	Western red-cedar
Larix occidentalis	Western larch
Libocedrus decurrens	Incense-cedar
Picea engelmannii	Engelmann spruce
Picea pungens	Colorado spruce
Pinus cembroides	Mexican pinyon pine
Pinus contorta	Shore pine, lodgepole pine
Pinus flexilis	Lumber pine
Pinus monticola	Western white pine
Pinus ponderosa	Ponderosa pine
Pinus radiata	Monterey pine
Pinus sabiniana	Digger pine
Pseudotsuga menziesii	Douglas-fir
Sequoia sempervirens	Redwood
Sequoiadendron giganteum	Giant sequoia
Thuja plicata	Giant arborvitae

6-23

among themselves the offspring will show considerable variation. Consequently, a desirable hybrid is usually propagated asexually to insure reproducing the desirable characteristics of a plant.

In some hybrids, a shift in the genetic makeup occurs, such as doubling of chromosomes, so that the hybrid will breed true from seed. An example of this is *Aesculus* × *carnea*, the red horsechestnut, which is a hybrid between the common horsechestnut, *A. hippocastanum* of Europe, and the red buckeye, *A. pavia* of North America.

Plant hybridization by man was first recorded in the eighteenth century, though there is evidence to suggest it was practiced first much earlier. By the early part of the nineteenth century, professional and amateur plant hybridizers were developing many new plants. By 1829, at least 1,450 varieties or cultivars of roses had been created through hybridization and by the end of the first half of the nineteenth century an estimated 6,500 cultivars of roses had been developed, of which less than 10 percent can now be found. Outstanding plant hybridizers include Luther Burbank (1849–1926) who, in addition to his outstanding work on vegetables and fruits, developed many ornamental plants such as lilies, roses, and several herbaceous ornamentals. Later hybridizers of ornamentals include Victor Lemoine of France and Dr. Maney of Iowa State University.

Origins of Selected Woody Plants

The origins of woody plants that are frequently used today are both interesting and revealing. Because of the large number of plants used in landscape projects, it will be necessary to dis-

Figure 6-22. Pinus strobus *(eastern white pine) is native to eastern North America, where it sometimes forms pure stands. It grows to 100 or 150 feet.*

Figure 6-23. Deutzia × lemoinei *(Lemoine deutzia) was hybridized from* D. parviflora *and* D. gracilis *and introduced during the 1890s by Victor Lemoine. It flowers profusely in the spring but is less interesting at other times of the year.*

cuss only a few, but these will serve to give some perspective on the roles of exploration, introduction, hybridization, and selection. It is important to recognize that the processes by which the distribution and varietal array of plants have been increased by man are always going on and that the widespread availability of plants today results largely from these practices in the past.

Probably of all trees recognized primarily because of their use by man in landscapes, none is so venerable as the ginkgo. This species, *Ginkgo biloba*, was in existence when the dinosaurs were still roaming the Earth 125 million years ago. It has remained virtually unchanged since the Mesozoic Era and thus provides a link between present and prehistoric times. Furthermore, its fanshaped leaves mark it as the sole surviving species of the order Ginkgoales, other species being known only through fossil evidence. Originating in China, the ginkgo is now distributed in many parts of the world. The earliest recorded evidence of cultivation dates from the eleventh century in eastern China. But at about the same time the ginkgo was introduced into Japan, where ginkgos still exist that are nearly a thousand years old. It first became known beyond the Orient through descriptions in the early eighteenth century and was introduced from Japan into Europe later in that century. The first recorded introduction of the ginkgo into America was from England by William Hamilton in 1784. From this long journey the ginkgo has become one of the most respected street and city trees in the United States, noted among other features for its freedom from insect pests. But one undesirable feature of this tree is that the pistillate tree

6-24

Figure 6-24. Metasequoia glyptostroboides *(dawn redwood) was known, until recently, only through the fossil record of the Mesozoic Era. During the 1940s it was discovered growing in China and was introduced to the United States. It is related to the sequoias and the sequoiadendrons, but it is deciduous. It grows quite fast and may become too large for many sites.*

produces a very rancid smelling fruit. Consequently, the staminate tree is usually used as a landscape plant.

Plane trees, also important shade and street trees for urban areas, have a more complex history. There are three species of interest: the Oriental plane (*Platanus orientalis*); the American plane (*P. occidentalis*), generally also called sycamore or buttonwood in the United States; and the London plane (*P. × hybrida*). The London plane tree does not grow in nature and is believed to be a hybrid between the Oriental plane and American plane trees. The Oriental plane is found in southeastern Europe and western Asia, though probably it originated in the Mediterranean area of Europe; the American plane is found in eastern North America. It is believed that the London plane first appeared in cultivation in the seventeenth century as a chance seedling in some botanic garden in Europe where the Oriental and American plane trees were growing close together. There are also indications that other hybrids of these two species occurred independently in several countries. The London plane, as well as the Oriental plane, was probably introduced into America from Europe in colonial times. The Oriental plane is not hardy in the northern United States and many trees that are called Oriental plane in the north should really be called London plane trees. However, considerable confusion surrounds the identity of the London plane because of its similarities to its parents and to the various other hybrid forms, and this is compounded by confusion about the common name. We indicated at the beginning of this paragraph that plane trees are commonly called sycamores in America.

In Europe the name sycamore is restricted to the sycamore-maple, *Acer pseudoplatanus*. Another species, *Ficus sycomorus*, of northeastern Africa, is commonly called the sycamore-fig. Hence, the importance of scientific names is clearly illustrated by these species.

Another interesting and important group of trees are those in the genus *Acer*, comprising at least 150 species widely distributed over the northern hemisphere and a few in the southern hemisphere. The largest number of *Acer* species originated in eastern and southeastern Asia. From Japan come the Japanese maple (*A. palmatum*) and several lesser known species, among them the trident maple (*A. buergerianum*), painted mono maple (*A. mono*), and the nikko maple (*A. nikoense*); from Korea, Manchuria, and northern China come such species as Amur maple (*A. ginnala*) and Manchurian maple (*A. mandshuricum*); from China come the largest number, including the paperbark maple (*A. griseum*), which is closely related to the nikko maple, David maple (*A. davidii*), and the Henry maple (*A. henryi*). From Europe and western Asia come the well known Norway maple (*A. platanoides*), sycamore-maple (*A. pseudoplatanus*) and hedge maple (*A. campestre*). Native species of North America include the outstanding and widely planted sugar maple (*A. saccharum*), red maple (*A. rubrum*), and the less desirable but frequently used silver maple (*A. saccharinum*). Although related, the sugar maple and the silver maple are very different in growth habit and landscape value. The sugar maple is slow growing, majestic in form, brightly colored in the fall, and long lived, whereas the silver maple is very fast growing and is consequently structurally weak and short lived. By planting maples alone it would be possible to represent a large part of the world in a single landscape design. Moreover, many of the species, such as the Japanese and Norway maples, are well known for their many varieties, which extend the diversity of the genus *Acer* even further.

The origin of some woody shrubs is also quite interesting and worthy of consideration. One of the most popular shrubs in the United States during colonial times was the lilac. The common lilac (*Syringa vulgaris*) was introduced into Europe in the sixteenth century from Turkey, though it probably originated in the Balkans. Another species, the Persian lilac (*S. persica*), did not originate in Persia as the name implies but was brought to Persia from China along ancient trade routes. In the latter part of the eighteenth century the two species *S. vulgaris* and *S. persica* were accidentally or intentionally crossed to produce a hybrid, *S. × chinensis*, known as the Rouen or Chinese lilac. Until well into the nineteenth century, those three species and a few varieties (cultivars) were the only lilacs cultivated. During the last half of the nineteenth century and into the twentieth, numerous other cultivars were introduced so that by 1928 at least 450 had been listed and described, most of them coming from France, where at least 153 were developed through the efforts of the firm of Victor Lemoine. Most of these cultivars were selected from *S. vulgaris*, but by the beginning of the twentieth century many new species were introduced from China that, in addition to increasing the number of different lilacs, now provide parent material for lilac hybrids. The hybridizing done in this century has resulted in the hardy Preston lilac (*S. × prestoniae*), a cross

between *S. villosa* and *S. reflexa*. Many other hybrids have been developed or are in the process of development, as well. The combination of plant exploration and hybridization has been important in the creation of these new plants.

A shrub group of more recent interest and introduction is cotoneaster. Although some cotoneasters originated in Europe, most are natives of China, Tibet, and northern India. In the early part of the nineteenth century only about 4 species were known; these were increased to 12 by the end of the century through introductions coming mostly from India and a few, such as the fishbone or rock spray cotoneaster (*Cotoneaster horizontalis*), coming from China. The popular spreading cotoneaster (*C. divaricata*) and willowleaf cotoneaster (*C. salicifolia*) also originated in China, but were not discovered and introduced into the United States until the early part of this century by E. H. Wilson. A number of hybrid forms have been developed since then, usually by crossing an evergreen with a deciduous species. However, none of these hybrids have become well known or widely used.

Finally, the history of some conifers reveals further the way in which commonly used landscape plants have originated. Usually conifers refer to evergreens, but a few, such as larch and bald-cypress, are deciduous. The genus *Taxus*, commonly known as yew, is an excellent example of the complexity of conifers. Species of this genus are widely distributed in Europe, North America, eastern Asia, and Asia Minor. The common yew (*Taxus baccata*), sometimes called English or European yew, is of European origin, with as many as 50 cultivars. Another

6-25

major species is the Japanese yew (*T. cuspidata*), which originated in the eastern Asian countries of Japan, Korea, and Manchuria. Although this species was introduced into the United States in 1862 by Dr. George R. Hall, it wasn't until the twentieth century that it became popular. It is now probably the most popular evergreen for landscape use. There are a number of cultivars, including the dwarf yew (*T. c.* 'Nana'). Two hybrids are of particular interest. The Anglojap yew or middle yew (*T.* × *media*) is a cross between *T. cuspidata* and *T. baccata*. Selected cultivars of this hybrid, such as Hicks and Hatfield yew, are particularly valuable in landscape designs. Another hybrid, Hunnewell yew (*T.* × *hunnewelliana*), is a cross between *T. cuspidata* and the native Canadian yew (*T. canadensis*).

It is significant that the majority of plants used in landscape designs were introduced, selected, or hybridized only within the past two or three centuries. Landscape designers have just begun to scratch the surface in using available plant materials and in planning to use potential plant materials. Considerably more effort is needed, particularly in breeding new plants to meet the hard conditions of urban environments, utilizing all the new plant species that have been introduced over the past couple of centuries.

FOR FURTHER READING

Coats, M., 1965. *Garden Shrubs and Their Histories.* New York: E. P. Dutton and Co., Inc. 416 pages.

Li, H.-L., 1963. *The Origin and Cultivation of Shade and Ornamental Trees.* Philadelphia: University of Pennsylvania Press, 282 pages.

Wyman, D., 1956. *Ground Cover Plants.* New York: The Macmillan Co.

Wyman, D., 1969. *Shrubs and Vines for American Gardens.* New York: The Macmillan Co. Revised edition, 613 pages.

Wyman, D., 1955. *Trees for the American Gardens.* New York: The Macmillan Co.

Zion, R. L., 1968. *Trees for Architecture and the Landscape.* New York: Reinhold Book Corporation. 284 pages.

Zucker, I., 1966. *Flowering Shrubs.* Princeton: D. Van Nostrand Co., Inc. 380 pages.

Figure 6-25. Taxus baccata *var.* repandens *(spreading English yew) is a popular ground cover or low foundation plant.*

III

Arranging Plants in the Landscape

7

Basic Principles of Planting Design

7-1

When using plants in the landscape, anyone who designs a landscape applies some basic principles of design, which are common also to other design professions, including architecture, interior design, and other arts.* These principles consist in various uses of line, form, texture, color, repetition, variety, balance, and emphasis; all of these terms apply to any aesthetic composition or work of art. In planting design some specific functions must also be considered along with aesthetic development. These functional factors will be discussed in Chapter 8.

The design of the landscape has unique qualities that distinguish it from other works of art, however. Whereas a painting is created on the flat surface of a canvas and a piece of sculpture is intended to be viewed on a pedestal, the designed landscape can be walked through, around, and under. In most arts, the beholder has to focus his senses toward an aesthetic effect that has been produced in a condensed or restricted space, but in landscape design the beholder can experience the artistic effect in many diverse ways, because he is within the design. Its scale is his scale. In a properly designed landscape, scale can be measured in relation to the size of people and the sizes of the spaces they need for their activities.

Furthermore, the landscape composition

*In Chapters 7 and 8, when we talk of a "designer," we will be referring to landscape architects, landscape designers, and any others who use plants in design.

Figure 7-1. *Two evenly spaced rows of trees along a sidewalk provide an example of strong straight lines. With the cars on both sides, a tunnel effect is almost created.*

changes as one moves through it and is constantly modified by ever-changing shadows as the sun crosses the sky, by the movements of clouds, by the emergence and disappearance of vistas relative to the viewer, and by the changing nature of the plants: new leaves in the spring, the appearance and aroma of flowers and fruit, the transformations of color in the fall, and the bareness of branches in winter.

Adding complexity to the three-dimensional composition of the landscape is a multitude of other factors from the physical environment, discussed elsewhere in this book. In his efforts, the designer faces tremendous challenge to create a work of art that is aesthetically pleasing to all the senses, is functional, and is harmonious with the physical environment in which it must survive, too.

AESTHETIC BASES OF LANDSCAPE DESIGN

Line

When the designer wants to create or control patterns, he does so by making use of line. The lines he has envisioned may ultimately become edges and borders. In a landscape composition a carefully planned group of lines will direct the attention of the viewer to a focal point or a particular area of interest in the composition. Lines are also useful in controlling movement, either visual or physical, in straight or curved directions. Rows of plants such as hedges are one example of the use of lines, but a row of trees may also create a line that is different because of the size and character of the trees. Moreover, lines can be found in the edges of paving materials as well as in the

7-2

Figure 7-2. *The monotony of straight lines can be reduced by changes in the surface patterns of the paving material. The repetition of the light fixtures emphasizes the lines of the walk, but visually the lights are weaker than the paving and trees. This view is of the Locust Walk at College Hall, University of Pennsylvania.*

7-3

7-4

7-5

Figure 7-3. *Angled lines create a meandering effect that encourages shoppers to remain longer at this St. Louis shopping center.*

Figure 7-4. *Curved lines in paving and plant materials, Constitution Plaza, Hartford, Connecticut.*

Figure 7-5. *Meandering lines appear in nature at the point of abrupt transition between evergreen and deciduous growth. The line is accentuated by the strong color contrast between the dark green foliage of the evergreens and the light green (or bright yellow in the autumn) of the aspens. This view is in the Caribou National Forest, Idaho.*

7-6

7-7

patterns in the material itself. Other kinds of lines are emphasized with fences and walls.

Straight lines suggest direct movement without hesitation. Interconnecting straight lines create points at the intersections for hesitation, stopping, sitting, changes of views, and reflections back to the point of beginning. Meandering, curved lines invite slower movement and are useful in areas that should seem as natural as possible, such as a path through the woods.

Form

The result of the total mass of a plant is described with the term "form." The trunk, branches, and leaves together create a form. If the plant is tall and slender, it is said to have a vertical form. If it is low and spreading, it is said to have a horizontal form. But a group of vertical plant forms may be grouped together in sufficient quantity that the length of the group is greater than the height, and the group then appears to have a horizontal form. A hedge of upright yews is an example.

Some shrubs with dense foliage can be trimmed into sculptured forms called "topiary," a practice rather uncommon today because of high labor costs but quite popular in seventeenth-century Dutch and English gardens. Today, designers prefer the natural forms of plants, which can be described by a variety of terms. How natural plant forms can be used in landscape design is illustrated in Chapter 9.

Texture

A designer tries to emphasize various textures through his use of plants and other landscape

Figure 7-6. *The individual vertical forms of* Euonymus japonicus *appear as a horizontal form when placed together. The same effect can be created with many varieties of plants.*

Figure 7-7. *An example of topiary in a re-created eighteenth-century garden at Colonial Williamsburg, Virginia.*

7-8

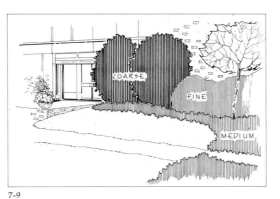

7-9

Figures 7-8, 7-9. *Three different textures were used for this project, with the medium texture as a ground cover visually unifying the others. Design for the offices of Yarway Corporation, Pennsylvania.*

7-10

materials. It is common to express the texture of plants in gradations from fine to medium to coarse. In an area that is to be planted with ground-covering plants, the large leaves of heartleaf bergenia (*Bergenia cordifolia*) present a coarse texture in contrast to Japanese pachysandra (*Pachysandra terminalis*), a plant with medium texture, and Irish moss or moss sandwort (*Arenaria verna* var. *caespitosa*), which has a fine texture. For contrast, pea gravel will provide a fine texture against the coarse texture of a group of large boulders averaging two or more feet in diameter.

Color

Most people, in one way or another, find that color has emotional impact. But human response to individual colors varies, and behavioral scientists find it difficult to measure and evaluate that response. In general, reds, oranges, and yellows are considered warm colors and seem to advance toward the viewer. Greens and blues are cooler colors and tend to recede in a composition. Dark blue, a cool color, may thus become a background color in compositions made up of several colors. Gray, being neutral, is best of all as a background when bright colors are used in the foreground. Numerous books have been written on color theory and a would-be designer does well to look into some of them if he does not know much about the nature of color.

In the landscape nearly everything expresses color, and colors seldom seem constant. There is almost an infinite variety of greens in leaves. Even in one species the green of the leaves undergoes a considerable change from the light, fresh color of an emerging new leaf

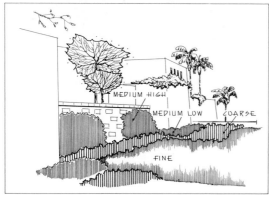

7-11

Figures 7-10, 7-11. *A fine texture is expressed in the grass with two medium textures at different heights against the wall and building, with coarse texture between them. The edges of the grass serve as a strong line in harmony with the angular lines of the building. This design was installed at the Sarasota office of the Arvida Corporation, Florida.*

in spring to the darker tones of midsummer and change completely from green to another color when fall arrives. Flowers and fruit also provide a wide variety of color. Winter colors tend to be more stark; bark colors and their variation will be more noticeable and will be accented by the color of persistent fruit, along with the greens of evergreen plants.

Nature's colors are nearly always superior to those manufactured by man and are subtler. Designers must be sensitive to color and know how to utilize it as one of the variables in designing the landscape.

Variety

A critical element in design is variety: too little leads to monotony and too much brings confusion. A very fine balance between extremes produces a pleasant sense of unity in a landscape composition. A planting design containing only junipers, even though these have a variety of forms and sizes, can be monotonous because the texture of junipers is so uniform. So far, in all the terms we have discussed, we have stressed that a variety of lines, forms, textures, and colors is needed to create an orderly, interesting landscape. But this does not mean that every shrub and every tree must be different within a design.

Repetition

Repetition gives the element of variety meaning and expression. It reduces the confusion that may result from excessive variety and introduces a sense of order to the viewer of the landscape. Designers frequently use the word "order" to describe a pleasing design.

7-12

7-13

7-14

Figure 7-12. *Texture is also altered by distance. A coarse texture at close view can become a finer texture as the distance increases, even though the plants are the same. This view is in Rocky Mountain National Park.*

Figure 7-13. *A variety of forms, colors, and textures, in both plants and paving. A small-scale design in a restored area of Philadelphia.*

Figure 7-14. *In large-scale areas, repetition is needed to prevent too much variety, but sufficient variety prevents monotony. A screen planting for a parking lot at Bernheim Forest, Kentucky.*

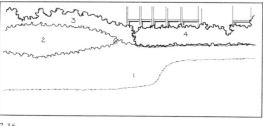

7-15

7-16

7-17

7-18

Figure 7-15. *A variety of color, massing, and height, against a background of white caststone. The repetition of individual plants provides the horizontal masses.*

Figure 7-16. *An analysis of the composition shown in Figure 7-15. (1) A mass of blue-green junipers that unifies the whole composition with its fine texture; (2) Mahonia aquifolium var. compacta—dwarf Oregon-grape—has a coarse texture and a light, glossy green color in the spring that is followed by dark green in late summer and purple in winter; (3) Euonymus japonica provides a year-round dark green; (4) Euonymus alatus var. compactus, the only deciduous plant of the four, has light green leaves in spring that darken as the season progresses and turn brilliant red in the fall.*

Figure 7-17. *Repetition in the line of trees emphasizes the curved line of the seat-wall.*

Figure 7-18. *Paving patterns and the railing create strong lines. The planting just beneath the railing is a simple horizontal mass that repeats the horizontal direction of the railing. Trees in the planters above and on the paving below the railing are repeated rhythmically in harmony with the paving pattern. Pepsico World Headquarters, Purchase, New York.*

Repetition is usually achieved by placing individual plants in groups or masses of a single species. In a large-scale landscape these masses, of varying sizes, may be repeated as the designer finds necessary.

Balance

Usually it is possible to perceive a central axis in a landscape composition. When weight, numbers, masses, etc., are distributed equally on both sides of the central axis, the composition is said to be in balance. It is on the basis of balance that landscapes are judged to be formal and informal, or symmetrical and asymmetrical. In a formal landscape, the distribution on either side of the axis is likely to be exactly the same, plant by plant. Except in a few public gardens, there are few formal landscape designs in existence today. Since World War II informality has been more popular. In informal landscapes the balance is likely to be equivalent rather than exact, and a large plant on one side of the axis may balance with a number of smaller plants on the other.

Emphasis

Through the use of emphasis, the eye is directed to one portion or object of the composition. This could be a single tree, a group of shrubs with unique character, or some structural feature, perhaps a fountain or a piece of sculpture. Secondary points of emphasis may be used too, whereby the eye is directed toward plants or other landscape features that have less contrast with the overall composition than the primary point or area of emphasis has.

7-19

7-20

Figure 7-19. *An example of formal or symmetrical balance, in the re-created garden of William Bryan, Colonial Williamsburg, Virginia.*

Figure 7-20. *An example of asymmetrical balance, at Bal Harbour Shops, Florida.*

Figure 7-21. *The use of sculpture for a point of emphasis in a garden. Voorhees Memorial Garden, Princeton University. Another area of this garden is shown in Figure 9-21.*

Figure 7-22. *A cluster of birches was placed as the focal point in this East Coast residential garden.*

Figure 7-23. *Emphasis was achieved in this composition by using one plant, a spreading English yew (Taxus baccata var. repandens). The pebbles provide a medium texture as a transition between the smooth concrete and the coarse yew.*

7-21

7-22

7-23

MAN'S PERCEPTION
OF THE LANDSCAPE

To perceive one's environment is to become aware of it through the senses of seeing, hearing, touching, smelling, and tasting (though taste is relatively unimportant in the perception of the landscape). Perception is also the process of communication by which an individual learns about himself and others and about other life and objects on the planet Earth. In the preceding paragraphs we spoke frequently of visual aspects of the landscape. Considering that other senses beside vision are important in perceiving the landscape, the "viewer" is actually a "participant" in the landscape.

Interaction of the Senses

Very little perception of the landscape occurs without some interaction of all the senses. As a means of examining this idea, think about the extent to which the following descriptions are made up of knowledge gained from sensory perception. All "landscape" is divided into natural and man-made categories. In scale, the natural landscape ranges from mountains and oceans to trees and ponds and to sticks, stones, and alpine flowers. The man-made landscape ranges in scale from city parks to village squares, from university campuses to shopping-center malls, from neighborhood miniparks to residential gardens.

What is perceived is dependent upon time, place, and particular sets of circumstances. Any landscape will contain some structural elements. Structural elements such as rocks and well-built buildings in the landscape change slowly through time. Plant life becomes established and semipermanent through time, changing seasonally, and emerging, living, and dying as part of the cycle of life. The atmosphere above any landscape changes constantly as the air shifts from place to place. Temperatures fluctuate and clouds soften the sun's shadows and lessen its heat.

All the senses interact during a walk in the autumn, after the leaves have started to fall. The eyes detect the movement of the leaves, both those that are falling and those being shuffled by the feet. At the same time, reinforcing the visually perceived data, the sense of touch is stimulated as leaves are stepped on and brush against the ankles and shoes. A light autumn drizzle begins: the freshly fallen leaves emit a dry, earthy odor.

Now imagine wintertime. It is a cold, crisp morning. A few inches of snow have fallen and the sun is shining. The visual sense is affected by the brightness of the sun's rays reflected from the snow. A slight breeze bites the cheeks and dries the nostrils. Some effort is required to move the feet through the snow. The sensation is reinforced by the crunching sound of the snow, detected by the ears. One's equilibrium is tested by occasional slick spots of ice.

Adaptation of the Senses

After prolonged exposure to certain sensations, such as odors, the body makes an adaptation; the mind responds less to a stimulus and it may even go unnoticed. A bouquet of flowers placed on the table in the dining room produces a pleasant odor throughout the room that will not be noticeable after a few hours because

7-24

7-25

adaptation has occurred. If one leaves the room for a few hours or takes a breath of fresh air outdoors and then returns to the room, the odor will be perceived again as if new. During its evolution, the human nervous system developed the ability to adapt to continuous, repetitive stimuli in order to keep the senses sharp for important new sensory information.

The sensory stimuli provided by the landscape are so varied that there is less monotony of perception or need for adaptation than in any other of man's physical environments. There are daily changes of the landscape in summer as flowers emerge and die to be replaced by fruit. Seasonal changes cover bare branches with leaves; the leaves, in turn, change from light green in spring to the brilliant colors of autumn. Whereas buildings remain static, the landscape is forever changing as plants grow and gain in size, modifying the scale of their surrounding spatial environment.

Modifications of Perception

As the landscape is perceived, the brain interprets the input. That interpretation is modified by previous experience. Once your finger has been painfully pricked by a rose thorn, your memory recall system, which is active during perception, is likely to caution you against blundering into other rose thorns.

Memory recall will also help one to enjoy pleasant experiences. Once one has had the extremely pleasant experience of walking through a natural landscape, such as a group of virgin woods in early spring when the wildflowers are in full bloom and the tree leaves are beginning to emerge, memory recall will influence you to repeat the experience when the same conditions recur the next year.

However, psychological theorizing has yet to explain the pleasurable feeling that comes when one walks through the serenity of some woods on a warm, fresh spring morning. It is just as difficult to explain the pleasure of the sounds of a Bach toccata reverberating in an ancient cathedral.

Night Effects

When night arrives, the amount of information the eyes receive is reduced even though the iris of the eye opens up to let in more light. The distance the eye can see at night varies according to the amount of artificial lighting available and the amount of natural lighting from the moon. Considerable distances can be seen during a full moon on an open snow-covered countryside.

Perception is altered by strong and long shadows. Further alteration comes during and after a rain, when wet surfaces reflect light in many directions.

Attention

A single person walking through the landscape will be affected more by his environment and will perceive more detail in it than will two or more persons who are involved with conversation while they walk. If one person is wandering slowly or meandering, several details are apt to catch his attention. If he has a goal in mind during his walk and is hurrying towards it, several things in the landscape will probably escape his attention.

Figure 7-24. *The sun is reflected brightly from the snow and provides strong contrast to the dark foliage of the conifers. Silence is broken by the sound of the snow-fed brook. A winter scene at Lake Tahoe, California.*

Figure 7-25. *Stand of old-growth redwood, Del Norte County, California. A forest such as this creates an incomparable feeling of serenity. The size of these trees is revealed by the human figure in the lower left of the photo.*

TOTAL DESIGN DEVELOPMENT

So far we have described some design principles and some aspects of man's perception of the landscape. Now it will be helpful to know how a skillful designer tries to combine all of these things into a total design development.

All of the design principles are combined to one degree or another in a planting design but the designer simultaneously gives consideration to the functional problems and needs of the landscape project. Then, aesthetic solutions to landscape problems are developed through a process that is more or less intuitive, depending upon the background, training, and experience of the designer. A designer with considerable experience may find that a design that is aesthetically successful comes largely by intuition.

Most planting designs are influenced by facilities either existing at the site or being designed as part of the project. The use the designer makes of line, form, texture, color, repetition, and emphasis must be closely coordinated with the use the architect has made of the same elements in the architecture at the site and with any land surfaces, walls, fences, paving materials and patterns, planters, pools, benches, etc. All must become part of the total landscape design of the site; as an integral part of the design, they provide three-dimensional relief to a landscape and cannot be separated during aesthetic and functional considerations of the use of plants.

Use of plant and landscape materials as design elements must also be coordinated with their use to fulfill functional needs of the project, which may or may not include the need

7-26

7-27

7-28

Figure 7-26. *All the elements of good design contribute to an effectively developed total composition. Here, contrast and variety in height are provided with ground covers, shrubs, and trees. The coarsest texture appears in the trees; their informality is preserved by using four trees of different heights, irregularly spaced. The ground cover creates a horizontal mass that repeats the roof line of the building and unifies the entire planting composition. Palm Aire, Florida.*

Figures 7-27 to 7-33. *On this and the next page, several views of a private residential garden on Long Island. The contrast of shadows, texture, and forms changes as one moves from one part of the garden to another.*

Figures 7-28, 7-29. *Subtle, undulating lines soften the flatness of the foreground (man-made ground forms), and clumps of bayberry provide additional interest in the composition. The view across the garden is terminated by a mix of deciduous and evergreen trees.*

7-29

7-30

7-32

7-31

7-33

146 / ARRANGING PLANTS IN THE LANDSCAPE

Figures 7-30, 7-31. *A study of the manner in which the long shadows of nearby trees (7-30) accentuate the undulating ground lines and provide contrasts of light and dark (7-31).*

Figures 7-32, 7-33. *The garden in winter. Winter provides additional patterns and contrasts to the design, which was created in total as a spatial display of motion and rhythm, subtlety, and serenity.*

Figures 7-34 to 7-38. *On this and the next page, several views of a Connecticut residential garden designed to stay in scale over many years, to possess a quality of space that is intimate, colorful, and welcoming, and to require little maintenance.*

Figure 7-34. *The entrance invites the visitor, through the openness of its low planting, simplicity of design, straightforwardness of the walk, and unity of materials: stone walk, exposed boulders, and junipers.*

Figure 7-35. *Contrast is achieved between the hardness of the rocks and the softness of the plants, yet there is unity or harmony between the horizontal and mounded forms of each. Plant materials include Japanese red pine (Pinus densiflora), eastern white pine (P. strobus), Japanese black pine (P. thunbergii), and Spanish fir (Abies pinsapo). Ground covers are shore juniper (Juniperus conferta), andorra juniper (J. horizontalis var. plumosa), and Sargent juniper (J. chinensis var. sargentii). Spreading English yew (Taxus baccata var. repandens) is used for accent and emphasis.*

7-34

7-35

7-36

7-37

7-38

Figure 7-36. *For detail and intimate interest along the walks, species of* Thymus, Arenaria, Sedum, *and* Festuca *were added. All of these are appropriate to the existing dry conditions and require little trimming or pruning to maintain scale.*

Figures 7-37, 7-38. *The curving or meandering nature of the walk as it disappears among the pines provides a sense of mystery and invites exploration. Permanence and mellowness result from the use of weathered, exposed rock and low plantings.*

for visual and physical barriers, climate control (of shade or of wind, etc.), noise control, erosion control, etc. How plants fulfill these functions is discussed in Chapter 8.

The functional aspects of a landscape design may dictate the location and size of plant masses on a site and may, indeed, affect the total aesthetic composition. Whatever their effect, the designer judges each part of the total design in terms of line, form, texture, color, repetition, and emphasis so that these design elements will still be successfully implemented to create a pleasing aesthetic effect on all of man's perceptual senses.

Plant Masses

The designer should try to achieve a transition in his design in order to relate large vertical plant masses to horizontal plants. A pyramidal effect can be created by using smaller plants in front of larger ones so that the plant mass will descend in size from the largest plant to the smallest. This technique also provides the advantage of covering up unsightly bare spots at the bases of large shrubs. The descending pyramidal effect is also used in isolated large masses in order to make a gradual transition from a high point in the center of the mass to a low level on the edges of the mass. Large plant masses usually have the pleasantest effect if viewed from a distance. Designing large plant masses close to both sides of a pedestrian corridor produces an uncomfortable feeling for most people.

A designer should try to provide transitions in texture. Abrupt changes from fine to coarse texture within a single plant mass will not be as aesthetically pleasing as a gradual transition, because the difference in texture will emphasize the individuality of plants rather than the unity of the plant mass. How often such transitions should occur depends upon the scale of the project and the effects being sought by the designer. In a small-scale project, one plant with very coarse texture might be utilized as a focal point in the composition. Gradual textural transitions would then be wanted between other plant masses in the composition so as not to attract the eye away from the point of emphasis in the composition. In a large-scale project, the point of emphasis may be a large mass of plants or a grouping of objects. Gradual textural transition throughout all subordinated plant masses may then be more important than a transition within each individual mass of plants.

Seasonal stability and variety is accomplished in plant masses through a mix of deciduous and evergreen plants (either coniferous or broadleaf evergreens). Climate dictates, through hardiness and availability, the possibilities of mixing plants within a particular composition. Greater choice of broadleaf evergreen material is possible in warm climates and they may largely dominate a composition. In cold areas the deciduous materials will dominate, and the evergreens will be principally coniferous. Only rarely should any design composition consist totally of evergreen or deciduous plants instead of a mix of both. If costs must be kept to a minimum, deciduous materials are less expensive and create a mature composition sooner since they grow faster.

7-39

7-40

Figure 7-39. *Effective use of plant mass. Here a pyramid effect ascends into the U formed by wings of a building. The pyramid is achieved by using three different heights of plants. Several of each are used to create the mass, thus providing some unity to the composition. Health Center, University of Oregon.*

Figure 7-40. *Effective use of a focal point, achieved by using one plant of very coarse texture.*

Leaf color can provide interest to plant masses. The transitions can be very subtle, as we discussed in regard to plant texture, or the color of individual plants can stand out as a point of emphasis. A plant like Japanese red maple (*Acer palmatum* var. *atropurpureum*) has a dramatic enough leaf color to become a simple specimen in a plant mass, thus serving as a focal point.

Through careful selection of plants it is possible to plan for flower color that changes in sequence between the individual plants of a large deciduous plant mass. Flowering will begin in early spring, to continue most of the season, perhaps to terminate in the fall with the bright crimson coloring of the leaves of winged euonymus (*Euonymus alatus*).

Scale

More variety and less repetition can be used in a small-scale design (such as a residential garden) in contrast to a large-scale design (such as an urban park), by using smaller masses of plants. The design effects must always be considered in relation to the scale or size of the area. In small-scale areas the viewing distance is short, and perception is thus changed considerably. Greater detail in individual plants can be observed at close range in small-scale designs. Subtleties in the changes of the color of leaves and flowers can be observed. Individual plants form masses in and of themselves in small areas where repetition can easily lead to monotony. Some people find that plants that are too large become overpowering. This is especially true of shrubs planted in small areas. This would not necessarily include trees that rise above a person to provide shade and

Figure 7-41. *Effective use of sculptures as points of emphasis in a garden setting, with plants of relatively uniform texture. Pepsico World Headquarters, Purchase, New York.*

shelter, which are therefore welcomed as protection. Plant fragrances are more important in small areas than in large areas, because people can detect and enjoy the fragrances that are close at hand.

Some Design Problems

A designer must learn to anticipate possible problems and to devise a landscape to eliminate them. Many problems can be solved through a wise selection of plants.

Designers usually prepare a plan based upon the average mature growth of plantings. This can create problems when, for instance, the designer specifies a shade-requiring ground cover such as pachysandra under what will eventually be a large shade tree. Although in a few years it will provide the needed shade, the tree, when installed, is too small to provide the shade needed for the ground cover.

In the early years of many projects, sun-loving shrubs grow well and look good, but as trees provide increasing shade, they become spindly, thin, and unsightly.

Most people select plants that are potentially much too large for the spaces they must occupy. After a few years, increasing maintenance is needed as pruning becomes necessary. In many cases the plant crowds a sidewalk or patio and makes the use of these uncomfortable or difficult.

Generally, most clients want immediate results from plants. They are reluctant to wait several years for the landscape design to mature, and thus the designer is forced to place plants closer together on his plan than his experience tells him is wise. The design looks mature sooner, but the longevity of the plants

is shortened. The plants will have to be replaced sooner because of the initial close spacing.

Maintenance becomes a problem when ground covers have been planted among roses or other shrubs. Maintenance workers find that pulling weeds is a painful and frustrating experience.

Narrow or crowded spaces and unsightly surfaces can be a problem. Vines can be considered for these, especially where a plant is wanted that will be leafy to a great height, such as against a tall building alongside which a sidewalk has left a narrow planting space. Vines will also climb unsightly power poles and television towers. Wire fences can also be covered by vines, and the designer can make good use of changes in color and texture with vines by using Boston ivy (*Parthenocissus tricuspidata*) on a light brick or stone wall. When space allows, a facing of junipers will provide additional contrast with color and texture. Shade can be created in a limited space by directing vines over garden structures, porches, and so forth.

Grass will not survive when beech trees and other trees that have low spreading branches are planted in open lawns. Sparsely leaved and high-branching trees like thornless honey locust (*Gleditsia triacanthos* var. *inermis*) are more desirable where a luxuriant lawn is wanted, because they let more light filter through to the grass below. In southern California, Hawaii, and Florida palm trees are well suited where light shade is needed.

Consideration of color contrast is needed when designing for planting against walls and fences. Yews will not show up nearly as well

7-42

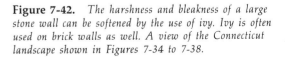

Figure 7-42. *The harshness and bleakness of a large stone wall can be softened by the use of ivy. Ivy is often used on brick walls as well. A view of the Connecticut landscape shown in Figures 7-34 to 7-38.*

against a red brick wall as they will against a wall made of buff brick or white cast stone. A silver or blue juniper will provide better color contrast against the red brick.

Some trees are notorious for their surface roots, which are especially troublesome in heavy clay soils. When planted too close to paving, these roots will eventually heave the paving upward.

SUMMARY

The designer must be constantly sensitive to all the complexities of plants, both functional and aesthetic, that may affect the results of his design efforts. The success of a designer's work of art is dependent on his mastery of all the physical and environmental factors that are present, but it is also dependent on the quality of the construction and maintenance that follows the design. If the landscape designer is retained by the client to provide inspection during construction, the quality of the use of lines, textures, color contrasts, repetition, variety, and emphasis can be achieved to the best advantage. The effect of the aesthetic elements is apt to fall short of expectations if the designer is not consulted about the maintenance of materials he has specified. Dead plants might be replaced with substitutions of other species that have a different form or color or texture, and the substitution would completely change the designer's composition. Thoughtless pruning may affect his composition as well. For instance, if the maintenance supervisor prunes individual privet and yew plants in the form of square boxes in an other-wise informal planting design, the harmony of plant forms is destroyed in the composition.

The quality of the landscape can be improved when the landscape contractor and landscape maintenance supervisor both understand thoroughly the basic principles of design. But there is also need for the designer to understand construction and maintenance problems thoroughly, and these are described elsewhere in this book.

FOR FURTHER READING

Hubbard, H. V., and T. Kimball, 1959. *An Introduction to the Study of Landscape Design.* Boston: Hubbard Educational Trust.

Simonds, J. O., 1961. *Landscape Architecture: The Shaping of Man's Environment.* New York: McGraw-Hill.

Walker, T. D., 1971. *Perception and Environmental Design.* West Lafayette, Indiana: PDA Publishers.

8

Functional and Aesthetic Values of Plants in Design

Too often landscape plants are thought of only for their beauty, without regard for their functional value, and the term "ornamental plants" is indicative of this limited concept. Yet plants can be used for much more than beautification; they can improve the quality of an environment functionally as well. In this chapter we will discuss some qualities of plants and planting designs that are chiefly functional and indicate what plants can satisfy the functions most aesthetically.

VISUAL CONTROL

Sometimes it is difficult to distinguish between the aesthetic and functional characteristics of plants. When planted to reduce the glare of oncoming headlights, highway median plantings would be serving a functional role, but at the same time they may also provide aesthetic improvement of the highway landscape. As a visual barrier to an objectionable scene such as an auto junkyard, the primary effect of plantings might be considered aesthetic, but at the same time these plants would also be serving a functional role. But plants are used so frequently to achieve visual control that we can easily speak of this use as being one of their primary functions. In addition to reducing glare and screening objectionable views, plantings also provide screening for privacy, they direct the view of the observer, and they define a space visually.

A significant but generally unrealized visual function of landscape plantings is to reduce the visual discomfort caused by glare

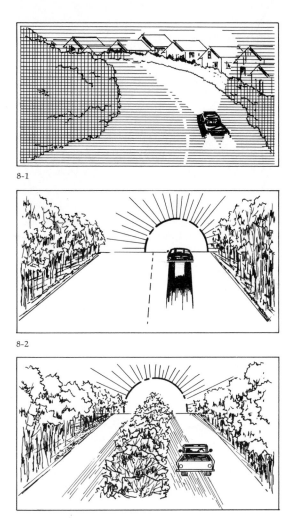

8-1

8-2

8-3

Figures 8-1 to 8-3. *Plants can be used as a visual screen against moving lights on a highway, for the comfort of residents near it (8-1) and drivers of vehicles (8-2 and 8-3). These uses of plants are aesthetic as well as functional.*

and reflection. By "glare" we are speaking of direct light from the sun or from artificial sources such as headlights, street lights, floodlights, neon signs, etc. The discomfort of these lights will depend on whether they are stationary or mobile, or constant or flashing. Reflected light is indirect light or light that has bounced off a surface; it has a different quality, which we can refer to as secondary glare. This is a general problem in urban areas where extensive paving and other reflective material is present. With the increasing use of glass and of smooth, polished building surfaces, reflection will become more serious. Reflection is not limited to urban areas though, for homes located near water or on beaches are also subjected to considerable reflection; moreover, homes located in northern climates catch reflected sun in the winter when there is considerable snow cover.

Plantings have frequently been used effectively to reduce glare from oncoming headlights by dense planting in median strips between the lanes of major highways. Dense planting of this kind is particularly important where curves in the road are such that headlight beams are aimed directly at the windshields of oncoming vehicles. Median plantings are sometimes so thick that the driver is unaware of the other lane of traffic. Likewise, plants can be used to reduce glare from the sun or from stationary artificial lights by locating plants of the proper height and density strategically between the source of the light and the area upon which the light shines, whether it is a bedroom or an outdoor living area. Usually the most effective control can be had by locating the plantings as close as possible to

the area upon which the light shines, since it is usually neither feasible nor desirable to block out the light at its source. If trees are planted too near light posts or beneath utility wires in an attempt to control glare originating there, they are nearly always in danger of being topped flat or otherwise "butchered" by unskilled street workers. The natural shape of the plant is lost and some species die from unattended wounds.

Reflected light can be reduced by intercepting the light either before it touches a reflective surface or after it has been reflected but between the reflective surface and the viewer. One is not always given a choice. Trees located over reflective paving will serve to filter the sunlight before it reaches the surface. But where a body of water forms the reflective surface it is difficult if not impossible to block the light before it strikes the surface, so the alternative is to place plantings strategically to filter reflected light before it reaches the viewer. When reflective building surfaces are the source of an uncomfortable glare, trees can be located relatively near the building to reduce the amount of light striking the lower portion of the building; these will also provide a filter for any light that is reflected from the building to an area near the trees. A designer needs to give considerable attention to the angle of the light source or the angle of reflection in order to select plants of the proper size and to plan their location effectively.

Another type of visual control achieved with landscape plantings is less remedial and more creative, and it might be classified as an architectural use of plants. We are referring to the plants that define outdoor "rooms"

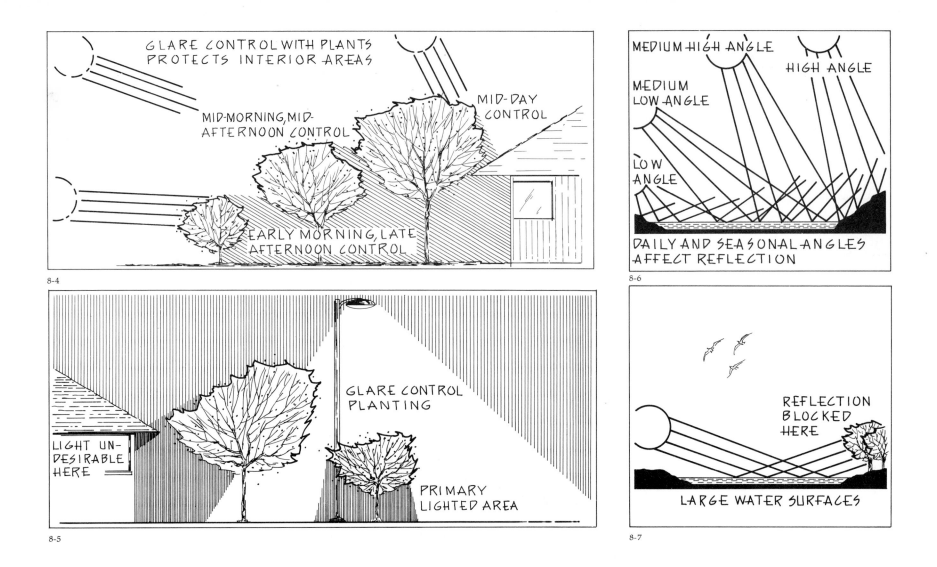

GLARE CONTROL WITH PLANTS PROTECTS INTERIOR AREAS

MID-MORNING, MID-AFTERNOON CONTROL

MID-DAY CONTROL

EARLY MORNING, LATE AFTERNOON CONTROL

8-4

LIGHT UN-DESIRABLE HERE

GLARE CONTROL PLANTING

PRIMARY LIGHTED AREA

8-5

MEDIUM HIGH ANGLE

HIGH ANGLE

MEDIUM LOW ANGLE

LOW ANGLE

DAILY AND SEASONAL ANGLES AFFECT REFLECTION

8-6

REFLECTION BLOCKED HERE

LARGE WATER SURFACES

8-7

Figures 8-4, 8-5. *Plants of varying heights and placement can control the brightness of both daytime light, which changes through the day as the sun changes (8-4), and nighttime glare from stationary artificial lights (8-5).*

Figures 8-6, 8-7. *Sun angles change seasonally, relative to Earth, thus changing the amounts and angles of glare (8-6). Plants are effective in screening glare from adjacent surfaces such as water when the sun is low (8-7).*

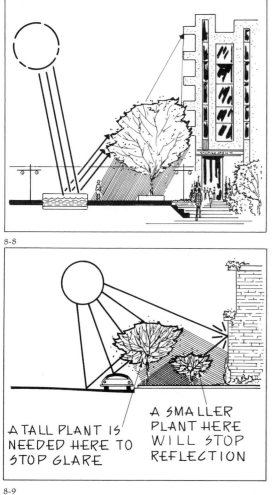

8-8

8-9

A TALL PLANT IS NEEDED HERE TO STOP GLARE

A SMALLER PLANT HERE WILL STOP REFLECTION

Figures 8-8, 8-9. *Trees of varying heights help reduce glare from paving and building surfaces, making travel by foot or in vehicles more comfortable.*

8-10

8-11

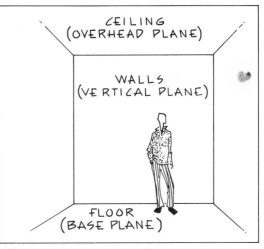

8-12

Figures 8-10, 8-11. *This use of plants invites the viewer to move toward a view by enframing it (8-10); the plants also define and enclose an area, creating an outdoor room (8-11), which opens onto the view shown in Figure 8-10.*

Figure 8-12. *The kind of space created by plants.*

visually through creation of plant "walls," "ceilings," and "floors." A wall of plants may be formed by a narrow hedge or a wider border-planting the width of two or three plants. Ceilings can be achieved by planting large-canopy shade trees or even medium-sized flowering trees. When used in conjunction with overhead arbors, vines may provide a similar effect. Various floors can be achieved by using grass in combination with ground covers or hard surface materials. Plants can be used in this way to serve as articulators of space and thus serve a primary design function. The designer should realize that, unlike architecture, space articulation with plants doesn't yield immediate results; there is a time lag between the execution of the design and the results of the design, while the plants grow.

Plants also provide a sense of privacy. In residential areas where homes are closely spaced, the need for privacy is acute. Although fences and other structural features can provide complete privacy in a limited space, plants can provide a more pleasant, less rigid screen if the space is available. Hedges make effective screens for privacy and require relatively little space. The density of the hedge planting can be determined either by plant selection or by careful pruning, or by both selection and pruning.

One of the frequent uses of plants is to screen objectionable views. In the 1965 Highway Beautification Act, a program entitled "Green Screen" was an attempt to make more effective use of plantings to screen auto junk-yards and other objectionable sights that desecrate the nation's roadsides. On a more limited scale, plantings can conceal unattractive

8-13

8-14

8-15

8-16

Figure 8-13. *Outdoor sculpture usually dominates nearby plantings. The plantings can be used to enclose a setting for the sculpture so that it is the focal point of a space.*

Figure 8-14. *As space articulators, plants define and create space—"rooms" with canopy planting ceilings or open spaces enclosed with screen planting walls. The resulting space might be small, where a few people can sit quietly, or large, like a plaza enclosed by plantings that separate it from areas having different uses or a different aesthetic character. Plants used in these ways might simultaneously provide privacy, screen glare, or create physical barriers that control pedestrians. Space articulation was carefully planned at Constitution Plaza, Hartford, Connecticut, shown here. Elsewhere in the book are views of other parts of this site.*

Figure 8-15. *An outdoor sitting area, or room, created with plants in raised planters. Constitution Plaza, Hartford, Connecticut.*

Figure 8-16. *Space is defined subtly here with mounds of green turf contained within raised precast edges, which double as sitting ledges. Trees help break what would otherwise be a plain, large total area and create smaller, more intimate shaded spaces. Note the excellent*

8-17

use of repetition in tree placement, mounding, edges, and paving, to create an effective design. Constitution Plaza, Hartford, Connecticut.

Figure 8-17. *Creating privacy through visual control.*

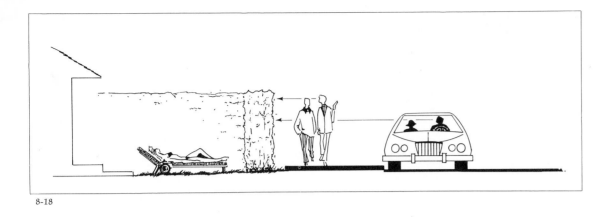

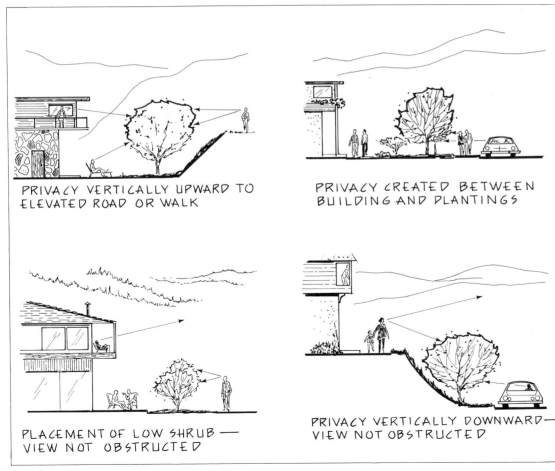

PRIVACY VERTICALLY UPWARD TO ELEVATED ROAD OR WALK

PRIVACY CREATED BETWEEN BUILDING AND PLANTINGS

PLACEMENT OF LOW SHRUB — VIEW NOT OBSTRUCTED

PRIVACY VERTICALLY DOWNWARD — VIEW NOT OBSTRUCTED

Figure 8-18. *A residential living area can be made private from an adjacent street or other public areas through effective screen plantings.*

Figure 8-19. *Effective visual screening of a parking lot by using low shrubs and a row of flowering crabapples.*

Figure 8-20. *The effectiveness of plant screens for privacy will be affected by plant size in relation to terrain. Small plants will block a view uphill without obscuring a view from above. Taller plants may be needed for complete screening, and this may increase the time before the screen develops fully.*

8-21

8-22

WORK AREA NOT
VISIBLE FROM ABOVE

8-23

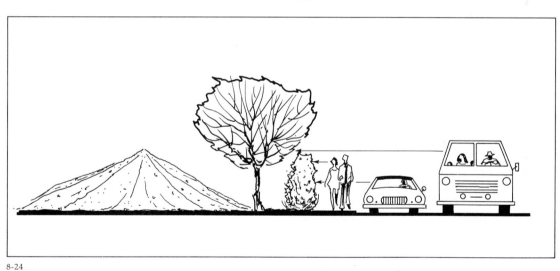

8-24

Figures 8-21 to 8-24. *Plant screens block various objectionable views: a service or utilities area (8-21), a construction equipment storage yard, junk pile, or sanitary land fill area (8-22, 8-23), and a quarry or mining area (8-24).*

areas on residential lots, such as the service area, which may be the location of trash receptacles, parking areas, or vegetable gardens or compost heaps, etc. Proper selection and placement of plants is always critical in achieving the desired effect.

Finally, plants can be used to direct a view toward the distant landscape. This may be done by placing plants so they reveal an outstanding view gradually as one moves through the plantings, or it may be done by framing or restricting the view with plants. This function of plants may be apparent to the viewer either from one stationary viewpoint or from several changing views perceived as one walks or drives through the landscape. On highways, vistas can be created either by thinning or by clear-cutting existing trees, or by installing additional plantings to create a channel through which the vista can be seen. Of course, the speed with which the vista will be seen will regulate the width and angle of the opening into it. A gap designed to be viewed from the highway will need to be wider than one designed for viewing from a trail through a park. These kinds of vistas provide views into a forest or woodland or through it to any unusual or attractive feature in the roadside landscape.

In general, effective screening and development of privacy require plantings that reach six feet or more in height. If year-round screening is important, evergreen materials should be considered.

Plantings for visual control need not become monotonous. Don't forget to plan for aesthetic effect even though the plants are intended to serve a functional purpose. Vary the species to provide some change in texture,

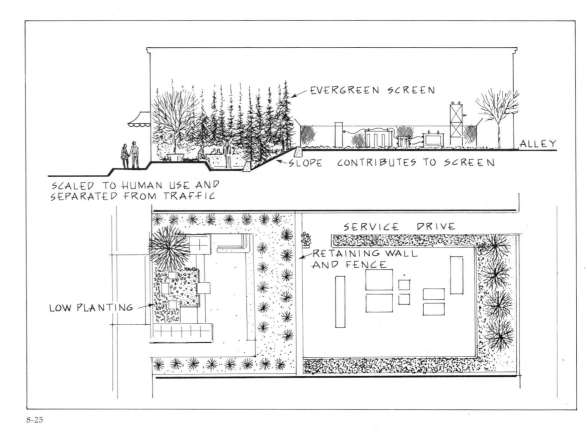

8-25

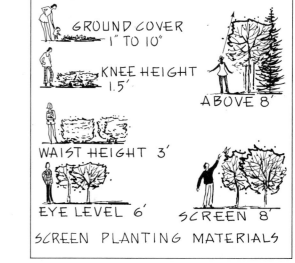

8-26

Figure 8-25. *In screening a utilities installation, a landscape architect might be able to create a minipark for the use of the community.*

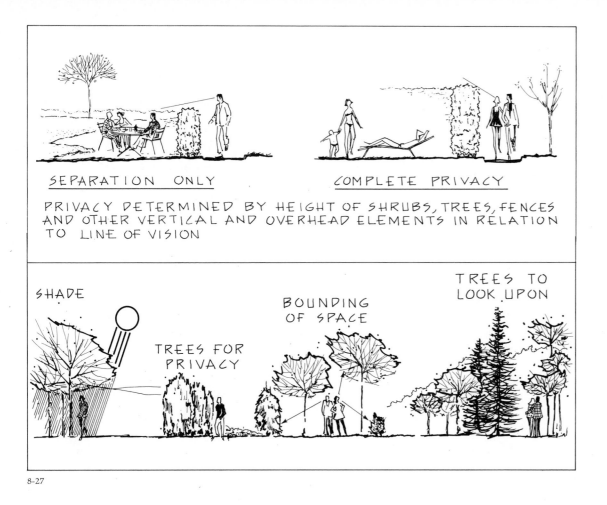

SEPARATION ONLY

COMPLETE PRIVACY

PRIVACY DETERMINED BY HEIGHT OF SHRUBS, TREES, FENCES AND OTHER VERTICAL AND OVERHEAD ELEMENTS IN RELATION TO LINE OF VISION

SHADE

TREES FOR PRIVACY

BOUNDING OF SPACE

TREES TO LOOK UPON

8-27

Figures 8-26, 8-27. *Selecting plants for visual control. Plant sizes affect spatial scale (8-26). Small spaces may seem crowded if plants are installed that are eight or more feet tall. Conversely, an eight-foot plant in a large space may seem too small to achieve the necessary privacy. To a certain extent the sizes of the plants determine their functions (8-27).*

color, and size. More variety is important in small spaces such as residential gardens than in large parks. Even less variety is required for highway plantings where high speed reduces a driver's ability to perceive detail. Indeed, too much variety of color, texture, and form along a highway may cause confusion and discomfort to the driver. But a designer can exercise considerable ingenuity to make screens interesting on other sites.

PHYSICAL BARRIERS

Plants can effectively control the movements of people and animals.

In general, plantings of three feet or less in height provide little physical control to mature adults and are more effective for the psychological control they suggest. It is especially difficult to select plants for this purpose, inasmuch as children and young adults find low plantings inviting to jump over and run through. However, plants with heights of from three to six feet offer a fair amount of control both for humans and animals. During rough play, young adults will jump and climb through plants of this size unless the plants are quite thorny and planted close together.

Thick, solid plantings of six feet or more in height will serve for both physical and visual control. Generally, plants should be selected so that in three to five years the branches will have intertwined to achieve the control that is wanted. The designer needs to indicate the appropriate planting distances in his drawings. If clients want more immediate effect and have the budget to afford it, large plant specimens can be selected and planted close enough to provide immediate control.

Barriers formed by plants can be used along property lines in lieu of fences or to divide one activity from another in a park. Plant masses along sidewalks will direct pedestrian traffic effectively toward some desired location and will prevent unnecessary destruction of turf areas across which people may otherwise walk in order to shorten a route. Barriers along parking lots can serve both to direct pedestrians and to screen the cars from view.

The design of barriers should follow the recommendations made previously for visual control with plants. Variety of form, texture, and color will create interest and reduce monotony.

CLIMATE CONTROL

One of the basic functional uses of plants in the landscape is to modify or control the microclimate. Trees have been used for windbreaks and in providing shade for centuries. Today, trees are of immediate importance in providing a more favorable microclimate for humans, particularly in urban areas where the replacement of vegetation with asphalt and concrete has increased temperatures significantly. Therefore, it is important for a designer to know how to use plants in ways that will modify the microclimate.

Comfort Zones

Inasmuch as a main concern in this chapter is climate control for human comfort, we need to establish criteria that will be applicable to

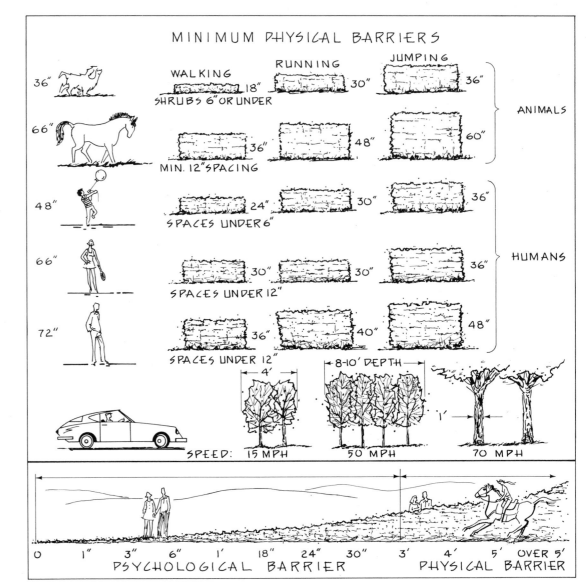

Figure 8-28. *The selection of plants to serve as physical barriers will depend on the use made of an area and the kind of control to be achieved. The lower panel summarizes the differences between psychological and physical barriers.*

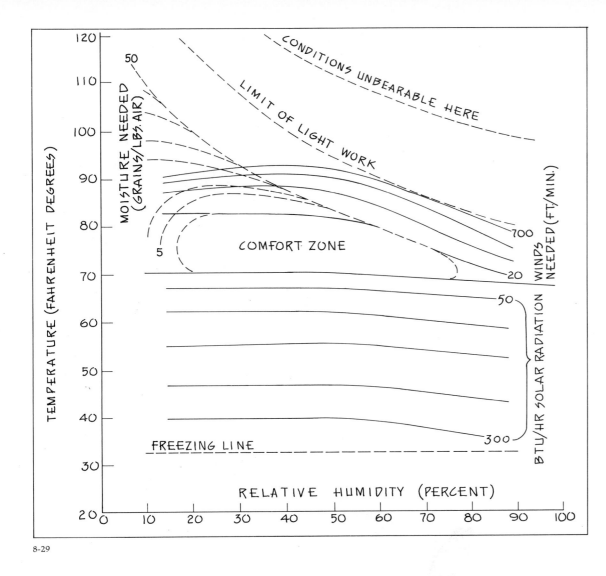

8-29

Figure 8-29. *The enclosed area in the center of this diagram represents a climatic zone where temperature, humidity, wind, and solar radiation combine to provide the greatest human comfort. Bioclimatic data can be plotted in order to determine how corrective measures, such as windbreaks or canopy plantings, can be best implemented. The data will vary throughout the year as the climate of the region in which the site is located changes. Month by month there would be little change in the bioclimatic data for Miami or Los Angeles and a great variation in the data for Minneapolis or New York.*

our discussion. The four climatic factors that affect human comfort are solar radiation, air termperature, air movement or wind, and humidity. Human comfort can be determined by making a plot of the relationship between these factors and observing the range that does not exceed the limits of what we may refer to as a "human comfort zone." The comfort zone will be slightly different for different people, and even more noticeably, it will differ between people from different geographical areas. For any given area, a general comfort range will be applicable. The relationship between temperature and humidity in determining human comfort zones, as applicable to moderate climate zones in the United States at elevations not exceeding 1,000 feet above sea level, is illustrated. If prevailing climatic conditions exceed the comfort zone, the use of plantings can at certain times provide the correction of climate needed to restore comfort conditions.

Solar Radiation and Temperature Control

The single most important factor affecting climate is solar radiation. Seasonal differences in radiation are due to the angle of the incidence of sunlight and daily differences are due to absorption and scattering of the radiation by the atmosphere and reflection by clouds. The radiation that strikes the Earth's surface is largely responsible for the temperature of the ground and the air above it. The nature of the soil surface will greatly determine how much of the radiation is absorbed and how much is reflected, and this in turn determines the soil-surface temperature and, ultimately, the surrounding air temperature. The more radiation a surface absorbs, the more it heats the surrounding air.

Vegetation, whether it is a grassy surface or a tree canopy, greatly increases the reflection of incoming radiation; in contrast, asphalt and other dark surfaces decrease the reflection and increase absorption. These differences, as well as the cooling effect of evapotranspiration, contribute significantly to the difference of air temperatures between a city block and a nearby park, which may be as great as 10°F. Even at night the air temperature in the city is usually from 5 to 10°F warmer than the suburban or rural countryside owing to the release at night of heat energy stored during the day, thus keeping the air warmer over areas of paving and buildings than over areas of heavy vegetation. Vegetation not only reflects more radiation, it also loses what radiation it absorbs more quickly, by reradiation, than building or paving surfaces do.

In a woodland or forest, the effect of vegetation on temperature is even more striking. Solar radiation strikes the top of the forest canopy where it is absorbed or reflected; very little heat is transmitted to the understory. Consequently, the air temperature above the canopy may be as much as 25°F higher than in the understory of the forest. At night, in contrast, the heat radiated from the ground is trapped beneath the canopy, so the air temperature is usually higher within the forest than it is in surrounding open areas of vegetation.

On a human scale, the direct effect of solar radiation on a person greatly influences the comfort or discomfort he experiences. Probably the most dramatic effect of vegetation

is the immediate comfort provided by the shade of a tree on a hot, sunny day. Similar radiation control is provided by vines on a trellis, or by groups of trees giving shade to a structure or to some area that is frequently used. The amount of shade can be controlled by the plants selected. If a heavy shade is desired, the Norway maple (*Acer platanoides*) has a broad canopy with dense foliage that provides complete shade. For lighter shade, a thornless variety of honey-locust (*Gleditsia triacanthos* var. *inermis*) is excellent because it has fine leaflets and open branches.

Although our discussion of radiation control has so far been directed towards its reduction, there are times, particularly during the colder months, when the heat of solar radiation is most welcome. Deciduous trees are quite useful at these times since they provide shade in the hotter months but drop their leaves in the fall, and thus permit radiation to penetrate to buildings beneath the trees during the colder months.

Wind Control

Wind currents have a direct influence upon the extremes of temperature and/or humidity that a person can comfortably stand. Frequently the air temperature and relative humidity do not exceed the comfort zone, but steady, severe wind creates an uncomfortable environment. On the other hand, wind currents can alleviate discomfort from prolonged high temperatures and high humidity. Therefore a designer may wish to use vegetation as a means of blocking, directing, or amplifying wind, thus modifying an uncomfortable microclimate.

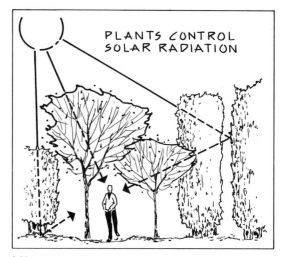

8-30

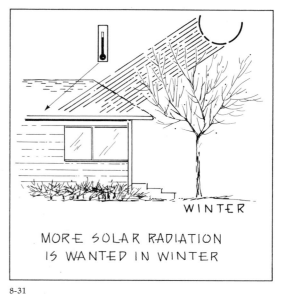

8-31

Figure 8-30. *Plants can obstruct and filter solar radiation or reduce its reflection. It is cooler beneath a plant that completely obstructs the radiation than it is beneath one that only filters it. Dark plants with small leaves will be effective in lessening the reflection of radiation.*

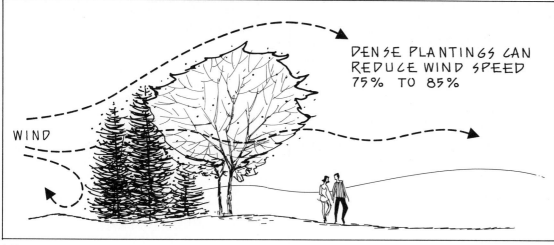

DENSE PLANTINGS CAN
REDUCE WIND SPEED
75% TO 85%

WIND

8-32

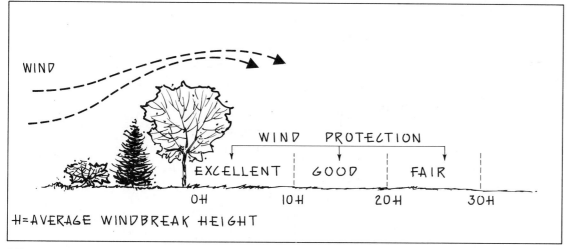

WIND

WIND PROTECTION

EXCELLENT | GOOD | FAIR

0H 10H 20H 30H

H=AVERAGE WINDBREAK HEIGHT

8-33

Figure 8-31. *The effectiveness of plant control of solar radiation and temperature will depend on the location of plants in relation to the sun and the time of year. In colder climates warmth during winter is desirable and can be achieved by using deciduous plants.*

Figure 8-32. *Using plants for wind control: the arrows indicate wind direction; the undulating arrow denotes reduced wind velocity. The zone of greatest protection occurs where the people are standing. Height and penetrability of plantings are more significant in reducing wind than the width of the plantings.*

Figure 8-33. *Areas of wind protection are related to the height of the planting.*

The use of plants for windbreaks is a well known and effective method of controlling wind. What extent of wind reduction can be achieved depends on the height, density, shape, and width of the plantings, but their height is the most important consideration. The height determines the size of the area adjacent to the windbreak in which there will be protection, with the amount of protection being relatively constant at the same horizontal distances when the heights of the trees in the windbreak are the same.

Next to height, wind reduction is most dependent on the density and shape of the windbreak. A moderately dense barrier is most effective and actually reduces wind over a greater distance than does a windbreak of higher-density plantings. Narrow windbreaks are as effective as wide ones, but single rows of trees are apt to be too sparse, and don't usually provide the density required, and they have the disadvantage of developing gaps more readily.

We stated earlier that wind protection will be constant at distances that are the same relative to similar tree heights. However, there are various zones of protection on either side of the area sheltered by a windbreak. Immediately in *front* of the barrier the wind is reduced. Just *beyond* the barrier, for a horizontal distance of about five times the height of the barrier, the greatest reduction of wind is measurable. Beyond that distance wind velocity begins to recover. Very slight reductions of wind may be measured up to a distance of 30 times the height of the windbreak. By placing windbreaks in a series, a continuous protection zone or shelterbelt can be created.

Plants can also be used to direct the flow of air to provide wind toward an area where it is desirable or away from an area where it isn't wanted. Wind flow can be diverted in this way by placing plant barriers in lines that are diagonal to the direction of the prevailing wind.

Since prevailing winds change directions seasonally, wind screens can serve as a windbreak in the winter and can direct breezes into an area during the summer. Hedges or deciduous canopy trees can also serve to direct and/or accelerate wind. By proper location of these planting barriers, optimum wind control can be realized. If the designer plans these barriers carefully they will have considerable aesthetic value. The designer should try to select plants providing a variety of color, texture, and form. If wintertime protection is important, the designer should select evergreens.

Control of Precipitation and Humidity

Plants are certainly not waterproof shelters, but they do provide some protection from rain during short showers. A considerable amount of precipitation collects on the foliage of trees before it passes through the foliage. Thus, trees do offer immediate temporary shelter from the rain.

The effect of plants on atmospheric humidity is of interest in any discussion of climate modification. Plants contain large quantities of water that are added to the air through transpiration. The more foliage, the greater is the amount of water added to the air.

Let us examine a given area to see how this is so. An acre of forested land may transpire 2,000 gallons of water on a hot day. The

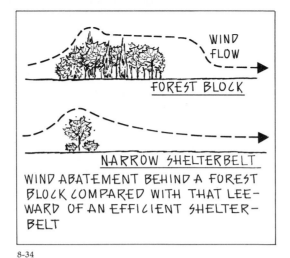

8-34

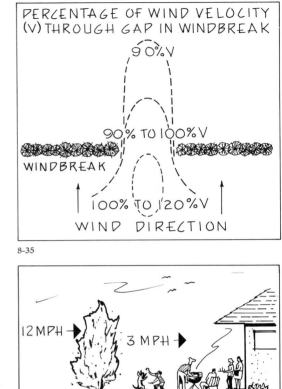

8-35

8-36

Figure 8-34. *The arrows indicate maximum wind velocity. The largest area of protection occurs if a narrow shelterbelt is used, because much of the wind reduction caused by the forest block is measurable in the forest rather than beyond it.*

Figure 8-35. *A gap in a windbreak funnels the wind and increases its velocity.*

Figure 8-36. *Strategic location of plantings near buildings will control wind around and over them and may affect interior ventilation.*

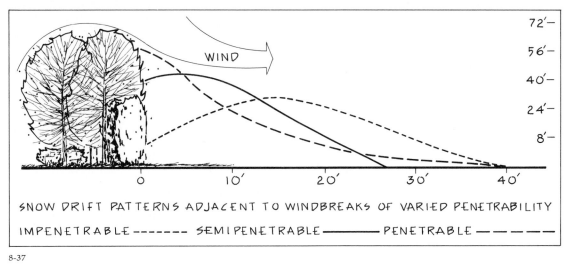

WIND

72'—
56'—
40'—
24'—
8'—

0   10'   20'   30'   40'

SNOW DRIFT PATTERNS ADJACENT TO WINDBREAKS OF VARIED PENETRABILITY

IMPENETRABLE ------- SEMIPENETRABLE ———— PENETRABLE — — —

8-37

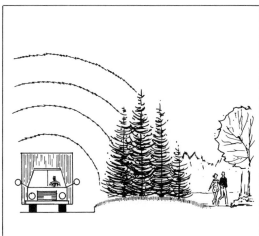

8-38

Figure 8-37. *In areas where it is important to control snow drifting, the density of a windbreak will be important.*

Figure 8-38. *In flat terrain wide plantings in mounded strips are needed to provide satisfactory noise control.*

evaporation process, by which transpired water is passed into the heated atmosphere, thus cooling it, and the shading of a forest canopy, both begin to explain the 25-to-30°F differences in forest air temperature that we cited earlier. It is no wonder that plants are sometimes called "natural air conditioners."

Another form of precipitation control provided by plants is in controlling snow placement or drifting, or snow retention. Some of what we said about the effect of plants on reducing wind is applicable to snow also, since wind causes snow to form drifts. By properly locating planting barriers, snow drifts on driveways and sidewalks can be prevented. Plants also shade snow and prevent it from melting. This use of plants is dependent on the use people make of an area. Snow can either be a hazard, if on roads, or an advantage, if on ski slopes. The proper location of plantings for snow control requires very careful planning, or undesirable effects may result.

Noise Control

Noise—unwanted sound—has become a problem of increasing concern in man's outdoor environments owing to urbanization and technology. Tremendous strides have been made in reducing noise within buildings by using building materials that control acoustics, but very little progress has been made in the landscape. But the possibility of using vegetation and other landscape features to reduce outdoor noise has been explored and merits consideration.

To understand how plants can reduce noise, it is necessary to understand some basic principles about sound energy. Sound travels in waves of different lengths, described in terms of their frequency, and its intensity or sound pressure is measured in decibels (dB). The loudness of sound, as perceived by the human ear, depends on both frequency and pressure. Higher frequencies, up to 4,000 cycles per second (cps), sound louder than lower frequencies. Sound pressure is measured on a logarithmic scale such that an increase of 10 dB is equal to 10 times the sound energy even though a noise at that level sounds only twice as loud to the human ear.

Sound is diminished as waves are absorbed by air or by objects, such as plants, or by diffraction as the waves come into contact with an object that deflects the sound and sends it in a different direction. The ability of plants to control noise is determined by the intensity, frequency, and direction of the noise as well as the location, height, width, and density of the planting. Another factor that greatly affects outdoor noise is climate, including wind direction and velocity, temperature, and humidity.

Generally, vegetation is most effective when used to reduce irritating high-frequency noises. Some plantings 25 to 50 feet wide can reduce noise at higher frequencies by 10 to 20 dB but are less effective in reducing noise of lower frequencies. Large pine and spruce plantings 50 to 100 feet wide are also capable of reducing some of the lower-frequency noise that is characteristic of traffic, by as much as 10 dB. Sound of the lowest frequencies, which are the most difficult to eliminate but fortunately the least annoying, are not affected by plantings. Plantings of a single species are not as effective as mixed plantings, because single-species plantings may muffle sounds of both

low and high frequencies, but will be ineffective in reducing sounds at frequencies midway between the high and low.

Some effective evergreens, which will provide year-round noise reduction, are arborvitaes, Douglas-fir, spruces, and pines, all of which must have foliage to the ground in order to be effective sound barriers. Less-dense evergreens, such as hemlocks, hollies, and junipers, are not as effective. Deciduous plants that provide relatively effective attenuation are thickets of sassafras and pawpaw, as well as mixed species, but only when foliage is present from the ground up. In addition to trees and shrubs, the presence of grass or other ground cover exerts a definite muffling effect on sound in comparison with hard surfaced areas, which tend to deflect sound.

The size and density of the plantings is critical in noise control, hedges and other narrow plantings being relatively ineffective. Plantings should be at least 25 feet wide and, preferably, wider than that. The height is also critical, since sound will travel over the top of a barrier that is low. Proper selection and spacing of plants, and proper land grading, can contribute significantly to the alleviation of noise.

Places in which plants can be used effectively to reduce noise are along highways, around industrial sites, in residential areas, and in parks and recreation areas. For example, highway noise can be greatly reduced by combining plantings with slopes or earth mounds that rise above the edges of the highway. Mounding by itself has been shown to reduce noise greatly; in combination with plantings, the effect of mounding is even greater. A sim-

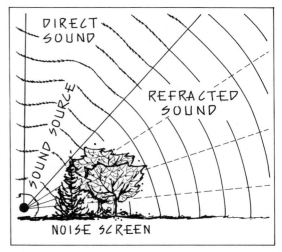

8-39

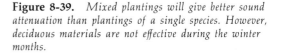

Figure 8-39. *Mixed plantings will give better sound attenuation than plantings of a single species. However, deciduous materials are not effective during the winter months.*

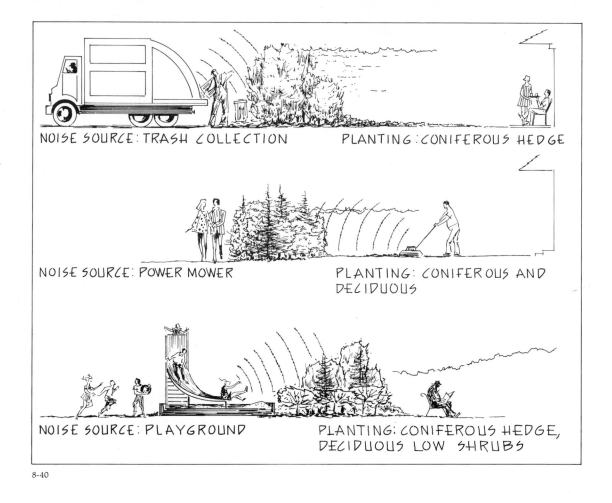

NOISE SOURCE: TRASH COLLECTION   PLANTING: CONIFEROUS HEDGE

NOISE SOURCE: POWER MOWER   PLANTING: CONIFEROUS AND DECIDUOUS

NOISE SOURCE: PLAYGROUND   PLANTING: CONIFEROUS HEDGE, DECIDUOUS LOW SHRUBS

8-40

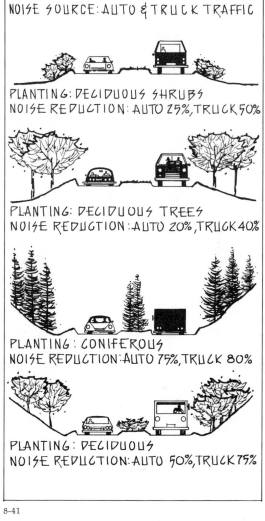

NOISE SOURCE: AUTO & TRUCK TRAFFIC

PLANTING: DECIDUOUS SHRUBS
NOISE REDUCTION: AUTO 25%, TRUCK 50%

PLANTING: DECIDUOUS TREES
NOISE REDUCTION: AUTO 20%, TRUCK 40%

PLANTING: CONIFEROUS
NOISE REDUCTION: AUTO 75%, TRUCK 80%

PLANTING: DECIDUOUS
NOISE REDUCTION: AUTO 50%, TRUCK 75%

8-41

Figure 8-40. *The effectiveness of sound control with plants will depend on the type, decibel level, intensity, and origin of the sound; the type, height, density, and location of the plantings; and wind direction, wind velocity, temperature, and humidity. Some sounds may be louder and more irritating than others depending on a person's perception.*

Figure 8-41. *The shape of the terrain adjacent to a highway and the kind of plants installed there will influence the amount of noise control.*

ilar approach would be worthy of consideration in other problem areas where there is need to control noise in the landscape.

It has been demonstrated that screen plantings of more than six feet in height, which eliminate visual contact with the source of noise, will psychologically reduce the irritating effects of noise even though the plants themselves may not reduce the decibel level measurably.

Air Filtration and Enrichment

The continual dumping of various gaseous and particulate pollutants (among the latter are dust and soot) into the atmosphere would gradually reach intolerable levels if some means of "cleaning the air" did not exist. Under natural conditions smoke, dust, and other solid pollutants are removed by dew, rain, and snow, as well as by sedimentation and by adsorption of the pollutants onto objects such as plants. Gases are absorbed by vegetation, soil, and water. Mixing the air merely dilutes it, and it is essential that means for removing impurities be present or life would soon become impossible over parts of the Earth.

Although one's first thoughts about air pollution are likely to be of its detrimental effects on plants, a neglected aspect of the relation between plants and pollution is the potential controlling effects that plants may have as a "natural filter" of the atmosphere. If it can be shown that plants are effective filters, then it would be wise to use vegetation in strategic areas as a way of cleaning the air for humans to breathe. Of course, pollution cannot be allowed to reach toxic levels or the plants

would not be able to survive. Thus, plants should be thought of as a secondary filter, primary filters being antipollution devices installed at the source of emission of the pollutant.

There is already evidence that plants do play an important role as secondary filters in removing various pollutants from the atmosphere. It is apparent that plants remove certain gases from the atmosphere from the very fact they are injured by these gases. Yet, plants can remove limited quantities of gases such as sulfur dioxide (SO_2) and hydrogen fluoride (HF) without showing any detrimental effect.

Based on studies of sulfur dioxide uptake in Douglas-fir it has been calculated that a 15-inch-diameter tree has the potential for removing 43.5 pounds of SO_2 per year if the concentration of SO_2 in the atmosphere is 0.25 ppm. If the concentration becomes higher the plants will be injured, but they can tolerate the lower concentrations indefinitely. Based on these calculations, an acre of this species could remove 3.7 tons of SO_2 annually, assuming the SO_2 content remained constant. Although these exact conditions do not exist, the significance of the use of vegetation as a potential secondary filter is apparent. However, without primary-pollutant controls, air pollution may reach levels that injure the plants, making them useless for any purpose.

There is also evidence that plants are effective in removing some pollutants from the atmosphere upon contact and remove larger particles by sedimentation as well as by adsorption. Hairy leaf surfaces on some plants trap airborne dust and soot quite effectively, as evidenced by the dirty foliage of some vegeta-

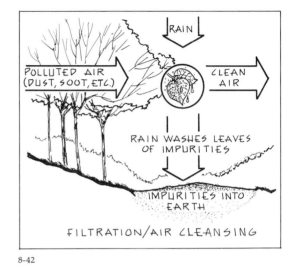

8-42

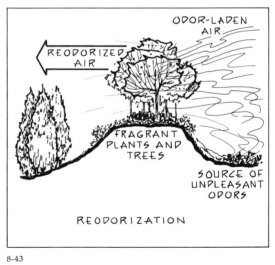

8-43

Figures 8-42, 8-43. *Plants serve a function by filtering air (8-42) and reodorizing air (8-43), and thus have an ability to lessen air pollution.*

tion. This will usually be cleaned quite naturally by rain, but sometimes, in some urban plantings, vegetation has to be washed with detergents. Atmospheric dust has been reduced by as much as 75 percent with a 200-yard-wide planting. Studies have also shown that ragweed pollen was reduced by 80 percent over a distance of approximately 100 yards into a dense evergreen forest.

Frequently we are reminded that plants enrich the atmosphere with oxygen. However, most of the oxygen generated by plants comes from the plants of the ocean. It is questionable that atmospheric oxygen is in danger of being depleted. Nevertheless, planting greenbelts around cities or along highways can add significant amounts of oxygen to the immediate environment, which will frequently contain a higher level of auto-exhaust fumes than is desirable.

Biological Means of Monitoring Air

In addition to their potential role in removing atmospheric contaminants, plants can provide a valuable function as indicators of toxic pollutants. If pollutants such as sulfur dioxide or hydrogen fluoride reach critical levels, some plants will be injured and will exhibit specific symptoms that can be diagnosed, as we pointed out in Chapter 5. Such plants can be placed as permanent monitors of air quality throughout a city or through a surrounding area to provide a biological measurement of toxic substances. These plants can be used in conjunction with instrumental methods of detecting pollutants. Plants that might be good monitors are described as sensitive indicators in Table 5-1, page 97.

EROSION CONTROL

Erosion is a serious problem, particularly where man disturbs the soil for construction and land development. Although slight erosion will cut away soil in the watersheds of forested areas, about five times as much occurs in agricultural areas and up to 25 times as much land is lost by erosion in suburban areas. Most of the suburban erosion happens between the time bulldozers first scrape the land and the time the denuded land has finally been revegetated.

Among places that are particularly susceptible to damage by erosion are recreation areas. Erosion is accentuated by the trampling of soils and may cause serious damage to lakeshores and campsites as well as endanger the quality of recreational waters. Roadbank erosion is also a serious problem, as roadbanks remain bare for long periods of time and are often difficult to revegetate. However, probably the largest amount of erosion occurs when land is cleared for the construction of new homes in subdivisions. The extent to which erosion will damage any one of the locations we have mentioned is dependent on a number of factors, including the structure of the soil, the slope of the land surface, and the amount of rainfall.

The best protection against soil erosion is a good cover of vegetation. Plants reduce the impact of rain on the soil and their roots help hold soil particles that may otherwise wash away. In addition, water filtration into the soil is greatest with vegetation; where water runoff is reduced in this way, erosion is also reduced.

Probably the most versatile and widely used vegetation for erosion control is grass.

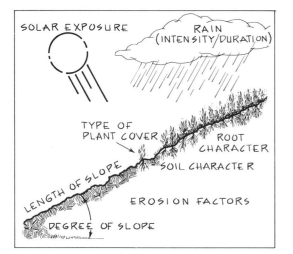

8-44

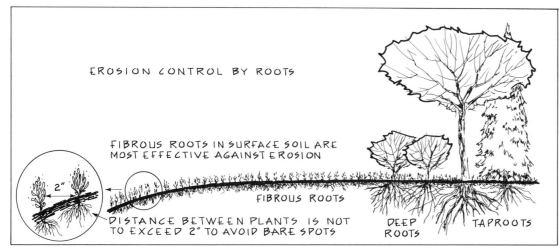

8-45

8-46

Figure 8-45. *Plant qualities can lessen soil erosion. Horizontal branches prevent water from running down tree trunks to erode their bases; rough bark impedes water; leaves hold water and break the impact of raindrops; fibrous roots near the soil surface retain the soil; dense vegetation reduces areas of bare soil. A plant density that leaves two-inch bare spots between plants is not adequate protection against erosion.*

Figure 8-44. *Many factors influence how extensively an area may be eroded. Plants are the best form of erosion control.*

Figure 8-46. *Concentrated use of this hiking trail along the top of a ridge in an Indiana nature preserve swept the litter away, exposing the soil to erosion during wind and rain storms. Exposed roots indicate the depth of the erosion.*

Table 8-1 A selection of plants that attract birds.

Botanical name	Common name
EASTERN	
Celastrus scandens	Bittersweet
Cornus spp.	Dogwood
Crataegus spp.	Hawthorn
Elaeagnus umbellata	Autumn-olive
Ilex spp.	Holly
Juniperus virginiana	Eastern red-cedar
Lonicera maackii	Amur honeysuckle
Lonicera tatarica	Tatarian honeysuckle
Malus spp.	Crabapple
Parthenocissus quinquefolia	Virginia creeper
Prunus spp.	Cherry
Pyracantha spp.	Firethorn
Rhus spp.	Sumac
Sorbus spp.	Mountain-ash
Vaccinium corymbosum	Highbush blueberry
Viburnum trilobum	American cranberry-bush
WESTERN	
Amelanchier spp.	Shadbush
Arbutus menziesii	Madrone
Berberis spp.	Barberry
Fremontodendron californica	Fremontia or flannelbush
Garrya elliptica	Coast silk-tassel
Heteromeles arbutifolia	Toyon
Mahonia spp.	Mahonia
Myrica californica	Wax-myrtle
Prunus spp.	Cherry
Rhus spp.	Sumac
Ribes spp.	Currant, gooseberry
Sambucus spp.	Elderberry
Symphoricarpos spp.	Snowberry, coralberry

There are over 15 million acres of established turf grasses in the United States, of which over 5 million acres are planted as residential lawns. Grass is not the only vegetation used for erosion control, for there is more extensive use of other ground covers such as crown vetch (*Coronilla varia*), particularly along highways where grass becomes monotonous. The most interesting plantings for erosion control are certain shrubs and trees, which, unfortunately, take considerable time to become established. Consequently, if slow-growing woody plants are to be used for this purpose, other temporary cover crops will need to be planted for immediate control, or else a mulch will be needed. Many a designer has wished that mulches were not so unattractive.

In recent years ground covers have become increasingly popular as a replacement for grass on the slopes of many site developments. Ground covers provide a contrast in color and texture, and thus they increase the aesthetic value of a project as well as control erosion. Covering a slope with low plants eliminates the difficult chore of mowing grass on sloping terrain. The most luxuriant ground covers are grown in those areas where the annual rainfall is greatest.

It is possible to create artificial mounds in some projects to relieve the monotony of flat terrain. The designer can then use ground covers for both erosion control and aesthetic appeal. On north slopes and in other shady locations, ground covers may be more successful than they are in bright sunlight. Mulches and herbicides are commonly needed with ground covers until they have become firmly established.

WILDLIFE HABITATS

Many plants are useful in providing food and shelter for birds and other wildlife. Large trees will attract a number of birds for shelter and nesting, and numerous kinds of shrubs provide cover for several wildlife species that will find shelter and feed on berries and nuts. Table 8-1 is a sampling of plants that attract birds.

AESTHETIC VALUES

As spring emerges each year large numbers of people flock from their homes to the parks and forests to see the wildflowers and the new leaves that are beginning to emerge on the trees. This annual homage to the beautiful displays of nature illustrates the attraction that plants hold in the life of man.

It is a refreshing respite from winter for a homeowner to discover the crocus appearing in the garden and coming into blossom, to be followed by yellow forsythia and then a multitude of other blossoms in subsequent weeks. This fascination with plant color may wane somewhat during the heat of summer, but as the leaves are suffused with the fiery colors of autumn the color-watch is renewed and man enjoys one last period of refreshment before winter returns.

Aesthetic values are generated not only from each individual plant, but also from the combination of such elements of the landscape as earth mounds and rolling topography. Masses of plants arranged in freeform, circular, and flowing patterns on similar forms of slopes and grades create a beauty that is unsurpassed. Some of these same aesthetic patterns occur in

8-47

8-48

8-49

Figure 8-47. *Lush, fresh green of springtime in one of the hardwood forest associations. Nantahala National Forest, North Carolina.*

Figure 8-48. *Because of their showiness, flowers provide perhaps the greatest aesthetic value of plants. Azalea in flower, Nantahala National Forest, North Carolina.*

Figure 8-49. *Blossoms of the flowering dogwood.*

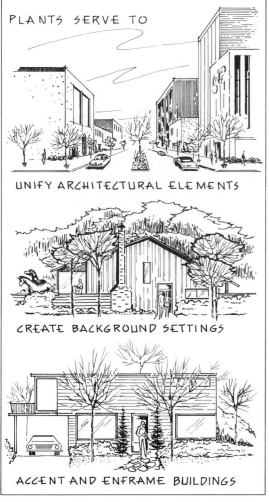

PLANTS SERVE TO

UNIFY ARCHITECTURAL ELEMENTS

CREATE BACKGROUND SETTINGS

ACCENT AND ENFRAME BUILDINGS

8-50

8-51

Figure 8-50. *Often the aesthetic effectiveness of plantings is dependent on the skill with which they are used in conjunction with architecture.*

Figure 8-51. *The use of mounding and planting here relieves the monotony of originally flat terrain and makes a small area seem large by inviting exploration.*

nature, where well worn or partially exposed rock outcroppings may alternate with wildflowers and tree masses, adjacent to a grassy meadow or surrounding a sparkling, clear lake with an undulating shoreline.

Changes in topography, in conjunction with changes in the height of plant masses, will create dimensional variations in the landscape, and most people find this pleasing. Few enjoy flat terrain if it is used monotonously. Designers are increasingly using earth mounds or land-sculpture to heighten the awareness of dimension in their planting designs. Other varietal changes can be achieved through the use of walls, fences, benches, and planters, in combination with plants. The hard materials provide immediate, permanent results while the plants modify and enhance the aesthetic values through their continuous growth and seasonal variety.

Moreover, in any well-designed landscape, harmonious relationships will be discernible between the colors, textures, forms, and lines of paving materials, structures, walls, etc., that the designer has used. The aesthetic values complement each other and convey a feeling of well-being and order.

Plants reflected in pools and ponds create patterns of light and shadow. Dark foliage creates a contrasting background for the white of a foaming fountain jet that shoots water several feet upward.

Shadows of plants create patterns of beauty on paving and walls, and these change by the hour as the Earth rotates. Patterns in summer will have sharp contrast with the bright sunlight, but the bare branches of winter will create intricate, more subtle patterns.

8-52

8-53

8-54

8-55

8-56

Figure 8-52. *Reflections of plants in water. Deerfield Lakes, Florida.*

Figure 8-53. *The regular pattern of shadows of tree foliage, branches, and trunks on the even paving surface seem to be repeated in the pattern of shadows in the sculpture at the right.*

Figures 8-54 to 8-66. *A landscape architect must be aware of the aesthetic qualities of plant parts that make each plant unique. This figure, showing leaves of the thornless honey-locust (Gleditsia triacanthos var. inermis), and the figures that conclude this chapter, all sample from the wide variety to be found in common landscape plants.*

Figure 8-55. *Exfoliation creates texture and color in the bark of the sycamore, or American planetree (Platanus occidentalis).*

Figure 8-56. *The bark of the black pine (Pinus nigra) is typified by its coarse texture.*

A unique kind of animation is expressed by plants as they respond to the wind. The slender, hanging branches of a weeping willow sway in a graceful way as the wind moves through them. The leaves of the quaking aspen shimmer or flutter even in a slight breeze.

When a wet snow falls in winter in neat little mounds on the branches of plants with dark bark, contrasting texture and new, unusual forms create a memorable beauty that occurs infrequently and disappears quickly.

The form of a large sycamore with patches of peeling bark is very majestic against a clear blue winter sky. Color is available during winter also from those plants that manage to retain their fruit. Some broadleaf evergreens turn from green to red or purple, providing other color changes. Plants provide the best color and textural relief to the drabness and monotony of winter.

Aesthetic values can be found in plant parts. Texture, color, and a feeling of design movement show in a wide variety of bark. The swirling patterns of knots are another element of design. Leaves provide a wide variety of forms and shape, most of them symmetrical in character. Subtle color changes and patterns are created by leaf veins. Some leaves are green above and powdery white below. Vivid color is provided by some, such as the Japanese red maple. When the sugar maple forests acquire their rich, warm autumn colors, few people can remain unmoved by the beauty.

Man has found it very difficult to duplicate the subtleties of colors and textures of flowers. Writers, poets, and artists over the ages have been enthralled with the beauty of flowers and have attempted to portray this beauty in a

8-57

8-59

8-61

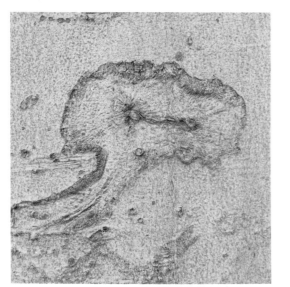

8-58

8-60

8-62

Figure 8-57. *The bark of* Melaleuca quinquenervia *is fine textured.*

Figure 8-58. *The smooth, blotched bark of the American beech* (Fagus grandifolia).

Figure 8-59. *Leaves of the American beech.*

Figure 8-60. *A flower and leaves of the sweet-bay magnolia* (Magnolia virginiana).

Figure 8-61. *Leaves of the pin oak* (Quercus palustris).

Figure 8-62. *Leaves of the linden* (Tilia *spp*).

8-63

8-65

8-64

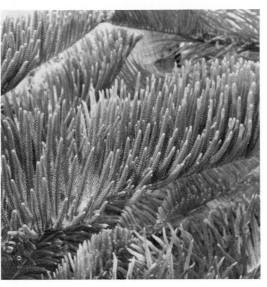

8-66

variety of ways. Firsthand contact with plants and their beauties is far superior to any written description or photograph.

The most successful functional and aesthetic uses of plants in design come about when the designer fully understands plants, their environments, and construction and maintenance problems. His efforts must then be followed by those of contractors who can faithfully install the materials according to plan and will freely communicate with the designer; finally, further work is needed by a maintenance supervisor who can understand the intent of the designer and who will care for, prune, and replace plants according to the design. If any one of this three-member team goes his own way without regard for the others, the functional and aesthetic values may be partially or even totally lost.

FOR FURTHER READING

Robinette, G. O., 1972. *Plants, People, and Environmental Quality*. Washington, D.C.: U.S. Government Printing Office.

Figure 8-63. *Leaves of the sugar maple* (Acer saccharum).

Figure 8-64. *Leaves of the Japanese maple* (Acer palmatum *var.* atropurpureum).

Figure 8-65. *Newly emerging candles on the Scots pine* (Pinus sylvestris).

Figure 8-66. *Foliage of the Norfolk Island pine* (Araucaria excelsa).

9

The Process of
Design with Plants

SITE ANALYSIS

The process of making a planting design, as practiced by the designer, is a very systematic one. After determining particular, unique needs and wants of the client, the designer must make a very thorough analysis of the site. It may be a site that the designer is already quite familiar with, if previously he prepared a master plan for the location of buildings, roads, parking areas, walks, patios, or other things, and the planting plan may be only a concluding phase of his work. In other projects an architect or engineer will have done the earlier planning of the site, leaving consideration of the landscape architect or designer until last. This working arrangement is less desirable because a number of mistakes may have been made that will affect the final aesthetic qualities of the site. Insufficient spaces may be left for planting, inadequate soil quantities may be on hand, or drainage may not have been anticipated.

A thorough site analysis should include, at least, the following:

1. Development of a site plan or plot plan showing the location of all structures and physical features, such as roads, walks, fences, walls, lakes, existing trees, and rock outcroppings. Utilities should also be located, both above and below the ground. Topographic characteristics that define warm and cold slopes, exposed and shaded areas, etc., are useful. The site plan should also show drainage patterns on the surface and notations about subsurface drainage and depth of the water table.

2. Determination of soil characteristics, such as soil pH, fertility, humus content, and compactability. A complete discussion of soils can be found in Chapter 13. On large sites soils may change drastically from one part of the site to another. One part of the site may be in a flood plain with a high water table, but another part may be an upper plateau with good drainage. Still another area may have a clay soil with good surface drainage but little permeability.

3. Climatic characteristics. The relation of the site to the total region needs to be studied. Cold-hardiness zone maps are generally helpful for such study. Microclimatic characteristics close to the site should be studied. Information about such factors as average temperature and rainfall can be secured from local meteorologists, but it is also useful to determine whether the site is exposed to prevailing winds or protected from them, and to determine the direction and intensity of these winds. Whether part or all of the site faces north or south will be important in determining what hardiness to plan for in plants. The choice of low plants and ground covers in some areas will be affected by the potential depth of the snow cover during the coldest portions of each winter. Some regions can expect a consistent cover of several inches of snow, but others may experience little or no snow, winter after winter. Less-hardy species will endure if they are protected by a consistent snow cover.

4. Functional and circulation characteristics. If the site is unoccupied at the time the site analysis is made, many of these characteristics must be determined with the help of the client

or else estimated. For sites in use, observation of vehicular and pedestrian circulation patterns over a period of time will help to ensure that potential plant locations are given the most efficient, functional uses. Other functional locations may be determined by standard practice; for instance, large trees are not compatible on the south and west sides of swimming pools and tennis courts, because leaf, flower, and seed litter in pools will result, and distracting shadow patterns on the courts will be caused.

5. Aesthetic factors. Determine the location of good views, and also the location of poor views that may require screening. It is always good to consult with the client about these. A client may prefer one view instead of another for reasons a designer cannot anticipate, and his personal likes and dislikes may require the designer to develop unique solutions because of a client's personal objections to neighbors or objects and structures on adjacent properties. For the most part, however, the designer's personal taste and judgment play a predominant role in evaluating the aesthetic characteristics of a site. Because of his training and experience, a designer will be capable of making judgments that will prove satisfactory to a majority of clients, most of whom will not be able to express why they like what they see but will admit they find it pleasant and enjoyable.

PLANT SELECTION

Having thoroughly analyzed the site, the designer begins the process of assembling a list of plants compatible with the findings of his site analysis. Other factors will also influence this selection. The availability of plants from established nursery sources is important. There is little value to selecting and using a plant in a planting plan if the landscape contractor finds it cannot be obtained. Whether or not good maintenance is available to the client will also influence plant selection. Those plants requiring extensive annual pruning and pest control will have to be minimized or eliminated from the design if good maintenance is not available. In nearly every project, cost becomes important and most clients are reluctant to plan for expensive maintenance, so the designer may have to select plants that require little maintenance to reduce cost. All clients should be persuaded to understand that some maintenance and some cost is necessary even when a project has been most carefully designed and planned to minimize it.

Occasionally clients will browse through a nursery catalog and ask the designer, "Can I have a plant like this one?" Usually they are attracted by the color of the flowers. Rarely do they understand that the plant must have some relationship to the total design. The plant they have seen in the catalog may not be hardy, or it may not be adaptable to the soils on the client's site. It then becomes the educational task of the designer to describe some basic principles of plant ecology, or to show a client plant examples already growing in the area of his site, and to orient him to the nature of design. This procedure may be needed more often in dealing with a residential client than with corporate or institutional clients, who may be quite accustomed to leaving all details of a delegated job to the professional they have engaged.

Dislikes of some plants will arise generally from unpleasant experiences. A child, having fallen into a clump of roses or a barberry bush, may dislike such plants permanently. It is always good to determine if a client has a dislike of some plant the designer plans to use. Some education of the client in the qualities of disliked plants may or may not be helpful.

PLANT CHARACTERISTICS AS A DESIGN DETERMINANT

Once he has assembled a list of plants to be used for the design of a project and has taken into account the information gained from the site analysis, the designer then considers the form, size, texture, and color of each plant to be used.

Form

There are a wide variety of forms. We mentioned the categories of horizontal and vertical forms earlier. These are the broadest categories. Trees and shrubs grow mainly in columnar, round or ellipsoidal, pyramidal, round-weeping or -drooping, and v- (or vase-) shaped forms. Some may have forms that combine these basic shapes. Horizontal form is characteristic of shrubs more than it is of trees, and some shrubs grow in horizontal-oval and mounded-to-flat form. Shrub forms may seem to hug the ground, whereas the forms of trees will be supported in the air on their trunks.

The vertical forms of individual plants will change to (or "read") as a horizontal form or

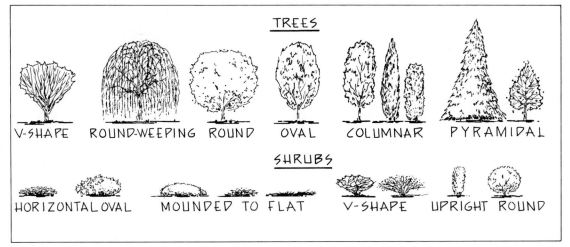

9-1

9-2

Figure 9-1. *Some of the most common tree and shrub forms. Various combinations of each of the forms can be found and there is a variety of plant sizes within each form.*

Figure 9-2. *When combined, individual plant forms become part of a horizontal mass. Here, the horizontal nature of the planting complements the lines of the architecture of the building.* Euonymus japonicus *with facing of* Taxus baccata *var.* repandens.

unit when the plants are placed together in a group for a mass planting.

Prime consideration must be given to the form of a plant when it is used as an individual specimen for a focal point or for emphasis in a design composition. Individual forms become less noticeable when several plants are closely spaced; then the form of a plant is likely not to express itself well or at all. A ground cover is an example in which forms of the individual plants of the same species are lost as part of the whole mass. Care must be taken never to use too many different forms together; too much variety of form will create a "hodge-podge" rather than a designed composition with aesthetic value.

The form of deciduous materials may change somewhat during the changing of the seasons. Where a strong oval form may be evident in a tree when foliage is luxuriant, only a very weak oval form will be perceived in winter, at which time the upright pattern of the branches at the center of the tree may be more dominant than the overall tree form observed in summer. Depending upon the circumstances, seasonal variations may have considerable effect on the design.

Size

What will be the ultimate or mature width and height of plants selected? Many plant listings or encyclopedias list these sizes. In most instances the sizes given are for full growth under ideal environmental conditions and may not represent growth potential of the site for which the design is being created. Therefore, the designer can find it helpful to consult with local nurserymen and horticulturists, and to rely on direct observation. Sometimes an accurate judgment of potential plant size is needed in conjunction with the spacing of plants. More will be said about size later in this chapter, under "Spacing of Plants."

Texture

The texture of each plant can be expressed in a number of ways. Texture varies also with the distance of the viewer from the plant and relates, usually by contrast, to adjacent textures. A plant with large leaves may express a coarse texture during summer, but in contrast to other plants during winter its branching pattern might be fine in texture. With some plants there is no difference. The large leaves of *Magnolia soulangeana* express a coarse texture and the bold branching pattern will also be coarse in winter. Tallhedge buckthorn (*Rhamnus frangula* var. *columnaris*) is coarser in texture during the summer than common privet (*Ligustrum vulgare*), which has small leaves, but their winter textures are practically identical.

Evergreens offer the advantage of consistent texture. Rhododendrons and yews are examples, respectively, of coarse and fine textures that will provide a year-round consistency in the design.

Color

Flowers, fruit, leaves, and branches are all sources of color and are all influenced by seasonal variations. In general, flowers on trees and shrubs are short lived, though their visual effect can be quite dramatic. A mass of forsythia in bloom during spring is an example;

9-3

Figure 9-3. *Skillful use of a variety of textures in a naturalistic project. An analysis of plant textures such as those shown in Chapter 7 was needed in planning this project. As a result, the textures combine naturally.*

it remains a popular plant though it offers little interest the remainder of the year.

Fruit value varies from plant to plant. Some fruit offers little contrast in color or showiness, but in other plants the fruit may be more dramatic than the flowers. If fruit color is dramatic or the fruit is persistent into fall and winter after the leaves have dropped, it becomes an important consideration in design. Pyracanthas are just one of many examples of shrubs with colorful and persistent fruit; species of this genus have berrylike fruit ranging from yellow-orange to scarlet and crimson, colors much more important than the flower colors of the shrubs.

The light, fresh green color of new leaves in spring can offer refreshing design possibilities. A deep contrast can be seen between the dark green of the past year's needles and the light color of the coming year's new growth in yew shrubs. The same is true among most conifers. Japanese red maple (*Acer palmatum* var. *atropurpureum*), begins the year with pale red leaves, which darken to purple as spring changes to summer. Plants that possess a leaf color dramatically different from the usual variations of green are useful for accents and points of emphasis in a design composition. Moreover, they reduce monotony and create a pleasant variety. As is true in using any element of design, too much variety of color will cause a design to look confused and disorganized and will destroy an otherwise pleasant aesthetic effect.

The fall coloring of leaves should also receive consideration. Winged euonymus (*Euonymus alatus*) presents an especially fiery display of color. This plant will always catch the eye and can easily occupy the center of a composition.

Branches are a useful source of winter color, though their color is apt to be less noticeable against the sky and thus can be given lower priority in a design than the other considerations just discussed. In a particular project, however, a plant such as red-osier dogwood (*Cornus stolonifera*), against a light grey fence, might become a central focal point in a garden during the winter. The dark brown branches of a nicely or artistically formed tree makes interesting contrast against the light brick or white cast stone walls of large buildings.

SPACING OF PLANTS

As living things, plants vary in size according to age. This ever changing factor presents problems to the designer. Some clients want a landscape that will look mature as soon as it has been installed, and if they can afford it in their budget, large-sized plants can be selected that may be several years of age. The general tendency is to place young plants too close together, without anticipating the ultimate size of the plant.

The designer should learn to think in terms of three common categories of plant size. Besides knowing the nursery size, the size at which plants are commonly sold, the designer plans for their full size at maturity (or old age), but he also familiarizes himself with their "average" mature size. Full size will vary according to the planting location and soil factors. Under ideal site and soil conditions a particular tree may grow to a height of 100 feet, but the particular characteristics of a site may restrict its growth to an ultimate height of 60 feet. If the tree is planted in a raised, enclosed planting bed, this will restrict its ultimate height even more, and it will probably shorten the tree's life-span as well.

Generally, most designers will base the plant spacing on their plans according to the average mature growth of the plants, and can thus achieve a design that looks full and mature before the plants reach their ultimate maturity. In some projects it is best to space the plants very close together for immediate effect. Hedges and privacy screens are examples of plantings in which a dense appearance is so important that the designer may plan for close spacing even of young plants.

THE USE OF FLOWERS IN PLANTING DESIGN

For the moment, let us confine our discussion to flowers such as perennials, annuals, and bulbs, instead of the flowers of trees, shrubs, or ground covers. Flowers require a great deal of maintenance, in return for which they provide considerable visual and aesthetic appeal, and most homeowners insist on providing some space for them in a garden design. The smaller or reduced scale of the residential garden allows intimate contact with flowers, which can be manipulated frequently and freely and given a kind of care not needed for other plants. However, most corporate, institutional, and governmental clients will limit the use of flowers to areas of special interest or positions of maximum exposure, because of the cost of their maintenance.

9-4

Figure 9-4. *Flowers used as a ground cover along a freeway.*

Generally, flowers should be planted against a background of shrubs or along a fence. In a planting bed the lowest flowers should be placed in front, with one or more masses of flowers of increasing height behind them. Plants should be selected so that a sequence of flower color will continue throughout the season, but attention should be given to avoiding clashes between adjacent colors that do not harmonize.

THE DESIGN PROCESS

The actual process of making a planting design begins after much of the other planning of a project has taken place. First comes the site analysis, as we described earlier, which is followed by a master plan. Buildings are precisely located, then designed by an architect. The landscape architect prepares the site plans for roads, walks, plazas, fountains, steps, wall, etc., in cooperation with engineers who are handling several technical details, including the design of underground utilities. Even though the landscape architect has kept his planting design in mind during the entire planning process and has thought about preserving existing trees on the site, developing his grading plans to avoid disturbing them, he begins to develop his planting drawings near the end of his "planning." Ideally the planting plan and sprinkling plans are prepared simultaneously and closely coordinated. The engineers will need to know some details of the sprinkling plan when they design the water mains.

The trend in landscape-architectural offices today is toward multidisciplinary staffing, so that several specialists are brought together to work on one project. The most successful planting designs will be created when designers, plant specialists, and maintenance specialists work together in reaching design solutions. The aesthetic value of a design will be increased and maintenance costs will be reduced to a greater extent than when a project is designed by one individual.

Utilizing the most up-to-date site plans, the designer makes an ozalid print of the site plan, places the print on his drafting board, and covers it with a sheet of light-weight sketching tissue.

Elevations of nearby buildings and perspectives of portions of the site should be used for coordinated study with the plan.

Using a soft pencil, the designer begins to place plant masses on his tissue sketches of plans and elevations. During this sketching, plant names are not applied. The designer studies these masses for their contribution to the composition. He may need to adjust their placement for the best combination of emphasis, repetition, and balance. Next he will think about the textures he wants to create, sketching these with appropriately varied widths of vertical lines. At the same time, the designer studies use of form, line, and color, comparing various combinations of these in turn on the plan and on elevations. Names and individual locations for each plant are now determined from the list previously prepared. If significant changes in the details of the site plan were made after the plant list was prepared, a cross-check is advisable to make sure the plants selected earlier still fit the particular environmental conditions created by sun, shade or wind, etc., on the site. Three, four, or more studies will be made on the lightweight sketching tissue before the final solution has been determined.

The next step—preparation of plans and specifications—is discussed fully in Chapter 10.

SOME GENERAL CONSIDERATIONS

In designing for plants, plants cannot be considered in and of themselves to the exclusion of all else. When they are placed on a site they can transform it, but it is important for the designer to remember that the site existed earlier, and its inherent or existing characteristics will control the success or failure of the finished site depending upon how well or how inadequately the designer understands and works with these characteristics.

A planting design for a large urban area dominated by buildings and paving can be bold and dramatic, but in rural, more natural settings, the design will need to be very subtle to fit into the existing landscape. In between these extremes is a wide variety of other sites requiring considerable intuitive ingenuity on the part of the designer before a design can be made that is satisfactory both functionally and aesthetically.

Some planting designs will have, as an important function, the remedy of bad site planning. Through lack of planning, many buildings are intrusions upon the natural landscape, poorly fitted to the site. The designer may be called upon to try to improve the site with the use of plants. Exposed foundations and crude grade-changes call for plant masses to create a smoother, more aesthetic transition

from building to site. Tall buildings can be made to fit their surroundings by the use of tall trees. Large expanses of windowless walls can be broken visually with columnar trees planted close to the walls. Shrub masses are effective around smaller buildings, creating a sense of lengthened horizontal dimensions and pulling the structure closer to the ground visually.

NATURALISTIC APPROACH TO DESIGN

Of increasing appeal to some people is the idea of a return to nature. To design landscapes that seem to have developed naturally requires a thorough knowledge of plant ecology. It also requires a tolerance by the client for a lack of neatness in the landscape, because a naturalistic design is not a manicured one. There is a vast difference between informal and naturalistic design. An informal design may make use of curved, irregular lines, but the finished appearance reveals attention to order and tidiness. However, in naturalistic design, such things as line, form, color, and texture appear only the way nature allows them. Only those plants that are compatible with each other and with the environmental conditions of the site are used, and these will survive without man's help.

As the naturalistic design matures, additional plants can be added. For instance, during maturity some areas of the site may have become shaded and the soil surface will have become built up with forest humus. Shade-loving ferns and wildflowers can be added where conditions have developed for which they are compatible.

9-5

9-6

Figure 9-5. *An effective naturalistic design. The slope beyond is left natural, and it complements and enhances the growth in the clearing.*

Figure 9-6. *A close-up of the site shown in the previous illustration. The lack of order is attractive because it is in harmony with nature.*

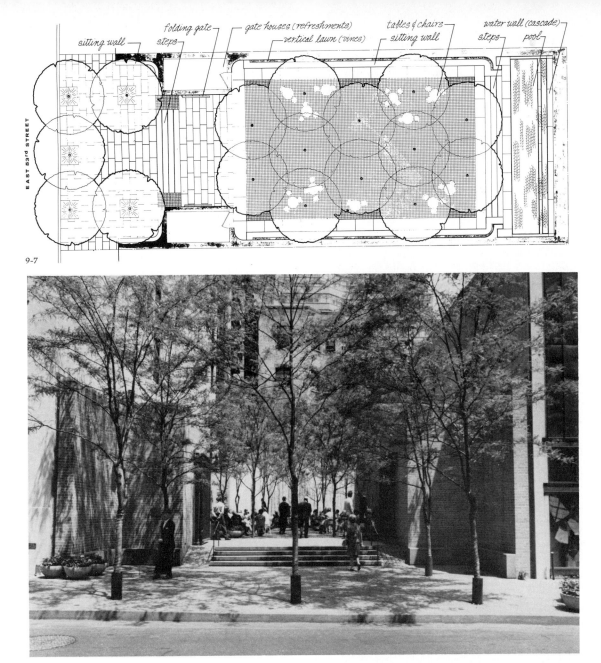

sitting wall — folding gate — gate houses (refreshments) — tables & chairs — water wall (cascade)

steps — vertical lawn (vines) — sitting wall — steps — pool

EAST 53rd STREET

9-7

9-8

Figures 9-7, 9-8. *A plan (9-7) and view (9-8) of Samuel Paley Plaza, a minipark in midtown New York. A wall of water terminates the view into the park. Extensive use of trees provides contact with nature in an urban area and offers shade.*

DESIGN CONSIDERATIONS OF SOME PROJECTS

The following examples of design projects are not all-inclusive but are intended to provide a general introduction to the variety and particular characteristics of the design problems a practicing designer can expect to encounter. Our emphasis here is on ways all the design elements we have discussed are used in a variety of projects, without studying more than their design qualities. Later in the book, in Chapters 19, 20, and 21, we will discuss typical projects in urban, suburban, and rural areas, for which many considerations, including planting design, will have to be integrated.

Parks and Recreation Areas

The use of shrubs, especially large masses, is often not wise in urban parks, even though they might be desirable. In many parks it is necessary for civil authorities to monitor park activities to insure the protection and safety of the people who use the park. Experience has shown that where shrub masses are used, even though they provide privacy, they also provide a screen for criminal activity. The designer may want to strive for the maximum amount of openness with his design.

Where the design of the park is informal, the tree planting should also express an informal quality. Random spacing and grouping of trees will yield the most successful results. In highly developed parks—those that are created largely out of architectural materials and in which the space for plants is minimal—the designer may have to use a different approach. Parks of this type are usually given

9-9

9-10

Figure 9-9. *Spanish River Park, a naturalistic oceanside park along the Atlantic in Boca Raton, Florida. The park covers a 45-acre area around which are located two residential developments and a water channel providing them with boat access.*

Figure 9-10. *A public area within Central Park Zoo, New York City. The steps lead toward an outdoor dining area.*

9-11

a modular design utilizing straight lines. Tree plantings in such parks will be more effective if designed formally to harmonize with the rest of the park design.

Roof Planting

There is increasing use of planting on the tops of structures above, at, or below street level. These gardens, parks, plazas, or whatever they might be called, pose special problems. Because planting beds will be entirely surrounded by some kind of container, temperatures are likely to reach extremes that will affect the hardiness of plants used, root zones will be restricted, and patterns of light intensity and reflection, shade, and air movement may all be quite unusual.

Moreover, there are structural problems that the designer should consider. Few structures are designed to support the weight of soil in the quantities needed for a luxuriant landscape.

Trees will have to be planted in raised containers over the supporting columns of the structure. Some designers have arranged soil mounds over the columns and placed a boxed tree at the center, an informal grouping of small shrubs on other portions of the mound, and ground covers over the rest.

On large structures, grass may be used to connect soil areas between supporting columns; for grass the soil layers can be thinner than for shrubs.

The availability of water and other utilities will limit what can be done. Consideration must be given to drainage and irrigation. Projects of this type that are actually parts of structures are usually heavily used areas and lighting

Figure 9-11. *A pool, gardens, and an open paved area for public use and civic events are all located above an underground two-level parking garage for 240 cars in Market Square, Alexandria, Virginia.*

9-12

9-14

9-13

Figures 9-12, 9-13, 9-14. *Several views of Constitution Plaza, Hartford, Connecticut. The variety and extensiveness of the planting in this elevated area is notable.*

Figure 9-13. *A fountain provides a focal point or emphasis in a large open plaza, around which are located planting beds and trees in raised containers.*

Figure 9-14. *Several planted terraces are used on different parts of Constitution Plaza. This one is adjacent to the fountain area shown in the previous illustration. Other views are shown in Chapter 8.*

is often needed so that the project can be used during evening and night hours. Carefully placed lights in concealed sources are successfully used and aesthetically pleasing. Designs of this kind are good places to make use of water, either in a splashing fountain or a reflection pool, both of which will enliven a small plaza without requiring a great amount of space.

Urban Center Areas

Closely related to roof planting in several of its problems is "street-scaping," or the revitalization of downtown areas, using plants as one of the components in this work. There are few streets in modern cities that do not have a multitude of utilities beneath the paving. Besides covering conduits for telephone and power cables, paving may have been laid over pipes for heating and cooling systems, water, and sanitary sewage and storm runoff systems. All combined, these can limit the amounts of soil available for the root zones of most plants. Securing sufficient information on underground utilities during site analysis is nearly always a problem inasmuch as few cities maintain maps. Some lines may have been installed privately without being placed on city maps. Quite often lines are changed during construction because of other hidden utilities or obstructions, thus making the city's drawings more inaccurate.

Designers often find raised planters convenient because these can be designed to provide sufficient soil space for planting. Irrigation in some form is generally a necessity.

Plant selection is crucial since the plants must tolerate air pollution, root restriction, heat, cold, wind, and other rugged conditions not common in other projects for which plants are used.

Frequently encountered problems of planting in urban environments are discussed in Chapter 19.

Housing Developments

In designing plantings for a low-cost housing development, the designer's choices will be severely restricted by his budget. For this reason, unfortunately, planting is usually kept to a minimum. Because of cost limitations, most of the plants selected are small in size and of inexpensive, deciduous species. They must be capable of surviving with little or no maintenance. Trees usually must be planted so sparsely that locating them carefully in the composition is critical. Selection of very durable species is also important.

When a large budget is available, as it often is for high-quality condominium developments, the designer has greater freedom to produce a planting plan that is both functional and aesthetic. Large plants can be used for a more immediate result. The creation of outdoor living spaces and installation of plant masses to screen noise, hide objectionable views, and provide privacy are some of the things that can be more easily designed for a project if the budget is large.

Schools and Campuses

In the past two decades there has been a surge of construction of educational facilities. Landscape architects have been involved in many phases of this work, including site selection, master planning, and site engineering, as well

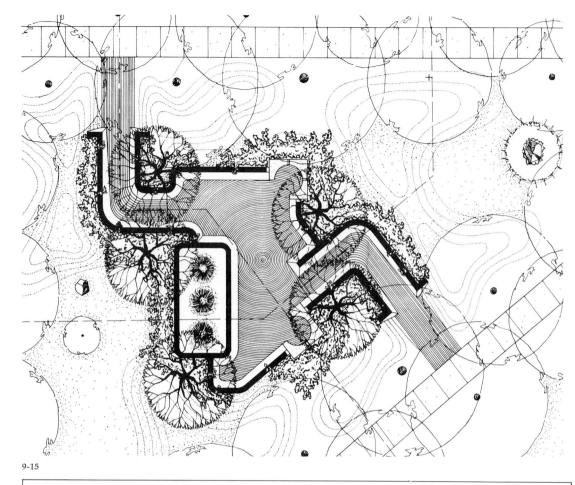

9-15

9-17

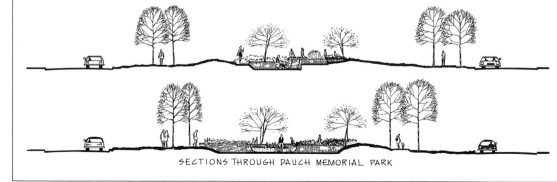

SECTIONS THROUGH DAUCH MEMORIAL PARK

9-16

Figures 9-15, 9-16, 9-17. *Dauch Memorial, Sandusky, Ohio. A small, well-designed urban park. The use made of plants, landscape materials, and variations in terrain in this park is quite similar to the way these were used in the park in Wilmington, Delaware, shown in Chapter 19.*

Figure 9-18. *A promenade in Ann Arbor, Michigan. This street was redesigned to increase the areas along it for pedestrians and plants.*

Figure 9-19. *A pedestrian mall in Louisville, Kentucky. What was formerly a street has been turned into an area for pedestrians.*

9-18

9-20

9-19

9-21

Figure 9-20. *Part of this mall in Lansing, Michigan was designed as a play area.*

Figure 9-21. *Wilderness condominiums. The units are attached, the way houses in a city might be, but the design of the landscape makes use of natural elements.*

Figure 9-22. *A community park developed on a quadrangle entirely enclosed by condominium units at Deerfield Lakes, Florida. A man-made lake, part of which is shown here, was excavated; the excavated soil was mounded to vary the terrain on which the buildings were built. The lake surrounds an island, reached by bridges. On the island is a swimming pool and clubhouse. The entire site covers 7 1/2 acres.*

9-23

9-24

9-25

Figure 9-23. *Reston, Virginia. A recently built, successful planned community. Creating a diverse, well-designed landscape for this new town was one of the important goals of its planners and developers.*

Figure 9-24. *Fox Lane Middle School, Bedford, New York. A good example of campus planning. An important goal was to fit buildings onto the site with the least disturbance of existing trees.*

Figure 9-25. *Planting on the campus of the University of California, Los Angeles. The strong, dominant lines of the building are softened by careful use of plants. In the foreground, a bed of agapanthus.*

9-26

9-28

9-27

Figure 9-26. *An area of the campus of Temple University, Philadelphia. Paving and planting have been used in a heavily travelled area and make an effective transition between the campus and surrounding city buildings.*

Figure 9-27. *A view of the Voorhees Memorial Garden, Princeton University, also illustrated in Chapter 7.*

Figure 9-28. *Educational Testing Service, Princeton, New Jersey. The campuslike setting here made use of existing groves of trees at the site.*

as planting design, with most of the work being done at new institutions of higher education, which often comprise several buildings on a campus. Elementary and secondary school districts have sought the services of landscape architects less frequently, relying instead on parent-teacher groups to provide the landscaping. This is especially true in rural areas.

There is about as much variety in planting design for schools as there are designers. Each school will have conditions that make a slightly different approach to arranging the plants necessary; many of the differences are dictated less by the site than by school-administrative preferences and cost factors. Because school buildings are large, designers will generally attempt to create a smaller, more human scale. If the shrub masses used are generally horizontal in character and are kept simple, this will make a large building seem lower. To complement the austere, geometric lines of modern architecture in a building with a large mass, large numbers of the same plant species can be used in continuous masses rather than smaller numbers of several species, as would be typical in a residential garden.

Corporate Headquarters

A trend among corporations in many areas of the country is to relocate their business offices in spacious suburban areas, away from crowded urban centers. In doing so, most of these clients have selected sites that provide opportunities for extensive landscaping. Water can be used to an extent that may not be possible in other projects, and bodies of water or small streams may be natural parts of the site, which the designer would want to develop for their aes-

9-29

9-30

9-31

9-32

9-33

Figure 9-29. *Pepsico World Headquarters, Purchase, New York. A large parklike landscape surrounds this office building, not far from New York City.*

Figure 9-30. *A garden court at the Pepsico World Headquarters.*

Figure 9-31. *An approach to the offices of Chemical Abstracts Service, Columbus, Ohio.*

Figures 9-32, 9-33. *An outdoor area for employees of Chemical Abstracts Service, Columbus, Ohio.*

thetic value. Outdoor areas for sitting and eating lunch should be a fundamental part of the planning, but depending on the needs of the client, a project might also contain elaborate recreation facilities, even swimming pools. The additional development and maintenance expenses at such sites have been justified by improved employee morale and public recognition of a favorable corporate image. During the past two decades some of the most significant building and landscape designs have been initiated by corporate clients.

Shopping Centers

The design of malls in shopping centers allows a designer to use more variety than he can in other projects of similar size and scale. Indeed, the more variety the better, for if a shopper feels encouraged to stop, or change his direction, or rest for a while, he will presumably stay in the shopping center longer, think of additional things to buy, and see shops he never noticed before. To help achieve these things, the designer tries to create the widest possible variety of experience, not only with plants, but also with paving patterns, the creation of small resting places and alcoves, mounds, raised planters, fountains, seating, and other things.

Since most shopping centers provide some protection from wind and frost, more exotic species can be used in the planting areas. Most trees selected are specimens and each can act as a focal point in a small space. In larger, open areas, informal masses of small trees or shrubs might be used. In general, shrubs should also be flowering, though some evergreens are important for winter color. Those shrubs that are brightly colored and fragrant are especially useful. Many successfully planted shopping center malls contain beds of flowers in which spring bulbs, summer annuals, and autumn chrysanthemums are rotated.

The cost of maintenance of flower beds is high, but many shopping center developers advertise the beauty of a well planted mall and use seasonal flower displays as an attraction for potential shoppers, who more than compensate them for the increased cost.

Cemeteries

There has been a transition during the past few decades from a complex and ornate expression of cemetery design to a simple one. Whereas cemeteries used to feature massings of shrubs and flowers in addition to tree plantings, around large headstones, today shrub plantings are kept to a minimum, headstones are kept flat, and the total area is given a sense of openness.

The main cause of this change is the cost of maintenance. Upright headstones and masses of shrubs and flowers are expensive to maintain, and a poorly maintained cemetery full of weeds and unmown grass is depressing. Lower cost can be realized by reducing shrub planting to a few locations at entrances and around buildings, by keeping trees few in number, and by developing large, open lawn spaces in which headstones are flush with the ground. Such a cemetery will be pleasant aesthetically. Best aesthetic quality is obtained when tree plantings are informal. Avoid straight rows or the excessive repetition of one species. A few trees with flower color will add the attraction of color, and those blooming near

9-34

Figure 9-34. *Bal Harbour Shops, Florida. Part of a shopping center—the outside of which was shown earlier, in Chapter 7—in which plants have been used throughout.*

the end of May will be especially pleasant.

The few shrub masses that may be necessary should generally have a strong horizontal form to fit the scale of a cemetery, though the precise character of the design will be dictated by any structural facilities at the site.

Selective Designing: Natural Landscapes

Sometimes the development of a planting design does not require preparing a planting plan and specifying new plants to be installed. Some large parks in wilderness areas of the country have plenty of existing vegetation. When a wilderness area is opened for public use, the need may not be for more planting but for the development of views from highways, visitor centers, and campgrounds. The design of such aesthetic effects can be accomplished by selective thinning or removal of plants. Low branches on trees can be pruned to provide a view between the trunks of large trees to a lake or a distant mountain peak. Where necessary, some trees and underplanting may be removed to reveal the vista, but care should be taken to retain some of the existing material to frame the view.

In their quest for neatness, many property owners who landscape new houses built in natural areas completely eliminate the undergrowth in favor of growing lawns. Grass cannot usually survive in the light that reaches the ground in wooded areas; the lawn fails, leaving the property owner frustrated. Many wooded natural areas, if left undisturbed, will maintain themselves. All such a "landscape design" requires is a willingness by the client to tolerate less neatness in the landscape and to derive increased enjoyment from the diversity nature offers with wildflowers and other forms of undergrowth, and with wildlife.

SUMMARY

Through his training in design, botany, horticulture, and ecology, coupled with some practical experience, the designer prepares himself to resolve complex planting design problems. There are many aspects of his work that pose problems he may not be able to resolve himself; for resolution of these he will need the services of others whose training and expertise will bring together the information and resources necessary for satisfactory, functional, and aesthetically pleasing landscapes.

FOR FURTHER READING

Eckbo, G., 1950. *Landscape for Living*. New York: Duell, Sloan and Pearce.

Robinette, G. O., 1972. *Plants, People, and Environmental Quality*. Washington, D.C.: U.S. Government Printing Office.

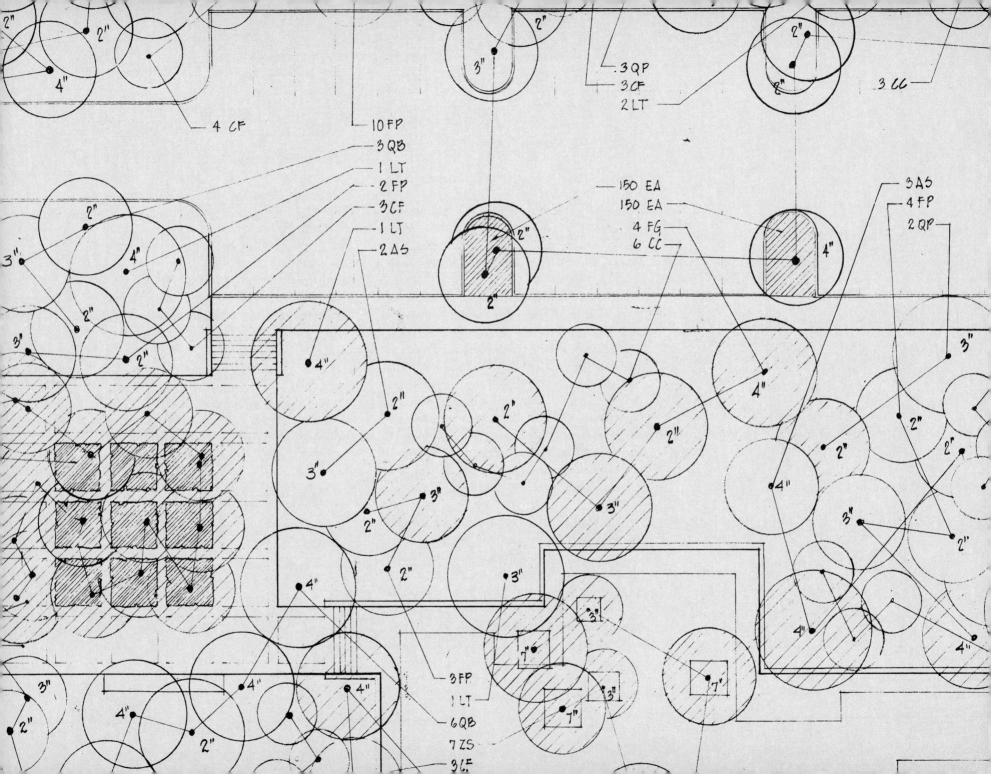

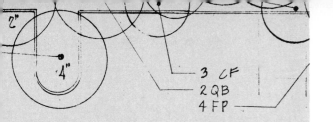

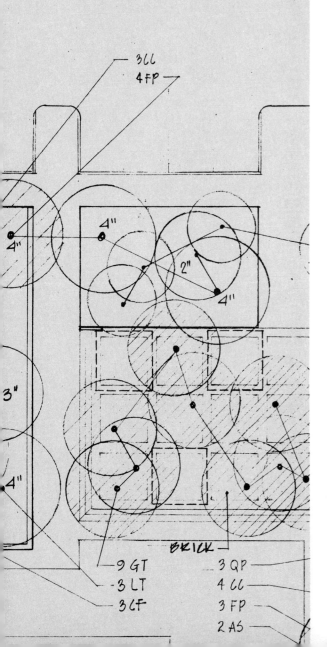

IV

Preparation and Implementation of Landscape Plans

10

Preparation of Planting Plans and Specifications

PLANS

A prerequisite to the preparation of planting plans or any other drawings is the development of drafting skills and an understanding of the common graphic symbolism used on plans. The elementary aspects of drafting will not be discussed here, because the skills are best acquired in a course where an instructor demonstrates them, monitors student progress frequently, and corrects errors and weaknesses quickly.

Professional designers prepare themselves through a number of college courses over a period of time generally exceeding three years. During that time, drafting and graphic skills are usually acquired in combination with background in a variety of problems in design, planting design, and construction. The designer's skills mature through internship, following graduation, for a period averaging from three to five years under the guidance of an experienced landscape architect or designer. The quality of workmanship on the drawings is as important as the quality of the design. Well-prepared, neat drawings make a positive impression upon both the client and the contractor.

Most states now require the registration or licensing of those who wish to call themselves landscape architects or practice landscape architecture (this varies from state to state), which means their plans and specifications must be stamped or bear a seal showing evidence of their compliance with the law. More information on registration can be found in

Figure 10-1. *A planting plan for a downtown urban park. The trees are planted in mounded grass areas along the sides and in planting areas provided in the paving. Note that the trees are informally grouped and irregularly spaced. The central focus of the park is the pool in the center. Several highrise office buildings have a view from above. Plants in this drawing are coded to the plant list at the lower right of the plan.*

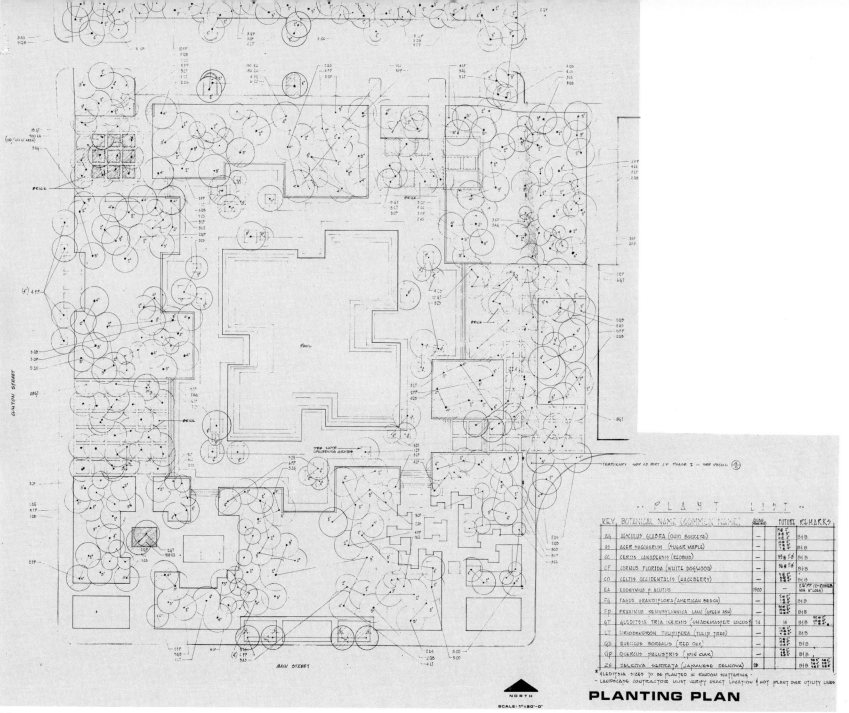

PLANTING PLAN

NORTH

SCALE: 1"=20'-0"

MAIN STREET

CLINTON STREET

POOL

BRICK

PLANT LIST

KEY	BOTANICAL NAME (COMMON NAME)	QUAN. (RANGE NO.)	FUTURE	REMARKS
AG	AESCULUS GLABRA (OHIO BUCKEYE)	—		B+B
AS	ACER SACCHARUM (SUGAR MAPLE)	—		B+B
CC	CERCIS CANADENSIS (REDBUD)	—		B+B
CF	CORNUS FLORIDA (WHITE DOGWOOD)	—		B+B
CO	CELTIS OCCIDENTALIS (HACKBERRY)	—		B+B
EA	EUONYMUS f. ACUTUS	1500		2'4" FF (3' PLANTED MIN. 5" LONG)
FG	FAGUS GRANDIFLORA (AMERICAN BEECH)	—		B+B
FP	FRAXINUS PENNSYLVANICA LANC (GREEN ASH)	—		B+B
GT	GLEDITSIA TRIACANTHIS (SHADEMASTER LOCUST)	14	14	B+B
LT	LIRIODENDRON TULIPIFERA (TULIP TREE)	—		B+B
QB	QUERCUS BOREALIS (RED OAK)	—		B+B
QP	QUERCUS PALUSTRIS (PIN OAK)	—		B+B
ZS	ZELKOVA SERRATA (JAPANESE ZELKOVA)	20		B+B

* GLEDITSIA SIZES TO BE PLANTED IN RANDOM SCATTERING.
- LANDSCAPE CONTRACTOR MUST VERIFY EXACT LOCATION & NOT PLANT OVER UTILITY LINES

10-1

10-2

10-3

Chapter 3. A number of states allow nursery-men and others who call themselves "landscape designers" to prepare planting plans. The preparation of planting plans for government projects in many states can be accomplished only by licensed (or registered) landscape architects.

Plans at best are very poor representations of the final completed project. They represent a view looking straight down from overhead, a view rarely if ever seen by the client. Most clients have difficulty understanding what they read on the plan or comprehending how the finished project will look on the basis of the drawing, but if the client is confident about the designer and trusts him, he need not feel insecure if he does not know what the graphic symbols mean. A good client will respect the abilities and reputation of his designer and will rely on his judgment and recommendations. The principal purpose of a plan is to convey the intent of the designer to the contractor, and drawings currently provide the best known means of serving this purpose.

The plans or drawings, combined with any drawings of planting details such as those illustrated in this chapter, along with the specifications, are part of the contract document used for a project. The preparation of specifications is discussed later in this chapter, and the specifications written for an actual project are reprinted in an appendix at the end of the chapter. Contracts are discussed in Chapter 12.

In projects where clients need a fuller visualization of the final appearance of a project than they see with the aerial plans, perspective sketches or renderings are useful.

Figures 10-2, 10-3. *Perspective sketches. When the client can see the trees and shrubs in relationship to the rest of the features of the garden, such as these sketches show, he will retain a better visualization of the potential of the finished project.*

10-4

Figure 10-4. *An above-ground perspective view of a proposed urban plaza design.*

Figure 10-5. *Part of a planting plan for a high income apartment complex.*

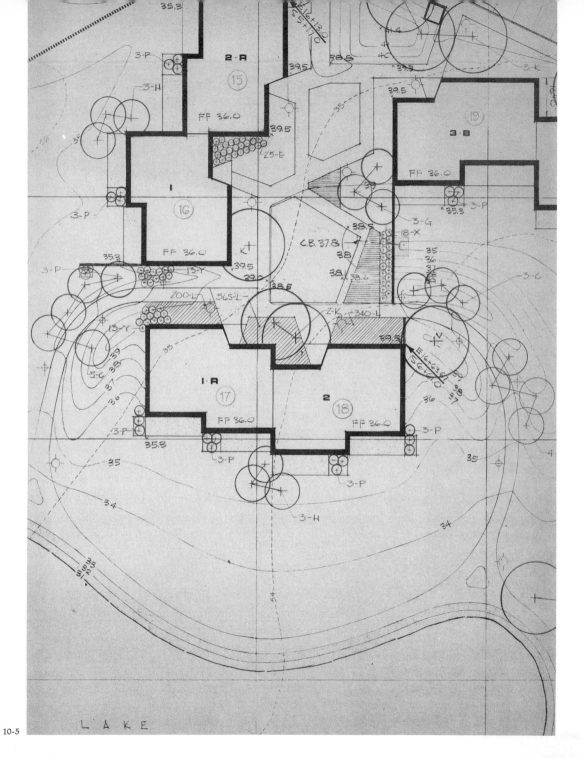

On the working drawings made as part of the planting plans, the exact location of each plant is shown. If there is room, the name of the plant should be written out; often an abbreviation is all there is room for. A designer should always work with the botanical name of a plant, providing a plant list, along with or as part of his drawings, on which are given the common name following the botanical name, total quantity, sizes, and other requirements for the plants.

Different symbols are used to illustrate a variety of plants. The scale of these drawings varies from project to project. It is difficult to show shrubs at a scale greater than 1 inch = 20 feet and the best scales are ⅛ inch = 1 foot or 1 inch = 10 feet. For showing the details of planting of perennials, annuals, etc., the best scale is ¼ inch = 1 foot.

It is rare that dimensions are placed on planting plans unless the location of a plant is quite critical. The contractor can usually place a scale or a measuring tape on the plan and determine the location of each plant with the accuracy needed.

When planting plans are prepared without specifications, a number of explanatory notes may be needed; otherwise these should be included in the specifications.

In a set of drawings one or more sheets following the planting plans will show various details. Some of these may include cross-sections through tree pits, staking arrangements, wells to protect existing trees when fill is added, and retaining walls to protect existing trees when the soil is cut below existing grades. In urban projects, trees may be planted in paved areas and raised planters.

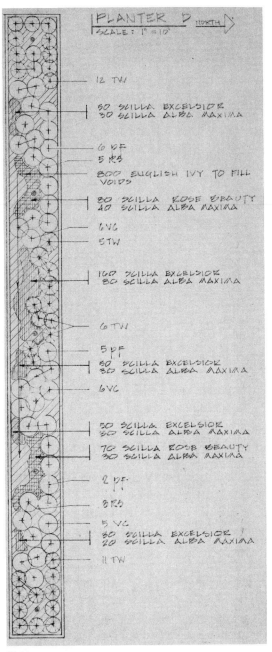

PLANTER D
SCALE: 1" = 10'
NORTH →

— 12 TW

— 50 SCILLA EXCELSIOR
30 SCILLA ALBA MAXIMA

— 6 PF
— 5 RB

— 800 ENGLISH IVY TO FILL
VOIDS

— 80 SCILLA ROSE BEAUTY
40 SCILLA ALBA MAXIMA

— 6 VC
— 5 TW

— 160 SCILLA EXCELSIOR
80 SCILLA ALBA MAXIMA

— 6 TW

— 5 PF
— 80 SCILLA EXCELSIOR
30 SCILLA ALBA MAXIMA

— 6 VC

— 80 SCILLA EXCELSIOR
30 SCILLA ALBA MAXIMA

— 70 SCILLA ROSE BEAUTY
30 SCILLA ALBA MAXIMA

— 2 PF

— 3 RB

— 5 VC
— 30 SCILLA EXCELSIOR
20 SCILLA ALBA MAXIMA

— 11 TW

10-6

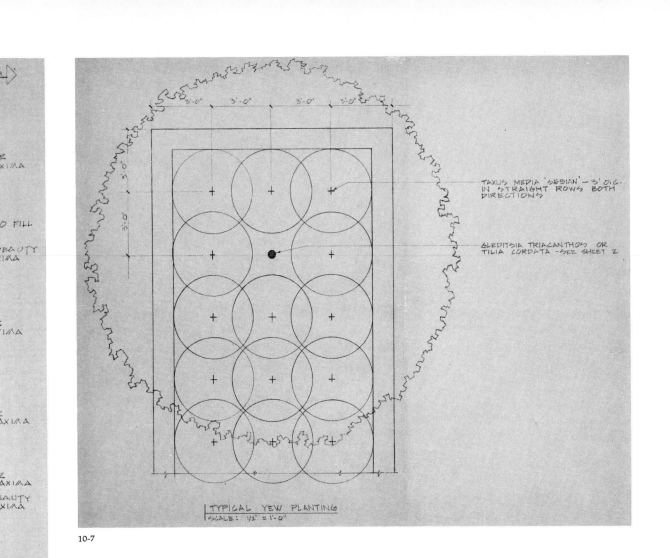

TAXUS MEDIA 'SEBIAN' — 3' O.C.
IN STRAIGHT ROWS BOTH
DIRECTIONS

GLEDITSIA TRIACANTHOS OR
TILIA CORDATA — SEE SHEET 2

TYPICAL YEW PLANTING
SCALE: 1½" = 1'-0"

10-7

Figures 10-6 to 10-8. *Partial planting plans for several raised planters in a downtown governmental office complex. The plants specified for Figure 10-6 are listed in Figure 10-11.*

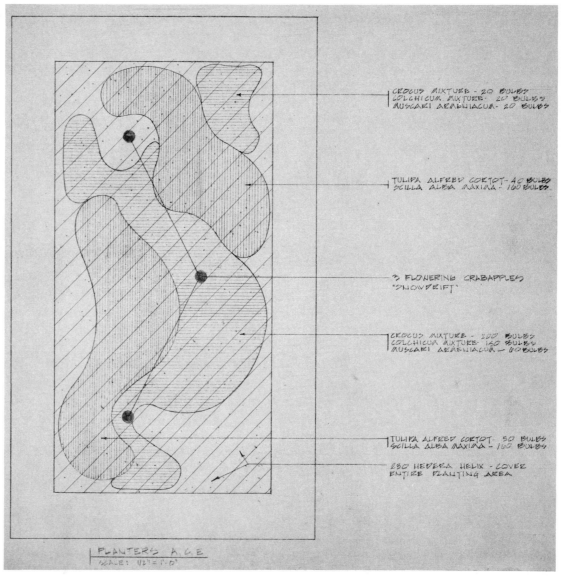

CROCUS MIXTURE - 20 BULBS
COLCHICUM MIXTURE - 20 BULBS
MUSCARI ARMENIACUM - 20 BULBS

TULIPA ALFRED CORTOT - 40 BULBS
SCILLA ALBA MAXIMA - 160 BULBS

3 FLOWERING CRABAPPLES
"SNOWDRIFT"

CROCUS MIXTURE - 200 BULBS
COLCHICUM MIXTURE - 160 BULBS
MUSCARI ARMENIACUM - 60 BULBS

TULIPA ALFRED CORTOT - 50 BULBS
SCILLA ALBA MAXIMA - 160 BULBS

230 HEDERA HELIX - COVER
ENTIRE PLANTING AREA

PLANTERS A.G.E.
SCALE: 1/2" = 1'-0"

10-8

Plant list

WOODY PLANTS

No.	Key	Botanical name	Common name	Size	Remarks
25	PF	*Pieris floribunda*	Mountain andromeda	24″–30″	B & B
17	RS	*Rhododendron schlippenbachii*	Royal azalea	24″–30″	B & B
28	VC	*Viburnum carlesi*	Fragant snowball	24″–30″	B & B
80	TW	*Taxus media 'Sebian'*	'Sebian' Japanese yew	24″–30″	B & B
9	MS	*Malus 'Snowdrift'*	Snowdrift crabapple	2″–2½″	B & B
2390		*Hedera helix*	English ivy	2¼″ pot	9″ O.C.

FLOWERING BULBS*	Number	Remarks
Colchicum giganteum	380	Top size; plant
C. 'Waterlily'	130	6″ deep
Crocus 'Blizzard' (white)	100	Top size; plant
C. 'Early Perfection'	400	2″ deep
C. 'Golden Goblet'	160	
Muscari armeniacum	240	Top size; plant 2″ deep
Scilla 'Alba Maxima'	1700	Top size; plant
S. 'Excelsior'	910	4″ deep
S. 'Rose Beauty'	680	
Tulipa kaufmanniana 'Alfred Cortot'	270	Top size; plant 2″ deep

*Bulb note: All bulbs shall be spaced irregularly and be planted in drifts within shapes shown on plane. Crocus (15 percent white, 25 percent violet, 60 percent yellow) should be planted in many drifts, keeping colors separate. Scilla and colchicum varieties should also be separated into many drifts within the shapes shown.

10-9

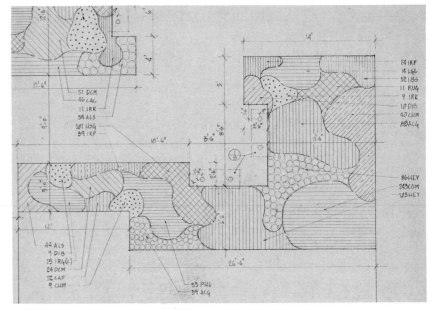

10-10

Figure 10-9. *A plant list prepared along with the drawing shown at Figure 10-6.*

Figure 10-10. *Portion of a flower garden planting plan prepared in conjunction with the plan for a downtown urban park shown in Figure 10-1. This plan was designed for display of color through as much of the growing season as possible. The plant list for this drawing is shown at Figure 10-11.*

Plant list

Key	Name	Quantity	Season	Color	Spacing	Height
ACG	*Achillea* 'Coronation Gold'	410	July–Aug.	Yellow	8"O.C.	3'
ACT	*Achillea taygetea*	14	June–Sept.	Yellow	8"O.C.	18"
ALS	*Alyssum saxatile (Aurinia saxatilis)*	467	May	Yellow	6"O.C.	1'
ASD	*Aster* (dwarf) 'Bonny Blue'	25	Aug.–Oct.	Lt. blue, lavender	12"O.C.	8"–10"
	A. 'Chorister'	25	Aug.–Sept.	White	"	18"
	A. 'Pacific Amaranth'	25	Aug.–Sept.	Purple, blue	"	15"
	A. 'Persian Rose'	23	Late Aug.–Oct.	Rose pink	"	12"–15"
AST	*Aster* (tall) 'Blue Feather'	7	Aug.–Sept.	Dark blue	"	22"
	A. 'Crimson Brocade'	10	"	Red	"	3'
	A. 'Lassie'	10	"	Pink	"	"
	A. 'Marie Ballard'	10	Sept.–Oct.	Powder blue	"	3'–4'
	A. 'Patricia Ballard'	10	Sept.–Oct.	Rose pink	"	3'
	A. 'Peerless'	10	Aug.–Sept.	Pale blue, lavender	"	24"–30"
CAC	*Campanula carpatica*	116	June–Oct.	Clear blue	8"–10"O.C.	8"–10"
CAP	*Campanula persicifolia* 'Grandiflora Alba'	8	July–Aug.	White	8"–10"O.C.	2'
	C. p. 'Grandiflora Caerulia'	18	July–Aug.	Blue	"	57"
CHM	*Chrysanthemum maximum* 'Aglaya'	44	July–Aug.	Double white	1'O.C.	—
	C. 'Thomas Killin'	128	July–Aug.	Sing. white/yellow	"	—
COM	*Convallaria majalis*	361	—	—	6"O.C.	—
DEB	*Delphinium belladonna* 'Clivedon Beauty'	67	June–Sept.	Blue	12"O.C.	3'–4'
DIB	*Dicentra eximea* 'Bountiful'	47	May–June (Sept.)	Pink	10"O.C.	20"
DCM	*Doronicum caucasicum* 'Magnificum'	150	April–May	Yellow	8"O.C.	15"
HED	*Hemerocallis* (dwarf) 'Primrose Mascotte'	10	July	Yellow	18"O.C.	20"
HEY	*Hemerocallis* (pink) 'Artemis'	3	July–Aug.	Orange-red	"	36"
	H. 'Magis Dawn'	6	June–Aug.	Rose-pink	"	"
	H. 'Mary Ann'	4	July	Pink	"	"
HEY	*Hemerocallis* (yellow) 'Fascinating'	45	June (late)	Chinese yellow	"	28"
	H. 'Hyperion'	45	July–Aug.	Citron	"	40"
	H. 'Magnificence'	46	Early July	Burnt orange	—	"
	H. 'Perpetual Motion'	80	June–Sept.	Apricot	—	—
HES	*Heuchera sanguinea*	360	June–Sept.	Pink	6"O.C.	18"
HSG	*Hosta subcordata* 'Grandiflora'	228	August	White	"	"
IBS	*Iberis sempervirens*	367	May	White	"	12"
IRG(A)	*Iris germanica* 'Harbor Blue'	63	May–June	Sapphire blue	12"O.C.	2'–3'
IRG(B)	*I. g.* 'Judith Meredith'	27	"	Bright pink	"	"
IRG(C)	*I. g.* 'Olympic Torch'	15	"	Bronze	"	"
IRG(D)	*I. g.* 'Rainbow Gold'	12	"	Yellow	"	3'
IRG(E)	*I. g.* 'Solid Gold'	10	"	Deep gold	"	2'–3'
IRK	*Iris kaempferi* 'Gold Bond'	20	June–July	White	10"O.C.	3'
IRP	*Iris pumila* 'Autumn Queen'	50	Apr.–May	White	6"O.C.	Border
	I. p. 'Jean Siret'	95	"	Chrome yellow	"	"
	I. p. 'Lieutenant Chavagnac'	50	"	Violet	"	"
IRS	*Iris sibirica* 'Royal Herald'	37	June	Purple	8"O.C.	36"
LGL	*Lavandula* 'Gray Lady'	48	July–Aug.	Blue	12"O.C.	18" Border
LIE	*Lilium* 'Enchantment'	44	—	Red	6"O.C.	36"–40"
PAB	*Papaver orientale* 'Cavalier'	42	—	—	12"O.C.	18" Border
	P. o. 'Watermelon'	43	—	—	"	"
PET(A)	*Petunia* 'Sugar Plum'	228	—	Pink–White	8"O.C.	—
PET(B)	*P.* 'Pink Cascade'	452	—	Pink	"	—
	P. 'Burgundy'	151	—	Burgundy	"	—
PHL	*Phlox paniculata* 'Balmoral'	185	July–Sept.	Pink (dark cent.)	10"O.C.	3'
	P. p. 'Dodo Hanbury Forbes'	185	"	Pink	"	"
RUG	*Rudbeckia* 'Goldsturm'	75	Aug.–Sept.	Gold	15"O.C.	"
	R. 'Robert Blum'	26	"	Pink	"	"
SAL	*Salvia* 'White Fire'	87	June–Oct.	White	12"O.C.	14"
SOL	*Solidago* 'Peter Pan'	80	July–Aug.	Yellow	8"O.C.	2½'
TEC	*Teucrium chamaedrys*	211	August	Blue	6"O.C.	12"

10-11

Figure 10-11. *A plant list prepared along with the drawing shown at Figure 10-10.*

Both plan views and cross-sections may be needed to show the details necessary for the contractor.

All drawings should be prepared on material such as vellum, linen, or mylar, which will remain tough even after a drawing has been handled for a time, and from which photocopies of the drawings can be made. The original drawings will always remain the property of the designer. It is possible to photocopy a second reproducible tracing on either sepia-paper or mylar, and this may be given to the client for his own use. Contractors sometimes also use such tracings for preparing "as-built" drawings which they return to the landscape architect following completion of the project.

Black-line or blue-line ozalid or diazo reproductions are generally made from the original drawings and are prepared in sets issued to contractors invited to bid on the project. After bid opening the sets of drawings are reclaimed by the landscape architect and re-issued to the successful bidder for his use during construction.

SPECIFICATIONS

Sources for Guidance

Many helpful suggestions for writing specifications are available from the Construction Specifications Institute (hereafter we will refer to it as CSI), in Washington, D.C. The institute publishes a *Manual of Practice*, as well as a number of other documents, and these are very useful as guidelines for the landscape architect. In "The CSI Format," a part of the manual containing model specifications, those for lawns and planting are listed at Section 0280 in Divi-

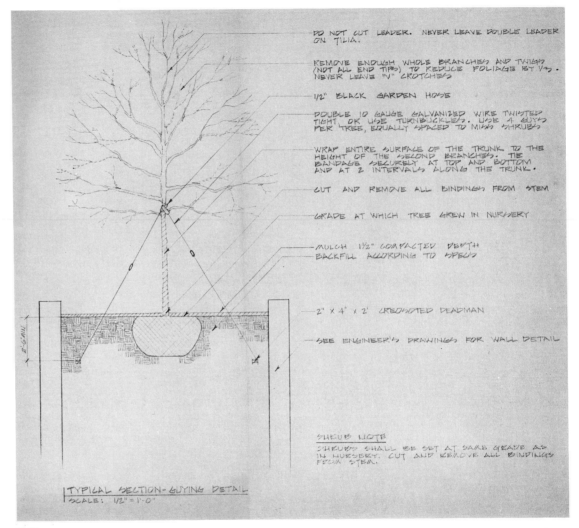

10-12

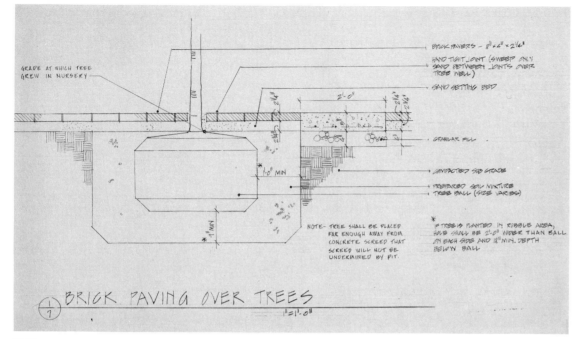

GRADE AT WHICH TREE
GREW IN NURSERY

BRICK PAVERS – 8" × 4" × 2½"

HAND TIGHT JOINT (SWEEP ONLY
SAND BETWEEN JOINTS OVER
TREE WELL)

SAND SETTING BED

2'-0"

GRANULAR FILL

1'-0" MIN

COMPACTED SUB GRADE

PREPARED SOIL MIXTURE
TREE BALL (SIZE VARIES)

1' MIN

NOTE- TREE SHALL BE PLACED
FAR ENOUGH AWAY FROM
CONCRETE SCREED THAT
SCREED WILL NOT BE
UNDERMINED BY PIT.

* IF TREE IS PLANTED IN RUBBLE AREA,
HOLE SHALL BE 2'-0" WIDER THAN BALL
ON EACH SIDE AND 18" MIN. DEPTH
BELOW BALL

BRICK PAVING OVER TREES

1" = 1'-0"

1/7

10-13

Figures 10-12, 10-13. *Two planting details typical of the kind that should be shown on drawings among the contract documents. A guy support detail for a tree installed in a planter (10-12); a detail for installation of trees in a paved area (10-13). Other planting details a landscape architect would include are shown in Chapter 14.*

sion 2, Site Work. Other specification lists that may be helpful are Section 0281, Soil Preparation; Section 0282, Lawns; Section 0283, Ground Cover and Other Plants; and Section 0284, Trees and Shrubs. Elsewhere in Division 2 are: 0210, Clearing of Site; 0220, Earthwork; 0250, Site Drainage; 0260, Roads and Walks; 0270, Site Improvements.

There are 15 other Divisions in "The CSI Format." Of these, Division 3 deals with specifications for concrete, and masonry is specified in Division 4.

In following the CSI suggestions, the planting specifications would consist of three parts: a general part, a discussion of products, and a discussion of execution.

Writing Specifications

Specification writing is not easy. These have a style all their own; writing specifications requires utmost care because these serve as legal documents. Using the right words to say what is intended can have considerable effect on the quality of work performed, especially in any instructions that call for the contractor to exercise judgment. Even a misplaced comma can have drastic consequences, so careless use of punctuation and words should be guarded against.

A person without experience in planting design and construction cannot be expected to write specifications for this kind of work. The person who has that experience but who has not previously written specifications can use past specifications from other projects as a reference source. The experienced writer will assemble standard specifications from his experience and will build on these and modify them as needed for each individual project or set of circumstances.

Like all writing, the specifications begin as an outline from a collection of notes. From these, one or more rough drafts are prepared.

The final draft should be neatly and accurately typed. It may be typed in the form of a carbon-backed master for spirit duplication, or a stencil for mimeograph duplication, or typed on sheets which are photocopied or used for offset printing. Spirit duplication is the least expensive method of reproduction, but it tends to look the worst. Mimeograph duplication produces a greater number of copies and looks better than the spirit process. Photocopying is good for small quantities; some processes and operators can produce very good quality copies. The best but most expensive process is offset printing. The quality is equal to the printed pages of a book. The finished specifications as they are printed are usually bound together in sets, once they have been duplicated, and are issued with the drawings to the bidders.

Too often landscape architects, because it is convenient or because of the pressures of time, use specifications prepared for previous projects without rewriting them. Each site will have its own unique problems, which must be dealt with, and accordingly it is advisable to write new specifications for each new project. The landscape architect who is striving to improve his work will find it helpful to solicit comments from each landscape contractor who constructs one of his projects. The comments may contain desirable suggestions about the specifications.

FOR FURTHER READING

Construction Specifications Institute, 1965. *CSI Manual of Practice.* CSI, 1150 Seventeenth Street, S.W., Washington, D.C. 20036. Revised edition, 1970.

Robinette, G. O., 1968. *Off the Board, Into the Ground.* Dubuque, Iowa: Kendell-Hunt.

Walker, T. D., 1972. *Perspective Sketches.* West Lafayette, Indiana: PDA Publishers.

Appendix 10-A
Specifications

Section 0280. Lawns and Planting

Part 1: General

1.01 Scope

a. Furnish labor, equipment, and materials necessary to complete the planting, maintaining, and guaranteeing of lawns and plants in accordance with the Drawings and as specified herein. The work to be completed in this section shall include the following:

1. Plants and Planting.

2. Lawns: seeding and/or sodding.

1.02 Agency Standards

a. **Nomenclature.** All plant materials used shall be true to name and size in conformity with the following standards:

1. *American Joint Committee on Horticultural Nomenclature.* 1942 Edition of *Standardized Plant Names.* (Published by Mount Pleasant Press, J. Horace McFarland Company, Harrisburg, Pa.)

2. *American Standard for Nursery Stock.* Copyright 1973. (Published by the American Association of Nurserymen, Inc., 230 Southern Building, Washington, D.C. 20005.)

Part 2: Products

2.01 Plant Materials

a. **Plant List:** A complete list of plants, including a schedule of quantities, sizes, and other requirements is shown on the

Reprinted with the permission of Walker, Harris, Associates, Inc., Landscape Architects.

Drawings. In the event that discrepancies occur between the quantities of plants indicated in the plant list and as indicated on the plan, the plant quantities indicated on the plan shall govern.

b. **Substitutions:** No substitutions shall be accepted, except with the written permission of the Landscape Architect.

c. **Quality:** All plants shall be typical of their species or variety. All plants shall have normal, well developed branches and vigorous root systems. They shall be sound, healthy, vigorous, free from defects, disfiguring knots, abrasions of the bark, sunscald injuries, plant diseases, insect eggs, borers, and all other forms of infections. All plants shall be nursery grown unless otherwise stated, and shall have been growing under the same climatic conditions as the location of this project for at least two (2) years prior to date of planting on this project. Contractor shall have the option of moving some selected trees from undisturbed portions of the site under the direction of the Landscape Architect in lieu of furnishing nursery grown materials. Plants which have been held in storage will be rejected if they show signs of growth during storage. Collected plants shall be taken from a subgrade favorable to good root development. All collected material shall be clean, sound stock and shall be free from decay.

d. **Measurements:** Size and grading standards shall conform to those of the American Association of Nurserymen unless otherwise specified. A plant shall be dimensioned as it stands in its natural position. Stock furnished shall be a fair average between the minimum and maximum sizes specified. Large plants which have been cut back to the specified sizes will not be accepted.

e. **Preparation of Plants:**

1. In preparing plants for moving, all precautions customary in good trade practice shall be taken. Workmanship that fails to meet the highest standards will not be accepted. All plants shall be dug to retain as many fibrous roots as possible. All plants shall be dug immediately before moving unless otherwise specified.

2. Balled and burlapped and balled and platformed plants shall have a solid ball of earth of minimum specified size held in place securely by burlap and a stout rope. Oversize or exceptionally heavy plants are acceptable if the size of the ball or spread of the roots is proportionately increased to the satisfaction of the Landscape Architect. Broken, loose, or manufactured balls will be rejected. Balled and platformed plants shall be securely tied with a stout rope to sturdy platforms equal in size to the diameter of the upper half of the ball of earth.

f. **Delivery:** All plants shall be packed, transported, and handled with utmost care to insure adequate protection against injury. Each shipment shall be certified by State and Federal Authorities to be free from disease and infestation. Any inspection certificates required by law to this effect shall accompany each shipment invoice or order of stock, and, on arrival, the certificate shall be filed with the Landscape Architect.

g. **Inspection:** No plant material shall be planted by the contractor until it is inspected and approved by the Landscape Architect or his representative at the site of the project. The Landscape Architect or his representative shall be the sole judge of the quality and acceptability of the materials. All rejected material shall be immediately removed from the site and replaced with acceptable material at no additional cost.

h. **Wrapping and Guying Details:** Materials used in wrapping, guying protection, etc., shall be as specified herein.

i. **Peat Moss:** Peat moss shall be imported Canadian sphagnum peat moss, brown, low in content of woody material, and be free of mineral matter harmful to plant life. Peat moss shall have an acid reaction of about 4.5 pH, and have a water absorbing capacity of 1100 to 2000 percent by weight. Peat moss shall be thoroughly pulverized before use except when used as a top dressing. No native or sedge peats shall be approved. Top dressing shall be sphagnum chunks similar to "Professional Bale" as manufactured by Premier Peat Moss Co., New York, New York.

j. **Herbicide:** Use [locally recommended herbicide].

2.02 Lawn Seeding Material

a. **Grass Seed:** Grass seed shall be fresh, recleaned seed of the latest crop, mixed in the following proportions by weight, and meeting the following percentages of purity and germination. Seed shall be delivered to the site in the original unopened containers which shall bear the vendor's guarantee of analysis.

Grass Seed Mixture

Seed and Proportion	Purity	Minimum Germination
20% Park Bluegrass	90%	85%
20% Delta Bluegrass	90%	85%
20% Merion Bluegrass	90%	85%
40% Manhattan Rye	90%	90%

Substitute Creeping Red Fescue for Rye in areas of shade.

b. Mulch shall be clean straw or other materials approved by the Landscape Architect.

c. Fertilizer shall be 10-6-4 or approved alternate, and shall be delivered to site in unopened containers bearing manufacturer's guaranteed analysis.

2.03 Sod Material (Alternate)

a. Sod shall be dense, well rooted sod, composed of 100% Bluegrass mix approximately two (2) inches high, grown in the general locality where it is to be used; it shall be free of debris, weeds, or other undesirable grasses. Submit mix to Landscape Architect for approval. The sod shall be cut out one (1) inch thick in uniform strips approximately 12" or 18" × 36", but not longer than is convenient for handling. Peat grown sod will not be acceptable.

b. Sod must be kept moist for protection and to facilitate handling. Sod shall be rolled in tight rolls or laid on boards or planks and lifted and transported to storage piles or carried to the point of installation without breaking or tearing. In all cases, sod must be lifted and loaded and unloaded by hand. Dumping from vehicles will not be permitted.

c. All sod shall be cut as required, and if possible shall be laid immediately. In no case shall sod remain in storage piles longer than three (3) days; sod shall be protected from wind and rain during such periods.

Part 3: Methods of Installation

3.01 Planting

a. **Time of Planting:** The Contractor shall start his planting when other divisions of

this work, including placing of topsoil to finished grade, has progressed sufficiently to permit planting. Thereafter, planting operations shall be conducted under favorable weather conditions during the next season or seasons which are normal for such work as determined by accepted practice in the locality of the project. At the Contractor's option and full responsibility, planting operations may be conducted under unseasonable conditions without additional compensation.

b. **Layout:** Planting shall be located where it is shown on the plan except where obstructions overhead or below ground are encountered or where changes have been made in construction. Prior to the excavation of planting areas or plant pits, or placing tree stakes, the Contractor shall ascertain the location of all utility lines, electric cables, sprinkling system, and conduits so that proper precautions may be taken not to disturb or damage any subsurface improvements. Should obstructions be found, the Contractor shall promptly notify the Landscape Architect or his representative who will arrange to relocate the plant material. Necessary adjustments shall be approved by the Landscape Architect or his representative.

c. **Setting Plants:** No planting holes shall be dug until the proposed locations have been staked on the ground, by the Contractor, and until such locations have been approved by the Construction Superintendent or his representative. Each plant shall be planted in an individual hole as specified for trees, shrubs, and vines. All holes shall be dug with straight vertical sides and crowned bottoms, or as directed. All plants shall be set to ultimate finished grade, so that they will be left in the same relation to the surrounding grade as they have stood before being moved. No filling will be permitted around trunks or stems. All ropes, wire, staves, etc., shall be removed from sides and top of ball and removed from hole before filling in, unless otherwise directed by the Construction Superintendent. Burlap shall be properly cut and removed from sides of ball. When depth is specified, it shall be understood as meaning depth below finished grade. A layer of topsoil three inches thick shall be applied on the bottom of each hole and then lightly tamped. Excess excavation from all holes shall be removed from the site.

d. **Backfilling of Planting Pits and Planting Beds:** Use planting mixture of 4 parts topsoil, 1 part approved commercial horticultural peat moss. Existing subsoil to be removed from site by Contractor. Planting pits and beds shall be backfilled carefully to fill all voids and to avoid breaking or bruising roots. Tamp backfill firm to prevent settlement. When pit is nearly filled, water thoroughly and allow water to soak away. If settling of the backfill occurs after watering, add more backfill to bring to level.

e. **Trees:** All trees shall be planted in holes at least two feet greater in diameter than their ball of earth or spread of roots. The depth of the holes shall be at least two feet, and as much greater as is necessary to accommodate the roots, so that when the tree is placed therein it will not be necessary to raise or lower it to bring it to the proper finished grade. Topsoil shall be tamped under the edges of balled trees after inspection by the Construction Superintendent. Topsoil shall be backfilled in layers of not over nine inches in depth and each layer watered sufficiently to settle before the next layer is put in place. Enough topsoil shall be used to bring the surface to finished grade when settled. A slight "saucer," with a minimum of a 4" lip, shall be formed around each tree to hold additional water.

f. **Shrubs:** All shrubs shall be planted in holes at least one foot greater in diameter than the ball of earth or spread of roots. The depth of the holes shall be at least one foot and as much greater as is necessary to set the plant properly at finished grade. After preparation of the hole as specified, the plant shall be planted in the center of the hole. Roots of bare rooted plants shall not be matted together, but arranged in their natural position with soil worked in among them. The hole shall be filled with topsoil and settled thoroughly by watering. Area in shrub beds between shrubs must be spaded and pulverized to a depth of six (6) inches. Arrangement of shrubs must meet with the approval of the Construction Superintendent. A slight "saucer" shall be formed around each plant to hold additional water. Shrubs shall not be planted closer than two (2) feet from the edge of shrub beds, nor closer than three (3) feet to walks or buildings.

g. **Vines:** All vines shall be planted in holes at least one foot in diameter and as much wider as is necessary to make them six inches wider than the size of pot or spread of roots. The depth of the hole and manner of planting shall be the same as specified for shrubs.

h. **Guying:** All trees over seven feet (7') in height, and all pine trees, shall immediately after setting to proper grade, be guyed with three sets of two strands, No. 12 gauge malleable galvanized iron, in tripod fashion. Wires shall not come in direct contact with the tree, but shall be covered with rubber hose at points of contact. Wires shall be fastened in such a manner as to avoid pulling crotches apart. Stakes shall be of 2" × 2" lumber three feet long, or other material approved by the Construction Superintendent. Wire shall be fastened to stake at ground line. Stakes shall not be driven where utility lines are within five feet of finished grade, but shall be placed by digging holes for them. A board 1½ inches wide and thirty inches long of uniform thickness shall be hung on each wire. All guying shall be done to the satisfaction of the Construction Superintendent. All guy stakes shall be placed outside the perimeter of planting pits.

i. **Wrapping:** The trunks of all trees shall be wrapped spirally with two thicknesses of crinkled paper cemented together with bituminous material (or approved cloth serving same purpose) in strips 4 inches (4") wide immediately after planting, in a neat manner to the satisfaction of the Construction Superintendent to the height of the first branches, or as directed. Wrapping shall be securely tied with lightly tarred medium or coarse sisal yarn twine.

j. **Mulching:**

1. After planting has been approved by the Construction Superintendent a layer of commercial horticultural peat moss, two inches (2") thick shall be placed on the finished grade about all plants. The boundaries of this mulch shall be six inches greater in diameter than that of the hole. All shrub beds shall be completely covered with a similar material. [If permitted by law, some herbicides may] be incorporated into the mulch and used on all plantings that are tolerant of the herbicide as shown on the [herbicide] label. The amount of [herbicide] to add to a particular volume of peat moss is dependent on the area covered

by that volume. The amount of [herbicide] to apply to one cubic yard of peat moss, assuming it covers 162 square feet at a two (2) inch depth, is six (6) ounces. The peat moss should be removed from the bale and thoroughly loosened before mixing the [herbicide]. The volume of peat moss is measured while in the loosened stage.

2. The [herbicide] is thoroughly mixed into the peat moss just prior to applying to the planting. Before applying the mulch containing the [herbicide], thoroughly water the planting. If the [herbicide] label does not clear it for use on a particular species, use pure peat moss.

3. Top dress the peat moss mulch with sphaghum chunks to a depth of 1½ inches.

k. **Watering:** Thoroughly water each plant immediately following planting.

l. **Pruning and Repair:** All plants shall be neatly pruned and/or clipped to preserve the natural character of the plants, and in a manner appropriate to the particular requirements of each plant, and to the satisfaction of the Landscape Architect. No plants shall be pruned or clipped prior to delivery except with the permission of the Landscape Architect. Broken or badly bruised branches shall be removed with a clean cut. All pruning shall be done with sharp tools in accordance with instructions of the Landscape Architect. Pruning cuts 2″ in diameter or larger shall be painted over with approved tree paint. All accidental damage to trees and shrubs occurring during the course of planting operations, which is not so great as to necessitate removal of a branch or replacement of a plant, shall promptly be treated as required

in accordance with recognized horticultural practices and the instructions of the Landscape Architect.

3.02 Seeding Procedure

a. Grass seed shall be sown in the Fall of [year] between August 20th and September 20th, or at other such times as approved by the Landscape Architect. Finish grading to the final 1½ inch shall be done by others.

d. Grass seed shall be sown evenly with mechanical spreader or by hand at the rate of four (4) pounds per one thousand (1,000) square feet. All seeding shall be done on days when the wind does not exceed a velocity of five (5) miles per hour and the seed shall be dry or moderately dry.

c. Spread fertilizer at a rate of fifteen (15) pounds per one thousand (1,000) square feet and incorporate into the topsoil uniformly.

d. After seeding, the surface of the soil shall be evenly raked with a fine-toothed rake or other procedures approved by the Landscape Architect.

e. Mulch shall be spread uniformly over all seeded areas at the rate of two (2) bales per one thousand (1,000) square feet.

f. Water mulch and seed bed thoroughly and immediately after completion of mulching. Soil shall be moistened to a depth of not less than four (4) inches. Contractor shall instruct Owner's representative on appropriate watering procedures during initial watering.

3.03 Sodding Procedures: (Alternate)

a. Sod shall not be laid unless soil is friable to a depth of six (6) inches.

b. A 25-5-10 fertilizer shall be incorporated into topsoil for new sodding at a rate of fifteen (15) pounds per one thousand

(1,000) square feet. At Contractor's option fertilizer may be spread after final rolling and before watering.

c. Finished grade shall be raked smooth, free from depressions or undulations, to the satisfaction of the Landscape Architect.

d. Rolling shall be done in two directions perpendicular to each other. The roller shall be a hand roller weighting not more than 200 pounds nor less than 150 pounds. After rolling repair and reroll any areas where depressions or other irregularities appear in the finished grade.

e. The soil surface shall be moistened immediately before sod-laying with a fine spray which will not cause disturbance of the finished surface.

f. Sod pieces shall be fitted tightly together so that no joint is visible and be firmly and evenly tamped by hand.

g. After sodding is completed and has been approved, it shall be rolled in the same manner as described in Paragraph **d.**

h. All sodded areas shall be watered immediately after final rolling with a fine spray to a depth of four (4) inches.

i. All sod shall be pegged on slopes steeper than 3 : 1.

Part 4: Maintenance, Inspection, Guarantees and Replacements

4.01 Plants:

a. The Landscape Architect shall prepare a maintenance schedule for the Owner. The Contractor shall review and approve the maintenance schedule. The Owner will assume the responsibility of maintenance including watering, fertilizing, spraying, weeding, cultivating, repairing and tightening guy wires, etc., upon completion of planting. The Contractor shall periodically inspect the project during the guarantee period and immediately notify the Landscape Architect and Owner of any irregularities or deficiencies which will affect his guarantee.

b. The Contractor shall also be responsible for resetting of any plants to an upright position or to proper grade, and for the removal and replacement of any dead plant material.

c. **Guarantee:** All plants shall be guaranteed to remain alive and healthy for the full twelve (12) months period. Replacements shall be guaranteed an additional twelve (12) months.

d. **Inspection for Beginning the Guarantee Period:** Inspection of the planting work, to determine its completion for beginning the guarantee period, will be made by the Landscape Architect, upon notice requesting such inspection by the Contractor at least seven (7) days prior to the anticipated date. All planting must be alive and healthy in order to be considered complete. Each phase of this project will be inspected separately.

e. **Final Inspection and Replacements:** Inspection of the planting to determine its final acceptance will be made at the conclusion of the guarantee period by the Landscape Architect. No plants will be accepted unless they are alive and healthy. The Contractor shall replace any plants which are dead or, in the opinion of the Landscape Architect, are in an unhealthy or unsightly condition, and/or have lost their natural shape due to dead branches. The cost of such replacement(s) shall be borne by the Contractor and shall be included in his bid price for this section of the work.

4.02 Lawn:

a. Final inspection to determine final acceptance of the lawn shall be made upon written request by the Contractor to the Landscape Architect at least seven (7) days prior to the anticipated date.

11

Cost Estimation for Landscape Construction

The execution of the landscape architect's plan is the next phase in the development of the landscape project. Now we need to consider the kind of work done by the landscape contractor, whom we described earlier as the second member of the landscaping "team." The landscape contractor will execute the plan of the landscape architect in the manner the landscape architect intends. It is necessary for the landscape architect and the contractor to have a thorough understanding of what effects should be evident in the landscape project, upon the completion of construction.

The landscape contractor receives the plan and specifications from the landscape architect or the contracting authority. He should examine the plans and specifications very thoroughly in considering what kind of work

will be required of him. The decisions he makes at this time are quite important, and his decision-making should be done in an orderly way. We will discuss the topics a contractor will have to decide on in the order we believe he should take them up:

1. Project selection.
2. Site evaluation.
3. Cost analysis.
4. Competitive bidding.
5. Submitting the bid.

Decisions about project selection, site evaluation, and cost analysis should be made for all projects regardless of whether a bid is required. On large projects that require the submitting of a bid, decisions will need to be made about all the items.

PROJECT SELECTION

Regardless of its size, a landscape construction firm cannot expect to bid on all available construction projects, nor should it bid on all. Some firms bid on undertakings even though the organization of the firm is such that it is totally incapable of completing the project to the satisfaction of the customer while making a profit for the firm. To maintain a reputation for good work along with a sound profit record, the wise landscape contractor will bid on, and accept, only those jobs his firm is particularly well qualified to carry out. But let us suppose that a contractor is well qualified and merely wonders if he should bid on the project. Being selective in submitting bids requires consideration of several factors even before spending any time in the initial phases of bid preparation.

The first factor to be considered is whether the work schedule of the firm will permit the new project to be completed within the time required by the contract specifications. Too often landscape contractors accept far more work than can be completed reasonably within the times allotted for each. Overscheduling of projects may result in workmanship that is poor because it was done too fast, in delayed completion owing to reassignments of personnel, and finally, customers who are dissatisfied. A reputation squandered in this way may reduce the amount of available work to such a point that the contractor may not be able to maintain a profitable business organization. Consider bids only if the time requirements of the contract can be met.

The size of the landscape project must be considered carefully. A job that is too small cannot be carried out efficiently by a large firm, which may employ specialized work crews who can work well at several large projects in sequence but who are used inefficiently on a variety of small tasks that may characterize a single, small project. Conversely, a large project should not be taken on by a firm that does not have the capability to complete it satisfactorily. Adequate manpower and the equipment best suited for the particular job are essential.

The contractor should be completely familiar with all the required installation techniques. If new procedures are required, he should make absolutely certain that his firm is equipped and prepared to handle such techniques without difficulty. Some landscape construction projects call for the building of earth mounds, which requires the obtaining of large quantities of topsoil and the movement of that soil into carefully planned shapes. This requires specialized techniques and equipment. The frequency with which such projects occur will determine if it is worth while for a firm to purchase the necessary equipment. Likewise, the installation of large turf areas, either by seeding or by sodding, may not be in the realm of the capabilities of a firm. The requirement by the landscape architect of extremely large plant specimens may eliminate some contractors because they lack the equipment required to move and install such plants.

Before preparing the bid the contractor should consult with the landscape architect if he knows of new procedures that would make the installation of the landscape materials more efficient or improve the quality of installation. This will provide time for the landscape architect to change his specifications to fit the new techniques. It is possible that the contractor will then be able to consider a project he would otherwise be inclined to turn down.

The contractor should examine the plant list too before deciding whether to accept a project. If he thinks the required plants are rare or in short supply, he should check sources of supply before continuing the decision-making process. Too many contractors submit bids on projects that require plant material they cannot readily obtain or that has increased greatly in price owing to increased demand for the plants. Locate a source, obtain a firm price, and establish a delivery commitment for all the required plant material.

Many times the landscape contractor is required to construct landscape features with materials other than plants, such as swimming pools, fountains, driveways, parking lots, sidewalks, walls, underground irrigation systems, and patios. Most landscape contractors will subcontract this type of work to specialists in each particular field. Yet the landscape contractor will be held responsible for the installation and acceptance of this work by the customer. Therefore, it is absolutely essential that the landscape contractor know all the details of the work he subcontracts and know, furthermore, that he has reliable subcontractors who will carry out the work within the time alloted in the contract specifications.

Consider the specifications and the required guarantee carefully. Some good contractors will not bid on highway landscape projects because they feel the installation techniques are unreasonable. Sometimes a single project will require procedures that may be so time consuming that other projects cannot be accepted until it is finished. The contractor must then decide if a project so time-consuming is worth undertaking.

The required guarantees on plant materials must be studied also. Many times the contractor is asked to guarantee large trees for two years or at least for two growing seasons. Some specifications in urban redevelopment areas require that the landscape contractor guarantee the plant material against loss due to vandalism. For some projects, meeting this requirement is nearly impossible, since the contractor cannot control the public use of the areas being landscaped. The contractor must give very serious consideration to whether he should even submit a bid on such a project.

The contractor will also want to give consideration to previous projects that he has done for the landscape architect. If the landscape architect constantly changes specifications *after* the contractor has been assigned the work, or is unclear in stating what he wants, the contractor may not want to bid on the project.

During the project selection, it is important to determine if the landscape work of the project will come under the influence of labor-union regulations. If so, the matters of pay scale, work schedules, and number of laborers required for a specific job must be dealt with. It is extremely important, also, when computing the cost data for the project, to determine whether unionized subcontractors are required for the necessary subcontracting work needed by the landscape contractor. The wrong time to have misunderstandings with labor unions is after landscape construction has started. Appendix 11-A at the end of this chapter shows a typical contract between a union and a landscape contractor.

Who will be the inspecting authority of the project is of prime importance to the contractor. Generally this is the landscape architect and previous knowledge of his ability as an inspection authority will be helpful to the contractor. The inspector has control over whether the work is accepted and payment is to be made, and he is expected to be knowledgeable about the development of plants at the landscape site. Inspection dates are important, also. The work should be inspected when the plants are at their best. Inspection too early in the season may mean that the inspector will needlessly reject plants slow to leaf out, though if the inspector is knowledgeable about plants he will to some extent consider such a factor when making his judgment. Likewise, inspection too late after installation may cause the rejection of plants suffering from excess leaf scorch, a condition that may not affect the future development of the plant. Leaf scorch occurs on many species of trees and shrubs after transplanting because of a water deficit in the plant. This is caused by a reduction of the size of the root system when the plant is dug. Sound inspection techniques by persons known to the construction firm may mean less unnecessary plant replacement and greater overall satisfaction of all parties.

The location of the project in relation to the location of the landscape contractor's base of operations is important. Jobs too far from home base can lead to difficulties. The move-ment of crews and supplies to and from the site becomes expensive. It is also harder to supervise the activities of subcontractors. Locating sources of plant material in an unfamiliar area can become time consuming, and shipping charges from nurseries far from either the site or the contractor's location increases the cost. If maintenance is required after installation, the contractor may tend to neglect to supervise it or to provide for that maintenance. Plant loss may result and replacement costs will soar. Profit quickly becomes loss.

Finally, payment procedures must be considered. Payment for one project should not be so slow that all available cash is tied up in it, for then future projects cannot be accepted because of a lack of cash. It is also wise to have a complete understanding of how payment is to be made; i.e., upon completion of installation, after final inspection, or perhaps in conjunction with both times. Moreover, on some projects a provision is made for the contractor to collect partial payments while work on the project progresses. If it is necessary for the contractor to borrow money to continue operations, the cost of obtaining those loans must be computed in the overall cost of the project.

Not all the pitfalls of bidding on landscape projects can be avoided merely by being selective in the projects that are being considered. However, careful selection of the project on the basis of the factors we have discussed will reduce the occurrence of large and unexpected financial losses. As a contractor becomes more experienced, he will take other factors into consideration before making a decision to bid on a project.

SITE EVALUATION

The cardinal rule is for a potential contractor to make an on-site evaluation. A study of the plan alone is not adequate, for often many surprising discoveries are made during installation that increase construction costs. Many specifications even require that an on-site study be made by the bidder. A good on-site study is one made with the landscape architect or a member of his firm.

Any good site study will include the taking of soil samples, which should be sent to a laboratory for chemical analysis. At the time the samples are being taken, examine the soil for texture and other physical characteristics. Cores should be taken from several locations to a depth of three feet or more. Examine the cores at various depths to determine if adequate drainage will occur during wet seasons. A moist sample that feels sticky and slick may have a high percentage of clay present. This indicates that water movement will be slow.

It is the duty of the landscape architect to carry out the soil analysis at the site and make the data available to prospective bidders. But in the event the contractor is preparing the planting plans as well as installing the plant material, he should take the soil samples and have the appropriate tests run.

If the plan calls for plants that will not tolerate heavy, moist soils, the contractor should discuss the problem with the landscape architect as soon as the results of the soil analysis are known—not after the bid has been made and the contract let. The landscape architect may be willing to change the design by using plants more adaptable to the condi-

tions present, or it may be necessary to modify the soil conditions. Any change in specifications must be made in writing—verbal changes are not acceptable. Modifying the soil condition is an added expense that must be calculated when bidding on a project. The landscape architect must be made aware if the contractor's bid does include the costs of such modifications, so that when competitive bids are examined, the cost is also included in those bids.

From the soil cores it is also possible to determine if the soil will be excessively rapid in drainage. If it is, extra waterings may be required during the plant establishment period and that cost must be included in the bid. Replacement of plants reduces the chances of realizing a reasonable profit from the project, regardless of the cause for the replacement.

Chemical modification of the soil at the landscape site is primarily based on the existing soil pH as determined by the soil-test results. Acid soils usually pose no problems for most woody ornamental plants, but soil pH that is too high may cause problems with specific plants both during their establishment and in the following years. If drastic modification of soil pH is required because of the kinds of plants selected, the cost of such modification must be included in the specifications, and hence in the estimations. Again, the landscape architect should inform contractors of the need for such a modification and specify the materials and rates necessary for the soil changes.

Examine entrances to and from the site. A site that possesses easy access to the entire work area is, of course, ideal. However, sites are not always ideal. If only one entrance is available at a large site, entering and leaving the project may be time consuming or even the cause of delays, all of which will increase the man-hours required to complete the job. Other construction activities may also slow the landscape contractor's work. Time spent by a laborer in nonproductive waiting is an expense that will eat into the possible profit from an undertaking if the cost is not calculated.

Water is the most essential single need of plants in the first year of establishment. Most large landscape contracts call for at least a one-year guarantee of survival of plant materials. In many areas of the country this means that supplemental waterings are necessary during the first growing season, and the availability of water at the site is of prime importance. We know of one large school project at which a contractor neglected to investigate the availability of water before contracting for the work. There was only one small water outlet on the property, and it was necessary for the contractor to haul water to the site, during the installation process, in tank trucks. Water was not hauled to the site during the summer when a mild drought occurred. There was a large plant loss and the expense for replacement of the dead plants fell to the landscape contractor. Not only did he lose his profit, he also incurred a large deficit on the job. The charges for any water provisions must be included in the cost estimation. The increase in the total bid might have lost the contract for the contractor, but then he would not have had to absorb a large financial loss. Of course, he would have been much better off to make a thorough site study, which would have revealed the lack of water at the site.

The nearness-to-completion of construction of architectural features at the site will influence the completion of the landscape construction of the project. As previously mentioned, the contractor should examine access to the site, and the amount of other construction also under way will influence the rate at which the landscape construction may be carried out. Perhaps of most importance in this regard are the *kinds* of construction jobs that are yet to be completed. Cleaning of building surfaces with acid may present a hazard to nearby landscape plants. Drifting acid fumes or direct splashes of acid onto plant material will result in severe foliage burn; heavy dosages can kill the plants. Physical damage to the installed plant material may also occur. The movement of construction equipment at the site poses a threat. If at all possible, the site should be cleaned up after construction, before plant installation.

If the landscape contracting and the prime construction contracting are done by separate contractors, the landscape architect should include in his specifications a starting date for landscaping that is well past the time designated for completion of construction. If the landscape work must be started before the finish of the construction of buildings, etc., the landscape contractor should not be held responsible for the damage done to landscape materials; the construction contractor is responsible. The landscape architect should spell this out in detail in the specifications and in the contract with the landscape contractor. Too often this is not done and the only recourse for the landscape contractor is to file a suit in court. The process in settling claims this way is long and costly.

It is also important to determine at the site if the microenvironmental conditions will be suitable for the required plant material. Problems that may occur are not always apparent. Recently, in a large metropolitan-area project, a landscape architect designed an attractive courtyard planting in an area seemingly well protected from winter weather. The choice of plant materials included a *Taxus* species that is not normally hardy in the open but can be used without difficulty in protected areas such as a courtyard. The plantings were on the western side of a large building, and though they were protected by a low wall from direct exposure to the prevailing northwest winds, when the winds hit the large wall, they were deflected to an easterly direction at markedly increased velocity. All things considered, the *Taxus* plants were actually planted in a very exposed site. Loss of the plants occurred during the first winter. The landscape contractor could have been held responsible for their replacement.

Plants used near high-speed roads, parking lots, and sidewalks may become victims of salt pollution in snowy areas of the country. If snow and ice are likely at a project, examine the required plant material list to see if any of the plants on it are particularly susceptible to salt injury. If some species are, the selection of more tolerant species should be discussed with the landscape architect before bidding. Any modifications in design that might reduce the chances of salt injury should also be discussed at this time. It is too late to modify specifications and plans after the contract has been let.

Ordinarily, it is the responsibility of the landscape architect—not the contractor—to be aware of microclimatic conditions at a site that might affect plant growth and development. However, it is to the advantage of the landscape contractor to be aware of possible problem areas and to call these to the attention of the landscape architect, particularly if the contractor feels that the design and specifications do not take into sufficient consideration the difficulties he might encounter.

The landscape contractor may find that his experience in making site studies before preparing cost estimations and bids will enable him to anticipate other factors for consideration at each site in addition to those discussed here. The examples we have given are of some factors the landscape contractor must consider when examining any site. Site evaluation before bidding is useful because changes in the design that might be beneficial can be discussed at this time with the landscape architect. Written changes in the specifications must be prepared before contract letting.

COST ANALYSIS

The preparation of a cost analysis on a project should be completed before preparing and submitting a bid. The cost analysis provides the landscape contractor with an estimation of his actual costs for a particular landscape project. Proper preparation of the cost analysis is absolutely essential if a realistic bid is to be submitted. If the cost evaluation is too low, it will probably mean that the contractor will be awarded the contract but will lose money on the project. If the evaluation is too high, it may mean that the bid submitted is not competitive and another firm will receive the contract.

Many small and even some large firms do not understand fully how all their business costs are incurred or how they should be calculated when preparing a cost estimation for the bidding process.

For simplification, we will divide our discussion of cost analysis into three segments: first, variable costs (or direct project costs); second, overhead (or fixed costs); and third, profit. These three items make up the bid, which is the total cost of the project to the customer or client.

Variable Costs (Direct Project Costs)

The variable costs of a business are those costs that change with a change in the activity of the business. The landscape contractor, when he submits a bid on a project, is anticipating a change in his business activity if he receives the contract. He must estimate what it will cost him to obtain all the materials and the labor he needs to complete the project. Variable costs include such items as subcontracting expenses, materials, freight, labor, operation of leased equipment, bid guaranty, and performance bonds. Purchase of equipment, rather than leasing, causes the cost of equipment to change from a variable cost to a fixed cost.

The landscape contractor may be responsible for other installations that are beyond the capabilities of his firm, and he will need to engage subcontractors. The landscape contractor must obtain a cost estimation, preferably a firm one, from the subcontractor for each particular phase of the project. The subcontractor's estimate is included among the variable costs.

Price quotes should be obtained for sub-contracting work. An example of a form that would be useful in obtaining such quotes is shown in Appendix 11-B. If the cost of the subcontracting work is large (a swimming pool is a large subcontracting job), it would be wise to sign a contract with the exact price stated in the contract. A sample of such a contract is given in Appendix 11-C.

If at all possible, the contractor should include an overhead value on the subcontracting work, inasmuch as the contractor has used his and his firm's time to obtain the subcontractor. (Overhead values are discussed next in this chapter.) Also, the landscape contractor assumes the responsibility for seeing that the subcontractor performs as agreed upon in the contract both have signed. Therefore, the landscape contractor is justified in including some management costs. Most companies calculate a certain percentage, such as 10 percent of the subcontractor's estimated cost, and add this to their estimate of the cost of using a subcontractor.

Materials costs include the expense of the plant materials as well as such construction materials as stone, railroad ties, concrete, fencing, etc., and those costs should be based on correct market value, not the purchase price. Sometimes the contractor grows his own nursery stock. If he is providing some or all the plant material in this way, still he must assign a realistic value to the material. The best way to do this is for him to determine the price that he would have to pay if he had to purchase all of the material from another source. If his growing costs are higher than the price he would have to pay to obtain plant material of the *same quality* from another nursery or supplier, he should question very closely the feasibility of producing his own nursery stock. Determining the costs of most materials is relatively easy, since the contractor will be using his regular, familiar sources of supplies. However, he should check when he makes a cost estimate to make absolutely certain that all supplies are available from those sources at the prices quoted by the supplier. It is not wise to use last year's nursery catalogues with the expectation of obtaining accurate prices for this year's plants.

Unusual plant materials should be located, also, and an exact price obtained for the specific size needed. If large quantities of plants are needed it may be wise to check in person at the nursery to make absolutely certain that all the plants are of the size and quality called for in the contract. Obtaining a commitment from the nurseryman on availability and cost is advisable.

Freight costs on most supply items must be computed from the point of origin either to the contractor's place of business or to the project site itself. Freight costs for large, heavy items can be a major factor in the cost computation. If it appears that very much time and labor will be required to move plants and supplies from the contractor's business location to the project site, an estimation of the time and cost of that journey should be computed and added to the freight cost estimate.

The labor expense that should be computed as a variable cost item includes that of the personnel directly involved in the actual installation of the landscape—the so-called production personnel, including the working foremen. To compute the total labor cost of the project, it is first necessary to estimate the man-hours necessary to do the job. At this time the completion timetable should be examined very carefully to determine if it will be necessary to require the personnel to work more than forty-hour work-weeks. If overtime is required, then the labor costs must be adjusted to include the increased wage-rate for overtime work. On certain governmental and industrial construction projects the wage-rates for all classes of employees are established. All contractors on those projects must then pay according to the established pay-scales or be in violation of labor laws, which violation may subject the contractor to trouble with the trade unions working for the contracting authority.

When computing an hourly wage-rate for the labor to be used at a project, be sure to include fringe benefits. Medical insurance to which the employer contributes, social security taxes, other retirement programs, vacation pay, and workmen's compensation payments are all fringe benefits and represent labor expense. Their amounts should be computed on an hourly basis and added to the base wage paid to the employee. Adding the fringe benefit costs per hour and the actual wage will provide the contractor with a true per-hour labor cost. Multiply this rate by the man-hours estimated for the project to arrive at the labor cost computation for the bid.

Equipment-operation costs should include the fuel expense and the maintenance expense necessary because of the work on the project. However, depreciation and major maintenance-work costs should be computed as overhead costs. The cost of the labor of operating the equipment should have been estimated in the total labor estimate unless it is necessary to hire special operators for the equipment. The expense of leasing special equipment for the project should also be added to the cost of equipment operation for the project.

A bid-summary form such as is shown in Appendix 11-D permits the contractor to itemize the cost of each material used on the project and to estimate the labor required for installation. Previous experiences will help the contractor determine what his replacement costs will be for a particular plant (some plants are more difficult to transplant than others). The bid-summary form is a work sheet, but it should be kept in the project file for future reference after the project is completed.

Data from the bid-summary form should be transferred to the bid/actual-cost comparison form (Appendix 11-E). Upon completion of the project, the actual costs can then be compared to the estimated (bid) costs, both for hours of labor and for materials. This comparison will tell the contractor how accurately he is able to estimate his costs and from this information he should be able to improve future cost estimations. When there are large differences between estimated and actual costs, the comparison form shows the reason for the difference. Landscape architects find this information very helpful when preparing their estimates for their clients.

To obtain actual labor costs for each task, each laborer should be asked to keep a record of his activities and to report the hours spent for each operation on a particular project. The job foreman should keep a record of employee time spent on each phase of the work on a project (see Appendix 11-F). It is also the job foreman's responsibility to ensure that employees report their times properly. Information from the labor-cost form is compiled on a master labor-summary form (Appendix 11-G). The total labor required for each task is recorded under the appropriate date, opposite the task involved. The total labor required to complete the task is recorded at the end of each month. This information is then compared with the cost-estimation information recorded on the bid/actual-cost comparison form (Appendix 11-E).

Accurate record-keeping is a very important phase of cost analysis. It must be done so that the contractor will be able to learn from each of his projects and will be able to make accurate estimates of his project costs.

On many large projects a bid guaranty is required. This is usually in the sum of five percent of the total bid amount and must be applied in the form of a certified check, bank draft, or a bid bond secured by a bonding company. The reason the contracting authority requires a guaranty on the bid is to protect itself from possible delays that would result from having to re-advertise for bids if the firm awarded the contract fails to start on the project or refuses the contract after submitting a bid. If this happens, the bid guaranty is forfeited to the contracting authority. If the money required for the bid guaranty must be borrowed, or if a bonding agency is used, the interest charged or the costs of bonding should be included in the variable cost figures.

Large projects may also require a performance bond if a firm is awarded the contract. Usually the bond is 100 percent or more of the contract total. This bond is held until the project is completed and is a guarantee that the contractor has performed all the tasks required by the construction contract and that all payments for subcontracted services, supplies, labor, equipment, and other services have been made. If payment for some phase of the work has not been made, the firm not being paid can bring a mechanic's lien against the project. To prevent this, all contractors must have a performance bond that will be forfeited in the case of nonpayment. The cost of such a bond should be determined in advance and added to the variable cost information.

On many projects, the client or the landscape designer requests changes after the work has started. The landscape contractor should receive proper compensation for such changes. He should obtain a change order properly filled out and signed by the owner and the landscape architect. This form will show the changes made and the costs incurred in making them (Appendix 11-H).

The total variable cost, the total of direct production costs for the project, can be computed by simply adding together all of the expenses described in the preceding paragraphs. This total will be the actual amount of cash needed to carry out the construction phases of the project.

Overhead

Fixed business costs may be defined as those continuing business costs that will be incurred whether or not the firm receives the contract for the project on which the bid has been submitted. Some firms assign the term "overhead"

to the fixed costs of business operations. It is these costs, or a portion of them, that most often are not properly accounted when preparing the cost analysis for a specific project. Overhead costs are of two types, those requiring cash outlay and those that are bookkeeping entries measuring such things as depreciation on property and equipment.

Overhead includes management expenditures. Too often the owner of a small construction firm does not include a salary for himself when computing his business costs. He should assign himself a fixed salary and not depend on the profits of the business to provide his personal income. The salary is one of the items included in the total cost analysis. Likewise, if the contractor's wife is the bookkeeper, secretary, or receptionist, she should be assigned a salary to be used in the cost computations. Management costs for large firms include such management personnel as nonworking foremen as well as the officers and business managers of the firm. Other personnel whose salaries are accounted for as overhead are the secretaries, bookkeepers, accountants, designers, etc. All of these staff members are nonproduction personnel and their pay continues whether or not the firm receives the contract for one specific project. Retainers for lawyers, accountants, etc., should also be included in the fixed-cost estimate.

Other fixed costs include the fringe benefits paid to nonproduction personnel, property costs, advertising, insurance, taxes, legal fees, etc. The fringe benefits include social security taxes, other retirement plans to which the employer contributes, unemployment compensation, disability insurance, medical-care insurances, profit-sharing plans, and vacation pay. These benefits should be totalled for each employee and added to his or her salary for a total employee-cost figure. This sum is used when making the cost analysis.

Property costs include many different expenses incurred by the firm in the course of normal operations over the year. The principal and interest payments on any real estate owned by the firm that is used directly in the operation of the construction phases of the business must be included in the cost estimation. The principal and interest payments must be calculated for all equipment that is purchased on time payment plans or leased on a semipermanent basis for many projects. The property and equipment owned by the company should have a depreciation value set at the time company funds are invested in the purchase of this property or equipment. A financial return of a portion of this investment must be realized through the income received from the completion of all landscape projects.

Various methods of figuring depreciation can be used to arrive at a cost estimation. A management consultant should be consulted about which method or methods should be used. However, there are times when, in bid preparation, it may be desirable not to include depreciation values when computing fixed costs. These instances will be discussed in Chapter 12.

Other property expenses, both real and equipment, include insurance, taxes, and upkeep or maintenance. Insurance is an expense that should be included in the overhead costs.

Likewise, property taxes, corporate taxes, and inventory taxes should be included. Real-estate taxes are an overhead cost that should be included in the cost estimate and not paid from the profits obtained on the year's landscape projects.

The overhead costs of the business operation are usually the most difficult to calculate when preparing the cost estimate for the particular project, because often the money has been spent and does not appear to be part of the investment for projects that may be under consideration. Costs of real estate are an example. The investment in real estate may have been made several years ago. However, some cost-accounting procedures should be developed so that these costs can be computed accurately when preparing a project cost analysis. Fixed costs become variable by leasing a piece of equipment for a specific project. Leasing costs can also be used to determine the value of equipment owned and to be used for a project.

Total Cost Analysis for the Project

To arrive at the total cost of the project it will be necessary to add the fixed costs to the variable costs. It is apparent that the entire year's overhead costs cannot be charged to one project. A project will occupy only a portion of the firm's work year and the overhead costs computed for a project should be based on that fraction of the year during which the firm worked at the project.

Firms that have been in business for several years know the approximate volume of business they will do in a year. It is possible then for them to determine what percentage of their total sales is needed to pay the fixed costs of the business operation. A firm whose total business costs are $250,000 (a figure that excludes what will later be set aside as *profit*) may use $100,000 of that to pay overhead costs. This means that for every dollar the company has expended for its work, 40 cents or 40 percent must be used to pay overhead. When this much is known, it is relatively simple to compute the overhead of a particular project. The variable costs calculated for a particular project should not simply be increased by 40 percent since the 40 percent value is based on the business costs of all the year's projects. It is necessary instead to use the total variable cost value, the other 60 percent of the total value of the year's projects. If the variable costs were $30,000 for one project, the simple ratio is: $30,000 is to 60 percent of the year's costs as the total cost of the project is to 100 percent. From the total cost would then be subtracted the 40 percent overhead. The problem is solved as follows:

$$\frac{\$30,000 \text{ variable costs}}{60\% \text{ of business costs}} = \frac{x \text{ total cost}}{100\% \text{ of business costs}}$$

$$60 x = 3,000,000$$

$$x = \$50,000$$

It should be noted that the variable costs of the project in this problem were increased by 66.7 percent once overhead was added to them, not the 40 percent that was determined from the total business costs. But when the annual rate of 40 percent is subtracted from the total $50,000 ($50,000 − $20,000), $30,000 remains, which is

the amount of the variable costs of the project. Using the percentage of total sales as a method for determining the amount of overhead to assign a particular project eliminates problems that would otherwise plague a seasonal business, and answers the need to know what fraction of the year's costs should be charged against each project.

Once the overhead rate that should be added to the variable costs has been determined for the particular business operation, it is a simple matter to multiply this rate by the variable, or production, costs to obtain the amount of overhead. Using the previous example, 67 percent of the variable cost of $30,000 is $20,000 and when the two figures are added together the total cost is the $50,000 arrived at by the previously described method of calculation. Always make certain that the rate is based on the total costs and that, when using variable-costs-data to determine the amount of overhead, the rate is increased proportionally.

Profit

Any business that operates merely to have enough income to match total costs will neither thrive nor survive if the income from the business operations is the only source of revenue available to the owner. A profit is not necessarily the entire reason for being in business, but it is a very important factor in staying in business. The amount of profit that the firm needs must be determined by the owners. There can not be a set amount or percentage, as each business is different in structure, etc. Once the total costs for a project have been determined, the profit percentage decided on by the owner is multiplied by the total cost and the result is added to the total cost analysis for a project.

Total Costs Including Profit

The final result of all the cost data plus the profit is the total cost for the project. This includes the variable costs for the project, the overhead determined from previous knowledge of company operations, and the amount of profit desired from the project. The total submitted for the bid should be competitive with those of other firms also bidding on the project if there is to be a chance of winning the contract. Competitive bidding as well as contracting procedures will be discussed in the next chapter.

FOR FURTHER READING

(Several of the following publications are revised periodically or as the occasion warrants.)

American Standard for Nursery Stock. American Association of Nurserymen, Inc. Washington, D.C.

Davidson, W. R., and A. F. Doody, 1966. *Retailing Management.* New York: The Ronald Press Co. 905 pages.

Landscape Designer and Estimator's Guide. National Landscape Association. Washington, D.C.

Operating Cost Study. Horticulture Research Institute, Inc. Washington, D.C.

Retail and Landscape Wage-Hour Summary. American Association of Nurserymen, Inc. Washington, D.C.

Tax Accounting Summary. American Association of Nurserymen, Inc. Washington, D.C.

Uniform Charts of Accounts. Horticultural Research Institute, Inc. Washington, D.C.

Appendix 11-A
Labor Agreement

This agreement, made and entered into by and between the [name of landscape contracting firm], Party of the First Part, and hereinafter referred to as "Employer", and [name of labor union], acting on behalf of its affiliated Local Unions, Party of the Second Part, hereinafter referred to as "Local Unions" or "Union", on this [date].

. . .

ARTICLE I. PURPOSE AND SCOPE
A.   It is the intent and purpose of the Parties hereto to set forth herein the basic agreement covering wages, hours of work, and conditions of employment to be observed between the Parties hereto, and to provide procedure for prompt equitable adjustments of alleged grievances to the end that there will be no work stoppages or strikes during the life of this Agreement.

B.   This Agreement shall cover all landscaping, such as planting (trees, flowers, shrubs), fertilization, pruning, drainage, mulching, soil preparation, transplanting, fencing for architectural features, irrigation, weed control, insect control, maintenance, and all appurtenances thereto.

C.   Excluded from coverage of this Agreement shall be all work which is now being done under another Agreement or Contract with [name of union], and all landscaping work being done under the predetermined rates set by the Davis Bacon Act.

ARTICLE II. UNION RECOGNITION
SECTION 1.   The Employer agrees to recognize and hereby does recognize the Union and its designated agents and/or representatives as the sole and exclusive collective bargaining agent on behalf of all of the Employees of the Employer, with respect to wages, hours and all other terms or conditions of employment.

SECTION 2.   Wherever used in this collective bargaining Agreement, the word "Employee" and/or "Employees" shall be defined herein as meaning any Employee covered by this Agreement and working within the jurisdiction of work as set forth in ARTICLE VIII.

ARTICLE III. UNION SECURITY
SECTION 1.   Subject to the provisions and limitations of the National Labor Relations Act, as amended, all present Employees, who are members of the Union on the effective date of this Agreement, shall continue their membership in the Union for the duration of this Agreement to the extent of paying an initiation fee and the membership dues uniformly required as a condition of acquiring or retaining membership in the Union. All Employees, who are not members of the Union, and all persons who hereafter become Employees shall become members of the Union on the thirty-first (31st) day following the effective date of this Agreement or on the thirty-first (31st) day following the beginning of their employment, whichever is later, and shall remain a member of the Union to the extent of paying an initiation fee and the membership dues uniformly required as a condition of acquiring and retaining membership in the Union, whenever employed under and for the duration of this Agreement.

SECTION 2.   The Union and the Employer both agree to conform with all Federal and State laws with respect to employment and job promotion and agree employment shall not be based on or in any way affected by Union Membership, by-laws, rules, regulations, constitutional provisions, or, any other aspects or obligations of Union membership, policies or requirements.

ARTICLE IV. MANAGEMENT RIGHTS
SECTION 1.   Subject to the terms of this Agreement, the Employer shall at all times have full responsibility and control of matters relative to the management and conduct of its business, the direction and supervision of its working force, and the right to hire, promote and transfer Employees. It is the prerogative of the Employer to decide if and how many *Foremen* may be required.

ARTICLE V. HIRING
SECTION 1.   In order to perform the work covered under this Agreement economically and efficiently, it is important to have experienced workmen. In the hiring of Employees, the Employer recognizes that the Union is a source of manpower and will therefore use it as a source when in need of Employees.

SECTION 2.   The Employer shall have complete freedom of selection in hiring and shall determine the qualifications of the men employed. The Employer shall have the authority to discipline or discharge any Employee for just cause, provided, however, that there shall be no discrimination on the part of the Employer against any workman or Employee, nor shall any such Employee be discharged by reason of any Union activity not interfering with the proper performance of his work. Further, the Employer and the Union both agree that there shall be no discrimination in the hiring, promotion, discipline, or discharge of workmen or Employees because of race, creed, color, national origin, age, or sex.

ARTICLE VI. UNION REPRESENTATION
SECTION 1.   The Business Manager and/or his representative of the Party of the Second Part are to be permitted to visit the job at any time for the purpose of transacting business in connection with the job and receive immediate admission to same.

ARTICLE VII. STEWARDS
SECTION 1.   When the Business Manager of the Party of the Second Part deems it advisable, he shall appoint a Steward on any given project. Said Steward is to be recognized by the Employer and he shall have the right to act on any grievance without discrimination. Said Steward shall also be retained on any given project as long as, or when any Employee or Employees are employed unless only a Foreman or Teamster Combination Man is all that is needed to complete the project.

SECTION 2.   In case the Steward cannot settle any dispute or grievance, the Business Manager shall be notified to take up with the Party of the First Part said grievance. For all purposes of this Agreement, it is understood that the duties of the Steward are limited to:

a. To insist that the provisions of this Agreement be complied with by the First and Second Parties.

b. To report to the Business Manager any question that he cannot settle with the Party of the First Part.

SECTION 3. Any other act by a Steward shall not constitute a breach or violation of this Agreement by the Union, Party of the Second Part, unless such action was authorized or ordered by the Union.

SECTION 4. A Steward (and/or Employee) who is called away from his job to take part in the conduct of Union business, i.e., delegate to Convention, Council, etc., shall automatically be granted unpaid personal leave for whatever period of time is necessary to complete the Union business.

ARTICLE VIII. PAY-DAY

SECTION 1. Pay shall be weekly and received by the Employee and/or Employees on the job and before the regular quitting time. When an Employee or Employees are laid off permanently, they shall receive their pay at the time of being laid off. Should an Employee be laid off and fail to recieve his pay at the time or should an Employee and/or Employees fail to receive their pay on the regular established pay-day and on the job, two (2) hours time at the regular rate of pay shall be allowed for each Employee required to report later for his pay. Should the Employee be required to wait for a period greater than twenty-four (24) hours, he shall receive four (4) hours pay at the regular rate of pay for reporting for his pay.

SECTION 2. Employees who voluntarily leave the Employer's employment may be paid at the next regular payday.

ARTICLE IX. HOURS OF WORK AND OVERTIME

SECTION 1. Eight (8) hours shall constitute a standard workday, exclusive of lunch periods, between the hours of 7:00 A.M. and 5:00 P.M. Forty (40) hours per week shall constitute a week of work, Monday through Friday inclusive. This work shall be paid at straight time rates.

SECTION 2. By mutual consent of the Employer, Employee, and the Union, an Employee may work on the Saturday following the Friday of the regular work week at straight time to make up to a forty (40) hour work week. No Employee is obliged to work makeup time and is not subject to discharge for refusing same. Makeup time applies to work lost due to inclement weather only.

SECTION 3. There shall be no work performed earlier than 7:00 A.M. except in an emergency situation.

SECTION 4. *Overtime Payment:* Time and one-half ($1\frac{1}{2}$) shall be paid at the rate of pay actually received by each Employee for any and all work performed over and above eight (8) hours of any work day and for any work performed over and above forty (40) hours per regular work week, except that double ($2\times$) time shall also be paid for work done on Sundays and the following named Holidays:

a. New Year's Day   d. Thanksgiving Day
b. Memorial Day   e. Christmas Day.
c. Fourth of July

SECTION 5. No work shall be performed on Labor Day except to save life or property and then this shall be paid at the rate of double ($2\times$) time.

SECTION 6. Any Employee reporting for work at the regular starting time, and for whom no work is provided, shall receive pay for two (2) hours at the stipulated rate for so reporting, unless he has been notified before the end of the last preceding shift not to report, provided weather conditions are favorable. Any Employee who reports for work, and for whom work is provided, shall receive not less than four (4) hours' pay, and if more than four (4) hours are worked in any one (1) day, shall receive not less than a full days (8 hours) pay, providing weather conditions are favorable.

ARTICLE X. SETTLEMENT OF DISPUTES

SECTION 1. It is agreed by the Party of the Second Part that in case any question should arise between the Parties of this Agreement, the members of said Local Unions, and/or men doing work which is under the jurisdiction of said Locals, shall continue to work until the [state] District Council has been notified and given sufficient time to take up for settlement such dispute, during which time it is strictly understood and agreed that in case individual members or groups of members of the Local Union and/or men doing work which is under the jurisdiction of said Local Unions, cease work or cause cessation of work in violation of the Agreement, that the Party of the Second Part will undertake every reasonable means to induce any and all Employees to return to their jobs.

ARTICLE XI. SAFETY AND SANITATION

SECTION 1. It is agreed that each Employee covered by this Agreement shall fully comply with all safety directives issued by his Employer and shall properly utilize all safety equipment provided by his Employer when so directed.

SECTION 2. Should the Employer, Party of the First Part, fail to comply with the Safety Code for the Construction Industry of the [state], after due notice by the Party of the Second Part, it will not be a violation of this Agreement, and will be termed legal, if a work stoppage occurs for the purpose of compelling the Employer to comply with the provisions of the aforementioned Safety Code.

SECTION 3. The Employer shall furnish at no cost to the Employee necessary protective equipment or clothing where needed for protection of health. Each Employee drawing such equipment shall be responsible for its return in the same condition it was issued excepting for ordinary wear and tear.

ARTICLE XII. WAGE RATES AND CLASSIFICATIONS

SECTION 1. All Employees shall be compensated in accordance with the Classifications and hourly Wage Rates set forth immediately following:

Classification	Effective April 1, 1974, Hourly Wage + $0.30 H&W[†] $0.30 Pens. $0.08 Trng.	Effective April 1, 1975, Hrly Wage + $0.35 H&W $0.30 Pens. $0.07 Trng.	Effective April 1, 1976, Hrly Wage + $0.35 H&W $0.35 Pens. $0.07 Trng.
Foreman	$5.50	$5.75	$6.00
Assistant Foreman	5.00	5.25	5.50
Machine Operator	5.00	5.25	5.50
Truck Drivers*	4.75	5.00	5.25
Laborers	4.50	4.75	5.00
Yard Office Work**	1.00 Less	1.00 Less	1.00 Less

[†See Articles XIII, XIV, and XV.]

*The "Truck Driver" Classification is applicable when trucks are used for the conveyance of materials incidental to the performance of the job.

**When off season or inclement weather conditions are present, the men may be asked to work at the Yard Office for $1.00 per *hour less* than their regular rate.

Section 2. All new Employees for the first thirty (30) days of employment shall receive the minimum rate of three ($3.00) dollars per hour.

Section 3. When new or different Classifications are needed for any job or jobs of the Employer, they shall be added to the above Classifications set forth in Section 1 of this Article by mutual agreement between the Party of the First Part and the Party of the Second Part.

Article XIII. Health and Welfare
Section 1. On work covered by this Agreement, the Employer agrees to pay into the [state] District Council of Laborers and Hod Carriers Welfare Fund, effective [date], thirty ($0.30) cents per hour for each hour worked by Employees covered by this Agreement, in addition to wages set forth herein, and, effective [date], an additional five ($0.05) cents per hour for each hour worked by Employees covered by this Agreement, in addition to the wages set forth herein. Payment shall be made on the dates, in the manner, form and in accordance with the rules and regulations as adopted by the Trustees of the herein mentioned Welfare Fund.

Section 2. The Employer agrees to be bound by the Agreement and Declaration of Trust entered into and dated May 25, 1953, establishing the [state] District Council of Laborers and Hod Carriers

Welfare Fund and Participating Employers and by any amendments to said Trust Agreement.

Section 3. The Welfare Fund shall be administered in accordance with all provisions of applicable law.

Article XIV. Pension
Section 1. Effective [date], the Employer agrees to pay into the [state] District Council of Laborers and Hod Carriers Pension Fund, thirty-five ($0.35) cents per hour for each hour worked by Employees covered by this Agreement, in addition to the wages herein set out. Payment shall be made on the dates, in the manner, form and in accordance with the rules and regulations as adopted by the Trustees of the herein mentioned Pension Fund.

Section 2. The Employer agrees to be bound by the Agreement and Declaration of Trust, entered into and dated June 1, 1962, establishing the District Council of Laborers and Hod Carriers Pension Fund and Participating Employers and by any amendments to said Trust Agreement.

Section 3. The Pension Trust Fund shall be administered in accordance with all provisions of applicable law.

Article XV. Training Trust Fund
Section 1. On work covered by this Agreement, the Employer agrees to pay into the [state] Laborers Training Trust Fund seven ($0.07) cents per hour for each hour worked by Employees covered by this Agreement in addition to wages herein set out. Payments shall be made on the dates, in the manner, form, and in accordance with the rules and regulations as adopted by the Trustees of the herein mentioned Trust Fund.

Section 2. The Employer agrees to be bound by the Agreement and Declaration of Trust, establishing the Laborers Training Trust Fund.

Section 3. The Employer, or his authorized representative, shall notify the Local Union, Party of the Second Part, of all Employees given employment covered by this Agreement within three (3) days from date of employment in order that the Union may obtain the required and necessary information

from the aforesaid individuals to properly register them in the Health and Welfare Fund, Pension Fund, and Training Trust Fund.

Article XVI. Permissible Work Stoppage
Section 1. It shall not be a violation of this Agreement should the Employees covered by this Agreement cease work for nonpayment of wages and/or nonpayment of contributions set forth in Article XIII, Article XIV, and Article XV, covering the Trust Funds under the respective Articles mentioned herein.

Article XVII. Subcontractor Clause
Section 1. All job site work covered by this Agreement shall be sublet subject to the terms and conditions of this Agreement.

Article XVII. Duration
Section 1. This Agreement shall be in full force and effect from [date] and shall continue in effect until [date]. Either Party, or the negotiating agent, desiring to terminate or change the Agreement at its termination date shall give written notice on or before [date], of such desire. If such notice is not given, the Agreement shall continue in full force and effect from year to year thereafter until one of the Parties serves a written notice on or before [month] 1st of any year thereafter.

Party of the First Part
[signatures]

Party of the Second Part
[signatures]

Appendix 11-B
Form for Subcontractor's Quote

Job name:		Date:
Contractor quoting:		
Quote given by:		
Quote received by:		
Quantity	Description	Price

Reproduced with permission of Landscape Design and Construction, Inc., Dallas, Texas.

Appendix 11-C
Subcontract: Job Contract

THIS AGREEMENT made the _____ day of _____, 19_____, by and between _____, hereinafter called "Contractor," and [name of landscape construction firm] hereinafter called "Company."

Contractor hereby agrees to furnish the labor, equipment, implements, machines, trucks and all other things necessary for and to do and perform the following:
[list].

Contractor further agrees to perform the work set out above as an independent contractor, free of control or supervision of Company as to means and method of performing the same; that all persons engaged in the performance of said work shall be solely the servants or employees of Contractor; that Contractor shall take out and keep in force and furnish Company acceptable certificates as to Employers' Liability or Workmen's Compensation insurance covering all persons performing such work and Public Liability insurance covering the classes of work done and all motor equipment used hereunder, all in amounts and under policies acceptable to Company.

Contractor shall defend, protect, indemnify, and save Company harmless from and against all claims, demands, and causes of action of every kind and character arising in favor of any person, including Contractor, Company's employees, Contractor's employees, or other persons, on account of personal injuries or death or damage to property in any wise incident to or arising out of work performed by Contractor hereunder, growing out of or incident to Contractor's operations hereunder, whether directly or indirectly due to Company's negligence, whether sole, joint, concurring or otherwise. Contractor

Reproduced with permission of Landscape Design and Construction, Inc., Dallas, Texas.

further agrees to pay Company for damages to its property and to indemnify and hold Company harmless against the payment of any and all taxes, penalties, interest, liens or indebtedness or claims against its property, or for work performed, or measured by the work performed, growing out of or incident to Contractor's operations hereunder.

Contractor agrees that Contractor is an employer, as that term is defined in the Federal Insurance Contributions Act and Unemployment Compensation laws of the state or states in which the work is to be performed. Contractor's identification-account number or numbers are as follows: [insert number].

Contractor agrees to furnish Company, upon request, other evidence of Contractor's compliance with said laws. Contractor will reimburse Company, upon request, for the amount of any and all such taxes plus penalty and interest assessed and paid by Company for or on behalf of Contractor and/or his employees.

Contractor agrees to comply with all federal, state, and municipal laws, ordinances, rules, and regulations applicable to any part of the service or work to be performed hereunder.

Company may first deduct any money due it before any sums of money shall be due and owing to Contractor under this contract.

Contractor may not assign this contract nor sublet the same or any part thereof, nor assign to any other person or persons all or any part of the remuneration due or which may become due to Contractor hereunder, without the written consent of Company, and the assignment of this contract or the subletting of any work to be performed hereunder, if so permitted by Company, shall not relieve Contractor of his or its obligations hereunder.

If performance of and payment under this contract is on any basis other than a turn-key basis (such as cost-plus, measured by time, classes of equipment used) and without limitation otherwise; then Company, at any time prior to or subsequent to making any payments to Contractor, shall have the right to audit the books, records, and invoices of Contractor involved in the performance of such contract to verify any and all charges so made by Contractor.

Contractor shall perform general landscaping construction work and other incidental landscaping work as ordered by Company from time to time. Such orders shall be in writing on Company's Work Order form. No work shall be started unless authorized representatives of the Company and the Contractor have agreed in writing on such Work Order as to the number of laborers and the rates to be applied by the Contractor or some other basis of payment for performing such work. Daily work reports shall be furnished by Contractor to the Company showing the number of hours of labor which Contractor furnishes and uses during each day of work.

Company agrees that, after inspection and approval of work done, it will pay Contractor within _____ days after receipt and approval of invoices for work performed pursuant to this Contract based upon the rates or other charges specified in Company's Work Order issued for such work.

If Contractor at any time shall fail to make prompt payment for labor, or disregard laws, ordinances, or requests of Company, or if Contractor shall fail, neglect, or be unable to provide adequate labor to perform the work, or shall fail to perform the work in a satisfactory and competent manner, Company shall have the right to terminate this Contract and any Work Order under this Contract forthwith.

WITNESS THE SIGNATURES of the parties hereto the day and year first above written.

[name of contractor]

By _____

[name of landscape construction firm]

By _____

Appendix 11-D
Bid Summary Sheet

No.	Description	Size	Source	Material cost (each)	Material cost (total)	Labor (each)	Labor (total)	Combined labor and material (each)	Combined labor and material (total)	Percent replacement	Total replacement	Subcontract
Job name: Date:												

Reproduced with permission of Landscape Design and Construction, Inc., Dallas, Texas.

Appendix 11-E
Bid-Actual Cost Comparison Form

Date:	Job name:					

Less cost of:	Sales price					Reason
	Bid		Actual		Difference	
Labor	$		$		$	
Plant material						
Other material						
Equipment rental						
Freight and other						
Subcontractors:						
Gross profit or loss	$		$		$	

Labor budget

Task:	Bid		Actual		Difference		Reason
	Hours	$	hrs	$	hrs	$	
Remove plants and turf		$		$		$	
Transplanting							
Grading							
SOIL PREP. — Excavation							
SOIL PREP. — Backfill							
SOIL PREP. — Tilling							
PLANTING — Pots							
PLANTING — 1 gallon							
PLANTING — 5 gallon							
PLANTING — B & B							
PLANTING — Divisions							
PLANTING — Trees							
PLANTING — Grass							
Edging: Steel, Wood							
Gravel, Boulders							
Pruning							
Espalier, Tree bracing							
Walls: Wood, Stone							
Cleanup							
Replacement							
Maintenance							
		$		$		$	

Appendix 11-F
Employees' Activities Form

Job name:		TASK	Remove plants & turf	Transplanting	Grading	SOIL PREP.			PLANTING							Edging: Steel, Wood	Gravel, Boulders	Pruning	Espalier, Tree bracing	Walls: Wood, Stone	Cleanup	Replacement	Maintenance			TOTAL HOURS
Job foreman:						Excavation	Backfill	Tilling	Pots	1 gallon	5 gallon	B & B	Divisions	Trees	Grass											
Date:																										
Time begin:	Time end:																									
Employee name																										
Total task production																										
Equipment hours and comments:																										

Reproduced with permission of Landscape Design and
Construction, Inc., Dallas, Texas.

Project name:	Month:	Day of the Month																															
	Budgeted hours	1	2	3	4	5	6	7	8	9	10	11	12	13	14	15	16	17	18	19	20	21	22	23	24	25	26	27	28	29	30	31	TOTAL TASK HOURS
TASK																																	
Remove plants & turf																																	
Transplanting																																	
Grading																																	
SOIL PREP. — Excavation																																	
SOIL PREP. — Backfill																																	
SOIL PREP. — Tilling																																	
PLANTING — Pots																																	
PLANTING — 1 gallon																																	
PLANTING — 5 gallon																																	
PLANTING — B & B																																	
PLANTING — Divisions																																	
PLANTING — Trees																																	
PLANTING — Grass																																	
Edging: Steel, Wood																																	
Gravel, Boulders																																	
Pruning																																	
Espalier, Tree bracing																																	
Walls: Wood, Stone																																	
Cleanup																																	
Replacement																																	
Maintenance																																	
TOTAL LABOR																																	

Reproduced with permission of Landscape Design and
Construction, Inc., Dallas, Texas.

Appendix 11-H
Change Order Form

Change order number:

_____   _____
Owner's Name   Date

_____   _____
Address   Original contract dated:

[Name of firm] is hereby authorized to perform the following changes in work:

	Additions		Deductions	
	$		$	
Total additions and subtractions	$		$	

The net change in the original contract is: Add $_____ Deduct $_____

This revision becomes part of, and in conformance with, the existing contract.

_____   _____
Owner or Representative   Landscape Architect

Date_____, 19_____   Date_____, 19_____

Reproduced with permission of Landscape Design and
Construction, Inc., Dallas, Texas.

12

Contracting Procedures and Bidding

THE ROLE OF THE LANDSCAPE ARCHITECT

Most landscape projects will need two sets of contracts: the first between the owner and the landscape architect, and the second between the owner and the landscape contractor.

On some large projects a team of design professionals may be involved, including, by themselves or in some combination, architects, engineers, and landscape architects. One member of the team will represent the group to the owner. This may or may not be the landscape architect. When it is not the landscape architect he will hold a subcontract to provide his services to the owner through another design professional. Usually when this occurs the project is bid in total and the landscape contractor becomes a subcontractor to a general contractor.

On large projects involving the work of only landscape architectural firms, two or more firms may combine in a consortium to provide their services effectively to the owner. Sometimes, when distance separates owner or project site from the landscape architectural firm, that firm will contract with another nearer the project to provide the planting plans since the latter will be more familiar with local conditions and can provide supervision and inspection for the project.

The first contract between the owner and landscape architect may take one of several forms depending on the circumstances. Preprinted forms are available to landscape architects from the American Society of Landscape Architects and might be used for small projects. The text of a standard form of agreement is reprinted at the end of this chapter in Appendix 12-A. The explanatory notes issued with the agreement are reprinted in Appendix 12-B. More commonly the landscape architect prepares a proposal for his professional services on his office letterhead which, when approved and accepted in writing by the owner, becomes a "letter of agreement" and is binding as a contract. A third possibility is to retain an attorney to prepare a formal written contract that would be prepared specifically for the project. Some governmental agencies will have their own contract forms that will have to be used when the landscape architect contracts his services to them.

In the contract or proposal of services the landscape architect or designer explicitly outlines the scope of his services and the fees to be charged. The services may include master planning, site analysis, working drawings (part of which would be planting plans), specifications, and supervision or inspection. The fees for these services will be determined in one of several ways or in a combination of ways: (1) as a lump sum, (2) as a percentage of construction cost, (3) as an hourly fee, and (4) as a per-unit cost. Billing for these services may be done on a monthly basis or as a percentage of the total fee at the completion of certain phases of the work.

The lump sum is most popular with private clients and others when there is not an established budget for computing a percentage fee. It gives the client an immediate figure to use in determining his cost while planning the project. The lump sum arrangement is generally the only approach used to establish fees for master planning.

Institutional, corporate, governmental, and private clients will use the percentage fee basis for projects where a budget has been established. If a college wants to construct a courtyard in a dormitory complex, it may have established a budget of $350,000. In the designer's negotiations with the college, they may have agreed on an eight percent fee. The designer will design within the budget limitations, providing layout drawings, construction details, planting plan, specifications, and supervision for a total fee payment of $28,000. Percentage fees are usually established on a sliding scale, with smaller percentages than described above for large projects, and higher percentages for small ones.

The hourly fee is not popular because the client is unable to determine his costs before they develop, and consequently, the hourly fee is not commonly used. It will generally be used for short-term consultation. It is generally figured by multiplying a payroll rate 2½ to 3 times. If the principal of a firm receives $10 an hour for his work, the firm will bill the client $25 or $30 per hour to cover *all* the costs of running the office for an hour, such as rent, secretarial help, supplies, utilities, the telephone, insurance, taxes, pensions, etc.

A per-unit cost may be used to design a subdivision at $10 per lot or to prepare a grading plan or planting plan for each unit in a 300 unit housing development at $35 per unit for each basic type of plan. Sometimes master planning will be done at a specific figure per acre.

After the landscape architect has completed those phases of his work that result in the completion of the plans and specifications—commonly referred to as the contract documents, which we discussed in Chapter 10—he is ready to begin the bidding procedure. The number of copies of the contract documents reproduced depends on the size of the project, the number of bidders, and the quantity needed by the successful bidder in order to execute the project.

For some projects, especially those where the owner is private rather than public, a prequalification procedure is used in selecting potential contractors. The process may be formal or informal. The formal process requires interested landscape contractors to submit a financial statement in which they list the kind and nature of projects previously contracted. This will enable the landscape architect to select those landscape contractors who have the size and financial capability to handle the proposed project and to determine the contractor's reputation on the basis of previous projects. The informal prequalification process is simple. The landscape architect selects potential bidders from among those landscape contractors he has had successful experience with in the past, or from among those he knows have established good reputations with other landscape architectural firms.

Bidding on public projects is usually more open, but the contract may be more stringent.

When contractors have not been prequalified, the procedures become more rigid and the inspection and supervision increases.

The "invitation to bid" may be issued by the landscape architect from his office (in the case of private work), or it may be advertised by a governmental agency (for public projects). Either way, contract documents can be secured from the landscape architect's office after leaving a cash deposit or certified check to insure return of the plans and specifications. The invitation for bids that the ASLA has prepared for the use of landscape architects, and the instructions for using them, are reprinted in Appendixes 12-C and 12-D.

The date and place of bid opening is established in the invitation to bid; at bid openings for public projects, the owner, landscape architect, and all contractors may be present. Bids generally must be submitted in a sealed envelope before a very rigid deadline and must be made on a preprinted "form of proposal." The bid form prepared by the ASLA is reprinted in Appendix 12-E. Each bid is opened and read aloud, as specified in the "instructions to bidders" (the ASLA form is reprinted in Appendix 12-G).

The bid opening on small, private projects may be quite informal. No date need be set and the bids will many times be opened at a conference attended by only the owner and the landscape architect.

The bids are held for a period of time during which the landscape architect reviews his cost estimates with the owner and compares them against the low bid. If the low bid is below the cost estimate, the contract between the owner and landscape contractor may be consumated.

The contract between the owner and the landscape contractor may be on a preprinted form furnished by the landscape architect (see Appendixes 12-I to 12-K), drawn by an attorney, furnished by a governmental agency, or it may simply be a "letter of agreement" in which the landscape architect outlines the services to be performed, all parties signing this agreement.

During construction, the landscape architect may provide several services. It is not unusual for a number of questions to arise about the interpretation of the plans and specifications. Generally the landscape architect's decision is final. Conditions on the site may change, requiring changes in the drawings and the issuance of a "change order" to the landscape contractor. (See Appendix 12-L.) Where costs may differ, these are negotiated, as we discussed in Chapter 11.

Other problems that might arise can include any of the following examples: the landscape contractor may complain because his work conflicts with that of other contractors, because still others were delayed in getting the project ready for him; the workmen, equipment, and materials of several contractors are getting in each other's way; changes are made by others without notification of the landscape contractor; plants are killed or injured by the cleanup procedures or chemicals used by other contractors.

Problems may arise because plants were omitted or incorrectly counted when designated on a plan, something inadvertently overlooked by the landscape architect. There may be inconsistencies between the plans and specifications, especially when projects are large and complex, that generally show up only when the project is under construction. If the landscape contractor is sharp and catches the inconsistencies or errors during the bidding procedure, an "addendum" can be issued by the landscape architect to correct the problem.

When disputes arise between the landscape contractor and the owner, or between the landscape contractor and another contractor, the landscape architect serves as an arbitrator until the differences are resolved. When a dispute cannot be resolved by all the parties above, it can be submitted to the American Arbitration Association, 140 West 51st Street, New York, New York 10020. This is a nonprofit organization set up to provide arbitration service. Claimants must pay a filing fee of $100 plus a percentage of the claim, both of which are set up only to cover the cost of administration.

Occasionally some projects will require considerable supervision by the landscape architect. Some examples of this kind of close supervision can include the following: the landscape architect may want to go to the nursery to select and tag specific plants to be used in a project; on the site he may want to orient each plant individually to achieve the particular aesthetic effect he wants to create; he may also prune both new and existing plants to enhance the appearance of individual specimens or to enframe particular views or focal points in the total landscape.

There is increasing use of land sculpture or the placement of soil in aesthetic forms for mounding, screening, privacy, noise control, etc. The landscape architect may closely supervise the placement of soil and its final grading in order to achieve the effect he intends.

Inspection of the rest of the work under progress will also be made periodically by the landscape architect. He or his representative will check to be sure plants are named, sized, and installed according to the plans and specifications, and that all other work conforms. Most projects generally require a guarantee period of one year or more. An inspection will be made at the beginning and end of the guarantee period. Most specifications will require the landscape contractor to replace all dead plants and others that may have become unsightly. Many times the contractor will be required to prune, water, mulch, fertilize, or otherwise maintain plants during the guarantee period to insure the successful planting of lawns, trees, shrubs, etc.

Coupled with the inspections, certification-of-progress statements will be made to the owner, which will enable the owner to make payments to the landscape contractor. After the final inspection at the end of the guarantee period, the landscape architect will issue a final acceptance notice, upon which the owner will make final payment to the landscape contractor. (See Appendix 12-M.) The project is then considered finished.

As can be seen, the landscape architect is concerned with the bidding and the contract-awarding procedure from the point of view of advising and protecting his client, who is the contracting authority. The landscape contractor is, of course, interested in the bidding processes since he must prepare a proper bid if he wants to be awarded the contract for the project.

To do this he must be competitive in his bidding.

COMPETITIVE BIDDING

The perfectly prepared cost analysis with a profit inclusion is little more than a practice exercise if the resulting bid on a landscape construction project is not accepted and the contract is awarded instead to another firm. Failure to have any specific contract awarded is not always of great importance, but failure to receive *any* contracts based on bidding means that the contractor is not submitting competitive bids. Some contracting firms depend on work for which bids are not required, but with the increase in large landscape construction projects, both public and private, most contractors are interested in obtaining a percentage of the work that does require the submitting of bids. In order to obtain this type of construction work, the firm must submit competitive bids.

There are several factors that must be considered when preparing a bid that is expected to be competitive with bids submitted by other firms. First, and perhaps the most important, is to know if the contract will be awarded solely on the basis of the lowest bid, or whether other factors such as quality of work, past performance on other projects, and the capability of the company to complete the project within contract specifications will be considered. If other factors are to be considered, the contractor must be aware of these factors and adjust his approach to obtaining the contract on the basis of these factors. It may be necessary to meet with the landscape architect and/or the contracting authority to "sell" the capabilities of the construction firm. Previously completed projects may be useful in displaying the firm's work. The landscape architect may be requested to make recommendations to the contracting authority about the acceptability of the various bidders, and the contractor, to be competitive, must make sure the architect is aware of his work.

For some nongovernmental projects the opportunity to match the acknowledged low bid may be afforded to a specific firm chosen by the landscape architect if the contracting authority has been favorably impressed with previous performances. It is necessary for a firm to be well established and to have its work well known to be accepted by the landscape architect who designed the project.

If the contract is to be awarded solely on the basis of the lowest bid, the contractor should, if at all possible, determine what other firms will be providing competitive bids. If the competing landscape construction companies have bid on other projects, study their bids and try to determine any bidding patterns that might be helpful in preparing a competitive bid. A composite comparison of all the bidding firms must then be prepared. It is not sufficient to underbid all but one firm since then the contract is still lost. As an example, some of the competitors may be characteristically high on plant materials but low on installation charges. A contractor may operate his own nursery and thus he will be able to bid low on the basis of "low-cost" plant material. A study of the competition's bidding patterns will permit the contractor to adjust his bid to be competitive.

How should the bid be adjusted? Most firms should be operated on the basis of making a profit on all projects. Too often the landscape contractor will sacrifice his profit in order to obtain the contract. To maintain a healthy industry the long-term goals of any firm should be to make a fair and honest profit on all landscape construction projects. To do this, all data about costs and profit must be included in the total amount bid on a specific job. However, there are times when, in order to be competitive, a contractor will want to submit a bid that does not include all costs. But because this is risky, we feel the reader ought to examine first other ways of preparing competitive bids.

In some instances a firm's fixed costs (overhead) may be too high. When these are added to the variable costs, the total for the bid is too high to be competitive. Inasmuch as the fixed costs represent money that has already been spent, if it is extremely important for the company to obtain the contract for a particular project, the rate of fixed costs may be reduced to make the bid more competitive. If several bids on different projects are too high because of high fixed costs, the company management should examine these costs very carefully and initiate money-saving programs at the firm to reduce them. Inefficiency in management is the usual cause of high fixed costs. Some firms have "too many chiefs and not enough Indians." Extravagant offices and physical facilities may account for higher expenditures than are necessary. Likewise, inadequate or poorly designed facilities can be highly inefficient. But regardless of why the fixed costs are high, in any company they must be cut eventually if they are so high that the company is not competitive either on bid or on nonbid work.

Other reasons for reducing the fixed-cost input in a bid on a specific job are: (1) to obtain a job that would give the company prestige; (2) to use the project, when completed, as advertising for future jobs; (3) the firm is new and needs the work to become established; and (4) the project may increase the amount of income for the firm for the year without measurable increase in fixed costs. In these instances, the fixed-cost input in the bid figure may be reduced to make the firm competitive.

It may be possible to reduce the variable costs, but the reduction should in no way be at the expense of the quality of work. All plant material and other supplies should measure up to specifications. A reputation damaged by shoddy or poor-quality work may cost more than the loss of one project. Ways of reducing variable or production costs are: (1) buying plants and supplies for more than one job at a time to obtain a better price; (2) through more efficient use of labor to reduce overtime work; and (3) by using subcontractors who are specialists on specific jobs that would otherwise be carried out at a higher cost by the landscape construction firm. The variable costs, the actual cash outlay for the project, are harder to adjust than the fixed-cost outlay.

Finally, the profit added to the project cost estimate should be examined. The profit on a job can be reduced or eliminated for the same reasons fixed costs can be reduced. However, many landscape contractors feel, psychologically, that it is a poor business practice not to include a profit figure in all project estimates, and rightly so, since all firms should be striving eventually for sound profits. Furthermore, many contractors feel that if the business is operating in a sound manner it should permit the owner to submit bids that include all cost factors plus a profit.

SUBMITTING THE BID

The type or format of the bid to be submitted depends on the type of landscape project. For most residential jobs no formal bid is submitted, but even when a bid is not required a cost analysis should be submitted to insure that the job is priced properly for the customer. It is wise to have a formal understanding about the cost of any job before work begins. This builds better customer relations and helps eliminate a major source of misunderstanding upon completion of the job. Large projects generally require that a specific procedure be followed when competing bids have been requested. If the procedures are not followed, this alone is sufficient reason not to consider the bid.

Governmental Projects

Generally, governmental projects have the most rigid procedures to follow when submitting the bid. The specifications for the particular project include a set of instructions to the bidders. Regardless of how many similar projects have been bid on previously, the contractor should read these instructions carefully, for each project will have its own set of rules that must be followed. A sample set of instructions to bidders, used on a federal housing project, is provided in Appendix 12-N.

Special bid forms must be used and the specifications will tell how many must be submitted. The bidding documents must be enclosed in properly labelled envelopes and sealed. Information about labelling is provided in the specifications; generally this will include the name of the bidder, the project name and number, and the date and time of bid opening. The date and time are needed to prevent premature opening of the bid, which would thus disqualify the bidder from further consideration.

It must also be mentioned here, again, that any changes or interpretations in the specifications must be agreed upon in writing before the deadline for submitting the bids. Some contracting authorities will require that requests for interpretations be made at least ten days before the date of the opening of bids. Any changes or additions to the specifications will be prepared by the contracting authority at least a week in advance of the bid opening. But it is the responsibility of the bidder to request the changes in the specifications from the contracting authority. They will not be sent automatically. The landscape architect must be consulted before specifications are changed.

Some projects will require any subcontractors to be listed. For some bids it will be necessary to list their qualifications in the same format the landscape contractor himself uses.

On some projects a bid guaranty (or bid bond) is required, as discussed in Chapter 11, at "Cost Analysis." This guaranty, in the form of a certified check or its equivalent, must accompany the bid. If it is necessary to submit a revised bid for a sum larger than the original bid, it will be necessary to increase the bid guaranty by the appropriate sum.

The specifications may also request that a noncollusion affidavit be submitted with the bid. (Appendix 12-O). This is an affidavit in which the contractor has sworn he has not consulted with other contractors about the amount of the bid and, therefore, has not attempted to fix the level of the bids submitted. If the landscape work is a subcontracted job, the landscape subcontractor may be required to submit such a document to the project's prime contractor.

For some bids, the landscape contractor may be required to submit a statement of his firm's qualifications to perform the work for which the bid is being submitted. This statement should include a list of similar projects that the firm has completed, equipment that is specialized for a particular operation, such as large tree movers, and the financial condition of the company, including appropriate credit references.

The bid should be submitted in perfect condition. Erasures may cause confusion and, if the bid is not clear, rejection may result. If erasures are necessary the changes should be made with an explanation over the signature of the bidder.

It is up to the bidder to make sure that the bid arrives on time. Late arrivals are usually not considered. It is recommended that the bidder be aware of the times of mail deliveries in the area and to make sure that the bid is posted in ample time for delivery before the bid opening is to take place. Also, any modifications of the original bid have to be received before bid opening takes place if they are to be considered.

When the bids are to be opened on a public project, the bidding firms may send representatives to the openings. The bids are read aloud. It is recommended that every bid opening be attended and that notes be taken on how competitive firms have bid on the project. This is a means of preparing a file on competing firms, and the information derived should be helpful in preparing competitive bids on future projects.

If for some reason the landscape contractor feels that he must withdraw the bid, this must be done before the bid opening and it must be done in writing. Telegraphing a withdrawal request is permitted by most clients, provided the request is made before the opening of the bids. The bid cannot be withdrawn after opening and explanations by the bidder that he made mistakes in the preparation of the bid are not considered proper reasons for withdrawing the bid then. If a mistake is discovered before the opening date, however, the bid may of course be withdrawn from consideration.

Awarding the Contract

The contract is awarded to the lowest bidder, provided he has submitted the appropriate documents, including the requested statement of his qualifications. After notification, the contractor will be required to submit a performance bond within a specified period of time. (Appendix 12-P.) We discussed the performance bond and the reasons for requiring one in Chapter 11. If the firm cannot produce such a performance bond within the prescribed period of time, the firm may lose the bid guar-

anty and be required to pay the difference between its submitted bid and the bid subsequently received after the contracting authority has re-advertised for new bids or taken the next higher bid.

If the firm's bid is not accepted, the bid guaranty is returned as soon as possible after bid opening and the awarding of the contract.

All the work of preparing a sound cost analysis and site evaluation will be lost if the simple directions given in the specifications are not followed in detail when preparing the bid documents. Follow the directions carefully and make sure the bid arrives in time for the opening. Be present at the opening and study all the bids submitted for future reference.

Nongovernmental Projects

Generally the bidding procedures for nongovernmental projects are not as rigid as they are for governmental projects. Often the bidding on nongovernmental projects is by invitation only. The landscape architect recommends to his client several contractors who he feels can do quality work. The landscape architect will mention in his specifications the bidding procedures to be followed. The requested procedures should be followed explicitly so that the bid is not rejected on a technicality. A contract will be let to the contractor with the best bid (not necessarily the low bid).

On many residential landscape sites the homeowner will obtain a plan from a landscape contractor. In return for the service of preparing a plan, the landscape contractor hopes the customer will use his services when it is time to install the required plant material.

If a landscape architect has been used by the homeowner, the landscape architect will assist in selecting a satisfactory landscape contractor. No formal bid procedures are followed, but it is wise to prepare an accurate cost estimate and to have a formal agreement for the work signed with the owner. This agreement will include total cost, payment plan, and estimated completion date, as well as the plant guarantees given by the landscape contractor.

SUMMARY

The awarding of the contract is where careful attention to proper cost analysis and bid preparation pays off. It is obvious that a good working relationship between the landscape architect and the landscape contractor will be beneficial to both parties and also to the client who hires both. After the contract is awarded, next will come preparation of the site and installation of the plant material by the landscape contractor.

FOR FURTHER READING

Landscape Architect's Handbook of Professional Practice, 1972. McLean, Virginia: American Society of Landscape Architects.

Appendix 12-A
Standard Form of Agreement Between Owner and Landscape Architect

This Agreement, entered into this _____ day of _____ 19_____, by and between _____

(Name of Owner)

_____

(Address of Owner)

_____ (hereinafter called the "Owner"), and _____ (hereinafter called the "Landscape Architect").

Witnesseth:

Article 1: Addresses

That the Owner does hereby employ the Landscape Architect to render professional services for the landscape improvement of the property at _____ _____ to the extent and kind defined in Article 2, below.

Article 2: Services

The professional service of the Landscape Architect shall be as follows: _____ [list].

Article 3: Payment

The Owner agrees to pay the Landscape Architect for professional services as follows: _____ [list].

Article 4: Items Supplied and Extra Work

a. The Owner shall furnish to the Landscape Architect at the Owner's cost and expense all necessary property line and topographic data applicable to the designated improvement. If additional topographic data are required beyond those first furnished, the additional topographic information shall be furnished by the Owner at the Owner's cost and expense.

Issued by the American Society of Landscape Architects. Reprinted with permission.

b. The Landscape Architect shall be reimbursed for blueprinting and duplication of other documents at the cost of reproductions, excepting, however, the first _____ sets which shall be furnished.

c. The Landscape Architect shall be reimbursed for authorized travel and living expenses related to this Agreement.

d. The services of _____ for the purpose of _____ shall be paid to _____.

e. If during the progress of the development of plans or during construction the Owner finds it desirable or necessary to cause the Landscape Architect to perform additional services other than those defined in Article 2 (and Article 4, if applicable), the payment for such additional work shall be _____ _____.

Article 5: Observation and Inspection

The Landscape Architect shall observe the work of the contractor or of the Owner's own staff by inspection at intervals of _____ when construction is in progress.

and/or,

The Owner shall supply full-time inspection by a competent individual or staff.

or,

The Landscape Architect shall supply a competent inspector at the rate of $_____ per _____.

Article 6: Abandonment of Improvement

If the Owner finds it necessary to abandon the project, the Landscape Architect shall be compensated for all work completed under Article 2 according to the schedule of payments designated under Article 3. Scheduled items not completed, but upon which work has been performed, shall be paid for upon basis of estimated extent of completion.

Article 7: Other Parties

a. It is mutually agreed that this Agreement is not transferable by either signatory to a third party without the consent of the other principal party.

b. Plans and specifications are instruments of service and remain the property of the Landscape Architect.

Article 8: Termination

a. This Agreement shall be terminated at any time by the Owner or the Landscape Architect upon giving thirty days' written notice. Termination by the Owner shall comply with Article 6.

b. This Agreement, unless previously terminated by written notice, shall be terminated by the final payment for the finished work.

Article 9: In Witness Whereof the parties hereto have executed this Agreement as of the day and year first above written.

Witness: _____

_____

Owner: _____

_____

(Typed Name and Title, if any)

_____

(Name of Authority, if any)

Landscape Architect: _____

Appendix 12-B
Standard Form of Agreement Between Owner and Landscape Architect: Explanatory Notes

The ASLA Committee on Standard Contract Forms has prepared the form of Agreement (or Contract) which accompanies these suggestions as to how it may be written. It is the Committee's intention and that of the Board of Trustees that the form of agreement is to be no more than a framework upon which the individual landscape architect may insert additional conditions as he may find necessary or believe them to be necessary. The form of agreement has a beginning and an ending, with flexibility between sufficient for the purpose.

Professional services in landscape architecture are varied and often so diverse that the Committee concluded a stereotyped form might have sufficient omissions and additions to present a hodge-podge of printed and written stipulations.

If an agreement is worth stating, it is obviously worth the study to be accurate and precise; once composed, a consistency of format is worth the nominal effort of typing in new material.

INTRODUCTION.   The opening lines of the agreement, above Article 1, are termed the Introduction.

When the Owner is a public authority or an institution (public or private), the official authorized to sign the contract may be designated on line 2 thus: "by and between The Board of Education, of the Summerfield School District, Anystate, acting through its President" (or "Chairman," or "Secretary," or "Business Manager," or otherwise provided locally).

On the last page, in Article 9, under signatures, the title of the official authorized to sign the contract should be given.

Authority for the Agreement: agreement for public or institutional work may require a statement that explains or justifies the employment of the landscape architect. A typical form for such purpose, as a revision of Article 1, could be: "ARTICLE 1. Whereas the Owner has, by Resolution No. _____ of 19_____" (or "by City Ordinance No. _____ of 19_____," or "in the minutes of its Meeting of _____, 19_____"), "employed the . . ." etc.

ARTICLE 1: ADDRESSES.   The mailing addresses of the property, or its precise location in the absence of a mailing address, should be stated. The Owner's address and site of the improvement are not always identical. Both addresses are important.

ARTICLE 2: SERVICES.   The progressive steps of rendering service may be entered here as item (a), (b), (c), etc. Each step requires accurate statement for the Owner's complete understanding. Also, the items listed here are the basis of payment shown in Article 3.

A typical statement of services might include: (a) preliminary plans; (b) general plan or working drawings; (c) specifications and contract; and (d) supervision. The variations are too numerous to indicate other progressions of service.

The form can be used for services on the basis of: a lump sum; percentage of a contract award; per hour, per day (diem), or for longer periods of time as agreed; consultation or preliminary visit (with or without written report); special investigations or research; expert witness (court proceedings).

Provision for payment for *additional work* not contemplated by an Owner at the signing of the contract, but later found to be necessary or desirable, *can* be stated in Article 2, but if they are stated in Article 4 such provision takes on the status of a contingency rather than a planned extension of services.

Generally public authorities, when funds are derived from a federal appropriation, write their own contract, which may include stipulations concerning: nondiscrimination; interest of local officials in the contract prohibited; interest of federal officials in the contract prohibited; assignability; interest of party of second part (the landscape architect) to be without conflict of interest; findings to be confidential; identification of documents; right of employees to collective bargaining; or other stipulations.

In the rare event the landscape architect must write the contract and include a series of stipulations peculiar to federal requirements, these can be identified in Article 2 and treated as indicated by the note.

Suplementary provisions and schedules required under some forms of professional service, particularly those of some public authorities, can be attached as a Schedule or as a series of Appendices 1, 2, 3, etc., and referred to in Article 2 thus: "Appendices 1 to x are included in this Agreement and shall have full force as here completely written."

ARTICLE 3: PAYMENT.   State here payments by specific sums or percentage of fee; if Article 2 is itemized, Article 3 should be identically itemized under subheadings (a), (b), (c), correlated with subheadings of Article 2.

The services in Article 2 should be fully descriptive, but the repeated identifications in Article 3 are best if brief, thus: "(a) Upon completion of the Preliminary Plan, as described" (or "as defined" or "as stated") in item (a) of Article 2, there shall be paid the sum of $_____."

ARTICLE 4: ITEMS SUPPLIED AND EXTRA WORK.
   a.   No comment
   b.   Strike out if not required, or if blueprints are furnished at no cost. Include when duplication of plans and documents is costly. If the practice is to furnish the first three to five sets to the Owner, so state.
   c.   Strike out if not part of the service.
   d.   Strike out if not required. When the services of others are to be supervised by the landscape architect but paid for by the Owner—engineers for sanitation or water problems or electric lighting, for instance, or makers of models or perspective renderings or an advertising brochure—this statement avoids misunderstandings. If these are part of the services to be rendered, state this under Article 2 with provision for payment in Article 3.

Issued by the American Society of Landscape Architects. Reprinted with permission.

e. See comment above under Article 2 regarding *additional work.* The inserted method of payment could be: (1) plan cost plus stated percentage for overhead; (2) based upon the addition to the contract award and compensation, and thus upon the terms of Articles 2 and 3; (3) a lump sum to be negotiated; or (4) some other method of local preference.

ARTICLE 5: OBSERVATION OR INSPECTION. Strike out if not applicable, or strike out inapplicable portions.

ARTICLE 6: ABANDONMENT OF IMPROVEMENT. Strike out if not needed.

ARTICLE 7: OTHER PARTIES.

a. Most professional service agreements are for personal service; the landscape architect acts as an agent of the Owner. The relationship cannot be transferred to a third party without consent of all three. When the landscape architect is a partnership or other form of plural responsibility, the agreement would usually continue after the death of one member of the firm. If continuation of the service is not agreeable, Article 8 can be invoked. When the landscape architect is an individual without associates, it may be necessary for him to form a temporary partnership to satisfy the legal continuation of professional service when a project entails a large sum of public funds or when the service extends over a long period of time. In such instances see your attorney—or perhaps better the client's attorney.

b. There is little probability that plans for most landscape projects can be used for a second project, but detail drawings and particularly specifications can be—and too frequently are—re-used by others than the author. Hence this provision.

ARTICLE 8. TERMINATION. Needs no comment.

ARTICLE 9: SIGNATURES. Obviously signature blanks are to be revised as may be necessary.

Appendix 12-C
Invitation for Bids

The _____ will receive bids for the

_____

until _____ AM/PM _____ time on the _____ day of _____ 19_____ at the _____ at which time and place all Bids will be publicly opened and read aloud.

Sealed Bids are invited upon the several items and quantities as follows:
[list].

Contract Documents, including Drawings and Specifications, are on file at the office of the Landscape Architect, _____ and at the _____ _____.

Copies of the Contract Documents may be obtained at the office of _____ on payment of $_____ for each set of Documents so obtained. Said sum is refundable upon return of all Documents in good condition not later than seven (7) days following opening of Bids. Plans may be examined without cost.

A certified check or bank draft, payable to the _____ or a satisfactory Bid Bond executed by the Bidder and an acceptable surety, in an amount equal to _____ percent (_____%) of the total Base Bid shall be submitted with each bid as a guaranty that if the Proposal is accepted the Bidder will execute the Contract and file acceptable Performance and Labor and Material Bonds within ten (10) days after award of the Contract.

The _____ hereinafter called the Owner, reserves the right to reject any and all Proposals and waive any formality or technicality in any Proposal in the interest of the Owner.

Bids may be held by the Owner for a period not to exceed thirty (30) days from the date of Bids for the purpose of reviewing the Bids and investigating the qualifications of the Bidders, prior to awarding the Contract.

Document 11A, © The American Society of Landscape Architects. Reprinted with permission.

Appendix 12-D
About Document 11A, Invitation for Bids

Advertisement for Bids: Laws governing work usually require that announcement of bidding be published as a legal notice in certain newspapers. This may be done in private work as a direct communication to each of a list of contractors. When this is done, the Invitation should be bound as a part of the contract documents.

Explanatory Notes for Using Form 11A— Invitation for Bids:

First [space]: Insert Owner's name.

Next [space]: Name, description and location of the project.

In entering the time and place of bid opening, be sure to state the time zone, such as "Pacific Daylight Saving Time" etc.

Under "Sealed Bids . . . as follows," state divisions of work, if divided and/or "one lump sum bid covering all work specified," or "Unit price bid covering all work specified."

After "the Office of the Landscape Architect," enter the Landscape Architect's name or firm name. After "and at the," enter other location or locations, at which the plans are on file, *if any.* Otherwise leave blank.

Refundable payment for set of Documents is normally equal to the cost of physical replacement of the documents plus an amount to cover the handling charges connected therewith. "A certified check . . . payable to the" (enter Owner's name) ". . . in an amount equal to" (this amount is normally 5 percent on large jobs, escalating on smaller jobs to 10 percent).

Issued by the American Society of Landscape Architects. Reprinted with permission.

Name of Project _____

_____

Location _____

_____

Gentlemen:

Pursuant to and in compliance with the advertisement for bids dated _____ 19_____, and Instructions to Bidders and other documents related thereto, the undersigned, having familiarized _____ self selves with the existing conditions on the site and the conditions under which the work is to be done, hereby proposes to furnish all labor, materials, equipment, and services to perform all specified work for the Site Improvement on the above named project in strict accordance with the Contract Documents and all addenda issued thereto at the prices price set forth on the accompanying bid form sheets attached hereto.

If written notice of acceptance of this bid is mailed, telegraphed, or delivered to the undersigned within _____ days after the opening of bids, or at any time thereafter before this bid is withdrawn, the undersigned agrees to execute and deliver a contract in the form specified and furnish the required bonds within _____ days after the prescribed forms are presented to him for signature.

Security in the sum of _____ ($_____) Dollars in the form of _____, is submitted herewith in accordance with the Instructions to Bidders.

a corporation
The bidder is a partnership and the name of an individual every person interested in this bid is as follows:

_____.

Document 11C, © The American Society of Landscape Architects, Inc. Reprinted with permission.

Notice of acceptance of this Bid shall be mailed to the undersigned at the following address:

By_____

Title _____

By _____

Title _____

Address _____

Phone No. _____

Furnish all bidders with identical forms, setting forth in detail all essential aspects of the bids. The form of the proposal is customarily bound in the specification book as one of the contract documents. Duplicates should be provided for contractor's copies. Additional copies should be available.

Actual dollar values should be set forth in words as well as figures. Where alternate bids and/or unit prices are required, these are also part of the proposal. If options or substitutes are permitted or requested to award of contract, these should also be provided for in connection with the proposal. The amount and type of bid bond or guarantee should be recorded, as well as the conditions regarding its return or forfeiture.

[Standard forms available from the ASLA:]

Bid Form:	ASLA Document 11C
Lump Sum Bid:	ASLA Document 11C-1
Unit Price Bid:	ASLA Document 11C-2

Issued by the American Society of Landscape Architects. Reprinted with permission.

Appendix 12-G
Instructions to Bidders

1. PROPOSAL FORM:

These Contract Documents include a complete set of bidding and contract forms which are for the convenience of the bidders and are not to be detached, filled out, or executed. Separate copies of Bid Forms are furnished for that purpose. These must be enclosed and sealed in an envelope which states on the outside: Sealed Bid for (Name of Project) _____.

2. INTERPRETATIONS AND ADDENDA:

No oral interpretation will be made to any bidder as to the meaning of the specifications and drawings. Interpretations, if made, shall be written in the form of an addendum and sent to all bidders to whom specifications have been issued.

3. EXAMINATION OF THE SITE:

Each bidder shall visit the site of the proposed work to fully acquaint himself with the conditions and difficulties attending the performance of the Contract. No additional compensation nor relief from any obligations of the Contract will be granted because of a lack of knowledge of the site or the conditions under which the work will be accomplished.

4. TIME:

Proposals will be received at _____ until _____ AM _____ Standard _____ time, _____ PM _____ Daylight Saving, _____, 19_____. No bids shall be permitted to be withdrawn after the time set for bid opening.

5. OPENING BIDS:

All bids received prior to the opening time shall be securely kept until the day and the hour above stated at which time all bids will be publicly opened

Document 11B, issued by the American Society of Landscape Architects. Reprinted with permission.

and read. No bids will be received after the above stated time.

6. RIGHT TO REJECT BIDS:

The Owner reserves the right to accept any part, or all of any bid, and to reject any and all or parts of any and all bids. Any proposal which contains items not specified, or which does not complete all the items scheduled for bid, shall be considered informal and $\begin{matrix} shall \\ may \end{matrix}$ be rejected on this basis.

7. SIGNATURE AND LEGIBILITY:

The prices for work and the names, addresses and signatures of the Bidders shall be clearly and legibly written. Signatures shall be signed in the space provided and in compliance with all legal requirements.

8. BID GUARANTEE:

Each proposal must be accompanied by a certified check, bank draft, or bid bond in an amount equal to _____ percent (%) of the amount of the bid. This guarantee shall be executed in favor of and guarantee to the Owner that the bidder will execute the Agreement and furnish the Performance and Labor and Material Bonds as required by the Contract Documents.

The aforesaid guarantee deposits of unsuccessful Bidders will be returned as soon as practical after the opening of the Bids.

9. EXECUTION OF CONTRACT AND DELIVERY OF BONDS:

The successful Bidder shall within _____ days after notice that his proposal has been accepted enter into a contract and deliver to the Owner a Performance Bond and a Labor and Material Bond each respectively issued by an approved surety company satisfactory to the Owner in an amount equal to the total price bid.

10. SPECIAL CONDITIONS:

_____
_____
_____
_____

Appendix 12-H
About Document 11B, Instructions to Bidders

The Instructions to Bidders, otherwise known as Notice to Bidders, contains information partially similar in nature to that included in the Invitation or Announcement for Bids, but goes into greater detail regarding legal aspects and requirements concerning preparation, submission and consideration of proposals, and overall framework of the project. A Schedule of Drawings may be included, and also Special Conditions of the job, unless published elsewhere.

Explanatory Notes for Using ASLA Document 11B—Instructions to Bidders [see also notes for use with the Invitation to Bid, reprinted in this book as Appendix 12-D.]

Paragraph 9. Execution of Contract and Delivery of Bonds. Fill in the number of days allowed after the bid acceptance until the signing of the contract and posting of the Performance Bond. Usually 5 or 10 days.

Paragraph 10. Insert any special conditions which pertain to this particular project. May include such items as union labor and/or State sales tax requirements; contractor's verification of topographic survey, and/or quantities of itemized units of work; statement of Bidder's qualifications required, etc.

Issued by the American Society of Landscape Architects. Reprinted with permission.

Appendix 12-I
Contract for Construction

THIS CONTRACT, entered into this _____ day of _____ 19_____ by and between _____ _____, a partnership corporation existing under the laws of the State of _____, an individual residing at _____,
(Street, City, State)
hereinafter called the "Owner," and _____ a partnership corporation existing under the laws of the State of _____, an individual trading as _____ of _____,
(Street, City, State)
hereinafter called the "Contractor," witnesseth:

In consideration of the mutual covenants existing between the parties, and the further consideration specifically set forth herein, the parties agree as follows:

ARTICLE I. STATEMENT OF WORK

The Contractor shall furnish all materials, labor, equipment and services, and shall perform all work for the property improvement at _____

_____
in strict accordance with the specifications dated _____, and addendum nos. _____ all prepared by _____ Landscape Architect, and the drawings dated _____ including revisions thru _____, all prepared by _____ Landscape Architect.

ARTICLE II. THE CONTRACT PRICE

The Owner shall pay the Contractor for the performance of the work called for under this Contract, a lump sum, in current funds, of _____ ($_____) Dollars.

ARTICLE II. THE CONTRACT PRICE (Alternate)

The Owner shall pay the Contractor for the _____

Issued by the American Society of Landscape Architects. Reprinted with permission.

performance of the work called for under this Contract, in current funds, subject to additions and deductions, as proved in the statement of the unit prices, and as hereinafter stated, the sum of _____ ($_____) Dollars, more or less; the final amount to be determined by the total work performed at the itemized unit prices bid.

ARTICLE III. TIME OF COMPLETION

The Contractor agrees to begin work covered by this contract within [a]_____ days after signing this Contract, weather permitting and to complete the work fully on or before _____. The time of completion shall not be extended except for unavoidable delays caused by but not limited to fires, floods, storms, strikes, accidents, illness, or other circumstances beyond the Contractor's control. The Landscape Architect shall be the sole judge of such "unavoidable delays," and the extent thereof, and in the event that such a determination is made and duly submitted to the parties in writing, the date of completion shall be extended by a length of time equal to that lost by such circumstances. For each and every day said work shall be delayed beyond the time specified herein, or beyond the extension of time as otherwise expressly provided, the Contractor shall pay to said Owner, as liquidated damages, the sum of _____ ($_____) Dollars.

ARTICLE IV. PAYMENT FOR WORK

From time to time as the work progresses, the Contractor, upon request, shall receive up to [b]_____ percent payment on the basis of unit prices bid for completed work upon certification by the Landscape Architect, and approval and acceptance by the Owner. The [c]_____ percent withheld shall constitute the final payment which shall be made upon final approval by the Landscape Architect.

ARTICLE IV. PAYMENT FOR WORK (Alternate)

On certification by the Landscape Architect,

[a]See "Special Notes for Use in Preparation," in Appendix 12-J.

The Owner shall within [d]_____ days of approval and acceptance pay the Contractor a lump sum in the amount of this Contract less any amounts advanced to the Contractor or otherwise paid out in behalf of the Contractor.

ARTICLE V. CONTRACT DOCUMENTS

The Contract Documents shall consist of the following component parts: [e]_____
  a. This Instrument.
  b. General Conditions and Supplementary Conditions.
  c. Instructions to Bidders and issued addenda.
  d. Technical Specifications as referred to in Article I of this Instrument.
  e. Drawings referred to in Article I of this Instrument.
  f. Itemized Unit Prices Bid.
  g. Performance Bond.
  h. Applicable Standard Details as required by the municipality wherein the work occurs.

It is expressly agreed that this written instrument and the other documents set forth in this Article and attached hereto, and which are made a part hereof as fully as if they were set forth at length herein, embody the entire contract between the parties. In the event that the provisions of any of the component parts of this contract conflict, the provision in the component part first enumerated in this article shall govern, except that addenda shall take precedence over the original construction documents as shall applicable standard details required by the municipality or as otherwise specifically stated.

IN WITNESS WHEREOF, the parties hereto have executed this agreement in duplicate in the State of _____ on the day and year first above written.

Witness:

[signatures and addresses].

Appendix 12-J
Contract for Construction: Explanatory Notes

The preparation of Contracts for Construction is generally a part of the obligation assumed by a Landscape Architect in his contract with a client.

The Contract for Construction is an agreement between the Owner and the Construction Contractor. There is a sequence in this arrangement for letting work that varies with the formality required by the Owner and the extensiveness of the work. In general, the sequence is as follows:

1. Advertisement for Bids.
2. Instructions to bidders.
3. Form of Proposal to do the work.
4. General Conditions which describe the conditions under which the work is to be done such as: superintendence, progress schedule, payments, work changes, care of the work, sanitary and safety facilities, use of premises, clean-up, inspection, etc.
5. Special Conditions which describe conditions peculiar to the particular job.
6. Description of the Work to be done under the contract:
   a. The drawings themselves.
   b. Written specifications supplementing the drawings.
7. Assurances of financial and technical abilities of the Contractor proposing to do the work.
8. The Contract for Construction, which is the legal document signed by Owner and Contractor. In the above Proposal the bidder stipulates his price and agrees to sign a contract if awarded the job. This is that contract.
9. Acceptance of Work by the Owner and release by the Contractor.

It should be noted that the formality of the procedure and documents should be commensurate with the size of the job. Simple jobs should have

Issued by the American Society of Landscape Architects. Reprinted with permission.

simple documents. Fussy, intensive, expensive jobs should have equally detailed and thorough specifications. Specifications should be kept to a minimum to avoid scaring the competing contractors and/or increasing the bid. However, there is a minimum amount of specifying and legal signing that can be done in order to protect yourself and your client in the event of suit or court case. It is essential that the contract (including drawings and specifications) be as simple, clear and concise as possible; that there be no ambiguity and that there is a clear understanding of the work to be done, the amount of payments, the way payments are to be made, and the date of completion.

Contracts for construction can be generally divided into two categories—those being done for a fixed lump sum; and those being done at a unit price basis on the actual amount of installed work. Always be sure that this is clearly stated. In many instances unit prices are itemized in lump sum bids in order to have a preconceived measure for additions or subtractions from the lump sum price where changes occur during the progress of the work.

SPECIAL NOTES FOR USE IN PREPARATION. The following items refer to the small letters in parentheses at the locations indicated, on the standard form of Contract for Construction:

ARTICLE III
  (a)Insert "ten" or other determined number of days.
ARTICLE IV
  (b)Insert "ninety (90%)" or other determined percentage.
  (c)Insert "ten (10%)" or other held back percentage to make total 100%.
ARTICLE IV (Alternate)
  (d)Insert "fifteen (15)" or other determined number of days.
ARTICLE V
  (e)On occasion small jobs will not require all of these enumerated documents. In such case omit from this list the documents which are not applicable.

Appendix 12-K
Contract for Construction: The ASLA Short Form Contract for Small Construction Contracts

THIS CONTRACT, entered into this _____ day of _____, 19_____ by and between _____, hereinafter called the "Owner," and _____, hereinafter called the "Contractor,"

WITNESSETH,

In consideration of the mutual covenants existing between the parties, and the further consideration specifically set forth herein, the parties agree as follows:

ARTICLE I. STATEMENT OF WORK

The Contractor shall furnish materials, labor, equipment and services, and shall perform all work as shown on the Drawings and described in the Specifications prepared by _____, Landscape Architects, for _____, at _____ _____.

ARTICLE II. THE CONTRACT PRICE

The Owner shall pay the Contractor for the performance of the work called for under this Contract, a lump sum, in current funds, of _____ ($_____) Dollars.

ARTICLE II. THE CONTRACT PRICE (Alternate)

The Owner shall pay the Contractor for the performance of the work called for under this Contract, in current funds, subject to additions and deductions, as provided in the statement of unit prices, and as hereinafter stated, the sum of _____ ($_____) Dollars, more or less; the final amount to be determined by the total work performed at the itemized unit prices bid.

Document 11-1-2, © The American Society of Landscape Architects. Reprinted with permission.

ITEM	QUANTITY	UNIT PRICE	AMOUNT

_____

_____

_____

_____

_____

_____

_____

_____

_____

_____

_____

TOTAL

ARTICLE III. TIME OF COMPLETION

The Contractor agrees to begin work covered by this contract within 10 days after signing this Contract, weather permitting and to complete the work fully, exclusive of maintenance, on or before _____.

ARTICLE IV. PAYMENT FOR WORK

From time to time as the work progresses, the Contractor, upon submission of requisitions, shall receive progress payments not to exceed _____ percent of the total contract price, such payment to be made on the basis of completed work upon certification by the Landscape Architect. The _____ percent withheld shall constitute the final payment which shall be made upon final approval by the Landscape Architect.

ARTICLE V. CONTRACT DOCUMENTS

The Contract Documents shall consist of the following component parts: This Instrument, General Conditions, Technical Specifications, and Drawings. It is expressly agreed that this written instrument and the other documents set forth in this Article and attached hereto, and which are made a part hereof as fully as if they were set forth at length herein, embody the entire contract between the parties; and no verbal alternatives or variations shall be binding on the parties or create any obliga-tions or liabilities not set forth or provided for herein.

ARTICLE VI. GENERAL CONDITIONS

1. *Drawings, Specifications, and Related Data*

   a. Contract Documents

   The Contract Documents shall include those enumerated in Article V above. The intent of the Contract Documents is that the Contractor shall furnish all labor, materials, equipment, and services necessary for the completion of the proposed work. The Contract Documents shall be signed in three counterpart copies by the Owner and the Contractor and each signer shall retain a copy and the third copy shall be filed with the Landscape Architect.

   b. Approvals

   All samples, shop drawings, or schedules required for approval shall be furnished by the Contractor as directed subject to approval by the Landscape Architect. The work shall be done in accordance with these approved items, and the Landscape Architect's drawings and specifications.

   c. Surveys, Permits, and Regulations

   Unless otherwise specified, the Owner shall furnish all surveys, at his expense. Permits, licenses, royalties, and lien fees necessary for the prosecution of the work shall be secured and paid for by the Contractor. Easements for permanent structures or permanent changes in existing facilities shall be secured and paid for by the Owner, unless otherwise specified to achieve proper conformity.

   The Contractor shall give all notices and comply with all laws, ordinances, rules, and regulations concerning the construction of the project as drawn and specified. If the Contractor finds that the Drawings and Specifications are at variance therewith, he shall immediately notify the Landscape Architect, who shall promptly make such changes as are necessary.

   d. Existing Conditions

   Existing conditions including surface features, soil boring data, and any underground utilities shown on the plans and/or referred to in the specifications are for informational purposes only and shall not be deemed as part of the plans and specifications. It shall be the Contractor's obligation to verify and augment such information and data to fully satisfy himself as to the conditions under which the work will be done. The Contractor shall maintain in operating condition all active utilities encountered in this construction. He shall contact all public utilities involved and have their representative locate their pipes, conduits, cables or other facilities before construction is started. The Owner and the Landscape Architect do not assume responsibility for location or disturbance of utilities or other existing features or conditions encountered on this project. Any replacement or relocation cost shall be the Contractor's responsibility, unless otherwise specified.

2. *Owner, Contractor, and Landscape Architect Relationship*

   a. Access to Work

   It shall be the obligation of the Contractor to provide proper facilities to permit the Owner and his representative to observe the work during any stage of the construction.

   b. Landscape Architect's Responsibility and Authority

   All work shall be done subject to the approval of the Landscape Architect. All decisions and questions which may arise as to the quality or acceptability of materials furnished, work performed, progress of the work, interpretation of drawings and specifications, and all questions as to acceptable fulfillment of the Contract by the Contractor shall be made by the Landscape Architect.

   All claims of the Contractor or the Owner shall be made to the Landscape Architect for decision. All decisions of the Landscape Architect shall be made in writing within a reasonable time and shall be final except where time and/or financial considerations are involved, which shall be subject to arbitration.

c. Arbitration

All claims subject to arbitration under the Contract shall be promptly submitted to arbitration upon demand by either party to the dispute. It is mutually agreed that the decision of the arbitrators shall be a condition precedent to any right of legal action that either party may take against the other.

Notice of demand for arbitration shall be in writing delivered in person or by certified or registered mail to the other party to the Contract. Simultaneously a copy shall be filed with the Landscape Architect. The notice of demand for arbitration shall be made within a reasonable time after the dispute but in no case shall such demand be made later than the time of final payment unless expressly stipulated otherwise in the Contract.

The Contractor shall not cause a delay of the work during any arbitration proceedings except by agreement with the Owner.

The procedure of arbitration shall be the standard form of arbitration procedure of the American Arbitration Association.

d. Separate Contracts

The Owner reserves the right to let other contracts in connection with the work under this contract. The Contractor shall provide reasonable access and opportunity for the other contractors to do their work and shall fit, connect, and coordinate his work with theirs so as not to cause them or him any undue delay or impediment to the prompt and proper performance and completion of the work by each.

e. Owner's Right to Do Work

The Owner, without prejudice to any other right or remedy he may have, shall have the right to prosecute the work in the event the Contractor fails to perform the work properly or fails to perform any provisions of the contract. A prerequisite of such action by the Owner shall be three (3) days written notice to the Contractor and approval of such action by the Landscape Architect. The amount charged the Contractor for making good such deficiencies shall be approved by the Landscape Architect and may be deducted from payments then or thereafter due the Contractor.

f. Owner's Right to Terminate Contract

In the event of any default by the Contractor, the Owner, without prejudice to any other right or remedy he may have, shall have the right to terminate the employment of the Contractor after giving the Contractor seven (7) days written notice. Such notice of termination shall be subsequent to default by the Contractor and after receiving written notice from the Landscape Architect certifying cause for such action. It shall be considered default by the Contractor whenever he shall:

1. Declare bankruptcy, become insolvent, or assign his assets for the benefit of his creditors.
2. Violate or disregard important provisions of the Contract or instructions from the Landscape Architect.
3. Fail to prosecute the work according to the agreed Schedule of Completion, including amendments and/or modifications thereof.
4. Fail to provide a qualified superintendent, competent workmen or subcontractors, or proper materials, or failure to make prompt payment thereof.

Upon termination the Owner may take possession of the premises and of all materials, tools, equipment, and appliances thereon and finish the work by whatever method he may deem expedient. In such case the Contractor shall not be entitled to receive any further payment until the work is finished.

In case the statement of accounts shows that the cost to complete the work including compensation for additional landscape architectural, managerial, and administrative services, is less than that which would have been the cost to the Owner had the work been completed by the Contractor under the terms of the Contract, the excess shall be paid to the Contractor. If such expense exceeds the unpaid balance, the Contractor shall pay to the Owner the difference, as certified by the Landscape Architect.

g. Contractor's Right to Stop Work or Terminate Contract

Upon the occurrence of any of the situations enumerated hereunder, the Contractor shall have the right to terminate the contract and recover from the Owner payment for all work executed including any proven loss sustained upon any equipment or materials and reasonable profit and damages, provided that seven (7) days written notice is given to the Owner and the Landscape Architect:

1. If the work should be stopped under order of any court or other public authority for a period of thirty (30) days through no fault of the Contractor or of anyone employed by him.
2. If the Landscape Architect should fail to issue any Certificate of Payment, through no fault of the Contractor within seven (7) days after formal request by the Contractor for payment.
3. If the Owner should fail to pay the Contractor within seven (7) days after the Landscape Architect has issued a Certificate of Payment or a Board of Arbitration has made an award.

h. Correction of Work

All work and materials condemned by the Landscape Architect as failing to comply with the Contract Documents shall be promptly removed, replaced, and/or re-executed by the

Contractor to bring it into compliance with the requirements. This shall be done at the expense of the Contractor without cost to the Owner and shall include making good all work of other contractors destroyed or damaged by such removal or replacement.

i. Liens

Before final payment is made the Contractor shall furnish the Owner with a full release of liens signed by all subcontractors and material men associated in any way with the work. These liens shall be accompanied by a notarized affidavit (sworn statement) to the effect that all claims of any character pertaining to the performance of the Contract, including subcontractors, material suppliers, and labor have been paid in full and that the acceptance of final payment is acknowledged as a release of the Owner from any and all claims arising under or by virtue of the Contract.

3. *Insurance and Protection*

The Contractor shall secure and maintain insurance coverages, in the amounts required and/or stipulated under paragraph 6 of this Article, protecting him from claims under Workmen's Compensation and Employer's Liability Insurance as required by law; Public Liability, Bodily Injury including death, and Property Damage which may arise in the course of carrying out the work under this contract. Certificates of such insurance shall be filed with the Owner and the Landscape Architect before commencing any of the work under this contract.

The Contractor shall adequately protect the work, adjacent property, and the public and shall be responsible for any damage or injury due to his act or neglect. The Contractor shall save harmless the Owner from and against any and all losses and/or claims brought or recovered against the Contractor or his subcontractors by reason of any error, omission, or act of the Contractor, his agents or employees in the execution of the work or the guarding of it.

The Owner may, at his own expense, obtain and maintain such insurance as will protect him from possible contingent liability to others for damages because of bodily injury or death, which the Contractor is required to insure against under provision of the Contract.

4. *Progress and Completion of the Work*

a. Schedule of Completion

Following the execution of the Contract by the Owner, the Contractor shall begin work within ten (10) days, unless otherwise notified in writing, and shall prosecute the work regularly and without interruption, weather permitting, so as to complete the work within the time stated in the Proposal.

b. Changes in the Work

If and as the need arises, the Owner may order in writing changes and/or extra work without invalidating the Contract. At the time of ordering such changes, additions, deletions, or modifications, the amount or method of compensation and any adjustment in the time of completion shall be determined and stipulated in writing.

c. Clean-up

The Contractor shall at all times keep the premises and public streets free from an accumulation of waste material or rubbish caused by his employees or work, and at the completion of the work he shall remove all his waste and excess material, rubbish, and equipment so as to leave the work and the premises neat and clean and ready for the purpose for which they were intended.

5. *Payments*

a. Method of Payment

Payments shall be made in accordance with Article 4 of the Contract. The payment of the final amount owing the Contractor shall

constitute a waiver of all claims by the Owner except:

1. Claims arising from failure to comply with the plans and specifications.
2. Claims arising from faulty work or materials appearing after substantial completion.
3. Claims arising by virtue of any special guarantee specified in the Contract.
4. Claims of the Owner previously made against the Contractor but as yet unsettled.

The acceptance of the final payment by the Contractor shall constitute a waiver of all claims by the Contractor except:

1. Claims previously made by the Contractor but as yet unsettled.

If the Owner should fail to pay the amount stated in any Certificate of Payment issued by the Landscape Architect or in any award by arbitration, the Contractor shall receive in addition to the amount certified to, interest thereon at the legal rate at the place of the work.

b. Payment Withheld

Any part or the whole of any payment may be withheld by the Landscape Architect to the extend he deems necessary and reasonable to protect the Owner should the Landscape Architect discover evidence of:

1. Defective work not corrected.
2. Claims filed against the Contractor.
3. Reasonable evidence indicating probable filing of claims against the Contractor.
4. Failure of the Contractor to make proper payments to subcontractors or for material or for labor.
5. A reasonable doubt that the Contract can be completed for the then unpaid balance.
6. Unsatisfied damage to another Contractor.

7. Unsatisfactory progress of the work by the Contractor.

When the above grounds are removed, the amount withheld because of them shall be paid to the Contractor, subject to and within the other terms of this Contract.

6. *Special Conditions of the Contract*
[list]

IN WITNESS WHEREOF, the parties hereto have executed this Agreement the day and the year first above written.

WITNESS

_____

_____

OWNER

_____

_____

WITNESS

_____

_____

CONTRACTOR

_____

_____

Appendix 12-L
Change Order

Date: _____ Change order no.: _____

Sheet ___ of ___

To Contractor: _____

Project: _____

You are authorized to make the following changes in this contract:
[list]

Previous contract total: _____ $_____

Contract shall be (increased) (decreased) by the sum of _____ $_____

Contract total including this change order: _____ $_____

The Contract time will be (increased by) (decreased by) unchanged _____days

Contractor acceptance: _____ Date: _____

Owner approval: _____ Date: _____

Landscape Architect: _____ Date: _____

Document B-107, © 1972 by The American Society of Landscape Architects. Reprinted with permission.

Appendix 12-M
Certificate for Payment

Date: _____ Certificate number: _____

Sheet ___ of ___

Project: _____

_____

Owner: _____

Contractor: _____

Contract date: _____

This is to certify that there will be due and payable from the Owner to the Contractor on _____ _____ the sum of: _____ dollars ($_____).

The status of account for this project is as follows:

Original contract sum: _____ $_____

Net change by change orders: _____ $_____

Contract sum to date: _____ $_____

Total completed and stored to date: _____ $_____

Retainage: _____% _____ $_____

Total earned less retainage: _____ $_____

Less previous certificates for payment: ___$_____

This certificate: _____ $_____

Certified by: _____

This certificate is not negotiable. It is payable only to the payee named herein and its issuance, payment, and acceptance are without prejudice to any rights of the Owner Contractor under their Contract.

Document B-109, © 1972 by The American Society of Landscape Architects. Reprinted with permission.

Appendix 12-N
Sample of Instructions to Bidders
on a Federal Housing Project

1. **USE OF SEPARATE BID FORMS**

Attention is directed to the fact that these Specifications include a complete set of bidding and contract forms. These are for the convenience of bidders, and are not to be detached from the Specifications, or filled out, or executed. Separate copies of Bid Forms are furnished for that purpose, in quadruplicate, three to be submitted with the bid and one to be retained by the bidder for his records. Only one of the three copies of the bid shall be signed. The other two shall be conformed copies only.

2. **INTERPRETATIONS**

No oral interpretation will be made to any bidder as to the meaning of the Specifications including Drawings. Every request for such an interpretation shall be made in writing to the Local Authority as [address of federal office issuing specifications]. Any inquiry received ten or more days prior to the date fixed for opening of bids will be given consideration. Every interpretation made to a bidder will be in the form of an addendum to the Specifications which, if issued, will be on file in the office at the Local Authority and the office of the Architect at least seven days before bids are opened. In addition, addenda will be mailed to each bidder, but it shall be the bidder's responsibility to make inquiry as to addenda issued. All such addenda shall become part of the Contract and all bidders shall be bound by such addenda, whether or not received by the bidders.

3. **ALTERNATIVE BIDS**

Alternative bids will not be considered.

4. **PROPOSALS**

a. All bids must be submitted on forms prepared by the Local Authority and shall be subject to all requirements of the Specifications, including the Drawings, and this Instruction to Bidders. Only the original shall be signed. Two additional conformed copies shall be submitted.

b. Bid Documents shall be enclosed in envelopes (outer and inner), both of which shall be sealed and clearly labeled with the words "Bid Documents," the project number, name of bidder, and date and time of opening so as to guard against premature opening of any bid.

c. A second inner *sealed* envelope marked "Data on Specialty Items" containing the information required by Section 9, below, shall be enclosed in the outer envelope.

d. The Local Authority may consider as informal any bid on which there is an alteration of or departure from the Bid Form hereto attached.

e. The Contract will be based upon the completion of the work according to the Specifications (including the Drawings), together with all Addenda thereto, under the lowest proposal submitted by a responsible bidder, irrespective of the options permitted by the Contract which the bidder chooses to use. The Local Authority has determined, by its inclusion of the options, that any of the requested options are equally acceptable. The bidder is, therefore, required to submit only his lowest proposal for the work to be performed inasmuch as no other will be considered.

5. **BID GUARANTY (OR BID BOND)**

a. The bid must be accompanied by a bid guaranty which shall not be less than five percent (5%) of the amount of the bid, and at the option of the bidder may be a certified check, bank draft, U.S. Government Bonds (at par value), or a bid bond secured by a guarantee company or a surety company in the form attached. No bid will be considered unless it is so guaranteed. Certified check or bank draft must be made payable to the order of the Housing Authority of [the city]. Cash deposits will not be accepted. The bid guaranty shall insure the execution of the contract and the furnishing of performance and payment bond or bonds by the successful bidder all as required by the Specifications.

b. Revised Bids, whether forwarded by mail or telegram, if representing an increase in excess of two percent (2%) of the original bid, must have the bid guaranty adjusted accordingly; otherwise the revision of the bid will not be considered and the original bid shall remain in force.

c. In case Bid Guaranty is the form of a certified check, bank draft, or U.S. Government Bonds, the Local Authority may make such disposition of the same as will accomplish the purpose for which submitted. Certified checks or bank drafts, or the amount thereof, and U.S. Government bonds of unsuccessful bidders will be returned as soon as practicable after the opening of Bids.

6. **COLLUSIVE AGREEMENTS**

a. Each person submitting to the Local Authority a bid for any portion of the work contemplated by the bidding documents shall execute an affidavit in the form herein provided, to the effect that he has not colluded with any other person, firm, or corporation in regard to any bid submitted. Such affidavit shall be attached to the bid.

b. Each person submitting a low bid for any subcontract work shall submit to the Contractor an affidavit in the form provided in Section 4 of the General Conditions.

c. Failure on the part of any bidder for either the prime contract or subcontracts to observe these provisions shall be cause for rejection of his bid.

7. **STATEMENT OF BIDDER'S QUALIFICATIONS**

Each bid and each conformed copy thereof must be accompanied by a statement on the form furnished for that purpose, a copy of which is included in the Specifications, of the bidder's financial resources, his construction experience, and his organization and equipment available for the work contemplated. The Local Authority shall have the right to take such steps as it deems necessary to determine the ability of the bidder to perform the work and the bidder shall furnish the Local Authority all such information and data for this purpose as the Local Authority may request. The right is reserved to reject any bid where an investigation of the available evidence or information does not satisfy the Local Authority that the bidder is qualified to carry out properly the terms of the Specifications.

8. OPTIONS

The attention of all bidders, whether prime or subcontract, is directed to the "List of Options" contained in the Special Conditions.

9. DATA ON SPECIALTY ITEMS

a. Each general bidder who includes in his bid the costs of the mechanical branches of the contract work shall submit, with his bid, in a separate sealed envelope identified on the outside by his name, project number, and marked "Data on Specialty Items," a breakdown of his overall bid showing the amounts included therein for the following subcontracts and work:

Amount of Site Improvements (Roads, Walks, etc.):	$_____
Amount of Lawns and Planting:	$_____
Amount of Plumbing Bid:	$_____
Amount of Heating Bid:	$_____
Amount of Interior Electric Wiring Bid:	$_____
Amount of Outside Utilities (Sewers, Water, Gas):	$_____
Amount of Electrical Distribution-Overhead:	$_____
All Remaining Work:	$_____
Total Overall Bid Price:	$_____

b. This information is required for analytical purposes, shall have no bearing upon the determination of the lowest responsible bidder, and will not be divulged to the public at bid opening.

10. CORRECTIONS

Erasures or other changes in the bids must be explained or noted over the signature of the bidder.

11. TIME FOR RECEIVING BIDS

a. Bids received prior to the time of opening will be securely kept, unopened. The officer whose duty it is to open them will decide when the specified time has arrived, and no bid received thereafter will be considered; except that when a bid arrives by mail after the time fixed for opening, but before award is made, and it is shown to the satisfaction of the officer authorized to make the award the nonarrival on time was due solely to delay in the mails for which the bidder was not responsible, such bid will be received and considered. No responsibility will attach to an officer for the premature opening of a bid not properly addressed and identified. Unless specifically authorized, telegraphic bids will not be considered, but modification by telegraph of bids already submitted will be considered if received prior to the hour set for opening; proved, that written confirmation of such modification over the signature of the bidder is placed in the mail and postmarked prior to the time set for bid opening.

b. Bidders are cautioned that, while telegraphic modification of bids may be received as provided above, such modifications, if not explicit and if in any sense subject to misinterpretation, shall make the bid so modified or amended subject to rejection.

c. Bidders are cautioned to allow ample time for transmittal of bids by mail or otherwise. Bidders should secure correct information relative to the probable time of arrival and distribution of mail at the place where bids are to be opened; and, so far as practicable, make due allowance for possible delays in order to avoid the necessity for investigations of claims that such delays in receipt of bids were due solely to delay in the mails as provided in this section.

12. OPENING OF BIDS

At the time and place fixed for the opening of bids, every bid received within the time fixed for receiving bids will be opened and publicly read aloud, irrespective of any irregularities therein. Bidders and other persons properly interested may be present, in person or by representative.

13. WITHDRAWAL OF BIDS

Bids may be withdrawn on written or telegraphic request dispatched by the bidder in time for delivery in the normal course of business prior to the time fixed for opening; provided, that written confirmation of any telegraphic withdrawal over the signature of the bidder is placed in the mail and postmarked prior to the time set for bid opening. Negligence on the part of the bidder in preparing his bid confers no right of withdrawal or modification of his bid after such bid has been opened.

14. AWARD OF CONTRACT: REJECTION OF BIDS

a. The Contract will be awarded to the responsible bidder who submitted the lowest proposal complying with the conditions of the Invitation of Bids, provided his bid is reasonable and it is to the interest of the Local Authority to accept it. The bidder to whom the award is made will be notified at the earliest practicable date. The Local Authority, however, reserves the right to reject any and all bids and to waive any informality in bids received whenever such rejection or waiver is in the interest of the Local Authority.

b. The Local Authority is prohibited from making any awards to contractors or approving as subcontractors any individuals or firms which are on lists of contractors ineligible to receive awards from the United States, as furnished from time to time by the FHA. The current list of ineligible contractors is available for inspection by prospective bidders at the offices of the Local Authority.

c. The Local Authority also reserves the right to reject the bid of any bidder who previously failed to perform properly, or to complete on time, contracts of a similar nature; who is not in a position to perform the contract; or who has habitually and without just cause neglected the payment of bills or otherwise disregarded his obligations to subcontractors, materialmen, or employees. In determining the lowest responsible bidder the following elements, in addition to those above mentioned, will be considered; whether the bidder involved (1) maintains a permanent place of business; (2) has adequate plant equipment available to do the work properly and expeditiously; (3) has suitable financial resources to meet the obligations incident to the work; (4) has appropriate technical experience. The Local Authority reserves the right to consider as unqualified to perform the work of general construction any bidder who does not habitually perform with his own forces the branches of structural concrete, masonry, and carpentry.

d. The ability of a bidder to obtain a performance bond shall not be regarded as the sole test of such bidder's competency or responsibility.

15. Estimates of Costs
The successful bidder may be required to cooperate with the Local Authority and the Architect in a breakdown of his bid price in order to show the division of costs between dwelling facilities, non-dwelling facilities and site improvements.

16. Performance and Payment Bond, Execution of Contract
a. Subsequent to the award and within ten days after the prescribed forms are presented for signature, the successful bidder shall execute and deliver to the Local Authority a contract in the form included in the Specifications in such number of counterparts as the Local Authority may require. Separate contract forms, in lieu of those found in the Specifications, shall be used for the purpose.

b. Having satisfied all conditions of award as set forth elsewhere in these documents, the successful bidder shall, within the period specified in 17*a* above, furnish a performance and payment bond in a penal sum of at least 100% of the amount of the contract as awarded, as security for the faithful performance of the contract and for the payment of all persons, firms, or corporations to whom the Contractor may become legally indebted for labor, materials, tools, equipment, or services, of any nature, employed or used by him in performing the work. Such bond shall be in the form of bond included in the Specifications and shall bear the same date as, or a date subsequent to the date of the contract.

c. On each such bond the rate of premium shall be stated, together with the total amount of the premium charged. The current power of attorney for the person who signs for any surety company shall be attached to such bond.

d. The failure of the successful bidder to execute such contract and to supply the required bonds within ten days after the prescribed forms are presented for signature, or within such extended period as the Local Authority may grant based upon reasons determined adequate by the Local Authority, shall constitute a default, and the Local Authority may either award the contract to the next responsible bidder or re-advertise for bids, and may charge against the bidder the difference between the amount for which a contract for the work is subsequently executed, irrespective of whether the amount thus due exceeds the amount of the bid guaranty.

**Appendix 12-0
Noncollusion Affidavit**

The Bidder, by its officers and by _____ _____, agent or representatives present at the time of filing this bid, being duly sworn, say on their oaths that neither they nor any of them have, in any way, directly or indirectly, entered into any arrangement or agreement with any other bidder, or with any public officer of the [state] whereby the affiant or affiants or either of them has paid or is to pay to any other bidder or any public officer any sum of money, or has given or is to give other bidder or public officer anything of value whatever; that the affiant or affiants or either of them has not entered, directly or indirectly, into any arrangement or agreement with any other bidder or bidders that tends to or does lessen or destroy free competition in the letting of the contract sought for by the attached bids; that no inducement of any form or character other than that which appears upon the face of the bid will be suggested, offered, paid, or delivered to any person whomsoever to influence the acceptance of the said bid or awarding of the contract; nor has this bidder any agreement or understanding of any kind whatsoever, with any person whomsoever to pay, deliver to, or share with any other person in any way or manner, any of the proceeds of the contract sought by this bid.

_____

_____

_____

_____

Subscribed and sworn to before me by _____ this _____ day of _____, 19_____.

_____

My commission expires:

_____

Subscribed and sworn to before me by _____ this _____ day of _____, 19_____.

_____

My commission expires:

_____

Appendix 12-P
Performance Bond

Know All Men by These Presents that _____ _____,
as Principal, hereinafter called the Contractor, and

_____
_____
_____,
as Surety, hereinafter called the Surety, are held and
firmly bound unto _____

_____
_____,
as Obligee, hereafter called the Owner, in the sum
of _____ Dollars ($_____) for the
payment whereof the Contractor and the Surety
bind themselves, their heirs, successors, administrators, executors and assigns, jointly and severally,
firmly by these Presents.

Whereas, the Contractor has by written agreement
dated _____, 19_____ entered into a Contract
with Owner for _____

_____
in accordance with drawings and specifications
prepared by _____

_____
_____
which agreement, hereinafter referred to as the
Contract, is by reference made a part of this bond as
is fully set forth herein.

Now, Therefore, the Conditions of This Obligation
are such that, if the Contractor shall promptly and
faithfully perform said Contract, then this obligation
shall be null and void; otherwise it shall remain in
full force and effect, and:

1. Whenever the Contractor shall be, and so
declared by the Owner, in default under the Contract, the Owner having performed the Owner's
obligations thereunder, the Surety may promptly

remedy the default, or shall promptly:

   a. Complete the Contract in accordance
with its terms and conditions, or

   b. Obtain a bid or bids for submission to
the Owner for completing the Contract in accordance with its terms and conditions, and upon
determination by the Owner and Surety of the
lowest responsible bidder, arrange for a contract
between such bidder and Owner, and make available as work progresses (even though there should
be a default or a succession of defaults under the
contract or contracts of completion arranged under
this paragraph) sufficient funds to pay the cost of
completion less the balance of the Contract price;
but not exceeding, including other costs and damages for which the surety may be liable hereunder,
the amount set forth in the first paragraph hereof.
The term "balance of the Contract price," as used
in this paragraph, shall mean the total amount payable by Owner to Contractor under the Contract
and any amendments thereto, less the amount
properly paid by Owner to Contractor.

   2. The Surety hereby waives notice of any
alteration or extension of time made by the Owner.

   3. Any suit under this bond must be instituted before the expiration of two (2) years from
the date on which final payment under the Contract
falls due.

   4. No right of action shall accrue on this
bond to or for the use of any person or corporation
other than the Owner named herein or the heirs,
executors, administrators or successors of Owner.

Signed and Sealed this _____ of _____ ad
19 _____.

In the presence of:
Witness:_____
Principal:_____(Seal)
Title:_____
Witness:_____
Surety:_____(Seal)
Title:_____

V

Landscape
Construction

13

Site Modification

Just satisfying the visible design requirements is only part of the landscape contractor's work. Conditions at the landscape site should provide a satisfactory environment for plant growth; the soil and the influence of nearby landscape features on the soil are of the utmost importance to the future development and growth of the newly installed landscape plants. Often the contractor will have to modify the site to provide proper moisture relationships, a suitable pH, and an adequate amount of soil for plant growth. Also, when construction is under way or such site modifications as grade changes are made, it may be necessary to protect existing plant materials. Later in this chapter we will discuss such techniques. Microenvironmental modifications, or planting techniques for individual plant specimens will be discussed in the next chapter, "The Planting and Establishment of Woody Plant Materials."

DRAINAGE SYSTEMS

Too often the drainage of water from the soil at the landscape site is ignored by the landscape architect and the landscape contractor. Any good farmer knows that a soil must be adequately drained if a high crop-yield is to be achieved. The same holds true for the growth and development of many of the woody plant species used on the landscape site. Both internal drainage and surface drainage should be considered when preparing the site for planting.

Internal drainage is controlled primarily by the soil type and by any physical damage that has occurred during the construction process. We recommend that landscape architects and landscape contractors consult the Soil Conservation Service to determine if there are drainage problems with the soil type at

Figure 13-1. *Poorly drained areas at a landscape site will limit the growth and development of plants on the site.*

Figure 13-2. *Types of drainage system designs that are adaptable to individual landscape sites. Notice the main lines and the various ways the laterals are tied into them.*

13-1

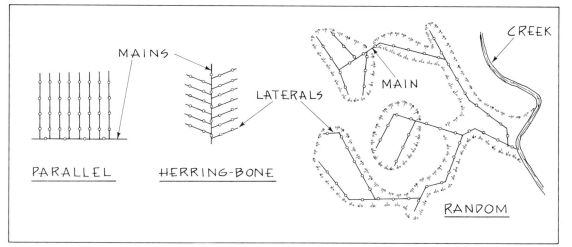

MAINS

LATERALS

PARALLEL

HERRING-BONE

CREEK

MAIN

RANDOM

13-2

the landscape site. The Service has data available and can make recommendations about installation of drainage systems for the soil type at the landscape site. However, if excess filling or disturbance of the soil has occurred, it will be necessary to supplement the SCS information with a first-hand study of soil conditions. If improvement of internal drainage is needed, a tile system should be installed before finishing the grading for turf establishment or installation of plant material, and after heavy construction has been completed. This should be installed in conjunction with a proper surface drainage system.

Tile Drainage System

The type of tile system to use and the technique of its installation will depend on the soil type, soil pH, the rate of drainage needed, and the use of the land over the system, for roadways, turf, etc. Before any installation begins, the entire site needs to be surveyed and grade levels need to be established. Low areas in which supplemental drainage will be needed should be defined. Also, if the system is to be tied into an existing drainage main at this time, the existing system should be examined thoroughly to insure that it is functioning properly, is in good repair, *and has the capacity to handle the increase in water that will be added*. The main is the line into which lateral lines drain. The main carries the water to a storm sewer or drainage ditch. Data from the grade and drainage survey will indicate whether the depth of the existing main is sufficient to permit proper installation of the new system. In other words, if the new system is to function properly, it must be installed so that the outlet drains well into the existing main. A new main must be installed for the new system if an outlet would be lower than the existing main.

The type of system will depend on the size and shape of the area to be drained. Wet areas may be drained by installing what is known as a random system, which will drain only those areas. If the area is flat and the soil is poorly drained, a complete system of parallel lateral lines, tied into an appropriately sized main, should be installed. Figure 13-2 illustrates the different systems that may be used depending on the drainage requirement of the site.

The rate at which the water must be removed from the soil to prevent plant injury is called the drainage coefficient. This rate varies with the soil type and with the plants to be grown. Unfortunately, information has not been compiled for landscape plant materials. Therefore, it is suggested that the data for truck crops be used if some of the required plant material is sensitive to poorly drained soils (See Tables 13-1 and 13-2). The rates for field crops should be adequate for turf areas and for plant material that is not sensitive to more moist soils. The tables give the amount (in inches) of water that should be removed per 24-hour period.

The soil type controls the minimum depth and spacing of lateral lines, the maximum grade that should be used, the size of tile that should be used, and the closeness-of-fit of individual tiles. For most landscape sites, minimum spacing of laterals probably should be made since the value of the site is much greater than the value of normal farm land; the cost of the additional installation is not very great, but the cost of improving the system after landscape plant material has become established is quite great. Table 13-3 lists both the spacings and the depths at which laterals should be installed. Shallow tiling may be damaged by movement of heavy loads over the soil surface and, in cold climates, by frost heaving. In warm climates it is possible to install tile lines at depths less than three feet if necessary, and if there is no danger from load damage. However, since roots of many woody plants penetrate to depths of 18 to 24 inches and more, it is not practical to install lines for large area drainage at depths less than two feet. Charts that provide specific information on tile depths and spacings for the individual soil types are available from the Soil Conservation Service in every state.

Always use high quality tile. Less costly tile may cause maintenance problems in the future. Clay tile is sold in three grades: standard quality; extra quality; and heavy duty. Concrete tile has the same ratings, except that the heavy duty concrete tile is called "special quality." Concrete tile should not be used if the soil pH is below 5.0.

Plastic tile is being used on many landscape sites, since it is easier and cheaper to install. Not all engineers agree as to the durability of plastic tile, but for tile of four inches or less in diameter, plastic should be as durable as either clay or concrete tile. However, its use under roadways and other areas of heavy vehicular traffic should be avoided.

The size of tile needed for laterals depends on the soil type. The minimum sizes recommended are:

Table 13-1 Drainage coefficients for land with complete surface drainage.

Soil	Coefficient (inches of water to be removed in 24 hrs)	
	Field crops	Truck crops
Mineral	⅜ to ½	½ to ¾
Organic	½ to ¾	¾ to 1½

Source: *Indiana Farm Drainage Guide*, ID-55, Cooperative Extension Service. West Lafayette, Indiana: Purdue University.

Table 13-2 Drainage coefficients for land with incomplete surface drainage.

Soil	Coefficient (inches of water to be removed in 24 hrs)	
	Blind inlets	Open inlets
FIELD CROPS		
Mineral	½ to ¾	½ to 1
Organic	¾ to 1	1 to 1½
TRUCK CROPS		
Mineral	¾ to 1	1 to 1½
Organic	1½ to 2	2 to 4

Source: *Indiana Farm Drainage Guide*, ID-55, Cooperative Extension Service. West Lafayette, Indiana: Purdue University.

Table 13-3 Spacing and depth for tile laterals.

Soil	Spacing (feet)	Depth (inches)
Clay	Less than 20	36 to 42
Clay loam	20 to 40	36 to 42
Silt loam	25 to 50	36 to 42
Muck	40 to 100	48 to 60

Source: *Indiana Farm Drainage Guide*, ID-55, Cooperative Extension Service. West Lafayette, Indiana: Purdue University.

13-3

Figure 13-3. *The installation of plastic tile or drainage pipe. This machine digs the trench to the proper depth and also lays the pipe. Note the survey stakes in the background. These are used as guides to keep the equipment digging the trench at the right depth.*

1. Four-inch tile for lines 1,300 feet or less in length.

2. Five-inch tile for silty and sandy soils if lines are 1,300 feet or more in length.

3. Six-inch tile for muck or peat soils.

What the minimum grade or slope should be depends on the tile size, but should not be less than 0.10 percent for a four-inch tile and not less than 0.07 percent for larger sizes of tile.

The tile mains must be large enough to handle the volume of water put into the system. The size can be determined by consulting a drainage chart that lists and compares various sizes of lateral tiles, the acreage drained, the rate of drainage required, and the tile grade or slope. As an example, let us suppose the drainage rate or drainage coefficient needed has been determined to be one inch of water in 24 hours and the area to be drained is 20 acres. The grade is 0.2 feet per 100 feet. Refer to the drainage chart in Figure 13-4. First locate the one-inch drainage coefficient column (lower right); move up the column to the 20-acre calibration. The 0.2 grade line (at the lower middle of the chart) intercepts the 20-acre line in the 10-inch area. This is the tile size needed for the main line. The maximum grade for tile mains depends on tile size and soil type. Table 13-3 shows the relation of soil type to tile spacing.

The key to any good tile drainage system is the outlet. The whole system can be a waste of time and money when the outlet is not properly installed. If the system is to drain from clay or clay loam soil into an open ditch or stream, the tile outlet of the main should be at least 12 inches above the low-water flow in the stream or ditch; from sandy soils the system

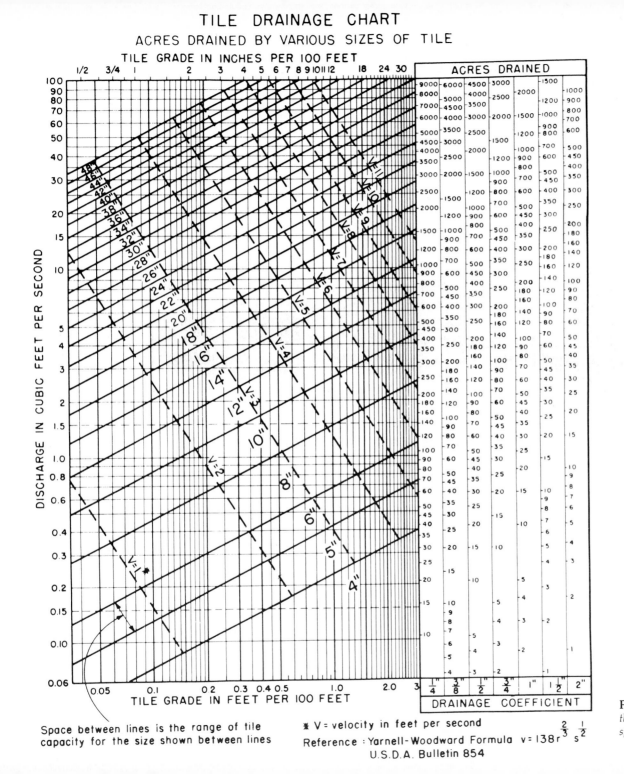

TILE DRAINAGE CHART
ACRES DRAINED BY VARIOUS SIZES OF TILE

Space between lines is the range of tile capacity for the size shown between lines

✳ V = velocity in feet per second

Reference: Yarnell-Woodward Formula $v = 138 r^{\frac{2}{3}} s^{\frac{1}{2}}$

U.S.D.A. Bulletin 854

Figure 13-4. *This chart may be used to determine the size of main line needed to drain an area of a specific size.*

13-5

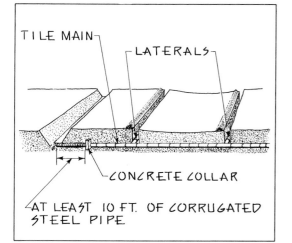

TILE MAIN
LATERALS

CONCRETE COLLAR

AT LEAST 10 FT. OF CORRUGATED
STEEL PIPE

13-6

Figure 13-5. *Use no more outlets on a tile system than necessary. If erosion under the outlet is a problem, use a concrete or metal backing for a spillway. The metal shield is installed at the edge of the ditch with about two feet of the main extending into the ditch. The main shown here will later be covered with fill soil.*

Figure 13-6. *Diagram showing proper installation of an outlet for permanent protection from erosion. The outlet should be equipped with a spillway. The concrete collar is used where the tile and the pipe meet.*

should drain from an outlet 18 inches above the low-water flow. The outlet should have a grating over the end to prevent small animals from entering. Also, the outlet should be constructed so that erosion and washouts do not occur. Figure 13-5 and 13-6 illustrates proper installation and grating technique. Use as few outlets as possible when designing the system.

At some landscape sites, open ditching is not feasible; then the installation of a French drain is necessary. A French drain consists of channels cut into soil in the same manner as open ditching, but the channels are filled with crushed rock or very coarse gravel. The surface may then be covered with topsoil to hide the underground waterway. It is suggested that a fiberglass mat be placed over the gravel before the soil is added, to prevent the soil from filtering down into the gravel and plugging the system. The French drain will not have the capacity to remove as large a volume of water as an open ditch and must be designed with this in mind.

The outlet must be low enough to permit placing the tile three or four feet below the soil surface in the lowest area that will need to drain down to the outlet. Clearly, this is not always possible; sometimes the installation of a pump and storage sump becomes necessary. The tile mains will drain into the storage sump, and when the water level reaches sufficient level it will be pumped to a higher main, which then drains to an outlet. Figure 13-7 is a cross-section of a typical drainage pump and storage sump. Information about what size of pump and storage area to use should be obtained from agricultural engineers at state agricultural colleges.

Correct installation methods should be followed in close detail to insure that the drainage is successful and that the system is useful for many years to follow. After land surveying has been completed and grade lines have been established, trench digging and tile laying should *start at the outlet and move to the inlet* end of the system. Special trench-digging and tile-laying equipment is available and should be used for large projects. The tile should be laid true to the survey line and at the proper grade. Smaller tiling jobs are often done by hand. For hand-laid tiling, the trench should be cut the width of the tile plus six inches. The tile should be fitted firmly in the bottom of the trench and at the proper slope or grade. There should not be sags or humps in the tile line.

The gaps left between individual tiles should be varied depending on the soil type. A tight fit is required for sandy soils; only 1/8-inch gap should be used on silt loam and clay loam. Tiles placed in a clay soil need a 1/8- to 1/4-inch gap to permit free water entry. Peat or muck soils require even a larger gap, of up to 3/8 inches.

Curves in the tile should be gradual with the tile being fitted by hand here unless manufactured tiles are available for curvatures. Careful fitting is required. A curve should not have a radius shorter than five feet.

As laterals and mains are installed, relief wells and breathers should be installed. Relief wells are vertical tiles that extend up to the soil surface and are installed at the bottom of sharp rises in the lines to take the pressure off the system when it is under a heavy water load. Breathers are installed in the same manner

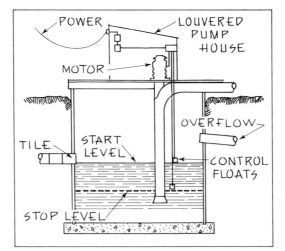

13-7

13-8

13-9

13-10

Figure 13-7. *A correct installation for a sump and storage pit for draining land that is lower than the main outlet. The pump house should have a hinged roof for accessibility. The walls of the storage area should be staves, blocks, or corrugated steel; the floor should be concrete.*

Figure 13-8. *Careful attention must be paid to tile installation to insure that a proper slope is achieved and that there are no depressions or rises in the line.*

Figure 13-9. *Installation of tile main requires equipment and techniques different from those used for laterals because the tile sizes are larger for mains than for lateral lines.*

Figure 13-10. *Installation of concrete tile by machine. Note the survey markers, used as guides.*

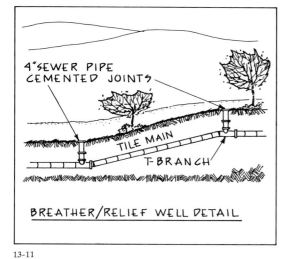

13-11

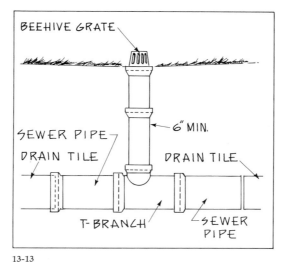

13-13

13-12

13-14

Figure 13-11. *Breathers or vents should be installed at the beginning of a steep section of main and at about every quarter mile on long mains. They improve the operation of the system, mark the location of the tile line, and serve as inspection holes.*

Figure 13-12. *The use of a fiberglass mat for blinding is a standard practice now. It can be installed by the same machine laying the tile.*

Figure 13-13. *An open inlet to a tile system used for surface drainage. The area around the inlet is sod to a radius of five feet or more. Note that flanged sewer pipes (cemented together) are used to secure the inlet to the tile system. Beyond the sewer pipe, drain tile is used in either direction. Flow is from left to right.*

Figure 13-14. *Surface inlet with sump used to drain gutters, parking lots, etc. The area at upper left will be covered with soil or turf or will be paved.*

as the relief wells and should be placed at 400- to 500-foot intervals in the lines. Breathers relieve the buildup of air pressure that may cause the tile to "blow out." The surface outlets of the relief wells and breathers should be placed so that they do not interfere with such maintenance practices as mowing. The openings should be covered with screens to prevent the entry of small animals or debris.

As the tile is installed, it should be covered with topsoil to insure water movement into the tile. In tight soils, straw or corncobs should be used as the initial covering. If the expense is warranted, the tile can be covered with a layer of coarse gravel and then a fiberglass mat covering, to prevent the soil from mixing with the gravel. The material for covering the tile is called blinding.

Manufactured T's and Y's should be used when connecting laterals to mains, breathers, surface inlets, etc. If these are not available, butt the tiles together, make sure the joining tile is of good fit, and cement the joints. Junction boxes should be used when two or more mains are joined together. The tiles may enter the junction box at more than one level.

When a tile line must pass under a roadway, special tiling techniques must be used. A metal pipe or extra-strength sewer tile should be used to keep the tile system from being crushed by the traffic on the roadway.

At many landscape sites, surface inlets are required. The construction of surface inlets to a tile system can complicate subsequent landscape maintenance, and therefore they should be installed correctly. If the quantity of water to be taken in at the surface is small, a direct inlet, constructed in the manner of the breather but covered with a "beehive" grate, can be used. To drain larger quantities of water, an open surface inlet with a sediment trap should be used. This is a more common inlet when draining parking lots and walkways.

Blind inlets—those that are hidden beneath the soil—will sometimes be used in landscape work. If one is needed it can be constructed in the same manner as a French drain, with the tile line being covered with gravel.

Always keep the tile system in good repair. A single broken tile or blow-out can obstruct an entire line, and it might even impede a major portion of the system. Keep the outlets open and functioning.

Surface Drainage

Surface drainage is the removal of water from some area by movement over the surface of the soil rather than by penetration to an internal tile system. Often, a good surface-drainage system will eliminate the need for the installation of an internal system; certainly good surface drainage should exist at the landscape site even if a tile system is to be installed. Whereas the tile systems for internal drainage can be installed by using the techniques for draining field crops, surface drainage at the landscape site presents some unique problems. This is especially true of drainage of water from large, paved parking lots, building roofs, and roadways. Too often the water collected in these areas is allowed to run freely over landscape beds and turf areas, and large volumes of water can compound the problems in both surface-draining and internal-draining systems. So it is to the landscape architect's advantage to know how to handle surface drainage of

water from large areas where, because of the nature of some of the landscape-construction features, water penetration is poor or non-existent. What we discuss in the next few paragraphs are generally good surface-drainage practices for landscaped areas.

DRAINAGE OF NONSOIL SURFACES

All building roofs should have guttering and downspouts installed to carry the water to central collecting points. Most large projects, at which numerous buildings are built, will have a storm-sewer system, and the water collected from building roofs should be fed into the storm sewer, not the sanitary sewer. Without guttering, the water from rainfall rushes off the roof onto the soil surface with great force. The soil is compacted and eventually the water cannot penetrate the surface easily. Also, it is a common practice for designers to plant rows of woody plants under a roof line, though to do so is not always acceptable aesthetically. These plants have a difficult time surviving the water falling directly on them and the wet, compacted soil conditions that result, as well as the ice that forms on them in the winter.

The runoff from the downspouts should, if not connected to a storm sewer, be directed to a turf area that permits a flow of water away from the building and away from any nearby landscape beds. The downspout should not be allowed to feed directly into a landscape bed, since possibly waterlogged conditions will still remain in a localized area around the outlet of the downspout. Some plants that are sensitive to wet soils, such as *Taxus* spp., have a difficult time surviving the wet soil at the outlet.

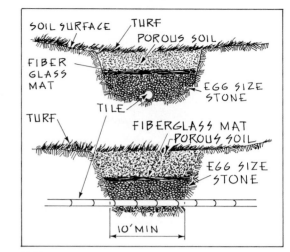

13-15

Figure 13-15. *Blind inlet using the French drain principle. The tile must be at a depth to permit water movement from the blind inlet to the main and the outlet of the drainage system.*

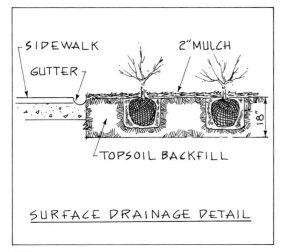

13-16

13-17

Figure 13-16. *Landscape bed constructed slightly higher than the walks or adjacent turf areas. The height increase and slope must be very slight to prevent movement of soil, mulch, etc., onto the walk or turf.*

Figure 13-17. *A sod waterway should be constructed to move surface water into desired drainage patterns and areas of the landscape site.*

Drainage from large paved areas can best be handled through the installation of a storm-sewer system at the time of construction. An adequate gutter system should be constructed to move the water to storm-sewer collection points and to prevent the water from flowing into nearby plant beds and turf areas. If gutters and curbings are not provided, not only is the soil in beds and turf areas forced to handle excess water, in northern climates the salt used to melt the snow and ice will be carried to them also. Check also the adequacy of gutter systems near small paved areas—roadways and even sidewalks. If salt is to be used in large quantities for ice removal, a means of carrying the water from the melted ice and snow to a storm sewer should be provided. Even in warm areas of the country where ice and snow are not problems, water drainage from sidewalks and roadways can be a problem.

It is a common but bad practice to have the soil surface graded lower than adjoining structural features, such as roads and walks. The technique should be avoided because it permits the collection of water in the lower plant beds and turf. Often it is practical to have the soil surface higher than the road or walk by building a slight mound. This may, however, cause a maintenance problem if the soil has a tendency to wash down onto the paved surface. All things considered, it is best to provide a road- or walk-drainage system and, if necessary, curbing.

DRAINAGE FROM LANDSCAPED SURFACES

Surface-drainage practices that should be followed for soil areas at any landscape site are relatively simple but effective. During the final grading, unwanted depressions or low pockets should be eliminated. The grade should be made lower in the direction that will move surface water away from structures and landscape features such as plant beds. The flow of water should be to a central surface-drainage system such as a sod waterway, or to the surface inlets to an internal drainage system. It is important that drainage patterns be coordinated with the drainage patterns of surrounding lands. Draining water onto someone else's property is not ethical and in most instances is not legal.

When designing drainage patterns for large areas or housing developments, a central waterway system should be provided for collection and removal of the water. In most areas of the country this can be a sod waterway, but in arid regions where flash flooding is a problem, an open ditch or storm sewer is essential. Eventually even the sod waterways must be tied onto a large-volume water-removal system, such as a ditch or a stream.

Sod waterways are really shallow drainage ditches constructed so as to be barely visible in the landscape. Figure 13-17 shows the installation of a sod waterway that can be used to provide surface drainage. The waterway must, of course, have proper slope to carry the water to the collection ditch or to some other outlet. The pattern or layout of the waterways will depend on the need and design of the site. The pattern may be formal, with a parallel system of waterways, or it may be random, with only low and troublesome areas being drained.

Good surface drainage of the landscape site will reduce the need for an internal drainage system or at least supplement the internal system's effectiveness, and at many projects it will be necessary to provide surface-drainage facilities for large paved areas and building roofs, to prevent excess water from collecting in plant beds and on turf areas.

IRRIGATION SYSTEMS

Providing water to landscape plantings is as important to plant development as providing good drainage. Irrigation has made it possible to grow plants in regions that were once arid wastelands, and irrigation systems have been used since the time of the ancient Egyptians, who lifted water manually from the Nile and poured it into irrigation ditches. The development of irrigation has progressed today to a point where large turf areas can be watered with automatic underground systems, with nozzles that pop up when the water pressure increases. Such a system can be controlled electronically to apply water only when needed.

There are many types of irrigation systems, and each is best suited for some particular water requirement for plant growth, or for some particular requirement of the site. Since there are so many systems on the market, it is suggested that an independent irrigation engineer be consulted about which system is best suited for the project. Remember that salesmen have a product to sell and they are not likely to recommend a competitive product even though it may do a better job. But an irrigation engineer can lay out the entire system and determine the water requirements, required equipment, and the approximate cost of the system. He will also be able to recommend alternative systems that cost less than the best system and explain their limitations and why they are cheaper. Some landscape architects are also skilled in the design of irrigation systems.

In the design of a system, careful consideration should be given to water distribution. Areas in the shade on the north and east sides of buildings will require less water than elsewhere. Systems serving these areas should be valved and controlled separately. The choice of sprinkler heads will also be dictated by plant types and characters. For instance, raised planters with low plants adjacent to a front entrance may best be irrigated by a bubbling or flooding head instead of a spray head that may block the entrance. The smaller, less noticeable shrub head will be preferred in shrub plantings. Riser height will be determined by the height of the planting, and it is best for aesthetic reasons to add or replace risers every year or two as plants grow, rather than install a riser that is too high.

It is recommended that the irrigation system, if it is to be of the underground type, be installed during the final grading process. Outlets for above-ground systems should also be installed at this time.

Many landscape maintenance supervisors prefer to maintain control of the rate and frequency of water applications and do not favor automatic controls. The time-clock method is particularly poor if soils are tight, since irrigation water will be applied by the automatic timer at a certain time even if it is not needed. Trees have suffered severe root damage when irrigation water controlled by a time-clock was applied after several days of exceedingly heavy rainfall. If the landscape maintenance supervisor is experienced enough to determine when the plants need water, without incurring an actual water deficit, turning on irrigation systems manually is the best. Some maintenance supervisors even prefer to water beds and planters by hand with a hose.

The frequency and rate of water application will be discussed in detail in Chapter 17, "Physical Care of Woody Plant Material."

SOIL-FERTILITY ADJUSTMENT BEFORE PLANTING

Before any planting of either woody plant material or turf is carried out at the landscape site, soil tests should be run to determine what fertilizer may be needed and how much the soil pH should be changed. Testing for these things actually needs to be done before the final grading so that the required fertilizer can be plowed down or at least disked into the soil. The need for a soil test cannot be stressed enough. Too often a standard fertilizer recommendation for all planting sites is written into the construction specifications for a project without the slightest knowledge of the true needs of the soil at the specific site. Also, the need for changing soil pH should be determined before planting, since the materials that change soil pH—lime or sulfur—are more effective if mixed into the soil rather than just applied to the surface. In fact, it is nearly impossible to lower significantly the pH of a calcareous-base soil (one originating from limestone) with the application of sulfur to the soil surface.

Once a soil test has been made, the proper fertilizer should be applied at the recom-mended rate. If a complete test is not run, at least the soil pH should be determined. The importance of proper soil pH was explained in Chapter 5 in connection with the discussion of the root-zone environment. Determine the soil pH best suited for the required plant material and then adjust the pH accordingly. If the soil is too acid (low pH), it can be made less acid by adding limestone. Ground limestone should be used, though more rapid pH changes can be obtained by using slaked lime or hydrated lime. For long-term landscape plantings, ground limestone will give better results.

The soil type determines the amount of limestone required to change the pH. Sandy soils have less buffer capacity, less resistance to acidity change, and require less lime per unit of pH change. The more clay present, the greater the buffer capacity, and the more lime required for increasing the soil pH. Highly organic soils have very high buffering capacity and often it is not practical to try to change their pH. Lime is added to organic soils to supply calcium rather than to effect a change in pH. Table 13-4 shows approximately what amount of limestone will be required to raise the soil pH to a desired level.

Sulfur is used to lower the soil pH. Again, the buffering capacity of the soil controls the amount of sulfur needed to decrease the soil pH by a given amount. Highly organic soils are nearly always acid and rarely need a decrease in pH. Soils with a limestone base have a high buffering capacity and it is very difficult to lower the pH in such soil. Generally it is much easier to increase soil pH with the addition of lime than it is to decrease it with sulfur. Table 13-5 shows the approximate amount of sulfur needed to lower the *p*H of various soil types.

The addition of sulfur to turf areas is recommended by some authorities; however, it should be done with caution as foliar burn of the grass can result. When temperatures are above 80°F and humidities are high, sulfur combines with water, forming acid. The result is a burning of the turf. Recovery takes several weeks or longer.

IMPORTANCE OF TOPSOIL CONSERVATION AT THE SITE

It is important to know about the principles of conserving the topsoil for future use, of providing an adequate amount of soil for plant growth, and of protecting plant material already growing at the site during the grading, and we will discuss each of these in this section. The techniques of grading, such as surveying procedures, equipment operation, etc., will not be covered. However, it is appropriate to point out that grading should be done only when the soil is properly moist. Working wet soils causes "puddling," which is one kind of destruction of the soil structure. This in turn may cause poor root aeration, which may result in poor growth for some plants.

During the initial phases of construction and preliminary grading, it is recommended that the top 6 to 12 inches of soil be removed if (1) the area is to be covered by a building or by paving, or (2) the grade to be cut away is greater than from 6 to 12 inches. This topsoil should be kept separate and stockpiled so that it can be used as the final soil just before the final grading. Too often the topsoil is buried

Table 13-4 Pounds of limestone needed to change soil reaction, by soil type.

| Change in pH desired in plow-depth layer | Pounds of limestone per acre of soil | | | | | |
	Sand	Sandy loam	Loam	Silt loam	Clay loam	Muck
4.0 to 6.5	2,600	5,000	7,000	8,400	10,000	19,000
4.5 to 6.5	2,200	4,200	5,800	7,000	8,400	16,200
5.0 to 6.5	1,800	3,400	4,600	5,600	6,600	12,600
5.5 to 6.5	1,200	2,600	3,400	4,000	4,600	8,600
6.0 to 6.5	600	1,400	1,800	2,200	2,400	4,400

Source: Knott, J. E., 1962. *Handbook for Vegetable Growers*. New York: John Wiley and Sons, Inc.

Table 13-5 Pounds of soil sulfur (99 percent) needed to change soil reaction, by soil type.

| Change in pH desired | Pounds of sulfur per acre of soil | | |
	Sandy	Loamy	Clay
8.5 to 6.5	2,000	2,500	3,000
8.0 to 6.5	1,200	1,500	2,000
7.5 to 6.5	500	800	1,000
7.0 to 6.5	100	150	300

Source: Knott, J. E., 1962. *Handbook for Vegetable Growers*. New York: John Wiley and Sons, Inc.

Figure 13-18. *Rough grading with a small grader. Note that soil conditions are dry enough to permit working of the soil without puddling.*

13-18

under tons of subsoil and rubbish and can never be recovered. When too thin a layer of topsoil is used as the final fill material, the results are usually poor, since there is not a good transition between the added topsoil and the subsoil. As a consequence, drainage may be poor and the roots of turf and shallow-rooted ornamentals may not penetrate the soil satisfactorily.

Filling and Mounding

It is now a common practice to change earth contours to provide some variation in flat terrain. The practice requires careful design to insure that drainage patterns are maintained and, most important from the point of view of design, that the best aesthetic value is achieved in the changed contour. Mounds provide effective visual and sound barriers. Use of mounds is sometimes necessary also to provide sufficient soil for the growth and development of large plant specimens. In extremely sandy soils, mounds of a more substantial topsoil have provided an area adequate for holding soil moisture and nutrients, to permit the growth and development of species that would not normally survive the sandy soil conditions.

In the development of urban shopping malls, landscaped areas are sometimes made over former thoroughfares, and this requires the addition of fill soils and mounds to provide adequate soil for root growth. The tops of some underground parking facilities have been landscaped with plant material, and the landscape architect may request the development of soil mounds.

With all such projects, a problem is presented by this type of planting—mainte-nance of normal soil temperatures. In northern climates, the winter soil temperatures may be kept too high by the heat radiating upward from an underground structure such as a parking garage. This may result in inadequate hardening of the plants, and low-temperature damage will occur. Providing an insulating layer of styrofoam or similar material between the garage roof and the soil before the soil is graded will help solve the problem.

Protecting Existing Plants

Existing plants, particularly large trees, are often considered very valuable at the landscape site. Often a building will be designed around a very fine specimen. The landscape architect often develops an entire landscape plan around existing plant material. For these reasons it is necessary to provide protection for these plants during construction of buildings and such land preparation as filling and cutting.

Root damage is the greatest danger to large trees. During construction it can occur in many ways. Trees with shallow roots, such as beech, are very susceptible to changes in soil conditions, and may even be injured or killed if the soil is compacted by continual movement of equipment over their shallow root systems. Severing a large number of roots will cause the decline of many tree species. This can occur when water, power, or gas lines are installed underground. Grade changes or the digging of a basement may destroy so much of its root system that a tree will die. But root damage can also occur indirectly, as it does when fill is added over the root system. The addition of fill soil changes the oxygen content of the soil air and at some sites the water table may rise when fill soil is added, reducing the amount of soil aeration further. The filling process may reduce their activity and indirectly affect the growth of the tree.

It is obvious that grade changes must be made and that filling around trees must be done. For valuable specimens that are to be saved for landscape purposes, it is important that a dry well be constructed to reduce the hazards to the tree. The dry well should be constructed if the fill soil is to exceed eight inches in depth. Some trees such as beech, sugar maple, and oak will not even tolerate eight inches of fill soil. Because of this, it is recommended that extreme caution be used when adding any fill around these trees and when any modification of a site might cause a change in soil aeration. Make sure that grade changes do not allow water to run to the bases of the trees. Never should stockpiles of fill soil or soil from excavations be piled on tree root systems.

It is too late to construct a dry well after a tree begins to show symptoms of root injury from the addition of fill soil. General symptoms are a premature dropping of foliage and a scorching of the leaf edges. Dry well construction should precede the filling operation.

The first step of construction is to remove sod, leaves, and debris from around the tree to a distance three feet beyond the drip line. Broadcast, at a rate of one pound per one inch of trunk diameter, a complete fertilizer such as 12-12-12 over the stripped area. (Fertilizers and fertilizer techniques are described near the beginning of Chapter 17.) Loosen the soil to a depth of two to three inches. Care should be taken not to damage the roots during this pro-

cess. Now the soil surface has been prepared for the installation of a tile-drainage system.

Four-inch, high-quality drain tile should be used. Tiles should be laid in a pattern as illustrated in Figure 13-19. A "spoked-wheel" pattern is the most commonly used. The tiles should be laid in the same manner as described for installing a tile system to provide internal drainage. The slope should be away from the tree trunk at a rate of 1/8 inch per foot. The joints should be tight and the tiles should be covered with a fiberglass mat to prevent the entry of soil and roots that might clog the systems. The outer perimeter of tiles should be at the drip line of the tree. Vertical vents should be installed in the same manner as breathers used in field systems. The tile system should be tied into a storm sewer or other drainage outlet.

Now a dry well can be constructed around the trunk of the tree. It must be large enough to allow for the future growth of the tree trunk. A space of only six to eight inches between the well wall and the tree trunk is adequate for large, old, slow-growing trees. The wall should taper slightly away from the trunk at the top of the wall. Of course the wall height is the level to which the fill soil will be added. A well constructed of cement blocks and faced with bricks often proves to be very satisfactory. The well can be loosely filled with two- to three-inch stones, which will reduce the maintenance problem of cleaning debris from the well.

After the well is built, the tile system and the fiberglass mat can be covered with stones three to six inches in diameter to a depth of eight to twelve inches. The top of the stone fill should be also covered with a fiberglass mat or with straw, much the way the French

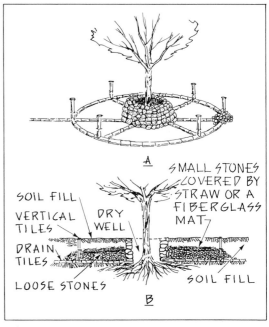

13-19

Figure 13-19. *A tile system protects a tree from a raised grade. In A, the tile is laid out on the original grade, leading from a dry well around the tree trunk. The well itself is made of large stones. At B, the tile system has been covered with loose stones to allow air to circulate over the root area, and these are covered with smaller stones, straw or matting, and fill.*

Figure 13-20. *A large tree well around several trees permitted several feet of fill soil to be added at a project where conservation of all existing trees was wanted. Canterbury Green, Fort Wayne, Indiana.*

13-20

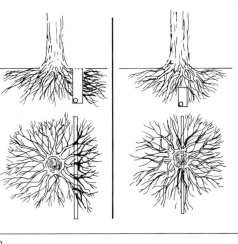

13-22

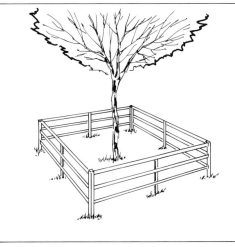

13-23

13-21

Figure 13-21. *A retaining wall can be used to protect tree roots when a cut is required near established trees. The soil immediately behind the retaining wall can be a mixture of peat moss and soil.*

Figure 13-22. *If tunneling is necessary, tunnel beneath root systems rather than across a side of them. Drawing at left shows trenching that would probably kill the tree. Drawing at right shows how tunneling under the tree will preserve many of the important feeder roots.*

Figure 13-23. *A simple barrier to protect a tree trunk and part of its root system from machanical injury during site modification.*

drain is constructed. This prevents the soil from filtering down into the space between the stones and plugging the system. The fill soil is then added to whatever grade level is needed. Care should be taken not to crush the tile with heavy equipment during the filling operation.

Filling only at one side of a tree can be handled basically by constructing half a system. It is necessary to provide retaining walls and to construct a partial dry well.

Lowering the soil level around a tree can be as injurious as filling. The excess cutting of roots will cause a portion of the tree or the entire tree to die. It is best to establish a retaining wall at the drip line of the tree so that as many roots as possible are retained within the original soil level.

Trenching near tree trunks in order to install utility lines can destroy an excessive number of roots, up to perhaps 40 percent of the total root mass. Inasmuch as the roots all radiate generally from the trunk, it is best to trench directly toward the tree trunk and tunnel under the tree when nearing the trunk, rather than trench past one side of the tree. Trenching toward the tree will destroy a minimum number of active roots.

EQUIPMENT INJURY

When heavy equipment is being used at the construction site, trees need protection from mechanical injury. The best method is to build a protective fence at the drip line of the tree. This not only prevents injury to the trunk but also prevents soil damage, since equipment cannot then be moved over the soil surface under the tree. If the tree has a large spread, it is not always possible to construct a fence at the drip line. Next best is to construct a triangular fence next to the trunk. This is similar to animal guards that are placed around trees in pastures. A third method, which protects only the trunk, is to place planks around the trunk, wiring them firmly in place. These planks will absorb the blows of construction equipment and reduce the chance of large bark wounds.

SITE PREPARATION IN AREAS THAT RESTRICT THE ROOT ZONE

Whether plants are being placed in containers, in paved areas, or in beds, the problems of developing a satisfactory environment for root growth are the same, for the restriction of the area for root development may result in deficient moisture. When the area for root development is restricted, this in turn limits the amount of root surface available for absorption of moisture. The problem becomes evident in midsummer on trees planted in sidewalks, raised containers, and beds that limit the area for root development. The first symptoms are leaf scorch due to lack of water. There is a premature loss of foliage. If the problem is not corrected, over a period of years the tree will lose vigor and decline. Restriction of the roots first begins to be evident when the tree reaches a size where it is too big for the soil volume in which it is planted.

There are several partial solutions to the problem. The most obvious one is to plant only trees that are small when mature. The top growth of such trees is usually nearly the same size as the root development. Another solution—actually a prevention—is to prepare the planting site properly before installing the plant. First and foremost is the installation of a proper drainage system. Each large planting hole in a bed or even each planting should have an individual tile system taking the water to a central removal system. A six- to eight-inch layer of crushed stone or rock should be placed over the tile in the bottom of the planting hole or the planter. A fiberglass mat should be used to cover the stone to prevent the soil from filtering into the stone and reducing the effectiveness of the drainage. The planting hole for small trees should be deep enough to allow addition of fill soil to at least 18 inches and up to 36 inches or more for larger trees.

The soil used to fill in around the tree or shrub root-ball should be of high quality, with good texture and drainage. It is recommended that one part sphagnum peat moss and one part coarse sand be mixed with two parts topsoil. Often horticultural-grade perlite (an expanded mineral) is used as sand replacement. Perlite can be particularly useful when a light-weight growing medium is needed. This mixture will provide an open soil that will hold moisture and at the same time provide excellent aeration. Three pounds of a complete fertilizer with an approximate analysis of 12-12-12 may be added to one cubic yard of the backfill mixture. Rapid root growth is possible in this mixture and common waterlogging problems that occur in planters when heavy, tight soils are used are eliminated.

Of course the problem of providing a water supply is always present when planting in areas that may restrict root development.

13-24

Figure 13-24. *Planks held firmly against a tree trunk by stapled wires will protect bark from much mechanical injury during site modification.*

It is all too evident that planting trees along city sidewalks where very little water-collecting area has been left is hazardous at best. The expense of installing an individual irrigation outlet for each tree is great, and so is the cost of labor to provide water by hand watering. In areas where the summers are even moderately dry, most sidewalk trees will survive only for a short time. Installing grids in the paved area around the tree will provide a larger surface area for absorption of water. The planting of drought-tolerant species is recommended. See Table 13-6 for a list of plants that will tolerate not only dry conditions but also other urban conditions that are torturous for plant materials.

On landscape sites where a high maintenance budget has been provided, the most satisfactory watering method is by hand, but the personnel must be experienced enough to know when the plants need water. It must be pointed out that the cost of hand watering is usually very great, and the method should be considered only if the client is willing to pay the cost. With light soil mixes, automatic watering may be used since the soil will drain rapidly even if excess rainfall has occurred. But it is imperative that good drainage be maintained if automatic watering is provided.

The use of mulch materials on the top of beds or planters will help reduce the water loss due to surface evaporation. Such materials as shredded bark, wood chips, crushed corncobs, stone, etc., have proven to be very satisfactory mulch materials. The mulch should be applied in a layer at least two inches thick.

It is also advisable to determine if soil temperature extremes will exist at any season of the year. If so, the use of sheets of styrofoam insulation will prove beneficial and add little to the cost.

MODIFYING ROOF-GARDEN SITES

The plantings in roof gardens require the same procedures as for planters. An additional problem exists here—that of soil weight. It is recommended that the soil mix be lightened by using one of the artificial soil conditioners, such as perlite. Table 13-7 shows the difference in weight of the different soil additives and the resulting weights when various mixtures are prepared. The lighter mixes have the disadvantages of requiring more water, and this may be a particular problem with narrowleaf and broadleaf evergreens in cold climates. Winter desiccation will injure plants unless water is provided during winter months. Coupled with this problem is that of wind damage. When winds flow around tall buildings—especially in metropolitan areas—the winds may behave very unpredictably, and it may be necessary to provide wind protection because of high wind velocities. The landscape architect should try to design the wind protection since the use of plastic barriers and other wind protections are usually unsightly and destroy the effectiveness of the landscape design.

SUMMARY

The landscape site should not only be modified for design purposes but also to provide a satisfactory environment for plant growth. The most

Table 13-6   A selection of plants for dry and sandy soils.

Botanical name	Common name
TREES	
Acacia longifolia var. *floribunda*	Gossamer Sydney acacia
Acer negundo	Box-elder
Ailanthus altissima	Tree-of-heaven
Albizia julibrissin	Silk-tree
Aralia elata	Japanese angelica-tree
Bauhinia spp.	Bauhinia
Betula davurica	Dahurian birch
Betula populifolia	Gray birch
Brachychiton spp.	Bottle-tree
Broussonetia papyrifera	Paper-mulberry
Casuarina spp.	Beefwood
Celtis australis	European hackberry
Ceratonia siliqua	Carob
Cupressus macrocarpa	Monterey cypress
Eucalyptus spp.	Eucalyptus
Ficus spp.	Figs
Fraxinus velutina	Velvet ash
Gleditsia spp.	Honey-locust
Grevillea robusta	Silk-oak
Juniperus spp.	Juniper
Keteleeria fortunei	Fortune keteleeria
Koelreuteria paniculata	Goldenrain-tree
Leptospermum laevigatum	Australian tea-tree
Maclura pomifera	Osage-orange
Melaleuca spp.	Melaleuca
Melia azedarach	China-berry
Olea europaea	Common olive
Parkinsonia aculeata	Jerusalem thorn
Pinus banksiana	Jack pine
Pinus canariensis	Canary pine
Pinus rigida	Pitch pine
Pinus torreyana	Torrey pine
Pinus virginiana	Virginia pine
Populus alba	White poplar
Populus fremontii	Fremont poplar
Prosopis glandulosa	Honey mesquite
Quercus kelloggi	California black oak
Quercus marilandica	Blackjack oak
Quercus montana	Chestnut-oak
Robinia spp.	Locust
Sassafras albidum	Sassafras

Botanical name	Common name
Schinus molle	California pepper-tree
Sophora japonica	Japanese pagoda-tree
Ulmus pumila	Siberian elm
SHRUBS	
Acanthopanax spp.	Acanthopanax
Acer ginnala	Amur maple
Amorpha spp.	False-indigo
Arctostaphylos uva-ursi	Bearberry
Artemisia spp.	Sagebrush
Atriplex spp.	Saltbush
Baccharis halimifolia	Groundsel-bush
Berberis mentorensis	Mentor barberry
Berberis thunbergii and vars.	Japanese barberry
Buddleia alternifolia	Fountain butterfly-bush
Callistemon lanceolatus	Lemon bottlebrush
Caragana spp.	Pea-tree
Ceanothus americanus	American ceanothus
Ceanothus thyrsiflorus	Blue-blossom
Chaenomeles spp. and vars.	Quince
Colutea spp.	Bladder senna
Comptonia peregrina	Sweet fern
Cornus racemosa	Gray dogwood
Cotinus coggygria	Smoke-tree
Cytisus spp.	Broom
Diervilla sessilifolia	Bush-honeysuckle
Elaeagnus angustifolia	Russian-olive
Epigaea repens	Trailing arbutus
Euonymus japonicus	Evergreen euonymus
Garrya spp.	Silk-tassel
Gaylussacia baccata	Black huckleberry
Genista spp.	Broom
Hamamelis virginiana	Witch-hazel
Hebe spp.	Hebe
Heteromeles arbutifolia	Toyon
Hypericum calycinum	St. Johnswort
Hypericum prolificum	Shrubby St. Johnswort
Indigofera spp.	Indigo
Juniperus communis	Common juniper
Juniperus conferta	Shore juniper

Botanical Name	Common name
Juniperus horizontalis and vars.	Creeping juniper
Juniperus virginiana vars.	Red-cedar juniper
Kolkwitzia amabilis	Beauty-bush
Lavandula spp.	Lavender
Lespedeza bicolor	Shrub bush-clover
Leucothoë racemosa	Sweet-bells
Ligustrum spp.	Privet
Lycium spp.	Box-thorn
Myrica spp.	Wax-myrtle and bayberry
Myrtus communis	True myrtle
Nerium oleander	Oleander
Physocarpus spp.	Ninebark
Pittosporum spp.	Pittosporum
Potentilla spp.	Cinquefoil
Prunus besseyi	Western sand cherry
Prunus maritima	Beach plum
Punica granatum	Pomegranate
Raphiolepis umbellata	Yeddo-hawthorn
Rhamnus spp.	Buckthorn
Rhus spp.	Sumac
Ribes alpinum	Alpine currant
Robinia hispida	Rose-acacia
Rosa carolina	Carolina rose
Rosa rugosa	Rugosa rose
Rosa setigera	Prairie rose
Rosa spinossima	Scotch rose
Rosa virginiana	Virginia rose
Rosmarinus officinalis	Rosemary
Ruscus aculeatus	Butcher's broom
Salix tristis	Dwarf gray willow
Salvia greggii	Autumn sage
Santolina chamaecyparissus	Lavender-cotton
Shepherdia argentea	Buffalo-berry
Shepherdia canadensis	Russet buffalo-berry
Sophora davidii	Vetch sophora
Spartium junceum	Spanish-broom
Tamarix spp.	Tamarisk
Vaccinium pallidum	Dryland blueberry
Vaccinium stamineum	Deerberry
Viburnum lentago	Nannyberry, sheepberry
Vitex agnus-castus	Chaste-tree
Yucca spp.	Yucca

Based on data in Wyman, D., 1965. *Trees for American Gardens.* New York: The Macmillan Co. Wyman, D., 1969. *Shrubs and Vines for American Gardens.* New York: The Macmillan Co.

Table 13-7 A Comparison of the weights of various soil mixes used in plant containers.

Material by volume	Pounds per cubic yard
Clay soil	2,000
Sand	2,500
Peat, semidry	300–1,000*
Perlite	125–200
Vermiculite	110
Baked clay particles	1,000
$\frac{1}{3}$ soil, $\frac{1}{3}$ sand, $\frac{1}{3}$ peat	1,500–1,800†
$\frac{1}{2}$ peat, $\frac{1}{2}$ sand	1,400†
$\frac{1}{2}$ peat, $\frac{1}{2}$ perlite	270†
$\frac{1}{3}$ soil, $\frac{1}{3}$ perlite, $\frac{1}{3}$ peat	1,000†

*Peat weight depends on type of peat and moisture. Peat will weigh 10 to 20 times its dry weight when saturated.
†Depends on type of peat used.

critical factor is to provide proper moisture relationships and soil aeration for the growth of plants. This can be accomplished by providing adequate surface and internal drainage at the site. Moveover, watering facilities such as irrigation systems or water outlets for hand watering of plant beds should be adequate.

Grade changes and the addition of soil are often necessary in creating elements of the design and providing sufficient soil for plant growth; an example is the mounding of soil in shopping mall projects. The grade changes—both filling and cutting—should be done in an orderly manner, and existing desirable plants should be protected to prevent injury. Mechanical injury, that caused by construction equipment, can be minimized with fencing or trunk protection.

Obtain soil tests and make appropriate fertility and pH changes before the final grading is done.

Make sure that good drainage is provided for plants growing in areas where the root zone is restricted. Provide good, well-drained soil mixtures for backfill and make sure that an adequate moisture supply is available.

FOR FURTHER READING

Black, C. A., 1968. *Soil-Plant Relationships*. New York: John Wiley and Sons, Inc. 792 pages.

Hanson, A. A., and F. V. Juska, 1969. *Turfgrass Science*. Madison, Wisconsin: American Society of Agronomy, Inc. 715 pages.

Knott, J. E., 1962. *Handbook for Vegetable Growers*. New York: John Wiley and Sons, Inc. 245 pages.

Indiana Farm Drainage Guide, ID-55, Cooperative Extension Service. West Lafayette, Indiana: Purdue University.

14

The Planting
and Establishment
of Woody Plant Material

The proper installation of the landscape plant material involves much more than just digging holes and setting plants in them. The landscape contractor is responsible, as far as possible, for developing a satisfactory microclimate for the optimum growth and development of the plant. A healthy and vigorous plant is required if the landscape is to achieve the desired effect. The healthy plant will also require less maintenance in the years following establishment, and the overall result is that the owner of the landscape site will be satisfied.

Proper installation is also of financial importance to the contractor. Replacements that are required at the contractor's expense often reduce or completely eliminate the profit that can be made on a particular project. Good planting methods are a part of good business management.

In the preceding chapter we described how to analyze the conditions at the landscape site before planting the site. Overall or gross modifications required at the site were also discussed in detail. In this chapter we will discuss the specific details about establishing individual plants and groups of plants. We will also describe how to handle the planting of areas that pose no problems as well as those where problems exist.

PLANTING ON SITES WHERE SOIL CONDITIONS ARE FAVORABLE

A site that has an optimum or at least an adequate environment for the growth of woody ornamental plants is a luxury that most landscape contractors rarely have. Some of the conditions that make a site ideal are well-aerated

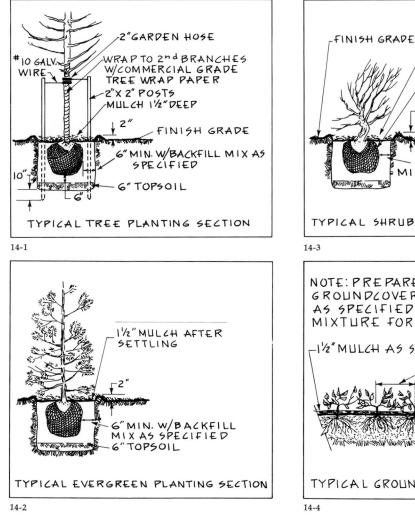

TYPICAL TREE PLANTING SECTION

14-1

TYPICAL EVERGREEN PLANTING SECTION

14-2

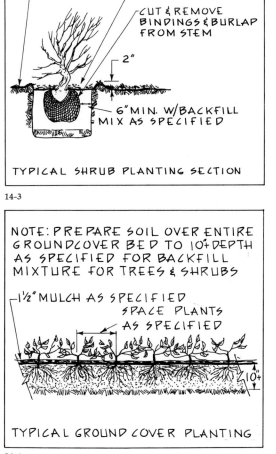

TYPICAL SHRUB PLANTING SECTION

14-3

TYPICAL GROUND COVER PLANTING

14-4

Figures 14-1 to 14-4. *Planting detail drawings are often included with the contract documents prepared by the landscape architect; at other times the planting details are left to the contractor. The specifications shown in these details for planting trees (14-1), evergreens (14-2), shrubs (14-3), and ground covers (14-4) are the minimum details that should be included on drawings. Actual planting detail drawings are shown in Chapter 10.*

soils with adequate moisture-holding capacity; surface drainage away from the planting area; and no need for protective devices against the natural or man-made elements. But even with the presence of ideal site conditions, specific procedures must be followed when installing plant material. Sometimes the contract or project specifications spell out in detail the installation methods that must be used, but more often than not the details of installation are left to the contractor. The following discussion will provide techniques that can be used when specific methods are not required in the contract.

The Planting Hole and Backfill

The planting hole is of real importance since this is the environment of the plant root system. Many plantsmen make many suggestions about how large the planting hole should be, but generally if the hole is 12 inches wider in diameter and 6 inches deeper than the soil ball, the size will be adequate. For very large specimens, such as trees of a four-inch caliper or more (the term "caliper" is derived from the use of a caliper to measure the trunk diameter) and large shrubs with a soil ball of three feet or more, the hole should be made up to 24 inches wider. The depth, six inches deeper than the soil ball, remains the same. If the large specimens are to be machine-dug and moved immediately to the site, different procedures will be used in preparing the planting hole. This will be discussed in the next section of the chapter.

For a commercial project, it is not practical to separate the topsoil from the subsoil when digging the hole, and if the soil condition is satisfactory, such separation is not even worth considering at all. The method of digging the hole ranges from digging manually with shovels to using tractor-mounted power-takeoff augers. Many contractors use hand-held power-driven augers for installing smaller plants. There are several sizes of augers, with a range of from 9 inches in diameter to 20 inches in diameter being available. Two men cannot easily handle the equipment when an auger is used that is of more than 20 inches in diameter. The tractor-mounted augers can be obtained in sizes of 36 inches or more. The holes dug with an auger usually require a little dressing with shovels before planting.

The addition of peat moss to the soil removed from the hole is desirable when preparing the backfill soil. At the well-drained site, use approximately one part peat by volume to two parts soil, and mix thoroughly. Add six inches of backfill mix before placing the plant in the hole. This should bring the top of the soil ball to the level of the surrounding soil. The planting depth should be such that the plant is at exactly the same depth after replanting as when growing in the nursery. Probably more plants are lost because they were planted too deep than for any other reason.

An acceptable amount of settling of the plant will occur with the use of six inches of backfill in the bottom of the planting hole. However, in certain sections of the country wet springs (the main planting season) are common. Then six inches of backfill in the bottom of the planting hole may result in excessive settling. A more practical approach if weather conditions of this type are prevalent is to excavate

14-5

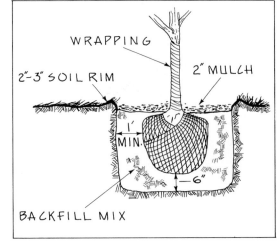

14-6

Figure 14-5. *A proper planting hole for small balled-and-burlapped or container-grown nursery stock should be about six inches larger than the root ball on all sides. The walls should be vertical. Prepared backfill is added around the plant. The burlap wrapping should be cut and folded down after the hole is two-thirds filled with soil. The strings that secured it should be removed from around the trunk.*

Figure 14-6. *A planting hole for larger sized plants (trees of 4-inch caliper and over or shrubs with root balls three feet or more in diameter) should have a diameter 24 inches larger than the root ball. A water basin rim should be constructed after planting. Likewise, mulch should be added and, in cold climates, tree trunks should be wrapped.*

14-7

Figure 14-7. *A tractor-mounted auger digging 20-inch diameter holes at a highway landscape site.*

the hole no deeper than the depth of the soil ball.

Caution should be used when planting in holes prepared by using an auger. Too often the plants are placed in the hole without regard for how deep the hole has been dug. It is quite common for operators of power augers to dig planting holes too deep. At one highway site several hundred spreading cotoneasters (*Cotoneaster divaricata*) in one-gallon containers were killed because they were placed in the bottom of planting holes that were several inches too deep, having been dug with a tractor-mounted auger. The tops of the soil balls were covered with from four to six inches more soil than had covered them while they were growing in the containers. The roots were smothered and the cotoneasters were lost. The cardinal rule in planting is this: *Never replant a plant at such a depth that after transplanting it is lower in the soil than it was before transplanting.*

Once the six inches of backfill has been added, carefully place the plant in the hole. Balled and burlapped material (commonly referred to as "B and B") must be handled carefully. If the soil ball on most species is broken for any reason, the plant will die. Always pick the plant up by the soil ball or container—never by the trunk or stem. Remove all plastic or metal containers before placing the plant in the hole. Small containers with tapered sides can be removed by turning the plant upside down and giving the top edge of the container a sharp rap. Catch the soil ball in the hands as it slips from the container. Do not break the soil ball apart. The larger-sized containers, of five gallon or more, should be cut away with

special cutters. If the plants have become overgrown in the container and the root mass is growing in a tight, compact circle around the soil ball, cut out the outer roots with a sharp knife in two or four places around the soil ball. Make the cut from the top to the bottom of the soil ball. The burlap should not be removed from the soil ball of B and B plants. Decomposable containers (papier-mâché) need not be removed from the soil ball.

Bare-root plants should have the packing material removed from the roots, and all damaged or dead roots should be removed. If possible, before planting, the roots should be soaked in water for at least 1 hour but not longer than 24 hours. Do not allow the roots to be exposed to the sunlight or dry out before planting. It is best to keep the bare roots covered with moist burlap or some reasonable substitute until actually planting each individual plant.

After the B and B plant or container-grown plant has been placed in the hole, fill in around the plant with the prepared backfill until the hole is two-thirds full. With the bare-root plant the soil should be worked gently in and around the roots while the plant is being supported. The most satisfactory way of firming the soil and removing air pockets is to fill the hole with water. If water is not available or it is not practical to use this procedure, firm the soil by hand around the plant ball or roots. However, be sure not to use excessive force, since soil compaction should be avoided, and because excessive packing defeats the purpose of adding peat moss to the backfill. Extreme caution should be used in firming wet backfill.

Before finishing the filling process, make absolutely certain the plant is straight and at the proper depth. Then complete the filling process with the backfill mixture. If the specimen is an individual it will be desirable to construct a ring two to three inches high at the edge of the outside diameter of the hole to form a water basin. Plants in beds probably will not require a water basin. Water the plant thoroughly as soon as the water basin is constructed. After the water has soaked away, fill the basin with a mulch material. Organic mulches such as peat moss, bark, wood chips, etc., provide the best environment for the future root development, but often a stone or other inorganic mulch will be called for by the designer.

It should be noted that no fertilizer was added to the backfill mixture. Often too much fertilizer is added and the newly developing roots are damaged. If it is apparent from your knowledge of the soil condition that fertilizer is needed, add a water-soluble material at the recommended rate during the final watering phase. Large areas should already have an established fertility level based on recommendations from soil test results before the planting of individual plants takes place. A fertility program should be begun late in the fall of the first growing season.

The use of "slow-release" fertilizers should be considered by the landscape contractor. These materials may be used at the time of planting and will supply some nitrogen to the plant throughout the growing season. The rates that should be used are recommended by the manufacturer and should not be exceeded. The cost of the slow-release fertilizers is sub-stantially higher than for regular fertilizer salts, and debate about whether plants fertilized in this manner harden sufficiently for winter still continues, yet little difficulty has been reported in overwintering plants fertilized with slow-release fertilizers.

Pruning and Supporting Newly Installed Plants

An initial pruning is needed immediately after planting. Container-grown and B and B plants require only the removal of all broken and damaged branches. Bare-root stock requires more severe pruning, since the root area has been markedly reduced during digging. For these plants, it is necessary to reduce the water loss by removing one-third to one-half of the leaf area. This pruning can be done by using the thinning process. Be sure not to ruin the natural growth habit of shrubs, and do not remove the central leader of trees. We will discuss pruning in detail in Chapter 17.

Most shrubs do not need to be supported after planting unless bare-root stock has been planted that is quite large, or very tall B and B specimens have been used. If so, use the same techniques for shrubs that we will describe for trees.

A general rule of thumb is to provide support for all bare-root trees over eight feet in height. Smaller B and B or container-grown trees usually do not need support. Trees that are quite large—six inches or more in diameter—should be supported. There are several methods for supporting smaller trees, any one of which is satisfactory. A single stake about three-fourths the height of the bare-root tree should be driven at a distance of two to four inches

14-8

Figure 14-8. *Douglas-fir bark mulch has been used here to reduce weed growth and help retain moisture in soil for newly planted trees. Note the wrappings on the newly planted trees.*

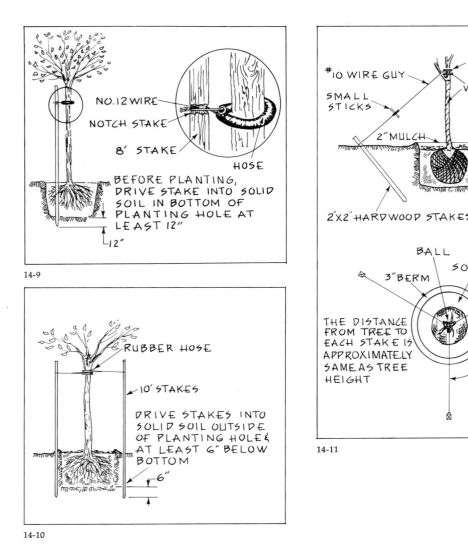

NO.12 WIRE

NOTCH STAKE

8' STAKE

HOSE

BEFORE PLANTING,
DRIVE STAKE INTO SOLID
SOIL IN BOTTOM OF
PLANTING HOLE AT
LEAST 12"

12"

14-9

RUBBER HOSE

10' STAKES

DRIVE STAKES INTO
SOLID SOIL OUTSIDE
OF PLANTING HOLE &
AT LEAST 6" BELOW
BOTTOM

6"

14-10

#10 WIRE GUY

RUBBER HOSE

SMALL
STICKS

WRAPPING

2" MULCH

30°-45°

30" MIN.

2"X2" HARDWOOD STAKES

BALL

3" BERM

SOIL MIX

THE DISTANCE
FROM TREE TO
EACH STAKE IS
APPROXIMATELY
SAME AS TREE
HEIGHT

120°

14-11

Figure 14-9. *Single-stake method of supporting small bare-root trees.*

Figure 14-10. *Double stakes used to support small bare-root trees.*

Figure 14-11. *Tree guy wires used to support small trees of three-inch caliper or more during the first year of establishment.*

from the center of the planting hole, so that the stake will be on the southwest side of the tree trunk. This should be done *before* the tree is placed in the hole. Then plant the tree according to the procedures described in the previous paragraphs. After the planting is completed, fasten the tree to the stake with a wire or a suitable substitute formed in a loose loop. Before fixing both ends of the wire at the stake, slip a short length of rubber hose onto the wire. The part of the wire in contact with the trunk should be covered with the rubber hose to prevent injury to the bark as the tree moves in the wind. The advantage of this method of support is that the stake is close to the trunk and does not cause maintenance problems. In turf areas, stakes and guy wires outside the perimeter of the planting hole can be troublesome, since they hinder mowing operations. Under no circumstances should this method of support be used on B and B or container-grown stock, for it is usually not possible to locate a stake close to the trunks of such stock before planting, and if driven through the soil ball, the stake will cause damage to the soil ball and the roots.

A more satisfactory method of supporting small trees is to use two parallel stakes driven solidly at least 18 inches into the firm soil about a foot beyond the planting hole. The height of the stakes after being driven into the ground should be approximately two-thirds that of the tree. The tree is then supported by wires attached to both stakes and looped loosely around the trunk. A rubber hose length can be used to protect the tree trunk.

A third method—the one most commonly used—is to fasten three guy wires to stakes or deadmen that have been fixed in firm soil around the edge of the planting hole at an equal distance from the hole. Stakes are generally used on smaller plants. They should be driven 18 to 30 inches into the ground at a 45-degree angle away from the tree trunk. It is absolutely essential that all three stakes be firmly implanted so that one or more of them will not pull out in high winds. The top of the stake is notched to hold the wire. The wire is then fastened two-thirds of the way up the trunk by a loose rubber-hose-covered loop. The other ends of all wires should be fastened equally tightly, without putting a strain on the trunk, to the implanted stakes.

On very large specimens, of over six-inch caliper, it is suggested that deadmen be installed in place of the stakes. The deadmen usually are made of eight-inch stock, either eight-inch logs or four-by-eight-inch lumber, three to four feet in length. Soil-anchor devices can also be used as deadmen, and so can 6-by-6-by-12-inch concrete blocks. The anchors have the advantage of being smaller and requiring less disturbance of turf during installation. They should be installed at a depth of not less than three feet depending upon the soil type and the size of the specimen being anchored. The larger the tree the deeper the deadmen should be set. The eight-inch width of the deadman should be placed so that it is at a 90-degree angle to the direction of the maximum pull—that is, it should be tilted slightly upward, facing the tree. An eye-bolt should be inserted in each deadman so that the cable may be attached, or else the cable may be passed around the deadman. The cable is attached to the tree

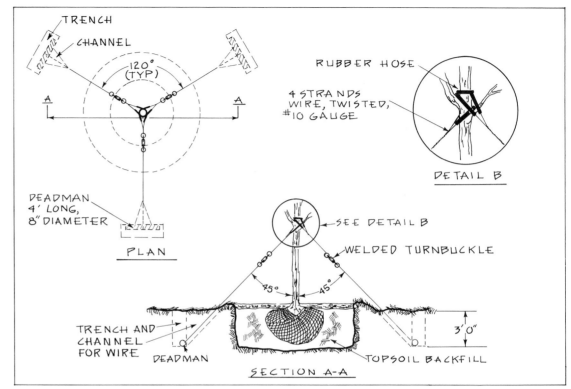

14-12

Figure 14-12. *Deadmen should be used for anchoring a large specimen. The details shown here would suffice in good soil. In light soils four deadmen or soil anchors might be needed instead of three. A soil rim, mulch, and tree wrapping should be added after planting, as described in the text.*

Figures 14-13, 14-14. *In the northern climates, after trees have been planted, the trunks should be treated with insecticide and then a wrapping should be applied for the first winter season. The wrapping is wound tightly from the bottom (14-13) to the first crotch or beyond (14-14) and the ends are tied with twine.*

14-13

14-14

in the manner described in the preceding paragraph. A loose loop is used, with heavy-duty rubber hose, to protect the tree trunk from physical damage. It is necessary to use turnbuckles in the cables to tighten the cables and to provide the required support for the tree during its establishment. If the soil types are light and the specimen is large, four guy wires and deadmen may be required.

There are variations in the methods described for supporting trees, which may be useful in specific circumstances. As an example, a three-stake frame can be used in place of the two-stake method where it is desirable to protect the tree from possible physical damage. Also, slight variations in the guying methods can be used, but the techniques for supporting the trees are the same. There is one variation that is *not* recommended; that is to screw eye-bolts into tree trunks, the guy wires then being fastened to these eye-bolts. There are two principle disadvantages to this procedure. First, the tree trunk may be weakened because of the deep penetration of the eye-bolts into the wood. Second, when the eye-bolts are removed they leave wounds that may be a means of entry into the trunk by insects and disease.

All supports should be removed from the small trees within one season after planting. The tree should have become established in this period of time, and it has been reported that growth is actually reduced if the supports are left in place for longer periods of time. Larger trees may take longer for establishment, so the supports should be removed from large trees immediately after establishment.

In cold climates, after the tree has been planted and supported, the tree trunk should be wrapped with tree-wrap paper or burlap. Before the wrapping is applied, the trunk should be treated with an insecticide to help prevent damage by borers. Check with the state entomologist or the Cooperative Extension Service specialist in entomology about current recommendations for control of borers. After the trunk is treated, apply the wrapping tightly to the trunk. This wrapping serves several purposes. On smaller trees, it reduces the water loss from the lenticels of the bark. More important, it reduces the winter temperature fluctuation of the trunk. Rapid variations in trunk temperatures result in frost cracks and sunscald. On bright, cold winter days, the trunk temperature rises several degrees above the air temperature. If the sun suddenly goes under a cloud or behind a building, the temperature drops rapidly, causing the death of the exposed tissue—i.e., sunscald. Or the bark will contract more rapidly on one side than the inner wood does, causing frost cracks to develop in the bark. The tree wrapping helps maintain an even temperature on the bark of the trunk, which is not exposed directly to the rays of the sun. The branches of well-established trees provide partial shade that reduces the danger of sunscald and frost cracks.

Another feature of tree wrapping is that it provides some barrier to insects that might attack the trunk. Also, it slows markedly the rate at which the insecticide treatment for borers is washed from the trunk. Trunk protection may also be provided by wire mesh, plastic, or solid metal guards. These are ineffective against borers, but will reduce the chances of trunk wounds that might otherwise be caused by vandals, vehicles, mowers, rodents, etc.

The planting of trees and shrubs is relatively simple when environmental conditions are satisfactory, and success can be achieved and plant losses reduced if the techniques we have outlined here are followed.

Preparation of the Site for Large Specimens

As mentioned in the preceding section, preparation of the planting hole for machine-dug large specimens presents unique problems. It is suggested that before the specimen is dug, the machine that will do the digging be taken to the planting site and used to excavate the planting hole. The hole will then be exactly the right size for the tree or shrub when it is brought to the site in the digging machine. Trying to dig the hole by hand results in unnecessarily high labor costs. The use of a backhoe, or other mechanical means, requires a skilled equipment operator to insure that the hole is of the right size. It is quite easy to dig a hole too deep with a backhoe. Large trees of certain species planted six to eight inches too deep probably will not survive. On the other hand, setting the plants in a machine-dug hole usually prevents improvement of the planting site through the use of a good backfill material.

If the plants are not to be set by machine and the holes are to be dug by hand or backhoe, a peat and soil backfill can then be used. It is important that the soil be firm in the bottom of the hole before the large soil ball is placed in the hole. Otherwise, excessive settling may result and the plant will be too deep, or the top of the soil ball will sink by one or two inches, causing a maintenance problem.

The newly planted specimen should be watered thoroughly with two or three inches of water at the time of planting. (From 1¼ to 1¾ gallons of water per square foot of soil surface is required if two to three inches of water is to be applied at planting time.) The water must be added slowly enough to insure good penetration with a minimum runoff. If above-ground irrigation is used, the amount of water that is applied in a given period of time should be measured. Check several locations in the irrigation pattern; you will be surprised at how long it takes to apply even one inch of water. The supporting of the tree is carried out as described previously, but deadmen should be used if at all possible, rather than stakes.

Reducing Transplant Shock in Large Specimens

The transplanting of very large specimens requires special techniques. The key difficulty in moving such specimens is the moisture stress that is developed because of loss of roots during the digging operation. The amount of water needed by the plant is determined by the number of leaves that the plant posesses, and the amount of water taken up to satisfy this need is determined by the number of roots. The balance between root and top cannot be greatly disturbed without throwing the plant into a severe moisture stress. The larger the plant, the greater the amount of root surface lost in transplanting and the more severe the moisture stress.

Several techniques may be used to reduce water loss by large plants during their trans-

14-15

Figure 14-15. *The placing of a large pine dug with a Vermeer tree spade into a hole dug with the same machine. The tree planting depth is more accurate if the hole is dug before the tree is dug.*

14-16

Figure 14-16. *Large specimens are often needed when replacements are made in mature landscape settings. To offset transplant shock, a large soil ball was left on this horsechestnut and the tree was transplanted in winter.*

planting. The use of antitranspirants (the principal water loss by the plant is through the transpiration stream) is widespread among many landscape contractors. The antitranspirants are of two types, one of which causes the stomata openings to close chemically and the other of which coats the leaf surfaces with a vapor-impervious material, thus reducing water loss through the leaves. Spraying antitranspirants on the foliage of large plants before transplanting them will reduce the water loss. But it is a mistake to believe that the benefit gained from antitranspirants is long lasting. Research indicates that after two to three days the effect begins to wear off. However, a second application can be made. Moreover, inasmuch as within two to three days after transplanting, new roots begin to develop, it is the reduction of water loss by the antitranspirants applied during those critical first days of transplanting that really matters. Follow the directions given by the manufacturer when applying the anti-transpirants. The coating antitranspirants must be sprayed on the *underside* of the leaves as well as the tops of the leaves. The greatest number of stomata openings of most plant species are located on the underside of leaf surfaces, so it is of very little benefit to spray only the upper surfaces of the leaves.

Remember that antitranspirants are only temporary reducers of the water demands of the plant. They are not water substitutes. It is necessary to supply adequate water to the plant during the establishment period. Also, the reduction of water loss should be continued beyond the period for which antitranspirants are effective. One way of reducing the water demands is to reduce the leaf area of the plant

by pruning. Removing up to a third of the total leaf area will reduce the amount of water lost by transpiration.

The transpiration rate is reduced when the relative humidity is high. The construction of a mist system throughout the plant can help to maintain a high humidity at the leaf surfaces and hence will reduce the amount of water lost by transpiration. The installation of a mist system is expensive. But if the transplanting of a very large specimen is required this may be the only method of preventing severe moisture stress, and the expense is then warranted. The system is constructed by using plastic pipe fitted with some type of mist nozzles. The selection of the nozzle type depends on the quality of water available. Water with a high mineral content will clog nozzles that have orifices that are too small. Select the nozzle type accordingly. The spread or diameter of the mist spray will be given in the specifications for the nozzle. Little or no overlap is needed but the nozzles should be close enough together to insure complete coverage. The system should be installed on the side of the plant that faces in the direction from which the prevailing winds blow. This will allow the winds to carry the mist throughout the tree.

The frequency of misting will depend upon the temperature and dryness of the climate. In the more arid regions of the country the misting may need to be nearly continuous. The leaf area should not be allowed to dry out for long periods of time, i.e., several hours. In more humid regions, misting is needed less frequently, but it must be frequent enough to keep the humidity in the tree high at all times during daylight hours. The misting should be stopped early enough in the day to allow the foliage to dry before nightfall. This will reduce the chances of the development of foliage diseases due to the high humidity surrounding the foliage. The quantity of water put out by the system must not be so great that the soil in which the tree is planted becomes waterlogged. Likewise, the soil should be checked frequently at a depth of from six to nine inches to make sure it has not become too dry because of the frequent light waterings.

The control of the mist system may be manual, but such labor is costly. The use of a time clock connected to a solenoid valve is the most practical control. The frequency of misting as well as a shut-off time can be set on the clock and the system will operate automatically.

As the tree becomes established it is suggested that the frequency of mistings be reduced to give the plant a chance to become accustomed to reduced humidity and moisture. This equilibration process should be done gradually, over a period of several weeks.

The use of antitranspirants and mist systems not only is beneficial when large specimens are moved, but many contractors have found the techniques useful when planting is to be done during the hot summer periods of the year. In some instances very large trees have been moved while in full leaf during the summer by using antitranspirants and by installing mist systems.

PLANTING ON SITES WHERE SOIL CONDITIONS ARE UNFAVORABLE

Unsatisfactory soil conditions are the most common problems encountered by the land-scape contractor at the site. Heavy soils, poorly drained soils, excessively rapid-draining soils, and foreign objects left over from construction are some of the unfavorable conditions found frequently at sites. The contractor must modify the soil environment so that the plants he installs not only surivive but also thrive. Planting techniques in heavy, poorly drained soils will be considered first.

Poorly Drained Soils

General planting procedures should be followed, with particular emphasis on the correct depth of planting: it is absolutely essential that the plant be installed at a depth exactly the same as the one at which it was growing previously. Avoid the mixing of any organic or inorganic soil conditioner in the backfill soil. Also, use the soil removed from the hole for backfill. Bringing in lighter, more porous soil for backfill should not be done. The more porous backfill mixes will cause the formation of a sump in the planting hole. Then, water will move into the hole and, because of the heavy, poorly drained soil forming the walls of the hole, the water will be trapped. In periods of excessive rainfall or when application of moisture has been too heavy, the planting hole fills with water and aeration is markedly reduced. If this condition persists for more than a few hours, plant injury may result, and if the waterlogging exists for longer periods, plants of some species will die.

Providing drainage of water from the planting site may be required. Area drainage was discussed as one of the topics in Chapter 13. The expense of this type of drainage may not be justified on the project and it will then

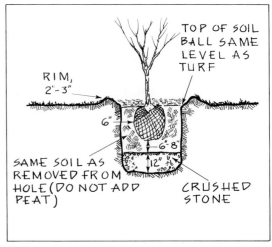

14-17

Figure 14-17. *Preparation of a sump under the planting hole in poorly drained soil to collect some of the water as it drains into the planting hole.*

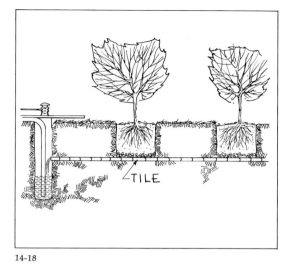

14-18

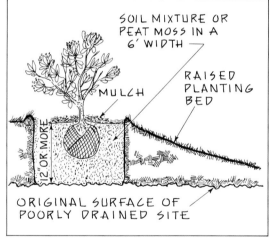

14-19

Figure 14-18. *A sump pump method of removing water from a landscape bed. Small stones or crushed gravel should be used at the bottom of planting holes. The sump pump method is expensive and so, is seldom used.*

Figure 14-19. *A raised bed may be used to establish plants that will not tolerate wet soils.*

be necessary to provide drainage for individual plants. There are several techniques that can be used, depending upon the severity of the drainage problem. The simplest is to provide a dry well in the bottom of the planting hole. To do this, dig the planting hole 12 to 18 inches deeper than required and fill the additional depth with coarse gravel or stone. This will provide a sump for the collection of water that drains into the planting hole. The technique will work only in areas of moderate or light rainfall and in soils that are only moderately tight.

A modification of the dry-well technique is to dig the hole deep enough that a well-drained stratum of soil is reached. The hole is then filled with gravel to the depth that will permit normal planting procedures. The dry well connects the hole to the well-drained stratum, forming a connecting channel for water movement from the hole. This technique can be used only if the permeable soil layer exists at a reasonable depth, such as 24 to 30 inches below the soil surface. Make sure that the water table level is not as high as the well-drained substratum.

If a very permeable layer exists at depths greater than three feet, it is possible at some sites to drive a six- to eight-inch-wide drainage channel from the bottom of the hole to the permeable layer. The drain channel should be filled with coarse gravel.

At many sites a permeable layer does not exist at any reasonable depth. Under these soil conditions, it is necessary to provide tile drainage from the individual planting hole or bed to a water-removal system such as a storm sewer. However, the discharging of drainage systems into public sewer systems must be cleared with the proper authorities before connection is made to the public system. Field tile can be used for this sytem. The tile should be laid at a depth slightly deeper than the planting hole, beginning beneath the hole and leading away from it. The tile under the planting hole should be covered with a four- to six-inch layer of coarse gravel or crushed stone. In areas of great rainfall or where heavy turf irrigation is used, two rows of tile, one running away from each side of the planting hole, may be desirable. Beds in which plants are growing close together may be drained this way, though if soils are very tight, it is necessary to run a tile under every row of medium- or large-sized shrubs, because in very tight soils, the lateral movement of water into drain tiles is slight.

An alternative method to using the storm sewer for disposing of the water collected in the tile system is to dig a sump at the end of a bed or a series of plants. The sump should be constructed by setting a large tile in a vertical position. The water collected in the sump can be pumped to the soil surface and away from the bed. This is an expensive procedure but at some sites it is the only way that a bed or planting site may be drained. The use of this procedure will be more common for beds in turf areas that are heavily irrigated.

Another solution, if the site cannot be easily drained, is to construct a raised planting bed. This technique requires building a soil mound to accommodate all or at least most of the eventual root development of the plant. A well-drained planting medium can be prepared by mixing one part peat moss to two parts well-well drained topsoil by volume. If the topsoil is not well drained the mix should consist of one part peat moss, one part sand, and two parts topsoil by volume. Recognizably, the cost of preparing a soil mix of this type may be prohibitive for some projects. If this is true, and soil must be brought in from somewhere else, be sure to exercise extreme care in selecting the fill soil to be used for the bed construction. It should be a type that is well drained, yet it should have adequate moisture-holding capacity. Heavy clay soils and light sandy soils should be avoided.

The soil surface should be worked up thoroughly with a rototiller before the bed is constructed. This will increase the bonding action of the soil surface with the soil mix that will be used to construct the raised bed. Before the bed is constructed it may be desirable to provide tile drainage at the bottom of the bed. This can be done simply by preparing a grid system of tiles laid on the newly tilled soil surface. The soil for the bed is then merely placed on top of the tile system. The drain system should be used if the plant material that will be installed in the raised bed is very sensitive to low-oxygen/high-moisture levels in the soil. Also, it will benefit the plants if the bed is given the same frequent irrigations that adjacent turf areas require.

The depth of the bed will depend in part on the type and size of plant that will be grown in it. Small plants with small soil balls, such as some azaleas and rhododendrons, require a bed that is 12 to 18 inches in depth. The bed should be 24 to 30 inches deep for larger trees and shrubs.

Inasmuch as the bed is raised, the retention of surface water may be reduced, and excessive drying out of the soil can result. To prevent this, the bed should be given a rim of soil two to three inches in height. This can be constructed in the same manner that the water basin for individual plants is constructed (as was described in the first section of this chapter). This rim will prevent excessive runoff of rainfall and irrigation water. If the bed is very large, with many plants, a water basin should be constructed for each plant. Water retention throughout the entire bed will be improved if an organic mulch is used.

Large beds of this nature may look more attractive if the edges of the bed are retained with a wall. Railroad ties are quite popular for this purpose, though flagstone or any other wall-construction material can be used. The landscape architect will specify the type of wall and the construction procedures to be followed in most of the projects he has designed. It may be desirable to blend the bed into a surrounding turf area. If this is done, the edge of the bed should slope gently to the turf area, with the slope starting at the water retention rim. The slope can be grassed over immediately after construction to prevent erosion of the edges.

For individual specimens such as trees, raised beds can also be used. The bed should be from two to three feet wider than the soil ball and the depth will depend upon the size and eventual development of the plant. The soil surface should be worked up before constructing the bed. A shallow hole can be dug to support the soil ball, if the drainage problem is not excessive surface water. The bed can then be constructed around the soil ball, after the plant has been set. A water-basin rim

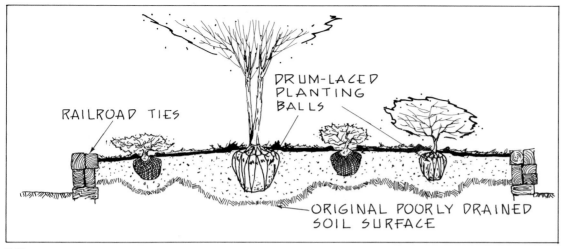

RAILROAD TIES

DRUM-LACED
PLANTING
BALLS

ORIGINAL POORLY DRAINED
SOIL SURFACE

14-20

Figure 14-20. *Use of retaining walls for construction of a raised planting bed. Railroad ties can be used for such walls and provide a neutrally colored architectural addition to the landscape. When soil balls have been drum-laced, as shown here, it is important to be sure that any cords that encircle the trunks are cut free before planting.*

should be constructed, and a mulch should be used.

Raised-bed techniques should be used for numerous plants that will not tolerate poorly drained soils. In many areas, it is common practice to use the method for planting rhododendrons, azaleas, and other ericaceous species. Certain of the dogwoods, particularly *Cornus florida*, develop better if the raised-bed planting technique is used than when they are planted in soil that has not been prepared for them. It is felt that many dogwoods do not survive urban planting sites because of heavy, poorly drained soils. *Taxus* spp. will not tolerate waterlogged soils, either; many *Taxus* plants have had to be replaced more than once because of this condition, and contractors should consider using raised beds for *Taxus* oftener at those sites where drainage is poor.

On construction sites where the topsoil has been removed, and all that remains is a nonfertile subsoil of low productivity, the use of the raised-bed planting technique provides a satisfactory environment for the development of roots and, hence, for the future growth of the plant. Highway sites frequently possess planting sites where soil conditions are poor, and raised beds offer a solution there to the problem of establishing woody ornamentals for landscape purposes.

Where the possibility of an artificial water table exists, the planting procedures should be the same as for heavy soils. The use of a drainage system is almost essential in areas where rainfall is moderate or heavy and the design calls for plants that will not tolerate wet soils. If a high artificial or "perched" water table may develop during wet spells, the tile-drainage system is the most efficient means for providing drainage from planting sites. The techniques for laying the tile are the same as described previously.

Excessively Drained Soils

Soils that contain a high percentage of sand may not have sufficient moisture-holding capacity to provide adequate water during periods of dry weather. The contractor should then try to improve the moisture-holding capacity of the soil through the addition of peat moss. Increasing the organic matter in the soil provides a satisfactory environment for the development of new roots. The improved soil mix will hold moisture for longer periods of time and will supply water to the plant more evenly during the period when new roots are developing.

The addition of one-third to one-half sphagnum peat moss by volume to two-thirds to one-half soil is recommended for the backfill. A less satisfactory choice would be hypnum peat or sedge peat. These peats are better than not adding any organic matter, but sphagnum peat is the best.

For plants that are especially sensitive to lack of moisture it is also desirable to plan on providing a means of supplying moisture beyond the natural supply of rainfall. A water basin should be constructed that is one to two feet wider in diameter than the planting hole. The rim should be three to four inches high. An organic mulch that holds moisture is preferred over an inorganic or stone mulch.

Support for trees is more difficult in lightweight, rapidly draining soils. The use of support stakes for smaller trees is preferred over guy wires since the small stakes holding the guy wires may pull out of sandy soil during periods of high wind. However, large specimen trees, of four inches in diameter or more, should be supported with guy wires. The guy wires can be attached to the tree as described in the first section of this chapter, but in sandy soils it is essential that deadmen be used rather than stakes. Make absolutely sure that the deadmen or other soil anchors are buried at least three feet deep so that they will not pull loose. It is essential that the tree be well established before removing the supports, and longer than one year may be required for the establishment of large trees.

Wrapping the trunk will reduce water loss during the winter months. The same techniques for wrapping can be used that are used for planting in other soil types.

Foreign Objects Left in the Soil after Construction

Almost every landscape contractor faces the problem of what to do about foreign objects left in the soil at any site where heavy construction has taken place. It is also a common problem at home sites. But now we need to qualify what we mean when we say "foreign objects," because what the contractor discovers most often is that the soil in some parts of a site seems foreign, and that a completely different soil condition may exist in one spot than at the rest of the site. As an example, sand may have been used for fill next to a foundation, and this will result in an excessively dry planting site. Large pieces of masonry, wood, etc.—the materials one immediately thinks of as foreign to the soil at a site—will also cause dry areas to develop during dry weather.

14-21

Figure 14-21. *The debris shown in this photograph should have been cleared away before the backhoe operator began his work. If the debris is filled over, it may alter the soil condition.*

In sandy spots, the techniques for planting in excessively well-drained soils should be used. If only a small area of sand is present, it is best to remove it and to replace it with fill soil of the type found on the rest of the site. Large objects such as cement blocks, pieces of wood, plasterboard, etc., should be removed just as one would normally remove large rocks when digging a planting hole for planting. The removal of such objects is essential if all plants are to grow at as equal a rate as possible. Also, the number of future replacements will be fewer and the maintenance that will be required in subsequent years will not be as great. Frequently, landscape maintenance personnel have unexpected trouble with individual plants and the cause of the problem can be traced to construction residue left at the planting site.

So far we have discussed what to do only about the debris that an insensitive builder felt it was somehow all right to mix in with the fill he used at the planting site. It seemed "clean" to him. The landscape contractor must, however, also be aware of any materials dumped during construction that might drastically change the chemistry of the soil. Bags of plaster and cement will, when dumped in one spot, cause a rapid increase in soil pH at that spot, which some plants will not tolerate. If the plaster or cement is not mixed in the soil but is left on the surface, the concentration of the material will be so high that the plant will be killed immediately.

Other hazards are oils, tars, creosote, etc., that have been dumped. These materials kill all plant life; the only way to avoid this misfortune is to remove all the contaminated soil and replace it with a fill soil of the type that is prev-alent at the site. Care should be taken to insure that all of the contaminated soil is removed rather than buried under additional fill soil, as is a common practice.

The prime contractor (the contractor who is responsible for building construction, etc.) should be responsible also for removal from the site of any construction debris that results from the construction. Often the debris is not removed, and in some instances the prime contractor has merely covered the debris with fill soil. The project has been accepted by the contracting authority before the landscape contractor starts his work. Regardless of who should have been responsible for cleaning away the rubble, the landscape contractor can protect himself as much as possible by making a thorough site investigation to determine what kinds of soil-damaging materials are being used, where they are being used, and whether they are present in excessive amounts. If he believes the debris will interfere with his work, he should call this to the attention of the landscape architect and/or the client. The bid should be adjusted accordingly so that the debris can be removed and the plant material can be properly installed.

PLANTING ON SITES
THAT ARE ADVERSE TO
PLANT GROWTH

Physical characteristics of the site such as excessive exposure to winds, surface drainage of water into the planting site, slope grades in excess of a one-foot drop in every five feet, and possible plant damage due to wounding by equipment or animals or vandals must be considered by the landscape contractor when installing plant materials. The first condition to be considered will be locations where excessive wind may be a problem.

Excessive Wind

Certain characteristics of architectual features, such as large flat walls and building corners that face the prevailing winds, increase the chances that the plant may be injured by wind. When the wind hits a flat surface or goes around the corner of the building, its velocity sometimes increases markedly. This increase in velocity is what injures the plant. Broadleaf evergreens are particularly susceptible to this type of injury during winter, because they have a tendency to dry out rapidly when wind velocities are high, when the soil is frozen deeply, and when conditions are dry. Then the broadleaf evergreen cannot obtain sufficient water; leaf burn will often result, and the plant may die if the drying conditions persist. Also, any plant that is of borderline cold-hardiness is less likely to survive if planted where the amount of wind is excessive, or the velocity of the wind is excessive, or where both the amount and the velocity are excessive.

Besides the obvious solution of not planting plant material that is sensitive to wind damage, the only other solution to the problem is to provide windbreaks of some kind. These windbreaks should be designed and placed by the landscape architect. The windbreaks may be plant materials or architectural features such as fences, walls, and screens, which should be placed so as to change the wind direction and speed.

Planting Where Surface Drainage Is Poor

The draining of surface water into any planting site should be avoided at all costs, as we mentioned earlier. Woody plant materials cannot be established where this drainage problem exists. The water should be diverted from the planting site. This can be done in several ways, such as providing a gutter to drain water away from the plant or plant bed if the surface of a roadway or walk is the source of the problem. The construction of a curb is another means of diverting water from a planting area. Details of how to handle surface drainage from large impervious areas such as parking lots, roofs, and roads are discussed in detail in Chapter 13.

Sometimes no way can be found to install plants where the soil will not be drenched by excess water running off of architectural surfaces. A planting technique that can be used if surface water cannot be diverted from the planting area is to make a raised bed as described previously in this chapter. Care should be taken to insure that the bed is of sufficient height that water will not stand in it. The bed should extend at least two to three feet beyond the outermost plants in the bed so that if water collects where the bed and turf (or some other surface) meet, very little of the soil nearest the plants will be waterlogged if the water moves laterally. For individual specimens it may be necessary to recontour the site to move the water away from the individual plant. At some sites, a raised bed may be constructed that can be covered with turf later, after the plant has been established. Again, it is important that the bed be of sufficient size to prevent lateral movement of water to soil containing the plant roots.

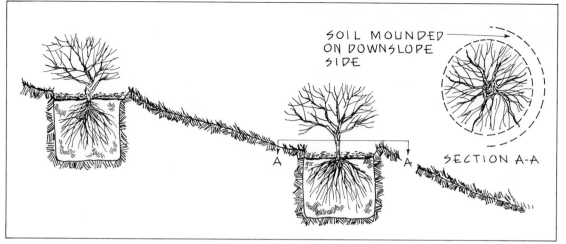

SOIL MOUNDED
ON DOWNSLOPE
SIDE

SECTION A-A

14-22

Figure 14-22. *The planting technique to be used for planting shrubs and trees on slopes.*

If the raised bed is in a turf area, the sides should not rise abruptly but should be gently sloped instead to facilitate easy mowing and prevent "skinning" of the edges of the raised bed with the mower.

Planting on Steep Slopes

Planting on slopes requires special techniques so that a water-collection basin may be constructed. Otherwise, the water will run off, and the plant may not receive the water it needs for establishment and growth. The planting hole can be dug the same way a planting hole is dug for a normal planting. However, it is necessary to prepare a soil mound on the downside of the hole. This mound helps to form a level area around the plant and makes the formation of a water basin possible. Other planting techniques such as mulching, watering, supporting, etc., are the same as described for planting under normal conditions.

The same technique can be used when several plant beds must be installed on slopes. A series of small terraces will help to provide the areas for water collection. It should be pointed out that on slopes of greater than a one-foot fall for every two feet, the use of the mound to provide an ample, level water basin is nearly impossible; hence, extensive terracing may be necessary. But when a steep slope allows it, a small water basin can be constructed on the lower side of the hole. Heavy mulching is recommended.

Planting in Paved Areas or Nonporous Containers

Planting in urban environments requires some special techniques. In planting, adequate drainage must be provided as well as soil adequate for growth and development. Figure 14-23 shows the bottom of a large planter, the top being about 18 inches above the sidewalk and the bottom 24 to 30 inches below the sidewalk. Figure 14-24 illustrates the correct installation techniques to use in such a planter, and Figure 14-25 shows a healthy *Pinus sylvestris* (Scots pine) thriving in a planter where proper installation and drainage techniques were used.

Trees planted in paved areas should have an area around the base that permits water to enter the planting hole. In large courtyards, paving bricks can be fitted together carefully but without the use of mortar, to permit the movement of water between the cracks. The use of gratings also permits movement of water to tree roots. The planting technique described in Figure 14-24 can be used for a raised planter in an urban setting. If the planter is being installed on a site that is well drained, the French drain system in the bottom is not needed. However, on poorly drained sites it is imperative to have a drain if the plants are to thrive.

PLANT PROTECTION

Protecting the plant from inflicted injuries during establishment is of great importance. The types of plant-mechanical wounding that are usually encountered are damage from mowers, rodents, and vandals. Protection from damage by mowers is virtually impossible, if the mower comes in contact with the plant. However, the tree supports and the water-basin rims around planting holes generally will provide ample warning to mower operators—so long as the supports and rims have been con-

14-23

14-25

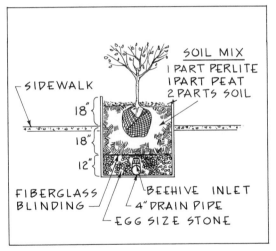

14-24

Figure 14-23. *The bottom of a planter with an internal drainage system. A beehive grate forms the inlet to the drain system.*

Figure 14-24. *The correct installation techniques for large planters in sidewalks. The same methods will be satisfactory for roof gardens, provided the bottom of the roof planter is waterproofed and the drain system is part of the root drainage system. In some instances the bottoms of large planters should be insulated to prevent the soil temperatures from becoming too warm in the winter.*

Figure 14-25. *A vigorous Scots pine (Pinus sylvestris) that has been correctly installed in a planter such as the one illustrated in the previous figure.*

14-26

14-27

14-28

Figure 14-26.   *The loose paving bricks used in this minipark permit water to move down to the tree roots. The paving extends right up to the trees, yet they receive the water they need.*

Figures 14-27, 14-28.   *A grating system that is easy to handle (14-27) and attractive and not an obstacle to pedestrians (14-28). It allows water to penetrate into the planting pit.*

structed with the thought that they can double as plant-protective measures. But planting trees and shrubs in turf areas without providing some means of keeping turf from growing close to the newly planted ornamental increases the chances of mower damage, because the operator of the mower will mow as close as possible to the plant to reduce the amount of hand trimming needed. Miscalculations often occur and result in plant injury.

Newly planted trees and some shrubs need protection from rodent damage, which occurs particularly in cold climates. The bark of the woody ornamental serves as a food source for animals during the winter months. Rabbits and mice cause the most damage, but browsing deer will also eat away the bark of young trees. There are three preventive techniques that can be used: mechanical barriers, baits, and repellants. Laws about use of baits vary throughout the United States and are constantly changing. The landscape contractor should investigate the regulations of the area in which the site is located before making use of these. It is much more advisable for the landscape contractor to install mechanical barriers at the time of planting. These consist of wire mesh screens that fit loosely around the trunk. The mesh should be ¼ inch or less so that mice cannot get through and the screens should fit tightly at the ground, with no gaps. A height of at least two feet is recommended so that rabbits cannot reach over the top of the protective screen. It must fit very loosely around the tree so as not to injure the trunk as the tree grows. As an alternative, a barrier can be made from a solid metal sheet, such as downspouting. The metal is fitted around the trunk and crimped after installation. The pro-

14-29

Figure 14-29. *Installation of a plastic rodent guard. The guard is preshaped and wraps around the trunk. Metal wire rodent guards are used in the same way.*

Figure 14-30. *Decorative tree-trunk protection along Nicollet Mall in Minneapolis, Minnesota.*

14-30

tective device should be removed with tin shears when the tree is well established and is at least two inches in diameter. A flexible plastic trunk guard has been developed recently that also provides protection against rodent damage.

Damage from vandals cannot be prevented if the vandal intends to damage the plant. The rodent-protective device made of solid metal will help if it is five or six feet in height, and it will deter cutting or carving of the trunk and the breaking over of the plant. In urban areas decorative trunk protections are sometimes used.

SUBSEQUENT CARE DURING THE ESTABLISHMENT PERIOD

The care that the newly planted plants receive during the establishment phases is often the responsibility of the landscape contractor, and how well he does his job will often determine whether the plants become well established and develop to their fullest potential. The most critical environmental factor that should be of concern to the contractor is the supply of available water during the establishment phase of the newly planted plant. For optimum growth it is essential that the amount of water available to the plant never be a limiting factor. However, the quantity of water must be carefully controlled, as too much water is often more detrimental to the plant than too little.

Ideally, water should be supplied by the contractor as required by the plant. However, in most cases this is not possible or practical. The frequency and amount of water needed by the plant is generally controlled by the soil type at the planting site. Lighter soils require more frequent waterings than heavier soils because of the lack of moisture retention by the lighter soils. Besides soil types, other factors that control the amount of water needed by the plant are the plant itself and climatic conditions. Some plants require less water than others. Generally, deciduous plants require more water than evergreens require during the active growing season. Plants with a high demand will require more water during hot, dry weather than if the temperatures are lower and humidities are higher. Some general, rule-of-thumb watering practices will be recommended, but nothing replaces the practical experience of being a careful observer to determine the water needs of landscape material.

If the two- or three-inch water basin has been constructed, it is recommended for well-drained loam type soils that this basin be filled at seven- to ten-day intervals throughout the growing season. It is important to supply water to the plant into the fall period so that the soil has an adequate moisture content during the winter. The water should be added during one watering period so that it will penetrate to a sufficient depth in the soil. Frequent, light waterings are of little value since soil penetration is slight and much water is lost through surface evaporation. If the planting area is to be watered by using an overhead irrigation system, one to two inches of water should be applied on a weekly basis. Again, this is for well-drained soils. The higher rate should be used for the lighter soils.

Plants that are being established in soils that drain with excessive rapidity, i.e., sands and sandy loams, should receive two one- to two-inch waterings per week. Again, this depends on the demands of the plant and the specific environmental conditions present.

Artificial waterings are used to supplement rainfall. If rainfall is adequate, no waterings are necessary. However, a four-inch rain does not mean that a two- to three-week supply of moisture will be retained by the soil. Runoff is not considered when precipitation is measured. Also, the excess water will drain rapidly from a well-drained soil. Waterings should be resumed in seven to ten days on well-drained soils if additional rainfall does not occur. Sandy soils may require even earlier applications. Again, the heavier soils should be checked for moisture before water is applied. Remember, brief summer showers are of little benefit. Know how much rain fell and in what period of time in order to plan the future irrigation program. Some trees will require supplemental waterings for up to six years after planting. Most plants, however, are established in one to two growing seasons and the waterings of normal maintenance are all that are required.

Insect and disease control for newly planted trees and shrubs should be carried out in the same manner as for established plants. The insect and disease control program is discussed in Chapter 18, on maintenance.

The first-year fertility program is limited to a fall application of fertilizer when spring or summer planting has been done. Fertilization should be done after dormancy has begun in areas where there is a cold season. This will prevent the development of a late flush of growth that might otherwise occur if fertilization were to be done late in the growing season; the soft, new growth cannot harden properly before cold weather occurs and winter injury can result. However, if fall planting has been done, a mid-spring treatment is best. In warmer climates the plants should be growing for at least two to three months before fertilizers are applied.

The easiest and most satisfactory method of fertilization is to broadcast dry fertilizer over the surface of the shrub bed or around the tree. The rate is based on the amount of nitrogen required, with a standard recommendation of two pounds actual nitrogen per 1,000 square feet being commonly used.

SUMMARY

Trees and shrubs that are not properly planted rarely develop to their fullest potential and the effect planned by the landscape architect is never achieved. It has been said that as much money or more should be spent on preparing the planting hole than on the plant itself. If, during the initial landscape construction phases, more attention would be given to planting, fewer maintenance problems would occur in the future growth and development of plants on the site.

FOR FURTHER READING

Robinette, G. O., 1968. *Off the Board, Into the Ground*. Dubuque, Iowa: Wm. C. Brown Book Co. 367 pages.

Sunset Magazine and Sunset Books (editors), 1967. *Sunset Western Garden Book*. Menlo Park, Calif.: Lane Magazine and Book Co. Revised edition, 1973. 448 pages.

Wyman, D., 1971. *Wyman's Gardening Encyclopedia*. New York: Macmillan. 1222 pages.

15

Installing Turf,
Ground Covers,
and Herbaceous Plants

The establishment of turf is required of the landscape contractor in many of his construction projects. The techniques and equipment for this are somewhat specialized, but once the principles are understood, installation of turf is relatively simple. Turf can be installed in one of three ways, i.e., by seeding, by sodding, and by sprigging or plugging. Several factors control the selection of the method to be used, and the landscape architect or the contracting authority or both must be aware of these factors when preparing the specifications for the turf at the landscape construction project.

TURF ESTABLISHMENT

Selecting the Best Procedure for Installation

Probably the factor given most consideration in turf establishment is that of economics. At nearly every project, an instant lawn would be the most desirable lawn, and through the use of sod, a lawn can be had nearly instantaneously. However, sodding is the most costly of all installation procedures. Generally, sodding costs are from five to seven times greater than those incurred when seeding is used and from three to four times greater than for sprigging and plugging. This means that eventually the customer must decide whether obtaining an "instant" turf cover warrants that additional cost or not.

To help him reach the decision about what kind of turf is best for his needs, the customer should be furnished with information on the rapidity with which he can expect a turf cover when the other installation methods are used. Also, the client or the contractor must consider the season of installation as well as other climatic conditions, such as the hardiness temperature zone in which the project is located, the amount of rainfall, availability of irrigation water, and soil conditions. Of course, if sound installation techniques are used with a good-quality product and good maintenance, sodding will provide "instant" cover and an established turf in from two to three weeks. The use of sprigs or plugs takes substantially longer, but if these are planted with a knowledge of the conditions listed above, the turf areas should become covered with grass in approximately two months. Complete cover, with a usable turf, will require up to four months when installed by seeding. Again, growing conditions must be ideal.

COOL-SEASON GRASSES

The climatic season is particularly critical if seeding is to be used. In the northern sections of the United States, mostly cool-season grasses are used, which means the seed germinates in cool weather and growth is best during cool weather. In fact, when the soil temperature rises above 80 to 90°F during the summer, active growth of established cool-season grasses ceases. The best times of the year for seeding cool-season grasses are from early to mid spring and from early to mid fall in the northern states. Obviously, cool-season grasses are not grown in southern climates. The optimum time for planting will depend upon the latitude of the location of the project. Thus, if cover is required during mid summer, seeding with cool-season grasses will not be very successful, and sodding should be installed instead, as it will be the only satisfactory way of achieving cover. The inexperienced contractor should obtain time-of-seeding information from the turf specialist of the Cooperative Extension Service. This specialist is usually located at the State Agricultural Experiment Station, which is a part of the state's college of agriculture.

WARM-SEASON GRASSES

Likewise, warm-season grasses have special temperature requirements for seeding. Soil temperatures should remain at an average of about 60°F for the best growth. This limits the seeding period to the time between late spring and mid summer. Late seedings do not allow enough time for the warm-season grasses to become established before cold weather comes. Of course, the problem of cold weather does not occur in the deep south and in southern California, where seeding can be carried out for longer periods of time. But seeding can cause problems if done too early in less-warm climates: where warm periods are of sufficient length to permit germination but are followed by cold weather, damage will be done to the newly emerged seedlings. Warm-season grasses are particularly susceptible to permanent cold-injury during the developing seedling stage. Again, check with local turf specialists to determine the optimum seeding times for warm-season grasses.

SPRIGGING, PLUGGING, AND STRIP SODDING

Sprigging is the spreading of live plant parts over the areas to be established in turf. The technique is limited mainly to use with warm-season grass species. The restriction on timing is not quite as severe as with seeding, but sprigging should be completed in time to allow the newly developing grass plants to become estab-

15-1

lished before cold weather occurs. Plugging is occasionally used, mainly for the warm-season grasses, though because weeds grow rapidly in the bare areas between plugs, the technique is not popular. Strip sodding (the laying of sod strips with space between the strips) or sod plugging is not considered satisfactory for the establishment of fine turf areas in the northern climates because of the slow rate of coverage.

In special instances plugs or strips of sod are used to control erosion. Plugs of grasses adapted to sand dunes can be used to help control wind erosion in these problem areas. Installation of plugs requires special techniques, which are described in the book *Turfgrass Science* by A. A. Hanson and F. V. Juska. It is listed among other readings at the end of the chapter.

If the season will not permit seeding and if neither climate nor grass variety lends itself to sprigging, the only option left is the use of total sodding to insure complete and satisfactory cover.

The rainfall that occurs in the area, availability of irrigation water, and soil conditions all influence the selection of the grass or grasses to be used in establishing turf. This selection affects in turn, somewhat, the method of installation that should be used. For small- to medium-sized areas, sodding is probably the most reliable method and the use of sod should be encouraged. The overall cost may not be too much greater than the cost of seeding, since initial maintenance and weed-control costs are less, and particularly if poor seeding requires making one or more additional seedings. But for large areas, the cost of sodding may be prohibitive, and seeding is the only method that is practical.

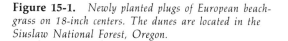

Figure 15-1. *Newly planted plugs of European beach-grass on 18-inch centers. The dunes are located in the Siuslaw National Forest, Oregon.*

Selecting the Right Species

Besides selecting the method for installation, the landscape architect must select the species of grass to be used on the basis of the characteristics he wants the turf area to have. We suggest that the reader study references on turf grasses to learn about the characteristics of the individual species. Such things as texture, growth habit, color, length of growing season, adaptability to climate or area, etc., should all be considered.

The most commonly used cool-season turf grasses are Kentucky bluegrass (*Poa pratensis*), and its varieties, and the red fescues (*Festuca rubra*). These grasses can be grown in nearly all sections of the country, though their use is limited in the Gulf Coast region of the southern United States. The warm-season grasses are Bermuda grass (*Cynodon dactylon*), and zoysia (*Zoysia japonica*). Bermuda and zoysia grasses are used to some degree in the Midwest, but their most common use is in areas farther south. St.-Augustine grass (*Stenotaphrum secundatum*) is limited to use in the South because of its lack of winter hardiness. Other warm-season grasses are also used in the South along the Gulf Coast, though to a more limited degree than those mentioned above. Also, different grass species are used for specific problem areas such as dune control, low light intensity, and drought areas. If the project is to be constructed in a problem area, consult turf references and turf specialists about the proper grass for the site. When an extremely fine-textured grass is needed, such as for golf greens, creeping bent grass (*Agrostis palustris*) is commonly used.

Table 15-1 Physical characteristics of important turf grasses.

Species	Texture	Uniformity	Turf quality Wear resistance	Shade tolerance
Kentucky bluegrass (*Poa pratensis*)	Fine	Good	Moderate	Low
Red fescue (*Festuca rubra*)	Fine	Good	High	Medium
Bermuda (*Cynodon dactylon*)	Medium	Good	High	Low
Zoysia (*Zoysia japonica*)	Fine	Good	High	High
St. Augustine (*Stenotaphrum secundatum*)	Coarse	Fair	Low	High

15-2

Important physical characteristics of the common turf grass species are of prime importance. Texture, uniformity, wear resistance, shade tolerance, and the length of the season the turf will remain green are all important considerations. Table 15-1 presents information on these characteristics for the five main turf grass species.

The cool-season grasses will remain green until heavy freezes occur and resumption of growth starts in the spring when soil temperatures reach approximately 40°F. This is true, of course, if adequate moisture is supplied during periods of drought. The warm-season grasses listed in Table 15-1 will turn brown immediately after the first frost.

The selection of specific varieties of each species will depend, first, on the suitability of that variety for use in the region where the project is located and, second, on the availability of seed. Recommendations for local conditions should be followed.

Site Preparation

Regardless of the establishment technique used, the site preparation is generally the same for all grasses. An orderly process should be followed when preparing the site, as this will save time and reduce installation costs. In their chapter in *Turfgrass Science*, Musser and Perkins suggest an eleven-item sequence to be followed in seedbed preparation, or for site preparation for sodding or sprigging. Their sequence of events is as follows:

1. Clearing and trash removal.
2. Location of borrow pits.
3. Stockpiling topsoil, and rough grading.
4. Installation of drainage and irrigation systems.
5. Subgrade fitting.
6. Placing topsoil.
7. Application of lime, basic fertilizer, and soil modifying materials.
8. Deep tillage and preliminary smoothing.
9. Application of starter fertilizer.
10. Final grading and smoothing.
11. Seedbed firming, if necessary.

Items 1 through 6 have been discussed in detail in our Chapter 13, "Site Modification." The techniques are the same, regardless of whether one is preparing the site for shrub and tree installation or for the development of a turf area. The most important fact here is to develop the site for turf establishment in an orderly fashion so that the best possible growing conditions for turf grasses are achieved at the site.

Once Item 6, the placing of topsoil, is completed, soil tests should be made to determine, first, the *p*H, and second, basic nutrient levels of the soil. The best *p*H is 6.5, and if below 6.2 lime should be added. The amount of lime required depends on the *p*H at the time of testing, and on the soil type. Table 13-4, in Chapter 13, gives suggested lime rates for different soil types. Remember that if large quantities of acid peat moss have been added to improve soil conditions, more lime will be required to raise the *p*H, because the peat moss has a high buffer capacity. Likewise, the use of large amounts of sand of a limestone origin will raise the *p*H, and lime may not be required. Using lime without making a soil test should be avoided. Some landscape architects write planting specifica-

Figure 15-2. *A landscape scraper being used to establish grade levels and break the subsoil surface before fill soil is added.*

tions that require lime for establishing turf areas even though the architect has not the slightest knowledge of the soil pH at the site. This practice is ridiculous; the preparer of the specifications should know better.

A pH of above 8.0 is not sufficiently acidic for most commonly used turf grasses. If grasses are used that do not tolerate a high pH condition, the acidity of the soil must be increased; that is, the pH must be lowered to an acceptable level, at or below 7.5. The lowering of soil pH is discussed in detail in Chapter 13. Soil pH should be modified at this particular phase of turf installation. Modification is more difficult after completion of installation, and sometimes it is nearly impossible if the pH must then be lowered a great amount.

Basic nutrients should also be added, according to the soil-test results, if these are needed to bring the soil levels to an acceptable level for turf establishment. The amounts and ratios of fertilizers will, of course, depend on the basic fertility needs determined by the soil test, the turf grass to be grown, climatic conditions such as rainfall and temperatures, the use of irrigation, and the soil type. Table 15-2 gives some suggested rates for the three basic elements, with the rate being based primarily on the nitrogen present in the fertilizer. The phosphorus and potassium levels recommended are the same as those for fertilizers with a 1 : 2 : 1 or 1 : 3 : 1 ratio.

The high rates should be used if soil tests reveal low fertility and, of course, the amounts should be reduced if the basic soil-fertility levels determined by testing are high. Often the testing laboratory will make specific recommendations for establishing turf if this is requested when the sample is submitted.

The fertilizer and lime, once it is spread evenly over the soil surface, should be thoroughly mixed in to a depth of six inches. This can be accomplished most easily with the use of a rotovator or a disk-cultivator. The size of the equipment needed depends, of course, entirely upon the size of the area to be covered with turf. This step is the deep-tillage portion (Item 8) mentioned earlier in the installation schedule. The soil surface should also be smoothed after the incorporation of the fertilizer. Although this is a preliminary smoothing, care should be taken to insure that proper contours and grades are maintained. A final removal of all foreign material, including stones larger than permitted in the specifications, should be done at this time.

The starter fertilizer application (Item 9) is made to the bed surface to insure that adequate fertility will be available to the seedlings or the sod during the time required for its establishment. Fertilizers should be used that are high in nitrogen, such as 3 : 1 : 1 or 2 : 1 : 1 mixtures. If the soil amounts of phosphorus and potassium are already satisfactory, only nitrogen need be added as the starter material. The rate of addition depends on the solubility of the fertilizer being used. Soluble or readily available forms of nitrogen should be used at the rate of 1 to 1½ pounds per 1,000 square feet, or 40 to 60 pounds per acre of actual nitrogen. Care should be taken not to use higher rates because fertilizer burn may damage emerging seedlings. The low-soluble, or "slow-release" fertilizers can be used at the higher

Table 15-2 Nutrient additions for turf site preparation.

| | Material needed (in pounds) | |
Element	per 1,000 sq ft	per acre
Nitrogen	2.5 to 4.0	100 to 160
Phosphorus (P_2O_5)	5.0 to 8.0	200 to 320
Potassium (K_2O)	2.0 to 3.0	80 to 120

Based on data in Vengris, J. 1969. *Lawns.* Fresno, Calif.: Thomson Publications.

15-3

15-4

Figure 15-3. *A Howard Rotovator, used to prepare a seedbed after rough grading has been done.*

Figure 15-4. *A landscape rake used to prepare seedbeds for turf grass seeding.*

rates of 4 to 5 pounds per 1,000 square feet or from 160 to 200 pounds per acre of actual nitrogen. The amounts depend on the material being used. Follow the manufacturer's recommendations to avoid injury to the new grass. The advantage of using slow-release fertilizers is that they meet the nutritional requirements of the grass over the entire establishment period. The disadvantage is that the slow-release fertilizer materials are generally several times more expensive than the conventional forms. The final results may justify the additional expense, but this can be determined only by experience.

The final grading and smoothing is a fairly delicate process and must be carried out with precision if the best results are to be achieved. It is absolutely essential that all grade stakes be reset at their proper location and level if they have been disturbed during the other phases of construction. All low places where water may not drain properly must be eliminated and the specified contours and slopes should be completed. On small areas (of a quarter acre or less), hand raking is done and use of leveling boards is commonly made because the area is too small to maneuver tractor-drawn equipment effectively. For large areas, the use of leveling equipment is not only practical but also essential for an economical installation. It will be necessary to hand-rake and smooth the soil around established plantings, trees, landscape features, and buildings.

Smoothing the bed surface is necessary if the establishment method is by seeding or sprigging. The smoothing or firming operation should be carried out when the soil is loose

and friable. Heavy, wet soils will become excessively compacted by the use of firming equipment. On loose, light soils, the firming as well as the smoothing can be done with light rolling equipment. When the seeding is to be done manually with gravity-feed or broadcast seeders, a light rolling of loam soils may be necessary if the surface is loose after final grading. When mechanical seeders are used, the equipment usually is equipped with firming parts that do the job adequately.

Gentle firming—but not compaction—of the planting bed should be done even if the planting technique is not seeding but sodding, sprigging, or plugging. This will help reduce the chances of low spots developing because of soil settling. All eleven of the site-preparation steps should be carried out regardless of the installation method to be used. This will help insure a good soil base for the turf area, and future problems and maintenance will be reduced.

Grass-Seed Planting

SEED MIXTURES

The importance of using high quality, certified grass-seed should not be overlooked since the best seedbed preparations are of little benefit if poor-quality seed is used. Low-price, poor-quality seed should be avoided. The savings to the contractor will be lost if reseeding is required. Actually, the cost of seed of the very best varieties represents only a small percentage of the total site-preparation costs. Therefore, it is false economy to purchase cheap seed of an unknown quality. Use only certified seed that is free from weed seed and has a high germination percentage.

The precise seed mixture should be specified by the landscape architect and/or contracting authority. Because this is not always done, often the landscape contractor must make the selection. Here, again, a turf specialist for the state or area should be consulted; however, there are some general recommendations that can be followed. A mixture should contain at least 60 percent of the permanent species desired. This does not mean that if a bluegrass turf is desired the seeding mixture should contain at least 60 percent bluegrass seed, because usually more than one kind of seed is mixed together. It means that 60 percent of the mixture should contain bluegrass and possibly another permanent species with the appearance of bluegrass, such as red fescue. Mixes containing high percentages of temporary grasses such as annual ryegrass (*Lolium* spp.) and redtop (*Agrostis alba*) should be used only to establish quick cover when seeding must be done at improper times. This seeding should be followed by an overseeding with a good permanent grass mixture.

It is also necessary to know what ratio of permanent grasses is desirable for the particular site. Such site conditions as the amount of shade present, usage of the turf, and drainage must all be considered when the mixture is selected. There are a large number of seed mixtures available commercially, and the best mixture for the particular project is probably available.

The seeding rate varies with the purity of the seed and the germination percentage. To achieve a satisfactory stand of seedlings, the seeding rates given in Table 15-3 should be followed. The higher rates should be used if quicker cover is needed or if establishment conditions are not optimum.

PLANTING TIMES

The timing for seeding has been mentioned already in the discussions about selecting installation procedures and grass species. But more needs to be said about the times for seeding. It must be pointed out that many construction projects call for seeding of turf areas during other than optimum seasons. The results obtained are often less than satisfactory and, if at all possible, the contractor should discourage the attempt to seed turf areas during seasons when growing conditions are poor. Usually the causes of the problem are delays in completing construction, which in turn push the seeding dates into unfavorable seasons. The contracting authority rarely if ever understands the conditions necessary for plant growth and seed germination, and usually insists that the seeding be carried out regardless of the season. This is often true of highway construction, and the results are often poor stands and insufficient covering of seeded areas.

For best results, sow seed during the prime season for germination and subsequent growth of the seedlings. This will vary with the species being grown and the geographic location of the project. Vengris in his book (see reading list) suggests that late August through September is the right time for seeding cool-season grasses in the northern parts of the United States. A second choice is early spring but not later than mid-May. Late seeding means poor germination and growth of the seedlings during

Table 15-3 Seeding rates for commonly used turf grasses.

| Grasses | Seed to be sown (in pounds) | |
	per 1,000 sq ft	per acre
Kentucky bluegrass (*Poa pratensis*)	2 to 3	80 to 120
Red fescue (*Festuca rubra*)	3 to 5	120 to 200
Bermuda, hulled (*Cynodon dactylon*)	2	80
Ryegrasses (*Lolium* spp.)	5 to 6	200 to 240
Red top (*Agrostis alba*)	1 to 2	40 to 80

15-5

the warm period of the spring and summer. Also, warm-season weed grasses and other broadleaf weeds germinate to compete with the new grass seedlings before they can become established. Seedings in late summer to early fall and very early spring permit the establishment of vigorous grass seedlings that can compete more favorably with the new weeds that come as the temperatures increase in the early summer. Exact seeding times should be determined from information supplied by state or local turf grass specialists.

Warm-season grasses should be seeded in March to May for best results in the South, and the time should be delayed from March towards May as one moves North. Bermuda grass is commonly seeded, but generally zoysia is propagated vegetatively by sprigging. Zoysia seed can be obtained in small quantities; it should be seeded the same time as Bermuda seed.

METHODS OF SEEDING

There are several pieces of equipment that can be used to distribute grass seed uniformly over the prepared seedbed. Generally the equipment used will depend on the size of the area being seeded. All operate in more or less the same way, but the size and method of moving the equipment varies; the larger units are self-propelled or pulled with a tractor; the manually operated equipment are well suited for small areas.

The equipment will distribute the seed in one of three ways, i.e., by drilling, by gravity feed, or by broadcast. A grass-seed drill sows the seed in rows, covers the rows, and firms the soil. This means that all three operations of

seeding can be done as one operation. The disadvantage of using seed drills is that the grass-seed is sown in narrow strips with wide, bare bands of soil in between. It is necessary to reduce weed growth in the bare areas until the grass has filled in.

The gravity-feed distributors are merely hoppers on wheels that have adjustable openings in the bottom to control the flow of seed onto the seedbed. The size of the openings is adjustable and should be calibrated to insure that the proper amount of seed is being distributed. Generally, a small agitator in the bottom of the hopper prevents the seed from sticking together and plugging some of the distribution holes. The size of such distributors ranges generally from a (manually pushed) spreader that distributes a 2-foot band to a hopper 20 feet wide, or even wider, which is pulled by a tractor. Some of the more advanced and expensive gravity-feed units are designed to cover the seed and firm the soil after the seed is sown. If time and costs permit, the equipment should be calibrated to distribute one-half of the seed over the entire area. Two applications are then made, the first in one direction, and the second across it in a direction at 90 degrees from the first.

The broadcast spreaders use an impeller that throws the seed horizontally onto the seedbed. The seed falls onto the impeller from a hopper, through an adjustable opening. The spreader can be calibrated by adjusting the size of the hopper feed opening. The size of broadcasting equipment varies from a small unit carried on a strap around one's neck to a large tractor-mounted unit with an impeller that is turned at a uniform rate by an electric

Figure 15-5. *The Brillion Precision Seeder sows grass seed in rows and covers the seed after sowing.*

motor. The impeller on the small hand-carried models are turned manually. The smaller units distribute the seed over a 6-foot band and the large, electrically powered units can spread a 20-foot-wide band. The disadvantages of an impeller are that if mixtures are used, there is a tendency for the impeller to throw the heavier seeds farther, resulting in an uneven distribution of the different grasses in the mixture. Also, the covering and firming steps are separate operations that require extra time, labor, and equipment. It is especially important to apply the seed in two cross-directions with an impeller also, to insure uniform distribution, as previously described.

The development of hydroseeders and hydromulchers allows the contractor to seed steep slopes and hard-to-reach areas without difficulty. The grass seed is mixed in a water slurry with or without a mulching material. The hydroseeder pumps the mixture under high pressure onto the slope or into otherwise inaccessible areas. The advantages of a hydroseeder may outweight the disadvantages. The mulch material acts as a seed covering; fertilizer can be added to the slurry so that the nutrition required for initial seedling development is also applied. Moreover, the water used by the hydroseeder serves as the initial watering for the newly seeded area. But the distribution patterns are not good enough for seeding fine turf areas, and the cost of the hydroseeder is much higher than the cost of other seed-distribution equipment.

COVERING AND MULCHING

The covering of the seed is of crucial importance, in particular the depth of the covering.

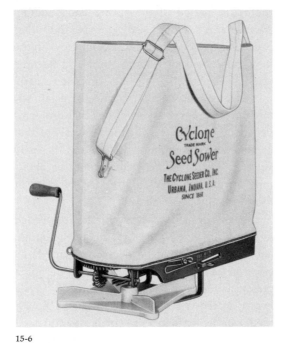

15-6

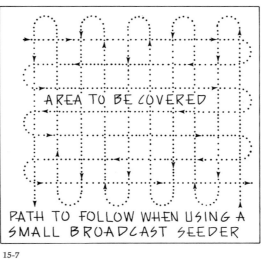

15-7

15-8

Figure 15-6, 15-7. *A broadcast seeder (15-6) will provide even distribution of seed if it is used across an area in two directions (15-7).*

Figure 15-8. *Seeding large areas with a helicopter. A broadcast spreader is attached to the underside of the aircraft; the hopper is on the side.*

15-9

Small seed such as the Kentucky bluegrass should be covered to a depth of ¼ inch and the larger-seeded grasses such as ryegrass should be covered up to ½ inch deep. On small areas, the covering may be accomplished by hand raking. Care should be taken not to redistribute the seed into uneven patterns. Firming can be done as required with a small hand-pushed roller. If the site is excessively wet, firming should not be done until the soil has dried out somewhat, to avoid compaction and crusting of the seedbed surface. On large areas, covering may be done with a variety of drags or with a shallow-set spike-tooth harrow. Again, be careful not to redistribute the seed into uneven patterns. Tractor-pulled rollers or an agricultural cultipacker may be used to firm the finished seedbed. Do not firm the soil if it is too wet.

To achieve more satisfactory results, we recommend the use of a mulch. The most critical time in the establishment of the turf area is during the germination and early seedling-growth stages. The seedling is hypersensitive to moisture stress and any drying of the soil surface will result in the injury or even the death of seedlings. Excessively wet soils provide conditions satisfactory for the development of diseases, such as "damping-off," which will reduce the stand of grass seedlings. Damping off is a fungus disease that attacks seedlings at the soil line, destroying the stem there and killing the seedling. A mulch will help prevent this and maintain the required environmental conditions for seed germination and seedling development.

Mulch materials that have been used range from wheat straw to commercially prepared

Figure 15-9. *A hydromulcher applying a mixture of lovegrass* (Eragrostis *spp.*), *lespedeza* (Lespedeza sericea), *fertilizer, and wood cellulose fiber mulch to a road bank with a slope steeper than 1 to 1, near East Ellijay, Georgia.*

cellulose mats. Wood chips, sawdust, shredded bark, peat moss, hay, and crushed corncobs have all been used. The wood products generally are more expensive than straw, though sawdust and shredded bark are sometimes cheaper at particular locations. Some seedling growth problems have been experienced when hardwood barks have been used, probably because of the presence of high quantities of tannic acids. Except for small areas, peat moss is too expensive to use as a mulch for turf seeding. The availability of crushed corncobs is rapidly declining because much of the corn grown is now shelled in the field and the cob is left in the field. Hay can be used, but should be avoided unless its source is known to have been free of weed seeds.

Cellulose fiber and fiberglass mats are satisfactory for small areas or steep slopes, where extra attention is required to hold the seed in place and reduce the chances of erosion. Installing the mats requires much more labor and their cost is much higher, per unit of area covered, than the cost of straw. The use of burlap is an old practice and this can still be used in very small areas, but the material and installation costs are high.

All in all, straw still remains the best mulch material for newly seeded turf. But sources of large quantities of straw are increasingly more difficult to find in many sections of the country, and increases in shipping costs are making the transporting of straw to nonwheat-producing regions nearly prohibitive. If the straw is readily available, it should be applied at the rate of from 1½ to 3 tons per acre. Of course, the higher rate should be used if the straw is wet. The straw may be spread by hand on small

areas but for large acreage or steep, difficult-to-reach slopes, a straw blower should be used. The straw blower separates the straw in the bale and chops it into approximately six-inch pieces. The straw is then blown onto the seeded areas. It is necessary to hold the straw onto the soil surface to prevent the wind and water erosion from removing it from the seedbed. Some straw blowers are equipped to spray a nonphytotoxic asphalt material onto the straw during the blowing phase. This binds the straw together and helps anchor it to the soil surface. For small areas and small slopes, the straw may be tied down by binder's twine or other string that is run between stakes on each side of the newly seeded area.

Vegetative Planting

The planting of plant parts, sprigging, is restricted nearly entirely to the warm-season grasses. This is the primary means for establishing zoysia turf, though sometimes bent grass is also established by using vegetative means. Vegetative propagation will produce turf identical to that of the parent plant. Genetic variations occur only to the extent that there are variations in the parent material.

It is as important to be aware of the quality of the planting stock as it is to be aware of the seed quality when the seeding method is used.

Depending upon the grass, the stolons or sprigs are usually from four to eight inches in length and should contain two or more nodes for the development of new sprouts. Good-quality stock should be purchased from a reliable source and obtained immediately before planting. If the landscape contractor is prepar-

15-10

Figure 15-10. *A straw blower used to mulch a seeded highway slope. A nonphytotoxic asphalt is applied to hold the straw down.*

15-11

Figure 15-11. *Planting and covering sprigs by machine. The roller firms the soil after planting.*

ing the planting material from sod at the site, the rate of preparation of material should coincide fairly closely with the planting rate. The plant material should not be allowed to dry out while waiting to be planted. But merely packaging the plant material in order to retain moisture can be damaging, too, unless precautions are taken. Holding actively growing plant parts in tightly sealed packages for more than 24 hours may result in serious damage to the stock unless refrigeration is used. The reason for this is that the material is respiring, and heat is given off. Temperatures will increase to very high levels in the packages and will either kill the material or so severely injure it that it will not develop into vigorous plants. However, it is possible to keep sprigs or stolons of some grasses for several weeks, so long as they are stored in polyethylene bags and are refrigerated. If packaging is loose, care should be taken not to allow the material to dry out, however. Dry, shrivelled stolons or sprigs will produce poor grass. Freshly obtained material is best.

In planting sprigs or stolons, the planting method depends upon the size of the area to be planted. Small areas can be planted by hand, with the sprigs being placed either in rows or in a broadcast manner. The row method is suggested for more arid regions where the soil surface dries out rapidly. The planting depth of from three to four inches places the sprigs at a soil depth where moisture remains more constant. The soil should be lightly firmed over the row after planting to insure good soil contact with the stolons. The spacing of rows depends entirely on the type of grass being planted. Bermuda grass and St.-Augustine grass are both planted in 12-inch rows with the sprigs

being from 8 to 12 inches apart in the row. Zoysia is much slower to fill into a tight turf and six-inch rows with the sprigs six inches apart in the row is suggested. Vengris suggests the use of an aerifying machine to prepare holes in a seemingly random pattern. The sprigs are inserted into the holes by hand and the soil is firmed after planting.

For larger areas, machines have been especially designed that plant sprigs in rows. The row is made, the sprigs are dropped into the row and are covered, and the soil is firmed. A broadcast surface application is also used in nonarid regions where the soil surface does not dry out rapidly. The sprigs are broadcast by machine uniformly over the area at a rate of from 100 to 400 bushels per acre depending on the grass being established. Vengris suggests the use of a manure spreader for spreading Bermuda grass stolons over a large area. The stolons are covered lightly with a shallow disking or are covered with from ¼ to ½ inch of soil dressing. The surface should be firmed after covering.

Sprigs or stolons that have been planted either in rows or in a broadcast pattern should be mulched in the same manner as the seeded areas. Straw is again the best mulch to use. The area should be watered immediately after planting.

Sod Plugs

The use of plugs or strip sodding is best limited to regions where conditions are ideal for turf establishment, so that the space between the sod strips or plugs will fill in rapidly. For the most part, few turf areas in landscape construction projects can be established by using plugs or sod strips because the fill-in time is slow. Exceptions to these considerations can be made in projects where erosion on slopes or dunes must be controlled. The use of plugs, plant divisions, and sod strips of special grasses adapted to the conditions present can be used to help establish a cover to hold the slope or the dune in place. The particular plant used depends on the climatic conditions present. As an example, beach grasses that tolerate salt spray will need to be planted along the seashore if it is necessary to control dunes.

Plugs are cut from established sod areas and range in size from two to four inches in diameter. The plugs in the new area should be 12 to 16 inches apart (from center to center) for Bermuda grass and St.-Augustine grass, but zoysia, because of its slower spreading rate, should be planted on six-inch centers. The soil should be firmed around the plugs, and the area should be watered immediately after planting. A mulch will help establish environmental conditions that will encourage rapid filling between plugs.

The site for planting the plugs will need to be prepared in exactly the same manner used for seeding. This careful preparation is necessary to insure a level, smooth turf and to provide the proper soil conditions for establishment of a tight, vigorous turf.

Sodding

Sodding is the most expensive and least troublesome method of providing a superb turf cover in a very short establishment period. The term "instant grass" is truly an accurate description of sodding. The use of sod, because

15-12

15-13

15-14

Figure 15-12. *Sod properly cut 3/4 inch thick so that it will knit to the soil rapidly.*

Figure 15-13. *Sod transported to the landscape site on pallets.*

Figure 15-14. *Laying sod in straight lines with tight joints. The roller is used to insure good contact of the sod with the soil.*

of the excellent results that are obtained, is becoming more and more common.

Buying sod requires the same care and precaution as buying seed mixtures and sprigs. To achieve optimum results, only well-grown, certified sod of the desired variety should be purchased. It is wise to investigate the sod source before purchase, particularly if the project calls for large amounts of sod. Check with other customers of a sod farm to determine if they were satisfied with that firm's product. Then examine the sod at the farm to determine if it will meet the specifications required by the landscape contract. Determine also that the grower has enough sod of the quality that is needed to fill the requirements for the project. The use of sod from pastures and meadows should be avoided, as it is not of the new, improved varieties, and in many instances it will introduce serious weed problems.

The best sod is freshly cut, transported immediately to the project site, and laid immediately. Sod that is not used for one or two days should not be allowed to dry out, as it will then become dormant and may take several weeks to return to active growth. Some growers have vacuum cooling equipment to insure that the customer receives the sod in good condition. Stored sod should be unrolled grass side up and kept watered. Light waterings are best. The old method of cutting sod so that it retains from 1½ to 2 inches or more of soil is no longer used. It has been determined that Kentucky bluegrass sod that is cut with from ½ to ¾ inches of soil will "knit," or become established on the planting bed soil much faster than the thicker-cut sod. Sod is commonly cut from 12 to 24 inches in width and from four to six feet in length. The longer lengths are generally rolled and the shorter are sold flat, stacked on pallets.

The sod should be laid on the soil bed, which should be prepared in the same manner as for seeding, with the first row or course being placed in a precisely predetermined straight line. This may be a line running perpendicular to a street, walk, or driveway, or parallel to a property line. Some sod is laid in a diagonal manner in relation to the street. The important thing is to establish a straight line, regardless of its direction. The line can be marked with a tightly stretched string or with precisely laid boards. The following rows or courses are laid tightly to the first with the joints being staggered, just as if one were laying courses of brick. Care should be taken to fit the joints very tightly together; for fine lawns, fill soil is worked into the joints so that a smooth turf is achieved. There should never be any overlapping of joints; the laying process should always be carefully supervised to avoid overlapping thin-cut sod.

After the sodding is completed, it should be given a light rolling to make certain that all pieces of the sod are laying smooth and in good contact with the soil of the planting bed. On relatively steep slopes it is suggested that the sod layers be pinned firmly in place. Heavy rains may cause the sod to slip down the slope before it becomes established.

Initial Maintenance of Turf Areas

Water is of prime importance in establishing a turf area. If proper watering techniques are followed, establishment is almost assured, barring any unusual conditions. The water requirements for newly seeded areas are very demanding. The upper surface should not be allowed to dry out until all the seed has germinated and the seedlings have become established. This means frequent, light waterings are necessary for a period of up to 30 days depending on the rate of germination of the grasses used in the seeding mixture. During windy, dry periods it will be necessary to water two or three times per day. The droplet size should be small and almost of a mist nature, if possible, to prevent washing out the seed and to avoid soil compaction. If the surface dries out, the grass seedlings will die, because they are particularly vulnerable to moisture stress during the critical germination period. Once the seedlings are well established and relatively deep rooted, the frequency of waterings may be reduced. More normal watering practices should then be followed, i.e., water applications should be heavy enough to insure at least six-inch soil penetration. Since mulch is generally used when stolons have been sown, the frequent light waterings are not required, but care should be exercised nonetheless to insure that the soil under the mulch does not dry out excessively before establishment takes place.

The watering of sodded, plugged, or sprigged areas should be accomplished in such a manner that the upper two or three inches of soil does not dry out markedly. Enough water should be applied to penetrate the soil at least six inches at every watering. The frequency of this watering will be determined by the soil type, amount of rainfall, and winds.

The first mowing of seeded areas should be done when the grass is from one to two inches taller than the normal mowing height. The bent grasses are normally cut very short, to less than one inch, so the initial mowing should be done when the grass has grown to two inches or more, whereas Kentucky bluegrasses are normally mown to two inches; therefore, their initial cutting will be after the seedlings have reached a height of from three to four inches. The surface should be dry and firm before the initial mowing to prevent compaction and rut formation caused by the mower. Mowing of sodded areas should begin as soon as the sod has become established. Mowing heights are whatever is recommended for the particular type of grass being grown.

Control of weeds is of great importance during the establishment phase. The weed control recommended for established turf areas may be put to practice for newly sodded areas once the sod is well established. If high-quality sod has been used it will be nearly weed free, and there is hardly any need for using herbicides before complete establishment is achieved. However, in seeded areas, the problem of weed control is more difficult. Follow current recommendations and use herbicides that will not injure the young grass seedlings. More effective herbicides may be used once the turf is established (after one year).

Try always to use these proper techniques for turf establishment. Too often, poor site preparation is done by the contractor and poor-quality turf is the result. By following carefully the 11 steps for site preparation that we mentioned near the beginning of the chapter, good turf can be achieved.

15-15

ESTABLISHING GROUND COVERS

It is a common practice to try to establish and grow ground covers in areas unsuited for turf grasses. Though this is one of the principal reasons for using ground covers, it is a mistake to believe that ground covers will tolerate and thrive under any conditions that will not support grass. The requirements for good growth and development of ground covers are specific and must be present at the landscape site if success is to be achieved. The environmental requirements for different ground covers vary greatly, and it is very important that the landscape architect and the landscape contractor be familiar with the specific requirements for various ground covers.

Soil Preparation

Most often, proper preparation of the soil at the planting site is neglected since the mistaken opinion is held that all ground covers will grow any place regardless of the soil condition. Many ground covers, such as *Pachysandra terminalis* (Japanese spurge), require well-drained soils and if planted in heavy clay soils fail to develop to their fullest potential. *Vinca minor* (common periwinkle) is a fine, vigorous ground cover that fills in very rapidly when planted in well-drained soil that has a *p*H of 6.5 or below. When planted in heavy clays or in excessively wet areas, it is susceptible to diseases, and the result is usually very poor stands and failure to fill in. Disease is found also in well-established, vigorous beds of vinca, usually, but because soil conditions permit rapid growth, the attack of disease is blunted and the plants thrive.

15-16

Figures 15-15, 15-16. Euonymus fortunei *'Coloratus' (15-15) is a vigorous ground cover that thrives under most conditions if the site is prepared properly (15-16).*

The same details of site preparation used for turf establishment should be used in the preparation of an area for installation of ground-cover plants. The landscape contractor should determine the optimum soil conditions required for good growth of the specified ground cover. The main factors to consider are physical characteristics, such as drainage, aeration, moisture-holding capacity, and the soil pH. A good reference such as *Ground Cover Plants*, by Donald Wyman, will provide this information for most commonly used ground covers. If the contractor is able to make the choice of what ground covers to use, he should of course choose the species most adaptable to the naturally occurring conditions.

Planting beds on relatively level planting sites should be worked to at least a depth of from six to eight inches. Soil conditioners such as peat moss and sand should be mixed into the bed at this time. Care should be taken not to change the grades established during the finished grading process. Grade stakes should not be disturbed, and any that are disturbed should be reset at the proper location and height. Final grading of the site can proceed as outlined in Chapter 13. If the area is poorly drained because of a tight, heavy soil or a shallow hardpan, a tile system should be installed before planting. This will save time and expense later and will reduce the chances of numerous plant losses because of poor soil conditions. Moreover, if the soil at the planting site is of poor quality, a good grade of fill soil should be used, as recommended for turf areas. Fill soil should be added to a depth of at least six inches and, if possible, put down in two applications. After the first application the fill soil should be worked into the subsoil to help provide a good transition between the two soil types. After this step is completed, the final layer of topsoil should be added. This will help to eliminate, though it will not completely eliminate, the chances of an artificial water table being established.

On steep slopes where ground covers are to be used, the bed preparation must be somewhat different. Deep working of soil with soil additives must be done with caution. If this process is carried out and heavy rains occur before planting and mulching, excessive erosion may result. Every site condition is unique, and the contractor must use his judgment about whether procedures for soil preparation that are described for level areas may also be applicable to a particular slope. All that may be possible is to prepare a good backfill mix to use in the individual planting holes. The planting techniques used for small shrubs would be appropriate if the project has the budget for the expense of such procedures. Generally, however, small potted plants are used and are planted by hand, using a trowel to dig small holes.

Fertilizer should be applied after determining the needs from soil-test results. For most ground covers the use of from 75 to 100 pounds of actual nitrogen per acre will be beneficial if applied at planting time. Actually, a complete fertilizer with an analysis ratio of 1 : 2 : 1 or 1 : 3 : 1 should be added, with the rate being based on that much actual nitrogen. If soil tests show an extremely low level of phosphorus, an additional application of phosphorus in the form of superphosphate should be made. For best results, the fertilizer should be added before the working of the soil. This will insure mixing of the fertilizer into the planting bed.

Planting Techniques

There are many techniques used to plant ground covers, and usually the selection is predetermined partially by the selection of ground cover species. As an example, if small shrubs such as *Cotoneaster apiculata* (cranberry cotoneaster) or selections of *Juniperus hortizontalis* (creeping juniper) are to be used, the planting techniques for balled-and-burlapped or container-grown stock should be used. *Vinca minor* may be planted as rooted cuttings, as plant clumps dug from established beds, or individually as potted plants. *Coronilla varia* (crown vetch) is planted by sowing seed on steep slopes as well as by planting divisions of mature, established plants. Each of the techniques will be described in more detail except for the planting of balled-and-burlapped stock, which was described in Chapter 14.

Many ground covers may be planted by using rooted cuttings, i.e., *Hedera helix* (English ivy), *Vinca minor*, *Pachysandra terminalis*, etc. The spacing will depend on two factors, the growth habit of the ground cover itself and the rapidity at which cover is desired. Generally, rooted cuttings are planted closer together than potted plants or clumps of the same species. To achieve cover in a normal length of time it is necessary to plant cuttings about four to six inches apart. A marking system, such as a grid prepared by using marker boards with nails, should be used to make sure rows are straight and that plants are accurately spaced.

15-17

Figure 15-17. Pachysandra terminalis *in a landscape bed.*

The roots of the cuttings should be protected from drying conditions during the planting operation. Do not remove a greater number of cuttings from the packaging than can be planted in a few minutes. Be sure to plant the cuttings at the proper depth: do not bury the crowns or plant the cuttings too deep. Firm the soil by hand around each cutting so that the soil is in good contact with the roots. After an area is planted, water it immediately to settle the soil around the roots completely and to prevent drying of the roots. If very large areas are being planted, it is recommended either that each cutting be provided with water as it is planted or that sections of the area be watered as soon as planting of a section is complete, and watering at both times can be recommended as well. Mulching will be beneficial to the establishment of the cuttings and is almost essential if planting is done on a steep slope. The mulch will reduce the chances that serious erosion will occur before the ground cover cuttings are well established or before slope control is achieved through complete filling in.

Planting potted material requires following approximately the same procedures as for rooted cuttings. Site preparation is the same. If the plants are growing in pots of plastic or clay, which must be removed before planting, the plants should be watered thoroughly long enough before planting to permit easy removal of the pot without disturbing the soil ball and the root mass, but close enough to planting time that adequate moisture is retained by the soil ball. The plants should be planted at approximately the same depth as they were when growing in the pot, and care should be taken not to plant too deep, for covering the plant crowns may result in substantial losses. But on the other hand, with potted material it is easy not to plant deep enough, and the top of the soil ball will then be above the level of the landscape bed. This can be particularly troublesome when peat-potted material is planted too high. Peat pots will tend to dry out, and the future root development will be restricted by the dry, impervious barrier of the pot wall. Also, when using peat-potted material, it is recommended that only those plants with good root penetration of the pot walls be used. The plants in peat pots should be watered thoroughly before planting, for if the watering procedures are followed carefully before planting, the administration of an initial watering phase is not quite as critical as it is with rooted cuttings. However, it is absolutely essential that the newly planted area be watered the same day it is planted. A mulch should also be used.

The divisions or clumps from established plants should not be allowed to dry out before or during the planting operation. The procedures used for cuttings would apply almost entirely for the planting of divisions and clumps. In our earlier discussion of vegetative planting of turf we described techniques that may also be used when establishing a ground cover through use of root cuttings or other plant parts. There are no basic differences in the procedures used between turf and ground-cover establishment.

Seeding of ground covers is most often carried out on slopes that are too steep to plant effectively with growing plants, or where areas

15-18

Figure 15-18. Lespedeza sericea *established by seeding on a highway slope in Missouri.*

are too large and the cost of the plants required for them becomes limiting. Highway slopes and banks at industrial or public facility sites are commonly seeded with ground covers such as crown vetch, *Lespedeza* spp., some alfalfa species, and the trefoils.

The rate of seeding depends on the plant species being seeded, site conditions, and the rapidity with which the cover is desired. For some plants, such as crown vetch, that are slow to germinate, it may be desirable to mix seed of a temporary cover crop, such as annual ryegrass, to hold the slope until the crown vetch is established. Some alfalfas may be used for this purpose. It has been reported that crown vetch may take from two to three years for a good percentage of germination to occur. Usually the most effective results are obtained if the seeds are covered in some manner. Hydromulch seeding is one technique that has been used quite successfully on highway slopes. On smaller areas, raking-in may cover the seed with enough soil to permit good germination. A cover with a mulch material such as straw will aid in germination, though the mulch should not be too deep. The rate of from 1½ to 3 tons per acre, the same rate of application used for turf seedings, is quite satisfactory for this purpose too. The mulch will help maintain an even moisture supply during the critical stages of seed germination. Watering may be necessary during periods of drought during the first season of seedling development of the ground cover; therefore an examination of the site periodically during the first season is warranted in most climates so that the moisture supply will not be neglected.

Initial Weed Control

Ground covers do not cover the entire soil surface immediately after being planted. The properly prepared planting bed provides nearly optimum conditions for weed seeds to germinate, and in the first or second growing season, the competition by weeds with the newly planted ground cover is fierce. Once the ground cover is established, it will generally compete favorably with the weeds, and eventually, if proper care of the bed is maintained, the cover will eliminate most weeds by the simple process of being more competitive for light, water, and space. However, the weed problem during those first seasons is so severe that many persons do not want to plant ground covers. The problem is partially solved with the use of a mulch, such as shredded hardwood bark or crushed corncobs, which reduces the weed growth markedly. The mulch must be heavy enough to cover the soil surface, i.e., it must be a depth of one inch or more. But of course it cannot be so deep that ground cover plants are buried.

The use of herbicides in newly established ground-cover beds is limited mainly because of the sensitivity of many of the ground covers to herbicide injury. It is advisable to check current recommendations by the Cooperative Extension Service. However, when an appropriate herbicide can be obtained, it is worth using; some herbicides have proven effective when repeated applications were made during the growing season.

ESTABLISHING ANNUAL AND PERENNIAL FLOWERS

Preparation of the planting bed for most annual and perennial flowers is very much the same as the procedures used for ground covers. If heavy, compacted soil exists at the site it is absolutely necessary to incorporate organic materials such as peat moss or well-rotted manure to a depth of at least six inches. One common error is to use too little peat moss because of its high cost. To achieve satisfactory results it is necessary to add 20 to 30 percent peat moss by volume to the heavy soil. Therefore if the soil is to be worked to a depth of from six to eight inches, it will be necessary to cover the bed with a layer of peat moss two inches deep before the deep cultivation required in bed preparation is done.

Internal drainage of the bed is critical for most annuals and perennials. Few species will tolerate heavy, waterlogged soils for any period of time without ceasing to thrive and to grow well. The addition of peat moss and sand to the soil may be necessary if a heavy soil exists, but care should be taken to avoid developing an artificial water table. It may be necessary to install a tile system if the site has particularly poor drainage. Also, be sure to construct the planting bed so that surface water from surrounding areas does not drain into the bed. Proper grading during site modification will usually eliminate this problem.

If at all possible, make soil tests on the soil in the planting bed before planting and preferably after the bed has had peat moss, manure, and/or sand incorporated. If the soil is acid (*p*H below 6.0), it is necessary to add lime to raise the *p*H to 6.5 for most annuals and perennials. The fertility needs of the soil can also be determined from the soil-test results. In the absence of soil-test results, the addition of from one to two pounds actual nitrogen per 1000 square feet of a complete fertilizer with an analysis ratio of 1 : 1 : 1 or 1 : 2 : 1 will be beneficial. This initial fertilization should be done before the working of the soil to insure good incorporation of the fertilizer.

Annual flower plants usually are available as individually potted plants, in small trays or packs, and in large flats. Seeds of a few annuals can be planted in beds, but plants are oftener used for landscape work since they will establish faster. Individually potted plants are usually of the best quality and suffer little or no transplant shock. Therefore, transplant losses are nearly nonexistent among potted plants. Plants grown in small blocks or flats, if not too large at transplanting time, are usually of good quality, and by cutting the soil blocks so that the roots of the plants are disturbed to a minimum, transplanting losses are very slight. The poorest-quality plants are those grown in large flats without adequate space for development.

Perennials are generally purchased as dormant roots, individually potted plants, or divisions of active growing plants. Generally the species of perennial being grown determines what condition it will be available in, i.e., potted, clump, etc. Planting techniques are the same as for ground cover and annuals. It is important that the proper soil conditions be established for the specific plant being grown. Initial care is generally the same for perennials as it is for ground covers and annuals.

Planting techniques for turf, ground covers, and herbaceous plants are no less precise than the requirements for trees and shrubs. Therefore, proper attention to planting details will help produce a good-quality produce for the customer.

FOR FURTHER READING

Cumming, R. W., and R. E. Lee., 1960. *Contemporary Perennials.* New York: The Macmillan Co. 363 pages.

Hanson, A. A., and F. V. Juska, 1969. *Turfgrass Science.* Madison, Wisc.: American Society of Agronomy, Inc. 715 pages.

Sunset Magazine and Sunset Books (editors), 1967. *Sunset Western Garden Book.* Menlo Park, Calif.: Lane Magazine and Book Co. Revised edition, 1973. 448 pages.

Vengris, J. 1969. *Lawns.* Fresno, Calif.: Thomson Publications. 229 pages.

Wyman, D., 1956. *Ground Cover Plants.* New York: The Macmillan Co. 175 pages.

Wyman, D., 1971. *Wyman's Gardening Encyclopedia.* New York: The Macmillan Co. 1222 pages.

VI

Maintaining the Landscape

16

Maintaining the Landscape Site

Getting the right job done at the right time is the most important rule of landscape maintenance. As will be pointed out several times in the following chapters, timing is the critical item in carrying out nearly all maintenance practices for trees and shrubs in the landscape. This chapter will be concerned first with how a maintenance schedule should be determined for a site and then with how to determine the time needed to carry out the required maintenance practices. From the latter information it is then possible to estimate the maintenance costs for a particular site.

DEVELOPING THE MAINTENANCE SCHEDULE

The maintenance schedule is the guide for executing maintenance practices at the correct time. A well-developed schedule permits the landscape maintenance supervisor to use his work crews with the greatest efficiency, to utilize his equipment effectively, to order his supplies well in advance of the time when they will be used, and to carry out the required maintenance when it will be of most benefit to the landscape plants. One of the most important benefits of preparing and following a schedule is that a sound maintenance budget can be developed for the site. The development of the budget will in turn permit decisions to be made by the landscape maintenance supervisor when questions of the costs of operations arise. Then priorities can be established with a full knowledge of what each operation costs.

How should the schedule be developed? The first step is to classify the different areas of the landscape site, basing the classifications on the degree of maintenance wanted for each area. Areas can be classified as needing high,

Figure 16-1. *A high level of maintenance is required to maintain a well landscaped home at its optimum: this is a general view of the Connecticut residential landscape shown in detail in Chapter 7. Through careful planning and plant selection, it was possible at this site to reduce the amount of maintenance necessary.*

Figure 16-2. *A roadside rest stop near Lincoln, Nebraska: an example of a site that requires a medium to high level of maintenance. Weed removal in landscape beds and frequent mowing of the turf are maintenance requirements.*

16-1

16-2

medium, or low maintenance, and this is determined primarily by the use of the area. High-maintenance areas would contain such things as carefully manicured turf, shrubs, ground covers, and flower beds; and well cared-for trees. Areas of this type are found around residences, office buildings, some industrial sites, some college campuses, etc. Medium-maintenance areas are found in most parks, high-use recreation areas, most industrial sites, highway roadsides, and some schools. Schools will often have areas that need both high and medium maintenance. Turf will not be mowed as frequently or be kept as weed free in medium maintenance work; trees and shrubs will receive only moderate care, such as limited pruning and pest control; and the use of annual flowers and ground covers will be limited.

Low-maintenance areas will be primarily found in natural landscape sites. Maintenance will consist of trash pickup; maintenance of trails, roadways, parking lots, and other physical facilities; here, any turf areas need infrequent mowing; and little or no care will be needed for trees and shrubs except when it is necessary to remove dead plants or plants that are detrimental to the use of the site. Many large parks will contain all three kinds of maintenance work. A great deal of maintenance will probably be done around visitor centers, gardens, etc., but the major recreation areas and camp areas will be maintained through a medium amount of work. Little maintenance is usually needed in isolated natural areas and undeveloped sites.

Of course a main factor in determining the kind of maintenance to be carried out in an area will be the budget. Costs are many times greater for intensive maintenance than for low or minimal maintenance. It is wise to develop a primary maintenance schedule and cost estimate for the site during initial planning phases. The landscape architect should be able to inform his client of the approximate cost of maintaining the site in future years. Cost data are available for most maintenance operations, but many landscape architects do not take advantage of the information when preparing the design. The result is often an overplanted, overdeveloped landscape that cannot be properly maintained because of budget limitations. The landscape architect must consider long-term maintenance and the ability of the client to maintain the site. To ignore this when preparing site plans will mean that clients are disappointed when they discover their landscape has declined because of poor maintenance.

Once the amount of maintenance has been determined for an area, the next step should be to make a complete list of all landscape plants in that area. It is from this list that the necessary maintenance practices, such as pruning, mowing, fertilizing, and spraying for pests, can be determined. It is suggested that plants be grouped in the following categories, based on flowering time, foliage, or use. Hereafter, we will have occasion to refer to some of the groups listed here.

SHRUBS

Group I: Deciduous—nonflowering, or inconspicuously flowering

Group II: Deciduous—early flowering (before June 30 or early summer)

Group III: Deciduous—flowering in summer (after June 30) and fall, or prized for fruit

16-3

Figure 16-3. *A natural landscape requiring very little maintenance. This winter view is in Yellowstone National Park.*

Group IV: Evergreens—broadleaf

Group V: Evergreens—narrowleaf

TREES

Group I: Deciduous shade trees

Group II: Deciduous—small early-flowering (before June 30) trees

Group III: Deciduous—small summer (after June 30) or fall flowering trees

Group IV: Conifers

HERBACEOUS PLANTS

Group I: Ground covers and vines

Group II: Perennials and annuals

Certain maintenance activities will be carried out on the plants in any particular category and group at a certain time. The third phase of preparing the schedule is to determine exactly what practices will need to be done to obtain the maintenance that is wanted. To obtain this information, it will be necessary for the landscape maintenance supervisor to consult several sources of knowledge about a wide variety of subjects. Of concern will be the physical care of the plants, which includes pruning, fertilizing, and watering. Pest control knowledge is essential for areas of high and medium levels of maintenance. Included under pest control will be insect, disease, and weed control. For the maintenance of some projects even rodent control will be of importance to the landscape maintenance supervisor. Care of turf areas requires specialized information that should be studied and used when preparing the schedule.

Sources of information about plant maintenance are numerous, and as many as possible should be utilized. There are several references listed at the ends of Chapters 17 and 18 that

will be of value both in the physical care of woody plants and for pest control. The latest recommendations by Cooperative Extension Service specialists in pest control and horticulture should also be sought. The latter source will help the landscape maintenance supervisor determine what pesticides are available for his use. More details of how to obtain specific information are given in Chapters 17 and 18.

Once it has been determined when and what maintenance practices are to be undertaken for a particular site, the landscape maintenance supervisor is ready to prepare his schedule. This schedule will include all maintenance for the trees, shrubs, herbaceous plants, and turf on the site, as well as the physical care of landscape features. Care of landscape features might include pool or pond care; snow removal from walks, roads, and parking lots in northern climates; resurfacing parking lots; maintaining irrigation systems; and so forth.

Appendix 16-A, page 351, is a typical maintenance schedule for a midwestern site. The appendix is based on a schedule prepared for a site on which moderate- to high-priced condominiums had been built; a high level of maintenance was wanted. Note that the schedule is prepared by the month; each month is divided into weekly periods.

KEEPING RECORDS

Once the schedule is prepared, the landscape maintenance supervisor needs to establish a record-keeping system. Record keeping should be as simple as possible and, at the same time, should provide all the information the landscape supervisor may need. The records can remind the supervisor how long a particular maintenance job took, who performed the work, when the work was done, and what equipment and supplies were necessary to complete the job.

The forms in which the records are kept should be simple so that all an employee needs to do is to fill in the number of hours spent on a project during a particular day. The supervisor or foreman at the site can summarize the records for the week and month. Accurate records of this type will permit accurate cost information to be computed not only for a particular maintenance activity but also for maintaining the total landscape site. Also, the quality and quantity of an employee's work can be checked.

Total cost information is determined by compiling the records of all employees who worked on a particular project, for example, at pruning shrubs. The total hours multiplied by the employee's total wage rate will then yield the cost of pruning shrubs. The total hourly cost or wage rate of an employee would include all fringe benefits plus vacation pay plus the cost of supervisory wages. Computing this hourly rate is much the same as described for computing the wage rate for employees working for a landscape contractor (see Chapter 11). It is relatively simple then to total the labor costs for all maintenance projects conducted at a particular site. To this information must be added the cost of supplies, such as pesticides, fertilizers, gasoline for equipment operation, small expendable hand tools, etc. Included also should be the overhead expense of doing business, which includes the cost of supervisory personnel, secretaries, and depreciation on

equipment and buildings. Again, Chapter 11 gives a more complete breakdown on computing overhead costs. If the landscape maintenance supervisor has kept good records, he should be able not only to compute the total costs for the maintenance project, but also to extract the cost of each individual operation. This will help him and his client determine which maintenance practices should be continued and at what level, on the basis of the cost of each.

Table 16-1 shows the overhead costs of a typical maintenance budget. Of course, every business operation would be somewhat different, but this breakdown illustrates the many items that must be included in an overhead cost computation.

A large firm, one that specializes in maintaining industrial, office building, and large residential sites, can also determine the time required to complete common landscape maintenance operations (see Table 16-2).

It should be pointed out here that the times listed in the table do not include times for travel, for setting up, or for cleaning up equipment. The times are for the actual operation itself—nothing more. The time for travel and for setting up and cleaning equipment will depend on how far the maintenance supervisor's base is from the project and what pieces of equipment are needed for the work. Information of this type can be helpful to the landscape architect, because he can tell a client whether or not maintenance of a particular planting design will be costly. It is helpful to the landscape maintenance supervisor when he is computing maintenance costs for a subsequent site for the first time.

Table 16-1 Typical maintenance budget.

Item	Percent of overhead	Percent of total budget
Wages (maintenance crews)		45
Equipment operation		2
Supplies and equipment, etc.		5
Subtotal		52
Overhead (itemized)		
Supervisory salaries	27	13
Office operation	6	3
Payroll tax and insurances	6	3
Unemployment compensation	4	2
Accounting costs	13	6
Equipment depreciation	14	7
Interest on loans	2	1
Property insurance	5	2
Rent (property)	2	1
Utilities	2	1
Public relations, including dues, subscriptions, etc.	2	1
Vehicle operation and maintenance	4	2
Equipment repairs and maintenance	4	2
Equipment rental	2	1
Miscellaneous	2	1
Lost time (vacation, sick leave, etc.)	5	2
Subtotal	100	48
Total		100

Data: Wayne Doede, Columbus, Indiana.

Table 16-2 Time required to complete some landscape maintenance operations.

Operation	Minutes	Operation	Minutes
TURF		TREES	
Mowing (and catching clippings)		Spraying (not included are times for filling, mixing, and travel)	
Small area (1,000 square feet) with hand-maneuvered 20-inch mower	15	Small (three-inch caliper)	25
Large area (one acre) with rider-operated 60-inch rotary mower	30	Large (eight-inch caliper)	10
Edging (100 feet)		Pruning (heavy)	
By hand	45	Small (three-inch caliper)	15
By mechanical edger		Large (eight-inch caliper)	60
Curbs	20		
Other edges	20	Watering	(Variable)
Fertilizing		SHRUBS	
Small area (1,000 square feet) with rotary spreader	5	Spraying	
Large area (one acre) with rotary spreader	30	Small (three to four feet-	1
		Large (seven to eight feet)	2
Spraying		Pruning	
Small area (1,000 square feet) with a back-carried tank	10	Small (three to four feet)	5
Large area (one acre) with a 300 gallon tank		Large (seven to eight feet, for rejuvenation)	30
Spray gun operated by two men for one hour	120	Watering	(Variable)
Spray hawk with boom on sprayer, in open area	105	GROUND COVER	
		Spraying 1,000 square feet	10

The maintenance schedule should be evaluated on a weekly or biweekly basis, and each operation should be recorded, to ascertain if it was successfully completed within the allocated time. At the end of the year the schedule should be modified, the modification being based on the previous season's results, so that a more realistic schedule is developed for the following year.

PERSONNEL

The most important part of the landscape maintenance operation is the employee actually doing the work. The best equipment and best supplies will not by themselves maintain a landscape site. Only qualified and well-trained personnel can complete the necessary maintenance of the plant material on a landscape site. To obtain employees who will be willing to work exceedingly long hours (on occasion) and who will take pride in their work, it will be necessary to pay a wage rate that permits the employee to achieve a satisfactory standard of living. Low pay scales destroy incentive and result in unusually rapid employee turnover.

The key employee in most maintenance firms is the crew chief or foreman. He will control to a large extent the quality and the quantity of work completed by his crew. Therefore, he should be a well trained, loyal employee who can lead men. He should be a permanent employee who is well paid and made to feel that his needs are considered whenever the firm plans its activities. Good foremen are extremely difficult to find, and the good landscape maintenance supervisor will make an extra effort to keep his foremen satisfied with their jobs.

Too often, an untrained or unskilled person is hired to help maintain plant material and is started on a job without any training by the landscape maintenance supervisor or by the crew foreman. A short training course in some of the basic principles of landscape maintenance will pay dividends in better workmanship and more enthusiasm for the job. When the new employee is asked to do an unfamiliar task, he should be shown how first by a skilled person. The time taken to do this will yield benefits in higher-quality work.

Opportunities for employment in landscape maintenance are increasing, and firms specializing in landscape maintenance are being established in several regions of the country. The main emphasis of these firms is on lawn care. However, because of increased demand for it they are also undertaking other maintenance work for homeowners and at some commercial and industrial sites. Their main work is at the operations most closely allied with turf care, so they specialize in fertilization and pest control, though some will undertake pruning too. In recent years consultants in landscape maintenance have set up businesses too. Future opportunities for persons interested in landscape maintenance seem assured.

Finally, many landscape management situations are at the site of a public facility, a school, a business building, or some other institution where it is not possible for a maintenance supervisor to operate a business for profit. Incentive plans are rare in these instances; however, a good landscape maintenance supervisor will, if at all possible, provide some sort of incentive plan to reward his key personnel for their good workmanship. An effort should be made to keep key personnel employed year-round even though, at least in the northern climates, business is very seasonal.

EQUIPMENT

There is a vast amount of equipment on the market to assist in the maintenance of the landscape site. There are many makes of the same type of equipment, such as mowers. The equipment manufacturer or his distributor will generally be able to demonstrate the equipment, and firsthand comparisons can be made. Besides demonstrations, evaluations can be made of the past performance of other pieces of equipment from the same manufacturer that might be owned by a maintenance firm. Contact with other firms and persons in the landscape management business should also be made to determine what equipment they like for jobs similar to the ones you will have to do.

Whether to buy equipment new or used is always a decision that must be made. Generally, if the equipment must withstand rugged, straining work, new equipment is a better buy, particularly if good service is available from the dealer. If it is anticipated that the equipment will be used instead for light, undemanding work and the piece is an especially good buy, then the used item should be purchased.

Another factor—perhaps the most important—is the frequency with which the equipment will be used. If only limited use is anticipated, the landscape supervisor has two options open to him. First, he may find it more economical to lease the equipment for the

16-4

16-5

16-6

16-7

Figure 16-4. *The use of reel type gang mowers permits high-quality mowing of large areas.*

Figure 16-5. *This reel type mower cuts a narrower swath than that cut with the mower shown in Figure 16-4. Note that the cutting units are in front of the wheels. This prevents the wheels from flattening the grass before it is cut.*

Figure 16-6. *Rotary type mowers are faster than reel type mowers; however, some maintenance workers believe that the quality of mowing is not as good. This mower cuts a 60-inch swath and is able to cut close to fences and other landscape features.*

Figure 16-7. *Leaf pickup can be expensive when done by hand raking. Leaf removal from large turf areas is best accomplished by using large leaf vacuums, such as this one.*

Figure 16-8. *Small vacuum units can be used to remove leaves and trash from small landscape areas. A thatching unit can be attached; the unit will dislodge and remove thatch that has accumulated.*

16-8

period of time it is needed; or second, he may contract the entire job done to another firm who already owns the specialized equipment needed for the work. Both of these possibilities should be investigated before purchasing any piece of large equipment.

SUMMARY

The development of a maintenance schedule for a landscape site is essential if the site is to be cared for properly. The schedule serves as a guide to the landscape supervisor to help him make sure that all maintenance tasks are carried out at the correct time. Besides making a schedule, the supervisor should keep accurate records to assist in the preparation of accurate cost accounting for the maintenance of the site.

Finally, well-paid, trained personnel are essential in the operation of any landscape maintenance organization. The key person is the crew chief or foreman. Every attempt should be made to keep him employed on a year-round, permanent basis. He should, moreover, be encouraged to attend workshops and short courses, and to read pertinent publications to keep himself up to date about maintenance procedures. It is good for employee morale to encourage all employees to develop their skills.

FOR FURTHER READING

Conover, H. S., 1958. *Grounds Maintenance Handbook*. New York: McGraw-Hill Book Co. 501 pages.

Sunset Magazine and Sunset Books (editors), 1967. *Sunset Western Garden Book*. Menlo Park, Calif.: Lane Magazine and Book Co. Revised edition, 1973. 448 pages.

Appendix 16-A
A landscape maintenance schedule

JANUARY AND FEBRUARY*

WEEKS 1, 2, 3, AND 4

Overhaul equipment for spring season.

Remove snow and ice as necessary. Use only enough salt to do a satisfactory job. Avoid excessive salt use.

Prune trees in Group I as needed when temperatures are above 40°F. [Various groups of woody plants are listed later in this table. Be sure to follow the pruning guidelines mentioned in Chapter 17.]

Prune shrubs in Groups I, III, IV, and V when temperatures are above 40°F. (Follow the pruning guidelines.)

Apply mulch to landscape beds as needed to replace or replenish to the required depths.

MARCH

WEEKS 1 AND 2

Turf

Overseed thin areas in turf. Use same seeding mixture called for in the original planting specifications. However, the rate of application should be reduced to one pound per 1,000 square feet.

Trees and Shrubs

Apply dormant-oil-spray pesticide to nonsensitive plants. Check current recommendations by entomologists on the phytotoxicities of various insecticides before applying them to plants. Dormant oil should be applied before leaf and flower buds start to expand and when temperatures are above 45°F. If scale insects have been a problem, use a summer oil on oil-sensitive plants.

---

*[This schedule was devised for the maintenance of a condominium development in central Indiana. Except for generalizing the pesticide recommendations, few adjustments have been made to adapt the schedule for general use. The arrival of spring would, of course, be earlier at sites on the West Coast or in the South, and later in the North.]

Fertilize shrub beds with a 2 : 1 : 1 ratio (analysis 22-11-11) at a rate of from 2 to 3 pounds actual N per 1,000 square feet (from 10 to 15 pounds of 22-11-11 analysis for 1,000 square feet). Do not allow fertilizer to fall onto turf areas.

Complete pruning of trees and shrubs that flower *after* June 30 and all evergreens except pines.

Apply preemergence herbicide to shrub beds. Use herbicide currently recommended. Follow directions given by the manufacturer closely. Do not use on plants not listed on the herbicide label. Read the label thoroughly.

WEEKS 3 AND 4

Turf

If crabgrass is a problem, apply a currently recommended preemergent crabgrass herbicide during the last week in March. Follow rates and application methods given by the manufacturer.

Fertilize turf areas with a high-nitrogen fertilizer, with a ratio of approximately 3 : 1 : 2. However, this may be difficult to find. Economically, the best fertilizer would have an analysis of 22–11–11 and be applied at a rate of 1 pound actual nitrogen per 1,000 square feet or 45 pounds N per acre. This is 5 pounds of 22–11–11 analysis fertilizer per 1,000 square feet, or 200 pounds per acre.

If the season is advanced, the first mowing may be necessary at this time.

Trees and shrubs

Continue and complete work described for previous two weeks.

APRIL

WEEKS 1 AND 2

Turf

Apply broadleaf-weed herbicide to established turf areas. Follow herbicide application directions. Calibrate equipment before each application. Use currently recommended broad spectrum herbicides such as 2,4-D in combination with 2,4,5-TP (silvex) at the rate of 1 pint of each per acre. Do not allow this to drift onto shrub beds and neighboring plantings. *Do not use dicamba.*

Mowing should be done as needed. Do not mow the grass shorter than 2 inches, and in areas where fine manicuring of the turf is not necessary (areas seeded to fescues), the mowing height may be increased to 2½ to 3 inches. Collection of clippings is desirable but because of the size of the area this may not be possible.

If turf diseases are present, apply recommended fungicide. See the publication *Lawn Diseases in the Midwest*[†] for identification and treatment. If in doubt as to the problem, contact the horticultural agent of the Cooperative Extension Service for advice.

Trees and Shrubs

Examine trees and shrubs for damage from winter storms, etc. Remove and/or repair all damaged limbs.

WEEKS 3 AND 4

Turf, Trees, and Shrubs

Continue and complete work for the previous two weeks.

Prepare beds that will have annual flowers. Add from two to three inches of peat moss or well-rotted manure, and 20 pounds of 12–12–12 analysis fertilizer per 1,000 square feet, regardless of whether peat moss or manure is used. Using a rototiller, deeply till the peat moss or manure and the fertilizer until thoroughly mixed in the soil. Do not work the soil when excessively wet.

MAY

WEEKS 1 AND 2

Turf

Mowing will probably need to be done twice a week during periods of high rainfall or in areas

---

[†][North Central Region Extension Service Publication 12, 1966. Ames, Iowa: Extension Service, Iowa State University. Readers in regions having mild winters may find the following publication, which contains a bibliography, useful: University of California Agriculture Extension Service, 1971. *Lawn Planting and Care in Ventura County*. Ventura, Calif.: Agriculture Extension Service.]

where irrigation is used. In areas where high-quality turf is wanted, do not cut off more than one inch of the grass at each mowing. Do not cut shorter than two inches.

Crabgrass control should have been completed by now.

If grubs are a problem, apply a currently recommended pesticide effective against soil insects no later than the first week in May. Use it as recommended on the label, and follow all the precautions given there.

Trees and Shrubs

Begin pruning all early-flowering trees and shrubs immediately after flowering is completed. Follow the directions given in pruning publications. [Some guidelines for pruning are given in Chapter 17 of this book.] Prune on an annual basis to maintain plants in a natural shape. The trees and shrubs of the early flowering groups are listed later in this table as "Shrubs: Group II" and "Trees: Group II."

Inspect trees and shrubs for any insect and disease pests. Remove any weeds from landscape beds.

WEEKS 3 AND 4

Turf

Continue mowing as needed. No irrigation will be necessary unless the spring is excessively dry. A period of two or more weeks without rain may make it necessary to apply up to one inch of irrigation water on the turf areas. Check publications about what irrigation techniques are most satisfactory for turf areas.

Make second fertilizer application during this period. The most economical choice would be urea (analysis 45–0–0). Apply 2 pounds per 1,000 square feet or 85 pounds per acre. Do not apply at a higher rate.

Check turf for diseases, but apply fungicide only if needed.

Trees and Shrubs

Plant annual flowers as required. Be prepared to water new plants during the establishment phase. Use currently recommended herbicides that can be applied immediately after planting. Apply according to the directions on the labels.

Continue pruning early-flowering trees and shrubs.

Remove weeds from shrub beds and inspect plant material for pests. An all-purpose spray may reduce the chance of insect and disease problems on the new trees and shrubs. Follow all safety precautions when spraying. Do not be careless. Be aware of the residents in the buildings; though the materials recommended are completely safe, the residents do not know this, and they may think your application is haphazard. Keep them informed of your program.

Prune conifers only if a thick Christmas-tree-like growth is wanted. [See Chapter 17 and pruning publications for the techniques.]

JUNE

WEEKS 1, 2, 3, AND 4

Turf

Mowing will continue to be needed twice a week in well-manicured turf areas. Less-frequent mowings will be required in the areas seeded with fescues.

During this period it is important to notice the soil moisture. The grass has been actively growing during the spring, when there is adequate moisture, and it will be susceptible to drought injury if June is a dry month. Irrigate the fine turf areas as required.

Trees and shrubs

Continue any pruning that is required of early-flowering ornamentals.

Inspect evergreens for mites and spray as needed. Inspect plants for scale insects. Close attention should be paid to any *Euonymus* species.

Weed beds as required.

If scale insects are present, spray as required.

Apply herbicide to shrub beds if weed growth starts to return. Use same material as in early spring. Clean out weeds before spraying.

Water shrubs and trees if the season has been excessively dry. Use one inch of water per application per week.

JULY

Weeks 1, 2, 3, and 4

Turf

Mow as needed. If turf is to remain green all summer, it will be necessary to pay particular attention to the sufficiency of water. Irrigate as needed.

Trees and Shrubs

Check plants for aphids, scale insects, and mites, and spray as needed. A second application of the all-purpose spray may help prevent an insect problem from developing.

Provide water for newly planted trees and shrubs as needed. Established older plants should be watered if the season has been dry. Use at least one inch of water for each application.

Weed landscape beds as needed.

AUGUST

Weeks 1, 2, 3, and 4

Turf

Mow as needed. Irrigate whenever rainfall is not adequate. Do not allow the turf to become dormant because of a lack of water in areas where fine lawn is desired.

Fertilize during the latter part of August as described for Weeks 3 and 4 in the month of May. Apply fertilizer only to those areas being irrigated.

Inspect lawn for diseases, but apply fungicide only if it is necessary.

Trees and Shrubs

Maintain adequate moisture for newly planted trees and shrubs. Water any established plants as needed.

Do not fertilize any woody plants until after their dormancy begins (October).

Continue to check plants for pests and control as required.

Remove weeds from beds.

SEPTEMBER

Weeks 1 and 2

Turf

Apply broadleaf-weed killer to turf. Do not allow this to drift onto nearby landscape plants. *Do not use dicamba.*

Overseed any thin areas with same mixture called for originally. Use one pound per 1,000 square feet.

Continue to water as required. Mowing should continue at the prescribed two-inch height.

Trees and Shrubs

Examine plants for pests, and spray as required, but do not use pesticides unless necessary.

Maintain the weeding of beds.

Weeks 3 and 4

Turf

Apply fertilizer as described for the month of May.

Continue to mow as required.

Trees and Shrubs

Begin to rake early-falling leaves.

Water only fall-planted trees and shrubs.

If chickweed is a problem in ground cover beds and shrub beds, apply a herbicide expressly manufactured to control chickweed. Check with the Cooperative Extension Service personnel to see what they recommend for this.

OCTOBER

Weeks 1, 2, 3, and 4

Turf

Mow as needed. Water only if the autumn has been dry.

Trees and Shrubs

Fertilize trees that might not be receiving fertilizer in conjunction with your applications to other plants (trees utilize some of the fertilizer applied to the turf). Use the broadcast method to apply an analysis 22–11–11 fertilizer at the rate of from 10 to 15 pounds per 1,000 square feet. Fertilize to at least three feet beyond the drip line.

Water plants as required. This must be done if the autumn has been dry to improve overwintering chances of plants.

Leaf removal should be carried out throughout the month.

Continue to keep beds weed-free.

NOVEMBER

Weeks 1, 2, 3, and 4

Prepare all equipment for winter storage.

Turf

Make the last mowing of the year during the first week in November.

Trees and Shrubs

Complete work outlined for October.

DECEMBER

Weeks 1, 2, 3, and 4

Turf

Finish any leaf removal (late-falling oak leaves should not be left to form a heavy mat over the turf during winter).

Prune late-flowering plants, evergreens, and trees listed among the trees of Group I and among the shrubs of Groups I, III, IV, and V.

Calculate supply needs for next season and order now. Discounts are usually available for early orders.

Take vacations; give permanent crew vacation time.

Plants at the site are categorized as follows:

SHRUBS

Botanical name	Common name

Group I: Deciduous—nonflowering, or inconspicuously flowering

Berberis mentorensis	Mentor barberry
Berberis thunbergii var. atropurpurea	Red-leaf Japanese barberry
Berberis thunbergii var. atropurpurea 'Nana'	Dwarf red barberry
Cornus baileyi	Bailey dogwood
Cornus stolonifera 'Flaviramea'	Yellow-twig dogwood
Cornus stolonifera 'Kelseyi'	Dwarf red-osier dogwood
Cotoneaster adpressa var. praecox	Early creeping cotoneaster
Cotoneaster apiculata	Cranberry-cotoneaster
Elaeagnus umbellata	Autumn-olive
Euonymus alatus 'Compactus'	Dwarf burning-bush
Viburnum trilobum 'Compactum'	Dwarf cranberry-bush

Group II: Deciduous—early flowering (before June 30 or early summer)

Chaenomeles japonica	Dwarf Japanese quince
Chaenomeles speciosa	Flowering quince
Forsythia intermedia 'Spectabilis'	Showy forsythia
Rhododendron catawbiense	Catawba rhododendron
Rosa rugosa	Rugosa rose
Viburnum burkwoodii	Burkwood viburnum
Viburnum carlesii	Korean spice viburnum

Group III: Deciduous—flowering in summer (after June 30) and fall, or prized for fruit

Cotinus coggygria	Smoke-tree
Pyracantha coccinea 'Lalandii'	Lalande firethorn
Viburnum dilatatum	Linden viburnum

Viburnum opulus	European cranberry-bush
Weigela florida 'Eva Rathke'	Eva Rathke weigela

Group IV: Evergreens—broadleaf

Euonymus fortunei 'Sarcoxie'	Sarcoxie wintercreeper
Euonymus fortunei var. vegetus	Bigleaf wintercreeper
Ilex glabra	Inkberry
Viburnum rhytidophylloides	Lantanaphyllum viburnum

Group V: Evergreens—narrowleaf

Juniperus horizontalis 'Bar Harbor'	Bar Harbor juniper
Taxus cuspidata	Japanese yew
Taxus media 'Nigra'	Nigra yew
Taxus media 'Wardii'	Ward's yew

TREES

Botanical Name	Common Name

Group I: Deciduous shade trees

Acer palmatum 'Atropurpureum'	Bloodleaf Japanese maple
Acer rubrum	Red maple
Acer saccharum	Sugar maple
Betula nigra	River birch
Carya ovata	Shagbark hickory
Celtis occidentalis	Hackberry
Cercis canadensis	Redbud
Cercis canadensis var. alba	White redbud
Fagus sylvatica	European beech
Fraxinus americana	White ash
Fraxinus pennsylvanica	Green ash
Fraxinus quadrangulata	Blue ash
Gleditsia triacanthos 'Shademaster'	Shademaster honey-locust
Hamamelis virginiana	Common witch-hazel
Juglans nigra	Black walnut
Ostrya virginiana	Ironwood, American hop-hornbeam

Platanus occidentalis	American sycamore
Quercus alba	White oak
Quercus imbricaria	Shingle oak
Quercus macrocarpa	Bur oak
Quercus palustris	Pin oak
Quercus rubra	Red oak
Salix babylonica	Weeping willow
Salix pentandra	Laurel willow

Group II: Deciduous—small early-flowering (before June 30) trees

Cornus florida	Flowering dogwood
Cornus florida var. rubra	Pink flowering dogwood
Malus floribunda	Japanese flowering crabapple
Malus scheideckeri	Scheidecker flowering crabapple

Group III: Deciduous—small summer-flowering (after June 30) or fall-flowering trees [the site for which this maintenance schedule was devised had none of these].

Group IV: Conifers

Pinus strobus	White pine
Tsuga canadensis	Canada hemlock

HERBACEOUS PLANTS

Botanical name	Common name

Group I: Ground covers and vines

Clematis jackmannii	Jackman clematis
Euonymus fortunei 'Coloratus'	Purple-leaf wintercreeper
Hedera helix	English ivy
Pachysandra terminalis	Japanese spurge
Vinca minor	Myrtle or periwinkle

Group II: Perennial flowers

Bergenia cordifolia	Heartleaf bergenia
Hosta lancifolia	Japanese hosta

17

Physical Care
of Woody Plant Material

Water, fertility levels, and pruning are three major factors that man can control greatly in the maintenance of landscape plant materials. Each is of importance in the development and growth of the plant for the landscape. Water is the most critical during the establishment of the plant; fertility levels and pruning are not so critical. However, adequate soil nutrient levels are essential if, after establishment, the plant material is to develop fully and require a minimum of maintenance. Pruning is the most essential of all subsequent maintenance practices and will, when done properly, help keep the landscape plants healthy and vigorous.

WATER

Water is the most essential of all the factors that influence plant establishment on the landscape site. Recommendations on watering are also the most difficult to make universally, as varying soil types and conditions at the site control to a great extent what watering techniques should be used. However, some general recommendations can be made.

The most important factor in watering woody ornamentals is to apply enough water to insure a 6- to 10-inch soil penetration. This may require from one to two or more inches of water per week, depending on soil type. Light, sandy soils require more frequent waterings. The water should be applied in one application at a rate that will permit maximum soil penetration with a minimum of runoff. On sandy soils it may be necessary to apply water twice a week with one inch or more being applied each time. The waterings should be applied as supplements to rainfall. Watering should be done immediately after a rain shower to bring the quantity of water up to one inch or more.

If rainfall is not adequate, weekly waterings will be necessary in most climates to insure establishment of most shallow-rooted ornamentals. This is particularly true for ground covers, annuals, and perennial plants. Most plant material being established will benefit from such a watering program.

For established plant material the same application techniques should be used (adequate amounts at each watering). However, it may not be necessary to water as frequently. The soil should be checked periodically to determine if water is needed. This is done by obtaining a sample of soil from a depth of six to eight inches. Squeeze the sample; if it sticks together, water is not needed. However, if it crumbles, enough water should be applied to penetrate eight to ten inches. Water on a regular basis until adequate rainfall occurs.

Watering turf areas requires techniques that are to some degree different. Watering should be done more frequently, in one-inch amounts, and these should be applied to penetrate to a six-inch depth. Care should be taken not to apply water at night in areas of high humidity. The turf remains wet too long and chances of diseases developing are increased. Of course, at some landscape sites night waterings are essential since traffic in the area during the daylight hours prevents watering. In arid areas night watering is done to reduce the loss by evaporation.

Some care should be taken when using time clocks to activate watering systems. Water applied in this way after periods of heavy rainfall may cause the soil to become waterlogged,

and root injury can result. Also, when watering turf, take care not to overwater nearby landscape beds. If possible, the turf watering system should be separate from the watering systems of landscape beds. The beds should be constructed so that water from the turf areas will not drain into them.

The crucial factors in watering are these: (1) apply enough water to soak the soil to a depth of six inches or more; (2) apply at a rate that minimizes runoff; (3) water newly planted material regularly; (4) do not ignore the moisture needs of established plant material; and (5) do not overwater established plant material.

FERTILIZER APPLICATIONS TO WOODY PLANT MATERIAL

A good fertility program will help maintain the vigor and health of woody plant material at a landscape site. Even mature specimens benefit from regular applications of fertilizer. Trees and shrubs that are healthy and growing vigorously are less susceptible to attack by insects and diseases.

Too often the landscape maintenance supervisor ignores the mineral-nutrient requirements of his trees and shrubs. He may be operating under the old adage that trees will grow where nothing else will. Although the tree might survive, it might not develop into the fine specimen that is wanted unless a sound fertility program is carried out.

However, fertilizers are not a substitute for sunlight and water, but make up just one of the environmental factors that must all be in balance if the landscape plant is to develop to its fullest potential. A good fertilizer program will help insure that deficiencies of essential mineral elements are not limiting plant growth.

Composition and Action of Fertilizers

There are many fertilizer materials on the market and selecting the right one to give maximum benefit for the money invested can be a problem. It is important to remember that there are no "miracle" fertilizers that will provide an optimum supply of nutrients for many years with one application. Moreover, a salesman will promote his product as the best material for a specific project. It is wise to investigate several sources of fertilizers and to check the validity of various claims of performance with an unbiased source before purchasing large quantities of fertilizers.

The analysis of any true fertilizer material must be given on the container label. A complete fertilizer contains three major elements essential for plant growth—nitrogen, phosphorus, and potassium. A fertilizer with an analysis of 6-12-4 contains 6 percent nitrogen, 12 percent P_2O_5 (phosphorus), and 4 percent K_2O (potassium) by weight. The nitrogen content is always given first, followed by phosphorus and potassium, in that order.

A careful inspection of the analysis on the label should be made. Many organic fertilizers have very low nutrient levels and their cost becomes exceedingly high in comparison with their total nutrient value. One of the considerations when buying fertilizer is the total analysis, which is important once it has been determined the ratio of nutrients is satisfactory. As an example, if a uniform ratio of 1 : 1 : 1 is desired, and a material has an analysis of 12-12-12, and its price is x dollars per ton, it is a better buy than a material with an analysis of 10-10-10 at the same price per ton. The fertilizer with the lower analysis would have to cost approximately 20 percent less before the price per unit of nutrient supplied would be the same.

Two factors besides price should be considered when buying fertilizers: (1) the availability to the plant of the nutrients in the fertilizer is important; (2) so is the effect of the fertilizer on soil pH. Readily available fertilizers are those that can provide a source of nutrients to the plant immediately because the fertilizer salts used are water soluble. This may or may not always be desirable. For some needs such as turf fertilization programs, it may be desirable to use a more slowly available nitrogen form to provide fertilizer to the plant for a longer time, and a water-soluble fertilizer might not be wanted. In other fertilization programs, if an acid soil reaction is desired for a particular plant species, an acid-reacting fertilizer should be used. However, for most needs, the materials that will be useful will be neutral in reaction, and their overall influence on soil pH will be minor.

SOLUBLE FERTILIZERS

The mineral fertilizer materials that are readily available and neutral in reaction are those made from a strong base salt and a strong acid salt. As an example, a potassium source, muriate of potash (KCl), is formed by a reaction of a strong base, potassium hydroxide, with a strong acid, hydrochloric acid, and the resulting salt is neutral. Another example would be a nitrogen source: sodium nitrate. Commonly used agricultural fertilizers such as those with a

12-12-12 analysis are usually prepared from neutral salts and have very little influence on the soil pH. These materials are readily available to the plant because the salts themselves are very soluble in water. However, they are not properly called water-soluble fertilizers because the carrier (the filler) that is used is not soluble.

The water-soluble fertilizers on the market are used mostly by greenhouse operators and container stock growers, who inject the fertilizer into irrigation water. Water-soluble fertilizers have basically the same salts as the more conventional dry fertilizers; however, the nonsoluble carrier has been eliminated. Moreover, in water-soluble fertilizers, the phosphorus source is a more expensive water-soluble salt. There is little, if any, difference in the availability of the phosphorus to the plant. The water is the carrier rather than a dry clay particle or, in some materials, vermiculite. The use of water-soluble fertilizers in a landscape fertility program for plant material that has been established cannot be justified because of the high cost of the fertilizer.

Liquid fertilizers that are slightly acidic in reaction are those manufactured by reacting phosphoric acid and ammonium hydroxide. This reaction produces a salt with a strong acid and a weak base. Moreover, the fertilizer that is produced contains two forms of ammonium phosphate that are acidic in reaction. The potassium is added as muriate of potash (KCl). The analysis ratio is approximately 1 : 3 : 0. This liquid fertilizer is not any more available to the plant than the dry fertilizer, but it can be applied directly to the fields without a carrier, from large tank-trucks, and so it is useful at large farms. However, it is of little value to most people in landscape management.

The acidic reaction fertilizers that should be used primarily on such plants as rhododendrons and azaleas are usually more expensive but are necessary in areas where water sources may be alkaline. Ammonium sulfate is commonly used for this purpose. Ammonium sulfate should not be confused with aluminum sulfate, but it often is. Aluminum sulfate has no fertilizer value and is used primarily for pH change. It should be pointed out here that some plants are sensitive to high levels of aluminum; therefore it is suggested that some means of reducing soil pH be used other than application of aluminum sulfate.

Besides ammonium sulfate, ammonium phosphates are other acidic fertilizers that can be purchased in the dry form, but they are quite expensive. They do provide a source of phosphates and nitrogen, and they do have an acidic reaction. However, the phosphorus becomes tied up at the surface soil when surface applications are made and consequently has little value as a surface application.

SLOW-RELEASE FERTILIZERS

There has been a search for several years for fertilizer materials that will release nutrients over long periods of time. Many materials have been sold sometimes with unwarranted claims about their long-term nutrient values. Phosphorus materials are less soluble and do not move in the soil, so once initial levels have been built up, their depletion is slow. The retention of potassium, although not as great as that of the phosphates, is still satisfactory after a fairly long time. However, there is little response by woody plants to potassium fertilization, and in some areas, such as the Rocky Mountain area, potassium isn't needed since it is abundant naturally. So the limiting element in immediate or prolonged fertilization of woody ornamentals is nitrogen. Whether or not a fertilizer releases nitrogen slowly often depends on the water-solubility of the fertilizer material. The water-solubility must be low if the nutrients are to be released slowly, because as more rainfall or more irrigation water is added, more of the fertilizer material is dissolved and becomes available to the plant. Besides low solubility the release rates of some fertilizers are dependent on the particle size. Finer particles are more soluble because of a greater ratio of surface area to weight. The effective nutrient supply time of some low-solubility fertilizer materials is increased by manufacturing the fertilizer in coarser grades.

Low-solubility has sometimes been obtained by coating fertilizer materials with a plastic coating that acts as a membrane. The presence of water with low fertilizer salt concentration on the outside of this membrane causes the fertilizer material on the inside to pass outward, through the membrane. Again, available surface area would affect release rates, so small particles supply nutrients faster than large particles. This technique is moderately successful, but, as we said earlier, its success is based on the amount of water available during the growing season. In wet periods, the breakdown rate is much more rapid.

ORGANIC FERTILIZERS

There are also organic sources of fertilizer materials. Recently the emphasis on the ecologically sound, nonpolluting procedures has aroused more interest in these. One material that is not a slow-releasing material but is often thought to be, is urea. This synthetic organic compound has the characteristics of a mineral rather than an organic source of nitrogen. It is highly soluble, though pelleting gives it some slow-release effect. It will not supply nitrogen except for a relatively short time. The conversion by which urea is effective is from urea to ammonia to nitrate. It is a mistake to believe that high concentrations of urea will not cause soluble salt damage (excess fertilizer burn).

A complex of urea and formaldehyde gives a slower-releasing material. The ratio of urea to formaldehyde determines the amounts of nitrogen that are available to the plant and also the solubility of the material. Currently there are urea-formaldehyde complexes on the market that will supply nitrogen over a one-season period. In some, the urea and formaldehyde are combined with the supply of phosphorus and potassium, and these are all pressed into the form of a large tablet. This tablet is then used in the initial planting stages and is frequently used for container-grown stock. Pellets have limited contact with the roots. Pellets may also be used with some effectiveness in landscape plantings.

There are, furthermore, the pure organic forms of fertilizer material such as blood, tankage, castor-bean pomace, etc., which supply nitrogen that is initially in a protein form. The breakdown by microorganisms is from protein to amino acids, to ammonia, to nitrite, and finally to nitrate. The breakdown is generally controlled by the organic material itself, by soil temperature, and by moisture. Generally, these materials are not satisfactory for fertilizing trees and shrubs in the landscape site. The cost per unit of nutrient is extremely high; the materials should not be considered for use unless they are specifically requested by the customer.

Fertilizer Techniques

It is important to determine whether a fertility program is needed for mature landscape plantings. A general rule of thumb is that if a complete fertilization program is being carried out for turf the trees and shrubs will not need additional fertilizer so long as the fertilizer is also applied to the plant beds. But never use turf fertilizer-herbicide mixes in plant beds.

As the growth of a tree tapers off before maturity, the terminal growth should be from six to nine inches per year, and for newly planted or actively growing trees growth should be from 9 to 12 inches annually. If the growth rate is less than this, the tree would probably benefit from a fertility program.

Recommendations about the time and rate of application vary greatly. There are two basically different determinations about the best time for tree fertilization. Some research suggests that for northern climates, an April or May application will make the most efficient use of any nitrogen supplied, with October and November being suggested as second best. The reverse order is suggested by recent research based on soil temperatures at the root zone. Soil temperatures are warmer in the fall, and more absorption of fertilizer will occur when temperatures are warmer. In southern or west coast climates where the temperatures are mild the year round, applications should be made before the growing season starts.

Nitrogen is the key element and should be applied at least every two years. Application of phosphorus and potassium every three to five years is probably adequate for satisfactory growth.

There are two basic techniques for applying fertilizer; so-called deep root-feeding, and surface application. Research has indicated generally that surface applications will provide the same benefits to the tree as deep root-feeding. However, surface applications have certain disadvantages. The turf is often stimulated under the tree and the turf will be much greener here than in surrounding turf areas. The tree will appear to be growing in a little oasis. However, for fertilization of shrub beds and trees where high absorption rates are not needed or where the stimulation of the turf area is not disadvantageous, the surface application is easier to make and it can be done with less labor, and consequently, with less cost.

It is recommended that a rectangle be staked out or at least visually laid out slightly beyond the drip line of the tree. The addition of nitrogen should be at the rate of two pounds of nitrogen per 1,000 square feet. This rate should be used at each application if spring and fall applications are made. Table 17-1 gives the rates for application of nitrogen fertilizer based on their nitrogen analysis. Any complete analysis fertilizers would also be applied based at a rate based on the amount of nitrogen in the fertilizer.

Table 17-1 Pounds of nitrogen-source fertilizers to add to obtain two pounds actual nitrogen per 1,000 square feet.

Fertilizer	Analysis	Pounds per 1,000 sq ft
Urea	45–0–0	4
Ammonium nitrate	33.5–0–0	6
Ammonium sulfate	21–0–0	10
Sodium nitrate	16–0–0	12

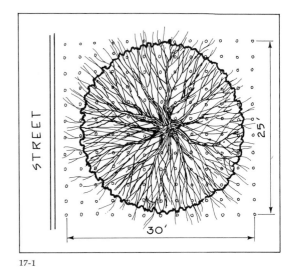

17-1

Figure 17-1. *A uniform method of applying fertilizer by the deep root feeding method. The total amount of fertilizer to be applied is divided by the number of holes and an equal amount is placed in each hole. The holes are from 2 to 2½ feet apart.*

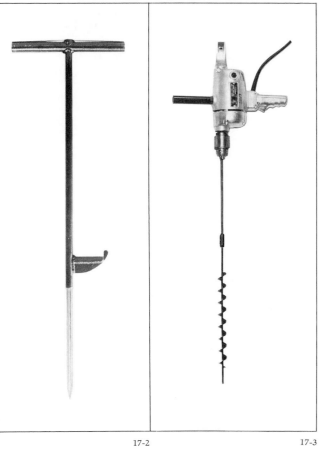

17-2   17-3   17-4

Another recommendation often made is to feed trees 0.5 pounds total nitrogen for each inch of trunk diameter. When following this recommendation, take care not to apply the fertilizer at a rate more concentrated than two pounds total nitrogen per 1,000 square feet of surrounding turf. When applying a complete fertilizer, it is suggested that a ratio of 2 : 1 : 2 be used; again, the rate should be based on the amount of nitrogen in the analysis.

Dry fertilizer can also be injected into soil either dry or after it has been dissolved in water. Placement of the holes can be in a circular arrangement outward as far as the tree limbs spread. Or a rectangular area can be laid out past the drip line of the tree and the holes evenly spaced on two-foot centers with approximately 250 holes per 1,000 square feet. The depth of the holes should not be much greater than 18 inches since most of the feeder roofs of many trees are within two feet of the surface. The diameter of the holes should be two inches. Turf plugs should be kept intact so that they may be used after the fertilizer is added. The total amount of fertilizer is then divided by the number of holes, and equal amounts of fertilizer are put in each hole. The hole is then filled with sand and the turf is replaced on the top. This technique is time consuming and expensive, but it does eliminate the problem of a green turf oasis under the tree.

Dry fertilizer is sometimes injected by blasts of air—a technique that requires use of special equipment. Sand is often used as a carrier; the technique has the additional benefit of improving soil aeration.

The use of liquid injection can be made if the equipment is available. Approximately

Figures 17-2, 17-3. *Two tools can be used to drill the holes shown in Figure 17-1: A punch bar (17-2) or a soil auger (17-3).*

Figure 17-4. *This machine drills about four holes per minute, inserts the fertilizer, and fills the holes automatically.*

200 gallons of water is recommended per 1,000 square feet. The holes should be spaced 2½ feet from center to center; approximately 30 pounds of 20-20-20 analysis fertilizer is recommended per 200 gallons of water. In an area of 1,000 square feet there will be approximately 160 injection sites; 1½ gallons of solution should be injected into each hole. Some caution should be taken in using liquid injection methods. Apply no more than 1½ gallons per hole, and do not force the liquid into the hole at great pressure, for this may create air holes around the root system of the tree being fed.

The major concern thus far has been with the major nutrient—principally the nitrogen requirements—of the woody ornamentals. Generally, few of the minor elements are limiting to the growth of most woody species. However, an exception is true with high-pH soils. Iron chlorosis can develop in many species grown in such soils. Common examples are the ericaceous plants and pin oak, *Quercus palustris*. Iron chlorosis is generally thought to be due to the low solubility of iron in high-pH soils. However, damage to root systems such as that caused by the low oxygen levels in waterlogged soils may also cause chlorosis symptoms.

There are several solutions to iron chlorosis and generally these can be classified as permanent, semipermanent, and temporary. Of course, a permanent solution is to correct the problem of high pH in the soil before planting. The area treated should be large enough to allow for the future root development of the plant. Too often the soil pH is adjusted only for the backfill in the planting hole, or in an area only slightly beyond the hole, without any regard for the future development of the tree

17-5

17-6

17-7

Figure 17-5. *A soil needle, used to inject water soluble fertilizer below the soil surface.*

Figures 17-6, 17-7. *A hole is bored into a tree that is suffering from iron chlorosis (17-6). A capsule containing iron is inserted into the hole (17-7). The capsule contains a soluble form of iron.*

Table 17-2 Soil applications of an iron sulfate-sulfur mixture for control of chlorosis in trees and shrubs.

Diameter of tree 4 feet above ground (inches)	Total amount of the iron sulfate-sulfur mixture per tree (pounds)	Two-inch diameter holes in ground		Total amount of the iron sulfate-sulfur mixture per hole (pounds)
		Number of holes	Depth of holes (inches)	
1	1	4	12	0.25
2	2	4	12	0.5
3	4	6	15	0.75
4	6	8	15	1.0
5	10	10	15	1.0
6	12	12	15	1.0
7	14	14	18	1.0
8	16	16	18	1.0
9	18	18	18	1.0
10	20	20	18	1.0
15	30	30	18	1.0
20	40	40	18	1.0
25	50	50	18	1.0

or shrub. The tree roots grow out of this planting area into areas where high pH has not been treated and iron chlorosis develops sometimes 5 to 10 years or more after planting.

To lower soil pH, use sulfur and acidic fertilizers. In limestone base soils, changing soil pH at depths of from 18 to 24 inches with fertilizers is nearly impossible; in those soils, the trees should be fed by the deep root method, with ferrous sulfate (iron sulfate) and sulfur. The rates are given in Table 17-2. Chelated iron may be used in place of ferrous sulfate. Chelated iron may give more satisfactory results in any kind of soil if used in a soil injection or in a deep root-feeding than it will if applied to the surface. The response to these techniques is slow but fairly permanent.

Sometimes a tree has declined greatly because of iron chlorosis to such a great extent that a quicker response is needed. Trunk injections of ferrous sulfate or capsules containing iron chelate can provide a response within three weeks. The treatment may last for up to five years. At the same time, soil treatments should also be made.

In early spring when the new growth is expanding, a foliar spray with ferrous sulfate or iron chelate solution will provide an immediate response. It is only temporary, since the iron does not move in the plant beyond the foliage that has been sprayed; the new growth not treated will be chlorotic. This method should be used only to provide an immediate response, and a more permanent means of correcting the chlorosis should be initiated immediately.

Fertility programs for the woody plants in the landscape should be carried out on a regular basis. Soil tests and growth observations should be used as a means of determining the fertility needs of the plants. Rates should be based on the nitrogen level in the fertilizer.

Modifying Soil pH

As stated in previous chapters, the soil pH controls to a large degree the availability of many of the essential mineral elements. It was suggested that the pH be modified to fit the requirements of the landscape plants before their installation. It is obvious that though this is the most desirable means of adjusting pH it is not the practice commonly followed. Consequently it may be necessary to change the soil pH at the landscape site years after the plant installation has been completed.

The need for a soil test before adding lime or sulfur to change the soil pH cannot be overemphasized. Too frequently lime or sulfur is applied to a soil without the slightest knowledge of the existing soil pH. In some sections of the country, such as the Northeast, the pH of many soils, but not all, are already low, below 5.5, and the addition of sulfur is of no benefit. In fact, for certain plants this practice may even be harmful. Within a very short distance of some soil with low pH there may be another soil with a pH of 6.5 or higher. The need for a reduction in pH in this soil is apparent if so-called acid-loving plants are to be grown, but without a soil test there is no way of knowing whether the soil pH is too high or too low for good growth. It is absolutely essential to have a soil test or at least a pH determination made at least biannually. Do not blindly add lime or

sulfur to soils just because someone makes a general recommendation or because the practice is carried out on an adjoining site.

The modification of soil pH on established landscape plants is done in the same manner as described for pH modifications before planting (see Chapter 13). The amounts of lime required to raise the pH or of sulfur to lower it depend on the magnitude of change and the soil type. The same rates should be used that were given in Tables 13-4 and 13-5 in Chapter 13.

When applying sulfur over established turf, certain precautions should be followed. The sulfur can combine with water and this will form a dilute acid. If air temperatures are above 80°F and the humidity is high, the formation of acid on turf grasses will cause a burning of the foliage. Unless the rates of application are excessively high, the turf will eventually recover from the injury. For safety, it is recommended that two pounds per 100 square feet (870 pounds per acre) be the maximum amount of sulfur applied at one time and that applications be made several weeks apart. The number of applications required can be determined from Table 13-5 by dividing the recommended rates by 2 (pounds per 100 square feet) or by 870 (pounds per acre).

The pH requirement of the landscape plant must also be considered. Compare the results of the soil test with the plant requirements to determine if a change is required. Table 17-3 lists some commonly used landscape plant material and the soil pH-range at which the growth can be expected to be close to optimum.

Table 17-3 Some trees and shrubs for which soil-reaction adaptations may be needed because they grow better in a pH range other than 6.5–7.5.

Botanical name	Common name	Most favorable pH range	Botanical name	Common name	Most favorable pH range
Abies spp.	Fir	4.0 to 6.5	*Ostrya virginiana*	American hop-hornbeam	6.0 to 6.5
Acer pensylvanicum	Striped maple	4.0 to 5.0	*Oxydendrum arboreum*	Sour-wood	4.0 to 6.0
Acer rubrum	Red maple	4.5 to 7.5	*Picea* spp.	Spruce	4.0 to 6.5
Acer spicatum	Mountain maple	4.0 to 5.0	*Picea pungens*	Colorado spruce	6.0 to 6.5
Aesculus hippocastanum	Horse-chestnut	6.0 to 7.0	*Pinus* spp.	Pine	4.0 to 6.5
Aesculus pavia	Red buckeye	6.0 to 6.5	*Pseudotsuga menziesii*	Douglas-fir	6.0 to 6.5
Betula lenta	Sweet birch	4.0 to 5.0	*Quercus coccinea*	Scarlet oak	6.0 to 6.5
Carya ovata	Shagbark hickory	6.0 to 6.5	*Quercus falcata*	Spanish red oak	4.0 to 5.0
Castanea dentata	American chestnut	4.0 to 6.0	*Quercus macrocarpa*	Bur oak	4.0 to 5.0
Castanea pumila	Chinquapin	4.0 to 6.5	*Quercus marilandica*	Blackjack oak	4.0 to 5.0
Chamaecyparis spp.	False-cypress	4.0 to 7.5	*Quercus palustris*	Pin oak	5.5 to 6.5
Chamaecyparis thyoides	White-cedar	4.0 to 5.5	*Quercus phellos*	Willow-oak	4.0 to 6.5
Chionanthus virginicus	Fringe-tree	4.0 to 6.0	*Quercus prinus*	Chestnut-oak	6.0 to 6.5
Cornus florida	Flowering dogwood	5.0 to 6.5	*Quercus rubra*	Red oak	4.5 to 6.0
Franklinia alatamaha	Franklinia	4.0 to 6.0	*Quercus stellata*	Post oak	4.0 to 6.5
Gordonia lasianthus	Loblolly bay	4.0 to 6.0	*Robinia pseudoacacia*	Black locust	5.0 to 7.5
Halesia tetraptera	Silverbell	4.0 to 6.0	*Salix repens*	Creeping willow	4.0 to 5.0
Ilex opaca	American holly	4.0 to 6.0	*Sorbus americana*	American mountain-ash	5.0 to 7.0
Juniperus communis var. *saxatilis*	Mountain juniper	4.0 to 5.0	*Stewartia malacodendron*	Stewartia	4.0 to 6.0
Juniperus horizontalis	Creeping juniper	4.0 to 6.0	*Styrax americana*	Storax	4.0 to 6.0
Kalmia latifolia	Mountain-laurel	4.0 to 6.5	*Symplocos tinctoria*	Common sweetleaf	4.0 to 6.0
Liquidambar styraciflua	Sweet-gum	6.0 to 6.5	*Tsuga canadensis*	Canada hemlock	4.0 to 6.5
Magnolia spp.	Magnolia	4.0 to 7.0	*Tsuga caroliniana*	Carolina hemlock	4.0 to 5.0
Nyssa sylvatica	Sour-gum	5.0 to 6.0			

Data from P. P. Pirone, 1972. *Tree Maintenance*. New York: Oxford University Press.

PRUNING TREES AND SHRUBS

Pruning is one of the most essential maintenance practices. The proper pruning of plants will increase their longevity and usefulness in the landscape for many, many years. If the pruning is done properly, it will help maintain the plant forms that were intended by the landscape architect when he chose a plant for a certain location. However, pruning is often ignored for years until the plants have become overgrown; then it is nearly impossible to bring them back to the intended shape. Ideally, yearly pruning should be done on any landscape site to maintain the plant material within the desired size and shape. Following are some guides about why, when, and how to prune correctly.

Why To Prune

The primary reason for pruning is to maintain or occasionally to reduce the size of the tree or shrub in the landscape. This prevents overgrowth, keeps the plant in the form that has been planned for, and permits new growth to develop vigorously. Pruning is also done to remove dead or broken branches, which is often simply a cosmetic process and at other times is of help in bringing the plant back to a vigorous and healthy condition. On newly planted trees and even on some established trees, pruning may be done to remove weak branches and/or numerous branches that may form weak crotches.

Such plants as rhododendrons and azaleas require the removal of old flower heads after the flowers have withered and before the formation of fruit, to promote flower bud development for next season. On a large landscape site having many rhododendrons and azaleas it is nearly impossible to carry out this practice.

When plants have been permitted to overgrow an area it is often necessary to rejuvenate them to restore new vigor and to reduce their size. The process requires drastic removal of many large branches and, except in a few species, this should be done gradually for several years rather than all at once. Not all shrubs used in a landscape can be rejuvenated. However, lilac, privet, forsythia, and some spireas are a few of the plants that can be pruned in this manner.

It may be necessary to prune in order to remove limbs that hang low over walkways or roads, or that extend into the area of power lines, or that constitute some other danger.

Finally, pruning is sometimes done to shape plants in unnatural forms, most often in hedges and screens. In formal gardens sheared hedges can be used with special effectiveness, and many of the gardens of the past were typified by such pruning and, when it was in style, by topiary. Topiary was done not only by pruning but also by wiring shrubs to form animals and various other objects. Evergreens pruned in globes and squares today are in poor taste at most landscape sites. Plants should be allowed to develop into their natural shape except when used for hedges, screens, or accent plants.

When To Prune

To obtain maximum benefit and beauty from trees and shrubs, it is important to know when to prune. Here are several rules that, if followed, will guide landscape personnel in the proper times for pruning.

Table 17-4 A selection of trees and shrubs which may be pruned both before and after bloom.

Botanical name	Common name
Cornus stolonifera	Red-osier dogwood
Cotoneaster apiculata	Cranberry cotoneaster
Cotoneaster divaricata	Spreading cotoneaster
Cotoneaster multiflora	Multiflora cotoneaster
Mahonia aquifolium	Oregon-grape
Spiraea bumalda	Anthony Waterer and Frobel spirea
Symphoricarpos albus	Snowberry
Symphoricarpos chenaultii	Chenault coralberry
Weigela florida	Rose weigela

1. Trees and shrubs that flower early in the spring should be pruned *immediately after* flowering. Trees and shrubs that fall into this category set their flowering buds on the previous season's growth and the buds overwinter on this older growth. *Note*: Pruning before flowering or late in the previous season will reduce the number of the buds and some of the beauty of the shrub or tree will be lost.

2. Trees and shrubs that flower from early summer through the fall should be pruned during their dormant season. These plants develop their flower buds on the current season's growth.

3. A few plants may be pruned lightly before and after flowering to increase their flowering production. Plants in this category are found in Table 17-4.

4. The fruits of some plants are prized quite highly for their fall color and because they provide a source of food for birds. Even though these plants flower heavily in the spring, they should be pruned lightly each season after fruit production. In this way the fruit production of one season can be enjoyed and the number of flowers that will develop and flower the next spring will be reduced only slightly.

5. Evergreens are grown in large quantities in many landscapes, yet the pruning of them is often neglected. Annual pruning of them is important and may be done anytime the wood is not frozen. When frozen, the wood becomes brittle and will break; pruning then will result in poorly shaped plants and undesirable wounds. Pruning should be done on broadleaf evergreens as well as needle evergreens.

6. There are a few trees in particular that fall into the so-called bleeder class. If these are pruned during the period of sap flow, a great amount of sap is lost. This is not injurious to the plant, contrary to popular belief; however, it may be objectionable if the sap drips on sidewalks, cars, etc. Therefore, late fall pruning is best for these trees. Trees in this group are maple, birch, dogwood, elm, walnut, and yellowwood (*Cladrastis lutea*).

7. In the northern regions of the U.S., in hardiness zones 5 and north (where the average minimum temperature is –20°F or colder), late summer pruning and early fall pruning should be avoided since this might encourage the plant to develop new soft growth before the winter season. This new soft growth may not have time to harden and winter damage could result.

How To Prune

The key to proper pruning is to have the proper tools and know how to use them. Tools should be in good condition and of good quality, and they should be kept sharp. Moreover, tools that are left dirty after a pruning operation can transfer disease and may not make clean cuts. Of the many tools used in pruning operations, each has a specific function. The small hand shears usually range from six to nine inches long and should be used to cut branches that are not thicker than ½ inch in diameter. A larger kind of hand shears are loppers, which have handles usually 20 to 36 inches in length and can be used on limbs up to 1 inch in diameter and slightly larger. Loppers are sometimes useful for removing old mature branches in the centers of shrubs, which are hard to reach with

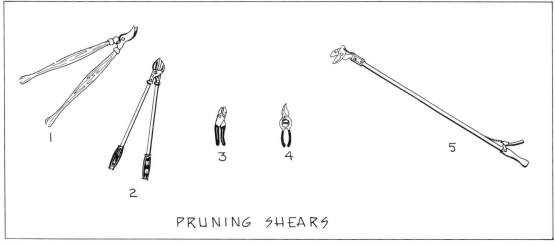

PRUNING SHEARS

17-8

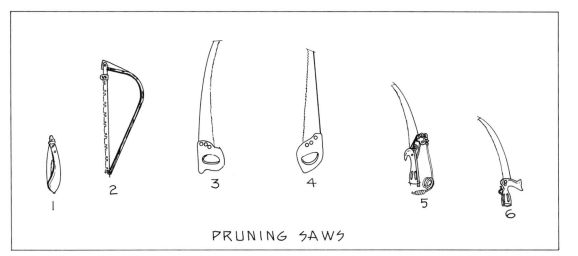

PRUNING SAWS

17-9

Figure 17-8. *A selection of pruning shears. One blade of the hook-and-blade lopper (1) holds a branch; the other slices through it. The blade of the blade-and-anvil lopper (2) slices through a branch against a flat plate. Next are small blade-and-anvil shears (3) and small hook-and-blade shears (4). At the right, an extension blade-and-anvil pruner for light pruning beyond arm's length (5).*

Figure 17-9. *A selection of pruning saws. Curved blades cut when pulled; straight blades cut when pushed. The folding light-weight curved saw (1) can be worn on a belt. The bow saw (2), useful on heavy limbs or logs, is held at the broad end; the narrow end will push branches out of the way while the saw cuts. The curved saw (3) and the straight saw (4) are for large limbs. Two attachments (5 and 6) can be used with extension poles: a combination shear and curved saw (5) has cord-operated shears; the crook of the curved saw attachment (6) will pull dead branches. Telescoping extension poles are made of wood or metal. Never use metal poles near electric wires.*

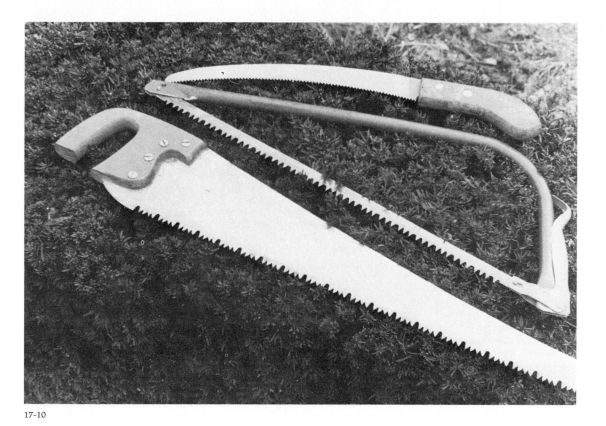

17-10

other tools. Also in the group of cutting tools are the hedge shears. These usually have blades 6 to 12 inches long and are designed to be used for trimming and clipping. These are the shears to use when one wants to give a shrub a sculptured formal appearance. They should never be used to remove branches or internal shrub growth. The blades are designed to come together tightly along the cutting edges with no looseness, and they are not made for cutting thick twigs or for pruning shrubs into natural forms. This tool should be used for hedges only.

All of the tools above are intended for work with small trees or with shrubs. Another group of tools is useful for larger woody plants.

Power loppers are available that can remove quite sizeable limbs. In some cases, logs of from six to eight inches have been cut with power loppers. The power equipment is of benefit to someone who is doing a great amount of pruning, but its cost cannot be justified for routine maintenance at most landscape sites.

Pruning saws come in various sizes and shapes, and each has a specific purpose. The small, curved saw can be used to remove small limbs and to reach into the internal parts of the plant. This saw can be mounted on a pole to remove limbs high up in a tree. Pole pruners are also available that work with the action of a lopper, with extensions that reach 10 to 15 feet in the air. Larger saws can, of course, be used to remove larger limbs, and for very large work chain saws are available. Pruning saws have very coarse teeth and don't become gummed up easily. The teeth remove a large bite, and this helps to reduce the binding effect of the green wood beneath its own weight as

Figure 17-10. *Use the proper tool, sharp and of high quality, for each pruning job. These pruning saws should be used only on limbs of more than* ³/₄ *inches in diameter. Pruning saws have coarse teeth which do not gum up, but they may be too coarse for smaller limbs, which will be torn instead of cut.*

it is being cut. Saws should always be kept sharp so that they can be used efficiently.

PRUNING DECIDUOUS TREES AND SHRUBS

The most important fact to remember about pruning trees and shrubs is to follow the shape that is suggested by their natural growth habits. Often deciduous shrubs are sheared into squares, globes, cones, etc., and the effect wanted by the landscape architect is lost. This "haircut" pruning also results in dense, thick growth on the external parts of the shrub, which causes the internal parts to become shaded out and weakened, and this in turn will result in poor growth. Correct pruning is a thinning technique by which the length of the various branches is reduced, not all branches to the same length, however. Remove some of the heavy old growth in the interior parts of the shrubs, too.

When making the individual cuts approximately ¼ inch above an active bud, choose a bud that is facing to the outward part of the plant to encourage development of the shoots in an outward direction. Cutting a branch ¼ inch beyond the bud will ensure that stubs are not left. Cuts should be made close to the trunk so that the wounds will heal properly. All wounds over one inch in diameter should be treated with a tree wound dressing. Do not use common tars or house paints for this. Some landscape maintenance personnel find it advantageous to apply tree-wound dressing from a spray can. The wound is simply sprayed immediately after cutting. Even though the materials cost more, the savings in labor more than make up the cost of this technique.

17-11

17-12

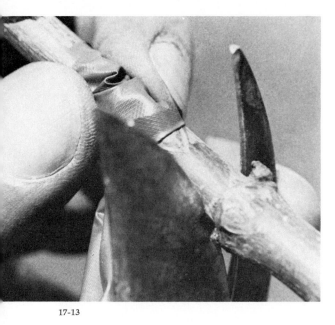

17-13

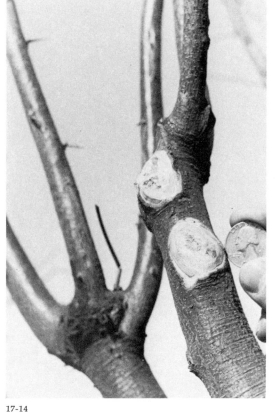

17-14

17-15

Figure 17-11. *Avoid "haircut" pruning. This leaves a thick tangle of branches which causes the interior of the plant to become shaded.*

Figure 17-12. *Always prune so that the natural shape of the plant is enhanced. Cut the branches to varying lengths.*

Figure 17-13. *Cut a branch ¼ inch above an active bud located where growth is wanted. This will promote new growth in that direction. The ribbon merely marked branches to be removed by pruning.*

Figures 17-14, 17-15. *Treat all wounds one inch or more in diameter (17-14) with tree wound dressing that contains an asphalt compound and fungicide (17-15).*

Generally, the evergreen has a very pleasing natural shape. Use the same pruning techniques described for deciduous shrubs. This should be done for both broadleaf and narrowleaf evergreens. Prune by thinning. It is important to remember to prune on an annual basis and keep the shrub within bounds. When evergreens become overgrown, heavy pruning is required. The nongreen portions of an evergreen will not produce new growth. The plants should not be cut back to this nongreen portion. Prune evergreens annually, and reduce the new growth by a half, or more. This will keep the plant in an active and vigorous growing condition, and it will not become overgrown.

Conifers require a little different pruning technique. If the job to be done by pruning is to give just a few trees at the site a very tight growth habit, it is advantageous to pinch the new candles when they are approximately two inches long. Half of the new candle should be removed. Shears should be avoided for this because they damage the needles, which will then have brown tips. If there are a large number of evergreens at the site, it is not practical to pinch the candles out. Shearing should then be done when the new candles have hardened, approximately six weeks after they have started to elongate in the spring. The central leader or the main leader candle of the tree should not be removed in its entirety. However, sometimes it is necessary to shorten this candle or the space between branches will be excessive. Cut the leader, when it has hardened, approximately midpoint in its length, and make the cut at an angle. A straight cut will cause the devel-

17-16

17-17

Figure 17-16. *Do not cut branches back to the old nongreen portions of a shrub or a large tree. The nongreen stubs will not send out new growth.*

Figure 17-17. *In the spring, prune evergreen foliage by removing half of a candle (the new growth) when it is approximately two inches long. Be sure to pinch candles out rather than use shears.*

Figure 17-18. *To make a tree more compact, cut the leader at an angle about half-way down. New buds will sprout at the cut.*

17-18

17-19

17-20

opment of a "bird nest" effect as several buds start to grow.

PRUNING LARGE TREES

Too often one sees large trees that have been deformed through pruning or topping. Topping is an undesirable practice, one that should never be done regardless of the situation. The topping of trees has been promoted by the ignorant as a rejuvenation technique; and this is just not true. Topping ruins the shape of the tree as numerous water sprouts develop from the soft growth, and the tree is weakened. In many trees that have been topped out, large wounds decay, and the tree may die.

To remove branches from large trees often requires work high in the tree. It is desirable to use specialized equipment, such as bucket lifts, for this. Precautions should be taken for the safety of men working in the trees.

On large branches an inch and more in diameter, the double-cut technique should be used. The first cut is made approximately six inches from the tree trunk on the underside of the limb, and the cut is made approximately half way up through the branch. Then move out about one or two inches farther and make the second cut on the top side; the branch will break away. This prevents splintering that might occur if the first cut is made flush with the trunk. Now the stub should be removed and the edges of the wound rounded off with a sharp knife so that the wound will heal rapidly. The wound should be covered with tree-wound dressing. On these large wounds, it is sometimes necessary to renew the dressing on an annual basis until they have healed.

Figure 17-19. *These trees are ruined and will never regain their natural growth habit.*

Figure 17-20. *Use proper equipment for high work. Buckets are the safest for this type of work.*

17-21

17-22

17-23

17-24

Figures 17-21 to 17-24. *Use the double cut method (17-21) for branches and limbs of more than one inch in diameter. The limb will fall without tearing the bark near the cut (17-22). A third cut should be made to remove the stub (17-23) as close as possible to the trunk (17-24). This limb may have been removed because its steep angle formed a weak crotch.*

17-25

Certain shrubs such as lilac, forsythia, spirea, and privet can be rejuvenated by pruning. The rejuvenation of privet hedges or plants may be accomplished in one year. The plants should be cut down to two or three inches of the ground. The new growth that comes back can then be shaped into the desired plant or hedge. For other plants, such as lilac or forsythia, the rejuvenation process should be done over a three-year period, with approximately a third of the old heavy growth being removed each year. The new growth that occurs as a result of the pruning should be cut back to varying lengths to force it to thicken each year. This process should bring new vigor to these overgrown plants. Not all plants can be rejuvenated, and a knowledge of which plants can be is required before the process can be carried out.

Peegee hydrangea (*Hydrangea paniculata* 'Grandiflora') can be cut back in the same manner as privet and this should be done on an annual basis. Such pruning is a basic requirement to force the plant to develop heavy, vigorous shoot growth.

Good screening plants should be full all the way to the ground so that the view of whatever is being screened will be totally obscured. However, such hedges are often improperly pruned; the hedge is pruned with a wide top and narrow base. This will cause upper branches to shade the lower portions of the hedge, and a leggy, thin screen planting will result. Proper techniques require that the hedge be pruned narrow at the top and wide at the base. This will permit the sun to reach the lower portions of the plant and the plants will be full to the ground, giving

17-26

Figure 17-25. *In a properly pruned hedge the top is sheared slightly more narrow than the base. This is a hedge of* Euonymus alatus *at the Morton Arboretum, Lisle, Illinois. The hedge has been sheared to a formal shape.*

Figure 17-26. *The top of an improperly pruned hedge is wider than the base. The wide top shades the lower portion of the hedge. The hedge then becomes leggy and thin at the bottom. This hedge was intended as a screen. Improper pruning defeated the purpose of the planting.*

the right effect. This simple technique will be more effective for screen plantings than will the technique by which the natural growth habit is followed.

SUMMARY

The correct use of water for growing plants at a landscape site is essential. The amount of water needed and the frequency with which it should be added will vary with the individual site. Careful observation of soil moisture conditions is required of the landscape contractor during the establishment phase and of the landscape maintenance supervisor during the subsequent development of the plant material.

Adjustments in soil pH are best made before installing the plant material at the landscape site, but if the soil pH is adjusted after planting, the rate of addition of lime or sulphur should be based on soil test results. Likewise, the addition of fertilizers should also be done after soil test results are obtained and evaluated. Fertilizing in the years following establishment of woody plants at the site should be done as required. Plant growth is a good indicator of fertilizer requirements. The plants will respond mostly to nitrogen fertilization.

A few simple points about pruning should be remembered. The most important thing, except with hedges that may form screen plantings, is to prune the plant in its natural shape. Allow a plant to develop as it would in nature. This effect is generally desired by the landscape architect. Pruning to an unnatural shape may be required for some plants; this should be noted in the original landscape design. Prune at the proper time so that the plant will provide the greatest effect in the landscape. Prune on an annual basis so the plant will not become overgrown. Use the correct techniques of pruning described in the previous paragraphs. Never top large shade trees as an attempt at rejuvenation of them.

FOR FURTHER READING

Frese, P. F. (editor), 1966. *Pruning Handbook.* Brooklyn: Brooklyn Botanic Garden. Special edition of *Plants and Gardens*, Vol. 14, No. 3. 81 pages.

Neely, D., and E. B. Himelick, 1966. *Fertilizing and Watering Trees.* Urbana, Illinois: Illinois Natural History Survey. 20 pages.

Pirone, P. P., 1972. *Tree Maintenance.* New York: The Oxford University Press. 574 pages.

Soil Improvement Committee of the California Fertilizer Association, 1975. *Western Fertilizer Handbook.* Danville, Illinois: Interstate Printers and Publishers. Fifth Edition. 200 pages.

18

The Control of Insects, Diseases, and Weeds

Controlling insects and diseases that attack the plant material in the landscape is of the utmost importance. Since insects and diseases can pose a threat to survival of the woody plants, it is one of the functions of the landscape maintenance supervisor to make sure they are controlled. This requires a knowledge of the current pesticide recommendations and the correct application techniques. Care in the use of pesticides is also absolutely essential so that they will not cause ecological damage.

Weed control is a different matter. Weeds generally pose no immediate threat to the survival of the plant material. However, manual control of weeds is probably the greatest labor expense in maintaining the landscape so that it has a satisfactory appearance. Therefore, the use of herbicides (chemical weed killers)

becomes essential in order to reduce labor costs without sacrificing the appearance of the site. Thus a knowledge of herbicide use is essential for the landscape maintenance supervisor.

It should be noted here that describing specific insect and disease problems of ornamental plants is beyond the scope of this book. There are many good references that do this in detail, and some are listed at the end of the chapter. What we will try to do, in the following section, is to discuss the importance of using the proper pesticide (whatever it might be) in whatever is the correct dosage, when the time is right. As we will mention later, recommendations about controlling insects and disease may vary depending upon climatic differences. The availability of pesticides will be dependent on federal and state regulations governing their use. Although we may have occasion to use a brand name or a common pesticide type for purposes of illustration, we do so to explain some detail that is true of all brands and not because one brand can be given a standard recommendation. Pesticides are periodically issued and withdrawn from use. We feel we cannot emphasize enough the importance of consulting with knowledgeable *local* specialists before specifying for use, or using, any pesticide.

INSECT AND DISEASE CONTROL

Correct diagnosis of the problem is the first and most important factor in disease and insect control. Symptoms of insect damage or disease injury may often appear to be very similar. To further complicate matters, some herbicide injury may resemble disease or insect damage. Frequently a plant is weakened from a physiological disorder and the disease or insect that attacks is of a secondary nature. To correct the problem, the landscape maintenance supervisor must correct some maladjustment in the plant's environment so that the plant is growing vigorously. But on the other hand, simply applying a fungicide to a plant that is infested with insects is also a waste of time and money.

Since correct diagnosis of the problem may be difficult, it is wise to consult experts in insect and disease control. Horticulturists should be consulted if physiological disorders or herbicide injuries are suspected. Most states will have specialists in these areas of expertise on the staff at the State agricultural college or at the State Agricultural Experiment Station. One method of contacting specialists is through the local agricultural agent in the Cooperative Extension Service office.

Once the problem is identified, the next phase of insect and disease control is to select the correct pesticide and to apply it at the proper time. It is important that the most up-to-date pest control recommendations be consulted. With the increased interest in environmental quality has come tighter controls on pesticide usage. Certain pesticides have been banned because it has been discovered they are ecologically harmful. The landscape maintenance supervisor has a responsibility to his clients and the public in general to apply only approved pesticides.

Once the proper pesticide has been selected, it must be applied properly and at the correct time. Proper application is not difficult if the user will adhere to some basic principles of usage. First the equipment should be of a size adequate to do the job. It is recommended that a power sprayer have a minimum delivery capacity of from 10 to 25 gallons per minute and develop pressure of not less than 125 pounds per square inch. The sprayer should have an air delivery rate of not less than 10,000 cubic feet per minute. The sprayer must meet these minimum requirements if complete coverage of foliage in dense, tall trees is to be achieved. It is apparent that specialized equipment, in good working order, is needed for insect and disease control. Often the landscape maintenance supervisor needs such equipment for only a few hours each year and it will be more economical for him to contract the spraying with a custom pesticide applicator. The custom applicator will have the equipment and

Figure 18-1. *High-pressure sprayers of this type will reach the tops of large shade trees. Good coverage is essential for good control. Note the protective clothing worn by the applicator.*

18-1

trained operators necessary to do the job properly. Also, he will have the licenses that are required before one applies pesticides.

Some safety precautions should be taken when applying any pesticide. The first is to read the label thoroughly and follow all precautions given on the label faithfully. If protective clothing is required, make sure that all operators—including the person mixing the pesticide—wears what is required. The following are safety rules for pesticide users:

1. *Always read* the label before using sprays or dusts. Read all warnings and cautions each time you open the container.

2. *Never smoke* while spraying or dusting.

3. Avoid inhaling sprays or dusts. When directed to, by the label, wear protective clothing and masks.

4. Avoid spilling sprays or dusts on skin or clothing. If they are spilled, remove clothing and wash the skin *immediately*. Also wash the clothing thoroughly.

5. Wash hands and face and change to clean clothes after spraying or dusting. Also wash clothing each day before wearing them again.

6. To prevent possible plant injury, use separate equipment for applying herbicides.

7. *Always dispose* of empty insecticide containers in such a way that there is no possible hazard to humans, animals, or valuable plants.

8. Cover food and water containers before treating areas around livestock or pets. Don't overlook fishponds; they should not be contaminated.

9. When spraying, never stand downwind so that you are in the drift patterns of the spray.

10. Never spray in high wind; make sure that the spray does not drift onto other properties.

11. Do not spray when children or pets or unsuspecting adults are likely to be hit by the spray or its drift.

12. Know where the local poison control center is and how to contact it.

13. If symptoms of illness occur during or shortly after spraying or dusting, call a physician or take the person who is ill to a hospital immediately.

Protective masks are required when using many pesticides. The cartridges through which the air is filtered contain different ingredients for different pesticides. Make absolutely certain that the mask contains the correct cartridge for the pesticide being used.

Safe Storage of Pesticides

One phase in the use of pesticides that often receives little attention by the user is that of storage. In all but the remotest areas of the country it is easy to lose track of the comings and goings of people where pesticides are kept, and this necessitates that the pest control operator take special precautions to ensure that pesticides are stored securely. Because of the close proximity of many landscape sites to housing developments, many unauthorized persons, mainly children, have access to sheds or cabinets where pesticides are stored. Always assume that the liability of protecting children from accidental poisoning lies with the person who has stored the pesticide for eventual use on plants. To protect all parties concerned, the following storage procedures should be followed.

1. Store all pesticides (insecticides, fungicides, and herbicides), in their original containers. Labels should never be removed.

2. Read the label concerning proper storage conditions, shelf life, etc. Destory old chemicals in the way recommended for them. Don't keep them in storage.

3. Pesticides should be stored in some building other than the main building at a site.

4. Use a locked, secure building, and/or storage cabinets.

5. Post adequate warning signs on the storage building.

6. Do not store feed, seed, and other farm supplies in the same shed with pesticides.

7. Do not store 2,4-D type weed killers in the same building other pesticides are stored in.

Check the way pesticides are stored. Proper storage procedures can prevent an accident that might cost a life.

Phytotoxicity

Some pesticides are phytotoxic; that is, they will injure certain ornamental plant species. To determine if a certain pesticide will injure a plant it is wise to check two sources of information. First, read the label carefully. Often plants that are susceptible to injury by the particular pesticide will be listed on the label. Second, check the current pest control recommendations prepared by the State Cooperative Extension Service specialists. Their recommendations will often list not only the plants that specific pesticides will injure but, also, the conditions under which such injury will occur. Be absolutely sure to check the phytotoxicity lists before using a pesticide. It does not do much good to kill the pests on a tree or shrub if the pesticide used causes severe injury to the plant.

Application Timing

It is very important that the pesticide be applied when the pests are susceptible to the pesticide. Many insects and diseases can be controlled by pesticides only at critical times in their life cycles. Scale insects are a prime example of an insect that is most susceptible to control with insecticides during a particular phase of its life cycle. During the susceptible stage the scale insects have not covered themselves with the hard, waxy coat that will resist insecticide penetration at a later time. To be most effective, the insecticide must be applied during the few days when the scale insects are in the crawler stage of growth. Likewise, most diseases are more effectively controlled with a fungicide if it is applied during a period in their cycle when they are susceptible to control. Thus, timing is very important.

Check local recommendations about the best time for application, since life cycles of insects and diseases vary with the climate just as flowering times of some plant species vary with climatic conditions. Time of application may vary between a few days and several weeks depending on the section of the country in which the landscape site is located.

WEED CONTROL

Weed control with herbicides is a relatively new science, and there are few references that pertain specifically to weed control at developed landscape sites. Therefore, we feel we should devote special attention to this topic.

Weed control is a major budgetary item in the landscape maintenance program. While the use of herbicides has simplified weed control in other kinds of agriculture, their use in landscape plantings has not been fully developed because of the specific problems unique to the landscape site. It is necessary to understand what these problems are and how they may be solved before using herbicides in landscape plantings.

Each spring the farmer plows under any new and old weed growth left over from the previous season's crop and hence starts the season with a seedbed relatively free of weeds. The spring flush of weed growth can thus be partially or completely eliminated. He then can use preemergence herbicides to control weeds for several additional weeks. By this time his crop has reached sufficient size to compete favorably with the weeds. The farmer has another advantage in that he plants only one crop in a very large area; application of one herbicide or a combination of herbicides is easily done. With only one crop being grown, it is also easily possible to select an herbicide that will not injure the crop but will control the weeds. Finally, a great number of herbicides are available to farmers because the large acreages of agronomic crops being planted offer an attractive market for the development of new herbicides by chemical companies.

In comparison, the landscape maintenance supervisor cannot avail himself of any of these advantages when considering the use of herbicides. It is obvious that the landscape bed cannot be plowed each spring to provide a clean seedbed. The herbicides must be applied to the landscape early in the spring before the weed growth starts or after all weed growth has been removed by hand cultivation, and this is expensive because of the labor required. Herbicides applied to landscape beds must be persistent for the entire growing season, from early spring to early fall, a period of from six to eight months. The landscape plants generally are not competitive enough to crowd out weed growth the way an agronomic crop does. Furthermore, in many landscape designs many different plant species grow together in one bed. This makes it difficult to find an herbicide that will control a wide range of weeds without at the same time injuring some individuals of the wide variety of ornamental plants being grown in the bed. The advantage is lost that the farmer gains by planting only one crop such as corn or cotton in a large area.

It is difficult to apply herbicides to small, irregularly shaped areas such as some landscape beds since no equipment has been developed to do the job. Worse, it is nearly impossible even to estimate what will be an accurate application of the herbicide in small, irregular areas, and accurate applications are absolutely essential if satisfactory weed control is to be successful. It is also necessary, when applying the herbicide, to keep a sharp line of demarcation between the landscape bed and the surrounding turf area. Movement or drift of the herbicide from the landscape bed into the surrounding turf may result in serious injury to the turf.

Finally, since total acreages are low, the chemical companies are not likely to develop

18-2

Figure 18-2. *When using herbicides it is necessary to have a sharp line of demarcation between a landscape bed and surrounding turf area.*

new herbicides specifically for use in the landscape situation. So far there has not been, nor is it likely there will be extensive work done to increase the number of ornamental species listed on any one herbicide label.

Herbicide Characteristics

It is necessary to understand some of the characteristics of herbicides before putting them to use in landscape beds. Herbicides are classified as either preemergence and postemergence materials. Preemergence herbicides must be applied before the weed seedlings emerge. If weed growth has started, the effectiveness of herbicides is generally very limited. Postemergence herbicides are applied to weeds that are already growing. Most postemergence materials will not work when used as if they were preemergence herbicides.

The terms preplant and postplant are also commonly used when discussing herbicides, but these words refer to the crop that is to be protected, not the weeds. Preplant means the herbicide should be applied before the crop is planted, and though this term does not mean much when considering possible use of herbicides around established woody ornamentals, it is important if herbicides will be used in beds of annual flowers that are planted every year. Likewise, postplant means the herbicide should be applied after the crop is planted. The delay period between planting and herbicide application is of particular importance, for reasons that will be discussed in more detail later in this chapter.

Herbicides are commonly sold in one of three formulations, i.e., as granules, as wettable powder, or as a liquid. If the desired herbicide is available in two or more of the formulations, the one to choose will depend mostly on what method of application the landscape maintenance supervisor has chosen. Granular materials are usually designated with a number and the letter G. The number stands for the percentage of active ingredient and the letter G refers to the granular formulation. A material designated as 4G contains 4 percent of the active herbicide and 96 percent of a carrier, by weight. The granular formulation should be applied in the dry form with a gravity feed spreader or an impeller spreader. If pesticide laws permit, it may be possible to mix granular herbicides with a mulch material.

The wettable powders are usually labelled with a number and the letters W or WP. An herbicide with the designation 50W contains 50 percent of the active ingredient and 50 percent inert materials. A wettable powder must be mixed with water and applied as a spray. Liquids have several different designations because of differences in the specific formulations. Some are true liquids, which means that the active ingredient is dissolved in a liquid carrier that can in turn be diluted with water. Some materials must first be dissolved in carriers, which can then be diluted with water; however, they are emulsions that stay in suspension once they have become mixed with water. These materials are called emulsifiable concentrates. The liquids are usually designated in terms of active ingredient per volume. An example is an herbicide designated with the term "two pounds per gallon," which means that each gallon contains two pounds of the active herbicide. All liquids must be applied as a spray.

How Do Herbicides Kill Plants?

Although the specific ways in which some herbicides kill weeds are not known, the general effect of the more common materials is known. Some herbicides inhibit or stop the process of photosynthesis; a new seedling is then unable to produce the carbohydrates that it needs to supply the energy for its future growth. The weed seeds germinate and emerge, but they die as soon as they have used the food reservoir in the cotyledons (seed leaves). This is important to know because, if weed seedlings are observed, it does not mean that the weed control has been unsatisfactory inasmuch as the seedlings may die before true leaves develop.

Other herbicides are root and/or bud inhibitors, which means simply that they prevent root and shoot development. Plants sensitive to the herbicide will be unable to develop root systems, or their buds will fail to grow into shoots. This is also very important to know because, if a landscape plant has been injured inadvertently, the injury may not be readily apparent inasmuch as the inhibition of root development may result only in an overall stunting of the plant growth. If there are no untreated plants for comparison, the user may not even be aware of the damage.

Some materials are growth regulators, and in many of these the actual method by which they kill weeds is unknown, except that the regulators disturb processes vital to the development of the plant and the abnormal growth processes eventually cause the death of the plant. Finally, a contact herbicide such as paraquat acts as a plant desiccant; that is, it causes a tissue sprayed with the herbicide to lose water. The plant dies of dehydration.

The user of herbicides should also know what weeds will be controlled by his herbicide program. It is nearly useless to treat a problem caused by a profusion of weeds of a certain kind by applying an herbicide that will not control the specific weed species involved. Most herbicide manufacturers list the weeds that are controlled on the herbicide label. Other sources of information are the current recommendations published by the State Cooperative Extension Service. If the weed species present are not known, the user should send a specimen to a specialist for identification. The Cooperative Extension Service should be of help in identifying unknown weeds.

Read the Label

The label placed on the herbicide container provides a wealth of information for the user. It is extremely important that the user read this label before purchasing or using the herbicide. The label gives some of the information we have discussed in the preceding paragraphs, such as the herbicide concentration, its formulation, and some of the weeds it will control. One of the most important sections of the label is that portion that lists the ornamental plants that are tolerant of the herbicide. In some rare instances ornamental plants *injured* by the material will be listed as being *tolerant* of the herbicide. It is always good to corroborate a manufacturer's claims about the tolerance of ornamentals by determining what the experience of other authorities on herbicide usage has been; Cooperative Extension Service specialists

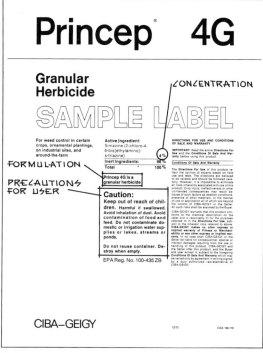

Princep® 4G

Granular Herbicide

SAMPLE LABEL

(handwritten annotations) CONCENTRATION · FORMULATION · PRECAUTIONS FOR USER

For weed control in certain crops, ornamental plantings, on industrial sites, and around-the-farm

Active Ingredient:
Simazine (2-chloro-4,6-bis[ethylamino]-s-triazine) ... 4%
Inert Ingredients ... 96%
Total ... 100%

Princep 4G is a granular herbicide

Caution:
Keep out of reach of children. Harmful if swallowed. Avoid inhalation of dust. Avoid contamination of food and feed. Do not contaminate domestic or irrigation water supplies or lakes, streams or ponds.

Do not reuse container. Destroy when empty.

EPA Reg. No. 100-435 ZB

CIBA–GEIGY

18-3

Princep® 4G — *(handwritten)* HOW TO USE

General Information

Princep 4G is a herbicide that should be applied before weeds emerge or following removal of weed growth. It controls a wide variety of annual broadleaf and grass weeds when used at selective rates in agricultural crops and ornamental plantings. When used at higher, nonselective rates in noncrop areas, it also controls many perennial broadleaf and grass weeds.

Since Princep enters weeds mainly through their roots, rainfall or irrigation is needed to move it into the root zone.

Princep 4G is noncorrosive to equipment, nonflammable, and has low electrical conductivity.

Directions for Use

Selective Weed Control

Fruit Crops

Blueberries

Cranberries

Grapefruit and Oranges

Nonselective Weed Control on Noncrop Land

Princep® 4G — *(handwritten)* PRECAUTIONS FOR CROP USE · RATES · CROP CLEARANCE

Nurseries, Christmas Tree Plantings, and Shelter Belts

Established Nursery Stock

Shelter Belts and Christmas Tree Plantings

Apply Princep 4G to these species of trees and shrubs, as recommended above:

American Elm, Arborvitae, Austrian Pine, Balsam Fir, Barberry, Blue Spruce, Boxelder, Bush Honeysuckle, Caragana, Cotoneaster, Dogwood, Douglas Fir, Fraser Fir, Hemlock, Honey Locust, Juniper, Mugho Pine, Norway Spruce, Oregon Grape (Mahonia spp.), Red Cedar, Red Oak, Red Pine (Norway Pine), Red Spruce, Russian Olive, Scotch Pine, Siberian Elm, White Cedar, White Pine, White Spruce, Yew (Taxus spp.)

Agricultural Division
CIBA-GEIGY Corporation
Greensboro, NC 27409

Figure 18-3. *A sample pesticide label that shows what information is given on the label.*

at the State agricultural college can be helpful. Information supplied by this source generally is unbiased and much more reliable than information obtained from other users or suppliers.

Besides crop lists, the label provides information on any application methods that must be used before the herbicide will provide the maximum weed control. Such factors as the volatility of the herbicide are of prime concern to the user. Herbicides that are volatile must be incorporated in the soil by mechanical means or with irrigation. If this is not done, the herbicide vaporizes into the air and its weed-control capabilities are lessened or are entirely lost. The directions of how and when the incorporation must be carried out are given on the label. However, if the herbicide is non-volatile, incorporation may be detrimental to its effectiveness. The label will note this.

Spraying techniques are also given on the label, such as the minimum and maximum amounts of water to mix with the herbicide in order to spray an area of a given size. For some materials, labels indicate the amount of granular material to use for small areas. This information can be readily adapted for use when applying the herbicide to small landscape beds.

Finally, the label gives any precautions that should be taken when using the chemical. These precautions pertain not only to the plants but to the user, also. Follow those safety precautions; they are there for your protection. Furthermore, heed the storage procedures listed for insecticides and fungicides in the previous section. Never store herbicides in the same cabinets or storage areas with insecticides, fungicides, or seed.

Note: Always read the label on any herbicide carefully and follow the directions when applying the herbicide.

Using Herbicides among Landscape Plants

Some of the problems of using herbicides among landscape plantings, which we alluded to at the beginning of this section, can be solved so that the herbicides presently available can be used. Some broad-spectrum (controlling of many different weed species) long-lasting herbicides are available, as we said, that will control most weeds for the entire growing season, for six to eight months. They can be applied in the very early spring or late fall and eliminate the spring flush of weed growth. Materials that are not as broad in their weed control nor as long lived will not provide control into the summer months if applied before weed growth starts in the spring. In extreme southern and southwestern areas of the country more than one application of an herbicide may be necessary because of the extended growing season of the weeds.

Perennial weeds are a problem in many landscape plantings, and unfortunately they are often introduced with the ornamental plants because of infestations at the nursery. Very few preemergence herbicides are capable of controlling perennial weeds simply because the perennial weeds are already established and growing actively. Most perennial weeds have underground plant parts that provide food reserves for future growth. If an herbicide will control perennial weeds, it may be necessary to apply the herbicide for two or more seasons to obtain semipermanent control.

How to use an herbicide when several different ornamental species are being grown

Table 18-1 Amount of 4G herbicide to add to one cubic yard of mulch, and the area it will cover.

Depth of mulch (inches)	Area covered by 1 cubic yard (square feet)	Amount of 4 percent granular herbicide (ounces per cubic yard)
1	334	12
2	162	6
3	108	4.5
4	81	3

in the same landscape bed has not been determined completely. Some herbicide labels contain a very complete list of ornamental plants that are tolerant to the herbicide, but the tolerance extends to a great number of weed species too, and the number of weed species controlled is therefore limited. As previously stated, the market for plant-specific herbicides is small, and herbicide companies are not likely to undertake the research necessary to increase the number of ornamental species included on labels of the long-lasting, broad-spectrum herbicides already developed for essentially agricultural use. The safety of using the herbicide on a particular species is of prime importance; therefore, make a test application for one or more seasons before using on a large scale.

Herbicide-Mulch Combination

[*There is little difference between incorporating an herbicide with the soil in the way described on an herbicide label and incorporating the same herbicide with a mulch in the way described in the following paragraphs. However, at present the Environmental Protection Agency does not permit the use of any pesticide in ways other than are described on the labels of pesticide containers. The lack of instructions on the label may make it illegal to apply the following technique. Therefore, before the reader uses the technique he should check current EPA regulations to determine if any herbicides may be used in this way.*]

One procedure has been developed to make application easier and more accurate when using herbicides in irregularly shaped small areas surrounded by turf. A broad-spectrum herbicide that is highly volatile can be mixed with a mulch material for application to

these landscape beds. The mulch material dilutes further the granular herbicide, and with this very diluted mixture of herbicide and mulch it is possible to apply the herbicide uniformly over the landscape bed. A sharp delineation or line can be kept between the turf bed and the landscape bed treated with herbicide-mulch. This combination minimizes the danger that the herbicide will erode from relatively steep slopes onto lower areas where the herbicide might injure plants and turf. The rate at which the herbicide is applied is controlled by the depth of the herbicide-mulch combination. If the depth is doubled, the rate at which the herbicide is applied to the landscape will also be doubled unless, of course, the amount of herbicide mixed into the mulch is reduced by half. Table 18-1 gives the amounts of a 4 percent granular herbicide to be mixed with one cubic yard of mulch material, and the area covered by one cubic yard of mulch, when it is applied in layers of various depths.

Mixing the herbicide with the mulch may be done very easily. Small quantities of mulch, such as a few cubic yards, can be mixed by hand. The mulch should be spread in a pile 12 to 18 inches high and the herbicide should be spread evenly over the top of the mulch. The pile should then be turned immediately several times; remember that the herbicide is volatile. Large quantities of mulch can be mixed in a cement mixer or in some other mechanical mixer. Once the herbicide has been mixed in the mulch, the danger of vaporization of the herbicide is basically eliminated. It is possible to store the herbicide-mulch combination for a period of several months, if it is stored in a large, deep pile, covered with polyethylene film.

When applying the herbicide-mulch combination, estimate the size of the area to be covered and apply the correct quantity of the combination to give the wanted depth over the entire area. Be especially careful in this. It is difficult to judge the difference between one-inch and two-inch depths of mulch. Usually more mulch is applied than is needed, and this means too much herbicide has been applied to the landscape bed. However, research results have shown that the two-inch depth (with the correct herbicide concentration for that depth) is the most efficient means of achieving nearly complete weed control. In the second season, control of from 85 to 95 percent of the weeds can be expected. As mentioned previously, perennial weeds require several applications of herbicides to effect complete control. A second and even a third application of the combination will be required in successive years before control of the perennial weeds can be achieved.

The best mulches to use in combination with herbicides are those of a coarse material, for which shredded bark, ground corncobs, wood chips, pea gravel, etc., will all serve well. The surface of a fine material such as peat moss stays moist longer, and blown-in weed seeds then have a good medium for germination during the season. The surface of a coarser material dries out more readily and provides less-favorable conditions for germination. The herbicide will not provide satisfactory weed control if used with stones larger than pea gravel because of the volatility of the herbicide. The large stones do not provide a vapor barrier and the herbicide vaporizes.

Most preemergence herbicides of low volatility do not work well when mixed with a mulch material, since the mulch dilutes the herbicide and the overall effect is a marked reduction in the herbicidal properties of the material. However, use of the low-volatility materials on the surface of the landscape beds before a mulch is applied will provide satisfactory weed control. But the problem of making a uniform application at the right rate is not solved.

A few words of warning are in order about herbicide mulches. The use of the mulch enhances the herbicidal properties of most materials and it is easy for plants sensitive to an herbicide to be injured. If the herbicide-mulch combination is used, annuals and perennial flowers cannot be planted together. Nor can bulbs be planted.

Application of Herbicides to Small Landscape Beds

The use of herbicides without mulches can be accomplished if the shape and size of the landscape bed will permit the use of small hand sprayers or, for application of granular materials, small impeller spreaders. It is very important that the right application techniques be used. Applying herbicides is different than the spraying done for insects and diseases. With insecticides and fungicides, their concentration in the spray water controls the rate of application and the materials are generally applied until they run off the foliage. Generally covering an area more than once with insecticide or fungicide sprays does not cause a problem. When applying herbicides, it is necessary that over-

18-4

Figure 18-4. *Calibration of the hand sprayer is essential before applying herbicides.*

18-5

lapping be avoided, and it is generally not necessary to apply a saturation spray to assure complete saturation of the soil surface.

Calibration of the application equipment is absolutely necessary in order to know that exactly the prescribed amounts of herbicides are being applied to the landscape bed. Not only should the equipment be calibrated, but the user carrying the equipment should also pace the movements he will be making while using the equipment. Since the speed that the equipment moves is of prime importance to the calibration process, it is essential that each man who will be using the equipment run his own calibration procedures and record the settings and other information he obtains. Then the proper settings can be made for the application of granular herbicide or for the right quantities of wettable powder or liquid herbicide to be added to the spray water. Following is a step-by-step procedure for calibrating a hand carried or back pack sprayer, one designed for continuous pumping.

CALIBRATING THE HAND SPRAYER

1. Add a measured quantity (for example, one gallon) of water to sprayer.

2. Spray an area with the measured quantity of water until the sprayer is empty.

   a. Walk at the rate to be walked when actually applying herbicide.

   b. Hold the nozzle at the level it will be held when applying herbicide.

3. Determine the area covered (width of spray band times the length of the sprayed area).

4. Determine how much water the sprayer

Figure 18-5. *Spraying a large turf area for weeds. Note the complete coverage at the ground level, with little or no drift. Large weed sprayers such as this also need calibration, with each nozzle being checked for flow and distribution.*

would deliver to an acre on the basis of the data from 2 and 3.

a. *Example:* Spray width (1.5 feet) times the length sprayed (400 feet) = 600 square feet covered with one gallon of water. Divide the area of one acre by the square feet covered to obtain the total number of gallons that would be delivered to one acre:

$$\frac{43{,}560 \text{ (square feet/acre)}}{600 \text{ (square feet covered by 1 gallon)}}$$

$$= 72.5 \text{ gallons/acre}$$

5. Determine the amount of herbicide needed per acre.

a. *Example:* Recommended rate for diphenamid is 4 pounds per acre. Recommended rate for Enide 50W is 8 pounds of material per acre.

6. Determine the amount of herbicide needed in each gallon of water to be used in the sprayer that has just been calibrated.

a. *Example:* Sprayer delivers 72.5 gallons per acre. Eight pounds of Enide 50W are needed per acre. Divide the amount of water into the pounds of herbicide needed.

$$\frac{8 \text{ pounds}}{72.5 \text{ gallons}} = 0.11 \text{ pounds/gallon}$$

To convert to ounces per gallon, multiply by 16: 16 × 0.11 = 1.76, or 1¾ ounces per gallon.

It is absolutely essential that the sprayer be calibrated accurately so that the rate of delivery of the water can be determined. The amount of water used is the only variable in the calculations, and it is important that this variable be determined accurately.

The impeller granular spreader is cali-brated by using a plastic bag to catch the granular herbicide. It is then weighed and the rate is computed. It should be remembered that it is very difficult to use equipment for granular application in beds that have turf borders.

CALIBRATING THE
GRANULAR APPLICATOR

1. Set applicator dial (or dials) to give the rate of delivery of granules that is suggested in the spreader manufacturer's instructions. In a small test area spread granules with the spreader to determine the width of the area over which they will be impelled.

2. Fill the hopper with the granules that will be used. Fit the hopper with a bag, bucket, or other container so that the granules expelled during the calibration procedure will be retained.

3. Travel across an area for the distance required to cover 1/40 acre (1,000 square feet). To determine how far this should be, divide the width covered during the test application into 1,000.

4. Weigh the granules collected in the bag and multiply by 40 to find the amount of granular herbicide that would be needed for an acre. It may be more, or less, than the rate the spreader manufacturer recommends.

5. Adjust the settings and recalibrate until the right delivery rate is obtained.

Weed Control around Specimen Trees and Landscape Features

The herbicide-mulch combination can be used without difficulty around individual trees and shrubs, so long as the applications are not in violation of pesticide regulations. The procedures described in the preceding discussion of herbicide mulches should be followed.

Another technique that can be used is to spray around the base of the tree with a contact herbicide that will kill the existing green vegetation around the tree trunk. The contact herbicide is generally nonselective and will kill all the green plants it comes into contact with. The calibration techniques described previously for small sprayers must be followed. Sometimes it is possible to mix a preemergence herbicide with the contact killer to provide longer-lasting control after the effects of the contact herbicides have diminished. Be sure to check current recommendations about herbicide combinations before mixing any herbicide. Most contact herbicides used on landscape plantings do not have soil-residual properties and regrowth of weeds will start to occur within a few days after their application. Thus the preemergence herbicide will prove helpful.

SUMMARY

Use of insecticides and fungicides must be made according to label recommendations. Follow them closely to protect the user, the public, and plant, and animal life. It is your obligation to use pesticides responsibly.

Read the herbicide label and follow its directions about the timing, incorporation, and other details of application precisely. Furthermore, check the label to make sure that landscape plants you want to protect will tolerate the herbicide once it is applied. Current recommendations of the weed control specialists in the Cooperative Extension Service should be followed and questions concerning specific problems of weed control should be directed to them. However, we recommend that anyone working in landscape maintenance learn to use herbicides in the landscape with confidence. The savings in the cost of maintaining the landscape site will be great and the overall appearance of the site can be improved.

FOR FURTHER READING

Pirone, P. P., 1972. *Tree Maintenance.* New York: The Oxford University Press. 574 pages.

Pirone, P. P., and B. O. Dodge, 1970. *Diseases and Pests of Ornamental Plants.* New York: The Ronald Press. 546 pages.

Roberts, D. A., and C. W. Boothroyd, 1972. *Fundamentals of Plant Pathology.* San Francisco: W. H. Freeman and Co. 402 pages.

Shurtleff, M. C., 1966. *How to Control Plant Diseases in Home and Garden.* Ames, Iowa: Iowa State University Press. 649 pages.

Weaver, R. J., 1972. *Plant Growth Substances in Agriculture.* San Francisco: W. H. Freeman and Co. 594 pages.

VII

Integrative Landscaping

19

Planning, Establishing, and Maintaining the Urban Landscape

In the next three chapters we will be considering the interrelationships of design, establishment, and maintenance practices as they apply to specific types of landscapes. These we have arbitrarily classified as urban, suburban, and rural. Within each of these classifications there are specific landscape settings that will need to be analyzed and discussed. However, we intend to do this briefly, and inasmuch as these chapters will integrate material already covered, we will use detail only if a topic was not mentioned in an earlier chapter.

DESCRIPTION OF THE CHARACTERISTICS OF URBAN SITES

A common characteristic of the urban landscape is the intense use of the land, since land is expensive and space is limited. This in turn creates a compactness and sense of confinement in cities that can be oppressive. The scale of urban buildings and urban spaces frequently fails to relate to human scale. This was not always so, and in parts of some older cities it is still possible to find buildings and spaces left over from a time when "scale" was measured in terms of the pedestrian, not the automobile. Frequently, in urban redevelopment projects, creating or preserving space for the use of pedestrians is an important goal. It is in the midst of special limits to space and scale that properly selected plants can play a significant role in creating a more pleasant urban environment.

The lack of space is a factor that must be considered when placing and establishing plants in the urban environment. One of the typical problems is that space is restricted for plant growth, primarily root environments, but

19-1

Figure 19-1. *The civic center in Bethlehem, Pennsylvania. The plaza shown here, landscaped for the use of pedestrians, is located above an underground parking garage. The center is a redeveloped site along the Lehigh River, in the oldest part of the city.*

frequently there is not adequate space for branch development either. Raised planters or tree wells are common ways of installing plants in the city. The problems associated with these are many and require special attention.

The climate of cities is another factor to be considered. The high density of residential, commercial, and industrial buildings in cities greatly affects the climate of the city, and it also affects the immediately adjacent countryside, though to a lesser extent. Although some climatic differences are favorable for plants in the city (for example, during winter, nighttime minimum temperatures are higher in the city than in the country), the overall effect of climatic differences is to make urban conditions injurious to plants. The most serious climatic problem is air pollution; but it would be less of a problem in cities if cities did not function as "heat islands," producing and absorbing greater quantities of heat than does the countryside. Urban heat tends to trap dust particles above a city; the pollution reduces sunlight by as much as 15 to 20 percent in addition to being harmful to people and plants. Sunlight is also reduced because of an increase in fog, which condenses on dust particles in the air. Likewise, cloudiness is greater over metropolitan areas on days when fewer or no clouds form over rural areas. Although the relative humidity is less in urban than in rural areas, when rain falls, cities receive more rain than the surrounding countryside does. The "heat island" quality of urban areas explains why temperatures are much higher in cities than in the surrounding countryside, particularly at night. As we indicated, higher minimum temperatures may be desirable in winter, but high temperatures in

the summer usually cause increased stress on people and plants. Because the climate of cities can create human discomfort, it is an attractive challenge to try to alleviate the problem with plantings; unfortunately, the same conditions create stress for plants.

Another problem that is more prevalent in the city than elsewhere is vandalism. In densely populated areas it is difficult to anticipate how people will use or abuse plants, and there are bound to be some people intent on damage. This is particularly true in city parks, some of which are designed, ironically, to give city dwellers the access to foliage that is in such short supply in cities. Often this discourages some communities from attempting even to grow trees. However, vandalism is not insurmountable. Making proper selection, using larger-sized plants, and protecting them with barriers can alleviate this problem.

THE FUNCTION OF PLANTS IN THE URBAN LANDSCAPE

Trees provide a primary contact with the natural world in urban areas that are dominated by man. Where so much of the land surface is paved with concrete and asphalt, it is refreshing to experience the various textures and softening effect of green leaves, as well as the cooling shade of trees. The patterns of texture and shadow created by tree forms are visually effective in helping to alleviate the sterile, harsh quality of many urban structures. At the same time, plantings help counteract many of the stresses to which humans are subjected in cities, such as noise, high temperature, and air pollution.

Plants do not by themselves make the urban landscape. They are just one of the many elements that must all be related to each other in the organization of outdoor space. Unfortunately, when landscape plans are developed, plants are frequently the last feature included in the plan and the first item removed if money is lacking. Yet, to make a proper use of plants in a design it is necessary to think of them as no more or less important than other elements. Plants provide the means of integrating all the man-made features of an area with the area surrounding it.

In fact, as important as plants are, there are some urban sites where plants are not suitable, and others at which the architect chooses, with great success, to make a handsome design without plants. Frequently climatic extremes or pollutants, such as the salt used on roadways in the winter, make plantings a poor investment. Recently, some efforts have been made to use plastic "plants" where real plants will not normally grow, as a way of simulating the effect of vegetation. Usually, this is totally unsatisfactory. If green foliage is of such desirability in an inhospitable area that plastic sprigs are installed, it would be a worthwhile investment to redesign the area so that real plants can be used.

The use of plants in the urban landscape requires relating groups of plants to nearby buildings or other adjacent urban features. Observation of various measures of scale is one of the most critical design principles to adhere to in urban areas. Trees are the most useful plant form to use in city landscaping because they are of an intermediate scale and help bring tall, massive buildings into human

19-2

19-3

Figures 19-2, 19-3. *Site of the Headquarters of the United Nations, along the East River in Manhattan. The lawn covers an underground garage. The area available for landscape use was increased additionally by building a walkway (19-3) above a highway along the river's edge.*

Figure 19-4. *Planting was made an integral part of The Oakland Museum in downtown Oakland, California. The museum is built on several levels descending across a sloping site. The entire structure supports a series of roof gardens. These are accessible from various galleries in the museum.*

scale. The vertical lines of tall buildings will seem to be less domineering if they are viewed through or beyond a group of trees, the lower branches of which form a foliage canopy for pedestrians. The trees actually seem to reduce the vertical lines visually. Canopies of foliage significantly reduce the oppressive effect frequently experienced in cities.

A major function of plants in the city is to provide a continuous, unifying pattern throughout the urban landscape. Too often the only features that accomplish this unification are roads and sidewalks. Even if the only use of trees in urban areas were along city streets, a vital function would be served. That is not to suggest that every street has to have trees. In a project so large that it entailed devising a planting plan for an entire city, a landscape architect might choose to use trees to define one or more major thoroughfares and to use alternate patterns of planting on secondary streets.

Using plants along roads and sidewalks as a means of unifying the city landscape makes use of roads and sidewalks that already contribute toward this goal. Of a different class and, as a project, far vaster, would be to unify parts of the city with the surrounding landscape by means of parks in a system that would run throughout the city. The scale of such undertakings is so large that even though they are desirable they are seldom accomplished, and those systems that have been implemented are usually quite renowned.

In small cities and in newly built towns the concept of a greenbelt is more easily realized. Greenbelts or large areas of land allocated for vegetation, open land either reclaimed from other uses and planted or already existing, can serve a vital role in integrating the city with surrounding rural areas. It is nearly every planner's dream that the city of the future should be woven into a fabric of vegetation that consists of planted pedestrian walks, boulevards, and landscaped roadways, with vegetation widening at the edge of the city into greenbelts that extend outward to the rural landscape. A metropolitan region would be designed as a large regional park, providing intimate planted areas right among the urban dwellings and at the same time offering other open spaces within short traveling time.

PLANTS FOR URBAN LANDSCAPES

The criteria for selection of plants for the city should be the same used for other landscape situations; namely, to select plants (a) to fit a particular landscape need and effect, (b) that are adaptable to the environment, (c) by considering all the characteristics of the plant, including its mature size and shape, and (d) that require relatively little maintenance. The major difference in selecting plants for urban areas is the extremely hostile environment they must endure. This may mean eliminating many plants that fully meet other design requirements.

The environmental stresses that urban plants must tolerate have been enumerated elsewhere in this book. These are not static stresses but vary from city to city, as well as within any one city. They also change from year to year. Many of the plants that were once considered tolerant of city conditions no longer are. This may be because of new types of stress, such as pollution from gasoline engines, which

did not become a serious problem until after 1940. Lilac was classified as being tolerant of city conditions before these pollutants appeared, but since lilac species are very sensitive to pollutants, they can no longer be recommended for city use. Other plants also fall into this category. It is important to reevaluate plants constantly as to their adaptability to urban environments. Do not rely completely on any list of plants that are recommended, for they will provide only a general guide. It is more useful to observe the performance of plants yourself for a particular location in the city; the environmental conditions of that location should be the primary consideration. You will probably discover that air pollution is not equally distributed throughout the city, nor is salt toxicity a problem everywhere. Data will be helpful in making judgments about which plants can grow successfully in each situation. In your observations, you will also notice that the longevity of plants in cities will probably not be as great as in natural areas, and that more frequent replacement will be necessary, particularly if plants are grown in containers or raised beds. As you become more experienced, you will most likely conclude that to classify plants as tolerant of city conditions is slightly misleading, and that it would be more appropriate to indicate the particular stress tolerances of each plant, such as tolerance to specific air pollutants (information that has yet to be determined by research), or whatever other stress a plant is subjected to in a particular urban location.

In addition to tolerance of urban stress, another important criterion when considering urban plants is the amount of maintenance

Figure 19-5. *Promenade in Ann Arbor, Michigan. The trees provide a canopy that gives the street a uniform scale. The raised flower planters, benches, and varied paving materials provide repetition of the design. The unity of the street is more noticeable than the variations between different buildings along the street; thus the appearance of the business area is improved.*

required. Plants that have insect or disease problems that require frequent spraying should be avoided because of the cost and inconvenience of spraying in urban areas. Furthermore, plants that drop messy fruit and other litter should be used only where the litter can be removed easily or where it will not be troublesome if it is not removed. Of course, plants with poisonous fruit or dangerous thorns should be used with caution.

Generally, deciduous trees will be the primary plant used in urban areas. They give form, provide enclosure, and add an element of unity to the divergent styles of associated buildings. Shrubs, on the other hand, should be used less because of the maintenance required. They tend to trap litter and annual pruning is required to keep them attractive and healthy. Flowers should be restricted to limited areas for which there is adequate maintenance care.

STREET AND MALL PLANTING

It is interesting to note how many streets in towns and cities derive their names from such trees as walnut, elm, oak, maple, etc. Ironically, if originally the name was descriptive, today it may only be symbolic, for there may not remain a single tree on the street that bears the name. Yet, the frequency with which such names are found is a reminder of a relationship between trees and streets that has endured for centuries. Trees have always been placed along streets, either to provide shade for horses in earlier times or, when urban planners designed broad, straight boulevards leading from one impressive building or monument to another, to provide a visual asset and to create a sense

19-5

of unity and stability. The trees that are used along city streets today may be the only attempt made in a large city to maintain vegetation in a particular urban environment. The importance of street trees cannot be stressed enough as a means of giving character and softening the harshness of city streets.

This is realized in some towns, and street trees are often considered of such importance that town or city ordinances directly or indirectly affect their planting and maintenance. Ordinances can be either negative or positive in their method of control. An ordinance can be positive in that the city may take full control of all street trees, their planting, their maintenance, and their removal. An ordinance can be negative in that a property owner may be prohibited from removing or cutting trees without obtaining a permit, or from planting trees that create problems, such as cottonwood, the seeds of which are a nuisance. Most cities in which street trees are planted have street tree commissions that decide and implement such policies.

The tree selected will depend to some extent on the amount of ground space available. If space is limited, smaller trees should be selected, or else pruning will be essential to maintain the root-to-top balance. Where space is not limited, it is recommended that larger trees, preferably at least two to three inches in diameter and larger (regardless of the species), be specified because these will give a finished, well-established appearance to a planted area sooner. Larger trees also have a better chance of survival in the midst of people and vehicles.

The spacing and arrangement of trees along city streets deserve particular considera-

19-6

19-7

19-8

19-9

19-10

Figures 19-6 to 19-10. *Several views of a governmental complex for a small city: Ocala, Florida. The plantings create a permanent parklike setting that is appropriate for this city, not far from the Ocala National Forest.*

19-11

19-12

19-13

19-14

Figures 19-11 to 19-14. *Installation of American sycamore trees along Market Street in San Francisco. A two-mile length of the thoroughfare was renovated following construction of a subway tunnel. The project called for more than 800 trees to be placed in single and double rows along wide brick sidewalks. An automatically operated irrigation system was installed when the tree wells were built. Gratings were placed over the well openings after planting. The gratings were later lined with screen to make them rodent proof.*

tion. Before the automobile, trees were generally planted uniformly at regular intervals right next to the curb. Although the pattern is sometimes used today, it is not considered wise for a number of reasons. First, from the standpoint of safety of automobile drivers as well as of trees, there should be greater room between the curb and tree in case an auto runs off the road. As for uniform, regularly spaced plantings, the problem is in maintaining symmetry. If a tree becomes diseased or dies, then it is very difficult to replace it with a tree that will maintain the symmetry. Furthermore, as was realized with the loss of the American elm (*Ulmus americana*), which was widely used along streets because of its arching branches, if a single species is used for a street planting, there is the risk of losing the entire planting. (Although it might be difficult to persuade a public works commission in a large city, or a city's street commission, of the wisdom of replanting streets with American elm, that tree is in fact as endangered by possible extinction through lack of use as it is by Dutch elm disease. It deserves to be planted from time to time by landscape architects whose clients are willing to risk that in mixed plantings its chances of survival may be higher than when it is used in great numbers by itself.) There are projects for which a uniform tree-planting design will be considered worth the high cost and risk, but more frequently it is useful to vary a row of trees in some way.

The spacing between trees can be varied, as well as the species, in order to introduce variations in height, form, and texture. These will overcome the drabness that generally exists in the cityscape and will also allow the landscape architect to emphasize particular views. Moreover, diversity of species helps provide ecological stability by reducing the danger that a planting will be totally lost to blight or some other condition to which all plants of the same species are susceptible. Flexibility of design also allows smaller trees to be used in conjunction with smaller buildings. In general, today there is a trend towards using smaller trees along city streets in contrast to the giant elms and other large trees that were once used.

However, if uniform plantings are desired along city streets, certain precautions should be taken. To overcome the possibility of losing all of the street trees in a city because of disease or some other factor to which all the trees are equally sensitive, it is recommended that many different species be used throughout the city for those designs that include many streets. This can be achieved by assigning a different dominant species to different streets. In regularly spaced plantings, trees should usually not be planted opposite each other (thus leaving gaps between pairs of trees and crowding the tops of opposite trees) but should be alternated to allow for greater development of the tops and a more even appearance. Spacing should be at least 50 feet and preferably 75 feet apart, except for very small species, which can be planted closer together. Close planting creates maintenance problems, such as the need for heavy pruning or even tree removal.

The size of the planting pits required when planting a row of trees depends on the maximum growth of the trees but each pit should be no less than five feet in diameter and preferably eight feet or more. The pit should be excavated to at least four feet, but only after checking to determine whether any utilities will be in the way. If steam conduits or tunnels run below the area, it may be necessary to provide insulation for the roots.

Very often a plan will require the placement of trees where there is no possibility of providing adequate tree pits because of underground utilities or tunnels. In such situations, the use of above-ground plant containers provides an alternative solution. Containers also reduce or eliminate the problem of salt injury to roots since, being above ground level, they will not accumulate salt. But the use of containers has many limitations. In addition to the high costs of purchase and maintenance, the primary limitation is the small size of the tree that can be grown effectively and economically in containers. Plants in containers are usually under additional stresses, including inadequate moisture and excessively high and low soil temperatures, all of which reduce survival and performance considerably. Selection of plants for containers is critical, and even when carefully selected, there is a need for much more maintenance than is needed when other methods of planting are used.

There are many trees that can be used as street trees. Those best suited depend greatly on a practical consideration, their size in relation to available space, and on an aesthetic consideration, whether the street is narrow or wide. As in so many other urban landscape matters, frequently it is easier to say which trees should not be used than it is to recommend trees. Some trees may be prohibited by local ordinance owing to such problems as: the tree is weakwooded and splits or breaks

easily; the roots clog drains and sewers; the tree is messy and creates a nuisance; the tree is very susceptible to disease or insect pests; or the tree has dangerous thorns. Some examples of trees that are frequently prohibited are listed in Table 19-1.

It is essential that overhead utility lines be considered when planting street trees. One of the major maintenance problems with street trees is to keep them clear of utility lines by frequent, costly prunings. Unfortunately, when pruning is done for this purpose it usually must consider aesthetics secondarily. Dealing with the utility line problem before trees are planted offers alternative solutions. The most desirable solution is to convince the city and public companies to install all their utilities underground. Not only does this eliminate the problem, but it also removes one of the offensive visual pollutants that blight most cityscapes. If this cannot be accomplished, then low-growing trees should be used that will not interfere with the lines, or if larger trees are desired, they should be located so that they will not be directly below overhead lines. Otherwise, pruning or chemical growth retardants will be necessary to keep the branches from interferring with the lines.

Associated with utilities is the problem of preventing trees from interfering with street lighting and traffic signals. Street trees and street lighting occupy substantially the same space, but through cooperation and proper design and maintenance there can be harmonious joint use of that space. The use of smaller trees and taller light poles with arms that extend the lamp out over the street has reduced the conflict considerably. The use of columnar and

Figure 19-15. *Street tree planting must be planned so as to avoid interference with power lines or light poles. Some trees are more suitable than others because of their shapes. Light poles that clear the foliage of the tree are desirable, too.*

Table 19-1 A selection of trees frequently not allowed in new street plantings.

Botanical name	Common name	Problem
Acer negundo	Box-elder	Weak wood; weedy
Acer saccharinum	Silver maple	Weak wood
Aesculus hippocastanum	Horsechestnut	Blight-prone leaves; fruit is messy and poisonous if eaten; weak wood
Carya spp.	Hickory	Weak wood
Catalpa spp.	Catalpa	Leaves and seeds produce litter
Crataegus spp.	Hawthorn	Host to numerous insect pests; thorns are troublesome
Eucalyptus globulus	Blue gum	Weak wood; roots are greedy; produces litter
Fraxinus spp.	Ash	Weedy; susceptible to scale infestations
Gleditsia triacanthos (thorn-bearing)	Honey-locust	Thorny; seed pods create litter
Juglans nigra	Eastern black walnut	Roots produce a substance toxic to other plants; fruit creates litter and will stain concrete
Morus spp.	Mulberry	Fruit creates messy litter
Populus spp.	Poplar	Short-lived; disease-prone; roots invade drain tiles
Prunus spp.		Susceptible to disease and insect pests
Robinia spp.	Locust	Host to insect pests
Salix spp.	Willow	Weak wood; susceptible to numerous insects and diseases
Ulmus fulva	Slippery elm	Susceptible to disease and storm damage
Ulmus pumila	Siberian elm	Weak wood

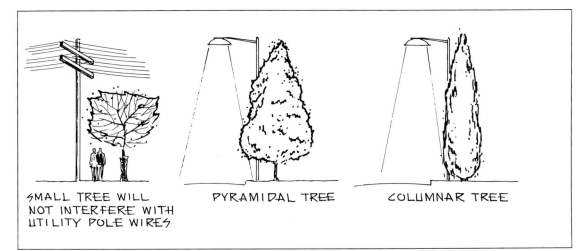

SMALL TREE WILL NOT INTERFERE WITH UTILITY POLE WIRES   PYRAMIDAL TREE   COLUMNAR TREE

19-15

pyramidal tree forms can reduce this problem somewhat also. When necessary, careful pruning can alleviate most problems, although this should be kept to a minimum. The relationship between tree size and form with regard to the location of street lighting or utility wires is illustrated in Figure 19-15.

Once the trees are selected and located, the planting and subsequent care becomes of critical importance. The design, of course, determines the kind and amount of care that will be necessary. For example, tree pits should be covered with a grating or with porous construction material, such as cobblestone or brick, or with molded concrete or welded metal grates, so that the soil will receive water but not be compacted by pedestrian traffic. To prevent vandalism, tree guards may be necessary. Where dogs are present, a galvanized metal guard should be installed at the base of the tree.

Pruning of trees is more important in cities than in other environments. Selective pruning can maintain openness that permits development of foliage on the interior of the crown and not just on the peripheral ends of the branches. Pruning may be necessary just to keep the trees within the sizes required by city ordinances. Pruning may also be used to achieve certain architectural effects, which are quite common in Europe and are used to some extent in this country. *Pleaching* and *pollarding* are two methods of pruning to accomplish architectural effects. Training trees to interlace with other trees to form an archway is called pleaching. Trees that are pollarded have their main branches cut back to near the trunk to form a crown of many small dense branches. Whenever pruning of either type is practiced, much closer spacing is possible and may even be necessary in order to keep the planting design in a good scale. The maintenance costs are quite high when these kinds of pruning are done.

Mall tree-planting considerations need not differ greatly from street tree-plantings; malls do offer several alternatives for design that have greater flexibility, however. The design of a mall tends to emphasize the role that trees and sometimes shrubs have in defining space. In contrast to street trees, which have a linear quality or hedge effect, tree groups can be employed either in symmetrical masses or in more loosely arrayed green space in order to define spaces in the mall. The development of malls, particularly of shopping malls, has recently become more important in the cities of the United States than it was in the past. Some cities have created malls in downtown business areas by closing streets to traffic and converting them to use by pedestrians through landscaping with trees, shrubs, and flowers, as we discussed in Chapter 9.

As some cities undertake redevelopment of deteriorating areas, spaces once occupied by buildings now removed are frequently set aside as open space. During the 1960s in New York many such spaces were utilized as miniparks, most only a little larger than a city lot, and these provided just enough space for the installation of a few benches and trees, or a fountain, or some other park facilities. The minipark concept is now gaining acceptance in many other cities around the United States. Generally, in lots occupied formerly by buildings, there is sufficient soil depth away from the streets and

19-16

Figure 19-16. *Plaza in Canton, Ohio.*

DELAWARE AVENUE

HARRISON STREET

PENNSYLVANIA AVENUE

19-17

Figures 19-17, 19-18. *A plan and view of Fountain Plaza, Wilmington, Delaware.*

19-18

19-19

19-20

19-21

Figure 19-19. *Public Mall, Cleveland, Ohio. Beneath the mall are located an exhibition hall and a parking garage. The location of the reflecting pool was chosen so that minimum weight would be placed above large underground rooms.*

Figure 19-20. *The open space shown here was gained through redevelopment of the Central Business District of Wichita, Kansas. Projects of this kind enable a city to create large open areas where none may have existed previously, for the use of people and for planting.*

Figure 19-21. *In another area of the redeveloped Central Business District of Wichita, street trees and container plantings have been used to create a small plaza before an office building.*

Figure 19-22. *Plaza at 77 Water Street, lower Manhattan, New York. Closely spaced honey-locusts provide a shady canopy that encourages sitting and relaxing.*

19-22

utility lines to grow trees successfully once the soil has been filled and graded.

In the largest cities, where skyscrapers are being built, many of these are designed to occupy less than the whole site, so that room will be left to provide a small plaza setting, including space for tree planting. Where the space under this street level plaza is not developed as a parking garage or as a basement, most likely there is adequate soil space for tree planting. Through careful coordination during the design of the project, planters can be built over supporting columns in plazas above most parking lots to form roof gardens that provide soil space for planting. Plants in such settings are subjected to adverse conditions that require careful selection of those species that will be hardy and tolerant of various pollutants.

If all members of the landscape industry team up to solve urban landscape problems, the resulting solutions will be unique and imaginative.

FOR FURTHER READING

Cullen, G., 1961. *Townscape.* London: Architectural Press.

Ecko, G., 1961. *Urban Landscape Design.* New York: McGraw-Hill.

Halprin, L., 1963. *Cities.* New York: Reinhold.

McHarg, I. L., 1969. *Design with Nature.* Garden City, New York: The Natural History Press.

Newton, N. T., 1971. Design on the Land: The Development of Landscape Architecture. Cambridge, Mass.: Belknap Press.

20

Suburban Landscape

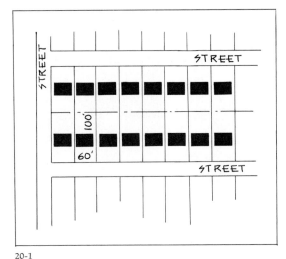

20-1

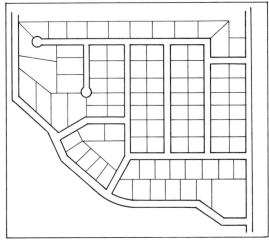

20-2

Since the Second World War a dramatic transformation of the nation's land has taken place as increased numbers of urban dwellers have moved to the suburbs. The replacement of the city with the suburb for the location of so many residences has gradually shifted the pattern of industrial and business site locations, also, from the inner city to suburbia. Simultaneously, the inner cities have deteriorated because many of the people and businesses who once used downtown urban areas now conduct most of their activities in the suburbs. According to the 1970 census, suburbs now exceed cities in numbers of sites of both jobs and homes.

The outstanding characteristic of suburban scenery is the existence of open space and other amenities of the countryside within relatively dense residential areas. Although this would seem ideal, too frequently open space has been more illusory than real, for houses are packed too close to each other. Subdivisions are developed without careful planning for the optimum use of open space and natural recreation sites. A business that is necessary to the life of a suburban neighborhood may not require a large building, but the parking lot built beside it may need to be immense. Much existing vegetation often disappears, leaving a relatively bare landscape. Thus the open, country-like effect sought by suburban residents is often destroyed in the very process of developing the suburb.

Many of the problems in the suburban landscape are caused by stereotyped planning, because of zoning restrictions that either require houses to be spaced in a certain way or

Figure 20-1. *A subdivision design with straight streets and small lots is an approach to land development that is used too frequently.*

Figure 20-2. *When land is subdivided as shown in the previous figure, the lots are often used for monotonous row housing.*

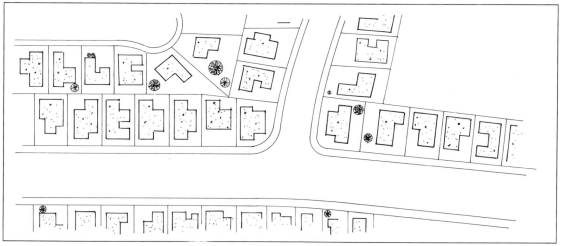
20-3

20-4

do not prevent inappropriate land use, because of economic priorities that make open space unprofitable, and because of a general lack of sensitivity to the natural landscape. Few plans allow spacious outdoor living space; houses are located in the middle of small lots, and the remaining space consists of small useless areas. Generally more space is allocated for a spacious front yard and a driveway than to the area that would be most usable and private for recreation and leisure. Developers frequently space houses at regular intervals, side by side and back to back, with the primary consideration that of placing the greatest number of salable homes in the smallest space. Natural topography is frequently destroyed to facilitate the location of roads and other engineering functions. Trees are removed for ease of construction. Thus, it is apparent that the suburban residential site is not ideal in its usual form.

PLANNED RESIDENTIAL DEVELOPMENTS

In recognition of the consequences of uncontrolled urban sprawl, the concept of planned communities has been given serious consideration and been implemented in some places across the country by foresighted developers. Two outstanding early planned communities, built with public funds during the New Deal, include Greenbelt, Maryland, and Norris, Tennessee. More recent well-known planned communities include Columbia, Maryland, and Reston, Virginia.

A primary feature of these communities is well-planned placement of open space. In contrast to ordinary subdivisions, where the only open space is in private lots or in streets laid

Figure 20-4. *A crowded, uninteresting mobile home park. Although an attempt at planting has been made, the mobile homes are placed in a monotonous grid pattern.*

Figure 20-3. *Lots that are too small leave insufficient open space around each house.*

20-5

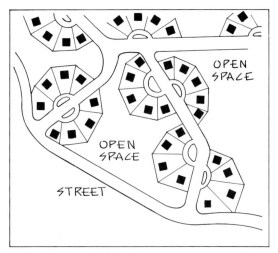

20-6

Figure 20-5. *The way uncontrolled urban sprawl sometimes begins can be seen in this photo. The housing development has been built on parcels of land previously used for farming. The residents must travel elsewhere to work and shop, or for recreation. The surrounding farmland may ultimately be used for more of the same kind of houses.*

Figure 20-6. *Cluster designs provide for the preservation of open space, because housing units are located close together on small areas of land and large areas of land are left available for use by all the residents of the development.*

Figure 20-7. *Curved roads and preservation of some open space will provide a more attractive mobile home park.*

Figure 20-8. *A swimming pool in a community park in Palm Aire, Florida.*

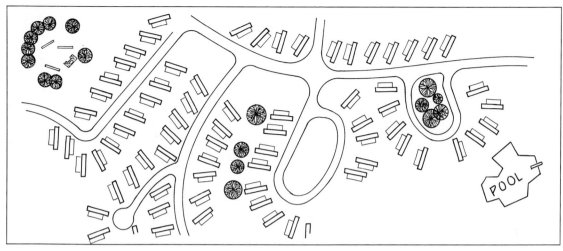

20-7

20-8

out in monotonous grid patterns, common open space can be set aside in a well-planned residential development for parks, recreation areas, golf courses, or for spacious expanses of greenery. Often this open space is located in areas that are not suitable for building yet can contribute greatly to enhancing the natural environment of the nearby residential sites. Intentional preservation of open green space makes it possible for a landscape planner to give greater attention to the shape of the land, existing vegetation, and other natural features which are frequently ignored in subdivision planning when the placement of open space is a secondary rather than primary goal.

The use of parkways or green corridors to link the town center with schools, parks, and residential areas is another way of maintaining green open space and creating continuity between the circulating system and various functional areas of a community. A well-planned parkway may contain not only right-of-way for vehicular transportation but areas to either side for pedestrian walks, bicycle paths, and bridle trails, which have a functional value as well as a pleasing visual effect. Trees and other plantings may need to be added to supplement existing vegetation, which should be preserved when possible.

Rather than to isolate parks, a community with open spaces can try to link these with large-scale greenbelts and other public open spaces. Greenbelts are being used increasingly to control urban sprawl and maintain open space. They may extend from urban areas through suburban areas or planned communities and out into the open country, along some natural topographic path such as a river, or they may provide buffer zones between these areas. Often greenbelts contain recreation areas, particularly in conjunction with planned residential areas, but they may also be designed purely for the conservation of green space.

On a lesser scale, development of clusters of residences allows the preservation of common open space that would otherwise be divided up between private lots. By reducing front yard space to a small outdoor area in front of each residence, the remaining sizable land area beyond can be allocated to use by the entire neighborhood, and a residential area of relatively high density can be realized without depriving any resident of an outdoor living area. Cluster developments of this kind do not have the "squeezed" effect that is usual when high density housing is built.

A primary objective of cluster development is to increase population density without sacrificing environmental amenities. It is not surprising then that in some outstanding cluster developments can be seen the integration of single-family dwellings with townhouses, garden apartments, and highrise apartments. It is likely that the kinds of people who live in such developments will be more varied than in conventional subdivisions. This variety can be achieved without losing most of the desirable features of the typical single-family subdivisions. The use of townhouses and apartments in planned residential areas adds variety and visual appeal to a neighborhood and increases the amount of open space by making some building areas more compact. When one examines housing needs for the future, integrated cluster developments appear to be one of the more important solutions.

20-9

Figure 20-9. *Careful siting of homes in a wooded area.*

A form of cluster housing that is rapidly increasing in popularity is the condominium. This type of development provides for private ownership of homes or apartments, with open space and recreation facilities held in common ownership. A homeowner's association is established to which each homeowner contributes financially to provide for the maintenance of the condominium project. The home or apartment owner can leave his home for six months without concern, because the grounds around his condominium unit are being maintained by the association. In addition, he has ready access to playgrounds, swimming pools and tennis courts that he could not otherwise afford.

The landscape requirements for planned residential developments are quite different from those for single dwellings. To begin with, the landscape work requires a plan for the total area. Plans of this scale usually emphasize the general, large-scale relationships of buildings, the circulation of people and traffic, and open space. Consequently, the planting design—microscale planning—may not receive the consideration necessary for a totally effective design. Although anyone's primary perception of his environment may be of the relationships of larger spaces, he is also affected by the planting he encounters in his immediate, micro-environment. A balanced approach to both macro- and micro-design is demanding of even the most skillful designers, but essential. With large-scale landscape designing such as is needed in planning a residential community, it is of the utmost importance that design, installation, and maintenance be handled as a team effort.

THE RESIDENTIAL LANDSCAPE

Landscaping is considered a vital step in establishing a home in suburbia. Unfortunately, the suburban residential landscape is often unplanned; yet somehow, more often than not it seems stereotyped in appearance. Immediately after his house is completed, the homeowner rushes to the nursery to buy a half dozen evergreens and two fast-growing shade trees for the front yard. Frequently that is the extent of the concern and planning he gives to landscaping.

A large part of the cost of a suburban home is the land on which the house is built. Like the house, outdoor space is an investment and it is very important that this space around the house be as carefully planned as the interior space. Otherwise, it would be just as wise to invest in less land or even consider living in an apartment. Because of increased land and construction costs a larger number of young couples and families are choosing to live in apartments or condominiums or similar forms of cluster housing.

Basic Design Concepts

An important concept in residential landscape design is a division of a lot into functional zones. The area around a house can be divided into three or four main functional areas: a public area, a service area, a living area, and sometimes a private, secluded area. These functional areas should be located near the same functional areas within the house. For example, an outdoor service area should be close to the garage, laundry, and other work areas of the house. Likewise, there should be easy access

20-10

20-11

Figure 20-10. *A residential garden planned to create an interesting relaxation area. The bridge and gravel provide a unique way of handling the flow of drainage water across the property.*

Figures 20-11, 20-12. *Plants provide enclosure and privacy for this Philadelphia residence.*

20-12

from a family's interior living area to its outdoor living area. The public area outdoors will lead to an indoor area that is used with guests.

As each of these areas is defined, each should be designed in a manner similar to interior space. That is, each area should be considered as one or more outdoor rooms each with a floor, walls, and ceiling. In other words, outdoor space is no less enclosable than interior space. The floor of an outdoor area provides the walking surface, the walls provide privacy and define space, and the ceiling provides shelter from the elements. Of course, the plant materials chosen for any of these uses should be selected for their ability to enrich the landscape, also.

The complete landscape approach outlined above will provide a usable as well as attractive landscape, in contrast to the cosmetic treatment for which foundation plantings are often used. The emphasis given to each area should also reflect the amount of use the area is likely to have. Thus the outdoor living area should receive the highest priority because of its greatest use, even if the outdoor living area is toward the back of the house. Usually, however, it is the public area that receives the greatest attention. Likewise, the amount of land allocated to each area should have a relation to use and not just appearance.

The public area contributes to the appearance of the neighborhood and serves as the entrance to the house. Plants are often overpowering when the main attractions of this area are showy flower beds. This should not be so. Landscape plantings should provide a setting that enhances the aesthetic value of the house. In other words, the house should be the main

20-13

Figure 20-14. *A rock garden at the residence shown in the previous figure. A rock garden is one solution to the problem of landscaping a slope. It may require more maintenance than other kinds of landscapes; a homeowner who elects this solution may look upon such maintenance as a desirable and relaxing recreation.*

Figure 20-15. *Functional zones for residential landscape planning. The uses made of the lot relate to uses of the interior of the house.*

Figure 20-13. *Lush entrance planting for a home in the Pacific Northwest.*

20-14

20-15

attraction and not the landscape. Plants in this area should be selected that will be interesting in all seasons, attractive but not dominating.

The outdoor living area ought naturally to be the largest area, and it ought to have the best climatic exposure. Trees will be important in providing a favorable microclimate. Proper placement of the house is necessary first to achieve the best exposure for both winter and summer comfort, but trees can greatly enhance this seasonal modification of the microclimate even if the house is not ideally placed. As most outdoor leisure activity will take place in this area it is important that adequate space be provided, and that it be visually attractive.

The service area includes such unattractive features as clothes lines, the doghouse, the vegetable garden, the compost pile, etc. It may not need to be very large, and it may be either necessary or desirable to conceal it with planting or enclose it with a fence. On the other hand, a homeowner who likes to raise pets and wants his children to play away from the street may want to develop the service area, perhaps with landscape materials other than plants, before he perfects a public area in front of his house.

Reducing Maintenance

An important concept in most residential landscapes is keeping maintenance low. Even though most people have more leisure time now than in the past, the majority of homeowners do not want to be immobilized by landscape chores. They want all the pleasures of gardening, which may involve some creative participation, but they want the landscape to look attractive without becoming a slave to keep it that way.

There are ways of reducing maintenance, particularly in the planning stage. The use of paving or other hard surfacing in place of grass is an easy way but use of paving is often overdone. Simple layouts with large open areas are also easier to maintain than a landscape with many specimen plants or flower beds. Of course, the most important consideration in reducing maintenance is in the selection of maintenance-free plants. The more exotic the choice and arrangement of plants, the more maintenance will be required. Where possible, cooperation with nature will reduce many of the maintenence problems.

Certain plantings require more maintenance than others. Lawns require constant care and consume considerable time in regular mowing. Whatever lawn pattern is used should facilitate easy mowing by being free from obstacles. Mowing strips—narrow bands of concrete or lumber (railroad ties are ideal for this)—will help by providing a track for the mower wheel at the edge of a lawn and will separate the lawn from other landscape areas. Herbaceous flowering plants also require considerable maintenance, but the use of low-maintenance perennials such as daylilies will greatly reduce the problem. Plantings that require frequent trimming, clipping, or pruning should be avoided if low maintenance is a requirement. If a hedge effect is desired without considerable pruning, select plants that are relatively dense and uniform without having to be pruned. Finally, avoid plants that require constant spraying, rejuvenating, feeding, or other cultural practice.

20-16

Figure 20-16. *Walkway or public entry into a portion of a multifamily housing development in Houston, Texas.*

20-17

Using Plants in the Residential Landscape

As one begins to construct the exterior rooms of a residential lot, plants become one of many kinds of landscape materials that can be used for the floor, walls, and ceiling. They are not always the best choice, for many times fences or other construction materials will do the job better, particularly if space is limited. Sometimes a combination of plants and construction materials is superior to either fences or other materials by themselves.

SURFACES

The floors or surfaces of these exterior spaces can be landscaped with vegetation, hard surfacing, or with a combination of these. Grass is considered the most versatile and durable of the various forms of ground cover plants. Besides being tolerant of hard wear, it provides a uniformly textured, pleasantly colored surface. Maintenance is high but can be reduced by proper design, such as by use of mower strips between lawn and planting beds. In some areas, traffic will be too great for grass and some type of paving should be used in its place. For shady areas where grass does not do well or on steep slopes where mowing is difficult, various plants that grow as ground covers can be used effectively. Interesting and practical surface patterns can be created with combinations of these materials.

ENCLOSURES

Walls or enclosures control the view into and out of the outdoor space, control movement of people and animals, and may reduce the environmental stresses from wind, noise, and

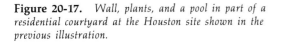

Figure 20-17. *Wall, plants, and a pool in part of a residential courtyard at the Houston site shown in the previous illustration.*

sun. The size and density of the enclosure will be determined by its location and function in the landscape. It may need to be high and dense to screen away an ugly view in an adjacent lot or low and open if a pleasant view can be had across sloping terrain in the distance. In most suburban neighborhoods, some screening is essential for privacy. In addition to these obvious functions, enclosures also define the space of the outdoor room.

Enclosures for these outdoor rooms require an imaginative selection and arrangement of plants or other materials. If space is not a limiting factor, shrub borders can be very effective aesthetically and they will provide privacy. The planting enclosure may be a formal or informal hedge, or it may be a shrub border of various species. If a fence is used, plants such as vines or shrubs can be espaliered against it. Like interior walls, exterior enclosures have to be considered structurally as well as in terms of their surface treatment. Often, flowering shrubs or herbaceous flower beds provide the visual accent to an enclosure, much as a carefully selected painting will accent a living room wall.

SHELTER

Outdoor space is, of course, distinguished from indoor space by the absence of a roof; i.e., outdoor space will be open to the sky. Yet shelter is often helpful, even if it is not necessarily expected in the outdoor living area. Partial or complete shelter may be needed for protection from climatic extremes of sun, rain, wind, or snow, or it may reduce the problems associated with glare, dust, and noise. As with enclosures, this shelter may be supplied by

20-18

Figures 20-18, 20-19. *Two different styles of entrance courtyards at multifamily housing developments in Houston, Texas.*

20-19

plantings or structures or by some combination, such as vines on structures.

Trees can provide an interesting canopy or ceiling that provides shelter as well as defines space. Deciduous trees have a special feature, in that they provide shade in the summer when it is needed but allow the sun to penetrate during the winter. The number of trees needed will depend on tree size and the amount of space to be sheltered. Most residential lots have limited space and it may not be advisable to install more than two or three large trees for the reason that the landscape will look cluttered. An alternative approach is to create a small grove of trees, taking care to see that this is balanced with other landscape elements and that the trees are not spaced so far apart that they seem to have been planted randomly.

Vines may also provide a vegetation canopy similar to trees when grown on a supporting structure. They are very versatile in restricted spaces since they require very little ground space and can be trained to shade particular areas. Their value depends to a great extent on proper selection; you should recognize their limitations as well as their assets. In selecting a vine, such characteristics as method of climbing, height and spread, vigor in relation to pruning requirements, as well as esthetic qualities, all should be considered. For example, knowing that Chinese wisteria (*Wisteria sinensis*) grows to be a very large, heavy vine, one should use it only with strong supportive structures, but silver fleece vine (*Polygonum aubertii*) is less weighty and can be used on lesser structures. Without careful selection, vines can cause such problems as constant litter and deterioration of a roof.

20-20

20-21

Figure 20-20. *A small, carefully designed residential garden. The wall enclosing the garden provides privacy all the way to the edges of the property. This use of space is ideally suited to urban sites where space must be economized, but it is a technique that makes it possible to place the units of suburban cluster developments closer together also, with the result that the size of commonly shared open areas can be increased.*

Figure 20-21. *Multifamily housing development at Nuns Island, Montreal, Canada.*

In addition to the functional use of plants in the residential landscape, flowering plants are important for enrichment of the landscape. Properly placed flower beds can provide points of accent and seasonal interest in a planting border or patio area. They also satisfy the ambitions of garden enthusiasts and provide cut flowers for interior decoration. Regardless of their purpose, flower beds should be integrated into the total landscape scheme rather than treated as something separate, separate treatment being what they receive so frequently.

Herbaceous flower borders should be used in conjunction with a background planting or structure. Not only does this provide a strong background for the flowers—a kind of framework—the permanent structural design material will remain when the flowering plants die down to the ground. The background should not compete for interest with the flowers but should be something subtle and simple, such as a fine-textured hedge, fence, or wall.

Herbaceous plants can effectively supplement any permanent landscape structures and plantings but do not in themselves provide constant visual interest or a form that is continuous through the landscape. Consequently, the landscape should be designed to be effective without these plants, which should then be added for accent or seasonal color. Keep these plantings simple, striving for maximum effect during a particular season in different areas of the landscape. For maximum effect with minimum care, select perennials that do not require frequent divisions, and use them with other perennials and just a few annuals. Bulbs can be used effectively either with the herbaceous perennials or among the shrubs. By proper selection, flower borders can be planned that will reach full flower here and there around the landscape in the spring, midsummer, or fall.

Like the selection of woody plants, the selection of herbaceous plants requires consideration of a number of requirements, including environmental factors as well as suitability of design. There is considerable versatility and variability in herbaceous plants, but of course these are limited by maintenance needs and the duration of their effect. Every residential landscape does not need them, but for those people interested in doing some gardening, the well-planned flower border can provide a fascinating opportunity for creative gardening.

SCHOOLS, CAMPUSES, AND CHURCHES

The increased number of new schools and churches built in suburban areas during the 1950s and 1960s caused increased attention to be given to the landscape development around new buildings of these kinds. This reflects a growing public concern for improving the appearance of all public buildings. Landscaping costs, including design and establishment, are generally included as a part of the initial budget rather than added later, if money is available.

Schools

The importance of landscaping on school grounds cannot be overemphasized. Schools are the primary public environment of the younger generation and help shape their attitudes about the environment in which they live. A neglected school landscape communi-

20-22

Figure 20-22. *Chelmsford Junior High School,
Chelmsford, Massachusetts.*

cates seriously negative attitudes about the outdoor environment. Schools can exert a major impact on the appearance of a community and set standards for other buildings. This has been dramatically demonstrated in Columbus, Indiana, where emphasis on the total integration of the architecture and landscaping of schools has aroused all the citizens to an interest in the community's total appearance. Columbus is something of an exception but all the more enviable for the fact that outstanding architects and landscape firms have been invited to design the town's main buildings.

Generally, school landscapes should be designed for ease of maintenance as well as spaciousness. Because of the large scale of most school sites, trees should be a dominant feature in the landscape, yet frequently only foundation plantings are emphasized. The selection of species should include major consideration of native plants, because such plantings can be used for teaching purposes as well as for their appearance. Some schools that have vocational horticulture programs may require (and certainly can benefit from) plant selections that lead toward the creation of an arboretum. This allows the school grounds to become an outdoor teaching laboratory.

Suburban high schools, like most public buildings, have considerable space allocated for parking. A landscape design that requires an immense area for parking can be improved if several smaller parking lots are formed in various locations not far from major entrances to the building. The importance of trees around parking areas cannot be overemphasized. Tree selection is crucial in this situation. Qualities that need to be considered are lack of messi-

20-23

Figure 20-23. *Play equipment constructed with natural materials, which combine well with the wooded setting.*

ness, low maintenance, an attractive appearance, and tolerance of heat, dirt, and pollutants.

There is increased possibility of vandalism on school grounds. Consequently, trees with smooth bark such as beech, which might be engraved, should generally not be selected. Moreover, the trees that are planted should be sufficiently large that they will withstand abuse they might receive from rowdy children. In Chapter 9 we discussed the use of plants around school buildings to unify building masses and to give them a comfortable scale.

Campuses

The college campus offers a unique opportunity to create an attractive landscape in a parklike setting. Because of the permanence of most campuses and the extent of plantings, greater emphasis can and frequently is placed on the design as well as the maintenance of the landscape. This does not assure a landscape of high quality, as is evidenced by the sterility of the design of some campuses.

During the past 25 years college campuses have expanded and changed in ways never imagined by their founders. The effect of the rapid change has been particularly noticeable in the campus landscapes, which have been in a state of flux. Many landscape plantings that were once considered permanent can suddenly become theatened. The college is given money to extend a building, and a fine old grove of trees becomes an obstacle rather than an asset. If the campus is large or draws its students from the surrounding community, parking lots are paved over lawns. Much of the tree removal could be avoided by long-range cam-

pus planning or by placing a higher priority on existing trees during site planning for new buildings.

A primary function of landscape plantings on a college campus is to provide continuity or to tie various visual qualities of the campus together. This is particularly crucial on large, sprawling campuses but is also necessary on smaller campuses with extreme diversity in the age and style of the architecture of buildings. In some ways the diversity of a university campus poses problems of the kind that have to be dealt with in city landscaping. Large trees are effective in creating visual continuity on the campus just as they are among diverse city buildings. On the campus they can be used in treelined walks. These are best handled by planting only a few tree species. Ground covers and shrubbery can also be used to provide continuity.

In recent decades cars have invaded college and university campuses and in many instances dominate them. Where sensitive landscape architects have been consulted, the cars have been kept in peripheral areas, earth mounds and plantings being used to screen the areas from view. In more recent years a second invasion, this one of bicycles, has occurred. Bicycles require separate circulation routes and bicycle storage facilities. Again, plants are effective in isolating bicycle parking areas and screening them from view. Because of their close proximity to buildings, most bicycle areas must be enclosed with hedges or with other narrow plant masses to minimize the use of space.

Where such features as woods, rock outcroppings, or sloping topography occur on campuses, natural areas can be created for

20-24

Figure 20-24. *Campus of the Educational Testing Service, Princeton, New Jersey.*

Figures 20-25 to 20-28. *Views of parts of the campus of the University of California, Los Angeles. Broad walkways, large turf areas, and numerous gathering or sitting areas all make the campus more useful to the students.*

20-25

20-27

20-26

20-28

both study and leisure use. Through careful design, maintenance can be kept to a minimum, allowing most of the area to remain as natural and undisturbed as possible.

In addition to fulfilling an aesthetic function, planting on campuses can be of value for teaching purposes. Consequently, the use of the campus as an arboretum is an idea that has been effectively implemented on a number of campuses, with varying degrees of success, Michigan State University's campus in East Lansing being a particularly successful example. There are many problems in such an undertaking, including the manpower needed to keep accurate records of plant acquisitions and locations, as well as the maintenance problems in working with material that is intentionally quite diverse. Close coordination is needed between the design staff and the curator of the arboretum. Some planting design concepts useful in school landscaping are included in the discussion of school design in Chapter 9.

Church Landscapes

The church is another contemporary structure the needs of which must be given careful consideration when its landscape is created. Probably no institutions in present-day society hold the heritage and symbolic dimension to the extent the churches and synagogues do. Consequently, these should reflect man's relation to the landscape in the most profound way.

Early churchmen were very conscious of the art and science of landscape work, and the monastic orders preserved and perpetuated much of the ancient knowledge of gardening through the Dark Ages. It is interesting to note

20-29

20-30

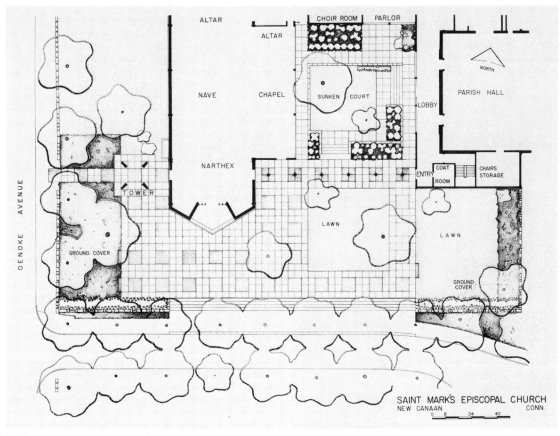

ALTAR

ALTAR

CHOIR ROOM   PARLOR

NORTH

NAVE   CHAPEL

SUNKEN COURT

PARISH HALL

LOBBY

NARTHEX

COAT
ROOM

CHAIRS
STORAGE

ENTRY

TOWER

LAWN

LAWN

GROUND COVER

GROUND
COVER

OENOKE AVENUE

SAINT MARK'S EPISCOPAL CHURCH
NEW CANAAN   CONN.
0   8   24   40

20-31

Figures 20-29 to 20-31. *Two views and a plan of Saint Mark's Episcopal Church, New Canaan, Connecticut. Existing trees were carefully preserved and only a minimum of additional planting was needed.*

that in Rome various popes have maintained beautifully landscaped gardens within the walls of the Vatican, which until recently were strictly private. The emphasis placed on the gardens and grounds of earlier church facilities no doubt reflected different attitudes or relationships to the landscape than are practical today. Whereas in the past the small churchyard was considered a place for meditation, religious processions, outdoor marriages, and funerals in the church cemetery, today's urban and suburban churches often think only in terms of maintaining an impressive physical plant that will attract and retain members in the religious fellowship. This is not surprising when one notes the cultural shift from an earlier, tradition-bound religious orientation to the present secular image made necessary for reasons of materialism.

How can churches today develop a consciousness of their role in establishing a religious dimension to contemporary life that will be evident even in the church landscape? First, the congregation must see clearly that the landscape, like the church interior, can serve various symbolic, social, and solitary or meditative functions.

The symbolic function of the church landscape can best be accomplished if the landscape provides a suitable environment for liturgical events such as outdoor worship, weddings, funerals, memorials, baptisms, processions, and others that would be conducted outdoors. Although these events do not usually take place outdoors, it may be that the undesirability of the site is more to blame than the pleasantness of being indoors. Sites openly exposed to the noise and visual distractions of urban areas are

20-32

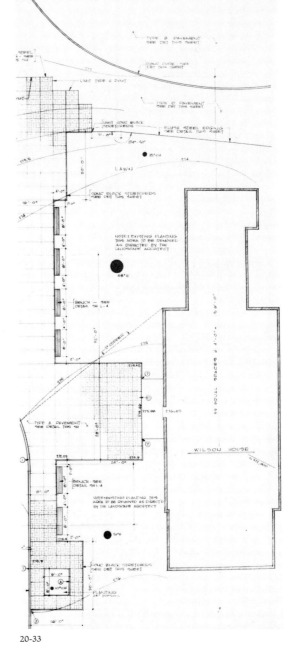

20-33

Figures 20-32, 20-33. *A view and a plan of First
Baptist Church, White Plains, New York.*

seldom conducive to most liturgical events. However, it is possible to design a walled garden in the yard of an urban church and to place it so that it can be seen beyond glass walls along the side of a chapel. Unfortunately, the only symbolism in most churchyards comes about through use of plants with religious significance and in numbers that have some symbolic significance. Such efforts seldom serve the functional religious roles mentioned above because they fail to provide the definition of space and privacy that can make churchyards as usable as church interiors.

The social needs of the church should receive as much attention, through landscaping as the aesthetic needs receive. The social needs include space for parking, circulation and entry for people, congregating spaces, and area for social activities, which in good weather may include picnics, festivals, recreation for church school children, or any other typical outdoor social activities. Such areas can be designed to serve the neighborhood too, and not only the congregation.

The solitary meditative function can be fulfilled when the landscape provides areas for meditation, contemplation, prayer, or study in the serenity that frequently can only be found in an outdoor setting. This function obviously requires privacy to the extent that most sites are unable to provide. This does not necessarily mean that a separate area has to be found for this particular activity, only that any landscape designed for this purpose should be designed rigorously to satisfy requirements of quietness, subdued lighting, and protection from the wind.

INDUSTRIAL LANDSCAPES

In contrast to the time when most industries were bleak, dirty factories designed only to suit functional considerations and without regard for the comfort of employees, many new industries today are placing greater emphasis on site location in order to fulfill aesthetic considerations. The trend can be traced back to several sources. The first is an emphasis on improving public image, employee morale, and working conditions. "Clean" industries, such as those manufacturing electronic equipment, have also become more prevalent. Many industries are now located in the suburban landscape, beyond urban areas, with considerable open space surrounding them. Except for the area allocated to parking, most of the open space is usually landscaped in a parklike manner. In fact, some industrial sites today are landscaped in a manner not too different from the estates of the nineteenth century.

A typical building housing a suburban industry or an industrial corporation head-quarters will generally be located quite a distance back from major roads. This allows for attractive development of a public view of the building, one that will project an impressive image of the industry. Parking will generally be located to the rear or to the sides of buildings, effectively screened from the view of employees as well as passing motorists. Although the plantings installed to form such screens do not completely block the view, they greatly subdue the ugliness and sterility that are characteristic of most parking areas, and can reduce the glare that is reflected from metal and paving surfaces.

20-34

20-35

20-36

Figure 20-34. *Sidewalk landscaping before the offices of Ohio Bell Exchange, Columbus, Ohio.*

Figure 20-35. *View of grounds at Mercury Rosemead Assembly Plant, Los Angeles.*

Figure 20-36. *Hershey Medical Center, Hershey, Pennsylvania. The landscaping of the interior courtyard of this hospital makes use of water and white marble disks, and for contrast, anthracite coal chips. The plants are delicate birches, underplanted with dense, dark green English Ivy.*

20-37

20-38

Figures 20-37, 20-38. *An existing outdoor space was reconstructed to form a sculpture garden, which also serves in part as a dining terrace.*

Considerable area is devoted to the establishment of fine lawn areas and, consequently, considerable maintenance is required. In this setting of turf, large specimen trees as well as small flowering trees are used extensively in parklike arrangements. Entrance areas and drives are usually handled with special care, frequently by using formal planting hedges and occasionally some flowers.

The maintenance of the grounds of many industrial sites is often handled by full-time employees who may or may not be trained in maintenance practices. Some firms hire landscape contractors as permanent maintainers of the landscape. Whatever provisions are made for maintenance, a comprehensive schedule such as the one we included in Chapter 18 is helpful to insure the regular care needed for a trouble-free landscape. Because of the large area turf usually occupies, it is a critical feature in the maintenance program. Irrigation is commonly used to keep the turf in an active growing condition so that it will hold its color all summer. Regular fertilization, weed control, insect and disease control are all essential to provide the uniform appearance desired on these large surfaces. Mowing will be a costly operation at these sites and will generally require large equipment. As we mentioned in Chapter 9 and have shown in numerous illustrations in the book, the kinds of landscape problems present at industrial or corporate office landscapes will differ greatly depending upon the particular site.

SHOPPING CENTERS

With the creation of suburbs and greater dis-

tance between suburban homes and downtown shops, suburban families began to patronize local shopping facilities. General stores along once rural roads gave way to long strips of specialty businesses along major roads; then planned shopping centers resulted which competed with stores in the city. The shopping center differs from other commercial facilities in that generally it is designed to minimize the amount of space required for a large number of shops, some effort has been made to unify the entire complex with an overall design, and plants are used for spectacular effects in a way that would be inappropriate elsewhere. This use of plants is made both in open, protected court areas and beneath high glass roofs. Besides permanent plantings, a variety of rotated floral displays, sculpture, and fountains are used in some shopping center malls to provide a pleasant environment for the shopper. We discussed some aspects of planting designs that are suitable for shopping centers in Chapter 9.

Careful maintenance is required to keep the plantings—among which will be a great number of flowers—in top condition at all times. Natural light levels in enclosed malls are generally not high enough for plant health, growth, and survival. Arrangements with greenhouse facilities are necessary to insure that these plants will be rotated constantly, to keep them in a desirable condition. Because the environment of the enclosed mall is thoroughly controlled, more exotic plants can be used.

SUMMARY

In contrast to the urban and rural landscapes, the greatest attention to the design and maintenance of landscaped areas has been in suburban neighborhoods. The nation's suburbs are its most affluent communities, and suburban landscape development is controlled by the private sector, whereas public monies are generally required when landscape improvement is attempted in urban and rural areas. As governmental units and agencies become aware of the need for careful landscape planning in every area of the nation, funds may become available to assist those members of the landscape industry who feel a commitment to remedy the problems caused by uncontrolled suburban growth.

20-39

Figure 20-39. *Site of the 1939–1940 New York World's Fair.*

20-40

FOR FURTHER READING

Dober, R. P., 1963. *Campus Planning*. New York: Reinhold.

Dober, R. P., 1969. *Environmental Design*. New York: Van Nostrand-Reinhold.

Eckbo, G., 1956. *The Art of Home Landscaping*. New York: F. W. Dodge.

Eckbo, G., 1960. *Landscape for Living*. New York: F. W. Dodge.

Rutledge, A. J., 1971. *Anatomy of a Park*. New York: McGraw-Hill.

Nelson, W. R., Jr., 1963. *Landscaping Your Home*. Urbana, Illinois: Cooperative Extension Service.

Figure 20-40. *A Japanese hill-and-pond garden at the Brooklyn Botanic Garden.*

21

The Natural Landscape

Because of the tremendous success of agricultural technology the nation's food supply is produced today by fewer people than in the past and on less farm land than was used in the past. Many small rural farms have disappeared. The families who lived on them have moved to urban or suburban areas, and this has released much rural land for new uses. One of the important questions facing the United States in the twentieth century is what purpose these rural lands should serve.

In the past the importance of preserving great wilderness areas was recognized through the creation of National Parks and Monuments. Yellowstone National Park was the first of these. It was established in 1872. People travel on holidays and vacations from large metropolitan areas all over the country to visit these parks and monuments today. The stress caused by the large number of people who drive, camp, and hike in these areas is nearly more than the parks can withstand; sometimes restrictions are required to protect the most popular of these parks from overuse.

If the number and variety of rural parks close to cities were greater, people would not have to travel as far to experience natural areas. State and county park systems serve this need because they are more numerous than the national parks, but they too are being overused. Because of high land taxes, farm land nearest the cities is usually the first land to be converted into housing subdivisions. Much is rich agricultural land and might best be protected as such in order to maintain productive lands but also to allow urban dwellers to experience a

Figures 21-1, 21-2. *The pattern of fields, homes, hedgerows, and roads in today's rural landscape. While the efficiency of agricultural technology has increased, it has become more difficult to farm profitably the small properties that make these views so picturesque.*

21-1

21-2

relationship with the rural or agricultural lands that support them. Another possibility is to convert abandoned farm land as it becomes available, when it is not being used for farming, into outdoor recreation areas or greenbelts.

CHARACTERISTICS OF THE RURAL LANDSCAPE

As we consider the rural landscape it may be helpful to distinguish between those lands that are preserved as wilderness or are completely natural and those in which there is management of the land. There are very few areas left unaffected by man and every precaution must be taken to preserve those that remain. However, of primary concern in this chapter is the managed rural landscape, which is directly effected through human effort.

There is a tendency to assume that man and his technologies are menaces to the natural landscape. This is not necessarily so. If man participates as a technologist in managing the landscape in accord with ecological principles, it is possible that land use for the benefit of man can be accomplished without destroying the natural landscape. For example, the intensified, multiple uses of land that are essential to meet the needs of a population that is growing and requiring a higher standard of living can be accomplished by achieving maximum land fertility, and this can best be done by applying technological knowledge. By land fertility we do not mean high levels of soil fertility to support a single agricultural crop (though this is a part of land fertility) but rather fertility or productivity of *all* natural elements and inhabitants on the land at the highest

Figure 21-3. *Some natural landscapes are best left untouched by man. The terrain at Glacier Bay, Alaska, shown here, is almost devoid of vegetation.*

21-4

Figure 21-4. *High rocky cliffs and sparse vegetation at the Grand Canyon, Arizona.*

Figure 21-5. *The dramatic beauty of Yosemite Falls, Yosemite National Park, California. The park is easily reached from the densely populated central areas of California. In recent years the park has been in danger of overuse.*

21-5

sustainable level. Rural lands on which this goal has been achieved might combine agriculture, cattle grazing, wildlife habitats in small wooded areas, and timber production in larger areas, as well as unintensive recreational use.

Two qualities of rural land will influence any landscape work in it. It is spacious; it requires, therefore, that maintenance be kept to a minimum. The best success in rural landscape work can be accomplished by simulating the natural landscape and recognizing the ecological principles that govern it. In managing such a landscape it should be realized that plants selected and maintained in cultivation generally require continued protection. If any landscape is left untended over an extended period there will be a tendency for natural vegetation to overtake it. Realizing these principles, it makes sense to select and arrange plants in any rural projects as they would occur there naturally. With this approach less management will be required to maintain the plantings. An ecological approach to planting design will be easier if one has analyzed and described the native plant communities in an area before designing additional plantings.

WOODLANDS AND FORESTS

Woodlands are a vital part of the land because they are scenic and contain places for recreation, and because they provide timber. There is no reason why woodlands cannot simultaneously serve both the vacationer in search of peace of mind and the lumberer in search of profit, with proper management. Many of these woodlands are close to suburban residential areas as well as along well traveled roads in

21-6

21-8

21-7

Figure 21-6. *The vertical repetition of Douglas-fir complements and provides relief to the rugged mountain scenery at Mt. Baker National Forest, Washington.*

Figure 21-7. *Trees are sparse and grass predominates in this upper watershed of the Little Missouri River, Custer National Forest, North Dakota.*

Figure 21-8. *Water scenery in the Rockies: Upper Mesa Falls on the Snake River, Targhee National Forest, Idaho.*

Figure 21-9. *Water scenery along White River, in the Ozark National Forest, Arkansas. The river feeds the Missouri and ultimately the Mississippi. In rural landscape design, thinning or pruning of trees near view areas can be done selectively so that outstanding scenery is revealed to the viewer.*

Figure 21-10. *Water scenery at Potomac Gorge, Virginia.*

21-9

21-10

rural areas, so it is essential that they be developed and maintained as attractive, vigorous, productive, well-managed woodlands. Multiple use of these woodlands can be made through timber production, watershed use, open space preservation, and recreation, as well as through preservation because of unique aesthetic or microclimatic qualities.

Some of the land on the outskirts of cities that can no longer be farmed economically is being converted back to woodlands in areas that have foreseen the need for open space planning, and if this were done more often, enough land would be gained to serve as greenbelts around large metropolitan areas. To develop the amenities of a woodland requires using plant materials that have the attributes of rapid growth, stability and variety, enough density to provide a visual screen but not to prevent walking through, and of providing habitats for interesting animals.

Woodland Design

If abandoned pastures or other unplanted areas are to be developed as woodland the establishment of certain plant species can ultimately determine the character of the woods. Selected tree plantings can alter the composition of species in areas occupied by undesirable trees as well as supplement the regeneration that will eventually occur naturally. The addition of adaptable flowering trees and shrubs can greatly enhance any woodland. Shade-tolerant evergreens, planted in conjunction with deciduous species, will also create a more varied and interesting woodland. Generally, the most successful treatment will be a planting that most nearly resembles a plant association

21-11

21-12

Figure 21-11. *Cabin sites at Twin Falls State Park, West Virginia.*

Figure 21-12. *Spanish-moss hanging from the limbs of live-oak trees along a road built by the U.S. Forest Service in Francis Marion National Forest, South Carolina.*

21-13

21-14

native to the area. However, it is what a designer can add successfully and unobtrusively to the association that will determine whether his efforts are highly regarded or overlooked.

The outline of any tree plantation should flow with the contours and topography of the area. In the actual shaping of the woodland, leave some views open by keeping some land unplanted. Along a road or other place from which a view can be had it is helpful to keep plantings some distance away. The woodland should be integrated with the total landscape view by preserving natural features such as rock outcroppings and relating the woods to them.

If a woodland or forest exists but is made up of the monotonous and uniform plantings characteristic of commercial plantations, plants can be added at the edges for interest and variety. These edges can be made more interesting by substituting groups of other species than are present in the forest, which have different characteristics. It is important to limit the number of species in these border plantings, however, or they will seem as chaotic as the forest they enclose seems monotonous. For the greatest interest with few species, use dark-colored plants toward the inside of the border and light-colored ones in more prominent locations. These boundaries should merge and curve harmoniously in relation to the topography.

Woodland Management

As a woodland develops, the ultimate forest stand can be greatly influenced by removal of inferior saplings in favor of species with special aesthetic qualities. This culling operation,

Figure 21-13. *A sand pathway defined with plantings of* Pinus densiflora.

Figure 21-14. *Western red-cedar trees in the Kootenai National Forest, Montana. Western red-cedar grows rapidly and is a valuable source of timber.*

which can be done mechanically or chemically, can enhance a woodland by enabling specimens or groups of outstanding species such as a few conifers or flowering trees to grow fully and freely in the midst of a hardwood stand.

Pruning the lower branches in timber stands before they have become large reduces the chances for fire to spread and produces clear lumber free from knots. This same practice can greatly improve the appearance of a woodland. Removal of any dead lower branches improves the visibility into the woodland, besides being neater. On the other hand, trees along the edge of a forest with full-leaved branches to the ground would best be preserved. Too much pruning looks artificial and does not achieve a natural effect.

Thinning is commonly done in woodland management to achieve a better quality of wood. It can also improve the appearance of an area by removing undesirable trees, and this removal in turn reduces crowding, thus improving the growth of the preferred trees. Variation in tree height can also be achieved by selective thinning. Thus, by including the criteria of aesthetics in thinning, the interests of timber producers and the public are both served.

An approach similar to thinning is improvement cutting, which is the removal of inferior dominant trees to encourage growth of more desirable, less dominant trees. In effect, improvement cutting is a way in which the forest succession is adjusted slightly. The removal of some dominant trees increases the light intensity on the woodland floor, stimulating growth of desirable seedling shrubs and trees, as well as herbaceous plants. Many times the trees that will be favored for aesthetic pur-

poses are also those with the highest value as timber.

A critical problem in the aesthetic management of woodlands occurs during harvesting operations. It is difficult to make a harvested forest attractive. But thoughtless clear-cutting can create hideous scars over a vast forest, and ugliness this extensive can be reduced. The appearance of clear-cut areas can be greatly enhanced if their shape is irregular rather than square or rectangular. Irregular shapes are, after all, the shapes of nature. A solution more satisfactory than clear-cutting is light or partial cutting in a forest every 5 or 10 years. Another major problem in harvesting is what to do about the harvest residue, or "slash." It can be cut and scattered, or placed in piles, but the preferable use of it is as pulpwood, firewood, or mulch. Whatever use is made, the harvesting should be conducted during the dormant season when the leaves are absent; this will reduce the amount of residue.

Thus, the design and management of woodlands can accomplish both aesthetic and productive objectives. With aesthetic considerations exerting greater importance today, it is essential that when man supplements woodlands and forests along highways and in other public areas they not be unattractive. Many times the natural vegetation of an area requires no attention. But other times, particularly in tree plantations, there is room for considerable improvement. Making multiple use of woodlands in the future will mean that greater attention to aesthetic factors will be needed, and this will require the coordination of the work of the forester, the landscape architect, and the ecologist.

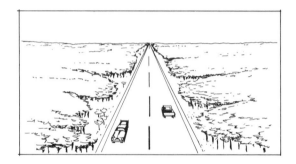

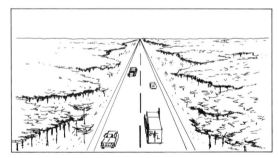

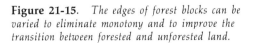
21-15

Figure 21-15. *The edges of forest blocks can be varied to eliminate monotony and to improve the transition between forested and unforested land.*

21-17

21-16

21-18

Figure 21-16. *Patterns resulting from clear-cut timber harvesting near Mount St. Helens, Washington.*

Figures 21-17, 21-18. *A forested slope shown both before (21-17) and after (21-18) timber was harvested with careful attention to the aesthetic appearance of the slope.*

MANAGEMENT OF RIGHT-OF-WAYS

Controlling vegetation along roadsides and under utility lines that cut through wooded areas is a major operation. In the United States, more than 70,000,000 acres of land lie along right-of-ways. With the availability of herbicides, a way has been found to control undesirable vegetation, partially, by general and indiscriminate foliage applications, which often fail to kill the plant roots. Consequently, continued re-application of these herbicides is required, and these tend also to kill many desirable plants. By killing most herbaceous and woody shrubs unintentionally, those plants are destroyed that would naturally have provided competition for undesirable trees.

Only undesirable vegetation that may directly or indirectly interfere with the utility lines should be eliminated when these in right-of-ways are managed. Existing shrub vegetation should be preserved as a ground cover to minimize the regeneration of trees, as well as because it supports wildlife. Studies have shown that selective control of undesirable vegetation at the same time that low shrubs and herbaceous covers are retained is effective in preventing tree growth; by contrast, in areas where the shrub cover had been reduced by nonselective herbicide spraying, seedlings had little competition and proliferated.

In controlling vegetation along utility right-of-ways, it is desirable to create a transition zone between the area directly under the wires and the adjacent woodlands. If properly controlled, a cross-section of the vegetation, from top to ground, would take the form of a valley. In the center of the valley, directly under

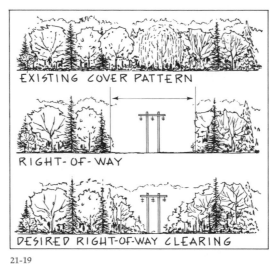

21-19

21-21

21-20

Figures 21-19. *The top view illustrates the vegetation pattern in a forest before a right-of-way is cleared. Typical right-of-way clearance is illustrated in the middle view. The transition from low to tall vegetation shown in the bottom view is a better solution to right-of-way management.*

Figure 21-20. *Steel towers erected to support a power line. Their placement, color, and alignment do not blend with the landscape.*

Figure 21-21. *Wood poles were used to support the power line shown here, little vegetation was cut, and the power line was carefully aligned with the topography to blend better with the landscape. Compare this right-of-way with the one shown in the previous figure.*

21-22

Figure 21-22. *This stucture, containing microwave equipment of the Mountain Bell System at Vail, Colorado, was carefully designed to complement the landscape. It blends with the massive mountain scenery of the area better than exposed steel cross members would.*

21-23

Figure 21-23. *A scar created by the installation of a pipeline. A right-of-way 100 feet wide was cleared in order to lay pipe 30 inches in diameter. Until vegetation restores itself, there is danger of soil erosion. The scar will be visible long after the right-of-way vegetation has returned.*

21-24

21-25

Figure 21-24. *A pipeline laid with minimum damage to the natural landscape. The pipe was pulled into place by cable, thus preventing damage to the site by trucks and other heavy equipment. The sod was carefully removed and stored.*

Figure 21-25. *The trench shown in Figure 21-24 was filled and the sod was replaced after the pipe was laid. Very little change in the landscape is visible.*

21-26

Figure 21-26. *Use of a helicopter for installing utility lines and recreation equipment at a ski resort, to minimize damage to the landscape.*

the wires, a trail 8 to 10 feet wide is maintained as grass so that the wires will be easily accessible for inspection and repair. Grass should also be used around the bases of poles and towers. Directly adjacent to the grass strip, only shrubs less than three feet in height and a few scattered tall shrubs should be allowed to remain. Along the sides of the right-of-way, between the wires and the resumption of the forest, all tall or potentially tall trees should be removed, but shrubs and small trees should be allowed to persist to prevent encroachment by the taller trees. At the edge of the "valley" and the beginning of the forest, tall-growing trees should be removed before they are high enough to fall into the wires.

This method of managing the right-of-way is both ecologically and aesthetically sound. Not only does it recognize the stabilizing effect of vegetation as a natural competitor to other plants and as a habitat for wildlife, it also inflicts a less obvious scar on the landscape and helps to integrate right-of-way clearings into the adjacent woodlands.

MANAGING THE MEADOW

One of the most pleasant rural scenes is a rolling meadow dotted here and there with a few trees, or a pasture in which cows or horses are grazing. As large parks and recreation areas are developed, portions of such lands should be included in them, to be maintained as grassland vistas across which one may be able have scenic views of water or of hilly woods extending into adjacent forests. The meadow itself may be merely a vehicle for a view of something beyond it. If properly managed, meadow flowers will supplement the grasses in these meadows to create a spectacular sea of color. Spring bulbs can also be naturalized into a meadow for a more exotic effect.

If one does not already exist and is wanted, a meadow can be created by clearing areas in which woody vegetation grows or by acquiring an abandoned pasture. Whatever its origin, the land should be cleared of unwanted perennials by mechanical or chemical methods or with a combination of both methods. The procedures outlined in the section on management of right-of-ways in woodlands will be applicable here.

Maintaining an area as a meadow requires annual care, and this can be provided by using one of the following schemes:

1. Mowing will probably be the most effective method for preventing the regeneration of woody vegetation yet at the same time allowing meadow flowers to flourish. Cutting the grass once or twice a season encourages such plants as violets, bluets, daisies, and orange hawkweed to grow. The only times of the year when these mown meadows might seem unsightly is immediately after mowing, particularly if the hay is not removed. Yet if mowing takes place at times when the grass is actively growing, the vigorous regrowth will soon cover the unsightly stuble and hay.

2. Another method already hinted at is grazing. At one time pastures with grazing cattle were common sights. Cattle or other grazing animals can maintain a pasture and are interesting to watch in the landscape. Indeed, cattle have a very distinguished history in connection with special landscapes. When Dutch and English painters used land shapes as the subjects of paintings in the seventeenth and eighteenth centuries, they often included cows in their paintings. The English naturalist landscape gardeners often used grazing land in their landscape designs, devising the "ha-ha," a grassy ditch, as a way of controlling the cattle without fences. Grazing animals are used today on large estates and in at least one city park—Grant Park in St. Louis.

3. Still another approach to meadow control is with fire. Although fire is dangerous if it should get out of control, it is both effective and inexpensive. It should be used only where conditions are such that a fire will not get out of control and where there is sufficient manpower and equipment in the event that it does. Burning once a year will control woody shoots and will result in a well kept meadow.

4. Finally, meadows can be maintained by the use of herbicides. Broadleaf herbaceous and woody plants can be effectively controlled by foliar or basal (root affecting) sprays of 2,4-D or 2,4,5-TP, either mixed with water or oil. Once the perennials are controlled the established grass should effectively compete with most broadleaf weeds. The few woody or herbaceous weeds that might invade these grasslands can be controlled by spot application. Meadows are generally small and are likely to be walked through or at least viewed at close range. The effort required for spot application will be worth while.

21-27

Figure 21-27. *Highways frequently scar the landscape. The trees have been cleared to a uniform distance from the highway along either side. Variations in the width of the clearing would have lessened the monotonous appearance of the right-of-way.*

Figure 21-28. *Deep cuts and broad fill areas are often used to shorten a highway route.*

LANDSCAPE PLANTINGS
ALONG THE HIGHWAY

The Importance of Good Highway Design

During their driving, whether for business or for pleasure, millions of Americans view the landscape along the nation's highways daily. The appearance of anything viewed by this many people should be aesthetically pleasing, but highways must also be designed carefully for reasons of highway safety.

The most important consideration in highway landscape planning is the location of the road so that it will take advantage of the greatest existing scenic values, including vegetation. Too often highways are laid out by engineers to achieve safety, convenience, and economy without regard for natural beauty, which may either be destroyed or merely treated as if it did not exist. Before a highway is designed, a landscape architect should make a thorough site analysis to determine desirable scenic features that need to be preserved. Protecting "scenery" may mean that it would be preferable to route a highway past a village that will lose more than it will gain if it is bisected by a highway. The site analysis should be part of the data that is used in finally deciding the highway route. Because it may take from 15 to 25 years for a stand of trees to establish itself, the primary goal in any planting design should be to conserve the existing plantings. Not only should these existing plantings be preserved, supplemental landscaping should be aimed at enhancing rather than replacing these natural plantings. This may require establishing native vegetation that grows rapidly and easily in an

21-28

21-29

21-30

21-31

Figure 21-29. *In arid areas, construction scars are slow to heal and may become permanent parts of the landscape.*

Figures 21-30, 21-31. *Aesthetics and safety were important in the design of this highway. Monotony was reduced by using gentle curves, increased median widths, and frequent changes in grade. Existing vegetation was preserved wherever possible: The Garden State Parkway, New Jersey.*

21-32

21-33

Figures 21-32, 21-33. *Backroads bypassed by high-speed roadways are frequently used for leisurely travel, becoming more scenic as the roadside vegetation matures.*

area on some road cuts within that area rather than introducing a grass that has not proven itself there.

Highway beauty involves more than planting trees and shrubs along the roadside or providing access to off-the-road scenic areas for the motorists. To be aesthetically superior, the highways must also reflect, by their location and design, a recognition of existing social environments and the relation of the inhabitants there to the history and natural heritage of the area through which the roads pass. The highway should unite and integrate the communities with the surrounding landscape. Too often highways become ugly scars on the rural landscape or concrete jungles in urban areas. Unfortunately, it is futile to attempt to cover up the ugliness with landscaping. Landscaping should be an integral phase of the total highway design and should not be used just as a cosmetic treatment to conceal something that was badly conceived in the first place. This requires collaboration between the engineer and the landscape architect from the earliest stages of a highway design to its completion.

Changing Highway Needs

More than 2,000 years ago, trees were planted along roadsides to guide and shade the traveler. Centuries later, the early American settlers planted trees along roadsides for shade, to increase property values, and for their beauty. As long as travel progressed only as fast as a horse, the old roads, their widths dictated by the earlier plantings, were adequate. With the advent of the automobile, roads were regraded, or widened, or relocated altogether. Although

21-34

Figure 21-34. *Rest areas along limited access highways provide several useful functions besides relief from the monotony of high-speed travel. When thoughtfully designed they provide an optimum of function and comfort. This rest area is near Artois, California.*

trees are still important along highways, the ways they are used are different. No longer are trees located close to the road for shade, except along urban streets. In fact, some highway designers question the value of having any trees along high-speed highways because of their danger as an obstacle if a vehicle runs out of control. However, trees and shrubs and other kinds of landscape plantings are probably more important than ever before in providing interesting roadside scenery and therefore a safer highway, particularly inasmuch as they can overcome the monotony of long-distance driving.

Today the landscape architect needs to be able to control a great expanse of land adjacent to a highway in order to create, enhance, or protect interesting or beautiful views that in turn keep a driver alert. However, adequate adjacent land areas are not usually included in the land acquisition for highway development. Instead, a very narrow right-of-way is acquired to either side, or a median strip is obtained as a substitute for land adjacent to the highway, and this creates rigid limitations for the designer. Faced with limited space and rigid regulations on tree placement, he frequently resorts to planting rows of trees along the edge of the right-of-way. This not only fails to develop the roadside attractively, it tends to accentuate the "corridor" effect that already exists and is so monotonous. Faced with the fixed-width median, the landscape architect sometimes resorts to a uniform planting pattern in the median because this is necessary to reduce the glare of headlights, but in doing this, again he accentuates the monotonous corridor effect.

Figure 21-35. *Randolph Collier Rest Area, Humboldt County, California.*

21-36

21-37

21-38

Figure 21-36. *Crestview Rest Area, Mono County, California.*

Figure 21-37. *The Corning Rest Area, in Tehama County, California is located in what was once an olive orchard.*

Figure 21-38. *This highway rest area in Nebraska is located among large cottonwood trees that are native to the area. They offer excellent protection against solar radiation.*

Figure 21-39. *A footbridge in a rest area along a highway near Lincoln, Nebraska. The bridge connects two picnic areas on either side of Blue River.*

Design Concepts

The general principles of design that should be implemented at highway sites are simplicity, scale or proportion, balance, rhythm, contrast, and unity. What actually happens in highway design is that many of these principles are practiced effectively, yet at the same time others are abused. For example, the principle of rhythm is certainly present in highway development but usually at the expense of contrast. In fact, if there is one element of design that is inadequately handled in most highway projects, it is contrast or, as we have suggested, the need to relieve monotony. Another principle that is frequently abused is that of scale. The landscape architect often locates islands of shrubs in interchanges and along right-of-ways which are generally out of scale with the total highway environment, particularly when one views these at 55 miles per hour. If the shrubs are too large and too close to the roadway, a clump of them will startle a driver. If they are too small, they will have a comical appearance. The problem of unity in highway design is also critical, and as already pointed out, the most important task of the highway designer, in terms of aesthetics, is to integrate or unite the highway into the total environment, whether this is rural or urban.

The problem of monotony is particularly acute in flat areas of the country. Any highway scenery continued for too long a time becomes tiring and is a deterrent to highway safety. This holds true for solid woodland, long avenues of trees, or field after field of corn. Variety or contrast is essential for beauty. Therefore, occasional open spaces will enhance the beauty of the woodlands seen from the road. But where openness dominates the highway view, it is necessary occasionally to close the landscape view with patches of woodland or with the addition of mass plantings. Ideally these should not be far off in the distance but should be near the road so that they will provide a pleasant surprise to someone driving through them. This requires bringing the woodland fairly close to the highway and perhaps even across the median, using shrubs there rather than trees for safety purposes.

Using plants to alleviate monotony is not the only way highway vegetation is related to highway safety. In planning roadside landscapes, proper placement of vegetation is critical to avoid creating traffic hazards. Some of these possible hazards include (1) obstruction of vision, (2) danger of collisions with tree trunks, (3) skidding caused by fallen leaves, and (4) uneven and slow melting of snow and ice in shady areas.

Less obvious, but also important for highway safety, is the location of vistas that are created along roadways. These should not be located on curves where drivers, distracted by a sudden vista, may not concentrate on a turn. Wide-angle vistas along straight stretches of road are much safer. The width of an opening will depend to a great extent on the speeds that will be used on the highway.

Conserving existing plantings is by far a more suitable method of achieving foliage along the roadside than to install new plantings. Yet dense woodland plantings for mile after mile without variation can become very monotonous. There are many ways woodlands can be managed to create a more attractive, visually stimulating, safe roadside. Thinning woodlands along the edge of the highway will allow a motorist to see into the woods. Clear-cutting, although more drastic, may be more effective in some places in opening up a view. It may be necessary to eliminate straight, abrupt tree borders by clearing as well as by adding plantings. It is obvious that all of these management practices should not be done just once but will require continual care. The use of herbicides should be of considerable value in maintaining the desired effects.

The potential impact of highway land-scaping is frequently lost by doing limited plantings along an entire highway rather than extensive landscaping at selected sites. One reason highway interchanges are extensively landscaped is to add variety; highway inter-changes are also one of the few kinds of areas along a highway in which sufficient space has been set aside for developing interesting plant-ings. The method of landscaping these inter-changes has changed dramatically during the past few years. In the past, islands of shrubs were extensively used and these created small, low patches of vegetation that added little in-terest to the interchange. Now, the trend is toward using large trees and evergreens in mass plantings that will be visible from quite a distance. These are more effective because they fit the scale of the total highway environment and add the important element of contrast.

Properly placed on highway right-of-ways, vegetation can also be functional. Plantings can contribute to the control of soil erosion, reduc-tion of headlight glare, creation of a uniform appearance to the highway so that traffic will flow steadily, control of wind and drifting snow,

formation of crash barriers, absorption of dust, noise, and fumes, screening of unsightly areas, provision of shade at turnout areas, and other functions. Ideally, plants used for these pur-poses will be integrated with the total design so that they contribute to the aesthetics of the highway site as well.

Selection and Establishment of Plants Along Highways

In preparing a site for a highway, not only is the existing vegetation often removed, but much of the topsoil that would support new plantings is also removed. Consequently, such roadsides are poorly suited to support vegeta-tion and special attention must be given to procedures of selection and establishment. To avoid this situation, topsoil should be removed and stockpiled before road grading work be-gins. After final grading, this soil can be used as topsoil in areas to be seeded and for backfill in planting operations. If the subsoil has not been compacted and adequate topsoil is available, then planting can be handled in the usual manner.

Unfortunately, the planting sites along new highways usually resemble a gravel pit or strip mine. Not only is the topsoil and sometimes the subsoil removed but considerable compac-tion is caused by the heavy construction equip-ment. If this has occurred, drastic changes in planting procedures are needed. Using good topsoil for backfill during planting will not counteract the problem. Poor drainage is fre-quently a problem on these sites and adding topsoil to a planting hole that will not drain solves nothing. On the other hand, the site may be too well drained so that not enough moisture

Figures 21-40 to 21-43. *Roadside plantings, used at these sites to reduce the monotony of paving, to lessen the vastness of the space required by an interchange, to soften the grayness of concrete walls, and to cover bare slopes. Some of these uses of plants aid also in attenuation of sound and in prevention of soil erosion.*

21-40

21-42

21-41

21-43

can be retained to support plant growth. Both kinds of drainage problems are prevalent on highway roadsides, sometimes at the same interchange.

One approach to planting in adverse soil conditions is to use adaptable grasses, such as Canadian bluegrass (*Poa compressa*), creeping red fescue (*Festuca rubra*), and bahia grass (*Papsalum notatum*) in the Deep South. These do an adequate job in retaining soil and stabilizing the right-of-way, but do little towards alleviating the monotony of the roadside. Moreover, the cost of keeping grass mowed is an expensive operation.

Ironically, not only is mowing costly, it prevents that natural vegetation from developing which would eventually add interest and beauty to the roadsides. Too often the concept of maintenance is that neatness equals beauty. Although the roadsides may be unsightly at first, the development of natural vegetation ultimately will be more interesting and help integrate the highway into the surrounding landscape. The native plants of an area are usually also more resistant to erosion, are adaptable, and require relatively little maintenance.

Herbaceous ground covers other than grass are being used more and more along roads today. One of the most effective and popular is crown vetch (*Coronilla varia*) and its cultivars 'Emerald', 'Chemung', and 'Penngift'. This is a long lived, winter hardy, drought resistant legume that grows well in poor soil and prevents soil erosion at the same time it provides an interesting pink-flowering effect in the summer. Unfortunately, there is a tendency to use crown vetch as the only substitute for grass, so that it, like grass, is becoming monotonous

along many highways. Other herbaceous legumes that need to be considered and used more extensively either as permanent or temporary covers are adaptable species of *Lespedeza*, alfalfa (*Medicago sativa*), and trefoil (*Lotus* spp.). Nonleguminous herbaceous species, such as daylily (*Hemerocallis* spp.), and butterflyweed or milkweed (*Asclepias* spp.), also have a place in the roadside landscape for a splash of color. Many plants that are considered weeds in other locations may be excellent choices for roadside plantings.

Efforts to plant shrubs and trees along roadside frequently fail because of inadequate attention to soil conditions. The most important consideration in dealing with this problem is proper selection of plants. Highway sites should not be treated like a residential landscape. Only those plants that can tolerate the most adverse soil conditions should be used. They should be able to tolerate extremely low fertility and low moisture. Some of the plants best for adverse highway conditions would probably not be used very frequently in other landscapes.

Establishment of woody plants is extremely difficult on highway sites. There are many problems in addition to poor soil, although that is the most critical. Providing enough water immediately following installation and during the first season is quite difficult. Road salt in cold climates is frequently a severe problem. And finally, mower damage is particularly troublesome when plants are young.

All of these problems make the establishment of woody plants on roadsides very risky and costly. Landscaping contracts usually require a one-year guarantee on all plantings, so

21-44

Figure 21-44. *Strip mine devastation.*

the cost of plant losses must be included when estimating landscape contracts. Unfortunately, the high cost of highway landscaping, in conjunction with less than satisfactory plant performance means that insufficient quantities of plants grow along roadsides, and this has left many of the nation's highway roadsides much worse off than they would be with adequate planting.

PLANTING IN STRIP MINES, PITS, AND QUARRIES

Surface mining and other mineral extraction procedures have created serious environmental problems that require special attention in this book. As vegetation is removed from large areas, the exposed soil is subjected to increased water runoff and erosion. The residues that wash away from these eroded areas cause damage to streams and turn clear waters muddy. In addition, these large denuded areas are left as ugly scars on the landscape, many times in areas highly exposed to view from nearby highways.

Rehabilitation of such areas is very difficult because the site consists of newly exposed rock and raw subsurface materials. It is helpful in any mining or quarrying process if the topsoil and subsoil over the mineral deposit, called the overburden, be retained as a base for reestablishment of vegetation later as well as for shaping the surrounding landscape. Preferably the topsoil should be separated from the subsoil when the overburden is removed, for the best planting conditions later, but this is seldom done. Consequently, the soil conditions at each site have to be considered individually and planting plans made accordingly.

Vegetation in these areas can serve to stabilize soil and to keep it from eroding into surrounding waterways, to screen unsightly areas, to control dust, and generally to improve the appearance of the site. Since plantings take years to develop, the planning and establishment of vegetation should be initiated early in the mining operation, to continue throughout the process, rather than begun only after mining has terminated.

Revegetation of Strip-Mined Land

Strip-mining is usually associated only with coal, but other minerals, such as phosphorus, are also extracted in the same manner. The site conditions will be quite different depending on what mineral deposit is sought there but also different between sites with similar mineral bases. The soils that are produced by strip-mining are variable and complex, since they will most likely consist of a mixture taken from many rock strata. Therefore, each site must be carefully evaluated, and any trees selected should be the ones most adaptable to the conditions found to exist there.

Some important site factors that should be considered are: the physical characteristics of the soil, including the percentage of stone, soil texture, structure, and consistency; the soil pH, particularly when it is less than 4.0; and topography.

In selecting a vegetation cover, either a dense ground cover or some selection of trees and shrubs may be considered, but it is best not to use all of these together because they will compete with each other. Grasses or legumes

21-45

Figure 21-45. *New regulations require strip mine operators to regrade a mine site after mining and to prepare the site for reclamation. Regrading has begun here; the snow highlights scars that have yet to be removed through further grading.*

21-46

21-47

21-48

Figures 21-46 to 21-48. *Strip mines reclaimed to provide a variety of new uses.*

such as crown vetch, alfalfa, and clover have all been used successfully, especially on slopes. Trees and shrubs are generally considered more desirable, and deciduous species perform best. If conifers are used they should be planted alone. Planting a "nurse" plant, such as the legume black locust (*Robinia pseudoacacia*), in mixed plantings may result in better growth of many associated deciduous species.

Various methods of planting these large areas have been tried. Direct seeding of woody plants has generally not been successful. Planting seedlings by hand appears to be most feasible. The success of any planting depends on species, quality of planting stock, season of planting, method of planting, and spacing. Failure to account for any one of these matters is more serious in a strip-mine planting than in ordinary plantings.

Even if plans for landscape development of the site were prepared when mining began, site preparation is necessary before planting. Slope stability cannot be accomplished by planting alone; thus slopes must be graded down. The amount of grading depends to a great extent on the use of the land. If the land is to be farmed rather than reforested, smooth grading will be necessary. The less grading done, the less compaction of the soil will take place.

Plantings around Gravel Pits and Quarries

In considering the use of vegetation around pits and quarries, the primary objective should be to improve the appearance of the area during and after operations. Screen planting will be most important, particularly around the edge of the mine site. If it is known that an area will be mined, screening materials should be planted

21-49

21-50

21-51

21-52

Figures 21-49, 21-50. *Barrow pits can be designed to fit into the remaining landscape. Big Bend Lake, in Cook County, Illinois, shown during excavation and after.*

Figures 21-51, 21-52. *Beck Lake, in Cook County, Illinois, during excavation and after.*

before the operation begins because of the time required to achieve sufficient size. Plants should be of size and density to achieve the screen needed as quickly as possible.

The factors to consider in designing planting screens are the density needed, the height and location of the objects to be screened, and the shape and height of plants during the time the screen is needed. A screen does not need to be a continuous dense mass of trees and shrubs. Instead, variation in plant selection and arrangement would be more desirable.

Plantings that control dust are quite helpful along roadways as well as around the processing plant and the pit. In particular, trees will help contain dust in the area.

Where excavation has taken place, it will be necessary to grade the slopes and to improve any badly drained places in the pit area. Then at least a six-inch layer of topsoil and subsoil should be distributed over the land to be revegetated. It will be necessary at most sites to provide initial maintenance until the plants are well established.

SUMMARY

The increased emphasis today upon maintaining the quality of man's environments has led to a realization that environmental impact statements must be prepared when new projects are begun. Perhaps this will mean that in the future everyone—not just ecologists, or soil engineers, or members of the landscape industry—will understand why the way the land is used is so important. When this is understood, the natural landscape has a chance to survive. As man's leisure increases and he learns the value of respecting the natural landscape, he will begin to use it with a greater sensitivity, and thus he will insure a quality of life for himself and for nature previously thought not possible.

FOR FURTHER READING

Kenfield, W. G., 1966. *The Wild Gardener in the Wild Landscape*. New York: Hafner Publishing Company.

McHarg, I. L., 1969. *Design with Nature*. Garden City, New York: Natural History Press.

United States Department of Agriculture, Forest Service, 1973, 1974. *National Forest Landscape Management*. Washington, D.C.: U.S. Government Printing Office. Volume I (1973); Volume II (1974).

Acknowledgments and Indexes

Acknowledgments

(Illustrations not listed here were supplied by the authors or drawn for this book.)

Frontispiece, Hertzka and Knowles, and Skidmore, Owings, and Merrill, associated architects; photo: Crown Zellerbach.

PART I.

1-2, 1-3, U.S. Forest Service.
1-4 to 1-6, National Park Service.
1-7, 1-8, U.S. Forest Service.
1-9, National Park Service.
1-10, U.S. Forest Service.
2-1, *Monumenti dell'Egitto e della Nubia* (1832), Ippolito Rosellini. Courtesy of The New York Public Library.
2-2, *Histoire de l'art dans l'antiquité* (1882), Georges Perrot and Charles Chipiez.
2-3, *The Architecture of Ancient Rome* (1927), William J. Anderson and Richard Spiers.
2-4, 2-5, Italian Cultural Institute.
2-6, 2-7, Spanish National Tourist Office.
2-8, 2-9, Bancroft Library, University of California, Berkeley.
2-10, Italian Cultural Institute.
2-11, *The Art of Garden Design in Italy* (1906), H. Inigo Triggs.
2-12 to 2-16, Italian Cultural Institute.
2-17, *Jardins Francais créés à la Renaissance* (1955), Alfred Marie.
2-18, *Jardins de France* (1925), P. Pean.

2-19, French Government Tourist Office.
2-20, 2-21, Historic Urban Plans.
2-22, French Government Tourist Office.
2-23, *Garden Craft in Europe* (1913), H. Inigo Triggs.
2-24, The Metropolitan Museum of Art.
2-25, *Vitruvius Britannicus* (1771), Colen Campbell. Reproduced by permission of the University of California, Berkeley.
2-26, *English Homes, Period IV,* Vol. II (1929), H. Avray Tipping.
2-27, reproduced by permission of Faber and Faber, Ltd.
2-28, 2-29, *English Homes, Period IV,* Vol. II (1929), H. Avray Tipping.
2-30 to 2-32, British Tourist Authority.
2-33 to 2-35, Consulate General of Japan.
2-36 to 2-41, *Gardens of Japan* (1928), Jiro Harada.
2-42, 2-43, Colonial Williamsburg Foundation.
2-44, Dumbarton Oaks, Trustees for Harvard University.
2-45, Olmsted Associates, Inc.
3-2 to 3-6, Edward D. Stone, Jr., and Associates.
3-7, 3-8, Johnson, Johnson, and Roy, Inc.
3-9, California State Department of Transportation.

3-10, Sketch for Big Creek Park, by Jerry Fuhriman; T. D. Walker, Landscape Architect.
3-11, Maas and Grassli.
3-12, Sasaki, Dawson, DeMay Associates, Inc.
3-13, Walker, Harris Associates, Inc.
3-14, Laboratory for Applications of Remote Sensing, Landscape Architecture, Purdue University
3-15, Laporte County Landscaping Service, Inc.
3-16, Purdue Photographic Service.
3-17, Ford Tractor Operations.
3-18, Cal-Turf.
3-19, Nebraska Department of Roads.
3-20 to 3-27, Laporte County Landscaping Service, Inc.
3-28, A. E. Bye and Associates.
3-29, Jacobsen Manufacturing Co.
3-30, Sasaki, Dawson, DeMay Associates, Inc.
3-31, 3-32, Vermeer Manufacturing Co.
3-33, 3-34, F. A. Bartlett Tree Expert Co.
3-35, F. E. Myers & Bro. Co.

PART II.

4-2, U.S. Forest Service.
4-3, Montana Highway Commission.
4-4, U.S. Forest Service.
4-5, 4-6, National Park Service.
4-7, 4-8, U.S. Forest Service.
4-9, 4-10, National Park Service.
4-11 to 4-13, U.S. Forest Service.
4-14, USDA.
4-15, U.S. Forest Service.
4-24, A. E. Bye and Associates.
4-25, USDA, Soil Conservation Service.
4-26, USDA, Soil Conservation Service.
5-1, after *Plants in Action,* Machlis and Torrey; W. H. Freeman and Company; Copyright © 1959.
5-2, National Park Service.
5-3, after General Electric.
5-4, USDA, Soil Conservation Service.
5-5, 5-7, USDA
5-9, Virginia Polytechnic Institute.
6-4 to 6-12, 6-15, 6-17 to 6-22, 6-24 Harrison L. Flint.
6-25, Pierre.

PART III.

7-2, George E. Patton, Inc.
7-4, Sasaki, Dawson, DeMay Associates, Inc.
7-5, U.S. Forest Service.
7-7, Colonial Williamsburg Foundation.
7-8, George E. Patton, Inc.
7-10, Lane L. Marshall and Associates.
7-12, National Park Service.
7-18, E. D. Stone, Jr., and Associates.
7-19, Colonial Williamsburg Foundation.
7-20, E. D. Stone, Jr., and Associates.
7-21, Clarke and Rapuano, Inc.

7-22, 7-23, A. E. Bye and Associates.
7-24, USDA.
7-25, U.S. Forest Service.
7-26, E. D. Stone, Jr., and Associates.
7-27 to 7-38, A. E. Bye and Associates.
7-40, Don Normark.
7-41, E. D. Stone, Jr., and Associates.
7-42, A. E. Bye and Associates.
8-10, 8-11, George Schenk.
8-14 to 8-16, Sasaki, Dawson, DeMay Associates, Inc.
8-47 to 8-49, U.S. Forest Service.
8-52, E. D. Stone, Jr., and Associates.
8-53, A. E. Bye and Associates.
9-3, A. E. Bye and Associates.
9-4, California State Department of Transportation.
9-5, 9-6, A. E. Bye and Associates.
9-7, 9-8, Zion and Breen Associates, Inc.
9-9, E. D. Stone, Jr., and Associates.
9-10, Clarke and Rapuano, Inc.; photo: J. Gass.
9-11, Lester A Collins.
9-12 to 9-14, Sasaki, Dawson, DeMay Associates, Inc.
9-15 to 9-17, William A. Behnke Associates; James H. Ness, Associated Landscape Architect.
9-18 to 9-21, Johnson, Johnson, and Roy, Inc.
9-22, E. D. Stone, Jr., and Associates.
9-23, USDA.
9-24, The Architects Collaborative, Inc.; photo: Ezra Stoller © ESTO.
9-25, Cornell, Bridgers, Troller, and Hazlett.
9-26, George E. Patton, Inc.
9-27, 9-28, Clarke and Rapuano, Inc.
9-29, 9-30, E. D. Stone, Jr., and Associates.
9-31 to 9-33, Labrenz Riemer, Inc.

PART IV.

10-1, Browning, Day, Pollak Associates, Inc.
10-2, 10-3, Office for Capital Programs, University of Illinois.
10-4, Maas & Grassli.
10-5 to 10-9, 10-12, 10-13, Browning, Day, Pollak Associates, Inc.

PART V.

13-1, 13-3, USDA, Soil Conservation Service.
13-4, USDA.
13-5, 13-8 to 13-10, 13-12, 13-14, 13-17, . USDA, Soil Conservation Service.
13-18, Ford Tractor Operations.
13-20, USDA, Soil Conservation Service.
14-7, R. E. McNiel.
14-8, Nebraska Department of Roads.
14-11, 14-12, adapted from *Off the Board, Into the Ground,* G. Robinette; Kendall/Hunt Publishing Co., Copyright 1968.
14-13, 14-14, Purdue Research Foundation.

14-15, Vermeer Manufacturing Co.
14-21, Ford Tractor Operations.
14-26, A. E. Bye and Associates.
14-29, R. A. Hayden.
15-1, U.S. Forest Service.
15-2, Servis Equipment Co.
15-3, Howard Rotavator Co., Inc.
15-4, Servis Equipment Co.
15-5, Brillion Iron Works.
15-6, Cyclone Seeder Co., Inc.
15-8, USDA.
15-9, USDA, Soil Conservation Service.
15-10, Finn Equipment Co.
15-11, 15-12, Cal-Turf, Inc.
15-13, Ford Tractor Operations.
15-14, Cal-Turf, Inc.
15-15, 15-16, Harrison L. Flint.
15-17, Cunningham Gardens, Inc.
15-18, USDA, Soil Conservation Service.

PART VI.

16-1, A. E. Bye and Associates.
16-2, Nebraska Department of Roads.
16-3, National Park Service.
16-4, Jacobsen Manufacturing Co.
16-5, Hahn, Inc.
16-6 to 16-8, Jacobsen Manufacturing Co.
17-1 to 17-3, Illinois Natural History Survey.
17-4, Ferti-Feeder, Inc.
17-5, Illinois Natural History Survey.
17-10 to 17-19, Purdue Research Foundation.
17-20, Mobile Aerial Towers, Inc.
17-21 to 17-24, Purdue Research Foundation.
17-25, The Morton Arboretum.
17-26, Purdue Research Foundation.
18-2, Nebraska Department of Roads.
18-3, CIBA-GEIGY Corporation.
18-5, F. E. Myers & Bro. Co.

PART VII.

19-1 to 19-3, Clarke and Rapuano, Inc.; photos:
    19-1, L. Williams; 19-2, 19-3, D. Plowden.
19-4, Daniel Kiley, Landscape Architect.
    Geraldine Knight Scott, Associate
    Landscape Architect. Photo by William
    Tenney.
19-5, Johnson, Johnson, and Roy, Inc.
19-7 to 19-10, Wallis-Baker and Associates.
19-11 to 19-14, photos: William Tenney.
19-16, Johnson, Johnson, and Roy, Inc.
19-17, 19-18, Edward R. Bachtle.
19-19, Clarke and Rapuano, Inc.; photo:
    L. Checkman.
19-20, 19-21, Oblinger-Smith Corporation.
19-22, A. E. Bye and Associates.
20-4, 20-5, USDA, Soil Conservation Service.
20-8, E. D. Stone, Jr., and Associates.
20-9, USDA, Soil Conservation Service.
20-10, Robert E. Goetz & Associates; photo:
    M. Mizuki.
20-11, 20-12, George E. Patton, Inc.

20-13, 20-14, George Schenk.
20-16 to 20-19, Bishop and Walker.
20-20, James C. Rose.
20-21, Johnson, Johnson, and Roy, Inc.
20-22, The Architects Collaborative, Inc.;
    photo: Louis Reens.
20-23, Royston, Hanamoto, Beck & Abey.
20-24, Clarke and Rapuano, Inc.
20-25 to 20-28, Cornell, Bridgers, Troller
    & Hazlett.
20-29 to 20-33, Vincent C. Cerasi
    and Associates.
20-34, Labrenz Riemer, Inc.
20-35, Cornell, Bridgers, Troller & Hazlett.
20-36, George E. Patton, Inc.
20-37 to 20-39, Clarke & Rapuano, Inc;
    photos: J. Gass.
20-40, Brooklyn Botanic Garden.
21-1, USDA, Soil Conservation Service.
21-2, U.S. Forest Service.
21-3 to 21-5, National Park Service.
21-6 to 21-9, U.S. Forest Service.
21-10, National Park Service.
21-11, The Architects Collaborative, Inc.;
    photo: Louis Reens.
21-12, U.S. Forest Service.
21-13, George Schenk.
21-14, U.S. Forest Service.
21-16, USDA.
21-17, 21-18, U.S. Forest Service.
21-19, Norman H. Malone.
21-20 to 21-26, U.S. Forest Service.
21-27, 21-28, Oregon State Highway Dept.
21-29, California State Department
    of Transportation.
21-30, 21-31, Clarke and Rapuano, Inc.; photos:
    Aero Service.
21-32, New Mexico State Tourist Bureau.
21-33, Missouri Resources Division.
21-34 to 21-37, California State Department
    of Transportation.
21-38, 21-39, Nebraska Department of Roads.
21-40 to 21-43, California State Department
    of Transportation.
21-44 to 21-48, Indiana Department of
    Natural Resources.
21-49 to 21-51, Forest Preserve District of
    Cook County, Illinois; photos: Chicago
    Aerial Survey.
21-52, Forest Preserve District of Cook County,
    Illinois; photo: George Hall.

Index of Plant Names

(References to illustrations are indicated in italics.)

Subject Index

(References to illustrations are indicated with italic page numbers)